Pearson New International Edition

Foundations of Financial Markets
and Institutions
Fabozzi   Modigliani   Jones
Fourth Edition

PEARSON®

Pearson Education Limited
Edinburgh Gate
Harlow
Essex CM20 2JE
England and Associated Companies throughout the world

Visit us on the World Wide Web at: www.pearsoned.co.uk

ISBN 10: 1-292-02177-2
ISBN 13: 978-1-292-02177-5

British Library Cataloguing-in-Publication Data
A catalogue record for this book is available from the British Library

Table of Contents

Introduction

LEARNING OBJECTIVES

After reading this chapter, you will understand

- what a financial asset is and the principal economic functions of financial assets
- the distinction between financial assets and tangible assets
- what a financial market is and the principal economic functions it performs
- the distinction between debt instruments and equity instruments
- the various ways to classify financial markets
- the differences between the primary and secondary markets
- the participants in financial markets
- reasons for the globalization of financial markets
- the distinction between an internal market and an external market
- the distinction between a domestic market, a foreign market, and the Euromarket
- the reasons why entities use foreign markets and Euromarkets
- what a derivative instrument is and the two basic types of derivative instruments
- the role of derivative instruments
- the typical justification for governmental regulation of markets
- the different ways that governments regulate markets, including disclosure regulation, financial activity regulation, financial institution regulation, regulation of foreign firm participation, and regulation of the monetary system
- the U.S. Department of the Treasury's proposed plan for regulatory reform
- the primary reasons for financial innovation

In a market economy, the allocation of economic resources is the outcome of many private decisions. Prices are the signals operating in a market economy that direct economic resources to their best use. The types of markets in an economy can be divided into (1) the market for products (manufactured goods and services), called the *product market*, and (2) the market for the factors of production (labor and capital), called the *factor market*.

Our purpose is to focus on one part of the factor market, the market for financial assets, or, more simply, the **financial market**. In this chapter, we will look at the role of financial markets, the "things" that are traded (i.e., bought and sold) in financial markets, the reasons for the integration of world financial markets, and the government's role in the regulation of financial markets. At the end of this chapter, we provide a brief overview of some of the reasons for financial innovation.

FINANCIAL ASSETS

We begin with a few basic definitions. An **asset**, broadly speaking, is any possession that has value in an exchange. Assets can be classified as *tangible* or *intangible*. A **tangible asset** is one whose value depends on particular physical properties—examples are buildings, land, or machinery. Intangible assets, by contrast, represent legal claims to some future benefit. Their value bears no relation to the form, physical or otherwise, in which these claims are recorded.

Financial assets are intangible assets. For financial assets, the typical benefit or value is a claim to future cash. This book deals with the various types of financial assets, the markets where they are traded, and the principles for valuing them. Throughout this book, we use the terms **financial asset**, *financial instrument*, and *security* interchangeably.

The entity that has agreed to make future cash payments is called the *issuer* of the financial asset; the owner of the financial asset is referred to as the *investor*. Here are just seven examples of financial assets:

- a loan by Bank of America (investor) to an individual (issuer/borrower) to purchase a car
- a bond issued by the U.S. Department of the Treasury
- a bond issued by Verizon Communications
- a bond issued by the City of New York
- a bond issued by the government of Japan
- a share of common stock issued by IBM
- a share of common stock issued by Honda Motor Company, a Japanese company

In the case of the car loan, the terms of the loan establish that the borrower must make specified payments to the commercial bank over time. The payments include repayment of the amount borrowed plus interest. The cash flow for this asset is made up of the specified payments that the borrower must make.

In the case of a U.S. Treasury bond, the U.S. government (the issuer) agrees to pay the holder or the investor the bond interest payments every six months until the bond matures, then at the maturity date repay the amount borrowed. The same is true for the bonds issued by Verizon Communications, the City of New York, and the government of Japan. In the case of Verizon Communications, the issuer is a corporation, not a government entity. In the case of the City of New York, the issuer is a municipal government. The issuer of the Japanese government bond is a central government entity.

The common stock of IBM entitles the investor to receive dividends distributed by the company. The investor in this case also has a claim to a pro rata share of the net asset value of the company in case of liquidation of the company. The same is true of the common stock of Honda Motor Company.

Debt versus Equity Instruments

The claim that the holder of a financial asset has may be either a fixed dollar amount or a varying, or residual, amount. In the former case, the financial asset is referred to as a **debt instrument**. The car loan, the U.S. Treasury bond, the Verizon Communications bond, the City of New York bond, and the Japanese government bond cited above are examples of debt instruments requiring fixed dollar payments.

An **equity instrument** (also called a **residual claim**) obligates the issuer of the financial asset to pay the holder an amount based on earnings, if any, after holders of debt instruments have been paid. Common stock is an example of an equity instrument. A partnership share in a business is another example.

Some securities fall into both categories. Preferred stock, for example, is an equity instrument that entitles the investor to receive a fixed dollar amount. This payment is contingent, however, and due only after payments to debt instrument holders are made. Another "combination" instrument is a convertible bond, which allows the investor to convert debt into equity under certain circumstances. Both debt and preferred stock that pay fixed dollar amounts are called **fixed-income instruments**.

The Price of a Financial Asset and Risk

A basic economic principle is that the price of any financial asset is equal to the present value of its expected cash flow, even if the cash flow is not known with certainty. By cash flow, we mean the stream of cash payments over time. For example, if a U.S. government bond promises to pay $30 every six months for the next 30 years and $1,000 at the end of 30 years, then this is its cash flow. In the case of the car loan by Bank of America, if the borrower is obligated to pay $500 every month for three years, then this is the cash flow of the loan. We elaborate on this principle throughout this book as we discuss several theories for the pricing of financial assets.

Directly related to the notion of price is the expected return on a financial asset. Given the expected cash flow of a financial asset and its price, we can determine its expected rate of return. For example, if the price of a financial asset is $100, and its only cash flow is $105 one year from now, its expected return would be 5%.

The type of financial asset, whether debt instrument or equity instrument, and the characteristics of the issuer determine the degree of certainty of the expected cash flow. For example, assuming that the U.S. government never defaults on the debt instruments it issues, the cash flow of U.S. Treasury securities is known with certainty. What is uncertain, however, is the purchasing power of the cash flow received.

In the case of the Bank of America car loan, the ability of the borrower to repay presents some uncertainty about the cash flow. But, if the borrower does not default on the loan obligation, the investor (Bank of America) knows what the cash flow will be. The same is true for the bonds of Verizon Communications and the City of New York.

In the case of the Japanese government bond, the cash flow is known if the Japanese government does not default. The cash flow, however, may be denominated not in U.S.

dollars but in the Japanese currency, the yen. Thus, while the cash flow is known in terms of the number of yen that will be received, from the perspective of a U.S. investor, the number of U.S. dollars is unknown. The number of U.S. dollars will depend on the exchange rate between the Japanese yen and the U.S. dollar at the time the cash flow is received.

The holder of IBM common stock is uncertain as to both the amount and the timing of dividend payments. Dividend payments will be related to company profits. The same is true for the cash flow of the common stock of Honda Motor Company. In addition, because Honda will make dividend payments in Japanese yen, there is uncertainty about the cash flow in terms of U.S. dollars.

Although there are various types of risks that we will discuss in this chapter and those to follow, we can see three of them in our examples. The first is the risk attached to the potential purchasing power of the expected cash flow. This is called **purchasing power risk**, or **inflation risk**. The second is the risk that the issuer or borrower will default on the obligation. This is called **credit risk**, or **default risk**. Finally, for financial assets whose cash flow is not denominated in U.S. dollars, there is the risk that the exchange rate will change adversely, resulting in less U.S. dollars. This risk is referred to as **foreign-exchange risk**.

Financial Assets versus Tangible Assets

A tangible asset such as plant or equipment purchased by a business entity shares at least one characteristic with a financial asset: Both are expected to generate future cash flow for their owner. For example, suppose a U.S. airline purchases a fleet of aircraft for $250 million. With its purchase of the aircraft, the airline expects to realize cash flow from passenger travel.

Financial assets and tangible assets are linked. Ownership of tangible assets is financed by the issuance of some type of financial asset—either debt instruments or equity instruments. For example, in the case of the airline, suppose that a debt instrument is issued to raise the $250 million to purchase the fleet of aircraft. The cash flow from the passenger travel will be used to service the payments on the debt instrument. Ultimately, therefore, the cash flow for a financial asset is generated by some tangible asset.

The Role of Financial Assets

Financial assets have two principal economic functions. The first is to transfer funds from those who have surplus funds to invest to those who need funds to invest in tangible assets. The second economic function is to transfer funds in such a way as to redistribute the unavoidable risk associated with the cash flow generated by tangible assets among those seeking and those providing the funds. However, as we will see, the claims held by the final wealth holders are generally different from the liabilities issued by the final demanders of funds because of the activity of financial intermediaries that seek to transform the final liabilities into the financial assets that the public prefers.

We can illustrate these two economic functions with three examples:

1. Joe Grasso has obtained a license to manufacture Rugrat wristwatches. Joe estimates that he will need $1 million to purchase plant and equipment to manufacture the watches. Unfortunately, he has only $200,000 to invest, and that is his life savings, which he does not want to invest, even though he has confidence that there will be a receptive market for the watches.

2. Susan Carlson has recently inherited $730,000. She plans to spend $30,000 on some jewelry, furniture, and a few cruises, and to invest the balance, $700,000.
3. Larry Stein, an up-and-coming attorney with a major New York law firm, has received a bonus check that after taxes has netted him $250,000. He plans to spend $50,000 on a BMW and invest the balance, $200,000.

Suppose that, quite by accident, Joe, Susan, and Larry meet at a social function. Sometime during their conversation, they discuss their financial plans. By the end of the evening, they agree to a deal. Joe agrees to invest $100,000 of his savings in the business and sell a 50% interest to Susan for $700,000. Larry agrees to lend Joe $200,000 for four years at an interest rate of 18% per year. Joe will be responsible for operating the business without the assistance of Susan or Larry. Joe now has his $1 million to manufacture the watches.

Two financial claims came out of this meeting. The first is an equity instrument issued by Joe and purchased by Susan for $700,000. The other is a debt instrument issued by Joe and purchased by Larry for $200,000. Thus, the two financial assets allowed funds to be transferred from Susan and Larry, who had surplus funds to invest, to Joe, who needed funds to invest in tangible assets in order to manufacture the watches. This transfer of funds is the first economic function of financial assets.

The fact that Joe is not willing to invest his life savings of $200,000 means that he wanted to transfer part of that risk. He does so by selling Susan a financial asset that gives her a financial claim equal to one-half the cash flow from the business. He further secures an additional amount of capital from Larry, who is not willing to share in the risk of the business (except for credit risk), in the form of an obligation requiring payment of a fixed cash flow, regardless of the outcome of the venture. This shifting of risk is the second economic function of financial assets.

Key Points That You Should Understand Before Proceeding

1. The difference between tangible assets and financial assets and how they are related.
2. The difference between debt instruments and equity instruments.
3. What is meant by the cash flow of a financial asset.
4. Three types of risk associated with investing in financial assets: purchasing power or inflation risk, default or credit risk, and exchange-rate risk.
5. The two principal economic functions of financial assets.

FINANCIAL MARKETS

A financial market is a market where financial assets are exchanged (i.e., traded). Although the existence of a financial market is not a necessary condition for the creation and exchange of a financial asset, in most economies financial assets are created and subsequently traded in some type of financial market. The market in which a financial asset trades for immediate delivery is called the **spot market** or **cash market**.

Role of Financial Markets

We previously explained the two primary economic functions of financial assets. Financial markets provide three additional economic functions.

First, the interactions of buyers and sellers in a financial market determine the price of the traded asset. Or, equivalently, they determine the required return on a financial asset.

As the inducement for firms to acquire funds depends on the required return that investors demand, it is this feature of financial markets that signals how the funds in the economy should be allocated among financial assets. This is called the **price discovery process**.

Second, financial markets provide a mechanism for an investor to sell a financial asset. Because of this feature, it is said that a financial market offers *liquidity*, an attractive feature when circumstances either force or motivate an investor to sell. If there were not liquidity, the owner would be forced to hold a debt instrument until it matures and an equity instrument until the company is either voluntarily or involuntarily liquidated. While all financial markets provide some form of liquidity, the degree of liquidity is one of the factors that characterize different markets.

The third economic function of a financial market is that it reduces the cost of transacting. There are two costs associated with transacting: **search costs** and **information costs**.

Search costs represent explicit costs, such as the money spent to advertise one's intention to sell or purchase a financial asset, and implicit costs, such as the value of time spent in locating a counterparty. The presence of some form of organized financial market reduces search costs. Information costs are costs associated with assessing the investment merits of a financial asset, that is, the amount and the likelihood of the cash flow expected to be generated. In an efficient market, prices reflect the aggregate information collected by all market participants.

Classification of Financial Markets

There are many ways to classify financial markets. One way is by the type of financial claim, such as debt markets and equity markets. Another is by the maturity of the claim. For example, there is a financial market for short-term debt instruments, called the **money market**, and one for longer-maturity financial assets, called the **capital market**.

Financial markets can be categorized as those dealing with financial claims that are newly issued, called the *primary market*, and those for exchanging financial claims previously issued, called the **secondary market** or the market for seasoned instruments.

Markets are classified as either *cash* or *derivative instruments* markets. (The latter is described later in this chapter.) A market can be classified by its organizational structure: It may be an *auction market*, an *over-the-counter market*, or an *intermediated market*.

All these classifications are summarized in Table 1.

Market Participants

Participants in the global financial markets that issue and purchase financial claims include households, business entities (corporations and partnerships), national governments, national government agencies, state and local governments, and supranationals (such as the World Bank, the European Investment Bank, and the Asian Development Bank).

Business entities include nonfinancial and financial enterprises. Nonfinancial enterprises manufacture products—for example, cars, steel, and computers—and/or provide nonfinancial services—including transportation, utilities, and computer programming.

Finally, while we have focused on market participants that create and/or exchange financial assets, a broader definition of market participants would include regulators of financial markets. We will discuss regulation further later in this chapter.

Table 1 Summary of Classification of Financial Markets
CLASSIFICATION BY NATURE OF CLAIM:
Debt market
Equity market
CLASSIFICATION BY MATURITY OF CLAIM:
Money market
Capital market
CLASSIFICATION BY SEASONING OF CLAIM:
Primary market
Secondary market
CLASSIFICATION BY IMMEDIATE DELIVERY OR FUTURE DELIVERY:
Cash or spot market
Derivative market
CLASSIFICATION BY ORGANIZATIONAL STRUCTURE:
Auction market
Over-the-counter market
Intermediated market

Key Points That You Should Understand Before Proceeding

1. The three economic functions of financial markets are to improve the price discovery process, enhance liquidity, and reduce the cost of transacting.
2. There are various ways that financial markets can be classified.
3. The market participants include households, business entities, national governments, national government agencies, state and local governments, supranationals, and regulators.

GLOBALIZATION OF FINANCIAL MARKETS

Because of the globalization of financial markets throughout the world, entities in any country seeking to raise funds need not be limited to their domestic financial market. Nor are investors in a country limited to the financial assets issued in their domestic market. Globalization means the integration of financial markets throughout the world into an international financial market.

The factors that have led to the integration of financial markets are (1) deregulation or liberalization of markets and the activities of market participants in key financial centers of the world; (2) technological advances for monitoring world markets, executing orders, and analyzing financial opportunities; and (3) increased institutionalization of financial markets.

Global competition has forced governments to deregulate (or liberalize) various aspects of their financial markets so that their financial enterprises can compete effectively around the world.

Technological advances have increased the integration of and efficiency of the global financial market. Advances in telecommunication systems link market participants throughout the world, with the result that orders can be executed within seconds. Advances in computer technology, coupled with advanced telecommunication systems, allow the transmission of real-time information on security prices and other key information to many participants in many places. Therefore, many investors can monitor global markets and simultaneously assess how this information will impact the risk/return profile of their portfolios. Significantly improved computing power allows the instant manipulation of real-time market information so that arbitrage opportunities can be identified. Once these opportunities are identified, telecommunication systems permit the rapid execution of orders to capture them.

The U.S. financial markets have shifted from domination by retail investors to domination by financial institutions. By *retail investors* we mean individuals. For example, when you or I buy a share of common stock, we are referred to as retail investors. Examples of financial institutions are pension funds, insurance companies, mutual funds, commercial banks, and savings and loan associations.

The shifting of the financial markets from dominance by retail investors to institutional investors is referred to as the *institutionalization* of financial markets. The same thing is occurring in other industrialized countries. Unlike retail investors, institutional investors have been more willing to transfer funds across national borders to improve portfolio diversification and/or exploit perceived mispricing of financial assets in foreign countries. The potential portfolio diversification benefits associated with global investing have been documented in numerous studies, which have heightened the awareness of investors about the virtues of global investing.

Classification of Global Financial Markets

Although there is no uniform system for classifying the global financial markets, an appropriate schematic presentation appears in Figure 1. From the perspective of a given country, financial markets can be classified as either internal or external. The **internal market** is also called the **national market**. It is composed of two parts: the **domestic market** and the **foreign market**. The domestic market is where issuers domiciled in a country issue securities and where those securities are subsequently traded.

The foreign market in any country is where the securities of issuers not domiciled in the country are sold and traded. The rules governing the issuance of foreign securities are those imposed by regulatory authorities where the security is issued. For example, securities issued

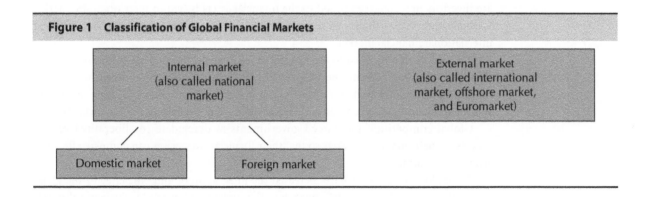

Figure 1 Classification of Global Financial Markets

Internal market (also called national market)

External market (also called international market, offshore market, and Euromarket)

Domestic market

Foreign market

by non-U.S. corporations in the United States must comply with the regulations set forth in U.S. securities law. A non-Japanese corporation that seeks to offer securities in Japan must comply with Japanese securities law and regulations imposed by the Japanese Ministry of Finance. Nicknames have developed to describe the various foreign markets. For example, the foreign market in the United States is called the *Yankee market*. The foreign market in Japan is nicknamed the *Samurai market*, in the United Kingdom the *Bulldog market*, in the Netherlands the *Rembrandt market*, and in Spain the *Matador market*.

The **external market**, also called the **international market**, allows trading of securities with two distinguishing features: (1) at issuance securities are offered simultaneously to investors in a number of countries, and (2) they are issued outside the jurisdiction of any single country. The external market is commonly referred to as the **offshore market**, or, more popularly, the **Euromarket**.[1]

Motivation for Using Foreign Markets and Euromarkets

There are several reasons why a corporation may seek to raise funds outside its domestic market. First, in some countries, large corporations seeking to raise a substantial amount of funds may have no choice but to obtain financing in either the foreign market sector of another country or the Euromarket. This is because the fund-seeking corporation's domestic market is not fully developed and cannot satisfy its demand for funds on globally competitive terms. Governments of developing countries have used these markets in seeking funds for government-owned corporations that they are privatizing.

The second reason is that there may be opportunities for obtaining a lower cost of funding than is available in the domestic market, although with the integration of capital markets throughout the world, such opportunities have diminished. Nevertheless, there are still some imperfections in capital markets throughout the world that may permit a reduced cost of funds. The causes of these imperfections are discussed throughout the book. A final reason for using foreign or Euromarkets is a desire by issuers to diversify their source of funding so as to reduce reliance on domestic investors.

Key Points That You Should Understand Before Proceeding

1. The three major factors that have integrated financial markets throughout the world.
2. What is meant by the institutionalization of financial markets.
3. What is meant by an internal market (or national market), domestic market, foreign market, and external market (or international market, offshore market, or Euromarket).
4. The motivations for U.S. corporations to raise money outside the United States.

| DERIVATIVE MARKETS

So far we have focused on the cash market for financial assets. With some contracts, the contract holder has either the obligation or the choice to buy or sell a financial asset at some future time. The price of any such contract derives its value from the value of the

---

[1] The classification we use is by no means universally accepted. Some market observers and compilers of statistical data on market activity refer to the external market as consisting of the foreign market and the Euromarket.

underlying financial asset, financial index, or interest rate. Consequently, these contracts are called **derivative instruments**.

Types of Derivative Instruments

The two basic types of derivative instruments are *futures/forward contracts* and *options contracts*. A futures or forward contract is an agreement whereby two parties agree to transact with respect to some financial asset at a predetermined price at a specified future date. One party agrees to buy the financial asset; the other agrees to sell the financial asset. Both parties are obligated to perform, and neither party charges a fee.

An options contract gives the owner of the contract the right, but not the obligation, to buy (or sell) a financial asset at a specified price from (or to) another party. The buyer of the contract must pay the seller a fee, which is called the option price. When the option grants the owner of the option the right to buy a financial asset from the other party, the option is called a **call option**. If, instead, the option grants the owner of the option the right to sell a financial asset to the other party, the option is called a **put option**.

Derivative instruments are not limited to financial assets. There are derivative instruments involving commodities and precious metals. Our focus, however, is on derivative instruments where the underlying asset is a financial asset, or some financial benchmark such as a stock index or an interest rate, a credit spread, or foreign exchange. Moreover, there are other types of derivative instruments that are basically "packages" of either forward contracts or option contracts. These include swaps, caps, and floors.

The Role of Derivative Instruments

Derivative contracts provide issuers and investors an inexpensive way of controlling some major risks. Here are three examples that clearly illustrate the need for derivative contracts:

1. Suppose that Verizon Communications plans to obtain a bank loan for $100 million two months from now. The key risk here is that two months from now the interest rate will be higher than it is today. If the interest rate is only one percentage point higher, Verizon Communications would have to pay $1 million more in annual interest. Clearly, then, issuers and borrowers want a way to protect against a rise in interest rates.

2. IBM pension fund owns a portfolio consisting of the common stock of a large number of companies. Suppose the pension fund knows that two months from now it must sell stock in its portfolio to pay beneficiaries $20 million. The risk that IBM pension fund faces is that two months from now when the stocks are sold, the price of most or all stocks may be lower than they are today. If stock prices do decline, the pension fund will have to sell off more shares to realize $20 million. Thus, investors, such as the IBM pension fund, face the risk of declining stock prices and may want to protect against this risk.

3. Suppose Sears, Roebuck plans to issue a bond in Switzerland and the periodic payments that the company must make to the bondholders are denominated in the Swiss currency, the franc. The amount of U.S. dollars that Sears must pay to receive the

amount of Swiss francs it has contracted to pay will depend on the exchange rate at the time the payment must be made. For example, suppose that at the time Sears plans to issue the bonds, the exchange rate is such that 1 U.S. dollar is equal to 1.5 Swiss francs. So, for each 7.5 million Swiss francs that Sears must pay to the bondholders, it must pay U.S. $5 million. If at any time that a payment must be made in Swiss francs, the value of the U.S. dollar declines relative to the Swiss franc, Sears will have to pay more U.S. dollars to satisfy its contractual obligation. For example, if 1 U.S. dollar at the time of a payment changes to 1.25 Swiss francs, Sears would have to pay $6 million to make a payment of 7.5 million Swiss francs. This is U.S. $1 million more than when it issued the bonds. Issuers and borrowers who raise funds in a currency that is not their local currency face this risk.

The derivative instruments that can be used by the two borrowers (Verizon Communications and Sears, Roebuck) and the one investor (IBM pension fund) in these examples to eliminate or to reduce the kinds of risks that they face.

Derivative markets may have at least three advantages over the corresponding cash (spot) market for the same financial asset. First, depending on the derivative instrument, it may cost less to execute a transaction in the derivatives market in order to adjust the risk exposure of an investor's portfolio to new economic information than it would cost to make that adjustment in the cash market. Second, transactions typically can be accomplished faster in the derivatives market. Third, some derivative markets can absorb a greater dollar transaction without an adverse effect on the price of the derivative instrument; that is, the derivative market may be more liquid than the cash market.

The key point here is that derivative instruments play a critical role in global financial markets. A May 1994 report published by the U.S. General Accounting Office (GAO) titled *Financial Derivatives: Actions Needed to Protect the Financial System* recognized the importance of derivatives for market participants. Page 6 of the report states:

> Derivatives serve an important function of the global financial marketplace, providing end-users with opportunities to better manage financial risks associated with their business transactions. The rapid growth and increasing complexity of derivatives reflect both the increased demand from end-users for better ways to manage their financial risks and the innovative capacity of the financial services industry to respond to market demands.

Unfortunately, derivative markets are too often viewed by the general public—and sometimes regulators and legislative bodies—as vehicles for pure speculation (that is, legalized gambling). Without derivative instruments and the markets in which they trade, the financial systems throughout the world would not be as integrated as they are today.

Key Points That You Should Understand Before Proceeding

1. The two basic types of derivative instruments: futures/forward contracts and options.
2. The principal economic role of derivative instruments.
3. The potential advantages of using derivative instruments rather than cash market instruments.

THE ROLE OF THE GOVERNMENT IN FINANCIAL MARKETS

Because of the prominent role played by financial markets in economies, governments have long deemed it necessary to regulate certain aspects of these markets. In their regulatory capacities, governments have greatly influenced the development and evolution of financial markets and institutions. As stated in a March 31, 2008, speech by Henry M. Paulson, Jr., Secretary of the U.S. Department of the Treasury:[2]

> A strong financial system is vitally important—not for Wall Street, not for bankers, but for working Americans. When our markets work, people throughout our economy benefit—Americans seeking to buy a car or buy a home, families borrowing to pay for college, innovators borrowing on the strength of a good idea for a new product or technology, and businesses financing investments that create new jobs. And when our financial system is under stress, millions of working Americans bear the consequences. Government has a responsibility to make sure our financial system is regulated effectively. And in this area, we can do a better job. In sum, the ultimate beneficiaries from improved financial regulation are America's workers, families and businesses—both large and small.

It is important to realize that governments, markets, and institutions tend to behave interactively and to affect one another's actions in certain ways. Thus, it is not surprising to find that a market's reactions to regulations often prompt a new response by the government, which can cause the institutions participating in a market to change their behavior further, and so on. A sense of how the government can affect a market and its participants is important to an understanding of the numerous markets and securities to be described in the chapters to come. For that reason, we briefly describe the regulatory function here.

Because of differences in culture and history, different countries regulate financial markets and financial institutions in varying ways, emphasizing some forms of regulation more than others. Here we will discuss the different types of regulation, the motivation for regulation, and the basic U.S. regulatory structure.

Justification for Regulation

The standard explanation or justification for governmental regulation of a market is that the market, left to itself, will not produce its particular goods or services in an efficient manner and at the lowest possible cost. Of course, efficiency and low-cost production are hallmarks of a perfectly **competitive market**. Thus, a market unable to produce efficiently must be one that is not competitive at the time, and that will not gain that status by itself in the foreseeable future. Of course, it is also possible that governments may regulate markets that are viewed as competitive currently but unable to sustain competition, and thus low-cost production, over the long run. A version of this justification for regulation is that the government controls a feature of the economy that the market mechanisms of competition and pricing could not manage without help. A shorthand expression economists use to

---

[2] It is in this speech that Secretary Paulson introduced what is known as the "Blueprint for Regulatory Reform" that we will describe shortly.

describe the reasons for regulation is **market failure**. A market is said to fail if it cannot, by itself, maintain all the requirements for a competitive situation.

Governments in most developed economies have created elaborate systems of regulation for financial markets, in part because the markets themselves are complex and in part because financial markets are so important to the general economies in which they operate. The numerous rules and regulations are designed to serve several purposes, which fall into the following categories:

1. to prevent issuers of securities from defrauding investors by concealing relevant information
2. to promote competition and fairness in the trading of financial securities
3. to promote the stability of financial institutions
4. to restrict the activities of foreign concerns in domestic markets and institutions
5. to control the level of economic activity

Corresponding to each of these categories is an important form of regulation. We discuss each form in turn.

Disclosure regulation is the form of regulation that requires issuers of securities to make public a large amount of financial information to actual and potential investors. The standard justification for disclosure rules is that the managers of the issuing firm have more information about the financial health and future of the firm than investors who own or are considering the purchase of the firm's securities. The cause of market failure here, if indeed it occurs, is commonly described as **asymmetric information**, which means investors and managers have uneven access to or uneven possession of information. This is referred to as the **agency problem**, in the sense that the firm's managers, who act as agents for investors, may act in their own interests to the disadvantage of the investors. The advocates of disclosure rules say that, in the absence of the rules, the investors' comparatively limited knowledge about the firm would allow the agents to engage in such practices.

Financial activity regulation consists of rules about traders of securities and trading on financial markets. A prime example of this form of regulation is the set of rules against trading by corporate insiders who are corporate officers and others in positions to know more about a firm's prospects than the general investing public. Insider trading is another problem posed by asymmetric information, which is of course inconsistent with a competitive market. A second example of this type of regulation would be rules regarding the structure and operations of exchanges where securities are traded so as to minimize the risk of defrauding the general investing public.

Regulation of financial institutions is the form of governmental monitoring that restricts these institutions' activities in the vital areas of lending, borrowing, and funding. The justification for this form of government regulation is that these financial firms have a special role to play in a modern economy. Financial institutions help households and firms to save; they also facilitate the complex payments among many elements of the economy; and in the case of commercial banks, they serve as conduits for the government's monetary policy. Thus, it is often argued that the failure of these financial institutions would disturb the economy in a severe way.

Regulation of foreign participants is the form of governmental activity that limits the roles foreign firms can have in domestic markets and their ownership or control of financial institutions.

Authorities use **banking and monetary regulation** to try to control changes in a country's money supply, which is thought to control the level of economic activity.

These types of governmental regulation of markets and financial institutions are mentioned here briefly in order to provide a comprehensive picture of the government's role in modern financial systems.

Regulation in the United States

The regulatory structure in the United States is largely the result of financial crises that have occurred at various times. Most regulations are the products of the stock market crash of 1929 and the Great Depression in the 1930s. Some of the regulations may make little economic sense in the current financial market, but they can be traced back to some abuse that legislators encountered, or thought they encountered, at one time. In fact, as noted by Secretary Paulson in his March 31, 2008, speech:

> Our current regulatory structure was not built to address the modern financial system with its diversity of market participants, innovation, complexity of financial instruments, convergence of financial intermediaries and trading platforms, global integration and interconnectedness among financial institutions, investors and markets. Moreover, our financial services companies are becoming larger, more complex and more difficult to manage. Much of our current regulatory system was developed after the Great Depression and it has developed through reaction—a pattern of creating regulators as a response to market innovations or to market stress.

The current regulatory system in the United States is based on an array of industry- and market-focused regulators. Again, we will discuss the complex array of regulation when we describe the various financial institutions and financial markets. A proposal by the U.S. Department of the Treasury, popularly referred to as the "Blueprint for Regulatory Reform" or simply Blueprint, would replace the prevailing complex array of regulators with a regulatory system based on functions. More specifically, there would be three regulators: (1) a market stability regulator, (2) a prudential regulator, and (3) a business conduct regulator. The market stability regulator would take on the traditional role of the Federal Reserve by giving it the responsibility and authority to ensure overall financial market stability. The Federal Reserve would be responsible for monitoring risks across the financial system. The prudential regulator would be charged with safety and soundness of firms with federal guarantees that we will describe in this book such as federal depository insurance and housing guarantees. The business conduct regulator would regulate business conduct across all types of financial firms. This regulator would take on most of the roles that the Securities and Exchange Commission and the Commodity Futures Trading Commission now have.

This change in regulatory structure is the long-term recommendation of the Blueprint. This may not occur for 10 or 15 years, if at all. If history is our guide, major regulatory changes do take that long to become legislation. For example, there is the major regulatory reform as of this writing: the Gramm-Leach-Bliley Act 1999. According to one source, portions of that legislation were first recommended by a special commission of the Reagan administration in the early to mid 1980s.

> ### Key Points That You Should Understand Before Proceeding
>
> 1. The standard explanation for governmental regulation of markets for goods and services.
> 2. What is being sought by regulation.
> 3. The major forms of regulation.
> 4. The "Blueprint for Regulatory Reform" proposed by the U.S. Department of the Treasury.

FINANCIAL INNOVATION

Categorizations of Financial Innovation

Since the 1960s, there has been a surge in significant financial innovations. Observers of financial markets have categorized these innovations in different ways. Here are just three ways suggested to classify these innovations.

The Economic Council of Canada classifies financial innovations into the following three broad categories:[3]

- *market-broadening instruments*, which increase the liquidity of markets and the availability of funds by attracting new investors and offering new opportunities for borrowers
- *risk-management instruments*, which reallocate financial risks to those who are less averse to them, or who have offsetting exposure and thus are presumably better able to shoulder them
- *arbitraging instruments and processes*, which enable investors and borrowers to take advantage of differences in costs and returns between markets, and which reflect differences in the perception of risks, as well as in information, taxation, and regulations

Another classification system of financial innovations based on more specific functions has been suggested by the Bank for International Settlements: *price-risk-transferring innovations, credit-risk-transferring instruments, liquidity-generating innovations, credit-generating instruments*, and *equity-generating instruments*.[4] Price-risk-transferring innovations are those that provide market participants with more efficient means for dealing with price or exchange-rate risk. Reallocating the risk of default is the function of credit-risk-transferring instruments. Liquidity-generating innovations do three things: (1) They increase the liquidity of the market, (2) they allow borrowers to draw upon new sources of funds, and (3) they allow market participants to circumvent capital constraints imposed by regulations. Instruments to increase the amount of debt funds available to borrowers and to increase the capital base of financial and nonfinancial institutions are the functions of credit-generating and equity-generating innovations, respectively.

Finally, Professor Stephen Ross suggests two classes of financial innovation: (1) new financial products (financial assets and derivative instruments) better suited to the circumstances of

---

[3] *Globalization and Canada's Financial Markets* (Ottawa, Canada: Supply and Services Canada, 1989), p. 32.
[4] Bank for International Settlements, *Recent Innovations in International Banking* (Basle: BIS, April 1986).

the time (for example, to inflation) and to the markets in which they trade, and (2) strategies that primarily use these financial products.[5]

For now, let's look at why financial innovation takes place.

Motivation for Financial Innovation

There are two extreme views of financial innovation.[6] There are some who believe that the major impetus for innovation has been the endeavor to circumvent (or **arbitrage**) regulations and find loopholes in tax rules.[7] At the other extreme, some hold that the essence of innovation is the introduction of financial instruments that are more efficient for redistributing risks among market participants.

It would appear that many of the innovations that have passed the test of time and have not disappeared have been innovations that provided more efficient mechanisms for redistributing risk. Other innovations may just represent a more efficient way of doing things. Indeed, if we consider the ultimate causes of financial innovation,[8] the following emerge as the most important:

1. increased volatility of interest rates, inflation, equity prices, and exchange rates
2. advances in computer and telecommunication technologies
3. greater sophistication and educational training among professional market participants
4. financial intermediary competition
5. incentives to get around existing regulation and tax laws
6. changing global patterns of financial wealth

With increased volatility comes the need for certain market participants to protect themselves against unfavorable consequences. This means new or more efficient ways of risk sharing in the financial market are needed. Many of the financial products require the use of computers to create and monitor them. To implement trading strategies using these financial products also requires computers, as well as telecommunication and Internet networks. Without advances in computer and telecommunication technologies, some innovations would not have been possible. Although financial products and trading strategies created by some market participants may be too complex for other market participants to use, the level of market sophistication, particularly in terms of mathematical understanding, has risen, permitting the acceptance of some complex products and trading strategies.

[5] Stephen A. Ross, "Institutional Markets, Financial Marketing, and Financial Innovation," *Journal of Finance* (July 1989), p. 541.
[6] Ian Cooper, "Financial Innovations: New Market Instruments," *Oxford Review of Economic Policy* (November 1986).
[7] Merton H. Miller, "Financial Innovation: The Last Twenty Years and the Next," *Journal of Financial and Quantitative Analysis* (December 1986), pp. 459–471.
[8] Cooper, "Financial Innovations," see Table 9. We add inflation to the first category described.

| Key Points That You Should Understand Before Proceeding |

1. The extent of the innovation in many financial markets, securities, and institutions over the last few decades.
2. The causes of innovation, such as the high level of volatility in prices and interest rates, the arrival of technology, the new intensity of competition, and the globalization of markets and institutions.

SUMMARY

In this chapter, we have explained the role of financial assets and financial markets. A financial asset (or financial instrument or security) entitles the owner to future cash flows to be paid by the issuer as well as to the liquidation value of the asset. The claim can be either an equity or debt claim. The price of any financial asset is equal to the present value of the cash flow expected. Because of uncertainty about the cash flow, in nominal and inflation-adjusted dollars, there is risk in investing in financial assets.

The two principal economic functions of a financial asset are (1) transferring funds from those who have surplus funds to invest to those who need funds to invest in tangible assets, and (2) transferring funds in such a way that redistributes the unavoidable risk associated with the cash flow generated by tangible assets among those seeking and those providing the funds.

Financial markets provide the following three additional functions beyond that of financial assets themselves: (1) they provide a mechanism for determining the price (or, equivalently, the required return) of financial assets, (2) they make assets more liquid, and (3) they reduce the costs of exchanging assets. The costs associated with transacting are search costs and information costs.

There are various ways to classify financial markets: money (or short-term) versus capital markets, debt versus equity markets, primary versus secondary markets, and cash versus derivative markets. Another classification is based on the type of organizational structure: auction versus over-the-counter versus intermediated markets.

The increased integration of financial markets throughout the world can be attributed to three factors: (1) deregulation or liberalization of major financial markets (market deregulation and institutional deregulation), (2) advances in telecommunications and computer technologies, and (3) institutionalization of financial markets. Global financial markets can be classified as the national market of a country, consisting of the domestic market and foreign market, and the external market (overseas or Euromarket).

A derivative instrument is a contract whose value depends on the value of the underlying financial asset. The chief economic function of a derivative instrument is to provide ways to control risk. Derivative markets may offer three advantages over cash markets: (1) lower transaction costs, (2) faster speed at which transactions can be completed, and (3) greater liquidity.

Regulation of the financial system and its various component sectors occurs in almost all countries. A useful way to organize the many instances of regulation is to see it as having four general forms: (1) enforcing the disclosure of relevant information, (2) regulating the level of financial activity through control of the money supply as well as trading in financial markets, (3) restricting the activities of financial institutions and their management of assets and liabilities, and (4) constraining the freedom of foreign investors and securities firms in domestic markets. The U.S. Department of the Treasury has proposed a major revamping of the regulatory system.

Financial innovation has increased dramatically since the 1960s, particularly in the late 1970s. While financial innovation can be the result of arbitrary regulations and tax rules, innovations that persist after regulations or tax rules have been changed to prevent exploitation are frequently those that have provided a more efficient means for redistributing risk.

KEY TERMS

- Agency problem
- Arbitrage
- Asset
- Asymmetric information
- Banking and monetary regulation
- Call option
- Capital market
- Competitive market
- Credit risk (default risk)
- Debt instrument
- Derivative instrument
- Disclosure regulation
- Domestic market
- Equity instrument (residual claim)
- External market (international market, offshore market, Euromarket)
- Financial activity regulation
- Financial asset

- Financial market
- Fixed-income instrument
- Foreign-exchange risk
- Foreign market
- Information costs
- Internal market (national market)
- Market failure
- Money market
- Price discovery process
- Purchasing power risk (inflation risk)
- Put option
- Regulation of financial institutions
- Regulation of foreign participants
- Search costs
- Secondary market
- Spot market (cash market)
- Tangible asset

QUESTIONS

1. What is the difference between a financial asset and a tangible asset?
2. What is the difference between the claim of a debtholder of General Motors and an equityholder of General Motors?
3. What is the basic principle in determining the price of a financial asset?
4. Why is it difficult to determine the cash flow of a financial asset?
5. Why are the characteristics of an issuer important in determining the price of a financial asset?
6. What are the two principal roles of financial assets?

7. In September 1990, a study by the U.S. Congress, Office of Technology Assessment, entitled "Electronic Bulls & Bears: U.S. Securities Markets and Information Technology," included this statement:

    Securities markets have five basic functions in a capitalistic economy:

    a. They make it possible for corporations and governmental units to raise capital.

    b. They help to allocate capital toward productive uses.

    c. They provide an opportunity for people to increase their savings by investing in them.

d. They reveal investors' judgments about the potential earning capacity of corporations, thus giving guidance to corporate managers.

e. They generate employment and income.

For each of the functions cited above, explain how financial markets (or securities markets, in the parlance of this Congressional study) perform each function.

8. Explain the difference between each of the following:

    a. money market and capital market

    b. primary market and secondary market

    c. domestic market and foreign market

    d. national market and Euromarket

9. Indicate whether each of the following instruments trades in the money market or the capital market:

    a. General Motors Acceptance Corporation issues a financial instrument with four months to maturity.

    b. The U.S. Treasury issues a security with 10 years to maturity.

    c. Microsoft Corporation issues common stock.

    d. The State of Alaska issues a financial instrument with eight months to maturity.

10. A U.S. investor who purchases the bonds issued by the government of France made the following comment: "Assuming that the French government does not default, I know what the cash flow of the bond will be." Explain why you agree or disagree with this statement.

11. A U.S. investor who purchases the bonds issued by the U.S. government made the following statement: "By buying this debt instrument I am not exposed to default risk or purchasing power

risk." Explain why you agree or disagree with this statement.

12. In January 1992, Atlantic Richfield Corporation, a U.S.-based corporation, issued $250 million of bonds in the United States. From the perspective of the U.S. financial market, indicate whether this issue is classified as being issued in the domestic market, the foreign market, or the offshore market.

13. In January 1992, the Korea Development Bank issued $500 million of bonds in the United States. From the perspective of the U.S. financial market, indicate whether this issue is classified as being issued in the domestic market, the foreign market, or the offshore market.

14. Give three reasons for the trend toward greater integration of financial markets throughout the world.

15. What is meant by the "institutionalization" of capital markets?

16. **a.** What are the two basic types of derivative instruments?

    b. "Derivative markets are nothing more than legalized gambling casinos and serve no economic function." Comment on this statement.

17. What is the economic rationale for the widespread use of disclosure regulation?

18. What is meant by market failure?

19. What is the major long-term regulatory reform that the U.S. Department of the Treasury has proposed?

20. Why does increased volatility in financial markets with respect to the price of financial assets, interest rates, and exchange rates foster financial innovation?

Financial Institutions, Financial Intermediaries, and Asset Management Firms

From Chapter 2 of *Foundations of Financial Markets and Institutions*, 4/e. Frank J. Fabozzi. Franco Modigliani. Frank J. Jones.

Financial Institutions, Financial Intermediaries, and Asset Management Firms

LEARNING OBJECTIVES

After reading this chapter, you will understand

- the business of financial institutions

- the role of financial intermediaries

- the difference between direct and indirect investments

- how financial intermediaries transform the maturity of liabilities and give both short-term depositors and longer-term, final borrowers what they want

- how financial intermediaries offer investors diversification and so reduce the risks of their investments

- the way financial intermediaries reduce the costs of acquiring information and entering into contracts with final borrowers of funds

- how financial intermediaries enjoy economies of scale in processing payments from final users of funds

- the nature of the management of assets and liabilities by financial intermediaries

- how different financial institutions have differing degrees of knowledge and certainty about the amount and timing of the cash outlay of their liabilities

- why financial institutions have liquidity concerns

- concerns regulators have with financial institutions

- the general characteristics of asset management firms

- the types of funds that asset management firms manage

- what a hedge fund is and the different types of hedge funds

I n this chapter, we discuss financial institutions and a special and important type of financial institution, a financial intermediary. Financial intermediaries include commercial banks, savings and loan associations, investment companies, insurance companies, and pension funds. The most important contribution of financial intermediaries is a steady and relatively inexpensive flow of funds from savers to final users or investors. Every modern economy has financial intermediaries, which perform key financial functions for individuals, households, corporations, small and new businesses, and governments. In the last part of this chapter, we provide an overview of the organizations that manage funds for financial intermediaries as well as individual investors: asset management firms.

FINANCIAL INSTITUTIONS

Business entities include nonfinancial and financial enterprises. Nonfinancial enterprises manufacture products (e.g., cars, steel, computers) and/or provide nonfinancial services (e.g., transportation, utilities, computer programming). Financial enterprises, more popularly referred to as **financial institutions**, provide services related to one or more of the following:

1. Transforming financial assets acquired through the market and constituting them into a different, and more widely preferable, type of asset—which becomes their liability. This is the function performed by **financial intermediaries**, the most important type of financial institution.
2. exchanging of financial assets on behalf of customers
3. exchanging of financial assets for their own accounts
4. assisting in the creation of financial assets for their customers, and then selling those financial assets to other market participants
5. providing investment advice to other market participants
6. managing the portfolios of other market participants

Financial intermediaries include **depository institutions** (commercial banks, savings and loan associations, savings banks, and credit unions), which acquire the bulk of their funds by offering their liabilities to the public mostly in the form of deposits; insurance companies (life and property and casualty companies); pension funds; and finance companies.

The second and third services in the list above are the broker and dealer functions. The fourth service is referred to as underwriting. Typically a financial institution that provides an underwriting service also provides a brokerage and/or dealer service.

Some nonfinancial enterprises have subsidiaries that provide financial services. For example, many large manufacturing firms have subsidiaries that provide financing for the parent company's customer. These financial institutions are called *captive finance companies*. Examples include General Motors Acceptance Corporation (a subsidiary of General Motors) and General Electric Credit Corporation (a subsidiary of General Electric).

Key Points That You Should Understand Before Proceeding

1. The services provided by financial institutions.
2. The special role played by a financial intermediary when it transforms assets acquired from customers or the market into its own liabilities.

ROLE OF FINANCIAL INTERMEDIARIES

As we have seen, financial intermediaries obtain funds by issuing financial claims against themselves to market participants, and then investing those funds. The investments made by financial intermediaries—their assets—can be in loans and/or securities. These investments are referred to as **direct investments**. Market participants who hold the financial claims issued by financial intermediaries are said to have made **indirect investments**.

Two examples will illustrate this. Most readers of this book are familiar with what a **commercial bank** does. Commercial banks accept deposits and may use the proceeds to lend funds to consumers and businesses. The deposits represent the IOU of the commercial bank and a financial asset owned by the depositor. The loan represents an IOU of the borrowing entity and a financial asset of the commercial bank. The commercial bank has made a direct investment in the borrowing entity; the depositor effectively has made an indirect investment in that borrowing entity.

As a second example, consider an **investment company** which pools the funds of market participants and uses those funds to buy a portfolio of securities such as stocks and bonds. Investment companies are more commonly referred to as "mutual funds." Investors providing funds to the investment company receive an equity claim that entitles the investor to a pro rata share of the outcome of the portfolio. The equity claim is issued by the investment company. The **portfolio** of financial assets acquired by the investment company represents a direct investment that it has made. By owning an equity claim against the investment company, those who invest in the investment company have made an indirect investment.

We have stressed that financial intermediaries play the basic role of transforming financial assets that are less desirable for a large part of the public into other financial assets—their own liabilities—which are more widely preferred by the public. This transformation involves at least one of four economic functions: (1) providing maturity intermediation, (2) reducing risk via diversification, (3) reducing the costs of contracting and information processing, and (4) providing a payments mechanism. Each function is described below.

Maturity Intermediation

In our example of the commercial bank, two things should be noted. First, the maturity of at least a portion of the deposits accepted is typically short term. For example, certain types of deposit are payable upon demand. Others have a specific maturity date, but most are less than two years. Second, the maturity of the loans made by a commercial bank may be considerably longer than two years. In the absence of a commercial bank, the borrower would have to borrow for a shorter term, or find an entity that is willing to invest for the length of the loan sought, and/or investors who make deposits in the bank would have to commit funds for a longer length of time than they want. The commercial bank, by issuing its own financial claims, in essence transforms a longer-term asset into a shorter-term one by giving the borrower a loan for the length of time sought and the investor/depositor a financial asset for the desired investment horizon. This function of a financial intermediary is called **maturity intermediation**.

Maturity intermediation has two implications for financial markets. First, it provides investors with more choices concerning maturity for their investments; borrowers have more choices for the length of their debt obligations. Second, because investors are naturally reluctant to commit funds for a long period of time, they will require that long-term borrowers pay a higher interest rate than on short-term borrowing. A financial intermediary is willing to make longer-term loans, and at a lower cost to the borrower than an individual investor would, by counting on successive deposits providing the funds until maturity (although at some risk—see below). Thus, the second implication is that the cost of longer-term borrowing is likely to be reduced.

Reducing Risk via Diversification

Consider the example of the investor who places funds in an investment company. Suppose that the investment company invests the funds received in the stock of a large number of companies. By doing so, the investment company has diversified and reduced its risk. Investors who have a small sum to invest would find it difficult to achieve the same degree of **diversification** because they do not have sufficient funds to buy shares of a large number of companies. Yet, by investing in the investment company for the same sum of money, investors can accomplish this diversification, thereby reducing risk.

This economic function of financial intermediaries—transforming more risky assets into less risky ones—is called *diversification*. Although individual investors can do it on their own, they may not be able to do it as cost-effectively as a financial intermediary, depending on the amount of funds they have to invest. Attaining cost-effective diversification in order to reduce risk by purchasing the financial assets of a financial intermediary is an important economic benefit for financial markets.

Reducing the Costs of Contracting and Information Processing

Investors purchasing financial assets should take the time to develop skills necessary to understand how to evaluate an investment. Once those skills are developed, investors should apply them to the analysis of specific financial assets that are candidates for purchase (or subsequent sale). Investors who want to make a loan to a consumer or business will need to write the loan contract (or hire an attorney to do so).

Although there are some people who enjoy devoting leisure time to this task, most prefer to use that time for just that—leisure. Most of us find that leisure time is in short supply, so to sacrifice it, we have to be compensated. The form of compensation could be a higher return that we obtain from an investment.

In addition to the opportunity cost of the time to process the information about the financial asset and its issuer, there is the cost of acquiring that information. All these costs are called *information processing costs*. The costs of writing loan contracts are referred to as **contracting costs**. There is also another dimension to contracting costs, the cost of enforcing the terms of the loan agreement.

With this in mind, consider our two examples of financial intermediaries—the commercial bank and the investment company. People who work for these intermediaries include investment professionals who are trained to analyze financial assets and manage them. In the case of loan agreements, either standardized contracts can be prepared, or legal counsel can be part of the professional staff that writes contracts involving more complex transactions. The investment professionals can monitor compliance with the terms of the loan agreement and take any necessary action to protect the interests of the financial intermediary. The employment of such professionals is cost-effective for financial intermediaries because investing funds is their normal business.

In other words, there are economies of scale in contracting and processing information about financial assets because of the amount of funds managed by financial intermediaries. The lower costs accrue to the benefit of the investor who purchases a financial claim of the financial intermediary and to the issuers of financial assets, who benefit from a lower borrowing cost.

Providing a Payments Mechanism

Although the previous three economic functions may not have been immediately obvious, this last function should be. Most transactions made today are not done with cash. Instead, payments are made using checks, credit cards, debit cards, and electronic transfers of funds. These methods for making payments, called **payment mechanisms**, are provided by certain financial intermediaries.

At one time, noncash payments were restricted to checks written against non–interest-bearing accounts at commercial banks. Similar check writing privileges were provided later by savings and loan associations and savings banks, and by certain types of investment companies. Payment by credit card was also at one time the exclusive domain of commercial banks, but now other depository institutions offer this service. Debit cards are offered by various financial intermediaries. A debit card differs from a credit card in that, in the latter case, a bill is sent to the credit card holder periodically (usually once a month) requesting payment for transactions made in the past. In the case of a **debit card**, funds are immediately withdrawn (that is, debited) from the purchaser's account at the time the transaction takes place.

The ability to make payments without the use of cash is critical for the functioning of a financial market. In short, depository institutions transform assets that cannot be used to make payments into other assets that offer that property.

Key Points That You Should Understand Before Proceeding

1. The difference between a direct investment and an indirect investment.
2. How a financial institution intermediates among investors and borrowers in the area of maturity, reduces risk and offers diversification, reduces the costs of contracting and information processing, and provides payment mechanisms.

OVERVIEW OF ASSET/LIABILITY MANAGEMENT FOR FINANCIAL INSTITUTIONS

To understand the reasons managers of financial institutions invest in particular types of financial assets and the types of investment strategies they employ, it is necessary to have a general understanding of the asset/liability problem faced. In this section, we provide an overview of **asset/liability management**.

The nature of the liabilities dictates the investment strategy a financial institution will pursue. For example, depository institutions seek to generate income by the spread between the return that they earn on assets and the cost of their funds. That is, they buy money and sell money. They buy money by borrowing from depositors or other sources of funds. They sell money when they lend it to businesses or individuals. In essence, they are spread businesses. Their objective is to sell money for more than it costs to buy money. The cost of the funds and the return on the funds sold is expressed in terms of an interest rate per unit of time. Consequently, the objective of a depository institution is to earn a positive *spread* between the assets it invests in (what it has sold the money for) and the costs of its funds (what it has purchased the money for).

Life insurance companies—and, to a certain extent, property and casualty insurance companies—are in the spread business. Pension funds are not in the spread business in that they do not raise funds themselves in the market. They seek to cover the cost of pension obligations at a minimum cost that is borne by the sponsor of the pension plan. Investment companies face no explicit costs for the funds they acquire and must satisfy no specific liability obligations; one exception is a particular type of investment company that agrees to repurchase shares at any time.

Nature of Liabilities

By the **liabilities** of a financial institution, we mean the amount and timing of the cash outlays that must be made to satisfy the contractual terms of the obligations issued. The liabilities of any financial institution can be categorized according to four types as shown in Table 1. The categorization in the table assumes that the entity that must be paid the obligation will not cancel the financial institution's obligation prior to any actual or projected payout date.

The descriptions of cash outlays as either known or uncertain are undoubtedly broad. When we refer to a cash outlay as being uncertain, we do not mean that it cannot be predicted. There are some liabilities where the "law of large numbers" makes it easier to predict the timing and/or amount of cash outlays. This is the work typically done by actuaries, but of course even actuaries cannot predict natural catastrophes such as floods and earthquakes.

Keep these risk categories in mind. For now, let's illustrate each one.

Type-I Liabilities

Both the amount and the timing of the liabilities are known with certainty. A liability requiring a financial institution to pay $50,000 six months from now would be an example. For example, depository institutions know the amount that they are committed to pay (principal plus interest) on the maturity date of a fixed-rate deposit, assuming that the depositor does not withdraw funds prior to the maturity date.

Table 1 Nature of Liabilities of Financial Institutions		
Liability Type	Amount of Cash Outlay	Timing of Cash Outlay
Type I	Known	Known
Type II	Known	Uncertain
Type III	Uncertain	Known
Type IV	Uncertain	Uncertain

Type-I liabilities, however, are not limited to depository institutions. A major product sold by life insurance companies is a **guaranteed investment contract**, popularly referred to as a **GIC**. The obligation of the life insurance company under this contract is that, for a sum of money (called a premium), it will guarantee an interest rate up to some specified maturity date.[1] For example, suppose a life insurance company for a premium of $10 million issues a five-year GIC agreeing to pay 10% compounded annually. The life insurance company knows that it must pay $16.11 million to the GIC policyholder in five years.[2]

Type-II Liabilities

The amount of cash outlay is known, but the timing of the cash outlay is uncertain. The most obvious example of a Type-II liability is a life insurance policy. There are many types of life insurance policies, but the most basic type is that, for an annual premium, a life insurance company agrees to make a specified dollar payment to policy beneficiaries upon the death of the insured.

Type-III Liabilities

With this type of liability, the timing of the cash outlay is known, but the amount is uncertain. An example is where a financial institution has issued an obligation in which the interest rate adjusts periodically according to some interest rate benchmark. Depository institutions, for example, issue accounts called **certificates of deposit (CD)**, which have a stated maturity. The interest rate paid need not be fixed over the life of the deposit but may fluctuate. If a depository institution issues a three-year floating-rate certificate of deposit that adjusts every three months and the interest rate paid is the three-month Treasury bill rate plus one percentage point, the depository institution knows it has a liability that must be paid off in three years, but the dollar amount of the liability is not known. It will depend on three-month Treasury bill rates over the three years.

Type-IV Liabilities

There are numerous insurance products and pension obligations that present uncertainty as to both the amount and the timing of the cash outlay. Probably the most obvious examples are automobile and home insurance policies issued by property and casualty insurance companies. When, and if, a payment will have to be made to the policyholder is uncertain. Whenever damage is done to an insured asset, the amount of the payment that must be made is uncertain.

Sponsors of pension plans can agree to various types of pension obligations to the beneficiaries of the plan. There are plans where retirement benefits depend on the participant's income for a specified number of years before retirement and the total number of years the participant worked. This will affect the amount of the cash outlay. The timing of the cash outlay depends on when the employee elects to retire, and whether or not the employee remains with the sponsoring plan until retirement. Moreover, both the amount and the timing will depend on how the employee elects to have payments made—over only the employee's life or those of the employee and spouse.

---

[1] A GIC does not seem like a product that we would associate with a life insurance company because the policyholder does not have to die in order for someone to be paid. Yet a major group of insurance company financial products is in the pension benefit area. A GIC is one such product.

[2] This amount is determined as follows: $10,000,000 (1.10)^5$.

Liquidity Concerns

Because of uncertainty about the timing and/or the amount of the cash outlays, a financial institution must be prepared to have sufficient cash to satisfy its obligations. Also keep in mind that our discussion of liabilities assumes that the entity that holds the obligation against the financial institution may have the right to change the nature of the obligation, perhaps incurring some penalty. For example, in the case of a certificate of deposit, the depositor may request the withdrawal of funds prior to the maturity date. Typically, the deposit-accepting institution will grant this request but assess an early withdrawal penalty. In the case of certain types of investment companies, shareholders have the right to redeem their shares at any time.

Some life insurance products have a cash-surrender value. This means that, at specified dates, the policyholder can exchange the policy for a lump-sum payment. Typically, the lump-sum payment will penalize the policyholder for turning in the policy. There are some life insurance products that have a loan value, which means that the policyholder has the right to borrow against the cash value of the policy.

In addition to uncertainty about the timing and amount of the cash outlays, and the potential for the depositor or policyholder to withdraw cash early or borrow against a policy, a financial institution has to be concerned with possible reduction in cash inflows. In the case of a depository institution, this means the inability to obtain deposits. For insurance companies, it means reduced premiums because of the cancellation of policies. For certain types of investment companies, it means not being able to find new buyers for shares.

Regulations and Taxation

Numerous regulations and tax considerations influence the investment policies that financial institutions pursue.

Key Points That You Should Understand Before Proceeding

1. What is meant by a financial institution being in the spread business.
2. The two dimensions of the liabilities of a financial institution: amount of the cash outlay and the timing of the cash outlay.
3. Why a financial institution must be prepared to have sufficient cash to satisfy liabilities.

CONCERNS OF REGULATORS

Here, we will provide a brief discussion of the risks that regulators have regarding financial institutions. These risks can be classified into the following sources of risk:

- credit risk
- settlement risk
- market risk
- liquidity risk
- operational risk
- legal risk

Credit risk is a broadly used term to describe several types of risk. In terms of regulatory concerns, credit risk is the risk that the obligor of a financial instrument held by a financial institution will fail to fulfill its obligation on the due date or at any time thereafter.

According to the International Financial Risk Institute, **settlement risk** is the risk that when there is a settlement of a trade or obligation, the transfer fails to take place as expected. Settlement risk consists of counterparty risk (a form of credit risk) and a form of liquidity risk.

Counterparty risk is the risk that a counterparty in a trade fails to satisfy its obligation. The trade could involve the cash settlement of a contract or the physical delivery of some asset. **Liquidity risk** in the context of settlement risk means that the counterparty can eventually meet its obligation, but not at the due date. As a result, the party failing to receive timely payment must be prepared to finance any shortfall in the contractual payment.

Market risk is the risk to a financial institution's economic well-being that results from an adverse movement in the market price of assets (debt obligations, equities, commodities, currencies) it owns or the level or the volatility of market prices. There are measures that can be used to gauge this risk. One such measure endorsed by bank regulators is **value-at-risk**, a measure of the potential loss in a financial institution's financial position associated with an adverse price movement of a given probability over a specified time horizon.

Liquidity risk, in addition to being a part of settlement risk, has two forms according to the International Financial Risk Institute. The first is the risk that a financial institution is unable to transact in a financial instrument at a price near its market value. This risk is called **market liquidity risk**. The other form of liquidity risk is **funding liquidity risk**. This is the risk that the financial institution will be unable to obtain funding to obtain cash flow necessary to satisfy its obligations.

An important risk that is often overlooked but has been the cause of the demise of some major financial institutions is operational risk. Well-known examples in the past two decades include Orange County (1994, United States), Barings Bank (1995, United Kingdom), Daiwa Bank (1995, New York), Allied Irish Banks (2002, Ireland), Enron (2001, United States), MasterCard International (2005, United States), and the terrorist attack in New York on September 11, 2001.[3] **Operational risk** is defined by bank regulators as "the risk of loss resulting from inadequate or failed internal processes, people and systems, or from external events."[4] The definition of operation risk includes **legal risk**. This is the risk of loss resulting from failure to comply with laws as well as prudent ethical standards and contractual obligations.

The Global Association of Risk Professionals (GARP) suggests classifying the major categories of operational risk according to the cause of the loss event as follows:

1. employee: loss events resulting from the actions or inactions of a person who works for a firm
2. business process: loss events arising from a firm's execution of business operations

---

[3] For a description of each of these examples, see Chapter 1 in Anna Chernobai, Svetlozar T. Rachev, and Frank J. Fabozzi, *Operational Risk: A Guide to Basel II Capital Requirements, Models and Analysis* (Hoboken, NJ: John Wiley & Sons, 2007).

[4] This is the common industry definition that has been adopted by the Bank for International Settlements. See Basel Committee on Banking Supervision, *Operational Risk*, Consultative Document, Bank for International Settlements, January 2001.

3. relationships: loss events caused by the connection or contact that a firm has with clients, regulators, or third parties. This category focuses on the interaction between a firm and other entities; relationship risks involve both parties

4. technology: loss events due to piracy, theft, failure, breakdown, or other disruption in technology, data or information. This category also includes technology that fails to meet the intended business needs

5. external: loss events caused by people or entities outside a firm; the firm cannot control their actions[5]

The five categories above apply to nonfinancial entities as well as financial institutions.

Several reports by regulators have recommended guidelines for controlling the risks of financial institutions described above. One key report is the "Derivatives: Practices and Principles" prepared by the Group of 30 in 1993.[6,7] Derivatives are used to control risks. Their use by end-users such as financial institutions and by dealers (commercial banks and investment banking firms) that are the counterparty for many types of derivatives is of great concern to regulators. As indicated by its title, the focus of the Group of 30 report is on derivatives. The report provides guidelines to help financial institutions and dealers in derivatives to manage derivatives activity in order to benefit from the use of these derivatives.

These guidelines fall into five categories: (1) general policies for senior management; (2) valuation and market risk management; (3) credit risk measurement and management; (4) systems, operations, and control; and (5) recommendations for legislators, regulators, and supervisors.

Key Points That You Should Understand Before Proceeding

1. The concerns of regulators involve credit risk, settlement risk, market risk, liquidity risk, operational risk, and legal risk.
2. Several reports by regulators have recommended guidelines for controlling the risks of financial institutions.

ASSET MANAGEMENT FIRMS

Asset management firms manage the funds of individuals, businesses, endowments and foundations, and state and local governments. These firms are also referred to as money management firms and fund management firms and those who manage the funds are referred to as asset managers, money managers, fund managers, and portfolio managers.

---

[5] Gene Álvarez, "Operational Risk Event Classification," published on the GARP website, www.garp.com.
[6] The Group of 30 is a private, nonprofit international organization seeking to "deepen understanding of international economic and financial issues, to explore the international repercussions of decisions taken in the public and private sectors, and to examine the choices available to market practitioners and policymakers."
[7] Two other key reports are the "Risk Management Guidelines for Derivatives" prepared jointly by the Basel Committee on Banking Supervision of the Bank of International Settlements and the International Organisation of Securities Commissions in 1994 and "Framework for the Evaluation of Internal Control Systems" prepared by the BIS in 1998.

Asset management firms are either affiliated with some financial institution (such as a commercial bank, insurance company, or investment bank) or are independent companies.

Larger institutional clients seeking the services of an asset management firm typically do not allocate all of their assets to one asset management firm. Instead, they typically diversify amongst several asset management firms, as well as possibly managing some portion of their funds internally. One reason for using several asset management firms is that firms differ in their expertise with respect to asset classes. For example, a client that seeks an asset manager to invest in common stock, bonds, real estate, and alternative investments (such as commodities and hedge funds) will use asset management firms that specialize in each of those asset classes.

Asset management firms are ranked annually by *Pension & Investments*. The ranking is based on the amount of **assets under management (AUM)**. On October 1, 2007, *Pension & Investments* reported that UBS AG (Switzerland) was the largest asset management firm in the world with AUM as of December 31, 2006, of almost $2.5 trillion, followed by Barclays Global Investors (United Kingdom) with AUM of about about $1.9 trillion. The eight largest U.S. asset management firms along with their global ranking and AUM are

Asset Management Firm	AUM (U.S. dollar millions)	Global Ranking
State Street Global Advisors	$1,748,690	3
Fidelity Investments	$1,635,128	6
Capital Group	$1,403,854	7
Vanguard Group	$1,167,414	9
BlackRock	$1,124,627	10
JPMorgan Chase	$1,013,729	12
Mellon Financial	$ 995,237	13
Legg Mason	$ 957,558	14

Asset management firms receive their compensation primarily from management fees charged based on the market value of the assets managed for clients. For example, if an asset manager manages $100 million for a client and the fee is 60 basis points, then the annual dollar management fee is $600,000 ($100 million times 0.0060). Management fees typically vary with the amount managed, the complexity of managing the asset class, whether the assets are actively managed or passively managed, and whether the account is an institutional account or individual account. Moreover, the management fee is typically higher for managing the assets of regulated investment companies than for other institutional clients.

While performance fees are common for hedge funds that we discuss later, asset management firms are increasingly adopting **performance-based management fees** for other types of accounts.[8] There are many types of performance-fee structures in the asset management industry. There can be a fee based solely on performance or a combination of a fixed fee based on assets managed plus a performance-based fee. An example of the latter is a fee structure whereby the asset manager receives 80 basis points of the assets managed

---

[8] Robert D. Arnott, "Performance Fees: The Good, the Bad, and the (Occasionally) Ugly," *Financial Analysts Journal* (July–August 2005), p. 10.

plus a fee of 20% of the return earned on those assets. The criterion for determining a performance-based fee varies. For example, the fee can be based on any positive return, the excess over a minimum return established by the client, or the excess over a benchmark (i.e., some index for the asset class) established by the client.

Types of funds managed by asset management firms include:

- regulated investment companies
- insurance company funds
- separately managed accounts for individuals and institutional investors
- pension funds
- hedge funds

Asset management firms are typically involved in managing the assets of several of the above. Below, we focus on just one type: hedge funds. The other types are discussed in more detail in later chapters.

Hedge Funds

It would be nice to provide a definition of what a hedge fund is by, say, using how it is defined by the federal securities law. However, there is no such definition available, nor is there any universally accepted definition to describe the 9,000 privately pooled investment entities in the United States called "hedge funds" that invest more than $1.3 trillion in assets.

The term *hedge fund* was first used by *Fortune* in 1966 to describe the private investment fund of Alfred Winslow Jones. In managing the portfolio, Jones sought to "hedge" the market risk of the fund by creating a portfolio that was long and short the stock market by an equal amount. Shorting the stock market means selling stock that is not owned with the expectation that the price will decline in the future. The point is that constructing the investment funds portfolio in that way, the portfolio was said to be "hedged" against stock market risk. Moreover, Jones determined that under the U.S. securities law his private investment partnership would not be regulated by the SEC if the investors were "accredited investors." The securities laws define an accredited investor as an investor who does not need protection offered other investors by filings with the SEC.[9] As of this writing, hedge funds are still not regulated by the SEC.

Let's look at some definitions for hedge funds that have been proposed. George Soros is the chairman of Soros Fund Management. His firm advises a privately owned group of hedge funds, the Quantum Group of Funds. He defines a hedge fund as follows:

> Hedge funds engage in a variety of investment activities. They cater to sophisticated investors and are not subject to the regulations that apply to mutual funds geared toward the general public. Fund managers are compensated on the basis of performance rather than as a fixed percentage of assets. "Performance funds" would be a more accurate description.[10]

---

[9] There are much more specific criteria set forth in the Securities Act of 1933 for an investor to be classified as an accredited investor. The details are not important for us in our discussion.

[10] George Soros, *Open Society: Reforming Global Capitalism* (New York: Publish Affairs, 2000), p. 32.

The President's Working Group on Financial Markets, a group created by then-President Ronald Reagan and consisting of the Secretary of the Treasury and chairpersons of the Board of Governors of the Federal Reserve Board, the SEC, and the Commodity Futures Trading Commission, provides the following definition:

> The term "hedge fund" is commonly used to describe a variety of different types of investment vehicles that share some common characteristics. Although it is not statutorily defined, the term encompasses any pooled investment vehicle that is privately organized, administered by professional money managers, and not widely available to the public.[11]

A useful definition based on the characteristics of hedge funds is the following provided by the United Kingdom's Financial Services Authority, the regulatory body of all providers of financial services in that country:

> The term can also be defined by considering the characteristics most commonly associated with hedge funds. Usually, hedge funds:
>
> * are organized as private investment partnerships or offshore investment corporations;
> * use a wide variety of trading strategies involving position-taking in a range of markets;
> * employ an assortment of trading techniques and instruments, often including short-selling, derivatives and leverage;
> * pay performance fees to their managers; and
> * have an investor base comprising wealthy individuals and institutions and a relatively high minimum investment limit (set at U.S. $100,000 or higher for most funds).[12]

From the above definition, we can take away the following four points about *hedge* funds. First, the word *hedge* in hedge funds is misleading. While that may have been appropriate in characterizing the fund managed by Alfred Winslow Jones, it is not a characteristic of hedge funds today.

Second, hedge funds use a wide range of trading strategies and techniques in an attempt to earn superior returns. The strategies used by a hedge fund can include one or more of the following:

* leverage, which is the use of borrowed funds
* short selling, which is the sale of a financial instrument not owned in anticipation of a decline in that financial instrument's price
* arbitrage, which is the simultaneous buying and selling of related financial instruments to realize a profit from the temporary misalignment of their prices
* risk control, which involves the use of financial instruments such as derivatives to reduce the risk of loss

---

[11] Report of The President's Work Group on Financial Markets, *Hedge Funds, Leverage, and the Lessons of Long-Term Capital Management*, April 1999, p. 1.
[12] Financial Services Authority, *Hedge Funds and the FSA*, Discussion Paper 16, 2002, p. 8.

Risk control is more general than hedging. In a hedge, one often thinks about the elimination of a risk. Risk control means that a risk is mitigated to the degree desired by the investor. Very few hedge funds employ "hedging" in the sense of the elimination of all risks.

Third, hedge funds operate in all of the financial markets described in this book: cash market for stocks, bonds, and currencies and the derivatives markets. Fourth, the management fee structure for hedge funds is a combination of a fixed fee based on the market value of assets managed plus a share of the positive return. The latter is a performance-based compensation referred to as an **incentive fee.**

Finally, in evaluating hedge funds, investors are interested in the absolute return generated by the asset manager, not the relative return. **Absolute return** on a portfolio is simply the return realized. The **relative return** is the difference between the absolute return and the return on some benchmark or index. The use of absolute return rather than relative return for evaluating an asset manager's performance in managing a hedge fund is quite different from the criterion used when evaluating the performance of an asset manager in managing the other types of portfolios discussed in this chapter.

Types of Hedge Funds

There are various ways to categorize the different types of hedge funds. Mark Anson uses the following four broad categories: market directional, corporate restructuring, convergence trading, and opportunistic.[13] A complete description of each category is difficult at this early stage in our understanding of financial markets and instruments, so we will give a general description here.[14]

Market Directional Hedge Funds. A **market directional hedge fund** is one in which the asset manager retains some exposure to "systematic risk." Systematic risk is simply the risk that cannot be eliminated by holding a diversified portfolio of financial instruments. Within the category of market directional hedge funds there are hedge funds that pursue the following strategies: equity long/short strategies, equity market timing, and short selling.

Corporate Restructuring Hedge Funds. A **corporate restructuring hedge fund** is one in which the asset manager positions the portfolio to capitalize on the anticipated impact of a significant corporate event. These events include a merger, acquisition, or bankruptcy. Hedge funds that fall into this category fall into three groups.

The first group includes hedge funds that invest in the securities of a corporation that is either in bankruptcy or is highly likely in the opinion of the asset manager to be forced into bankruptcy. The securities of such corporate entities are called *distressed securities*. The hope is to identify distressed securities that are undervalued relative to what the asset manager believes will result from the outcome of the bankruptcy proceedings.

The second group includes hedge funds that focus on what is called *merger arbitrage*. The underlying rationale for merger arbitrage is that in a merger the stock price of the target company usually trades below the price being offered by the acquiring company. Thus,

---

[13] Mark J.P. Anson, *Handbook of Alternative Assets*, 2nd ed. (Hoboken, NJ: John Wiley & Sons, 2006).

[14] For a discussion of the investment risks of hedge funds, see Ellen J. Rachlin, "Assessing Hedge Fund Investment Risk Common Hedge Fund Strategies," in Frank J. Fabozzi (ed.), *Handbook of Finance: Volume II* (Hoboken, NJ: John Wiley & Sons, 2008).

if the stock of the target company is purchased and the merger is in fact completed, there will be a profit equal to the difference between the price paid by the acquiring company and the market price at which the stock is purchased prior to the merger. The risk is that the merger will not be consummated and the stock price of the target company will decline.

The third group of corporate restructuring hedge funds includes hedge funds that seek to capitalize on other types of broader sets of events impacting a corporation. In addition to mergers and bankruptcy, such events include acquisitions, reorganizations, accounting write-offs, share buybacks, and special dividends.

Convergence Trading Hedge Funds. Certain relationships between prices and yields have been observed in sectors of the financial market. For example, the difference in the spread between the yields offered on two types of bond in the bond market might be within a certain range. If an assumed relationship between the prices or yields of securities are out of line and are expected to realign to the historical relationship, then there is an opportunity to capitalize on this expectation. When the relationship is such that the misalignment will generate a profit with absolutely no risk, the strategy employed to take advantage of the misalignment of prices or yields is referred to as an **arbitrage strategy**. In this strategy, the outcome is said to be a *riskless profit* and, hence, some market observers refer to this as a **riskless arbitrage strategy**, although the term *riskless* is redundant. Arbitrage opportunities as just described are rare, and when they do exist, they are usually eliminated quickly. A hedge fund that has as its objective taking advantage of such opportunities will find it difficult to stay in business.

In contrast, there are some perceived misalignments of prices or yields that may be more than temporary. They may in fact reflect a reconsideration by participants in the financial market of economic factors that have altered some historically observed relationship. In such cases, the risk of trying to capitalize on any misalignment of prices or yields is that there will not be the expected realignment of prices or yields. Because the asset managers of a hedge fund may use what is believed to be a "low-risk" strategy to capitalize on perceived misalignments of prices or yields, they unfortunately refer to this strategy as a **risk arbitrage strategy**. Since such strategies involve perceived misalignments of prices and yields to move back to or "converge" to the expected relationship, these hedge funds are referred to as **convergence trading hedge funds**.

The groups of hedge funds that fall into the category of convergence trading hedge funds are fixed-income arbitrage hedge funds, convertible bond arbitrage hedge funds, equity market neutral hedge funds, statistical arbitrage hedge funds, and relative value hedge funds.

Opportunistic Hedge Funds. **Opportunistic hedge funds** have the broadest mandate of all of the four hedge fund categories. Asset managers of hedge funds can make specific bets on stocks or currencies or they could have well-diversified portfolios. There are two groups of hedge funds that fall into this category: global macro hedge funds and funds of funds.

Global macro hedge funds are hedge funds that invest opportunistically based on macro-economic considerations in any market in the world. Probably the best-known hedge fund that falls into this group of hedge funds is the Quantum Hedge Fund. Here are two well-documented strategies that the asset managers of this hedge fund employed that produced significant profits. Based on macroeconomic conditions in 1992 in the United Kingdom, the hedge fund bet on the devaluation of the British currency, the pound sterling. The

British government did in fact devalue. In 1997, the hedge fund's macroeconomic analysis indicated that the currency of Thailand, the baht, was overvalued and would be devalued by the government of Thailand. The bet it made on the currency was right. The government of Thailand did devalue the baht.

Concerns with Hedge Funds in Financial Markets

There is considerable debate on the role of hedge funds in financial markets because of their size and their impact on financial markets that results from their investment strategies. On the positive side, it has been argued that they provide liquidity to the market. A study of the Federal Reserve Bank found that market participants described hedge funds "as a significant stability force" in the interest rate options markets.[15] Hedge funds have provided liquidity by participating in the municipal bond market.

The concern, however, is the risk of a severe financial crisis (i.e., systemic risk) due to the activities and investment strategies of hedge funds, most notably the employment of excess leverage. The best-known example is the collapse of Long-Term Capital Management (LTCM) in September 1998. Studies of LTCM indicate that it used leverage of 50. This means that for every $1 million of capital provided by investors, LTCM was able to borrow $49 million. The reason why LTCM was able to borrow such a large amount was because lenders did not understand or ignored the huge risks associated with that hedge fund's investment strategies. The loss of LTCM because of bad bets is not a concern per se since the investors in that hedge fund were sophisticated investors who took their chances in the hopes of reaping substantial returns. Rather, the problem was that the real losers of that hedge fund's activities were major commercial banks and investment banking firms that loaned funds to LTCM. In the view of the Federal Reserve, there were potential dire consequences from the potential failure of LTCM and it reacted by organizing a rescue plan for that hedge fund.

More recently, in June 2007, there was the collapse of the two hedge funds sponsored by the investment banking firm Bear Stearns: the High-Grade Structured Credit Strategies Enhanced Leverage Fund and the High-Grade Structured Credit Strategies Fund. This required the sponsor, Bear Stearns, to bail out the hedge fund.[16]

As a result of the LTCM failure, the President's Working Group on Financial Markets made several recommendations for improving the functioning of hedge funds in financial markets. The major recommendation was that commercial banks and investment banks that lend to hedge funds improve their credit risk management practices.

| SUMMARY

Financial institutions provide various types of financial services. Financial intermediaries are a special group of financial institutions that obtain funds by issuing claims to market participants and use these funds to purchase financial assets. Intermediaries transform funds they acquire into assets that are more attractive to the public. By doing so, financial

---

[15] Federal Reserve Board, *Concentration and Risk in the OTC Markets for U.S. Dollar Interest Rate Options*, p. 3.
[16] The funds primarily invested in subprime mortgages.

intermediaries do one or more of the following: (1) provide maturity intermediation, (2) provide risk reduction via diversification at lower cost, (3) reduce the cost of contracting and information processing, or (4) provide a payments mechanism.

The nature of their liabilities, as well as regulatory and tax considerations, determines the investment strategy pursued by all financial institutions. The liabilities of all financial institutions will generally fall into one of the four types shown in Table 1.

There are several sources of risk of concern to regulators in their regulation of financial institutions. These sources of risk include credit risk, settlement risk, market risk, liquidity risk, operational risk, and legal risk. Several reports by regulators have recommended guidelines for controlling the risks of financial institutions.

Asset management firms are involved in the management of funds for individuals, businesses, state and local government entities, and endowments and foundations. They generate income from fees based on the market value of the assets they manage and/or performance fees. One type of product line for an asset management firm is a hedge fund. While there are no universally accepted definitions for private investment entities that are referred to as "hedge funds," these entities have in common the use of leverage, short selling, arbitrage, and risk control in seeking to generate superior returns. Despite the term *hedge* in describing these entities, they do not completely hedge their positions. Asset managers of hedge funds receive performance-based compensation (incentive fee) plus a fee based on the market of the value of the assets. Hedge funds can be categorized as market directional, corporate restructuring, convergence trading, and opportunistic. The public policy concern with hedge funds has been the excessive use of leverage.

KEY TERMS

- Absolute return
- Arbitrage strategy
- Asset/liability management
- Assets under management (AUM)
- Certificate of deposit (CD)
- Commercial bank
- Contracting cost
- Convergence trading hedge funds
- Corporate restructuring hedge fund
- Counterparty risk
- Credit risk
- Debit card
- Depository institutions
- Direct investments
- Diversification
- Financial institution
- Financial intermediary
- Funding liquidity risk
- Guaranteed investment contract (GIC)

- Incentive fee
- Indirect investments
- Investment company
- Legal risk
- Liability
- Liquidity risk
- Market directional hedge fund
- Market liquidity risk
- Market risk
- Maturity intermediation
- Operational risk
- Opportunistic hedge funds
- Payment mechanisms
- Performance-based management fees
- Portfolio
- Relative return
- Risk arbitrage strategy
- Riskless arbitrage strategy
- Settlement risk
- Value-at-risk

QUESTIONS

1. Why is the holding of a claim on a financial intermediary by an investor considered an indirect investment in another entity?

2. The Insightful Management Company sells financial advice to investors. This is the only service provided by the company. Is this company a financial intermediary? Explain your answer.

3. Explain how a financial intermediary reduces the cost of contracting and information processing.

4. "All financial intermediaries provide the same economic functions. Therefore, the same investment strategy should be used in the management of all financial intermediaries." Indicate whether or not you agree or disagree with this statement.

5. A bank issues an obligation to depositors in which it agrees to pay 8% guaranteed for one year. With the funds it obtains, the bank can invest in a wide range of financial assets. What is the risk if the bank uses the funds to invest in common stock?

6. Look at Table 1 again. Match the types of liabilities to these four assets that an individual might have:
   a. car insurance policy
   b. variable-rate certificate of deposit
   c. fixed-rate certificate of deposit
   d. a life insurance policy that allows the holder's beneficiary to receive $100,000 when the holder dies; however, if the death is accidental, the beneficiary will receive $150,000

7. Each year, millions of American investors pour billions of dollars into investment companies, which use those dollars to buy the common stock of other companies. What do the investment companies offer investors who prefer to invest in the investment companies rather than buying the common stock of these other companies directly?

8. In March 1996, the Committee on Payment and Settlement Systems of the Bank for International Settlements published a report entitled "Settlement Risk in Foreign Exchange Transactions" that offers a practical approach that banks can employ when dealing with settlement risk. What is meant by settlement risk?

9. The following appeared in the Federal Reserve Bank of San Francisco's *Economic Letter*, January 25, 2002:

   > Financial institutions are in the business of risk management and reallocation, and they have developed sophisticated risk management systems to carry out these tasks. The basic components of a risk management system are identifying and defining the risks the firm is exposed to, assessing their magnitude, mitigating them using a variety of procedures, and setting aside capital for potential losses. Over the past twenty years or so, financial institutions have been using economic modeling in earnest to assist them in these tasks. For example, the development of empirical models of financial volatility led to increased modeling of market risk, which is the risk arising from the fluctuations of financial asset prices. In the area of credit risk, models have recently been developed for large-scale credit risk management purposes.
   >
   > Yet, not all of the risks faced by financial institutions can be so easily categorized and modeled. For example, the risks of electrical failures or employee fraud do not lend themselves as readily to modeling.

   What type of risk is the above quotation referring to?

10. What is the source of income for an asset management firm?

11. What is meant by a performance-based management fee and what is the basis for determining performance in such an arrangement?

12. a. Why is the term *hedge* to describe "hedge funds" misleading?
    b. Where is the term *hedge fund* described in the U.S. securities laws?

13. How does the management structure of an asset manager of a hedge fund differ from that of an asset manager of a mutual fund?

14. Some hedge funds will refer to their strategies as "arbitrage strategies." Why would this be misleading?

15. What is meant by a convergence traded hedge fund?

16. What was the major recommendation regarding hedge funds of the President's Working Group on Financial Markets?

Depository Institutions: Activities and Characteristics

LEARNING OBJECTIVES

After reading this chapter, you will understand

- the role of depository institutions

- how a depository institution generates income

- differences among commercial banks, savings and loan associations, savings banks, and credit unions

- the asset/liability problem all depository institutions face

- who regulates commercial banks and thrifts and the types of regulations imposed

- the funding sources available to commercial banks and thrifts

- the capital requirements imposed on commercial banks and savings and loan associations

- what are the Basel I and Basel II frameworks

Depository institutions include commercial banks (or simply banks), **savings and loan associations (S&Ls)**, savings banks, and credit unions. All are financial intermediaries that accept deposits. These deposits represent the liabilities (debt) of the deposit-accepting institution. With the funds raised through deposits and other funding sources, depository institutions both make direct loans to various entities and invest in securities. Their income is derived from two sources: (1) the income generated from the loans they make and the securities they purchase, and (2) fee income.

It is common to refer to S&Ls, savings banks, and credit unions as *thrifts*, which are specialized types of depository institutions. At one time, thrifts were not permitted to accept deposits transferable by check (negotiable), or, as they are more popularly known, checking accounts. Instead, they obtained funds primarily by tapping the savings of households. Since the early 1980s, however, thrifts have been allowed to offer negotiable deposits entirely equivalent to checking accounts, although they bear a different name (**NOW accounts**, share drafts). By law, the investments that thrifts are permitted to make have been much more limited than those permitted to banks. Recent legislation, however, has expanded the range of investments allowed by thrifts so that they can compete more effectively with banks.

Depository institutions are highly regulated because of the important role that they play in the country's financial system. Demand deposit accounts are the principal means that individuals and business entities use for making payments, and government monetary policy is implemented through the banking system. Because of their important role, depository institutions are afforded special privileges such as access to federal deposit insurance and access to a government entity that provides funds for liquidity or emergency needs. For example, deposits are currently insured up to $100,000 per individual account and $250,000 for retirement accounts (which has been increased to $250,000 and $500,000, respectively, through December 31, 2009). We will give examples of how depository institutions have access to emergency funds later in this chapter.

In this chapter, we will look at depository institutions—the nature of their liabilities, where they invest their funds, and how they are regulated. Before we examine the specific institutions, we begin with an overview of the asset/liability problem that a depository institution must manage.

ASSET/LIABILITY PROBLEM OF DEPOSITORY INSTITUTIONS

The asset/liability problem that depository institutions face is quite simple to explain—although not necessarily easy to solve. A depository institution seeks to earn a positive spread between the assets it invests in (loans and securities) and the cost of its funds (deposits and other sources). The spread is referred to as **spread income** or **margin**. The spread income should allow the institution to meet operating expenses and earn a fair profit on its capital.

In generating spread income a depository institution faces several risks. These include **credit risk, regulatory risk**, and **interest rate risk**. Credit risk, also called **default risk**, refers to the risk that a borrower will default on a loan obligation to the depository institution or that the issuer of a security that the depository institution holds will default on its obligation. Regulatory risk is the risk that regulators will change the rules so as to adversely impact the earnings of the institution.

Interest Rate Risk

Interest rate risk can be explained best by an illustration. Suppose that a depository institution raises $100 million via deposits that have a maturity of one year and by agreeing to pay an interest rate of 5%. Ignoring for the time being the fact that the depository institution cannot invest the entire $100 million because of reserve requirements, which we discuss later in this chapter, suppose that $100 million is invested in a U.S. government security that matures in 15 years paying an interest rate of 7%. Because the funds are invested in a U.S. government security, there is no credit risk in this case.

It would seem at first that the depository institution has locked in a spread of 2% (5% minus 7%). This spread can be counted on only for the first year, though, because the spread in future years will depend on the interest rate this depository institution will have to pay depositors in order to raise $100 million after the one-year time deposit matures. If interest rates decline, the spread will increase because the depository institution has locked in the 7% rate. If interest rates rise, however, the spread income will decline. In fact, if this depository institution must pay more than 7% to depositors for the next 14 years, the spread will be negative. That is, it will cost the depository institution more to finance the government securities than it will earn on the funds invested in those securities.

In our example, the depository institution has borrowed short (borrowed for one year) and lent long (invested for 15 years). This policy will benefit from a decline in interest rates but be disadvantaged if interest rates rise. Suppose the institution could have borrowed funds for 15 years at 5% and invested in a U.S. government security maturing in one year earning 7%—borrowed long (15 years) and lent short (one year). A rise in interest rates will benefit the depository institution because it can then reinvest the proceeds from the maturing one-year government security in a new one-year government security offering a higher interest rate. In this case, a decline in interest rates will reduce the spread. If interest rates fall below 7%, there will be a negative spread.

All depository institutions face this interest rate risk. Managers of a depository institution who have particular expectations about the future direction of interest rates will seek to benefit from these expectations. Those who expect interest rates to rise may pursue a policy to borrow funds for a long time horizon (that is, to borrow long) and lend funds for a short time horizon (to lend short). If interest rates are expected to drop, managers may elect to borrow short and lend long.

The problem of pursuing a strategy of positioning a depository institution based on expectations is that considerable adverse financial consequences will result if those expectations are not realized. The evidence on interest rate forecasting suggests that it is a risky business. We doubt if there are managers of depository institutions who have the ability to forecast interest rate moves so consistently that the institution can benefit should the forecast be realized. The goal of management is to lock in a spread as best as possible, not to wager on interest rate movements.

Inherent in any balance sheet of a depository institution is interest rate risk exposure. Managers must be willing to accept some exposure, but they can take various measures to address the interest rate sensitivity of the institution's liabilities and its assets. Regulators impose restrictions on the degree of interest rate risk a depository institution may be exposed to, as explained later in this chapter. A depository institution will have an asset/liability committee that is responsible for monitoring the interest rate risk exposure. There are several asset/liability strategies for controlling interest rate risk. While a discussion of these strategies is beyond the scope of this chapter, we can point out here that development of several financial instruments (such as floating-rate notes, adjustable-rate mortgages, and interest rate swaps) reflects the asset/liability problem that depository institutions seek to solve.

Liquidity Concerns

Besides facing credit risk and interest rate risk, a depository institution must be prepared to satisfy withdrawals of funds by depositors and to provide loans to customers. There are several ways that a depository institution can accommodate withdrawal and loan demand: (1) attract additional deposits, (2) use existing securities as collateral for borrowing from a federal agency or other financial institution such as an investment bank, (3) raise short-term funds in the money market, or (4) sell securities that it owns.

The first alternative is self-explanatory. The second has to do with the privilege we mentioned earlier. Banks are allowed to borrow at the discount window of the Federal

Reserve Banks. The third alternative primarily includes using marketable securities owned as collateral to raise funds in the repurchase agreement market, which we cover in later chapters.

The fourth alternative, selling securities that it owns, requires that the depository institution invest a portion of its funds in securities that are both liquid and have little price risk. By price risk, we refer to the prospect that the selling price of the security will be less than its purchase price, resulting in a loss. For example, while a 30-year U.S. government security is a highly liquid security, its price would change dramatically as interest rates rise. A price decline of, say, 25% would not be uncommon in a volatile interest rate environment. A 30-year government bond is therefore highly liquid, but exposes the depository institution to substantial price risk.

In general, short-term securities entail little price risk. It is therefore short-term, or money market, debt obligations that a depository institution will hold as an investment to satisfy withdrawals and customer loan demand. It does this chiefly by lending federal funds, an investment vehicle that we will discuss later in this chapter. The term to maturity of the securities it holds affects the amount that depository institutions can borrow from some federal agencies because only short-term securities are acceptable collateral.

Securities held for the purpose of satisfying net withdrawals and customer loan demands are sometimes referred to as **secondary reserves**.[1] A disadvantage of holding secondary reserves is that securities with short maturities offer a lower yield than securities with a longer maturity in most interest rate environments. The percentage of a depository institution's assets held as secondary reserves will depend both on the institution's ability to raise funds from the other sources and on its management's risk preference for liquidity (safety) versus yield.

Depository institutions hold liquid assets not only for operational purposes, but also because of the regulatory requirements that we discuss below.

Key Points That You Should Understand Before Proceeding

1. That a depository institution needs to earn a positive spread between the return on its assets and the cost of its funds, which it gets through deposits and other sources.
2. The source and impact of a depository institution's credit risk, interest rate risk, and regulatory risk.
3. The reasons for a depository institution's liquidity concerns and its ways of responding to these concerns.

COMMERCIAL BANKS

While today, we are aware of the role of the federal government in the regulation of commercial banks, prior to 1863, the federal government played almost no role in their regulation. Instead, banks were regulated only at the state level. Realizing the need for a

---

[1] Roland I. Robinson, *The Management of Bank Funds* (New York: Mcgraw-Hill, 1962), p. 15. The term *secondary reserves* is used because primary reserves are the reserves required by the Federal Reserve Board, which we will discuss later. If you looked at the balance sheet of a depository institution, you would not see the term *secondary reserves* on it. A depository institution invests in short-term or money market instruments for reasons other than liquidity and does not report the purpose for which it acquires securities.

stronger banking system, the U.S. Congress passed the National Bank Act in 1863 authorizing the federal chartering of national banks. The Office of the Comptroller of the Currency (OCC) was created and empowered with providing national bank charters and regulation of national banks. As a result, there existed state and national banks, a structure popularly referred to as "dual banking." The dual banking structure still exists today, with every state having its own state banking department responsible for regulating banks chartered by their state.

Realizing the need for banks to obtain liquidity during periods of economic stress, the federal government wanted to establish a banking system that would have an entity that banks could borrow from, sort of a "lender of last resort." The U.S. Congress accomplished this with the passage of the Federal Reserve Act of 1913. This legislation established the Federal Reserve System (FRS) as the central banking system. Banks that were members of the FRS were entitled to all the services that the FRS was empowered to provide by the legislation. We will discuss these services later in this section. The legislation required that all national-chartered banks become members of the FRS. State-chartered banks had the option to become members. Most state-chartered banks elected not to become members. Today state-chartered banks can be classified as state member banks and state nonmember banks. With the passage of the Depository Institutions Deregulation and Monetary Control Act of 1980 (DIDMCA), the reserve requirements that we shall discuss for member banks apply also to state-chartered nonmember banks.

Today, banks are regulated and supervised by several federal and state government entities. At the federal level, supervision is undertaken by the Federal Reserve Board, the Office of the Comptroller of the Currency, and the Federal Deposit Insurance Corporation.

As of the second quarter of 2007, there were 7,350 commercial banks operating in the United States. Only about 25% of the banks were national banks. Of the state-chartered banks, most were not members of the FRS. Despite the fact that national banks are small in number, they are the major holders of bank assets, more than 65%.

Banks are insured by the Bank Insurance Fund (BIF), which is administered by the Federal Deposit Insurance Corporation (FDIC). Federal depository insurance began in the 1930s, and the insurance program is administered by the FDIC. BIF was created by the Financial Institutions Reform, Recovery, and Enforcement Act of 1989 (FIRREA).

The asset size of banks in the United States as of the first half of 2007 is shown in Table 1. Although less than 7% of the banks have total assets in excess of $1 billion, these banks hold more than 85% of the total assets. The 30 largest banks in the United States as of September 30, 2007, are shown in Table 2.

Table 1 Asset Size Distribution for Commercial Banks as of the First Half of 2007		
Assets	No. of Banks	Percentage of Banks
Less than $100 million	3,197	43.50%
From $100 million to $1 billion	3,649	49.65
From $1 billion to $10 billion	413	5.62
Greater than $10 billion	91	1.24

Source: *Created from data obtained from the FDIC.*

Table 2	United States' Largest Banks (in millions of U.S. dollars)	
Rank	Name (City, State)	Consolidated Assets
1.	Citigroup (New York, N.Y.)	$2,220,866
2.	Bank of America Corp. (Charlotte, N.C.)	1,535,684
3.	J.P. Morgan Chase & Company (Columbus, Ohio)	1,458,042
4.	Wachovia Corp. (Charlotte, N.C.)	719,922
5.	Taunus Corp. (New York, N.Y.)	579,062
6.	Wells Fargo & Company (San Francisco, Calif.)	539,865
7.	HSBC North America Inc. (Prospect Heights, Ill.)	483,630
8.	U.S. Bancorp (Minneapolis, Minn.)	222,530
9.	Suntrust Banks, Inc. (Atlanta, Ga.)	180,314
10.	ABN Amro North America (Chicago, Ill.)	160,341
11.	Citizens Financial Group, Inc. (Providence, R.I.)	159,392
12.	Capital One Financial Corp. (McLean, Va.)	145,937
13.	National City Bank (Cleveland, Ohio)	140,648
14.	Regions Financial Corp. (Birmingham, Ala.)	137,624
15.	BB&T Corp. (Winston-Salem, N.C.)	127,577
16.	PNC Financial Services Group, Inc. (Pittsburgh, Pa.)	125,736
17.	State Street Corp. (Boston, Mass.)	112,345
18.	Fifth Third Bancorp (Cincinnati, Ohio)	101,389
19.	Keycorp (Cleveland, Ohio)	93,490
20.	Bancwest Corp. (Honolulu, Hawaii)	70,661
21.	Harris Financial Corp. (Wilmington, Del.)	64,475
22.	Northern Trust Corp. (Chicago, Ill.)	59,609
23.	Comerica Incorporated (Dallas, Tex.)	58,945
24.	Marshall & Ilsley Corp. (Milwaukee, Wis.)	58,327
25.	M&T Bank Corp. (Buffalo, N.Y.)	57,869
26.	Union Bank of Calif. (San Francisco, Calif.)	53,173
27.	Charles Schwab Corp. (San Francisco, Calif.)	49,003
28.	Zions Bancorporation (Salt Lake City, Utah)	48,703
29.	Commerce Bancorp, Inc. (Cherry Hill, N.J.)	48,231
30.	Popular, Inc. (San Juan, Puerto Rico)	46,985

Note: *As of September 30, 2007.*

Source: *Federal Reserve System, National Information Center.*

Bank Services

Commercial banks provide numerous services in our financial system. The services can be broadly classified as follows: (1) individual banking, (2) **institutional banking**, and (3) **global banking**. Of course, different banks are more active in certain of these activities than others. For example, money center banks (defined later) are more active in global banking.

Individual banking encompasses consumer lending, residential mortgage lending, consumer installment loans, credit card financing, automobile and boat financing, brokerage services, student loans, and individual-oriented financial investment services such as personal trust and investment services. Interest income and fee income are generated from mortgage lending and credit card financing. **Mortgage lending** is more popularly referred to as **mortgage banking**. Fee income is generated from brokerage services and financial investment services.

Loans to nonfinancial corporations, financial corporations (such as life insurance companies), and government entities (state and local governments in the United States and foreign governments) fall into the category of *institutional banking*. Also included in this category are commercial real estate financing, leasing activities,[2] and factoring.[3] In the case of leasing, a bank may be involved in leasing equipment either as lessors,[4] as lenders to lessors, or as purchasers of leases. Loans and leasing generate interest income, and other services that banks offer institutional customers generate fee income. These services include management of the assets of private and public pension funds, fiduciary and custodial services, and cash management services such as account maintenance, check clearing, and electronic transfers.

It is in the area of *global banking* that banks began to compete head-to-head with investment banking (or securities) firms. Global banking covers a broad range of activities involving corporate financing and capital market and foreign-exchange products and services. Most global banking activities generate fee income rather than interest income. At one time, some of these activities were restricted by federal legislation. More specifically, the Banking Act of 1933 contained four sections barring commercial banks from certain investment banking activities. These four sections are popularly referred to as the **Glass-Steagall Act**. After decades of debate regarding the need for such restrictions, the Glass-Steagall Act was repealed with the enactment of the **Gramm-Leach-Bliley Act** in November 1999, which expanded the permissible activities for banks and bank holding companies.

Corporate financing involves two components. First is the procuring of funds for a bank's customers. This can go beyond traditional bank loans to involve the underwriting of securities. In assisting customers in obtaining funds, banks also provide bankers acceptances, letters of credit, and other types of guarantees for their customers. That is, if a customer has borrowed funds backed by a letter of credit or other guarantee, its lenders can look to the customer's bank to fulfill the obligation. The second area of corporate financing involves advice on such matters as strategies for obtaining funds, corporate restructuring, divestitures, and acquisitions.

Capital market and foreign-exchange products and services involve transactions where the bank may act as a dealer or broker in a service. Some banks, for example, are dealers in U.S. government or other securities. Customers who wish to transact in these securities can do so through the government desk of the bank. Similarly, some banks maintain a foreign-exchange

---

[2] Leasing programs offered by some banks include vendor leasing, direct leasing, and leveraged leasing. For a discussion of these programs and the restrictions imposed on banks with respect to leasing activities, see Peter K. Nevitt, Frank J. Fabozzi, and Edmond J. Seifried, *Equipment Leasing for Commercial Bankers* (Philadelphia, PA: Robert Morris Associates, 1987).

[3] The factoring business involves a bank's purchase of accounts receivable.

[4] This means that the bank buys the equipment and leases it to another party. The bank is the lessor, and the party that uses the leased equipment is the lessee.

operation, where foreign currency is bought and sold. Bank customers in need of foreign exchange can use the services of the bank.

In their role as dealers, banks can generate income in three ways: (1) the bid–ask spread; (2) capital gains on the securities or foreign currency they have transacted in; and (3) in the case of securities, the spread between interest income by holding the security and the cost of funding the purchase of that security.

The financial products that banks have developed to manage risk also yield fee income. These products include interest rate swaps, interest rate agreements, currency swaps, forward contracts, and interest rate options. Banks can generate either commission income (that is, brokerage fees) or spread income from selling such products.

Bank Funding

In describing the nature of the banking business, we have focused so far on how banks generate income. Now let's take a look at how a bank raises funds. There are three sources of funds for banks: (1) deposits, (2) nondeposit borrowing, and (3) common stock and retained earnings. Banks are highly leveraged financial institutions, which means that most of their funds come from borrowing—the first two sources we refer to. Included in nondeposit borrowing are borrowing from the Federal Reserve through the discount window facility, borrowing reserves in the federal funds market, and borrowing by the issuance of instruments in the money and bond markets.

Deposits

There are several types of deposit accounts. **Demand deposits** (checking accounts) pay no interest and can be withdrawn upon demand. **Savings deposits** pay interest, typically below market interest rates, do not have a specific maturity, and usually can be withdrawn upon demand.

Time deposits, also called **certificates of deposit**, have a fixed maturity date and pay either a fixed or floating interest rate. Some certificates of deposit can be sold in the open market prior to their maturity if the depositor needs funds. Other certificates of deposit cannot be sold. If a depositor elects to withdraw the funds from the bank prior to the maturity date, a withdrawal penalty is imposed. A money market demand account is one that pays interest based on short-term interest rates. The market for short-term debt obligations is called the money market, which is how these deposits get their name. They are designed to compete with **money market mutual funds.**

Reserve Requirements and Borrowing in the Federal Funds Market

A bank cannot invest $1 for every $1 it obtains in deposit. All banks must maintain a specified percentage of their deposits in a non–interest-bearing account at one of the 12 Federal Reserve Banks. These specified percentages are called **reserve ratios**, and the dollar amounts based on them that are required to be kept on deposit at a Federal Reserve Bank are called **required reserves**. The reserve ratios are established by the Federal Reserve Board (the Fed). The reserve ratio differs by type of deposit. The Fed defines two types of deposits: transactions and nontransactions deposits. Demand deposits and what the Fed calls "other checkable deposits" (primarily NOW accounts) are classified as transactions deposits. Savings and time deposits are nontransactions deposits. Reserve ratios are higher for transactions deposits than for nontransactions deposits.

To arrive at its required reserves, a bank does not simply determine its transactions and nontransactions deposits at the close of each business day and then multiply each by the applicable reserve ratio. The determination of a bank's required reserves is more complex. Here, we will give a rough idea of how it is done. First, to compute required reserves, the Federal Reserve has established a two-week period called the **deposit computation period**. Required reserves are the average amount of each type of deposit held at the close of each business day in the computation period, multiplied by the reserve requirement for each type.

Reserve requirements in each period are to be satisfied by *actual reserves*, which are defined as the average amount of reserves held at the close of business at the Federal Reserve Bank during each day of a two-week reserve maintenance period, beginning on Thursday and ending on Wednesday two weeks later. For transactions deposits, the deposit computation period leads the reserve period by two days. For nontransactions deposits, the deposit computation period is the two-week period four weeks prior to the reserve maintenance period.

If actual reserves exceed required reserves, the difference is referred to as **excess reserves**. Because reserves are placed in non–interest-bearing accounts, there is an opportunity cost associated with excess reserves. At the same time, there are penalties imposed on banks that do not satisfy the reserve requirements. Thus, banks have an incentive to manage their reserves so as to satisfy reserve requirements as precisely as possible.

Banks temporarily short of their required reserves can borrow reserves from banks that have excess reserves. The market where banks can borrow or lend reserves is called the **federal funds market**. The interest rate charged to borrow funds in this market is called the *federal funds rate.*

Borrowing at the Fed Discount Window

The Federal Reserve Bank is the banker's bank—or, to put it another way, the bank of last resort. Banks temporarily short of funds can borrow from the Fed at its **discount window**. Collateral is necessary to borrow, but not just any collateral will do. The Fed establishes (and periodically changes) the type of collateral that is eligible. Currently it includes (1) Treasury securities, federal agency securities, and municipal securities, all with a maturity of less than six months; and (2) commercial and industrial loans with 90 days or less to maturity.

The interest rate that the Fed charges to borrow funds at the discount window is called the **discount rate**. The Fed changes this rate periodically in order to implement monetary policy.[5] Bank borrowing at the Fed to meet required reserves is quite limited in amount, despite the fact that the discount rate generally is set below the cost of other sources of short-term funding available to a bank. This is because the Fed views borrowing at the discount window as a privilege to be used to meet short-term liquidity needs, and not a device to increase earnings.

Continual borrowing for long periods and in large amounts is thereby viewed as a sign of a bank's financial weakness or as exploitation of the interest differential for profit. If a bank appears to be going to the Fed to borrow frequently, relative to its previous borrowing pattern, the Fed makes an "informational" call to ask for an explanation for the borrowing. If there is no

---

[5] Although altering the discount rate is a tool to implement monetary policy, along with open market operations and the changing of reserve ratios, today it is not viewed as a primary tool.

subsequent improvement in the bank's borrowing pattern, the Fed then makes an "administrative counseling" call in which it tells the bank that it must stop its borrowing practice.

Other Nondeposit Borrowing

Bank borrowing in the federal funds market and at the discount window of the Fed is short term. Other nondeposit borrowing can be short term in the form of issuing obligations in the money market, or intermediate to long term in the form of issuing securities in the bond market. An example of the former is the repurchase agreement (or "repo") market. An example of intermediate- or long-term borrowing is floating-rate notes and bonds.

Banks that raise most of their funds from the domestic and international money markets, relying less on depositors for funds, are called **money center banks**. A **regional bank** by contrast is one that relies primarily on deposits for funding, and makes less use of the money markets to obtain funds. Larger regional banks have been merging with other regional banks to form so-called **superregional banks**.

Capital Requirements for Banks

The capital structure of banks, like that of all corporations, consists of equity and debt (i.e., borrowed funds). Commercial banks, like some other depository institutions and like investment banks are highly leveraged institutions. That is, the ratio of equity capital to total assets is low, typically less than 8% in the case of banks. This level gives rise to regulatory concern about potential insolvency resulting from the low level of capital provided by the owners. An additional concern is that the amount of equity capital is even less adequate because of potential liabilities that do not appear on the bank's balance sheet. These so-called "off-balance sheet" obligations include commitments such as letters of credit and obligations on customized derivatives (such as swaps, caps, and floors).

The organization that plays the primary role in establishing risk and management guidelines for banks throughout the world is the **Basel Committee on Banking Supervision** ("Basel Committee"). This committee is made up of banking supervisory authorities from 13 countries.[6] The Basel Committee is one of four standing committees of the Bank for International Settlements (BIS) in Basel, Switzerland. The other three committees are the Committee on the Global Financial System, the Committee on Payment and Settlement Systems, and the Markets Committee. The four BIS standing committees publish background papers and reports to provide guidance for central banks throughout the world to foster monetary and financial stability.

The capital requirements that resulted from other guidelines published by the Basel Committee are referred to as **risk-based capital requirements**. In July 1988, the Basel Committee released its first guidelines in a document referred to as the **Capital Accord of 1988**.[7] Because the Basel Committee has since published other guidelines, the Capital Accord of 1988 is now commonly referred to as the **Basel I Framework**. The primary objective of the Basel I Framework was to establish minimum capital standards designed to protect against credit risk. In 1996, the Basel I Framework was amended to broaden its scope to include

---

[6] The countries are Belgium, Canada, France, Germany, Italy, Japan, Luxembourg, the Netherlands, Spain, Sweden, Switzerland, the United Kingdom, and the United States.

[7] Bank for International Settlements, *International Convergence of Capital Measurement and Capital Standard*, July 1988.

risk-based capital requirements based on market risk.[8] In 1998, the Basel Committee discussed the importance of operational risk as a substantial financial risk factor and beginning in 2001 published several guidelines and reports dealing with operational risk.[9]

During the two years that followed the publication of the amendment to Basel I for market risk, the Basel Committee decided to undertake a more comprehensive amendment to the Basel I Framework that would incorporate a diversity of risks faced by banks in formulating risk-based capital requirements. This led to a new capital accord released in June 2004 that is popularly referred to as the **Basel II Framework**.[10] The purpose of the Basel II Framework was to improve on the rules as set forth in the Basel I Framework by bringing risk-based capital requirements more in line with the underlying risks to which banks are exposed. Moreover, the Basel II Framework encourages banks to identify those risks not just today but in the future and to improve their existing risk management systems to manage those risks. That is, the Basel II Framework sought to promote a more forward-looking approach to capital supervision. The Basel II Framework, which went through a number of amendments since its release and was finalized in June 2006, is based on what the Basel Committee refers to as three "pillars": minimum risk-based capital requirements (Pillar I), supervisory review of capital adequacy and internal assessment process (Pillar II), and market discipline through public disclosure of various financial and risk indicators (Pillar III).

Moving from the guidelines to implementation by national banking authorities and banks is not simple. The Basel Committee has several subcommittees whose stated purpose is to promote consistency in its implementation of the guidelines. The four major ones are the Accord Implementation Group, the Capital Task Force, the Risk Management Group, and the Transparency Group. The purpose of the Accord Implementation Group is to promote the exchange of information on the practical implementation challenges of the two Basel frameworks. The Capital Task Force is responsible for considering substantive modifications to and interpretations of the two Basel frameworks. The objective of the Risk Management Group is to formulate new standards for risk management and methodologies for regulatory capital allocation models. The purpose of the Transparency Groups is to develop and review the disclosure principles described in Pillar III of the Basel Framework.

We will not review the risk-based capital requirements in detail. Instead, we will discuss simply the treatment of risk-based capital requirements for credit risk.

Credit Risk and Risk-Based Capital Requirements

Consider, for example, two banks, A and B, with $1 billion in assets. Suppose that both invest $400 million in identical assets, but the remaining $600 million in different assets. Bank A invests $500 million in U.S. government bonds and $100 million in business loans. Bank B invests $100 million in U.S. government bonds and $500 million in business loans. Obviously, the exposure to default losses is greater for Bank B. While the

---

[8] Bank for International Settlements, *Amendment to the Capital Accord to Incorporate Market Risks*, April 1996.

[9] See the following publications of the Bank for International Settlements: *Working Paper on the Regulatory Treatment of Operational Risk* (September 28, 2001), *Sound Practices for the Management and Supervision of Operational Risk* (December 20, 2001), *Sound Practices for the Management and Supervision of Operational Risk* (July 6, 2002), and *Sound Practices for the Management and Supervision of Operational Risk* (February 25, 2003).

[10] Bank for International Settlements, *Basel II: International Convergence of Capital of Measurement and Capital Standards: A Revised Framework*, June 2004.

Table 3	Credit Risk Weight Capital Requirement for Various Assets
Risk Weight	**Example of Assets Included**
0%	U.S. Treasury securities Mortgage-backed securities issued by the Government National Mortgage Association
20%	Municipal general obligation bonds Mortgage-backed securities issued by the Federal Home Loan Mortgage Corporation or the Federal National Mortgage Association
50%	Municipal revenue bonds Residential mortgages
100%	Commercial loans and commercial mortgages LDC loans Corporate bonds

capital adequacy standards take this greater credit risk into account, they do not recognize liquidity factors or the market price sensitivity to which a bank may be exposed.

The risk-based capital guidelines attempt to recognize credit risk by segmenting and weighting requirements. First, capital is defined as consisting of Tier 1 and Tier 2 capital. Minimum requirements are established for each tier. Tier 1 capital is considered **core capital**; it consists basically of common stockholders' equity, certain types of preferred stock, and minority interest in consolidated subsidiaries. Tier 2 capital is called **supplementary capital**; it includes loan-loss reserves, certain types of preferred stock, perpetual debt (debt with no maturity date), hybrid capital instruments and equity contract notes, and subordinated debt.

Second, the guidelines establish a credit risk weight for all assets. The weight depends on the credit risk associated with each asset. There are four credit risk classifications for banks: 0%, 20%, 50%, and 100%, arrived at on no particular scientific basis. Table 3 lists examples of assets that fall into each credit risk classification.[11]

The way the credit risk weights work is as follows. The book value of the asset is multiplied by the credit risk weight to determine the amount of core and supplementary capital that the bank will need to support that asset. For example, suppose that the book values of the assets of a bank are as follows:

Asset	Book Value (in millions)
U.S. Treasury securities	$ 100
Municipal general obligation bonds	100
Residential mortgages	500
Commercial loans	300
Total book value	$1,000

---

[11] There are special rules for determining the amount of capital required for off-balance sheet items. An off-balance sheet item is a position in interest-sensitive contracts and/or foreign-exchange-related products that is not reported on the balance sheet.

The risk-weighted assets are calculated as follows:

Asset	Book Value (in millions)	Risk Weight	Product (in millions)
U.S. Treasury securities	$100	0%	$ 0
Municipal general obligation bonds	100	20	20
Residential mortgages	500	50	250
Commercial loans	300	100	300
Risk-weighted assets	–	–	$570

The risk-weighted assets for this bank would be $570 million.

The minimum core (Tier 1) capital requirement is 4% of the book value of assets; the minimum *total* capital (core plus supplementary capital) is 8% of the risk-weighted assets. To see how this works, consider the hypothetical bank we just used to illustrate the calculation of risk-weighted assets. For that bank, the risk-weighted assets are $570 million. The minimum core capital requirement is $40 million (0.04 × $1 billion); the minimum total capital requirement is $45.6 million (0.08 × $570 million).[12]

One implication of the new capital guidelines is that it will encourage banks to sell off their loans in the open market. By doing so, the bank need not maintain capital for the loans (assets) sold off. Although the secondary market for individual bank loans has been growing, it has not reached the stage where a bank can efficiently sell large amounts of loans. An alternative is for a bank to pool loans and issue securities that are collateralized by the pool of loans. This is the process of asset securitization.

Key Points That You Should Understand Before Proceeding

1. Bank deposits are insured by government-sponsored insurance programs, and state-chartered banks may elect to join the Federal Reserve System.
2. Banks raise funds from deposits, from issuing debt and equity securities, and from their own earnings.
3. U.S. banks must keep a fraction of their deposits in assets that qualify as reserves.
4. Banks may borrow funds from the Federal Reserve System.
5. There are risk-based capital requirements and these requirements are set by the Basel Committee on Banking Supervision of the Bank for International Settlements.
6. The focus of the risk-based requirements as set forth in the Basel I framework was on credit risk; the Basel II framework extended risk-based capital requirements based on other risks.

SAVINGS AND LOAN ASSOCIATIONS

S&Ls represent a fairly old institution. The basic motivation behind the creation of S&Ls was the providing of funds for financing the purchase of a home. The collateral for the loans would be the home being financed.

---

[12] Other minimum standards imposed by the guidelines cover limitations on supplementary capital elements.

S&Ls are either mutually owned or have corporate stock ownership. "Mutually owned" means there is no stock outstanding, so technically the depositors are the owners. To increase the ability of S&Ls to expand the sources of funding available to bolster their capital, legislation facilitated the conversion of mutually owned companies into a corporate stock ownership structure.

Like banks, S&Ls may be chartered under either state or federal statutes. At the federal level, the primary regulator of S&Ls is the Director of the Office of Thrift Supervision (OTS), created in 1989 by FIRREA. Prior to the creation of OTS, the primary regulator was the Federal Home Loan Bank Board (FHLBB). The FHLBB no longer exists. The Federal Home Loan Banks, which, along with the FHLBB, comprised the Federal Home Loan Bank System, still exist and make advances (i.e., loans) to member institutions (S&Ls and commercial banks).

Like banks, S&Ls are now subject to reserve requirements on deposits established by the Fed. Prior to the passage of FIRREA, federal deposit insurance for S&Ls was provided by the Federal Savings and Loan Insurance Corporation (FSLIC). The Savings Association Insurance Fund (SAIF) has replaced FSLIC. SAIF is administered by the FDIC.

Assets

Traditionally, the only assets in which S&Ls were allowed to invest have been mortgages, mortgage-backed securities, and U.S. government securities. Mortgage loans include fixed-rate mortgages, adjustable-rate mortgages, and other types of mortgage designs. While most mortgage loans are for the purchase of homes, S&Ls do make construction loans.

As the structures of S&L balance sheets and the consequent maturity mismatch led to widespread disaster and insolvency, the Garn-St. Germain Act of 1982 expanded the types of assets in which S&Ls could invest. The acceptable list of investments now includes consumer loans (loans for home improvement, automobiles, education, mobile homes, and credit cards), nonconsumer loans (commercial, corporate, business, or agricultural loans), and municipal securities.

Although S&Ls had a comparative advantage in originating mortgage loans, they lacked the expertise to make commercial and corporate loans. Rather than make an investment in acquiring those skills, S&Ls took an alternative approach and invested in corporate bonds because these bonds were classified as corporate loans. More specifically, S&Ls became one of the major buyers of non–investment-grade corporate bonds, more popularly referred to as **junk bonds** or high-yield bonds. Under FIRREA, S&Ls are no longer permitted to invest new money in junk bonds.

S&Ls invest in short-term assets for operational (liquidity) and regulatory purposes. All S&Ls with federal deposit insurance must satisfy minimum liquidity requirements. Acceptable assets include cash, short-term government agency and corporate securities, certificates of deposit of commercial banks,[13] other money market instruments, and federal funds. In the case of federal funds, the S&L is lending excess reserves to another depository institution that is short of funds.

Funding

Prior to 1981, the bulk of the liabilities of S&Ls consisted of passbook savings accounts and time deposits. The interest rate that could be offered on these deposits was regulated. S&Ls were given favored treatment over banks with respect to the maximum interest rate

---

[13] The S&L is an investor when it holds the CD of a bank, but the CD represents the liability of the issuing bank.

they could pay depositors. They were permitted to pay an interest rate 0.5% higher, later reduced to 0.25%. With the deregulation of interest rates discussed earlier in this chapter, banks and S&Ls now compete head-to-head for deposits. Deregulation also expanded the types of accounts that may be offered by S&Ls—negotiable order of withdrawal (NOW) accounts and money market deposit accounts (MMDA). NOW accounts are similar to demand deposits. Unlike demand deposits, NOW accounts pay interest.

In the 1980s, S&Ls became more active in raising funds in the money market. For example, they were able to use the repurchase agreement market to raise funds. Some larger S&Ls have issued commercial paper as well as medium-term notes. They can borrow in the federal funds market and they have access to the Fed's discount window. S&Ls can also borrow from the Federal Home Loan Banks. These borrowings, called **advances**, can be short term or long term in maturity, and the interest rate can be fixed or floating.

Regulation

Federal S&Ls are chartered under the provisions of the **Home Owners Loan Act of 1933**. Federally chartered S&Ls are now supervised by the Office of Thrift Supervisor. State-chartered banks are supervised by the respective states. A further act in 1933 established the Federal Savings and Loan Insurance Corporation, which at that time insured the deposits of federally chartered S&Ls up to $5,000 and allowed state-chartered S&Ls that could qualify to obtain the same insurance coverage. We discuss some of the important legislation and the players below.

As in bank regulation, S&Ls historically have been regulated with respect to the maximum interest rates on deposit accounts, geographical operations, permissible activities (types of accounts and types of investments), and capital adequacy requirements. In addition, there have been restrictions on the sources of nondeposit funds and liquidity requirements. We mentioned liquidity requirements earlier.[14]

The maximum interest rate that is permitted on deposit accounts has been phased out by the Depository Institutions Deregulation and Monetary Control Act of 1980 (DIDMCA). While this allowed S&Ls to compete with other financial institutions to raise funds, it also raised their funding costs. For reasons to be described later, while banks also faced higher funding costs, their balance sheets were better constituted than those of S&Ls to cope with the higher costs resulting from interest rate deregulation.

Besides phasing in the deregulation of interest rates on deposit accounts, DIDMCA was significant in several other ways. First, it expanded the Fed's control over the money supply by imposing deposit reserve requirements on S&Ls. In return, S&Ls were permitted to offer NOW accounts.

Subsequent legislation, the Garn-St. Germain Act, not only granted thrifts the right to offer money market demand accounts so that S&Ls could compete with money market funds, but also broadened the types of assets in which S&Ls could invest. While S&Ls were first given permission by the FHLBB in 1979 to originate and invest in adjustable-rate mortgage loans, restrictions on the interest rate and other terms stymied their use. Two years later, the FHLBB removed some major impediments.

---

[14] Liquidity requirements are not imposed on banks because the majority of their assets are of less than five years' maturity.

Permission to raise funds in the money market and the bond market was granted by the Federal Home Loan Bank Board in 1975 (when it allowed the issuance of mortgage pass-through securities by S&Ls) and in 1979 (when it allowed the issuance of commercial paper and Eurodollar issues). FHLBB permission to form finance subsidiaries was granted in 1984. Through these subsidiaries, S&Ls were able to broaden their funding sources by the issuance of mortgage-related securities known as collateralized mortgage obligations.

Geographical operations of S&Ls were restricted until 1981, when the FHLBB permitted thrifts to acquire thrifts in other states.

There are two sets of **capital adequacy standards** for S&Ls, as for banks. For S&Ls, there are also two ratio tests based on "core" capital and "tangible" capital. The risk-based capital guidelines are similar to those for banks. Instead of two tiers of capital, however, there are three: Tier 1—tangible capital, Tier 2—core capital, and Tier 3—supplementary capital.

As with commercial banks, in addition to risk-based capital requirements based on credit risk there are risk-based requirements based on interest rate risk. For S&Ls, regulators have taken a different approach to measuring interest rate risk than regulators of commercial banks. In December 1988, the Federal Home Loan Bank Board, the predecessor to the Office of Thrift Supervision (OTS), stated that it intended to take into consideration interest rate risk exposure in establishing capital requirements. In December 1990, the OTS proposed a rule for dealing with interest rate risk exposure in setting capital requirements. In August 1993, the OTS finally adopted a rule that incorporates interest rate risk into risk-based capital requirements. The rule specifies that if a thrift has greater than "normal" interest rate risk exposure (where normal is defined by the rule), then there would be a deduction of the thrift's total capital for purposes of calculating its risk-based capital requirements. Interest rate risk exposure was specified in the rule as a decline in the net portfolio value (the value of the portfolio after deducting liabilities) resulting from a 200 basis point change (up and down) in market interest rates. What is deducted from the thrift's total capital is one-half the difference between the thrift's measured exposure and the "normal" level of exposure, which is defined as 2% of the estimated economic value of the assets.[15]

The Savings and Loans Association Crisis

The story of the growth of the S&L industry since the late 1960s and the ensuing S&L crisis can't be described in one short chapter, but a basic understanding of the downfall of this industry is possible.

Until the early 1980s, S&Ls and all other lenders financed housing through traditional mortgages at interest rates fixed for the life of the loan. The period of the loan was typically long, frequently up to 30 years. Funding for these loans, by regulation, came from deposits having a maturity considerably shorter than the loans. As we explained earlier in this chapter, this is the funding problem of lending long and borrowing short. It is extremely risky—although regulators took a long time to understand it. There is no problem, of course, if interest rates are stable or declining, but if interest rates rise above the interest rate on the mortgage loan, a negative spread will result, which must result eventually in insolvency. Regulators at first endeavored to shield the S&L industry from the need to pay high interest rates without losing deposits

---

[15] Federal Deposit Insurance Corporation, "Differences in Capital and Accounting Standards Among the Federal Banking and Thrift Agencies; Report to Congressional Committees." 2003.

by imposing a ceiling on the interest rate that would be paid by S&Ls and by their immediate competitors, the other depository institutions. But the approach did not and could not work.

With the high volatility of interest rates in the 1970s, followed by the historically high level of interest rates in the early 1980s, all depository institutions began to lose funds to competitors exempt from ceilings, such as the newly formed money market funds; this development forced some increase in ceilings. The ceilings in place since the middle of the 1960s did not protect the S&Ls; the institutions began to suffer from diminished profits, and increasingly from operating losses. A large fraction of S&Ls became technically insolvent as rising interest rates eroded asset market values to the point where they fell short of the liabilities.

But regulators, anxious to cover up the debacle of their empire, let them continue to operate, worsening the problem by allowing them to value their mortgage assets at book value. Profitability worsened with deregulation of the maximum interest rate that S&Ls could pay on deposits. While deregulation allowed S&Ls to compete with other financial institutions for funds, it also raised funding costs. Banks were better equipped to cope with rising funding costs because bank portfolios were not dominated by old, fixed-rate mortgages as S&Ls were. A larger portion of bank portfolios consisted of shorter-term assets and other assets whose interest rate reset to market interest rates after short time periods.

The difficulty of borrowing short and lending long was only part of the problem faced by the industry. As the crisis progressed, and the situation of many S&Ls became hopeless, fraudulent management activities were revealed. Many S&Ls facing financial difficulties also pursued strategies that exposed the institution to greater risk, in the hope of recovering if these strategies worked out. What encouraged managers to pursue such high-risk strategies was that depositors had no reason to be concerned with the risks associated with the institution where they kept their funds because the U.S. government, through federal deposit insurance, guaranteed the deposits up to a predetermined amount. Troubled S&Ls could pay existing depositors through attracting new depositors by offering higher interest rates on deposits than financially stronger S&Ls. In turn, to earn a spread on the higher cost of funds, they had to pursue riskier investment policies.

Key Points That You Should Understand Before Proceeding

1. S&Ls may be chartered by state or federal authorities.
2. The majority of assets owned by S&Ls are mortgages and mortgage-backed securities.
3. S&Ls may obtain funding from deposits and issuance of debt and equity securities.
4. The government regulates many aspects of an S&L's activities, including its capital structure.
5. The fundamental causes of the S&L crisis.

SAVINGS BANKS

Savings banks are institutions similar to, although much older than, S&Ls. They can be either mutually owned (in which case they are called mutual savings banks) or stockholder owned. While conversion of mutual to corporate structure was made easier by the Garn-St. Germain Act, most savings banks are of the mutual form. Only 16 states in the eastern portion of the U.S. charter savings banks. In 1978, Congress permitted the chartering of federal savings banks.

Although the total deposits at savings banks are less than those at S&Ls, savings banks are typically larger institutions. Asset structures of savings banks and S&Ls are similar. The principal assets of savings banks are residential mortgages. Because states have permitted more portfolio diversification than was permitted by federal regulators of S&Ls, savings bank portfolios weathered funding risk far better than S&Ls. Included in savings bank portfolios are corporate bonds, Treasury and government agency securities, municipal securities, common stock, and consumer loans.

The principal source of funds for savings banks is deposits. Typically, the ratio of deposits to total assets is greater for savings banks than for S&Ls. Savings banks offer the same types of deposit accounts as S&Ls. Deposits can be insured by either the Bank Insurance Fund or Savings Association Insurance Fund.

CREDIT UNIONS

Credit unions are the smallest and the newest of the depository institutions. Credit unions can obtain either a state or federal charter.[16] Their unique aspect is the "common bond" requirement for credit union membership. According to the statutes that regulate federal credit unions, membership in a federal credit union "shall be limited to groups having a common bond of occupation or association, or to groups within a well-defined neighborhood, community, or rural district." They are either cooperatives or mutually owned. There is no corporate stock ownership. The dual purpose of credit unions is, therefore, to serve their members' saving and borrowing needs.

Technically, because credit unions are owned by their members, member deposits are called shares. The distribution paid to members is, therefore, in the form of dividends, not interest. Since 1970, the shares of all federally chartered credit unions have been insured by the **National Credit Union Share Insurance Fund (NCUSIF)** for up to $100,000 and $250,000 for retirement accounts, the same as for commercial banks. State-chartered credit unions may elect to have NCUSIF coverage; for those that do not, insurance coverage is provided by a state agency.

Federal regulations apply to federally chartered credit unions and state-chartered credit unions that have elected to become members of NCUSIF. Most states, however, specify that state-chartered institutions must be subject to the same requirements as federally chartered ones. Effectively, therefore, most credit unions are regulated at the federal level. The principal federal regulatory agency is the **National Credit Union Administration (NCUA)**.

Credit unions obtain their funds primarily from the deposits of their members. With deregulation, they can offer a variety of accounts, including share drafts, which are similar to checking accounts but pay interest. Playing a role similar to the Fed, as the lender of last resort, is the **Central Liquidity Facility (CLF)**, which is administered by NCUA. CLF provides short-term loans to member credit unions with liquidity needs.

Credit union assets consist of small consumer loans, residential mortgage loans, and securities. Regulations 703 and 704 of NCUA set forth the types of investments in which a credit union may invest. They can make investments in **corporate credit unions.**

What is a corporate credit union? One might think that a corporate credit union is a credit union set up by employees of a corporation. It is not. Federal and state-chartered

---

[16] The Federal Credit Union Act of 1934 authorized the formation of federally chartered credit unions in all states.

credit unions are referred to as **"natural person" credit unions** because they provide financial services to qualifying members of the general public. In contrast, corporate credit unions provide a variety of investment services, as well as payment systems, only to natural person credit unions. As of 2000, there were 36 corporate credit unions ranging in size from $5 million to $30 billion. All but three corporate credit unions are federally insured. The U.S. Central Credit Union acts as the chief liquidity center for corporate credit unions by investing surplus funds from the other corporate credit unions.

SUMMARY

Depository institutions (commercial banks, savings and loan associations, savings banks, and credit unions) accept various types of deposits. With the funds raised through deposits and other funding sources, they make loans to various entities and invest in securities. The deposits usually are insured by a federal agency. Income is derived from investments (loans and securities) and fee income. Thrifts (savings and loan associations, savings banks, and credit unions) are specialized types of depository institutions. Historically, they have not been authorized to accept demand accounts, but more recently thrifts have been offering some types of deposits equivalent to checking accounts.

A depository institution seeks to earn a positive spread between the assets it invests in and the cost of its funds. In generating spread income, a depository institution faces credit risk and interest rate risk. A depository institution must be prepared to satisfy net withdrawals of funds by depositors and provide loans to customers. A depository institution can accommodate withdrawals or loan demand by attracting additional deposits, using existing securities as collateral for borrowing from a federal agency, raising short-term funds in the money market, or selling securities that it owns.

All national banks must be members of the Federal Reserve System. State-chartered banks may elect to join the Federal Reserve System. The services provided by commercial banks can be broadly classified as individual banking, institutional banking, and global banking.

There are three sources of funds for banks: (1) deposits, (2) nondeposit borrowing, and (3) retained earnings and sale of equity securities. Banks are highly leveraged financial institutions, meaning that most of their funds are obtained from deposits and nondeposit borrowing, which includes borrowing from the Fed through the discount window facility, borrowing reserves in the federal funds market, and borrowing by the issuance of instruments in the money and bond markets.

Banks must maintain reserves at one of the 12 Federal Reserve Banks, according to reserve requirements established by the Fed. Banks temporarily short of their required reserves can borrow reserves in the federal funds market or borrow temporarily from the Fed at its discount window.

The Basel Committee on Banking Supervision is the entity that establishes risk and management guidelines for banks throughout the world. The capital requirements that resulted from other guidelines published by the Basel Committee are referred to as risk-based capital requirements. These guidelines are set forth in the Basel I Framework and Basel II Framework. The purpose of the latter framework was to improve rules that were set forth in the Basel I Framework by bringing risk-based capital requirements more in line with the underlying risks to which banks are exposed and to promote a more forward-looking approach to capital supervision.

Like banks, S&Ls may be chartered under either state or federal statutes. At the federal level, the primary regulator of S&Ls is the Director of the Office of Thrift Supervision. The deposits of S&Ls are subject to reserve requirements established by the Fed. Federal deposit insurance for S&Ls is provided by the Savings Association Insurance Fund.

Much as in the case of bank regulation, S&Ls are regulated with respect to geographical operations, permissible activities, and capital adequacy requirements. S&Ls invest principally in mortgages and mortgage-related securities. Deregulation expanded the types of investments that S&Ls are permitted to make, as well as expanding the types of deposit accounts that may be offered and the available funding sources.

The asset structures of savings banks and S&Ls are similar. As some states have permitted greater portfolio diversification than is permitted by federal regulators of S&Ls, this is reflected in savings bank portfolios. The principal source of funds for savings banks is deposits. Deposits can be federally insured by either the BIF or SAIF.

Credit unions are depository institutions that have a "common bond" requirement for membership. They are owned by their members. Although they can be state or federally chartered, most credit unions effectively are regulated at the federal level by the National Credit Union Administration. The assets of credit unions consist primarily of small consumer loans to their members and credit card loans.

KEY TERMS

- Advances
- Basel I Framework
- Basel II Framework
- Basel Committee on Banking Supervision8
- Capital Accord of 1988
- Capital adequacy standards
- Central Liquidity Facility (CLF)
- Core capital
- Corporate credit union
- Credit risk (default risk)
- Credit union
- Demand deposit
- Deposit computation period
- Discount rate
- Discount window
- Excess reserves
- Federal funds market
- Glass-Steagall Act
- Global banking
- Gramm-Leach-Bliley Act
- Home Owners Loan Act of 1933
- Institutional banking
- Interest rate risk
- Junk bonds
- Money center bank
- Money market mutual fund
- Mortgage banking
- Mortgage lending
- National Credit Union Administration (NCUA)
- National Credit Union Share Insurance Fund (NCUSIF)
- "Natural person" credit union
- NOW (Negotiable Order of Withdrawal) account
- Regional bank
- Regulatory risk
- Required reserves
- Reserve ratio
- Risk-based capital requirements
- Savings and loan association (S&L)
- Savings bank
- Savings deposit
- Secondary reserves
- Spread income (margin)
- Superregional bank
- Supplementary capital
- Time deposit (certificates of deposit)

QUESTIONS

1. Explain the ways in which a depository institution can accommodate withdrawal and loan demand.

2. Why do you think a debt instrument whose interest rate is changed periodically based on some market interest rate would be more suitable for a depository institution than a long-term debt instrument with a fixed interest rate?

3. What is meant by:
   a. individual banking
   b. institutional banking
   c. global banking

4. a. What is the Basel Committee for Bank Supervision?
   b. What do the two frameworks, Basel I and Basel II, published by the Basel Committee for Bank Supervision, address regarding banking?

5. Explain each of the following:
   a. reserve ratio
   b. required reserves

6. Explain each of the following types of deposit accounts:
   a. demand deposit
   b. certificate of deposit
   c. money market demand account

7. How did the Glass-Steagall Act impact the operations of a bank?

8. The following is the book value of the assets of a bank:

Asset	Book Value (in millions)
U.S. Treasury securities	$ 50
Municipal general obligation bonds	50
Residential mortgages	400
Commercial loans	200
Total book value	$700

   a. Calculate the credit risk-weighted assets using the following information:

Asset	Risk Weight
U.S. Treasury securities	0%
Municipal general obligation bonds	20
Residential mortgages	50
Commercial loans	100

   b. What is the minimum core capital requirement?
   c. What is the minimum total capital requirement?

9. In later chapters, we will discuss a measure called duration. Duration is a measure of the sensitivity of an asset or a liability to a change in interest rates. Why would bank management want to know the duration of its assests and liabilities?

10. a. Explain how bank regulators have incorporated interest risk into capital requirements.
    b. Explain how S&L regulators have incorporated interest rate risk into capital requirements.

11. When the manager of a bank's portfolio of securities considers alternative investments, she is also concerned about the risk weight assigned to the security. Why?

12. You and a friend are discussing the savings and loan crisis. She states that "the whole mess started in the early 1980s. When short-term rates skyrocketed, S&Ls got killed—their spread income went from positive to negative. They were borrowing short and lending long."
    a. What does she mean by "borrowing short and lending long"?
    b. Are higher or lower interest rates beneficial to an institution that borrows short and lends long?

13. Consider this headline from the *New York Times* of March 26, 1933: "Bankers will fight Deposit Guarantees." In this article, it is stated that bankers argue that deposit guarantees will encourage bad banking. Explain why.

14. How did the Gramm-Leach-Bliley Act of 1999 expand the activities permitted by banks?

15. The following quotation is from the October 29, 1990 issue of *Corporate Financing Week*:

    Chase Manhattan Bank is preparing its first asset-backed debt issue, becoming the last major consumer bank to plan to access the growing market, Street asset-backed officials said. . . . Asset-backed offerings enable banks to remove credit card or other loan receivables from their balance sheets, which helps them comply with capital requirements.

    a. What capital requirements is this article referring to?

b. Explain why asset securitization reduces capital requirements.

16. Comment on this statement: The risk-based guidelines for commercial banks attempt to gauge the interest rate risk associated with a bank's balance sheet.

17. **a.** What is the primary asset in which savings and loan associations invest?

    b. Why were banks in a better position than savings and loan associations to weather rising interest rates?

18. What federal agency regulates the activities of credit unions?

The U.S. Federal Reserve and the Creation of Money

LEARNING OBJECTIVES

After reading this chapter, you will understand

- what a central bank is and the role of central banks

- the structure of the Federal Reserve System and the nature of the Fed's instruments of monetary policy

- the meaning of required reserves for banks, and the fractional reserve banking system of the United States

- the implementation and impact of open market operations and of open market repurchase agreements

- the role of the Fed's discount rate

- the different kinds of money and the definitions of key monetary aggregates

- the money multiplier, and how it generates changes in the monetary aggregates from changes in the banking system's reserves

- how banks and investors participate with the Fed in changing the level of the monetary aggregates

- how global trade and investment influence the Fed's monetary policy

In economies or groups of economies, the process by which the supply of money is created is a complex interaction among several economic agents, which perform different functions at different times. The agents are firms and individuals who both save and borrow, depository institutions that accept savings and make loans to firms, government entities, individuals and other institutions, and the nation's central bank, which also lends and buys and sells securities. This chapter gives a brief and general description of the complex process of creating the **money supply**. In so doing, the chapter highlights the role played by

U.S. depository institutions and by the financial markets that the process both uses and affects. We begin with a brief description of the role of central banks in general and then focus on the U.S. central bank.

CENTRAL BANKS AND THEIR PURPOSE

The primary role of a **central bank** is to maintain the stability of the currency and money supply for a country or a group of countries. To be a little more specific, let's look at the central bank of the United Kingdom, the Bank of England. On its website, it identifies as its role in financial stability as being as follows:

Risk Assessment: monitoring current developments both in the UK and abroad—including links between financial markets and the wider economy and, within financial markets, between different participants—to identify key risks to the financial system. For example, the Bank examines the overall financial position of borrowers and lenders, the links between financial institutions and the resilience and vulnerability of households, firms, financial institutions and international financial systems to changes in circumstances. The Bank also conducts risk assessment and research on the major developed countries and the main emerging-market economies.

Risk Reduction: reducing vulnerabilities and increasing the financial system's ability to absorb unexpected events. This can involve the promotion of codes and standards over a wide field ranging from accounting to improving legal certainty, and management of countries' external balance sheets.

Oversight of Payment Systems: oversight of the main payment and settlement systems in the UK that are used for many types of financial transaction—from paying wages and credit card bills to the settlement of transactions between financial institutions.

Crisis management: developing and coordinating information sharing within the Bank, with the FSA and HM Treasury, and with authorities internationally to ensure future financial crises are handled and managed effectively. In undertaking this work, the Bank advises on and implements policy measures to mitigate risks to the financial system.[1]

Here are excerpts from the central banks of three other countries:

Bank of Japan: The Bank of Japan Law sets forth that the objectives of the central bank of Japan, the Bank of Japan, are "to issue banknotes and to carry out currency and monetary control" and "to ensure smooth settlement of funds among banks and other financial institutions, thereby contributing to the maintenance of an orderly financial system." Furthermore, this law specifies that the Bank of Japan's principle of currency and monetary control is as follows: "currency and monetary control shall be aimed at, through the pursuit of price stability, contributing to the sound development of the national economy."

Bank of Canada: The Bank of Canada Act sets the principal role of the country's central bank, the Bank of Canada, to be "to promote the economic and financial welfare of

---

[1] http://www.bankofengland.co.uk/financialstability/functions.htm. In the quote, "FSA" is the Financial Services Authority and "HM Treasury" is Her Majesty's Treasury.

Canada." The mission statement is "The Bank of Canada's responsibilities focus on the goals of low and stable inflation, a safe and secure currency, financial stability, and the efficient management of government funds and public debt."

Reserve Bank of India: The preamble of India's central bank, the Reserve Bank of India, sets forth its basic functions of as ". . . to regulate the issue of Bank Notes and keeping of reserves with a view to securing monetary stability in India and generally to operate the currency and credit system of the country to its advantage."

One of the major ways a central bank accomplishes its goals is through monetary policy. For this reason, a central bank is sometimes referred to as a **monetary authority** (e.g., Monetary Authority of Singapore, Hong Kong Monetary Authority, and Bermuda Monetary Authority). In implementing monetary policy, central banks require private banks to maintain and deposit the required reserves with the central bank (we discuss reserve requirements later in this chapter). For this reason, a central bank is also referred to as a **reserve bank** (e.g., Reserve Bank of Australia, Reserve Bank of India, and South African Reserve Bank).

In discharging its responsibilities during a financial crisis or to avert a financial crisis, central banks perform the role of lender of last resort for the banking system. For example, the Bank of England states the following for its role as lender of last resort:

> In exceptional circumstances, as part of its central banking functions, the Bank may act as "lender of last resort" to financial institutions in difficulty, in order to prevent a loss of confidence spreading through the financial system as a whole. This role is set out in the Memorandum of Understanding, which also establishes arrangements for a Standing Committee of the three bodies to ensure effective exchange of information and to co-ordinate the response to a crisis.[2]

The central banks throughout the world are listed in the appendix to this chapter, which can be found online at www.pearsonhighered.com/fabozzi. In addition to the individual countries' central banks, there is the **European Central Bank (ECB)**. The ECB, which came into being on January 1, 1999, is responsible for implementing the monetary policy for the member countries of the European Union. The European System of Central Banks consists of the ECB and the central banks of the member countries.

There is widespread agreement that the central bank should be independent of the government so that decisions of the central bank will not be influenced for short-term political purposes such as pursuing a monetary policy to expand the economy but at the expense of inflation.[3] As stated in a speech by Frederic Mishkin, a governor of the U.S. Federal Reserve Board of Governors, on April 3, 2008: "Evidence supports the conjecture that macroeconomic performance is improved when central banks are more independent."[4] He provides examples from the Bank of England and Bank of Canada.[5] Moreover, this view is supported by several studies of central banks of industrialized countries.

---

[2] http://www.bankofengland.co.uk/financialstability/functions.htm.

[3] Further analysis and discussion regarding the issue of central bank independence can be found in James Forder, "Central Bank Independence and Credibility: Is There a Shred of Evidence?" *International Finance*, Vol. 3 (April 2000), pp. 167–85 and Alex Cukierman, "Central Bank Independence and Monetary Policy Making Institutions: Past, Present, and Future," *Journal Economía Chilena*, Vol. 9 (April 2006), pp. 5–23.

[4] "Central Bank Commitment and Communication" presentation at the Princeton University Center for Policy Studies," http://www.federalreserve.gov/newsevents/speech/mishkin20080403a.htm#f19.

[5] Further evidence is provided in Frederick S. Mishkin and and Niklas J. Westelius, "Inflation Band Targeting and Optimal Inflation Contracts," NBER Working Paper No. 12384, July 2006.

In 1975, as a result of the oil crisis and economic recessions being faced throughout the world, the United States formed an informal meeting of senior financial officials from five countries in addition to the United States: United Kingdom, France, Germany, Italy, and Japan. The group, which became known as the **Group of 6 (G6)**, decided to meet annually thereafter. The following year, Canada joined the group, which then became known as the **Group of 7 (G7)**. In 1998, Russia joined the group, which is now known as the **Group of 8 (G8)**. Although the G8 can concur on economic and financial policies and establish objectives, compliance is voluntary.[6]

THE CENTRAL BANK OF THE UNITED STATES: THE FEDERAL RESERVE SYSTEM

The most important agent in the money supply process is the Federal Reserve System, which is the central bank of the United States and often called just the Federal Reserve or "the Fed." Created in 1913, the Fed is the government agency responsible for the management of the U.S. monetary and banking systems. Most large commercial banks in the United States are members of the Federal Reserve System. The Fed is managed by a seven-member **Board of Governors,** who are appointed by the president and approved by the Congress. These governors have 14-year appointments (with one appointment ending every two years), and one governor is the board's chairman. The **Chairmanship of the Fed** is a highly visible and influential position in the world economy. The Federal Reserve System consists of 12 districts covering the entire country; each **district** has a Federal Reserve Bank that has its own president.

An important feature of the Fed is that, by the terms of the law that created it, neither the legislative nor the executive branch of the federal government should exert control over it. From time to time, critics charge that the Fed guards this autonomy by accommodating either the White House or Congress (or both) far too much. The Fed has substantial regulatory power over the nation's depository institutions, especially commercial banks.

It is worth noting here, before we discuss the Fed's tools for monetary management, that financial innovations in the past two decades have made the Fed's task more difficult. The public's increasing acceptance of money market mutual funds has funneled a large amount of money into what are essentially interest-bearing checking accounts. Another relevant innovation is the practice of asset securitization. Securitization permits commercial banks to change what once were illiquid consumer loans of several varieties into securities. Selling these securities in the financial markets gives the banks a source of funding that is outside the Fed's influence. The many hedging instruments have also affected banks' behavior and their relationship with the Fed. In general, that transformation amounts to reduced Fed control of banks and increased difficulty in implementing monetary policy.

---

[6] The G8 has in recent years dealt with other issues such as the prevention of HIV/AIDS, Middle East peace, reconstruction of Iraq, global security, and illegal logging.

INSTRUMENTS OF MONETARY POLICY: HOW THE FED INFLUENCES THE SUPPLY OF MONEY

The Fed has several tools by which it influences, indirectly and to a greater or lesser extent, the amount of money in the economy and the general level of interest rates. These tools are reserve requirements (whose use is somewhat constricted by Congressional mandate), open market operations, open market repurchase agreements, and the discount rate. These instruments represent the key ways that the Fed interacts with commercial banks in the process of creating money. Our discussion of these tools explains the impact of their use on a generally specified money supply. Later, we describe the money supply in more detail.

Reserve Requirements

Bank reserves play an important role in the U.S. banking and monetary system and are directly linked to the growth in the money supply. Generally, the higher the growth rate in reserves, the higher the rate of change in the money supply. Later in this chapter, we will discuss this linkage in some detail. At this point, we want to focus on the meaning and function of reserve requirements.

The United States has a **fractional reserve banking system**, which means that a bank must hold or "reserve" some portion of the funds that savers deposit in a form approved by the Fed. As a result, a bank may lend to borrowers only a fraction of what it takes in as deposits. The ratio of mandatory reserves to deposits is the **required reserve ratio**. For many years, the Fed had the authority to set this ratio. In the Depository Institutions Deregulation and Monetary Control Act (DIDMCA) of 1980, Congress assumed much of that responsibility, establishing new rules regarding this ratio to be applied to all depository institutions, including commercial banks, thrifts of various types, and credit unions.

In a key provision of the DIDMCA, Congress adopted a basic ratio of 12% for what are termed checkable or transactional accounts, that is, *demand deposits*, or accounts on which checks may be written often. For nontransactional but short-term deposit accounts—known as *time deposits*—the required reserve ratio is 3%. The 1980 law also authorizes the Fed to change the required reserve ratio on checking accounts to any level between 8% and 14%, and to raise it to 18% under certain conditions. In early 1992, the Fed reduced the ratio to 10% for banks with total checkable accounts at or above $46.8 million. For banks with smaller totals in these accounts, the required reserve ratio is 3%.

A bank must maintain the required reserves as either currency on hand (that is, cash in the bank) or deposits in the Federal Reserve itself. The more important form is the deposit, which serves as an asset for the bank and as a liability of the Fed. A bank has *excess reserves* if its reserves amount to more than the Fed requires. A bank's **total reserves** equal its required reserves plus any excess reserves. A bank whose actual reserves fall short of required levels can borrow excess reserves from other banks, or it can borrow reserves from the Fed itself, which we discuss later in this chapter.

Open Market Operations

The Fed's most powerful instrument is its authority to conduct **open market operations**, which means that the Fed may buy and sell, in open debt markets, government securities for its own account. These securities may be U.S. Treasury bonds, Treasury bills, or obligations of federal agencies. The Fed prefers to use Treasury bills because, in that large and liquid market, it can make its substantial transactions without seriously disrupting the prices or yields of bills. When it buys or sells, the Fed does so at prices and interest rates that prevail in these debt markets. The parties to the Fed's transactions may be commercial banks or other financial agents who are dealers in government securities.

The unit of the Fed that decides on the general issues of changing the rate of growth in the money supply, by open market sales or purchase of securities, is the **Federal Open Market Committee (FOMC).** The FOMC consists of the Board of Governors, the president of the Federal Reserve Bank of New York, and presidents of some of the other district Fed banks. This committee meets approximately every six weeks to analyze economic activity and levels of key economic variables. The variables may include short-term interest rates (such as the federal funds rate), the U.S. dollar's rate of exchange with important foreign currencies, commodity prices, and excess reserves, among other things.[7] After this analysis, the committee sets the direction of monetary policy until the next meeting. This direction is summarized in a brief "directive" at the time of the announcement after the meeting. The minutes of these meetings are published at a later time.

The implementation of policy, through open market operations, is the responsibility of the **trading desk of the Federal Reserve Bank of New York.** The desk transacts, in large volume, with large securities firms or commercial banks that are dealers, or market makers, in Treasury securities. While the desk does not buy and sell for profit, it functions as a rational investor, buying at the lowest prices and selling at the highest prices offered at the time of the transactions.

Fed purchases augment the amount of reserves in the banking system. If the seller is a commercial bank, it alters the composition, but not the total, of its assets by exchanging the securities for reserves at the Fed. If the seller is not a bank, much or all of the check with which the Fed pays will probably be deposited in a bank. The bank receiving the deposit would experience an increase in liabilities (the customer's deposit) and in assets (the growth in its reserve account at the Fed). In either case, the proceeds from selling the securities to the Fed raise the banking system's total reserves. Such an increase in reserves typically leads to an increase in the money supply. Individual banks whose reserves rise will generally make new loans, equal to the new deposit less required reserves, because loans earn interest while reserves do not. New loans represent growth in the money supply.

Conversely, the Fed's sale of Treasury securities reduces the money supply (or its rate of growth) because the funds that security dealers pay for the securities come from either deposits at banks or, if the dealers are banks, from the banks' own accounts. A reduction in deposits reduces reserves and leaves the banks less to lend.

Open Market Repurchase Agreements

The Fed often employs variants of simple open market purchases and sales, and these are called the **repurchase agreement (repo)** and the *reverse repo*. The Fed conducts these transactions, which are actually more common than the outright purchases or sales,[8] with

---

[7] D.S. Batten, M.P. Blackwell, I-S. Kim, S.E. Nocera, and Y. Ozeki, *The Conduct of Monetary Policy in the Major Industrial Countries*, Occasional Paper No. 70, International Monetary Fund (Washington: July 1990), p. 24.
[8] David M. Jones and Ellen Rachling, "Monetary Policy: How the Fed Sets, Implements, and Measures Policy Chokes," chapter 2 in Frank J. Fabozzi (ed.), *Handbook of Portfolio Management* (New Hope, PA: Frank J. Fabozzi Associates, 1998).

large dealers in government securities and, occasionally, with central banks of other countries. In a repurchase agreement, the Fed buys a particular amount of securities from a seller that agrees to repurchase the same number of securities for a higher price at some future time, usually a few weeks. The difference between the original price and the repurchase price is the return to the Fed for letting the dealer have the cash for the life of the agreement and, also, the cost to the dealer of borrowing from the Fed. In a reverse repo (also known as a *matched sale* or a *matched sale-purchase transaction*), the Fed sells securities and makes a commitment to buy them back at a higher price later. The difference in the two prices is the cost to the Fed of the funds and the return to the buyer for lending money.

An example will illustrate some of the points in a Fed repurchase agreement. Suppose the Fed wants to increase bank reserves for some reason over a short period of time, and it seeks out a financial institution that has $20 million in Treasury securities but no excess reserves. Suppose further that the institution wants to lend $20 million for seven days to a borrower. After some discussions, the Fed agrees to "buy" the securities from the institution at a price that reflects the current repo rate, and to "sell" them back in seven days, when the institution's borrower pays off that loan. The current annualized rate is 4.3%. The transaction would look like this: The Fed would buy the securities for approximately $19,983,292 and sell them back, seven days later, to the institution at the principal value of $20 million. The difference of nearly $16,708 is the interest the institution pays for the seven-day financing and the return to the Fed for lending that money. And for those seven days, the financial institution and the entire banking system can enjoy an increase in reserves, if, of course, the bank keeps the roughly $20 million in its account at the Fed.

The Fed uses repos and reverse repos to bring about a temporary change in the level of reserves in the system or to respond to some event that the Fed thinks will have a significant but not long-lived effect. A particularly good example of such an event is a large payment by the U.S. Treasury (as in tax refunds or Social Security benefits) that sharply but temporarily raises reserves at the banks. Of course, these temporary changes in the system's reserves alter the banks' ability to make loans and, ultimately, to prompt growth in the money supply for a short period.

Discount Rate

The Fed makes loans to banks that are members of the system. A bank borrowing from the Fed is said to use the *discount window*, and these loans are backed by the bank's collateral. The rate of interest on these loans is the *discount rate*, set at a certain level by the Fed's Board of Governors. As the rate rises, banks are understandably less likely to borrow; a falling rate tends to encourage them to borrow. Proceeds from *discount loans* are also reserves and increase the banks' capacity to make loans. Banks generally do not prefer to gain reserves in this way because the loans cost money as well as invite increased monitoring of the borrowing banks' activities. Accordingly, the flow of this borrowing has a very slight impact on the money banks have and can lend and, therefore, on the supply of money.

There is general agreement that the discount rate is the least effective tool at the Fed's disposal and its use in monetary policy has diminished over time. Today, changes in the discount rate function largely as the Fed's public signals about its intention to change the rate at which the money supply is growing.

DIFFERENT KINDS OF MONEY

Until now, we have spoken in general terms about the money supply. But we can be more precise and identify several different meanings of the word *money* and several different types of money.

First of all, money is that item which serves as a **numeraire**, or unit of account—in other words, the unit that is used to measure wealth. In the United States, the numeraire is the dollar; in Japan, it is the yen; and so on. Second, we call money any instrument that serves as a medium of exchange, that is, anything that is generally accepted in payment for goods, services, and capital transactions. In the United States, the medium of exchange encompasses currency, which is issued by the Treasury or the Fed, and demand deposits, which support payment by means of checks and are held at depository institutions such as commercial banks. The medium of exchange also performs the function of being a store of value, which means that the exchange medium can be used to carry resources over from the present to the future. Obviously, this function is impaired in times of high and unpredictable inflation.[9] Other accounts that resemble demand deposits include the NOW account (or Negotiable Order of Withdrawal account) and share drafts of credit unions.

Other assets that do not function in the role of medium of exchange have many properties in common with the numeraire. These properties include safety, divisibility, and high liquidity, which is the capacity of being transformed into the medium of exchange promptly and at negligible cost. Because of these properties, these assets are good substitutes for money, in particular, as stores of value. The assets of this type include *time deposits* at commercial banks or thrifts. These accounts earn interest over their specified lives, and the investor may not draw on the money in the account for a transaction, without incurring a penalty, until the deposit's maturity date. Other assets that are substitutes for money include balances in money market mutual funds.

MONEY AND MONETARY AGGREGATES

Monetary policy and the actions of the Federal Reserve System often concentrate on what are called **monetary aggregates**. The purpose of the aggregates is to measure the amount of money available to the economy at any time.

The most basic monetary aggregate is the **monetary base**. Also termed *high-powered money*, the base is defined as currency in circulation (or coins and Federal Reserve notes held by the public) plus the total reserves in the banking system. It is important to note that reserves make up the bulk of the base, which is under the control of the Fed. Thus, this aggregate is the one that the Fed is most able to influence with its various monetary tools.

The instruments that serve the role of **medium of exchange**—currency and demand deposits—are included in a monetary aggregate that is sometimes referred to as the narrow measure of the money supply and is labeled M_1. Thus, M_1 measures the amount of the medium of exchange in the economy.

M_2 is a more inclusive aggregate because it takes into account all the instruments that substitute for money in the capacity of storing value. Therefore, M_2 is defined as M_1 plus all dollars held in time and savings accounts at banks and thrift institutions, plus all dollars

---

[9] The *giro payment*, an alternative to the check, is used in many foreign countries. The giro payment is a direct order to the payer's bank to make a payment to a seller of some good or service. The check, of course, is an order to pay that is drawn on an account at the payer's bank and that the payer gives to the seller.

invested in retail money market mutual funds, plus some additional accounts such as overnight repurchase agreements. Some analysts also watch developments in two other monetary aggregates, which are labeled M_3 and L (for liquid assets). These aggregates equal M_2 plus certain other financial assets, including long-term time deposits, commercial paper, bankers' acceptances, and some Treasury securities.

The ratio of the money supply to the economy's income (as reflected by the gross national product or some similar measure) is known as the **velocity of money** in circulation. Velocity measures the average amount of transactions carried by a dollar. If the economy's velocity were stable, monetary policy could achieve any desired level of income by simply targeting the aggregate M_1. Unfortunately, velocity is not a stable relationship, and in fact, the linkages between the economy's income and the various aggregates vary considerably over time.

Typically, the monetary aggregates move in somewhat similar patterns, rising and falling at roughly the same rates and at roughly the same times. Table 1 shows the growth

Table 1	Annual Rates of Growth in Monetary Aggregates 1980–2007	
Year	M_1	M_2
1980	6.9%	8.5%
1981	6.9	9.7
1982	8.7	8.8
1983	9.8	11.3
1984	5.8	8.6
1985	12.4	8.0
1986	16.9	9.5
1987	3.5	3.6
1988	4.9	5.8
1989	0.8	5.5
1990	4.0	3.8
1991	8.8	3.1
1992	14.3	1.6
1993	10.2	8.5
1994	1.9	0.5
1995	−2.0	4.1
1996	−4.1	4.9
1997	−0.8	5.6
1998	2.1	8.6
1999	2.5	5.9
2000	−3.1	6.1
2001	8.7	10.4
2002	3.2	6.4
2003	7.1	5.1
2004	5.4	5.8
2005	−0.1	4.2
2006	−0.5	5.1
2007	−0.2	5.9

Note: *Annual changes are from December to December.*
Source: *Economic Report of the President 2007. 2005 data from www.Federalreserve.gov (Research and Data Section).*

rates for M_1 and M_2 during the period from 1980 to 2007. However, the differences among the changes in the aggregates are large and frequent enough to suggest that these aggregates are measuring different things. A major question in Fed policymaking (which we discuss below) has revolved around choosing the most appropriate definition of the money supply.

THE MONEY MULTIPLIER: THE EXPANSION OF THE MONEY SUPPLY

Our discussion of how the supply of money is created focuses on the linkage between the banking system's reserves and the aggregate M_1. The process we describe, the **money multiplier**, can be generalized to the other monetary aggregates, but the complexities involved in those processes are not relevant to our task now.

We begin by restating that the creation of the money supply, and changes in it, is a complex interaction of four parties: the Fed, banks, savers, and borrowers. The Fed provides reserves to banks and also requires banks to hold, as reserves, a portion of the deposits that the public holds at the banks. The banks, playing their key role in the money multiplier, lend the remainder of the deposits (or most of it) to borrowers at an interest rate that exceeds that of demand deposits. For any one bank, the remainder equals deposits less required reserves, which can be expressed as deposits times $(1 -$ required reserve ratio$)$. Clearly, the funds one bank lends to a borrower can become the borrower's deposits in another bank. The borrower's decision to hold wealth as deposits rather than cash also affects the money multiplier. Then, that second bank must keep a fraction of those new deposits as reserves and can lend out to other borrowers an amount equal to the deposits less required reserves.

We will illustrate this process with an extended example. Suppose the Fed's required reserve ratio is 12%, and deposits at Bank A are $100 million, while those at Bank B are $50 million. Bank A has reserves of $12 million and outstanding loans of $88 million, and Bank B has reserves of $6 million with loans to borrowers of $44 million. For Bank A, the loan amount to $88 million equals either $100 million of deposits less $12 million of reserves, or $100 million times $(1 - 0.12)$. For Bank B, loans of $44 million equal $50 million minus the 12% required reserves of $6 million. Thus, neither Bank A nor Bank B has any *excess reserves* (which equal total less required reserves). The level of reserves in the banking system has led M_1 to reach the level of (let us say) $900 billion, which equals $250 billion in currency and $650 billion in demand deposits. For this example, we assume that the amount of currency in the system will not change.

The Fed can increase the reserves by either lending to the banks or by purchasing government securities from the banks or other investors. (We ignore here the Fed's authority to change the required reserve ratio.) In this example, we suppose that the Fed buys $5 million of U.S. Treasury securities from a dealer who deposits the check, which is drawn on the Fed, with Bank A. Bank A's reserve account with the Fed has increased by $5 million and so have its (demand) deposits, its total reserves, and the overall level of M_1. But required reserves have risen only by $5 million $\times$ 0.12 or $600,000. This leaves an additional $4.4 million that the bank is free and eager to invest in order to improve its income.

We continue by assuming that a machinery manufacturing firm borrows all of the $4.4 million in a one-year loan, then buys equipment from a company that places all of that money in a checking account (or demand deposit) at another bank, which is Bank B. Bank A must transfer reserves for the amount of the loan to Bank B. The situation regarding

The U.S. Federal Reserve and the Creation of Money

Bank A is this: Its level of deposits remains unchanged at $105 million; its loans have increased by $4.4 million to $92.4 million; its reserves have fallen by $4.4 million from $17 million to $12.6 million; so, its ratio of reserves to deposits is again the required 12% and it has reached its capacity for making loans. Since Bank A's deposits are unchanged, M_1 is also unchanged from its new level of $900.005 billion.

After the transaction, Bank B's deposits have risen by $4.4 million, an increase that raises the amount of M_1 by an additional $4.4 million (or $9.4 million altogether, so far) to $900.0094 billion. Bank B has total reserves of $10.4 million and excess reserves equal to 88% of the $4.4 million in new deposits. Thus, Bank B can lend $3.87 million, keeping $528,000 as required reserves. If loans of $3.87 million are made to borrowers who place those loans as deposits with other banks, the process of creating money, in the form of M_1, will continue.

Where will the process end and what amount of new money, in the form of new demand deposits, will arise from the new reserves? In other words, what is the money multiplier? In this example, the Fed's open market purchase of $5 million of U.S. Treasury securities, along with the banks' incentive to make as many loans as they are permitted to do, has created demand deposits of $9.4 million at the first two banks involved. Still more deposits can be created at other banks. This process will continue as long as other banks use the ever smaller increases in demand deposits to make loans, which become additional demand deposits and excess reserves at still other banks, and so on. Although the process has no set limit in terms of time, there is a maximum number of dollars in new demand deposits that will spring from the new reserves.

This process is a form of a multiplier series that can be expressed in an algebraic formula. If we let ΔTDD be the total demand deposits created, ΔR be the reserves injected into the system by the Fed's purchase of Treasury securities, and REQ be the required reserve ratio, then the total of new deposits generated by the expansion of the initial injection of reserves would equal:

$$\Delta TDD = \Delta R + (1 - REQ) \times \Delta R + (1 - REQ)^2 \times \Delta R + (1 - REQ)^3 \times \Delta R \\ + (1 - REQ)^4 \times \Delta R + \ldots \tag{1}$$

Because there are many potential elements in this series, which can get cumbersome, it is best to use this simple version of it:

$$\Delta TDD = \Delta R / REQ \tag{2}$$

In the example, REQ equals 12% and ΔR equals $5 million. Hence, new total demand deposits (if banks lend as much as they can and keep no excess reserves) amount to $5 million/0.12, or $41.67 million. The money multiplier is, therefore, 8.33 ($41.67/5). As a result, total M_1 will reach $900.04167 billion when the process is completed, which equals the original $900 billion plus $41.67 million in new deposits. Equation (2) clearly shows that the eventual amount of the new demand deposits is negatively related to the required reserve ratio: As REQ falls, the change in TDD rises; and as REQ increases, the change in TDD declines. Thus, if everything in the example were the same, but REQ were 10% instead of 12%, the new demand deposits would reach $50 million.

Obviously, the process of reducing the money supply works in the opposite way. That is, if the Fed wants to drain reserves from the system and reduce the banks' lending ability, it sells securities. The reduction in reserves, as the public trades deposits for marketable securities, allows banks to make fewer new loans or to renew fewer old ones.

THE IMPACT OF INTEREST RATES ON THE MONEY SUPPLY

Interest rates actually influence the change in the money supply. This point emerges from an evaluation of two key assumptions made above.[10] First, banks are assumed to want to make all the loans they can. If, however, banks were to keep some excess reserves, they would make fewer new loans and generate fewer deposits at other banks, which would affect the amount of M_1 that the Fed's purchase of securities would generate.

One of the important factors in a bank's decisions about excess reserves is the level of market interest rates. High rates make excess reserves costly because they represent loans not made and interest not earned. If rates are low, banks may keep some excess reserves. Hence, the level of interest rates positively influences the amount of M_1 that any increase in reserves will create. Moreover, interest rates can also positively (but probably only slightly) affect the amount of reserves in the system: High market rates may prompt banks to borrow at the discount window in order to make loans, and these borrowed funds are part of reserves.

By the second assumption, borrowers retain none of their loans in cash, but rather deposit all cash flows—proceeds from sold securities, loans, and so on—into checking accounts. In contrast, if borrowers took some of their borrowings in cash, banks would receive fewer deposits and would have fewer reserves from which to make new loans. Accordingly, the public's demand for cash as a portion of its liquid wealth has an impact on the amount of M_1 that arises from the Fed's injection of new reserves.

The level of market rates shapes decisions about cash holdings. Many deposit accounts pay interest, so holding cash imposes an opportunity cost. The higher the rate, the greater the cost, and the more money investors will shuttle into deposits. But the rate on deposits is not the only relevant interest rate. The desired amount of deposits, from which transactions can be easily made, also reflects the rates of return from other assets. As those returns rise, investors would hold more in deposit accounts. For these reasons, the level of interest rates positively affects the size of the money multiplier and, hence, the amount of M_1 that any increase in reserves will produce.

An example will illustrate this point about the impact of rates on the money multiplier and the change in the money supply arising from an infusion of reserves by the Fed. The money multiplier from the previous example was 8.33 or (1/REQ), where REQ was 0.12. Let us now assume that the behavior of banks and depositors responds to interest rates. First, we will assume that the rate of return on bank loans is such that banks do not make all the loans they can but rather want to hold 1% of their deposits (TDD) in excess reserves (ER), with the result that the ratio (ER/TDD) equals 0.01. Second, let us suppose that the interest rate is at the level where the public will hold only 75% in checkable deposits (rather than 100% as before) and 25% in cash or currency. This means that the ratio (C/TDD) is 0.33. With these assumptions, the formula for the multiplier would now be this:

$$\frac{1 + (C/TDD)}{REQ + (ER/TDD) + (C/TDD)}$$

[10] Lucas Papademos and Franco Modigliani, "The Supply of Money and the Control of Nominal Income," chapter 10 in Benjamin M. Friedman and Frank H. Hahn (eds.), *Handbook of Monetary Economics* (Amsterdam: North-Holland, Elsevier, 1990), pp. 428–430.

Plugging in the actual values, we have a much lower multiplier, which is this:

$$\frac{1.33}{0.12 + (0.1) + 0.33} = 2.89$$

Remember, this multiplier is lower because households and banks do not deposit or lend, respectively, all that they can, and these drains from the money creation process reduce the multiplier effect of any increase in reserves.

THE MONEY SUPPLY PROCESS IN AN OPEN ECONOMY

Our discussion so far describes central bank activity in what economists call a *closed economy*. A closed economy is one in which foreign transactors—of either goods or financial assets—play a negligible role. In the modern era, almost every country has an **open economy**, where foreign firms and investors account for a large and increasing share of economic activity. This is especially true of the world's largest economy, that of the United States. Understanding of the money supply process, therefore, must include the influence of the foreign sector.

Monetarily, the crucial fact of significant foreign participation in the U.S. economy is that foreign central banks, firms, and individuals hold a substantial number of U.S. dollars. They do so for transactional reasons—buying and selling goods and services in the United States—and for investment purposes—treating the dollar as a financial asset. What makes the foreign holdings of dollars important is that the dollar's exchange rate with currencies of most developed countries floats according to demand and supply in the market. (Most central banks, including the Fed, try to keep exchange rates within politically acceptable ranges.)

Shifts in the dollar's exchange rates, obviously, affect the prices of domestic and imported goods, the revenues of U.S. companies, and the wealth of all investors in the country. As a result, the Fed accepts the responsibility to maintain some stability in the exchange rates. A major way to discharge this duty is to *intervene in the foreign exchange markets*. The Fed intervenes by buying and selling foreign currencies for its own account. (Most central banks of large economies own, or stand ready to own, a large amount of each of the world's major currencies, which are considered **international reserves**.)

If the Fed thinks the dollar's value is too high and a foreign currency's is too low, it can purchase some of the foreign currency with its own supply of dollars. A purchase involves increasing the outstanding number of dollars and thereby the monetary base. If the Fed thinks the dollar has too low a value relative to some other currency, it might sell some of its holdings of that currency for dollars. Thus, selling foreign currency entails a reduction in the monetary base. Intervention in the currency market is often a response to a particular international event. Moreover, the intervention usually involves a transaction with other central banks, which consists of an immediate exchange of currencies and an agreement for a future offsetting exchange. Thus, this kind of action allows the Fed to know the terms on which the currency deal will terminate and the time when it will terminate.

The dollar's exchange rates with important foreign currencies function as a major goal of monetary policy. That is, in forging and implementing policy; the Fed considers the effect of a change in the money supply on the relative value of the dollar in the foreign exchange market.

Dramatic evidence of the growing importance of international policy coordination on monetary matters occurred in two meetings of central bankers of the large industrial nations in the mid 1980s. In 1985, central bank chairmen and directors of the United States, Great Britain, France, Germany, and Japan (known as the Group of Five) met at the Plaza Hotel in New York. This is known as the Plaza Agreement. They agreed to coordinate policies in order to bring down the value of the U.S. dollar and to stabilize international exchange rates and trade. In 1987, at the Louvre Museum in Paris, central bankers from these five countries and Canada agreed to work together to keep exchange rates at their current levels. These efforts at international cooperation on monetary and exchange issues are generally seen as successful.[11]

Key Points That You Should Understand Before Proceeding

1. The Federal Reserve System is the central bank of the United States and responsible for the conduct of monetary policy.
2. The instruments of monetary policy, including reserve requirements, open market operations and repurchase agreements, and the discount rate.
3. The different kinds of money, such as the numeraire, the store of value, and the medium of exchange.
4. The various monetary aggregates and what they are supposed to convey to policymakers.
5. The nature of the money multiplier and how it links reserves in the banking system to monetary aggregates.
6. That interest rates affect the rate at which the money supply changes in response to actions by the Fed.
7. That the openness of an economy to participation by foreign firms, central banks, and individuals affects monetary management.

SUMMARY

The central bank of a country plays a key role in that country's economic and financial markets by implementing policies to stabilize the currency and controlling the money supply. The central bank may also act as a lender of last resort to the bank system in order to avert a financial crisis. Evidence suggests that a central bank can act more effectively by being independent of the government.

The Federal Reserve System is the U.S. central bank. Its tools of monetary policy include required reserves, open market operations and repurchases, and discount loans to banks. The Fed supplies reserves to the banking system, which participates, along with investors, in generating the money supply. The chief means of supplying reserves is open market operations: The Fed's purchase of government securities provides reserves, and the Fed's sale of securities reduces reserves. The money supply is composed of various types of money as well as demand and time deposits, which can be grouped into monetary aggregates. The fundamental aggregate is the monetary base, composed of currency plus total

---

[11] Frederic S. Mishkin, "What Should Central Banks Do," *Federal Reserve Bank of St. Louis Review*, November/ December 2000, 82, 6, pp. 1–13.

reserves in the banking system. M_1 equals currency plus all checkable deposits. Other aggregates include various time deposits.

The money multiplier is the process by which changes in bank reserves generate larger changes in the money supply. The banks use the added reserves to buy assets or to make loans; the seller or borrower redeposits these proceeds, which then support additional loans, and so on. The value of the multiplier depends on the required reserve ratio, the public's demand for cash, the banks' willingness to make loans, and the level of interest rates.

The growing international integration of economies requires that the Fed, along with other central banks, consider the impact of its monetary operations on foreign currency exchange rates. Thus, monetary policy must be considered from the standpoint of open economies, not the closed ones of years past.

KEY TERMS

- Board of Governors
- Central bank
- Chairmanship of the Fed
- District
- European Central Bank (ECB)
- Federal Open Market Committee (FOMC)
- Fractional reserve banking system
- Group of 6 (G6)
- Group of 7 (G7)
- Group of 8 (G8)
- International reserves
- L
- M_1
- M_2
- M_3

- Medium of exchange
- Monetary aggregate
- Monetary authority
- Monetary base
- Money multiplier
- Money supply
- Numeraire
- Open economy
- Open market operations
- Repurchase agreement (repo)
- Required reserve ratio
- Reserve bank
- Total reserves
- Trading desk of the Federal Reserve Bank of New York
- Velocity of money

QUESTIONS

1. What is the role of a central bank?
2. Why is it argued that a central bank should be independent of the government?
3. Identify each participant and its role in the process by which the money supply changes and monetary policy is implemented.
4. Describe the structure of the board of governors of the Federal Reserve System.
5. **a.** Explain what is meant by the statement "the United States has a fractional reserve banking system."
   b. How are these items related: total reserves, required reserves, and excess reserves?

6. What is the required reserve ratio, and how has the 1980 Depository Institutions Deregulation and Monetary Control Act constrained the Fed's control over the ratio?
7. In what two forms can a bank hold its required reserves?
8. **a.** What is an open market purchase by the Fed?
   b. Which unit of the Fed decides on open market policy, and what unit implements that policy?
   c. What is the immediate consequence of an open market purchase?

9. Distinguish between an open market sale and a matched sale (which is the same as a matched sale-purchase transaction or a reverse repurchase agreement).

10. What is the discount rate, and to what type of action by a bank does it apply?

11. Define the monetary base and M_2.

12. Describe the basic features of the money multiplier.

13. Suppose the Fed were to inject $100 million of reserves into the banking system by an open market purchase of Treasury bills. If the required reserve ratio were 10%, what is the maximum increase in M_1 that the new reserves would generate? Assume that banks make all the loans their reserves allow, that firms and individuals keep all their liquid assets in depository accounts, and no money is in the form of currency.

14. Assume the situation from question 13, except now assume that banks hold a ratio of 0.5% of excess reserves to deposits and the public keeps 20% of its liquid assets in the form of cash. Under these conditions, what is the money multiplier? Explain why this value of the multiplier is so much lower than the multiplier from question 13.

Monetary Policy

LEARNING OBJECTIVES

After reading this chapter, you will understand

- the goals of monetary policy, including price level stability, economic growth, stable interest rates, and stable foreign exchange rates

- that the operating targets of Fed policy are those monetary and financial variables that are affected by its tools in a predictable way

- that intermediate targets are economic variables that the Fed can affect indirectly through its work with operating targets

- that the federal funds rate and bank reserves have often been operating targets of monetary policy

- that the broad monetary aggregates have sometimes served as intermediate targets, as have certain interest rates

The Fed, in interaction with banks and other units of the economy, creates money and credit. There are also tools that the Fed can use to manage the rate of growth in the money supply.

This chapter examines the **goals of monetary policy**; that is, the conditions in the economy that the Fed seeks to bring about. Although the Fed cannot directly cause these conditions to exist, it can follow policies to target variables that it can influence with its tools. We also discuss monetary matters in some other major economies of the world.

From Chapter 5 of *Foundations of Financial Markets and Institutions*, 4/e. Frank J. Fabozzi. Franco Modigliani. Frank J. Jones.

GOALS OF MONETARY POLICY

The Fed, through such tools as open market operations, which change the reserves in the banking system, can prompt the banking system and depositors to implement desired changes in the money supply and in its rates of growth. The Fed manages the money supply in order to achieve certain economic goals. In this section, we identify some of the more commonly cited goals of Fed policy.[1]

Stability in the price level is a major goal of the Fed. Price stability gained new respect in the past 20 years as first inflation, then deflation, ravaged entire economies or major sectors such as farmland and commercial real estate. The standard way of measuring inflation is the change in a major price index. Table 1 shows the yearly percentage change in the Consumer Price Index between 1980 and 1999, and reveals that the high inflation marking the beginning of the 1980s had largely dissipated by the end of that decade. From this experience, policymakers and economists came to appreciate once more that unstable price levels retard economic growth, provoke volatility in interest rates, stimulate consumption, deter savings, and cause capricious redistribution of income and wealth with attendant social disturbances.

Inflation in advanced economies, however, is seldom (if ever) the result of excessive demand due to monetary or fiscal policy. Rather, a more important source of inflation is an economic shock in the supply of a crucial material, such as the oil shocks of the 1970s, which affected almost all countries. Evidence that the inflation at the end of the 1970s was not related to excessive demand for goods and services is that it occurred with high unemployment and gave the world a period of **stagflation**, which is a condition of both inflation and recession.

It is important to note that, when confronted with a supply shock, a central bank such as the Fed has two choices. First, the banking authorities can refuse to accommodate the higher price levels that follow the shock by matching them with an increase in the money

Table 1   Annual Percentage Changes in the Consumer Price Index from 1980–2007

Year	Rate	Year	Rate	Year	Rate
1980	12.5%	1990	6.1%	2000	3.4%
1981	8.9	1991	3.1	2001	1.6
1982	3.8	1992	2.9	2002	2.4
1983	3.8	1993	2.7	2003	1.9
1984	3.9	1994	2.7	2004	3.3
1985	3.8	1995	2.5	2005	3.4
1986	1.1	1996	3.3	2006	2.5
1987	4.4	1997	1.7	2007	4.1
1988	4.4	1998	1.6		
1989	4.6	1999	2.7		

Note: *Annual Changes are from December to December.*
Source: *Economic Report of the President 2007.*

---

[1] Ben Bernanke and Frederic Mishkin, "Guideposts and Signals in the Conduct of Monetary Policy: Lessons from Six Industrialized Countries," presented at the Seventh Annual Conference on Macroeconomics, March 1992.

supply. The results of nonaccommodation will initially tend to be higher interest rates and a decline in economic activity. For this reason, central banks and political authorities frequently have opted for the second choice, which is a policy of accommodation and increased growth in the supply of money. Unfortunately, this kind of policy permits the inflation to continue unchecked or possibly to accelerate.

High employment (or low unemployment) of the civilian labor force represents a second major goal for the Fed. While politicians often speak of the U.S. government's commitment to promoting "full employment," most people understand that an unemployment rate of zero is not possible. The reason is that **frictional unemployment**—the temporary unemployment of those changing jobs or seeking new or better ones—is both unavoidable and helpful to an economy. It is unavoidable because people do change jobs, and are likely to do so more readily as employment levels rise, and because some workers leave and enter the labor market constantly. Frictional unemployment is helpful because it allows a constant reallocation of labor and leads to increased efficiency in the workforce.

Given that zero unemployment is not a feasible aim, the appropriate goal of the Fed and other governmental policymakers is actually a high level of employment. A practical problem, however, is that economists and policymakers cannot agree on a suitable definition or specification of high employment. It does not help to specify a high level of employment as one that approaches 100% less the level of frictional unemployment, because there is also little agreement on the true rate of frictional unemployment.

For practical purposes, many observers consider that a civilian unemployment rate between 4% and 6% indicates an economy operating at or near a level of high employment. This figure allows for frictional unemployment and the effects of the rapid expansion in the workforce over the past several decades. That expansion occurred because of the entry into the workforce of many women, younger workers, and immigrants into the United States.

Table 2 provides yearly information on the U.S. level of unemployment from 1980 to 2007 and shows that relatively high employment occurred in the second half of the 1980s, the late 1990s and early 2000s.

Table 2   Annual Rates of Civilian Unemployment in the United States from 1980–2007

Year	Rate	Year	Rate	Year	Rate
1980	7.1%	1990	5.6%	2000	4.0%
1981	7.6	1991	6.8	2001	4.7
1982	9.7	1992	7.5	2002	5.8
1983	9.6	1993	6.9	2003	6.0
1984	7.5	1994	6.1	2004	5.5
1985	7.2	1995	5.6	2005	5.1
1986	7.0	1996	5.4	2006	4.6
1987	6.2	1997	4.9	2007	4.6
1988	5.5	1998	4.5		
1989	5.3	1999	4.2		

Source: *Economic Report of the President 2007.*

It is important to realize that high employment is one of the Fed's goals because, in certain circumstances, the Fed's policy can indirectly influence the level of employment. When the economy is operating sluggishly or below capacity, increases in the money supply can bring about economic expansion and employment because those increases can reduce interest rates, stimulate investment, encourage consumption, and lead to the creation of new jobs. A policy of expansion of the money supply is frequently described as an "easy money policy" because the Fed is said to ease the way for banks to acquire reserves and to extend loans. When the economy's output is close to capacity (given its stock of productive assets and population), however, easy money policies can be disadvantageous because they may kindle inflation and raise interest rates. Policymakers must often wrestle with the tough question of whether easing monetary policy will create higher employment or simply ignite inflation, or an undesirable combination of higher unemployment and higher inflation.

Economic growth, the third goal of the Fed, is the increase in an economy's output of goods and services. Clearly, this goal is closely related to the goal of high employment. As would be expected, there is very little agreement about the exact rate of growth that policymakers should try to achieve. Variously described as "sustainable" or "steady" or "reasonable," the economy's appropriate rate of growth has to be substantial enough to generate high employment in the context of an expanding workforce but low enough to ward off inflation.

Table 3 reports the annual growth rate in the gross domestic product (or GDP) over the past 28 years (through 2007). Note that the rate in two years (1984 and 1991) was slightly negative. Subsequently, growth exceeded a positive 3% in six years, but it never reached the stunning 7.3% level of 1984, although it was very high during 1998–1999. Interestingly, despite fairly sustained growth in the past 15 years, inflation has remained rather low. (See Table 1.)

Once more, economic growth is a Fed goal because its operations may be able to affect the level of growth. As we note in connection with employment, however, policies expanding the money supply and stimulating growth may be beneficial in some circumstances and detrimental in others, according to the economy's performance relative to its capacity.

The goal of stabilizing interest rates is directly related to the goal of growth and to the Fed's responsibility for the health of the nation's financial and banking system. Table 4 reports on yearly averages for the rates on Treasury bills (a short-term security) and on

Table 3 Annual Rates of Growth in U.S. Gross Domestic Product from 1980–2007

Year	Rate	Year	Rate	Year	Rate
1980	0.0%	1990	1.9%	2000	3.7%
1981	2.5	1991	−0.2	2001	0.8
1982	−1.9	1992	3.3	2002	1.6
1983	4.2	1993	2.7	2003	2.5
1984	7.3	1994	4.0	2004	3.6
1985	3.9	1995	2.5	2005	3.2
1986	3.4	1996	3.7	2006	2.9
1987	3.5	1997	4.5	2007	2.5
1988	4.2	1998	4.2		
1989	3.5	1999	4.5		

Source: *Economic Report of the President 2007.*

Table 4 Annual Average Rates of Interest on U.S. Treasury Bills and Bonds from 1980–2007

Year	Bills	Notes	Year	Bills	Notes	Year	Bills	Notes
1980	11.51%	11.46%	1990	7.51%	8.55%	2000	5.85%	6.03%
1981	14.03	13.91	1991	5.42	7.86	2001	3.45	5.02
1982	10.69	13.00	1992	3.45	7.01	2002	1.62	4.61
1983	8.63	11.10	1993	3.02	5.87	2003	1.02	4.01
1984	9.58	12.44	1994	4.29	7.09	2004	1.38	4.27
1985	7.48	10.62	1995	5.51	6.57	2005	3.16	4.29
1986	5.98	7.68	1996	5.02	6.44	2006	4.73	4.80
1987	5.82	8.39	1997	5.07	6.35	2007	4.41	4.63
1988	6.69	8.85	1998	4.81	5.26			
1989	8.12	8.49	1999	4.66	5.65			

Note: *Bills: Rates on new issues. Bonds: Yields on actively traded issues adjusted to constant 10-year maturity by the Department of the Treasury.*
Source: *Economic Report of the President 2007.*

Treasury bonds (a long-term asset). The table reveals that interest rate volatility over the early and mid-1980s was especially pronounced. This volatility has been troublesome to financial institutions such as commercial banks and thrift institutions. During the past 15 years, Treasury bills have been less volatile and Treasury bond rates have declined.

Note that the goal is to stabilize rates, not to prevent changes in rates. Obviously, interest rates move up and down with changes in economic conditions. Those movements may provide signals of important economic developments, and it would be making a mistake for the Fed to try to prevent such changes in rates. However, the Fed may help economic conditions by trying to moderate the impact of large moves in rates. Some increases in rates may reflect temporary or reversible developments, and the Fed can appropriately respond to these changes in a way that eliminates or greatly reduces such increases.

Stability in foreign currency exchange rates is the final goal that we will discuss. The foreign exchange market has become much more important in recent years, as the economies of the world have become more integrated, and foreign currency exchange rates have begun to affect ever larger segments of the economy. Because exchange rates are clearly dependent in some ways on the monetary policies of the major countries, the Fed has accepted the goal of stabilizing foreign exchange rates.[2] Of course, some fluctuations in exchange rates arise for economically sound reasons that monetary policy in one country cannot influence or control. A prime example of such a reason is a pronounced difference in the fiscal policies between two countries. In general, an important explanation of unstable rates among most of the world's major currencies has been the failure of the large industrial economies to coordinate their fiscal and monetary policies.

A chief disadvantage of unstable foreign currency exchange rates is that volatility in the prices of currencies inhibits the international trade that offers a host of benefits to all participating countries. Furthermore, both high and low exchange rates for the dollar are considered detrimental to the U.S. economy. High exchange rates (i.e., a "strong" dollar or

---

[2] Bernanke and Mishkin, "Guideposts and Signals in the Conduct of Monetary Policy: Lessons from Six Industrialized Countries," p. 11.

one with high value in terms of foreign currencies) reduce demand for U.S.-made products abroad and stimulate the import of foreign goods; the result is a trade imbalance. A "weak" dollar contributes to inflation, as U.S. buyers pay more for the many goods they do import. For these reasons, the Fed's goal of stability in the currency market often amounts to keeping the value of the dollar, in terms of the major foreign currencies, within some range that is considered politically acceptable and helpful to international trading, especially exporting.

During the late 1990s and early 2000s, due to the moderately strong U.S. dollar, strong U.S. economic growth, and weak or anemic economic growth in much of the rest of the world, the United States experienced a very large and increasing trade deficit.

TRADE-OFFS AND CONFLICTS AMONG POLICIES

This account of the widely accepted goals of monetary policy reveals a profound problem in the conduct of monetary policy. The goals are numerous, but the Fed's capabilities are limited to the simple menu of (1) trying to raise the rate of growth in the money supply by providing more reserves to banks, and (2) trying to reduce the rate of monetary expansion by reducing the reserves in the banking system. As a result, it is often the case that one of the goals may require a monetary policy that is inconsistent with some other goal. In other words, a monetary policy that furthers progress toward one goal may actually make attaining another either difficult or impossible.

For example, an easy money policy of expanding the money supply (that is, stimulating higher growth rates for one or more monetary aggregates) may appear to promote growth and low interest rates, but it may also raise the prospect of inflation, affect the exchange rate disadvantageously, and increase interest rates. Another example concerns the goal of price stability and the Fed's responsibility for the health of financial institutions. Suppose that, at a time of high inflation, many such institutions have invested according to inflationary expectations and have made many loans to firms dealing in real assets. Suppose, too, that the Fed decides it needs to take steps to curb the current inflation. In such a situation, the tight monetary policy that accomplishes this goal—a policy of reducing the rate of growth in the money supply—actually may imperil the institutions because the policy might well weaken the financial health of the firms that borrowed from the financial institutions.

Economists frequently describe this problem in this way: The Fed's policy necessarily represents trade-offs among its various goals, which have different levels of relative importance at different times, depending on the state of the economy. Another way of saying this is that the Fed, like any monetary policymaker, has numerous goals but focuses, at any time, on the goal that is most in danger of not being achieved.

GOALS AND TYPES OF TARGETS

A second problem in the implementation of monetary policy is that the Fed has no direct control over the goals that are the final objectives of its policies. The Fed cannot, with any of its monetary tools (open market operations, discount rates, etc.), directly influence such complex economic variables as the prices of goods and services, the unemployment rate, the growth in gross domestic product, and foreign exchange rates. We know the Fed can affect the rate of growth in the money supply only by means of its control of reserves in the banking system. As we discussed in the previous chapter, the Fed cannot fully determine changes in the money supply. The growth in the money supply depends to a substantial extent on the preferences, actions, and expectations of numerous banks, borrowers, and consumers.

The Fed seeks to achieve its goals through a form of chain reaction, which has the following chronology and structure. The Fed first employs one or more of its tools to affect what are called **operating targets**, which are monetary and financial variables whose changes tend to bring about changes in **intermediate targets**. Intermediate targets, which may include interest rates or monetary aggregates, are variables that have a reasonably reliable linkage with the variables, such as output or employment, that constitute the Fed's goals or *ultimate objectives*. Thus, the Fed exerts whatever influence it has on the intermediate targets in an indirect way, by means of its control over the operating targets. Thus, the Fed's power over the variables that make up its goals is quite indirect and dependent upon the linkages among the various targets and goals.

Although economists have argued many years about the identity of appropriate operating and intermediate target variables, there is no dispute about the chief characteristics of a suitable operating or intermediate target.[3] The first characteristic is *linkage*: An operating target must have an expected connection with the intermediate target, which itself must eventually affect the economy in a way that is consistent with the Fed's goals. The second characteristic is *observability*: Both operating targets and intermediate targets must be readily and regularly observable economic variables, so that the Fed can monitor its success in influencing their levels or rates of change. The third and final characteristic is *responsiveness*: To function as an operating target, a variable must respond quickly and in an expected way to the Fed's use of one or more of its tools; and an appropriate intermediate target is one that reacts, in an anticipated way and a meaningfully short time, to changes in the operating target.

Choosing the Operating Target

In some countries, a key foreign currency exchange rate may well function as an operating target. While the Fed has become more conscious of foreign exchange developments in the past 15 years or so, it has not adopted the dollar's exchange rate with any currency or group of currencies as an operating target. Rather, the Fed's monetary policy has directly targeted either short-term interest rates or some measure of bank reserves.

An important point about the operating target is that the Fed must choose either a short-term rate or the level of some reserves and cannot choose to target both kinds of variables.[4] To understand why the Fed must make a choice, we need to review what the Fed's tools allow it to do. Those tools—whether the secondary ones of discount loans and management of reserve requirements, or the primary tool of open market operations—enable the Fed to change only the level of reserves in the banking system. Obviously, a change in reserves also changes short-term rates because they are determined in the interbank market for excess reserves. Under most circumstances, the change in reserves is negatively related to the change in interest rates: As the Fed supplies more reserves and banks

---

[3] A formal treatment of the requirements for targets is available in Benjamin M. Friedman, "Targets and Instruments of Monetary Policy," Chapter 22 in Benjamin M. Friedman and Frank H. Hahn, *Handbook of Monetary Economics* (Amsterdam: North-Holland, 1990).

[4] William Poole, "Optimal Choice of Monetary Policy Instrument in a Simple Stochastic Macro Model," *Quarterly Journal of Economics* (1970), pp. 197–216.

gain more ability to make more loans and buy other assets, the short-term rates fall; as the Fed withdraws reserves and reduces the banks' lending capacity, the short-term rates rise.

Because of this inverse relationship, it might seem possible for the Fed to view each of these variables as a target and to set each of them at the same time. But, in fact, that is impossible. The reason is that the Fed cannot know or predict the *public's* **demand for money**, which is the aggregate demand for holding some of its wealth in the form of liquid balances, such as bank deposits. The public's desire to hold money depends on many factors, especially preferences and anticipations about future income and price inflation, among other things, and unexpected changes in those factors may well shift the public's desired holdings in significant ways. Therefore, the Fed cannot be certain how much impact any change in reserves will have on short-term rates. Without knowledge of what the rate will be for a given change in reserves, the Fed cannot simultaneously determine both the rate and the level of reserves.

In choosing its operating target, then, the Fed makes the decision to let the other variable fluctuate in response to changes in the public's demand for money. When an interest rate is the target, the Fed must let the growth in reserves vary as it strives to keep that interest rate at a certain level or to smooth its transition to a new (higher or lower) level. When some aggregate of reserves is the target, the Fed is forced to allow interest rates to change substantially, so that it can try to bring the level of reserves to that dictated by the Fed's policy. Of course, the Fed can change its target from time to time, in order to rein in the variable that has fluctuated while the Fed focused on the other. But, however often the Fed might change targets, it remains a fact that, at any one time, the Fed cannot target both rates and reserves.

Choosing the Intermediate Target

The best known of the intermediate targets is the money supply, measured by one of the more inclusive monetary aggregates that we described in the previous chapter. In the 1970s, many countries began to target the growth rates of one or more aggregates. The policy, at least as publicly stated, was to supply reserves at a pace that would lead to a selected rate of growth in the aggregates. The idea behind this policy was that the goals of central bank activity—growth, stable prices, and so on—would be realized if the money supply were to grow at a known and steady rate.

Over time, other intermediate targets have been specified, and they include foreign exchange rates, the level of national output (such as the gross national product), and the level of actual or expected inflation.[5] Furthermore, the array of interest rates—including rates available to consumers and investors—may also function as a target variable. We have said that a prime characteristic of a suitable intermediate target is that it is readily observable. Obviously, some of these candidates above do not fit that rule: Information on the GDP, for example, is available only on a quarterly basis, while measures of actual or expected inflation may be subject to considerable dispute.[6]

Interestingly, in recent years, many central banks have adopted inflation, despite certain problems in measurement, as a key intermediate variable. The reason is that the monetary aggregates have not had the kind of reliable and persistent relationship either with target variables or with goals that policymakers require. In most European countries, policymakers

---

[5] Bernanke and Mishkin, "Guideposts and Signals in the Conduct of Monetary Policy," p. 41.
[6] Friedman, "Targets and Instruments of Monetary Policy," p. 1203.

follow price indexes for sensitive commodities and make decisions about short-term rates and bank reserves on the basis of actual and expected inflation. In the United States, it is commonly said that former Fed Chairman Alan Greenspan carefully monitored the price of gold, among other commodities. Thus, the purchasing power of the domestic currency and the foreign exchange rate of the currency have become far more typical intermediate targets than monetary aggregates.

A REVIEW OF RECENT FEDERAL RESERVE POLICY

Targeting the Fed Funds Rate, 1970 to 1979

During most of the 1970s, the Fed viewed the federal funds rate either largely or exclusively as its operating target. Recall that *fed funds* refers to the excess reserves that commercial banks and other depository institutions keep in the form of deposits in the Federal Reserve System and lend among themselves for short periods of time, especially overnight. The rate on these interbank loans is the fed funds rate, and it is a good indicator of the banking system's supply of loanable funds. When banks have a lot of funds and lending capacity, the rate is low; the rate is high when the banking system has drawn its collective reserves close to the required level. It should be noted that the fed funds rate meets the first requirement listed above for an operating target: The rate is readily observable and continuously available because the market for fed funds is large and active.

The Fed targets the fed funds rate by its open market operations. As noted above, a requirement of a good operating target is that the Fed can exert substantial control over its level and changes. If the rate were to rise above the level that the Fed thought conducive to economic growth and high employment, the Fed would engage in open market purchases and inject reserves into the banking system. Through the workings of supply and demand, an increase in the reserves of the banking system would normally cause a fall in the fed funds rate, as many banks would have to borrow less to meet their reserve requirements. If the fed funds rate was too low, the Fed would sell securities and bring about a reduction in the growth of the banking system's total supply of reserves. This action would prompt a rise in the fed funds rate. Furthermore, the Fed has also used open market operations in its effort to smooth the transition of the fed funds rate from one level to another, as the rate varies with conditions in the economy.

The rationale for targeting the fed funds rate lies in the belief that changes in the rate can, over some time, affect the level of economic activity. (Recall, that linkage is also a prime requirement of a suitable operating target.) That is, if consumers, investors, and bankers believe that a given change in the fed funds rate is permanent and reflects a shift in Federal Reserve policy, such a change in rates can reverberate through the monetary and banking system, and cause a consequent change in the level of economic activity. Generally speaking, this version of monetary policy is associated with **Keynesian** economic theory, and it gives the Fed a great deal of discretion in the conduct of monetary policy.

In the Keynesian view, the Fed's decision to reduce the fed funds rate, by increasing the banking system's excess reserves, should have the following consequences. Banks, as the first economic units to be affected, will have more reserves and lower returns from lending in the fed funds market. As a result, the banks will reduce the cost of loans to businesses and consumers and the return (if any) available to investors on short-term deposits. Investors will now be confronted with lower yields on short-term assets, such as Treasury bills and certificates of deposit. Because of these lower yields, investors will reallocate their holdings from short-term to long-term securities, driving their prices up and raising the wealth of investors in financial securities. Declines in the general cost of funding will encourage firms to expand and increase their output. Consumers, seeing lower costs of borrowing, will increase their demand for more expensive purchases.

Overall, according to this view of the economy, a decline in the fed funds rate should lead to a higher level of output and employment in the economy. Obviously, if the Fed chooses to raise the fed funds rate and uses open market sales to reduce the system's excess reserves, the consequent rise in short-term interest rates will restrain the growth in economic activity. In an important sense, then, the array of short-term rates functions as the intermediate target (or one of the intermediate targets) in this view of monetary policy.

A cautionary note is in order here. Economists in the Keynesian tradition believe that declines in targeted rates can cause the sequence of events just described only if the economy is operating at less than full capacity and employment. If the economy is operating at full employment, these actions by the Fed will generally lead only to an increase in prices (that is, inflation) and interest rates.

A Monetarist Experiment, 1979 to 1982

One historic consequence of the policy of supplying reserves according to movements in the fed funds rate was that the Fed did not concern itself with the behavior of the level of reserves, or of the monetary base and other monetary aggregates, which expanded in an erratic way. On frequent occasions in this period of the 1970s, interest rates were on a rising path, in part because of the oil-price shock and the consequent inflation. The Fed responded to the rising rates by increasing reserves, as it tried to keep the rates from getting to what it considered a too high level. The expansion in the monetary aggregates was particularly rapid from 1975 to 1978, and that expansion (along with the oil shocks) led to serious inflation and a decline in the dollar's value. In 1979, for example, the rate of inflation was in double digits (i.e., above 10%), and the dollar's value, in terms of the Deutsche mark, fell almost 30% between 1975 and 1979.

In October 1979, as a response to inflation, then Chairman of the Fed Paul Volcker announced a new policy. The Fed would henceforth begin to target the banking system's **nonborrowed reserves**, which equal total reserves less those reserves created when banks borrow from the Fed through its discount window. The level of nonborrowed reserves meets the requirements for a good operating target to largely the same extent as the fed funds rate. Moreover, the Fed stated that its purpose in targeting nonborrowed reserves was to control the rate of growth in the money supply, as measured by the monetary aggregates.

This change in policy was widely viewed as a victory for the theory of **monetarism**, which favors a steady, predictable growth in reserves and the monetary base. Monetarists claim that policy that is based on known rules of growth in key monetary aggregates sustains stability in the price level, and that such stability fosters long-run economic growth and employment. Furthermore, monetarists had long criticized the **discretionary** policy whereby the Fed would change the rate of growth in reserves or aggregates in order to achieve short-run adjustments in interest rates or levels of economic activity. Monetarists believe that the "long and variable lags" between the start of a policy and its final impact on the economy make such adjustments unwise and potentially dangerous. This dispute on how best to conduct monetary policy is known as the controversy of "discretion versus rules."

The new Fed policy can be viewed as one where the monetary aggregates became intermediate targets, and the banking system's quantity of nonborrowed reserves was the operating target. Through its open market operations, the Fed has considerable control over this operating target. Movements in that target are, in turn, supposed to generate somewhat predictable changes in the levels of the intermediate targets, or monetary aggregates. The money multiplier, which we introduced in the last chapter, is the link between the reserves and the aggregates. Monetarists believe that the money multiplier is basically steady, so that the link between reserves and the monetary aggregates can be identified. Hence, the appropriate policy is to supply reserves (through open market operations) at that steady pace that will lead to a stable and reasonable rate of growth for the monetary aggregates. The changes in interest rates that may result from changes in money demand (which, in the monetarists' view, does not occur often or to a significant extent) should not be allowed to affect the policy on reserves.

Technically speaking, the Fed had claimed throughout most of the 1970s to be targeting certain aggregates, notably M_1 and M_2, and it had routinely published target ranges and expected growth paths for the aggregates. The Fed's devotion to such a policy was suspect, as the data repeatedly showed the aggregates growing at far faster rates than the Fed said it preferred. When faced with these high growth rates, the Fed often simply adjusted its planned growth path upward. Volcker's 1979 announcement seemed to suggest that the Fed would finally be seriously interested in the growth in aggregates. Indeed, the growth rate in the money supply was far smaller in this time than it had generally been in the 1970s. Also, the new policy stated that the Fed would let interest rates (particularly short-term rates) fluctuate far more freely than they had in the past. In fact, in late 1979 and through the early 1980s, rates of most maturities posted their highest levels in more than a hundred years and displayed a volatility that led to major changes in financial institutions and markets.

Back to the Fed Funds Rate, 1983 to 1991

The Fed did not remain committed to an aggregates policy very long.[7] By 1982, the tight monetary policy had banished the worst of the inflation, which seemed to reach a bottom of about 3% to 4%. Policymakers then faced the prospect of deflation and rising unemployment, which rose to around 10% in 1982. At the end of 1982, the Fed again let the monetary aggregates grow at a rather fast pace. Interest rates fell, employment rose, and economic growth resumed.

In 1983, the Fed adopted a new policy. This time, the Fed identified its operating target as the level of **borrowed reserves**, which are funds that the banks borrow from the Fed through its discount window. It is important to realize that the level of borrowed reserves in the banking system is closely and positively linked to the spread between the fed funds rate and the discount rate (the cost of borrowing at the discount window, which the Fed adjusts infrequently). When the fed funds rate goes up relative to the discount rate, all else being equal, the level of borrowed reserves rises because banks are more likely to borrow reserves from the Fed rather than from other banks. Thus, targeting borrowed reserves is equivalent to targeting the fed funds rate.

The Fed's policy beginning in 1983 was to keep the growth in borrowed reserves within some specified range. As a result, the Fed supplied reserves through open market purchases when borrowed reserves rose. Thus, the Fed was essentially supplying reserves when the fed funds rate rose. With this policy, the Fed was once more effectively targeting the fed funds rate,

---

[7] Franco Modigliani, "The Monetarist Controversy Revisited," *Contemporary Policy Issues* (October 1988), pp. 3–18.

while neglecting changes in the monetary aggregates. In 1987, the Fed admitted that fact and ceased to set targets for growth in M_1, substantially widening the acceptable ranges for growth in the larger aggregates, such as M_2 and M_3. From 1983 to the early 1990s, the Fed's chief operating target was the level of the fed funds rate. In fact, at the end of 1991, the Fed dramatically lowered short-term rates in a publicly announced effort to stimulate the economy.

Two Developments in the Mid 1980s

In the mid 1980s, however, two developments of note occurred. The first was the need for the Fed, which it publicly acknowledged, to become concerned with the level and stability of the U.S. dollar's foreign currency exchange rate. The U.S. dollar exhibited dramatic strength through the early 1980s, which made American exports very expensive. In 1985, the Fed implemented an expansionary monetary policy (that is, a policy of expanding aggregates), which drove down the dollar's value. In September 1985, the United States (with the Fed's support) entered into the Plaza Agreement, which was a plan for international coordination of monetary policies by the United States, Great Britain, France, (West) Germany, and Japan. (The Louvre Accord in 1987 was another effort toward coordination.) The result of these actions was a fast decline in the value of the U.S. dollar, which the Fed tried to stabilize in 1987. In a sense, then, the U.S. dollar's exchange rate began to function as a kind of intermediate target for Fed policy.

The second development was the shocking fall in equity prices around the world in October 1987. The Fed's immediate response to the crisis was to provide all necessary liquidity. The fall in prices also brought to the fore the need for stability in the financial markets, and the Fed began to treat that as one of its key objectives.

The Same Policy, but with a Twist, 1991 to 1995

The Fed successfully reduced rates across the maturity spectrum, from 1992 to the outset of 1994. The fed funds rate fell to 3%, and the yield on 10-year government bonds was also low, touching 5.72% in December 1993. During 1992 and 1993, economic expansion occurred at a fairly steady rate, with a falling civilian unemployment rate, a growing real GDP, and a modest rate of consumer price inflation.[8]

However, the Fed's expectations regarding the economic environment underwent a change in February 1994. For the first time in two years, the Fed pressured the fed funds rate upward, moving it from 3% to 3.25%. The explanation was the Fed's growing concern that robust economic growth might, at some point in the relatively near future, spark price inflation. The Fed was not paying much attention to the monetary aggregates, but rather Chairman Alan Greenspan and the Federal Open Market Committee (FOMC) were watching the prices of sensitive commodities and the level of industrial capacity being utilized. Thus, the Fed was still targeting rates in order to manage economic activity and to bring about both price level stability and continued expansion. Eventually, the Fed was to nudge rates up seven more times until February 1995, when the fed funds rate reached 6% and the discount rate grew to 5.25% (from its early 1992 level of 3%). These actions had the desired effects: Interest rates on debt of short and long terms to maturities rose and the rate of growth in the economy fell to low but generally positive levels. In 1995, the Fed did not change its mind, and target levels of short-term rates in late 1995 were at their end-of-1994 heights.

---

[8] "Monetary Policy and Open Market Operations during 1994," *Federal Reserve Bulletin* (June 1995), pp. 570–584.

The Last Half of the 1990s—Exploring the "New Paradigm"

Despite the seven Fed tightenings of 1994 and early 1995, the economy averted a recession and subsequently experienced strong and noninflationary growth. In fact, based on previous experience, economic growth was stronger than had been expected with little inflation. The explanation for this desirable strong growth–low inflation combination was the "new paradigm."

As of 1995, the conventional wisdom was that the maximum sustainable real GDP growth was approximately 2¼%, 1% due to increases in the labor force and 1¼% due to productivity increases. And (noninflationary) full employment was thought to be 5% to 5½%. During 1997/1998, with strong economic growth and unemployment decreasing below 4½%, Alan Greenspan and the Fed were faced with a dilemma: They had to decide whether to tighten monetary policy to slow economic growth, even though there were no inflationary forces, or to let the economy continue to grow at a rate that had been unsustainable by previous standards.

Greenspan and the Fed exhibited a combination of being cautious and experimental in their approach. Although their main policy tool was to change the fed funds rate (and to make public comments by Greenspan and other FOMC members), their approach was eclectic. They did not concentrate solely on the absolute level of the Fed funds rate, monetary aggregates, or commodity prices.

Greenspan decided to be vigilant but passive, and he permitted the economy to grow beyond what the "old paradigm" would have deemed feasible. In fact, the Fed eased the funds rate three times (by a total of 75 basis points) in 1998 due to a concern about a financial crisis. Another factor was a resulting global weakening due to the Russian default and the problem with a major hedge fund (Long-Term Capital Management) financial crisis.

Greenspan emphasized the traditional reasons for low inflation, including globalization (which reduced the pricing power of suppliers); the strong U.S. dollar; the U.S. trade deficit (by importing international goods, price pressures on U.S.–produced products were relieved); and immigration (which took pressure off domestic wage rates).

But the overriding explanation for this strong, noninflationary growth was a "new paradigm," which posited that productivity had increased due to the new technology and that accelerated capital expenditures were induced by the new technology. This *capital deepening* increased labor productivity and, thus, sustainable economic growth.

While the Fed was extremely tolerant of strong economic growth, it did enact six fed funds increases (from 4.75% to 6.50%) from June 1999 through May 2000. Overall, the Fed policy during this period could be described as nondoctrinaire, eclectic, and exploratory. For various reasons, Greenspan is credited with having orchestrated the longest postwar expansion, which began during April 1991 and continued until 2001.

In the U.S. stock market, the Fed witnessed the stock market bubble—or "irrational exuberance" as Greenspan called it—from 1995 to 1999. After growing by over 20% each year from 1995 through 1999 (reaching a peak of 1572 on March 24, 2000), the S&P 500 index declined each year from 2000 to 2002 (reaching a nadir of 777 on October 10, 2000), the "burst" of the bubble. In general, the Fed maintained a passive position during the bubble. Greenspan took the view that the role of the Fed was not to determine the correct level of the stock market.

As described earlier, during the last half of the 1990s, the Fed policy remained nondoctrinaire and eclectic. The Fed funds rate was the main (only) policy tool used. The money supply and reserve requirements were not used as policy tools.

Overall during Greenspan's tenure there were two recessions, during 1991 and a very mild recession during 2001 after the 9/11 terrorist attack. The Fed also engineered one soft landing during 1994–1995. Greenspan's conduct during the stock market bubble was the subject of some controversy. During December 1996, Greenspan said:

> How do we know when irrational exuberance has unduly escalated asset values. We should not underestimate . . . the interaction of asset markets and the economy. Asset prices, particularly, must be an integral part of the development of monetary policy.

From the time of these comments, the Dow Jones Industrial Average would more than double in the ensuing three years. As a result, "irrational exuberance" became the often-quoted description of the stock market's behavior during these three years.

But while at the time of Greenspan's comments, the Fed funds rate was 5.25%, it was not until almost two years later the Fed began to increase the Fed funds rate, starting from a rate of 4.75% during November 1998. Some critics assert that the Fed should have started to tighten earlier and more strongly.

Subsequently, the Fed was quite active with respect to the Fed fund rate. From June 1999 through May 2000, the Fed enacted six Fed funds rate increases (from 4.75% to 6.50%) in response to the strong stock market and the market-supported economy.

With respect to foreign currencies, the birth of the euro was monumental. The euro is a common currency among 15 members of the European Union (Belgium, Germany, Greece, Spain, France, Ireland, Italy, Luxemburg, The Netherlands, Austria, Portugal, Cyprus, Malta, Slovenia, and Finland). The euro was born on January 1, 1999, when the participating countries established exchange rates between their currencies and the euro (the euro currency and coins were formally put into circulation on January 1, 2002).[9] After the advent of the euro, the Fed no longer needed to focus on the conversion of individual currencies, such as in France and Germany.

After presiding as chairman of the Fed from August 1979 until August 1987, Paul Volcker was succeeded by Alan Greenspan. Greenspan presided from August 1987 until his retirement in January 2006. The last six years of Greenspan's tenure were eventful.

The Beginning of the Twenty-First Century

The 21st century began with the peak of the stock market in March 2000. After the stock market reversed and the bubble began to burst, the Fed decreased the Fed funds rate from 6.5% to 1.0% beginning in May 2000 to successfully avert a recession induced by the stock market. Later that year, that decline in the Fed funds rate helped avert a recession that could have been induced by the 9/11 tragedy.

By mid 2004, the Fed funds rate was 1%, a level the Fed viewed as inappropriately stimulative given economic conditions. During June 2004, the Fed began a series of 17 consecutive 0.25% increases in the Fed funds rate, to increase the Fed funds rate to 5.25% during June 2006. These increases were well communicated to the markets by the Fed before they were enacted. The increases were regarded by the Fed to be "measured"—that is, small in magnitude—and "accommodating"—that is, not significantly constraining to the economy—and, thus, did not upset the markets. Finally, on August 8, 2006, after the last of the 17 consecutive easings, the Fed refrained from another Fed funds increase. Subsequent Fed funds

---

[9] The initial exchange rate versus the U.S. dollar was $1.17 per Euro.

changes were, thus, no longer to be implemented to achieve a preconceived new level but would be "data dependent." The Fed had considered the previous 1% Fed funds rate as well below the "neutral rate" and that the new 5.25% level, once achieved, was regarded as a long-term neutral level. As of early 2007, the Fed remained "on-hold" due to balanced concerns regarding inflation versus economic growth, and a desired position for the Fed.

During January 2006, Alan Greenspan retired and was replaced by Ben Bernanke, who had previously been the chairman of the President's Council of Economic Advisors from June 2005 to January 2006. Bernanke mainly continued Greenspan's policies but was viewed as being more open with respect to communication about the Fed's policy and open to promoting more open discussion at the FOMC meetings. In addition, Bernanke was expected to advocate a more quantitative approach to policy, as opposed to Greenspan's subjective, eclectic approach.[10]

Bernanke became chairman during the final 25 basis point increases in the Fed funds rate to 5.25% on June 29, 2006, and maintained this rate through the remainder of 2006 and the first half of 2007. This balance of concern between inflation and economic growth, however, shifted toward a concern about economic growth during August 2007 with the early signs of what became the subprime mortgage crisis.

Due to concerns about the economy, the Fed decreased the Fed funds rate by 50 basis points on September 18, 2007, (the first decrease by more than 25 basis points since May 2000) and then by 25 basis points on two different dates (October 31, 2007, and December 11, 2007). The urgency about the economy and the financial system continued to intensify and the Fed took the unusual action of decreasing the Fed funds rate by 75 basis points between regularly scheduled FOMC meetings on January 22, 2008, and then by 50 basis points at its next scheduled FOMC meeting on January 30, 2008.

While these actions and subsequent actions by the Fed were considered by many analysts to be quite aggressive, others considered the Fed's actions as "too little, too late." They asserted that the seeds of the subprime mortgage crisis were sown during 2003–2005 when the Fed maintained very low rates and reacted to the crisis too late and with too little.

The crisis continued during March 16–18, 2008, with the rescue of the investment banking firm Bear Stearns. The Fed again eased the Fed funds rate by 75 basis points to 2.25% (thus, the Fed funds rate was reduced from 5.25% to 2.25% between August 2007 and March 2008) but this was not the headline activity. During March 2008, there were concerns that a bankruptcy of Bear Stearns was imminent and would significantly increase the systemic risk of the financial system and the economy. This potential bankruptcy was based on some fundamental business issues at Bear Stearns, mainly its exposure to subprime mortgages, its high leverage, and, most urgently, that Bear Stearns was being rejected by dealers in the short-term loan markets (the repo market). The Fed and the Department of the Treasury, thus, engineered a rescue by J.P. Morgan. On Sunday, March 16, just before the global market opened, the Fed agreed to lend $30 billion to J.P. Morgan to complete its acquisition of Bear Stearns. The loan was secured by assets such as mortgage-backed securities inherited from Bear

---

[10] See Jerry L. Jordan, "Money and Monetary Policy for the Twenty First Century," *Federal Reserve Bank of St. Louis Review* (November/December 2006), pp. 465–510; William Poole, "Understanding the Fed," *Federal Reserve Bank of St. Louis Review* (January/February 2007), pp. 3–13; Michael Ehrmann and Marcel Fratzscher, "Transparency, Disclosure, and the Federal Reserve," *International Journal of Central Banking*, Vol. 3, no. 1 (March 2007); and William Poole, "Data Dependence," *Federal Reserve Bank of St. Louis Review* (March/April 2007), pp. 77–81.

Stearns, which are difficult to value. If the assets deteriorated, the Fed would suffer the loss (and contrariwise the Fed would keep any gains).

This was the first time since the Great Depression that the Fed used its authority to lend to non-banks. This loan relied on a provision (Section 13(3)) of the Federal Reserve Act that gives the Fed the authority to lend, not just to banks, but to any corporation that cannot get credit elsewhere. It was last used in the 1930s when the Fed lent to small companies that were vulnerable during the banking crisis of the Great Depression.

During March 2008, the Fed introduced a new lending facility, called the Primary Dealer Credit Facility, for investment banks and securities dealers that would give them more ways to borrow against their securities holdings. The securities pledged by the investment banks, however, had to have market prices and investment-grade credit ratings. Loans could not be used. Commercial banks, on the other hand, traditionally borrowed from the Fed via a different borrowing facility, called the discount facility, wherein loans can be used. This new facility was used immediately.

As a result of this extreme problem and the Fed's strong response, the structure of the financial system—most importantly the relationships among the Fed, commercial banks, and investment banks—was being examined for a significant reform.

There were two key questions in the changes being considered in the financial regulatory structure. The first was whether the Fed should assess the risk across the financial markets regardless of the corporate form and to intervene (i.e., inject funds when appropriate). The second was whether, if the Fed was becoming the lender of last resort, it should become the regulator of last resort. If such changes occurred, the Fed would become the clear "top dog" among numerous financial regulators.[11]

Key Points That You Should Understand Before Proceeding

1. The Fed has numerous and complex goals related to conditions in the overall economy, which include price stability, high employment, economic growth, and stability in interest rates and the dollar's value in foreign currencies.
2. Policies that might further the attainment of one goal may make another difficult to realize.
3. The Fed is unable to realize its goals directly but must work through operating targets that it can affect and that, in turn, have some predictable influence on intermediate targets and the economy.
4. The Fed's operating targets have included the fed funds rate and various measures of reserves in the banking system; its primary tool has been open market operations.
5. Intermediate targets may include monetary aggregates, interest rates, or foreign currency exchange rates.
6. Keynesians adopt a monetary policy that largely calls for targeting short-term interest rates.
7. Monetarists adopt a monetary policy that largely calls for targeting reserves in order to achieve a steady growth in monetary aggregates.
8. The targets of Fed policy have changed several times in the past 25 years.

---

[11] See Robert M. Rasche and Marcela M. Williams, "The Effectiveness of Monetary Policy," *Federal Reserve Bank of St. Louis Review* (September/October 2007), pp. 447–480; William Poole, "Thinking Like a Central Banker," *Federal Reserve Bank of St. Louis Review* (January/February 2008), pp. 1–7; and William Poole, "Market Bailouts and the 'Fed Put,'" *Federal Reserve Bank of St. Louis Review* (March/April 2008), pp. 65–73.

SUMMARY

The goals of monetary policy include a stable price level, economic growth, high employment, stable interest rates, and predictable and steady currency exchange rates. Unfortunately, monetary policies involve difficult trade-offs, and policies that help to achieve one goal may make another less attainable.

Furthermore, the Federal Reserve has no direct control or influence on the complex economic variables that constitute the goals. Hence, it must identify intermediate targets that influence these variables and are, in turn, influenced by operating targets that are variables the Fed can control to a substantial extent. The intermediate targets may be interest rates, monetary aggregates, or possibly exchange rates. The level of bank reserves (borrowed or nonborrowed) and the level of the federal funds rate have served as operating targets from time to time since 1970. The Fed can effectively manage either this rate on interbank loans or the level of various measures of reserves by open market operations that control the flow of reserves to the banking system. However, the Fed cannot target both rates and reserves at the same time. Since 1970, the Fed's policy has alternated among targeting rates, targeting reserves, and an eclectic approach.

KEY TERMS

- Borrowed reserves
- Demand for money
- Discretionary
- Frictional unemployment
- Goal of monetary policy
- Intermediate target
- Keynesian
- Monetarism
- Nonborrowed reserves
- Operating target
- Stagflation

QUESTIONS

1. Name three widely accepted goals of monetary policy.
2. What keeps the Fed from being able to achieve its goals in a direct way?
3. Comment on this statement by an official of the Federal Reserve:

   > [the Fed] can control nonborrowed reserves through open market operations [but] it cannot control total reserves, because the level of borrowing at the discount window is determined in the short run by the preferences of depository institutions.

   Quoted from Alfred Broaddus, "A Primer on the Fed," Chapter 7 in Sumner N. Levine (ed.), *The*

   Financial Analyst's Handbook (Homewood, IL: Dow Jones-Irwin, 1988), p. 194.

4. Why is it impossible for the Fed to target, at the same time, both the Fed funds interest rate and the level of reserves in the banking system?
5. Explain the change in the Fed's targets that occurred with the 1979 Volcker announcement about inflation and the new Fed policy.
6. It is often said that you cannot hit two targets with one arrow. How does this comment apply to the use of monetary policy to "stabilize the economy"?
7. Describe the differences and similarities of the conduct of Chairmen Greenspan and Bernanke in managing Fed policy.

8. What are tools and responsibilities of the Fed in monitoring and affecting the level of the stock market?

9. Interpret the following, the concluding sentence in "The Effectiveness of Monetary Policy," by Robert M. Rasche and Marcela M. Williams, appearing in the *Federal Reserve Bank of St. Louis Review*, (September/October 2007), p. 477:

Finally, the case for consistently effective short-run monetary stabilization policies is problematic—there are just too many dimensions to uncertainty in the environment in which central banks operate.

Insurance Companies

LEARNING OBJECTIVES

After reading this chapter, you will understand

- the nature of the business of insurance companies

- the differences between the nature of the liabilities of life insurance companies and those of property and casualty insurance companies

- the different types of life insurance policies

- the different types of property and casualty insurance policies

- the types of assets in which life insurance companies and property casualty insurance companies invest

- the forms of insurance companies: stock and mutual

- the regulation of insurance companies

- recent changes in the insurance business and the factors contributing to those changes

Insurance companies provide (sell and service) insurance policies, which are legally binding contracts for which the policyholder (or owner) pays insurance **premiums**. According to the insurance contract, insurance companies promise to pay specified sums contingent on the occurrence of future events, such as death or an automobile accident. Thus, insurance companies are **risk bearers**. They accept or underwrite the risk in return for an insurance premium.

The major part of the insurance company underwriting process is deciding which applications for insurance they should accept and which ones they should reject, and if they accept, determining how much they should charge for the insurance. This is called the **underwriting process**. For example, an insurance company may not provide life insurance to someone with terminal cancer or automobile insurance to someone with numerous traffic violations. And in some cases, they may provide different classes of insurance with different premiums. For example, the company may insure but charge a smoker a larger premium for life insurance than a nonsmoker; and insure someone with a mediocre driving record, but charge more for automobile insurance than an individual with a better driving record. The underwriting process is critical to an insurance company.

Because insurance companies collect insurance premiums initially and make payments later *when* (e.g., the insured person's death) or *if* (e.g., an automobile accident) an insured event occurs, insurance companies maintain the initial premiums collected in an investment portfolio, which generates a return. Thus, insurance companies have two sources of income: the initial **underwriting income** (the insurance premium) and the **investment income**, which occurs over time. The investment returns result from the investment of the insurance premiums until the funds are paid out on the policy. The premium is a fairly stable type of revenue. Investment returns, however, may vary considerably with the performance of the financial markets.

The payments on the insurance policies are the major expense of the insurance company. These payments vary among the different types of insurance policies and companies. The payments may be very unstable, depending on the type of insurance. Another major type of expense is the operating expense of the insurance company. This expense tends to be quite stable.

Insurance companies' profits, thus, result from the difference between their insurance premiums and investment returns on the one hand, and their operating expense and insurance payments or benefits on the other. The type of risk insured against, which defines the type of premium collected and benefit paid, defines the insurance company. Table 1 summarizes the major risks that insurance companies will insure, many of which are elaborated on in this chapter.

Key Points That You Should Understand Before Proceeding

1. Insurance companies bear risk in return for a fee called the premium.
2. Deciding which risks to underwrite and how much to charge for bearing those risks is critical to an insurance company.

TYPES OF INSURANCE

Life Insurance

For life insurance, the risk insured against is the death of the "insured." The **life insurance company** pays the beneficiary of the life insurance policy in the event of the death of the insured. There are several types of life insurance, which will be examined later in this chapter.

Health Insurance

In the case of health insurance, the risk insured is medical treatment of the insured. The **health insurance company** pays the insured (or the provider of the medical service) all or a portion of the cost of medical treatment by doctors, hospitals, or others. This type of insurance has undergone significant changes in the past two decades. As a result, there has been a significant restructuring of the health industry, whereby the largest health insurance companies specialize

Table 1	Major Risks Insurance Companies Face	

LIFE INSURANCE	HEALTH INSURANCE	PROPERTY AND CASUALTY
• Term Insurance	• Medical	• Property
• Whole Life	♦ Indemmity	♦ Automobile
♦ Fixed	♦ HMO/PPO/etc.	♦ House
♦ Variable	• Dental	♦ Other
• Universal Life	• Other	• Liability
• Second to Die (Survivorship)		• Other

OTHER INSURANCE

- Liability
- Umbrella
- Disability
- Long-Term Care

MONOLINE INSURANCE

STRUCTURED SETTLEMENTS

INVESTMENT-ORIENTED PRODUCTS

- Guaranteed Investment Contracts (GICs)
- Annuities
  - Fixed
  - Variable
- Mutual Funds

in health insurance rather than sell health insurance in addition to other products, such as life insurance.

Until the past decade, the major type of health insurance available was *indemnity insurance.* According to indemnity insurance, the insurance company agrees to indemnify (reimburse) the insured for covered medical and hospital expenses. That is, the insurance company pays the medical provider (doctor, hospital, etc.) for the medical services provided to the insured. The provider is selected by the insured and can provide whatever service the provider deems appropriate.

Very often there is an annual minimum amount below which the issuer does not pay for the service, but the insured pays (a *deductible*). Typically, there is also a copayment (a "co-pay") required by the insured. For example, the insured pays 20% of the charge for the service and the insurer pays the other 80%.

Due to the lack of constraints and incentives for cost savings, the medical service insured by indemnity insurance became very expensive. In response, various forms of managed health care have been developed. In general, these forms of managed health care put constraints on the choice of the provider (doctor or hospital) by the insured and on the types of service provided by the provider. The various types of managed care, including health maintenance organizations (HMOs), preferred provider organizations (PPOs), and point of service organizations (POSs), are too diverse and complex to be considered here. It is accurate to assert, however, that no widely acceptable method has yet evolved. While indemnity insurance is still provided on both an individual and group basis, the various forms of *managed care* have become common.

There have been and continue to be nonprofit providers of health insurance, such as Blue Cross and Blue Shield, and federal government providers of health insurance, such as Medicare and Medicaid, as well as for-profit health care providers.

The two major classes of medical expense benefits are

Basic coverage: traditional hospital, surgical, and regular expense coverage; and
Major medical: designed to reduce the financial burden of heavy medical expenses resulting from catastrophic or prolonged illness or injury.

Property and Casualty Insurance

The risk insured by **property and casualty (P&C) insurance companies** is damage to various types of property. Specifically, it is insurance against financial loss caused by damage, destruction, or loss to property as the result of an identifiable event that is sudden, unexpected, or unusual. The major types of such insurance are

- a house and its contents against risks such as fire, flood, and theft (homeowners insurance and its variants)
- vehicles against collision, theft, and other damage (automobile insurance and its variants)

Liability Insurance

With liability insurance, the risk insured against is litigation, or the risk of lawsuits against the insured due to actions by the insured or others. Liability insurance offers protection against third-party claims, that is, payment is usually made to someone who experiences a loss and who is not a party to the insurance contract, not to the insured.

Umbrella Insurance

Typically, umbrella insurance is pure liability coverage over and above the coverage provided by all the policies beneath it, such as homeowner, automobile, and boat policies. The name *umbrella* refers to the fact that it covers liability claims of all the policies underneath it. In addition to providing liability coverage over the limits of the underlying policies, it provides coverage for claims that are excluded from other liability policies such as invasion of privacy, libel, and false arrest. Typically, users of umbrella policies have a large amount of assets that would be placed at risk in the event of a catastrophic claim.

Disability Insurance

Disability insurance insures against the inability of employed persons to earn an income in either their own occupation ("own occ" disability insurance) or any occupation ("any occ"). Typically, "own occ" disability insurance is written for professionals in white-collar occupations (often physicians and dentists) and "any occ" for blue-collar workers. Another distinction in disability insurance is the sustainability of the policy. Regarding sustainability, there are two types of policies. The first is *guaranteed renewable* (or guaranteed continuable) whereby the issuer has to sustain the policy for the specified period of time and the issuer cannot make any changes in the policy except that it can change the premium rates for the entire class of policy (but not an individual policyholder). The other type is noncancellable and guaranteed renewable (or simply *noncancellable*), whereby the issuer has no right to make any change in any policy during the specified period. Disability insurance is also divided between short-term disability and long-term disability, with six months being the typical dividing time.

Long-Term Care Insurance

As individuals have been living longer, they have become concerned about outliving their assets and being unable to care for themselves as they age. In addition, custodial care for the aged has become very expensive and is not covered by Medicare. Thus, there has been an increased demand for insurance to provide custodial care for the aged who are no longer able to care for themselves. This care may be provided in either the insured's own residence or a separate custodial facility. Many types of long-term care insurance are available.

Structured Settlements

Structured settlements are fixed, guaranteed periodic payments over a long period of time, typically resulting from a settlement on a disability policy or other type of insurance policy. For example, suppose an individual is hit by an automobile and, as a result, is unable to work for the rest of his or her life. The individual may sue the P&C company for future lost earnings and medical care. To settle the suit, the P&C companies may agree to make specified payments over time to the individual. The P&C company may then purchase a policy from a life insurance company to make the agreed-upon payments.

Investment-Oriented Products

Insurance companies have increasingly sold products that have a significant investment component in addition to their insurance component. The first major investment-oriented product developed by life insurance companies was the **guaranteed investment contract (GIC)**. According to a GIC, a life insurance company agrees, in return for a single premium, to pay the principal amount and a predetermined annual **crediting rate** over the life of the investment, all of which are paid at the maturity date of the GIC. For example, a $10 million five-year GIC with a predetermined crediting rate of 10% means that at the end of five years the insurance company pays the guaranteed crediting rate and the principal. The risk to the customer is that the return of the principal depends on the ability of the life insurance company to satisfy the obligation, just as in any corporate debt obligation. The risk that the insurer faces is that the rate earned on the portfolio of supporting assets is less than the guaranteed rate paid to the customer.

The maturity of a GIC can vary from one year to 20 years. The interest rate guaranteed depends on market conditions and the rating of the life insurance company. The interest rate will be higher than the yield on U.S. Treasury securities of the same maturity. These policies are purchased by individuals and by pension plan sponsors as a pension investment.

A GIC is nothing more than the debt obligation of the life insurance company issuing the contract. The word *guarantee* does not mean that there is a guarantor other than the life insurance company. Effectively, a GIC is a zero coupon bond issued by a life insurance company and, as such, exposes the investor to the same credit risk. This credit risk has been highlighted by the default of several major issuers of GICs. The two most publicized were Mutual Benefit, a New Jersey–based insurer, and Executive Life, a California-based insurer, which were both seized by regulators in 1991.

Annuity

Another insurance company investment product is an annuity. An **annuity** is often described as "a mutual fund in an insurance wrapper." What does this mean? To answer this question, assume that an insurance company investment manager has two identical common stock portfolios, one in a mutual fund and the other in an annuity. On the mutual fund, all income (that is, the dividend) is taxable, and the capital gains (or losses) realized by the fund are also taxable, although at potentially different tax rates. The income and realized gains are taxable whether they are withdrawn by the mutual fund holder or reinvested in the fund. There are no guarantees associated with the mutual fund; its performance depends solely on the portfolio performance.

Because of the insurance wrapper, discussed below, the annuity is treated as an insurance product and as a result receives a preferential tax treatment. Specifically, the income and realized gains are not taxable if not withdrawn from the annuity product. Thus, the "inside buildup" of returns is not taxable on an annuity, as it is also not on other cash value insurance products. At the time of withdrawal, however, all the gains are taxed at ordinary income rates.

The "insurance wrapper" on the mutual fund that makes it an annuity can be of various forms. The most common "wrapper" is the guarantee by the insurance company that the annuity policyholder will get back no less than the amount invested in the annuity (there may also be a minimum period before withdrawal to get this benefit). Thus, if an investor invests $100 in a common stock–based annuity and at the time of withdrawal (or at the time of death of the annuity holder) the annuity has a value of only $95, the insurance company will pay the annuity holder (or its beneficiary) $100. Many other types of protection or insurance features have also been developed.

Of course, insurance companies impose a charge for this insurance benefit—an insurance premium for the insurance component of the annuity. Thus, while mutual funds have an expense fee imposed on the fund's performance, an annuity has a *mortality and expense (M&E) fee* imposed. Annuities are, therefore, more expensive to the investor than mutual funds. In return, annuity policyholders get the insurance wrapper, which provides the tax benefit. Annuities can be either fixed annuities, similar to GICs, or variable annuities whose performance is based on the return of a common stock or bond portfolio.

Mutual funds and annuities distributed by insurance companies may have their investments managed by the insurance company investment department or by external investment managers, as discussed in the next section.

> **Key Points That You Should Understand Before Proceeding**
>
> 1. Life, property/casualty, and health are among the important categories of risks that insurance companies specialize in.
> 2. Insurance companies also sell investment products such as GICs (which are essentially zero coupon bonds) and annuities ("mutual funds in an insurance wrapper").

Monoline Insurance Companies

A very different type of insurance is monoline insurance. Monoline insurers guarantee the timely repayment of the bond principal and interest when a bond insurer defaults on these payments. Monoline insurers are called "monoline" because they provide their insurance services to only one industry, the capital markets. The insured securities have traditionally been municipal bonds, but they now include structured finance bonds, collateralized debt obligations (CDOs), collateralized loan obligations (CLO), asset-backed bonds, and other related products that we describe in later chapters in this book.

Monoline insurance companies make debt service payments on these bonds when the issuers cannot. Multiline insurance companies, on the other hand, often require a lengthy claims and submission and adjustment process.

Monoline insurance has existed since the 1970s. Ambac Financial Group Inc. began in 1971 and MBIA Inc. (previously the Municipal Bond Insurance Association) began in 1973. The Capital Markets Assurance Corporation was founded in 1987 primarily to insure asset-backed securities. In late 2007, Warren Buffett's Berkshire Hathaway Assurance entered the monoline insurance business for municipal bonds only. This entry was intended to capitalize on the subprime loan crisis.

Monoline insurers have been rated AAA and must have this high rating to be effective since they transfer their rating to the bond issue being insured. The insurers collect an insurance fee from issuers for providing insurance on their bonds; this insurance allows the bond issues to be rated AAA. The issuer then saves financing costs by issuing a AAA rated bond instead of a bond with their own lower rating. This savings exceeds the fee they pay for the insurance, providing a gain to the issuer. The monoline insurer insures many different bonds and by this diversification reduces the risk and the total cost of insuring these bonds.

Bond insurance has become an integral part of the capital markets, particularly in the municipal market wherein historically approximately one-half of municipal bonds have been insured.

INSURANCE COMPANIES VERSUS TYPES OF PRODUCTS

Whereas in concept these various types of insurance could be combined in different ways in actual companies, traditionally they have been packaged in companies in similar ways. Traditionally, life insurance and health insurance have occurred together in a *life and health insurance company* (L&H company). And property and casualty insurance have been combined in a P&C insurance company. Companies that provide insurance in both insurance products are called **multiline insurance companies**. Investment products tend to be sold by life insurance companies, not P&C companies. Tables 2 and 3 provide the 10 largest life insurance companies and P&C companies, respectively.

There have been some recent changes in the combinations of products by type of company, however. Health insurance has predominately, but not completely, separated from life insurance and become a separate industry. This change has been due mainly to federal regulation of the health insurance industry. Life insurance companies have also increasingly offered investment-oriented products, both annuities, variable and fixed, and mutual funds. Disability insurance is now sold primarily by pure disability companies but is also offered by some life insurance companies. Long-term care insurance is a fairly new line of

Table 2   Top 10 U.S. Life Insurance Companies

Company	12/31/07 Invested Assets ($000s)
1. Metropolitan Life Insurance Company	209,923,708
2. Teachers Insurance and Annuity Association of America	174,435,318
3. Prudential Insurance Company of America	148,745,800
4. Northwestern Mutual Life Insurance	131,563,104
5. New York Life Insurance Company	104,765,167
6. Massachusetts Mutual Life Insurance	74,280,405
7. American Life Insurance Company	62,806,167
8. Lincoln National Life Insurance	60,611,954
9. Principal Life Insurance Company	58,440,982
10. Allstate Life Insurance Company	56,871,650

Source: *ALIRT Insurance Research, LLC.*

Table 3   Top 10 U.S. Property & Casualty Insurance Companies

Company	12/31/07 Invested Assets ($000s)
1. State Farm Mutual Auto Insurance Company	99,103,876
2. National Indemnity Company	71,769,233
3. Allstate Insurance Company	39,953,260
4. Continental Casualty Company	34,431,958
5. Liberty Mutual Insurance Company	29,368,315
6. National Union Fire Insurance Company of Pittsburgh	27,710,067
7. Federal Insurance Company	26,690,512
8. Zurich American Insurance Company	24,244,071
9. State Farm Fire and Casualty Company	23,782,417
10. Nationwide 3Mutual Insurance Company	23,036,571

Source: *ALIRT Insurance Research, LLC.*

business and is offered by different types of companies, but mainly life insurance companies. In terms of specific product offerings, most companies are unique with respect to the combination of products they offer and how they offer them.

Key Points That You Should Understand Before Proceeding

1. Traditionally, L&H insurers have been distinct from P&C insurers. A few multiline insurers provide both types of insurance.
2. Increasingly, among L&H insurers, life, health, and disability insurance are being provided by separate companies.

FUNDAMENTALS OF THE INSURANCE INDUSTRY

A fundamental aspect of the insurance industry results from the relationship between revenues and costs. A bread manufacturer purchases its ingredients, uses these ingredients to make bread, and then sells the bread, all over a fairly short time frame. Therefore, the bread manufacturer's profit margin is easily calculated.

An insurance company, on the other hand, collects its premium income initially and invests these receipts in its portfolio. The payments on the insurance policy may occur much later and, depending on the type of insurance, may occur in a very unpredictable manner. Consequently, the payments are contingent on potential future events. For example, with respect to life insurance, it is certain that everyone will die. However, it is not known when any individual will die. The timing of the payment on any specific life insurance policy is, thus, uncertain. Although the payments on any single life insurance policy is uncertain, statisticians or actuaries can predict the pattern of deaths on a large portfolio of life insurance policies. Thus, while the payment on a single life insurance policy is uncertain, statistically the payment pattern on a portfolio of life insurance policies is less uncertain. And for a large portfolio of life insurance policies, the individual deaths are uncorrelated. At the other extreme, whereas payments on home insurance against hurricanes are singularly uncertain, the payments on a portfolio of homes are also uncertain. And payments on hurricane insurance are correlated with each other. If one house in South Florida is destroyed by a hurricane, for example, it is likely that many others will also be destroyed.

Thus, there are two very important differences between calculating profitability of bread manufacturers and insurance companies. The first is that the timing and magnitude of the payments are much less certain for an insurance company. The second is that there is a long lag between the receipts and payments for an insurance company, which introduces the importance of the investment portfolio.

These differences in the providers of bread and insurance lead to differences in the way consumers of bread and insurance view their providers. Purchasers of bread are not harmed if the bread manufacturer goes bankrupt the day after they buy the bread. However, while the purchaser of bread receives the bread immediately, the purchaser of insurance receives the payment on his or her insurance policy in the future and, thus, must be concerned about the continued viability of the insurance company. Therefore, the credit rating of an insurance company is important to a purchaser of insurance, especially for the types of insurance that may be paid well into the future, such as life insurance.

Key Points That You Should Understand Before Proceeding

1. The timing and magnitude of payouts to policyholders are highly uncertain for an insurance company.
2. Due to the lag between the premium receipts and policy payouts, the return on the investment portfolio is critical to an insurance company's profitability.

REGULATION OF THE INSURANCE INDUSTRY

According to the McCarran Ferguson Act of 1945, the insurance industry is regulated by the individual states, not the federal government. However, there has been increasing discussion of federal regulation. Insurance companies whose stock is publicly traded are also regulated by the Securities and Exchange Commission (SEC).

Model laws and regulations are developed by the **National Association of Insurance Commissioners (NAIC)**, a voluntary association of state insurance commissioners, for application to insurance companies in all states. Although the adoption of a model law or regulation by the NAIC is not binding on any state, states typically use these as a model when writing their own laws and regulations.

Insurance companies may also be rated by the rating agencies (Moody's, Standard & Poor's, A.M. Best, Fitch, and others) for both their "claims paying ability" and their debt outstanding, if any. Public insurance companies (discussed below) are also evaluated by equity analysts who work at investment banks and brokers or dealers, with respect to the attractiveness of their outstanding common stock.

The relationship between the premium revenues and the eventual contingent contractual insurance policy payments affects an important aspect of evaluating insurance companies. Insurance companies are monitored by their accountants and auditors, their rating agencies, and their government regulators. These monitors of the insurance companies are concerned about the financial stability of the insurance companies due, among other issues, to the lack of synchronicity between premiums and insurance policy payments and also the volatility of the payments. To assure financial stability, these monitors require insurance companies to maintain reserves or **surplus**, which are the excess of assets over liabilities. These reserves or surpluses are defined differently by regulators and accountants and have different names. Because for regulatory purposes, the treatment of both assets and liabilities is established by the state statutes covering the insurance company, surplus, by this measure, is called **statutory surplus** (or **reserves**) or STAT surplus. **Generally accepted accounting principles (GAAP) surplus** (or reserves) are defined by accountants for their purposes. While statutory and GAAP reserves are measured differently, their purposes are similar, although not identical.

Although specifying the definition of the assets is straightforward, defining liabilities is difficult. The complication in determining the value of liabilities arises because the insurance company has committed to make payments at some time in the future, and those payments are recorded as contingent liabilities on its financial statement. The reserves are simply an accounting entry, not an identifiable portfolio.

Statutory surplus is important because regulators view this as the ultimate amount that can be drawn upon to pay policyholders. The growth of this surplus for an insurance company also determines how much future business it can underwrite.

Key Points That You Should Understand Before Proceeding

1. Insurance companies are regulated by the individual states, typically using the laws developed by the NAIC as a model. They may also be rated by debt rating agencies.
2. Insurance companies whose stock is publicly traded are also regulated by the SEC, and perhaps evaluated by equity analysts.
3. The surplus (i.e., the excess of assets over liabilities) of an insurance company is measured differently for statutory and GAAP purposes, and is an important indicator of its financial standing.

STRUCTURE OF INSURANCE COMPANIES

Based on the previous discussion, insurance companies are really a composite of three companies. First, there is the "home office" or actual insurance company. This company designs the insurance contract ("manufactures" the contract) and provides the backing for the financial guarantees on the contract, that is, assures the policyholder that the contract will pay off under the conditions of the contract. This company is called the *manufacturer* and *guarantor* of the insurance policy. Second, there is the investment component that invests the premiums collected in the investment portfolio. This is the *investment company*.

The third element of an insurance company is the *distribution component* or the sales force. There are different types of distribution forces. First, there are the *agents* who are associated with the company. Agents sell only or mainly the company's own manufactured products. These agents typically are not employees of the company (although some companies also use employees as salespeople), but entrepreneurs financially associated with the company. There are also *brokers* who are not associated with any company but sell the insurance products of many companies. Brokers have traditionally operated individually but are increasingly operating in groups called *producer groups*. As deregulation progresses, commercial banks have also become a natural means of distribution for insurance and investment products. Banks are averse to "manufacturing" insurance products because of their inexperience; the risk borne by manufacturing insurance products; and the long payback period of some insurance products. On the other hand, insurance companies are attracted by commercial bank customer contacts. As a result, commercial bank distribution of insurance company products has grown considerably. This relationship is called **bankassurance**. More recently, the Internet has also been used by some insurance companies to distribute insurance products directly to clients. Internet distribution is very new and has considerable potential but is still in its infancy. This mode of distribution has been most successful in the more commodity-like insurance products, such as term life insurance and automobile insurance.

These three components of insurance companies traditionally have been combined in one overall company, but they are increasingly being separated and the three functions are being provided by different companies. First, as previously mentioned, many insurance companies use independent brokers or producer groups to distribute their products rather than their own agents. Many companies no longer have their own agents and sell all their products exclusively through brokers, producer groups, or on the Internet. Second, insurance companies are increasingly outsourcing parts of their investment portfolio or even the entire portfolio to external independent investment managers. Investment managers are also increasingly diversifying, that is, not specializing in managing any one type of assets such as pension fund assets, mutual funds, or insurance company assets, but managing several or all of them, including insurance company assets. Third, while the home office component of an insurance company seems to be the core of the insurance company, some home offices use external actuarial firms to design their contracts. And, more importantly, they may *reinsure* some or all of the liabilities they incur in providing insurance. According to the reinsurance transaction, the initial insurer transfers the risk of the insurance to another company, the **reinsurer**. There is an industry of reinsurers who accept the risk incurred by the primary insurance company. The financial guarantee on the insurance policy is, thus, provided by the reinsurer rather than the insurance company that originally provided or "wrote" the policy.

Given this fragmentation of functions in an insurance company, there has been discussion of a "virtual insurance company," whereby a small group of executives in the home office have external actuarial firms design the contract; reinsure all the insurance policies written; outsource all the investments; and use brokers to distribute their products. Some insurance companies are currently approaching being a virtual insurance company.

Key Points That You Should Understand Before Proceeding

1. The three key components of an insurance company are the design and financial guarantee of the insurance contract; the distribution of the product; and the investment of the premiums collected.
2. Traditionally, these components have been combined in a single company, but increasingly separate companies are performing these functions.

FORMS OF INSURANCE COMPANIES: STOCK AND MUTUAL

There are two major forms of life insurance companies: stock and mutual. A **stock insurance company** is similar in structure to any corporation or public company. Shares (of ownership) are owned by independent shareholders and are traded publicly. The shareholders care only about the performance of their shares, that is, the stock appreciation and the dividends. Their holding period and, thus, their view may be short term. The insurance policies are simply the products or business of the company.

In contrast, **mutual insurance companies** have no stock and no external owners. Their policyholders are also their owners. The owners, that is, the policyholders, care primarily or even solely about the performance on their insurance policies, notably the company's ability to pay on the policy. Since these payments may occur considerably into the future, the policyholders' view may be long term. Thus, while stock insurance companies have two constituencies, their stockholders and their policyholders, mutual insurance companies only have one, since their policyholders and their owners are the same. Traditionally the largest insurers have been mutual, but recently there have been many *demutualizations*, that is, conversions by mutual companies to stock companies.

The debate on which is the better form of insurance company, stock or mutual, is too involved to be considered in any depth here. However, consider selected comments on this issue. First, consider this issue from the perspective of the policyholder or perhaps the rating agency or regulator, not from the point of view of the insurance company. Mutual holding companies have only one constituency, their policyholder or owner. The liabilities of many types of insurance companies are long term, especially the writers of life insurance. Thus, mutual insurance companies can appropriately have a long time horizon in their strategies and policies. They do not have to make short-term decisions to benefit their shareholders, whose interests are usually short term, via an increase in the stock price or dividend, in a way that might reduce their long-term profitability or the financial strength of the insurance company. In addition, if the insurance company makes profits it can pass them on to its policyholders via reduced premiums. (Policies that benefit from an increased profitability of the insurance company are called *participating policies*, as discussed in the following text.) These increased profits do not have to accrue to stockholders because there are none.

Finally, mutual insurance companies can adopt a longer time frame in their investments, which will most likely make possible a higher long-term return. Mutual insurance companies, for example, hold more common stock in their investment portfolios. However, whereas the long time frame of mutual insurance companies may be construed as an advantage over stock companies, it can also be construed as a disadvantage. Rating agencies and others assert that, due to their longer horizon, mutual insurance companies may be less efficient and have higher expenses than stock companies. Empirically, rating agencies and others assert that mutual insurance companies typically have reduced their expenses after converting to stock companies. Overall, it can be argued that mutual insurance companies have such long planning horizons that they may not operate efficiently, particularly with respect to expenses. Stock companies, on the other hand, have very short planning horizons and may operate to the long-term disadvantage of their policyholders to satisfy their stockholders in the short run.

Consider now the issue of stock versus mutual companies from the perspective of the insurance company. What have been the motivations of mutual insurance companies to go public (issue stock via an initial public offering [IPO]) in recent years? Several reasons are typically given. First, with the financial industry diversifying, consolidating, and growing, insurance companies have concluded that they need to acquire other financial companies (insurance companies, investment companies, and other financial companies) to prosper or even survive. To conduct these acquisitions they have to have capital. Mutual companies cannot, by definition, issue stock and are limited in the amount of public debt they can issue—mutual insurance companies issue public debt via "surplus notes." In addition, internal surplus has been growing slowly for the insurance industry. Thus, many insurance companies have concluded that to expand as quickly as they deem essential, they have to be able to raise equity capital and, thus, go public. Second, some mutual insurance companies and their advisors believe that, at least at some times, stock is a better "acquisition currency" than cash (typically for reasons of taxes and financial accounting), even if the mutual insurance company has enough cash for the acquisition. Finally, company stock and stock options have become a more important form of incentive compensation in many industries, and many insurance companies have concluded that to attract, retain, and motivate the desired executives, they need public stock in their companies.

Whereas many mutual insurance companies go public for these reasons, other mutual insurance companies continue to prosper as mutuals. And while stock insurance companies can raise capital to acquire other companies, they also become vulnerable to being acquired by other companies. Mutual companies cannot be involuntarily acquired.

A new form of insurance company, which is a hybrid between a pure mutual and a pure stock company, has been approved by some states and implemented by some insurance companies in these states since their introduction in 1996. This form is called a **mutual holding company (MHC)**. According to the MHC structure, the upstream holding company is a mutual company (that is, there is no stockholder ownership) and also a holding company (that is, a mutual holding company but not an insurance company). Under the MHC structure, the mutual company forms a stock subsidiary and contributes some or all of its operating businesses to the subsidiary. Policyholders retain membership rights in the mutual holding company and contractual rights in the operating subsidiary. Up to 49.9% of the subsidiary's voting interest can be sold to the public to raise primary capital. The mutual holding company continues to hold a majority ownership in the downstream insurance company. The structure of an MHC is shown in Figure 1.

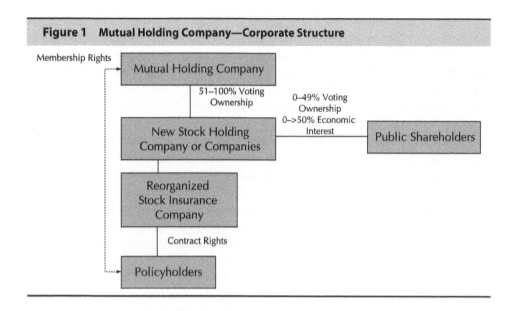

Figure 1 Mutual Holding Company—Corporate Structure

The participating life insurance is written by the downstream public life insurance company. Since the MHC board of directors has majority ownership of the life insurance company, it can and legally must operate the company in the best interests of the participating policyholders. Among the advantages of the MHC are

access to external funds, including equity
creation of acquisition currency, that is, common stock (which may be superior to cash for acquisitions)
expansion into new nonparticipating lines of business with these funds
retention of majority control of an insurance company
management ownership provides incentives to attract and retain top management

There are also tax advantages to a mutual insurance company becoming an MHC.

MHC laws have been approved by only a few states, and even where approved, the laws vary widely by state. The experience with MHCs is not yet sufficient to assess whether this form will be a viable and growing form of life insurance company structure. In fact, the Principal Financial Group, which converted from a mutual to an MHC during 1998, converted to a stock company.

Key Points That You Should Understand Before Proceeding

1. In terms of ownership, there are two main forms of insurance companies: stock and mutual. A hybrid form, the mutual holding company, has been approved in some states.
2. Traditionally, insurance companies have been mutual, but they are increasingly demutualizing due to the perceived benefits of having a publicly traded stock.

INDIVIDUAL VERSUS GROUP INSURANCE

All the insurance products mentioned in this chapter are sold to individuals. Some insurance products are also sold to groups, typically to the employees of specific companies through their employers, or educational, medical, or other professional associations. Among the major types of products distributed to groups are term life insurance, whole life insurance, medical insurance, disability insurance (short-term and long-term), and investment products such as mutual funds, annuities, and 401(k) products.

Insurance companies often have different distribution systems for individual and group products. They are typically different because individual product distributors deal with individuals and small company owners, and group product distributors deal with human resource departments of corporations and other organizations. In the P&C business, there is also a similar distinction between *personal lines of business* and *commercial lines of business*. Some P&C companies focus mainly or solely on personal lines such as automobile and homeowners insurance; others focus on commercial lines such as business property and liability insurance.

Key Point That You Should Understand Before Proceeding

1. Insurance products may be sold either to individuals (e.g., life, automobile) or to groups (e.g., disability, business property).

TYPES OF LIFE INSURANCE

This section elaborates on the types of life insurance products introduced earlier. There are two fundamentally different types of life insurance: **term life insurance** and **cash value life insurance**.

Term Insurance

Term insurance is *pure life insurance*. If the insured dies while the policy is intact, the beneficiary of the policy receives the death benefit. If the insured does not die within the period, the policy is invalid and has no value. There is no cash value or investment value for a term insurance policy. In addition, the policyholder cannot borrow against the policy.

With respect to the premium paid, there are two different types of term policies. The first is *level term*. For this type, the premium is constant over the life of the policy. For example, for a 10-year term policy, the premium will be the same for each of the 10 years. Obviously, given the increasing probability of dying with age, the insured overpays early in the life of the policy and underpays late in the policy's life. The second type is *annual renewable term*, whereby the policy provides guaranteed protection over the term of the policy (e.g., 10 years), but at an increasing premium. However, a maximum premium schedule is provided.

Cash Value or Permanent Life Insurance

There is a broad classification of life insurance, which is cash value or permanent or investment-type life insurance. A common type of cash value life insurance is called **whole life insurance**. In addition to providing pure life insurance (as does term insurance), whole life insurance builds up a cash value or investment value inside the policy. This cash value can be withdrawn and can also be borrowed against by the owner of the policy. Or, if the owner wishes to let the **policy lapse,** he or she can withdraw the cash value. This cash value develops because of the level premium approach to paying for this type of insurance. The actuarial cost of pure insurance increases with age, but the premium charged on this type of insurance is level. The policyholder is therefore overpaying for insurance early in the life of the policy and underpaying thereafter. The cash value builds up in the policy both for this reason and because the premium is greater than the premium for level term insurance. Growth in the cash value of the life insurance policy is referred to as the "inside buildup." A major advantage of this and other types of life insurance that have a cash or investment value is that *the inside buildup is not subject to taxation,* that is, not taxed as either income or capital gains. Neither is the beneficiary of the death benefit of a life insurance policy subject to an income tax. The death benefit of the policy may or may not be subject to estate tax, depending on how the beneficiary status is structured. Consequently, life insurance products have considerable tax advantages.

Life insurance and life insurance products are very complex. Only an overview is provided in this chapter.[1] There are two categories with respect to cash value life insurance policies. The first is whether the cash value is *guaranteed* or *variable.* The second is whether the required premium payment is *fixed* or *flexible.* Thus, there are four combinations (see Table 4), which we discuss below.

Guaranteed Cash Value Life Insurance

Traditional cash value life insurance, usually called whole life insurance, has a guaranteed buildup of cash value based on the general account portfolio of the insurance company. The insurance company guarantees a minimum cash value at the end of each year. This guaranteed cash value is based on a minimum dividend paid on the policy. In addition, the policy can be either *participating* or *nonparticipating.* For nonparticipating policies, the minimum dividend and the minimum cash value on the policy are the guaranteed amounts; that is, there is no upside. For the participating policy, the dividend paid on the policy is based on the realized actuarial experience of the company and its investment portfolio. The cash value may be above but not below the guaranteed level for participating policies. Thus, the actual performance of the policy may be substantially affected by the actual policy dividends over the guaranteed amount.

Table 4   Classification of Cash Value Insurance

	Guaranteed Dollar Cash Value Policies	Variable/Non-Guaranteed Policies
Fixed Premium	Whole life insurance	Variable life insurance
Flexible Premium	Universal life insurance	Variable universal life insurance

[1] For an excellent treatment of life insurance, see Ben G. Baldwin, *The New Life Insurance Investment Advisor,* revised edition (Boston, MA: McGraw Hill, 1994). See also *Life Insurance Fact Book,* American Council of Life Insurance, 2007.

Variable Life Insurance

Contrary to the guaranteed or fixed cash value policies based on the general account portfolio of the insurance company, variable life insurance policies allow the policyowners to allocate their premium payments to and among separate investment accounts maintained by the insurance company, within limits, and also to be able to shift the policy cash value among the separate accounts. As a result, the amount of the policy cash value and the death benefits depend on the investment results of the separate accounts the policyowners have selected. Thus, there is no guaranteed cash value or death benefit. Both depend on the performance of the selected investment portfolio.

The types of separate account investment options offered vary by insurance companies. Typically, the insurance company offers a selection of common stock and bond fund investment opportunities, often managed by the company itself and other investment managers. If the investment options perform well, the cash value buildup in the policy will be significant. However, if the policyholder selects investment options that perform poorly, the variable life insurance policy will perform poorly. There could be little or no cash value buildup, or, in the worst case, the policy could be terminated. This type of life insurance is called **variable life insurance**. Variable life insurance, which typically has common stock investment options, grew quickly beginning with the stock market rally of the late 1990s, but declined during the early 2000s.

Flexible Premium Policies—Universal Life

The key element of **universal life** is the flexibility of the premium for the policyowner. This flexible premium concept separates pure insurance protection (term insurance) from the investment (cash value) element of the policy. The policy cash value is set up as the cash value fund (or accumulation fund) to which the investment income is credited and from which the cost of term insurance for the insured (the mortality charge) is debited. The expenses are also debited.

This separation of the cash value from the pure insurance is called the "unbundling" of the traditional life insurance policy. Premium payments for universal life are at the discretion of the policyholder—that is, are flexible—except that there must be a minimum initial premium to begin the coverage. There must also be at least enough cash value in the policy each month to cover the mortality charge and other expenses. If not, the policy will lapse. Both guaranteed cash value and variable life can be written on a flexible premium or fixed premium basis, as summarized in Table 4.

Variable Universal Life Insurance

Variable universal life insurance combines the features of variable life and universal life policies, that is, the choice of separate account investment products and flexible premiums. Since the 1990s, term and variable universal life insurance have been growing at the expense of whole life insurance.

Survivorship (Second to Die) Insurance

Most whole life insurance policies are designed to pay death benefits when the person specified insured dies. An added dimension of whole life policies is that two people (usually a married couple) are jointly insured and the policy pays the death benefit not when the first person dies, but when the second person (the "surviving spouse") dies. This is called *survivorship insurance* or *second-to-die insurance*. This survivorship feature can be added to standard cash value whole life, universal life, variable life, and variable universal life policies. Thus, each of the four policies listed in Table 4 could also be written on a survivorship basis.

In general, the annual premium for a survivorship insurance policy is lower than for a policy on a single person because, by construction, the second of two people to die has a longer life span than the first. Survivorship insurance is typically sold for estate planning purposes.

Key Points That You Should Understand Before Proceeding

1. There are two key types of life insurance: term insurance, which does not have investment value; and cash value life insurance, which has investment value and can be borrowed against.
2. Cash value insurance products may be "guaranteed" or "variable"; with fixed or flexible premiums; and with or without a survivorship feature.

GENERAL ACCOUNT AND SEPARATE ACCOUNT PRODUCTS

The *general account of an insurance company* refers to the investment portfolio of the overall company. Products "written by the company itself" are said to have a "general account guarantee," that is, they are a liability of the insurance company. When the rating agencies (Moody's, Standard & Poor's, A.M. Best, and Fitch) provide a credit rating, it is on products written by or guaranteed by the general account. Such ratings are on the "claims-paying ability" of the company. Typical products written by and guaranteed by the general account are whole life, universal life, and fixed annuities (including GICs). Insurance companies must support the guaranteed performance of their general account products to the extent of their solvency. These are called **general account products**.

Other types of insurance products receive no guarantee from the insurance company's general account, and their performance is not based on the performance of the insurance company's general account but solely on the performance of an account separate from the general account of the insurance company, often an account selected by the policyholder. These products are called **separate account products**. Variable life insurance and variable annuities are separate account products. The policyholder chooses specific portfolios to support these products. The performance of the insurance product depends almost solely on the performance of the portfolio selected, adjusted for the fees or expenses of the insuring company (which do depend on the insurance company).

Key Points That You Should Understand Before Proceeding

1. The overall investment portfolio of an insurance company supports its general account products.
2. Separate account products depend solely on the performance of an account chosen by the policyholder.

PARTICIPATING POLICIES

The performance of separate account products depends on the performance of the separate account portfolio chosen and is not affected by the performance of the overall insurance company's general account portfolio. In addition, the performance of some general account products is not affected by the performance of the general account portfolio. For example, disability income insurance policies may be written on a general account, and while their payoff depends on the solvency of the general account, the policy performance (for example, its premium) may not participate in the investment performance of the insurance companies' general account investment portfolio.

Other general account insurance products *participate* in the performance of the company's general account performance. For example, whereas a life insurance company provides the guarantee of a minimum dividend on its whole life policies, the policies' actual dividend may increase if the investment portfolio performs well. (This is called the "interest component" of the dividend: The other two components are the M&E components discussed previously.) Thus, the performance of the insurance policy participates in the overall company's performance. Such a policy is called a *participating policy*, in this case, a participating whole life insurance policy.

Both stock and mutual insurance companies write both general and separate account products. However, most participating general account products are written in mutual companies.

Key Points That You Should Understand Before Proceeding

1. A participating policy pays a higher dividend than the guaranteed minimum if the general account portfolio performs well.
2. General account products may also be nonparticipating, with fixed payoffs.

INSURANCE COMPANY INVESTMENT STRATEGIES[2]

In general, the characteristics of insurance company investment portfolios should reflect their liabilities, that is, the insurance products they underwrite.

There are many differences among the various types of insurance policies. Among them are the following:

- the expected time at which the average payment will be made by the insurance company (technically, the "duration" of the payments)
- the statistical or actuarial accuracy of estimates of *when* the event insured against will occur and the *amount* of the payment (that is, the overall risk of the policy)
- other factors

In addition, there are tax differences among different types of insurance policies and companies.

The key distinction between life insurance and property and casualty insurance companies lies in the difficulty of projecting whether or not a policyholder will be paid off and how much the payment will be. Although this is no easy task for either a life or a P&C

---

[2] For a more detailed discussion of investment strategies, see Frank J. Jones, "An Overview of Institutional Fixed Income Strategies," in Volume 1 of *Professional Perspectives on Fixed Income Portfolio Management* (Hoboken, NJ: John Wiley & Sons, 2000), pp. 1–13.

insurance company, it is easier from an actuarial perspective for a life insurance company. The amount and timing of claims on property and casualty insurance companies are more difficult to predict because of the randomness of natural catastrophes and the unpredictability of court awards in liability cases. This uncertainty about the timing and amount of cash outlays to satisfy claims has an impact on the investment strategies of the funds of property and casualty insurance companies compared to life insurance companies.

Without investigating the details for the differences in the portfolios of different types of insurance products, the major differences in the portfolios of life companies and P&C companies are as follows. Life companies on average have less common stock, more private placements, more commercial mortgages, less municipal bonds, and longer maturity bonds. The difference in municipal bond holdings is due to the tax-exempt characteristic of these securities. The larger holdings of private placements and commercial mortgages indicate the yield orientation of life companies. This yield orientation is also consistent with the low holding of common stock for life insurance companies.

There are also differences in investment strategy between public (or stock) and mutual insurance companies of the same type. The major difference is that stock companies tend to have less common stock than mutual companies. The major reason for this difference is that common stock analysts, who make buy-hold-sell recommendations on all public companies for institutional and individual investors, consider mainly regularly recurring operating income in their calculation of income, not volatile returns. Coupon and dividend income tend to be stable, and capital gains tend to be unstable. Thus, these analysts have a bias favoring bonds, which have higher interest income, over stocks, which have higher capital gains and, over the long term, higher total returns. As a result, mutual insurance companies, which are not rated by common stock analysts, can focus on total return rather than just yield and have more common stock than public companies.

CHANGES IN THE INSURANCE INDUSTRY

There have been three major types of changes in the insurance industry in the past two decades:

- the deregulation of the financial system
- internationalization of the insurance industry
- demutualization

We discuss each of these changes in the following text.

The Deregulation of the Financial System

In 1933, Congress passed the Glass-Steagall Act. The act separated commercial banking, investment banking, and insurance. That is, a company could be involved in only one of these three types of business. One of the major intentions of this act was to prevent a single organization from having complete control over the sources of corporate funding, specifically lending to and underwriting the securities of a company. An initial celebrated outcome of this Act, which went into effect in 1935, was the breakup of the "House of Morgan," the business of J.P. Morgan. A Morgan son, two Morgan partners, and 25 employees left J.P. Morgan to set up the investment bank, Morgan Stanley. (J.P. Morgan subsequently became Morgan Guaranty Trust Company when it merged with the much larger Guaranty Trust Company in 1959.) Both the bank and the investment bank continue, although in significantly changed forms. J.P. Morgan was acquired by Chase Manhattan in July 2000 and has since been called J.P. Morgan Chase.

Over time, due to the evolution of the financial system, the implementation of the Glass-Steagall Act became more ambiguous, more difficult to implement, and, in the view of many, counterproductive. With this background, a recent landmark financial event was the revocation of the Glass-Steagall Act. On November 12, 1999, the **Gramm-Leach-Bliley Act (GLB)**, called the Financial Modernization Act of 1999, was signed into law. This act removed the 50-year-old "anti-affiliation restrictions" among commercial banks, investment banks, and insurance companies.

The GLB has facilitated and accelerated affiliations among these three types of institutions. The first mega-institution of this type is the combination of Salomon Brothers and Smith Barney, both investment banks; Travelers, an insurance company; and Citicorp, a commercial bank. This combined firm was founded in 1998 when Citigroup and Travelers merged, called simply Citigroup, and was involved in insurance, commercial banking, investment banking, and security brokerage. However, the synergies between insurance and banking did not work out well and in August 2002, Citigroup spun off Travelers as a separate subsidiary and three years later sold Travelers to Met Life. No companies have since attempted to combine insurance and banking on a large scale.

GLB is also asserted to be a reason for the accelerated demutualization of insurance companies. As indicated earlier in this chapter, demutualization permits insurance companies to acquire not only insurance companies but other types of financial institutions. And by demutualizing, insurance companies can acquire capital for acquisitions. The act certainly accelerated bankassurance, the sale of insurance products by banks, although at a slower pace than originally thought.

Even before the passage of the GLB bill, commercial banks were becoming involved in some aspects of commercial banking. For several years, in addition to selling mutual funds, banks have become successful at selling annuities, both variable and fixed, mainly manufactured by other investment managers. In addition, insurance companies have been entering one part of banking, namely trust banking. Many life insurance agents put some of their clients' assets and life insurance policies in trusts. As a result, several life insurance companies have obtained trust licenses.

Few insurers have planned to go into retail commercial banking. However, Metropolitan Life, after having become a public stock insurance company in March 2000, announced in August 2000 that it would acquire Grand Bank, N.A., in New Jersey and go into retail commercial banking, something that could not have been accomplished before the GLB bill was passed.

Internationalization of the Insurance Industry

Globalization has occurred in many industries, including the insurance industry. With respect to the United States, globalization operates in two directions. With respect to the first direction, U.S. insurance companies have both acquired and entered into agreements with international insurance companies and begun operations in other countries. With respect to the second, international insurance companies, mainly European, have become even more active in acquiring U.S. insurance and investment companies.

Among the reasons for the increased entry by international insurance companies into the U.S. insurance industry and other U.S. financial sectors are (1) the more rapid growth of the U.S. financial businesses relative to the international financial business, (2) the attractive demographics and income of potential U.S. clients, and (3) the less regulated environment of the U.S. insurance industry. Among the major international acquirers of U.S. insurance companies have been AXA Group (French), ING Group (Dutch), Allianze (German), Fortis (Dutch-Belgian), and Aegon (Dutch).

Demutualization

Since mid 1995, several insurance companies have changed from mutual companies to stock companies for reasons discussed previously in this chapter. Since insurance companies are regulated by states, such changes have to be preapproved by the state insurance regulatory department. Many industry observers believe that the recent demutualized insurance companies will either acquire other financial companies or will be acquired by other financial companies, or both.

Some states, as indicated above, have approved the mutual holding company status, and so the resident insurance companies had a choice of converting to a mutual holding company or a pure public stock company. Other states, including New York, have not approved the mutual holding company status, and so the only option remaining to a mutual company is to demutualize, that is, become a public stock company.

Key Points That You Should Understand Before Proceeding

1. The Glass-Steagall Act of 1933 prevented any one company from being simultaneously involved in commercial banking, investment banking, and insurance.
2. In response to a changing financial landscape, the Gramm-Leach-Bliley Act of 1999 removed the above restriction and is expected to accelerate mergers among formerly distinct financial institutions.

EVOLUTION OF INSURANCE, INVESTMENT, AND RETIREMENT PRODUCTS

Even prior to the Financial Modernization Act of 1999, there was an increasing overlap of insurance, investment, and pension products and the distribution of those products. The passage of this act has accelerated this convergence. This chapter as well as the next two discuss insurance companies, investment companies, and pension plans with their increasingly overlapping products.

Three decades ago, there were three distinct types of products for individuals: insurance, savings/investment, and retirement. The specific products in each distinguishable category were as follows. Insurance products included term life and whole life. Savings/ investment products included stocks, bonds, and mutual funds. Retirement products included Social Security (provided by the government), defined benefit and defined contribution plans (provided by employers), and **individual retirement accounts (IRAs)** (provided by investment companies).

During the past two decades, many products have been developed that fit into two or even three of these categories. Into which of these three categories, for example, does an IRA sold to a customer by a life insurance agent fit? Arguably, the correct answer to this question is all three categories. Figure 2 provides a summary of some of the products on the insurance/savings/retirement spectrum, which are really *hybrids*. We have discussed the various insurance products in this chapter. This section discusses products that are hybrid

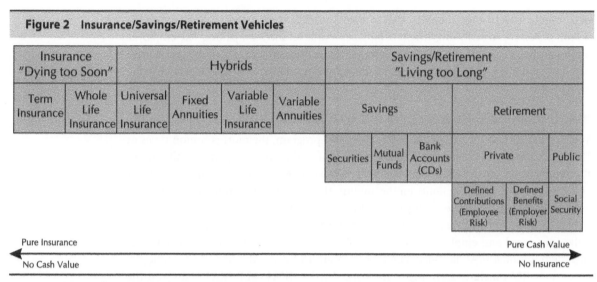

Figure 2   Insurance/Savings/Retirement Vehicles

Insurance "Dying too Soon"		Hybrids				Savings/Retirement "Living too Long"						
Term Insurance	Whole Life Insurance	Universal Life Insurance	Fixed Annuities	Variable Life Insurance	Variable Annuities	Savings				Retirement		
						Securities	Mutual Funds	Bank Accounts (CDs)		Private		Public
										Defined Contributions (Employee Risk)	Defined Benefits (Employer Risk)	Social Security

Pure Insurance   ←————————————————————————→   Pure Cash Value
No Cash Value   No Insurance

Source: *Frank J. Jones, "An Overview of Institutional Fixed Income Strategies," in Volume 1 of Professional Perspectives on Fixed Income Portfolio Management (Hoboken, NJ: John Wiley & Sons, 2000).*

retirement and savings products but which are often manufactured and distributed by insurance companies.

Products that are a hybrid of retirement and investment products and are often distributed by insurance companies and agents are 401(k)s, **Roth 401(k)s**, and variable annuities. These products are also often distributed by many insurance companies, and the insurance companies often include some of their own products within these categories. Because these plans are retirement plans, there are tax advantages to the investor.

Under the 1954 Internal Revenue Service (IRS) rules, *qualified plans* are tax-deferred plans set up by employers for employees. The employees pay taxes only when they withdraw the funds; that is, the contributions are not taxed, they are "before taxes." When employers make contributions to employee plans, the employers also, if they meet several requirements, receive a tax benefit (typically a tax deduction for the payment). Because these plans receive tax benefits and are intended for retirement, typically withdrawals prior to age 59½ are subject to a 10% (of principal) penalty tax, although there are some exceptions. In addition, withdrawals must begin by age 70½ to limit the duration of the tax advantage. 401(k) and Roth 401(k) plans are such qualified plans. The entire amount of all withdrawals is subject to taxation at the owner's income tax rate.

401(k) Plans and Roth 401(k) Plans

401(k) plans, which were authorized by the Revenue Act of 1978, are plans provided by an employer whereby an employee may elect to contribute pretax dollars to a qualified tax-deferred retirement plan. The employer offers a range of investment options from which the employee selects a vehicle to invest these funds. The company's own stock, if the company is public, is often one investment option. Most current employer 401(k) plans provide a diversified portfolio of mutual funds to their employees, typically including funds offered by one or more investment companies. 401(k) plans are offered to employers by several distribution systems, primarily investment companies and insurance companies. The employer often matches a certain portion of the employee's contribution. Because of the tax deferral privilege, there are limits on the amount the employee can contribute and also that the employer can match.

IRAs (Individual Retirement Accounts) and ROTH IRAs

While a 401(k) is an *employer-sponsored* retirement program, the most common types of IRAs are *personal* tax-deferred retirement plans; that is, they are set up at the initiative of the employee/investor. IRAs were created by the Employee Retirement Income Security Act (ERISA) of 1974. There are limits on the amount that may be invested in an IRA and the amount of earned income to qualify for an IRA investment.

Some IRAs, however, are employer sponsored. The various types of IRAs, both individually sponsored and employer sponsored, are as follows. Individually sponsored IRAs include traditional IRAs, non-deductible IRAs, **Roth IRAs,** and rollover IRAs. Employer-sponsored IRAs include Simplified Employee Pension IRAs (SEP IRA) plans and the Savings Incentive Matching Plan for Employees IRAs (SIMPLE IRA).

Traditional and Roth IRAs are vehicles for individuals to set up their own retirement plans outside their employment. Both types permit assets to accumulate free of taxes. In general, the Roth IRA, provided by the Taxpayer Relief Act of 1997, is similar to the traditional IRA, although the taxability of its contributions and withdrawals is reversed. Whereas contributions to traditional IRAs are tax deductible, contributions to Roth IRAs are made after tax (that is, are not tax deductible). On the other hand, with respect to distributions, traditional IRA distributions are taxed as ordinary income (that is, even capital gains and dividends are taxed as ordinary income), and distributions from Roth IRAs are tax free. Overall, traditional IRAs are taxed on the way out (at time of distribution), while Roth IRAs are taxed on the way in (at the time of investment).

In general, absent certain special circumstances (such as death, disability, or certain unemployment expenses), withdrawals from either IRA type prior to age 59½ are subject to a 10% IRS early withdrawal penalty. Some of the other rules on voluntary and mandatory distributions are very complex. Contributions to both Roth and traditional IRAs are limited to $5,000 per year ($6,000 if age 50 or older) during 2008, and even the ability to contribute this amount is phased out at higher incomes for both types of IRAs.

Rollover IRAs, also called "conduit IRAs," are used for rolling over eligible distributions from employer-sponsored retirement plans, such as 401(k)s. Rollover IRAs may be used when an individual is leaving an employer and wants to continue this retirement plan, that is, does not want to be subject to penalties or distribution/withdrawal taxes. The employees can roll over assets from an employer-sponsored program into a rollover IRA and subsequently roll them back to another employer-sponsored plan. Rollover IRAs are very similar to traditional IRAs.

Investors not eligible for traditional or Roth IRAs can invest in non-deductible IRAs. In these IRAs, contributions are after tax and gains are taxed at withdrawal, but the inside buildup is tax free.

SEPs and SIMPLEs are both qualified employer-sponsored IRAs wherein the contributions by the business are tax deductible to the business. The SEP is a type of IRA that allows an employer to make a tax-deductible contribution of from 0% to 25% of earned income per year, per participant, up to $46,000. SEPs are ideal for the self-employed or small business owner. According to the SIMPLE IRA, which became available during 1997, the employer must match employee contributions as low as 1% up to 3% of compensation; or must make a nonelective contribution of 2% of compensation to all eligible employees.

As can be seen with respect to both product design and distribution channels, the distinction among insurance, investment, and retirement products has become very blurred.

SUMMARY

In general, insurance companies bear risk from parties who wish to avert risk by transferring it to the insurance companies. The party seeking to transfer the risk pays an insurance premium to the insurance company.

Insurance companies pay the insured when and/or if the insured event occurs. Because insurance companies collect premiums initially and pay the claims later, the initial revenues are invested in a portfolio, and portfolio returns become another important revenue for the insurance company. Consequently, insurance companies are financial intermediaries that function as risk bearers.

The events insured can be death (insured by life insurance companies), health problems (health insurance companies), or housing or automobile damage (P&C insurance companies). In addition, there are different types of insurance for the different types of risks. Insurance companies have also become active in providing retirement and investment products. These different types of insurance liabilities reflect different types of risks and, therefore, the investment portfolios of these types of insurance companies differ significantly.

Insurance companies can be owned by stockholders (stock or public companies) or by their policyholders (mutual companies). Insurance companies are regulated by states, not the federal government. The regulations can vary significantly from one state to another.

The passage of the Gramm-Leach-Bliley Act (called the Financial Modernization Act of 1999) has eliminated the barriers between insurance companies, commercial banks, and investment banks, and various combinations of these types of companies will continue to evolve.

KEY TERMS

- 401(k) plans
- Annuity
- Bankassurance
- Cash value life insurance
- Crediting rate
- Generally accepted accounting principles (GAAP) surplus
- General account products
- Gramm-Leach-Bliley Act (GLB)
- Guaranteed investment contract (GIC)
- Health insurance company
- Investment income

- Individual retirement account (IRA)
- Life insurance company
- Multiline insurance companies
- Mutual holding company (MHC)
- Mutual insurance company
- National Association of Insurance Commissioners (NAIC)
- Policy lapse
- Premiums
- Property and casualty (P&C) insurance company
- Reinsurer

- Reserve
- Risk bearers
- Roth 401(k)
- Roth IRA
- Separate account products
- Statutory surplus
- Stock insurance company
- Surplus
- Term life insurance
- Underwriting income
- Underwriting process
- Universal life
- Variable life insurance
- Whole life insurance

QUESTIONS

1. **a.** What are the major sources of revenue for an insurance company?
   b. How are its profits determined?
2. Name the major types of insurance and investment-oriented products sold by insurance companies.
3. **a.** What is a GIC?
   b. Does a GIC carry a "guarantee" like a government obligation?
4. What are some key differences between a mutual fund and an annuity?
5. Why should a purchaser of life insurance be concerned about the credit rating of his or her insurance company?
6. **a.** Does the SEC regulate all insurance companies?
   b. If not, who regulates them?
7. Does the insurance industry have a self-regulatory group and, if so, what is its role?
8. What is the statutory surplus and why is it an important measure for an insurance company?
9. What is bankassurance?
10. **a.** What is meant by "demutualization"?
    b. What are the perceived advantages of demutualization?
11. Comment on the following quotation from Frank J. Jones, "An Overview of Institutional Fixed Income Strategies," in Volume 1 of *Professional Perspectives on Fixed Income Portfolio Management* (Hoboken, NJ: John Wiley & Sons, 2000):

    An important impediment to the use of the total rate of return objective by stock life insurance companies is the role of equity analysts on Wall Street. . . . These equity analysts emphasize the stability of earnings and thereby prefer stable income to capital gains. Therefore, they consider only income and not capital gains, either realized or unrealized, in operating income—an important measure in their overall rating. While this practice of not considering capital gains may be appropriate for bonds, it certainly is inappropriate for common stock and provides a significant disincentive to life insurance companies for owning common stock in their portfolios. . . . this equity analyst practice does a disservice to policyholders of stock life insurance companies since their insurance companies end up having inferior asset allocations.

12. What are term insurance, whole life insurance, variable life insurance, universal life insurance, and survivorship insurance?
13. Why are all participating policies written in an insurance company's general account?
14. Whose liabilities are harder to predict, life insurers or property and casualty insurers? Explain why.
15. How does the Financial Modernization Act of 1999 affect the insurance industry?

Investment Companies and Exchange-Traded Funds

LEARNING OBJECTIVES

After reading this chapter, you will understand

- the different types of investment companies: mutual funds, closed-end investment companies, and unit trusts

- how the share prices of mutual funds and closed-end funds are determined

- the structure of funds and the costs that they incur

- how investment companies can differ depending on their investment objectives

- the economic benefits that investment companies provide, including diversification and reduced costs of investing

- the meaning of a regulated investment company

- the structure of investment companies

- the taxation of mutual funds

- alternatives to mutual funds

- what exchange traded funds are

- the similarities and differences between exchange-traded funds and closed-end funds

- what separately managed accounts are

Investment companies are financial intermediaries that sell shares to the public and invest the proceeds in a diversified portfolio of securities. Each share sold represents a proportional interest in the portfolio of securities managed by the investment company on behalf of its shareholders. The type of securities purchased depends on the company's investment objective. Exchange-traded funds are similar to investment companies but have several advantages relative to investment companies.

TYPES OF INVESTMENT COMPANIES

There are three types of investment companies: open-end funds, closed-end funds, and unit trusts.

Open-End Funds (Mutual Funds)

Open-end funds, commonly referred to simply as **mutual funds**, are portfolios of securities, mainly stocks, bonds, and money market instruments. There are several important aspects of mutual funds. First, investors in mutual funds own a pro rata share of the overall portfolio. Second, the investment manager of the mutual fund actively manages the portfolio, that is, buys some securities and sells others (this characteristic is unlike unit investment trusts, discussed below). Third, the value or price of each share of the portfolio, called the **net asset value (NAV)**, equals the market value of the portfolio minus the liabilities of the mutual fund divided by the number of shares owned by the mutual fund investors. That is,

$$NAV = \frac{Market\ value\ of\ portfolio - Liabilities}{Number\ of\ shares\ outstanding}$$

For example, suppose that a mutual fund with 10 million shares outstanding has a portfolio with a market value of $215 million and liabilities of $15 million. The NAV is

$$NAV = \frac{\$215,000,000 - \$15,000,000}{10,000,000} = \$20$$

Fourth, the NAV or price of the fund is determined only once each day, at the close of the day. For example, the NAV for a stock mutual fund is determined from the closing stock prices for the day. Business publications provide the NAV each day in their mutual fund tables. The published NAVs are the closing NAVs. Fifth, and very importantly, all new investments into the fund or withdrawals from the fund during a day are priced at the closing NAV (investments after the end of the day or on a nonbusiness day are priced at the next day's closing NAV).

The total number of shares in the fund increases if there are more investments than withdrawals during the day, and vice versa. For example, assume that at the beginning of a day a mutual fund portfolio has a value of $1 million, with no liabilities, and there are 10,000 shares outstanding. Thus, the NAV of the fund is $100. Assume that during the day $5,000 is deposited into the fund, $1,000 is withdrawn, and the prices of all the securities in the portfolio remain constant. This means that 50 shares were issued for the $5,000 deposited (since each share is valued at $100) and 10 shares redeemed for $1,000 (again, since each share is $100). The net number of new shares issued is then 40. Therefore, at the end of the day, there will be 10,040 shares and the total value of the fund will be $1,004,000. The NAV will remain at $100.

If, instead, the prices of the securities in the portfolio change; both the total size of the portfolio and, therefore, the NAV will change. In the previous example, assume that during the day the value of the portfolio doubles to $2 million. Since deposits and withdrawals are priced at the end-of-day NAV, which is now $200 after the doubling of the portfolio's value, the $5,000 deposit will be credited with 25 shares ($5,000/$200) and the $1,000 withdrawn will reduce the number of shares by five shares ($1,000/$200). Thus, at the end of the day there will be 10,020 shares (25 − 5 new shares) in the fund with a NAV of $200, and the value of the fund will be $2,004,000. (Note that 10,020 shares × $200 NAV equals $2,004,000, the portfolio value.)

Overall, the NAV of a mutual fund will increase or decrease due to an increase or decrease in the prices of the securities in the portfolio. The number of shares in the fund will increase or decrease due to the net deposits into or withdrawals from the fund. And the total value of the fund will increase or decrease for both reasons.

To summarize, there are three important characteristics of open-end or mutual funds. First, the number of shares of these funds increases or decreases as investors increase their investment or liquidate shares. Second, the fund company facilitates these increases or decreases by selling new shares to or buying existing shares from the investor. Third, these new investments or liquidations occur via the fund company (not an external market) at a price equal to NAV.

Closed-End Funds

The shares of a **closed-end fund** are very similar to the shares of common stock of a corporation. The new shares of a closed-end fund are initially issued by an underwriter for the fund. And after the new issue, the number of shares remains constant. After the initial issue, there are no sales or purchases of fund shares by the fund company as there are for open-end funds. The shares are traded on a secondary market, either on an exchange or in the over-the-counter market.

Investors can buy shares after the initial issue (as discussed below) only in the secondary market. Shares are sold after the initial issue only on the secondary market. The price of the shares of a closed-end fund are determined by the supply and demand in the secondary market in which these funds are traded. The secondary market is one of the stock markets. Thus, investors who transact closed-end fund shares must pay a brokerage commission at the time of purchase and at the time of sale.

The NAV of closed-end funds is calculated in the same way as for open-end funds. However, the price of a share in a closed-end fund is determined by supply and demand, so the price can fall below or rise above the net asset value per share. Shares selling below NAV are said to be "trading at a discount," while shares trading above NAV are "trading at a premium." Newspapers list quotations of the prices of these shares under the heading "Closed-End Funds."

Consequently, there are two important differences between open-end funds and closed-end funds. First, the number of shares of an open-end fund varies because the fund sponsor will sell new shares to investors and buy existing shares from shareholders. Second, by doing so, the share price is always equal to the NAV of the fund. In contrast, closed-end funds have a constant number of shares outstanding because the fund sponsor does not redeem shares and sell new shares to investors (except at the time of a new underwriting). Thus, the price of the fund shares will be determined by supply and demand in the market and may be above or below NAV, as previously discussed.

Although the divergence of the price from NAV is often puzzling, in some cases the reasons for the premium or discount are easily understood. For example, a share's price may be below the NAV because the fund has large built-in tax liabilities, and investors are discounting the share's price for that future tax liability.[1] (We will discuss this tax liability issue later in this chapter.) A fund's leverage and resulting risk may be another reason for the share's price trading below NAV. A fund's shares may trade at a premium to the NAV because the fund offers relatively cheap access to, and professional management of, stocks in another country about which information is not readily available to small investors.

There are, however, "lifeboat provisions" in fund charters that require them to take action to reduce the discount on the share by buying back shares via a tender offer for the funds' stock, or doing an outright conversion to an open-end structure. If the fund manager does not believe it is in the best interest of the shareholders (or the fund management) to convert or tender an offer for shares, dissident shareholder groups can buy large blocks of stocks and initiate a proxy fight in order to liquidate the assets or "open-end the fund," in an attempt to increase the value of the fund to its NAV.

Under the **Investment Company Act of 1940**, closed-end funds are capitalized only once. They make an initial public offering (IPO), and then their shares are traded on the secondary market, just like any corporate stock, as discussed above. The number of shares is fixed at the IPO; closed-end funds cannot issue more shares. In fact, many closed-end funds become leveraged to raise more funds without issuing more shares.

An important feature of closed-end funds is that the initial investors bear the substantial cost of underwriting the issuance of the funds' shares. The proceeds that the managers of the fund have to invest equals the total paid by initial buyers of the shares minus all costs of issuance. These costs, which average around 7.5% of the total amount paid for the issue, normally include selling fees or commissions paid to the retail brokerage firms that distribute them to the public. The high commissions are strong incentives for retail brokers to recommend these shares to their retail customers, and also for investors to avoid buying these shares on their initial offering.[2]

The relatively new **exchange-traded funds (ETFs)**, which are discussed later in this chapter, pose a threat to both mutual funds and closed-end funds. ETFs are essentially hybrid closed-end vehicles, which trade on exchanges but which typically trade very close to NAV.

Since closed-end funds are traded like stocks, the cost to any investor of buying or selling a closed-end fund is the same as that of a stock. The obvious charge is the stockbroker's commission. The bid/offer spread of the market on which the stock is traded is also a cost.

Unit Trusts

A **unit trust** is similar to a closed-end fund in that the number of unit certificates is fixed. Unit trusts typically invest in bonds. They differ in several ways from both mutual funds and closed-end funds that specialize in bonds. First, there is no active trading of the bonds in the portfolio of the unit trust. Once the unit trust is assembled by the sponsor (usually a brokerage firm or bond underwriter) and turned over to a trustee, the trustee holds all the bonds until they are redeemed by the issuer. Typically, the only time the trustee can sell an issue in the portfolio is if there is a dramatic decline in the issuer's credit quality. As a result, the cost of operating the trust will be considerably less than costs incurred by either a mutual fund or

[1] Harold Bierman, Jr., and Bhaskaran Swaminathan, "Managing a Closed-End Investment Fund," *Journal of Portfolio Management* (Summer 2000), p. 49.
[2] Kathleen Weiss, "The Post-Offering Price Performance of Closed-End Funds," *Financial Management* (Autumn 1989), pp. 57–67.

a closed-end fund. Second, unit trusts have a fixed termination date, while mutual funds and closed-end funds do not.[3] Third, unlike the mutual fund and closed-end fund investor, the unit trust investor knows that the portfolio consists of a specific portfolio of bonds and has no concern that the trustee will alter the portfolio. While unit trusts are common in Europe, they are not common in the United States.

All unit trusts charge a sales commission. The initial sales charge for a unit trust ranges from 3.5% to 5.5%. In addition to these costs, there is the cost incurred by the sponsor to purchase the bonds for the trust that an investor indirectly pays. That is, when the brokerage firm or bond-underwriting firm assembles the unit trust, the price of each bond to the trust also includes the dealer's spread. There is also often a commission if the units are sold.

In the remainder of this chapter, our primary focus is on open-end (mutual) funds.

Key Points That You Should Understand Before Proceeding

1. The difference between an open-end fund (mutual fund) and a closed-end fund.
2. The meaning of NAV per share.
3. The difference between a closed-end fund and a unit trust.
4. The price of a share of a closed-end fund can trade at a discount or premium to its NAV.

FUND SALES CHARGES AND ANNUAL OPERATING EXPENSES

There are two types of costs borne by investors in mutual funds. The first is the *shareholder fee*, usually called the *sales charge*. This cost is a "one-time" charge debited to the investor for a specific transaction, such as a purchase, redemption, or exchange. The type of charge is related to the way the fund is sold or distributed. The second cost is the annual fund operating expense, usually called the *expense ratio*, which covers the fund's expenses, the largest of which is for investment management. This charge is imposed annually. This cost occurs on all funds and for all types of distribution. We discuss each cost in the following text.

Sales Charge

Sales charges on mutual funds are related to their method of distribution. The current menu of sales charges and distribution mechanisms has evolved significantly and is now much more diverse than it was a decade ago. To understand the current diversity and the evolution of distribution mechanisms, consider initially the circumstances of two decades ago. At that time, there were two basic methods of distribution, two types of sales charges, and the type of the distribution was directly related to the type of sales charge.

The two types of distribution were sales force (or wholesale) and direct. *Sales-force (wholesale) distribution* occurred via an intermediary, that is, via an agent, a stockbroker, insurance agent, or other entity, who provided investment advice and incentive to the client, actively "made the sale," and provided subsequent service. This distribution approach is active; that is, the fund is typically sold by the agent, not bought by the client.

The other approach is *direct* (from the fund company to the investor), whereby, there is no intermediary or salesperson to actively approach the client, provide investment advice

---

[3] There are, however, exceptions. Target term closed-end funds have a fixed termination date.

and service, or make the sale. Rather, the client approaches the mutual fund company, most likely by a "1-800" telephone contact, in response to media advertisements or general information, and opens the account. Little or no investment counsel or service is provided either initially or subsequently. With respect to the mutual fund sale, this is a *passive approach*, although these mutual funds may be quite active in their advertising and other marketing activities. Funds provided by the direct approach are bought by the client, not sold by an agent or the fund company.

There is a *quid pro quo*, however, for the service provided in the sales-force distribution method. The *quid pro quo* is a sales charge borne by the customer and paid to the agent. The sales charge for the agent-distributed fund is called a **load**. The traditional type of load is called a *front-end load*, since the load is deducted initially or "up front." That is, the load is deducted from the amount invested by the client and paid to the agent/distributor. The remainder is the net amount invested in the fund in the client's name. For example, if the load on the mutual fund is 5% and the investor invests $100, the $5 load is paid to the agent and the remaining $95 is the net amount invested in the mutual fund at NAV. Importantly, only $95, not $100, is invested in the fund. The fund is, thus, said to be "purchased above NAV" (i.e., the investor pays $100 for $95 of the fund). The $5 load compensates the sales agent for the investment advice and service provided to the client by the agent. The load to the client, of course, represents income to the agent.

Let's contrast this with directly placed mutual funds. In a directly placed fund, there is no sales agent and, therefore, there is no need for a sales charge. Funds with no sales charges are called **no-load mutual funds**. In this case, if the client provides $100 to the mutual fund, $100 is invested in the fund in the client's name. This approach to buying the fund is called buying the fund "at NAV"; that is, the whole amount provided by the investor is invested in the fund.

A decade ago, many observers speculated that **load funds** would become obsolete and no-load funds would dominate because of the investor's aversion to a sales charge. Increasingly financially sophisticated individuals, the reasoning went, would make their own investment decisions and not need to compensate agents for their advice and service. But, as discussed below, the actual trend has been quite different. Why has there not been a trend away from the more costly agent-distributed funds as many expected? There are two reasons. First, many investors have remained dependent on the investment counsel and service, and, perhaps more importantly, the initiative of the sales agent. Second, sales-force distributed funds have shown considerable ingenuity and flexibility in imposing sales charges, which both compensate the distributors and appear attractive to the clients. Among the recent adaptations of the sales load are **back-end loads** and **level loads**. While the front-end load is imposed at the time of the purchase of the fund, the back-end load is imposed at the time fund shares are sold or redeemed. Level loads are imposed uniformly each year. These two alternative methods provide ways to compensate the selling agent. However, unlike with the front-end load, both of these distribution mechanisms permit clients to buy a fund at NAV, that is, not have any of their initial investment debited as a sales charge before it is invested in their account.

The back-end load currently is a **contingent deferred sales charge (CDSC)**. This approach imposes a gradually declining load on withdrawal. For example, a common "3,3,2,2,1,1,0" CDSC approach imposes a 3% load on the amount withdrawn during the first year, 3% during the second year, 2% during the third year, and so forth. The sales charge is "deferred" because it is imposed at withdrawal and "contingent" because its level depends on how long it was held. There is no sales charge for withdrawals after the seventh year.

The third type of load is neither a front-end load at the time of investment nor a (gradually declining) back-end load at the time of withdrawal, but a constant load each year (e.g., a 1% load every year). This approach is called a level load. This type of load appeals to the types of financial planners who charge annual fees (called *fee-based* financial planners) rather than commissions, such as sales charges (called *commission-based* financial planners).

Many mutual fund families often offer their funds with all three types of loads (called "classes")—that is, front-end loads (usually called "A shares"); back-end loads (often called "B shares"); and level loads (often called "C shares")—and permit the distributor and its client to select the type of load they prefer.[4] Several other classes of load funds have also been developed. For example, the F class (also called by other letters) is available only to fee-based distributors who have a special agreement with the fund. F shares have no loads and lower expense ratios than A, B, and C shares.

As required by the National Association of Securities Dealers (NASD), the maximum allowable sales charge is 8.5%, although most funds impose lower charges. The sales charge for a fund applies to most, even very small, investments (although there is typically a minimum initial investment). For large investments, however, the sales charge may be reduced. For example, a fund with a 4.5% front-end load may reduce this load to 3.0% for investments over $250,000 and to 0% for investments of more than $1 million. There may be in addition further reductions in the sales charge at greater investments. The amount of investment needed to obtain a reduction in the sales charge is called a **breakpoint**; the breakpoints are $250,000 and $1 million in this example. There are also mechanisms whereby the total amount of the investment necessary to qualify for the breakpoint does not need to be invested up front, but only over time (according to a "letter of intent" signed by the investor).[5] Load funds that are placed in retirement accounts, such as 401(k)s or IRAs, typically waive the loads.

The sales charge paid by the client typically goes primarily to the individual distributor, with a small part going to the fund. How does the fund family, typically called the *sponsor* or manufacturer of the fund, cover its costs and make a profit? That is the topic of the second type of "cost" to the investor, the fund annual operating expense.

Annual Operating Expenses (Expense Ratio)

The *operating expense*, also called the *expense ratio*, is debited annually from the investor's fund balance by the fund sponsor. Operating expenses are deducted from NAV and therefore reduce the reported return. The three main categories of annual operating expenses are the management fee, distribution fee, and other expenses.

The *management fee*, also called the **investment advisory fee**, is the fee charged by the **investment advisor** for managing a fund's portfolio. If the investment advisor is a company separate from the fund sponsor, some or all of this investment advisory fee is passed onto the investment advisor by the fund sponsor. In this case, the fund manager is called a

---

[4] Edward S. O'Neal, "Mutual Fund Share Classes and Broker Incentives," *Financial Analysts Journal* (September/October 1999), pp. 76–87.

[5] Daniel C. Inro, Christine X. Jaing, Michael Y. Ho, Wayne Y. Lee, "Mutual Fund Performance: Does Fund Size Matter?" *Financial Analysts Journal* (May/June 1999), pp. 74–87.

subadvisor. The management fee varies by the type of fund, specifically by the difficulty of managing the fund. For example, the management fee may increase from money market funds to bond funds, to U.S. growth stock funds, to emerging market stock funds, as illustrated by examples below.

In 1980, the SEC approved the imposition of a fixed annual fee, called the **12b-1 fee**, which is, in general, intended to cover *distribution costs*, including continuing agent compensation and manufacturer marketing and advertising expenses. Such 12b-1 fees are now imposed by many mutual funds. By law, 12b-1 fees cannot exceed 1% of the fund's assets per year. The 12b-1 fee may include a service fee of up to 0.25% of assets per year to compensate sales professionals for providing services or maintaining shareholder accounts. The remaining 0.75% is used by the fund company for marketing. To be called a no-load fund, no 12b-1 fee can be imposed. The 12b-1 fees, as well as the operating expenses, are deducted from the NAV and, thus, reduce the reported return. Sales charges are not deducted from the NAV and do not reduce the reported return. The major rationale for the component of the 12b-1 fee, which accrues to the selling agent, is to provide an incentive to selling agents to continue to service their accounts after having received a transaction-based fee such as a front-end load. As a result, a 12b-1 fee of this type is consistent with sales-force-sold load funds, not with directly sold, no-load funds. The rationale for the component of the 12b-1 fee, which accrues to the manufacturer of the fund, is to provide incentive and compensate for continuing advertising and marketing costs.

Other expenses include primarily the costs of (1) custody (holding the cash and securities of the fund), (2) the transfer agent (transferring cash and securities among buyers and sellers of securities and the fund distributions, etc.), (3) independent public accountant fees, and (4) directors' fees. The sum of the annual management fee, the annual distribution fee, and other annual expenses is called the *expense ratio*. All the cost information on a fund, including selling charges and annual expenses, is included in the fund prospectus.

Table 1 shows the expense ratios from the current prospectuses of the three largest mutual funds: the Fidelity ContraFund Fund, the Vanguard S&P 500 Index Fund, and the American Growth Fund of America Fund. The first two are direct funds and the third is a sales-force fund. The Fidelity ContraFund and Vanguard S&P 500 Index funds are directly sold and, thus, have no 12b-1 distribution expenses. The American Growth Fund of America, on the other hand, is sales-force sold and has a distribution or 12b-1 fee. With respect to the management fee, index funds are easier to manage and, thus, the Vanguard S&P 500 Index fund has the lowest management fee.

Table 1   Annual Operating Expenses for Three Large Mutual Funds

Type of Expense	Fidelity ContraFund	Vanguard S&P 500 Index	American Growth Fund of America—A Shares
Management fee	0.71%	0.15%	0.27%
Distribution and/or service (12b-1) fees	0	0	0.25
Other expenses	0.18	0.03	0.12
Total	0.89%	0.18%	0.64%

Table 2 Shareholders Fees for Three Large Mutual Funds—A Shares

Type of Fee	Fidelity ContraFund	Vanguard S&P 500 Index	American Growth Fund of America—A Shares
Sales charge on purchases	0%	0%	5.75%
Sales charge on reinvested dividend	0	0	0
Redemption fee	0	0	0
Exchange fee	0	0	0

In addition to the annual operating expenses, the fund prospectus provides the fees, which are imposed only at the time of a transaction. (These shares are called A shares.) These fees are listed in Table 2 for the three large funds in Table 1. The Fidelity fund and the Vanguard fund are directly distributed and are pure no-load funds. The American fund is sales-force distributed and is a front-end load (A share) fund.

As we explained earlier, many agent-distributed funds are provided in different forms, typically the following: (1) A shares: front-end load, (2) B shares: back-end load (contingent deferred sales charge), and (3) C shares: level load. These different forms of the same fund are called *share classes*. Class B shares convert to A shares, which have lower annual expenses after the B shares back-end load period ends (typically five to seven years); C shares do not convert.

During 2006, $227 billion of new cash flowed into mutual funds with $166 billion flowing into no-load funds and $37 billion into load funds (the other $24 billion went into variable annuities). Of the amount that flowed into load funds, $51 billion flowed into front-end loads, $22 billion into level loads, and $12 billion into other loads (loads other than front, B level, and back), and there was an outflow of $49 billion from back-end loads, the fifth consecutive year of outflows from back-end load funds.

Table 3 provides an example of hypothetical sales charges and annual expenses of funds of different classes for an agent-distributed stock mutual fund. The sales charge

Table 3 Hypothetical Sales Charges and Annual Expenses of Funds of Different Classes for an Agent-Distributed Stock Mutual Fund

	Sales Charge			Annual Operating Expenses			
	Front	Back	Level	Management Fee	Distribution (12B-1 Fee)	Other Expenses	Expense Ratio
A	4.5%	0	0%	0.90%	0.25%	0.15%	1.30%
B	0	*	0	0.90	1.00	0.15	2.05
C	0	0	1	0.90	1.00	0.15	2.05

* 3%, 3%, 2%, 2%, 1%, 0%.

accrues to the distributor. The management fee accrues to the mutual fund manager. Other expenses, including custody and transfer fees and the fees of managing the fund company, accrue to the fund sponsor to cover expenses.

The A class of this fund has a 4.5% front-end load and an expense ratio of 1.30%. The B class has a back-end CDSC load that becomes 0% after five years and an expense ratio of 2.05%. The C class has a level load of 1% and an expense ratio of 2.05%.

For load funds with the various share classes, some periodicals provide the investment results for all the share classes and others provide the results only for the A class. In the latter case, the name of the fund is followed by an "A"; for example, "Amer Funds Growth Fund A" refers to the class A shares for the American Funds Growth Fund of America fund.

Which of these three classes of funds has the lowest total cost, sales charge plus expense ratio? The answer depends on the investor's planned holding period. For very short holding periods, such as one to two years, C class shares have the lowest total cost since they avoid the higher front-end and back-end loads of the A and B shares, respectively. For very long holding periods, such as 20 years, the A shares have the lowest total cost because the low expense ratio more than offsets the front load eventually. For intermediate time periods, such as six to 10 years, the B shares are the best because they pay no front-end load or back-end load. Exact calculations are necessary to determine which is the best share class over a given holding period. The SEC provides a mutual fund cost calculator, which permits such calculations.[6]

Multiple Share Classes

Share classes were first offered in 1989 following the SEC's approval of multiple share classes. During the 1990s, the number of share classes expanded even more quickly than the number of funds. Initially share classes were used primarily by sales-force funds to offer alternatives to the front-end load as a means of compensating brokers. Later, some of these funds used additional share classes as a means of offering the same fund or portfolio through alternative distribution channels in which some fund expenses varied by channel. Offering new share classes was more efficient and less costly than setting up two separate funds.[7] By the end of the 1990s, the average long-term sales-force fund offered nearly three share classes. Directly sold no-load mutual funds offer only one share class.

Key Points That You Should Understand Before Proceeding

1. The difference between a load and a no-load mutual fund.
2. The difference between a front-end load, a back-end load, and a level load fund.
3. The difference between a sales charge and an expense ratio.
4. The SEC Rule 12b-1 and the type of fund called a 12b-1 fund.
5. The components of the expense ratio.
6. The nature of a management fee.
7. The meaning of trading at NAV.
8. The definition of breakpoints.

---

[6] www.sec.gov/investor/tools/mfcc/rate-of-return.html.

[7] Brian Reid, *The 1990s: A Decade of Expansion and Changes in the U.S. Mutual Fund Industry*, Investment Company Institute, 6, no. 3 (July 2000), p. 15.

ECONOMIC MOTIVATION FOR FUNDS

Financial intermediaries obtain funds by issuing financial claims against themselves and then investing these funds. An investment company is a financial intermediary in that it pools the funds of individual investors and uses these funds to buy portfolios of securities. Recall the special role in financial markets played by financial intermediaries. Financial intermediaries provide some or all of the following six economic functions: (1) risk reduction via diversification, (2) lower costs of contracting and processing information, (3) professional portfolio management, (4) liquidity, (5) variety, and (6) a payments mechanism. Consider these economic functions as provided by mutual funds.

Consider first the function of risk reduction through diversification. By investing in a fund, an investor can obtain broad-based ownership of a sufficient number of securities to reduce portfolio risk. Although an individual investor may be able to acquire a broad-based portfolio of securities, the degree of diversification will be limited by the amount available to invest. By investing in an investment company, however, the investor can effectively achieve the benefits of diversification at a lower cost even if the amount of money available to invest is not large.

The second economic function is the reduced cost of contracting and processing information because an investor purchases the services of a presumably skilled financial advisor at less cost than if the investor directly and individually negotiated with such an advisor. The advisory fee is lower because of the larger size of assets managed, as well as the reduced costs of searching for an investment manager and obtaining information about the securities. Also, the costs of transacting in the securities are reduced because a fund is better able to negotiate transaction costs, and custodial fees and recordkeeping costs are less for a fund than for an individual investor. For these reasons, there are said to be economies of scale in investment management.

Third, and related to the first two advantages, is the advantage of the professional management of the mutual fund. Fourth is the advantage of liquidity. Mutual funds can be bought or liquidated any day at the closing NAV. Fifth is the advantage of the variety of funds available, in general, and even in one particular funds family, as discussed below. Finally, money market funds and some other types of funds provide payment services by allowing investors to write checks drawn on the fund, although this facility may be limited in various ways.

Key Points That You Should Understand Before Proceeding

1. A mutual fund can reduce risk through portfolio diversification.
2. A mutual fund can reduce a variety of costs related to investment and management of portfolios.
3. A mutual fund can provide liquidity.

TYPES OF FUNDS BY INVESTMENT OBJECTIVE

Mutual funds have been provided to satisfy the various **investment objectives** of investors. In general, there are stock funds, bond funds, money market funds, and others. Within each of these categories, there are several subcategories of funds. There are also U.S.–only funds, international funds (no U.S. securities), and global funds (both U.S. and international securities). There are also passive and active funds. Passive (or indexed) funds are designed to replicate an index, such as the S&P 500 Stock Index, the Lehman Aggregate Bond Index, or the Morgan Stanley Capital International EAFE Index (Europe, Australasia, and the Far East). Active funds, on the other hand, attempt to outperform an index and other funds by actively trading the fund portfolio. There are also many other categories of funds, as discussed below. Each fund's objective is stated in its prospectus, as required by the SEC and the "1940 Act," as discussed in the following text.

Stock funds differ by

- the average market capitalization ("market cap"—large, mid, and small) of the stocks in the portfolio
- style (growth, value, and blend)
- sector—"sector funds" specialize in one particular sector or industry, such as technology, health care, or utilities
- other ways

The categories for market cap, while not fixed over time, have recently been approximately:

- small—$0 to $2 billion
- mid—$2 billion to $10 billion
- large—more than $10 billion

With respect to style, stocks with high price-to-book and price-to-earnings ratios are considered "growth stocks," and stocks with low price-to-value and price-to-earnings ratios are considered value stocks, although other variables, such as the dividend yield, are also considered. There are also *blend stocks* with respect to style, that is, stocks midway between growth and value.

Bond funds differ by the creditworthiness of the issuers of the bonds in the portfolio (for example, U.S. government, investment-grade corporate, and high-yield corporate) and by the maturity (or duration) of the bonds (long, intermediate, and short). There is also a category of bond funds called municipal bond funds whose coupon interest is tax exempt. Municipal funds may also be single state (that is, all the bonds in the portfolio were issued by issuers in the same state) or multistate.

There are also other categories of funds such as asset allocation, hybrid, balanced, or target date funds (all of which hold both stocks and bonds), Balanced funds maintain a fixed proportion of stocks and bonds. For example, a "moderate" balanced fund may maintain a 60%/40% stock/bond mix and a "conservative" balanced fund maintain a 40%/60% stock/bond mix.

Another subcategory of the stock/bond hybrid category is the **target-date funds** (also **life-cycle funds**). Target-date funds are mutual funds that base their asset allocations on a specific date, the assumed retirement date for the investor, and then rebalance to a more conservative allocation as that date approaches. Target-date funds are designed to be "one-size-fits-all" portfolios for investors with a given number of years to retirement. Some investors choose not to manage their own retirement accounts and prefer a "set-it-and-forget-it" approach. The portfolio allocation varies by the number of years to retirement but not for other reasons specific to the investor. For example, in 2010, target-date funds with the following target dates might have the following stock/bond allocations.

Target Date	Stock/Bond Mix
2010	10%/90%
2020	40%/60%
2030	60%/40%
2040	90%/10%

Target-date funds are relatively recent additions to mutual funds and have grown rapidly. One reason for the growth is that target-date funds have been specified as one of the default options for the Pension Protection Act of 2006, according to which employers can direct their employee's funds if they do not make an allocation choice themselves.

The first generation of target-date funds had fairly simple asset allocations. For example, in 2010, a 30-year-old investor who planned to retire at 65 would invest in a 2045 target-date fund. A specific target-date fund might specify a 70%/30% U.S. stocks/bonds allocation. Such an allocation prompts two types of questions. First is whether 70%/30% is the optimal mix. Some observers assert that 70%/30% is too cautious for a 30-year-old—an 80%/20% might be more appropriate. Others would assert that this mix is too aggressive and a 60%/40% would be more appropriate. For example, in January 2008, the 2030 target-date funds from Fidelity, Vanguard, and T. Rowe Price were 81%, 86%, and 85%, respectively.[8] This issue could never be resolved in a "one-size-fits-all" product. To better address this issue, the risk tolerance on an individual investor basis must be considered.

There is also a category of money market mutual funds (maturities of one year or less) which provide protection against interest rate fluctuations. These funds can have some degree of credit risk (except for the U.S. government money market category). Many of these funds offer check-writing privileges. In addition to taxable money market funds, there are also tax-exempt, municipal money market funds.

Among the other fund offerings are *index funds*. Index funds, as discussed above, attempt to passively replicate an index. The number and type of index funds, and the amounts invested in them, have grown dramatically. ETFs, discussed later in this chapter, have provided significant competition to mutual fund index funds.

Several organizations provide data on mutual funds. These firms provide data on fund expenses, portfolio managers, fund sizes, and fund holdings. But perhaps most importantly, they provide performance (that is, rate of return) data and rankings among funds based on performances and other factors. To compare fund performance on an "apples-to-apples" basis, these firms divide mutual funds into several categories that are intended to be fairly homogeneous by investment objective. The Morningstar categories are shown in Table 4. By using these categories, for example, the performance of one Morningstar "large cap blend" fund can be meaningfully compared with another fund in the same category but not with a "small cap value" fund. Morningstar's ranking system, whereby each fund is rated from one star (the worst) to five stars (the best) relative to the other funds in its category, is well known.

Mutual fund data are also provided by the Investment Company Institute, the national association for mutual funds. Table 5 provides data on the assets of the major fund categories as reported by the Investment Company Institute.

---

[8] Jenna Gottlieb, "Benchmarks Sought for Target-Date Funds," *Financial Week*, January 28, 2008, p. 4.

Table 4   Morningstar Fund Categories

Morningstar	Morningstar
LG Large Growth	CS Short Term Bond
LV Large Value	GS Short Government
LB Large Blend	GI Interm Government
MG Mid Cap Growth	CI Inter-Term Bond MT
MV Mid Cap Value	CL Long Term Bond
MB Mid Cap Blend	GL Long Government
SG Small Growth	CV Convertibles
SV Small Value	UB Ultrashort Bond
SB Small Blend	HY High Yield Bond
DH Domestic Hybrid	
	MO Multisector Bond
FS Foreign Stock	IB International Bond
WS World Stock	EB Emerging Bond
ES Europe Stock	
EM Diversified Emerging Mkt	ML Muni National Long
DP Diversified Pacific Asia	MI Muni National Interm
PJ Pacific Asia ex-Japan	SL Muni Single St. Long
JS Japan Stock	SI Muni Single St. Interm
LS Latin America Stock	SS Muni Single St. Short
IH International Hybrid	MY Muni New York Long
	MC Muni California Long
ST Technology	MN Muni New York Interm/Short
SU Utilities	MF Muni California Interm/Short
SH Health	
SC Communication	
SF Financial	
SN Natural Resources	
SP Precious Metals	
SR Real Estate	

Key Points You Should Understand Before Proceeding

1. In order to meet investor needs, mutual funds offered in the market differ by a variety of measures such as asset category (stock vs. bond, etc.); management style (active vs. passive); market segment (small cap vs. large cap in stock funds, investment grade versus speculative grade in bond funds); and other such measures.
2. Organizations such as Morningstar and Lipper provide key performance data on mutual funds in ways that facilitate meaningful comparisons among them.

Table 5   Major Fund Assets by Major Fund Categories (as of January 2008)

	Net Assets ($ billion)	% of Total Assets	Number of Mutual Funds
Stock Funds	6,037.10	51.5	4,799
Hybrid Funds	690.80	5.9	489
Taxable Bond Funds	1,337.60	11.4	1,299
Municipal Bond Funds	379.60	3.2	672
Taxable Money Market Funds	2,804.40	23.9	556
Tax-Free Money Market Funds	478.50	4.1	260
Total	11,728	100	8,075

Source: *ICI Statistics & Research, Investment Company of America, February 2008 (www.ici.org).*

THE CONCEPT OF A FAMILY OF FUNDS

A concept that revolutionized the fund industry and benefitted many investors is what the mutual fund industry calls a *family of funds*, a group of funds or a complex of funds provided by the same fund company. That is, many fund management companies offer investors a choice of numerous funds with different investment objectives in the same fund family. In many cases, investors may move their assets from one fund to another within the family at little or no cost, and with only a phone call. Of course, if these funds are in a taxable account, there may be tax consequences to the sale. Although the same policies regarding loads and other costs may apply to all the members of the family, a management company may have different fee structures for transfers among different funds under its control.

Large fund families usually include money market funds, U.S. bond funds of several types, global stock and bond funds, broadly diversified U.S. stock funds, U.S. stock funds that specialize by market capitalization and style, and stock funds devoted to particular sectors such as health care, technology, or gold companies. Well-known management companies such as American Funds, Vanguard Group, and Fidelity Investments, the three largest fund families, sponsor and manage varied types of funds in a family. Fund data provided in newspapers group the various funds according to their families. For example, all the American Funds are listed under the American Funds heading, all the Vanguard funds are listed under their name, and so on.

Key Points That You Should Understand Before Proceeding

1. The meaning of the term *family of funds.*
2. The economic benefits that a family of funds can offer to investors.

Concentration in the mutual fund industry continues to increase. The three largest fund families are the American Funds with over $1.5 trillion in funds, followed by Vanguard and then Fidelity, both with over $1 trillion. At the end of September 2007, these three families held approximately 38% of all the U.S. mutual fund assets. And most of the new fund flows continue to go to these three. Interestingly, American Funds is a load family (with 5.75% load on its A shares), which offers only active funds; and Vanguard and Fidelity are no-load families, which offer a mix of passive and active funds. These funds seem to be growing quickly because of their strong brands and because there is believed to be economics of scale due to research costs and advertising. It becomes difficult for small and mid-sized firms to increase their expense ratios because investors and some of the mutual fund analysts like Morningstar are very expense-sensitive. Mergers and acquisitions continue to reduce the number of small and mid-sized firms. At the other end of the size spectrum, there are a number of small, niche firms that focus on one unique investing style.

INVESTMENT VEHICLES FOR MUTUAL FUNDS

Mutual funds may be included in several different investment vehicles. For example, the Vanguard S&P500 Index Fund, the Fidelity Contra Fund or the American Funds Growth Fund of America can be sold as a standard taxable investment instrument (as a no-load fund or a class A, B, C, F, or other load fund, whichever it is). This vehicle is often referred to as a *nonqualified vehicle* because it does not quality for tax advantages.

The same fund can also be included in a retirement plan such as a 401(k), Roth 401(k), IRA, or Roth IRA plan. These retirement plans are called *qualified plans* because they qualify for tax advantages. The same fund can also be included in a 529 educational plan or a variable annuity.

Each placement of these funds requires a separate portfolio on the fund family's books, but the portfolios are "look-alikes" and should have approximately the same returns.

MUTUAL FUND COSTS

Investors are very cost-sensitive. The competition among funds is very tough and costs are an important element of the competition. The Investment Company Institute (ICI) has developed a measure that combines a fund's annual expense ratio and the annualized sales charge investors pay for one-time sales loads (front and back). This measure is weighted by the assets in the funds. From 1980 to 2006, this measure declined from 2.32% to 1.07% for stock funds and from 2.05% to 0.84% for bond funds. There were three reasons for this decline. First, loads in general declined and investors have shifted, in general, to lower load funds. In addition, the use of funds in retirement plans has grown significantly and loads are usually waived on these funds. Second, the growth in no-load mutual funds, both the traditional direct sales and sales through fund supermarkets and discount brokers, also contributed to this decline. Finally, mutual fund expenses have also declined due to economies of scale and intense competition in the mutual fund industry.

The ICI provides data that permit investors to assess annual expenses independently of the sales charge or load. First, they calculate the simple average of annual expense ratios available in the market. They then calculate the average expense ratio mutual fund shareholders actually paid; this is the asset-weighted average expense ratio across all the funds. For 2006, the simple average expense ratio was 1.51% and the average expense ratio actually paid by shareholders was 0.87%. Thus, mutual fund shareholders actually paid expense ratios in the lower part of the range of the funds available in the market.

TAXATION OF MUTUAL FUNDS

Mutual funds must distribute at least 90% of their net investment income earned (bond coupons and stock dividends) exclusive of realized capital gains or losses to shareholders (along with meeting other criteria) to be considered a *regulated investment company* (RIC). If so, the fund is not required to pay taxes at the fund level prior to distributions of the returns to shareholders. Consequently, in practice funds always make these 90% distributions. Taxes are then paid on distributions only at the investor level, not the fund level. Even though many mutual fund investors choose to reinvest these distributions, the distributions are taxable to the investor, either as ordinary income or capital gains (long term or short term), whichever is relevant.

Capital gains distributions must occur annually, and typically occur late during the calendar year. The capital gains distributions may be either long-term or short-term capital gains, depending on whether the fund held the security for a year or more. Mutual fund investors have no control over the size of these distributions and, as a result, the timing and amount of the taxes paid on their fund holdings is largely out of their control. In particular, withdrawals by some investors may necessitate sales in the fund, which, in turn, cause realized capital gains and a tax liability to accrue to investors who maintain their holding.

New investors in the fund may assume a tax liability even though they have no gains. That is, all shareholders as of the date of record of the distribution receive a full year's worth of dividends and capital gains distributions, even if they have owned shares for only one day. This lack of control over capital gains taxes is regarded as a major limitation of mutual funds. In fact, this adverse tax consequence is one of the reasons suggested for a closed-end company's price selling below par value. Also, this adverse tax consequence is one of the reasons for the popularity of exchange-traded funds, to be discussed later.

Of course, the investor must also pay ordinary income taxes on distributions of income (e.g., bond interest payments). Finally, when the fund investors sell the fund, they will have long-term or short-term capital gains or losses, depending on whether they held the fund for a year or not.

Key Points You Should Understand Before Proceeding

1. Mutual funds must distribute at least 90% of their investment income in order to avoid taxation at the fund level.
2. Fund investors have no control over the size or timing of capital gains distributions, and consequently the associated tax liabilities.

REGULATION OF FUNDS

There are four major laws or acts that relate either indirectly or directly to mutual funds. The first is the Securities Act of 1933 ("the '33 Act"), which provides purchasers of new issues of securities with information regarding the issuer and, thus, helps prevent fraud. Because open-end investment companies issue new shares on a continuous basis, mutual funds must also comply with the '33 Act. The Securities Act of 1934 ("the '34 Act") is concerned with the trading of securities once they have been issued, with the regulation of exchanges, and with the regulation of broker-dealers. Mutual fund portfolio managers must comply with the '34 Act in their transactions.

All investment companies with 100 or more shareholders must register with the SEC according to the Investment Company Act of 1940 ("the '40 Act"). The primary purposes of the '40 Act are to reduce investment company selling abuses and to ensure that investors receive sufficient and accurate information. Investment companies must provide periodic financial reports and disclose their investment policies to investors. The '40 Act prohibits changes in the nature of an investment company's fundamental investment policies without the approval of shareholders. This act also provides some tax advantages for eligible RICs, as indicated below. The purchase and sale of mutual fund shares must meet the requirements of fair dealing that the SEC '40 Act and the NASD, a self-regulatory organization, have established for all securities transactions in the United States.

Finally, the Investment Advisors Act of 1940 specifies the registration requirements and practices of companies and individuals who provide investment advisory services. This act deals with registered investment advisors (RIAs). Overall, although an investment company must comply with all aspects of the '40 Act, it is also subject to the '33 Act, the '34 Act, and the Investment Advisors Act of 1940.

The SEC also extended the '34 Act in 1988 to provide protections so that advertisements and claims by mutual fund companies would not be inaccurate or misleading to investors. New regulations aimed at potential self-dealing were established in the Insider Trading and Securities Fraud Enforcement Act of 1988, which requires mutual fund investment advisors to institute and enforce procedures that reduce the chances of insider trading.

An important feature of the '40 Act exempts any company that qualifies as a "regulated investment company" from taxation on its gains, either from income or capital appreciation, as previously indicated. To qualify as an RIC, the fund must distribute to its shareholders 90% of its net income excluding capital gains each year. Furthermore, the fund must follow certain rules about the diversification and liquidity of its investments and the degree of short-term trading and short-term capital gains.

Fees charged by mutual funds are also, as noted above, subject to regulation. The foundation of this regulatory power is the government's de facto role as arbiter of costs of transactions regarding securities in general. For example, the SEC and the NASD have established rules as part of the overall guide to fair dealing with customers about the markups dealers can charge financial institutions on the sale of financial assets. The SEC set a limit of 8.5% on a fund's load but allows the fund to pass through certain expenses under the 12b-1 rule. Effective July 1, 1993, the SEC amended the rule to set a maximum of 8.5% on the total of all fees, inclusive of front-end and back-end loads as well as expenses such as advertising.

Some funds charge a 12b-1 fee, as authorized by the '40 Act. The 12b-1 fee may be divided into two parts. The first component is a *distribution fee*, which can be used for fund marketing and distribution costs. The maximum distribution fee is 0.75% (of net assets per year). The second is a *service fee* (or *trail commission*), which is used to compensate the sales professionals for their ongoing services. The maximum service fee is 0.25%. Thus, the maximum 12b-1 fee is 1%. While no-load funds can have 12b-1 fees, the practice has been that in order to call itself a no-load fund, its 12b-1 fee must be at most 0.25% (all of which would be a distrubution fee). In general, the distribution fee component of the 12b-1 fee is used to develop new customers while the service fee is used for servicing existing customers.

A rule called "prospectus simplification" or "Plain English Disclosure" was enacted on October 1, 1998, to improve the readability of the fund prospectus and other fund documents. According to the SEC, prospectuses and other documents were being written by lawyers for other lawyers and not for the typical mutual fund investor. This initiative mandated that prospectuses and other documents be written from then on in "plain English" for individual investors.

A reporting change has been that the portfolio holdings must be provided to shareholders on a quarterly basis, within 45 days after the end of the quarter.

Among the recent SEC priorities that directly affect mutual funds are the following:

1. Reporting after-tax fund returns. This pending requirement would require funds to display the preliquidation and postliquidation impact of taxes on one-, five-, and 10-year returns both in the fund's prospectus and in annual reports. Such reporting could increase the popularity of tax-managed funds (funds with a high tax efficiency).
2. More complete reporting of fees, including fees in dollars-and-cents terms as well as in percentage terms.
3. More accurate and consistent reporting of investment performance.
4. Requiring fund investment practices to be more consistent with the name of a fund to more accurately reflect its investment objectives. The SEC requires that 65% of a fund's assets be invested in the type of security that its name implies (e.g., health care stocks).
5. Disclosing portfolio practices such as "window dressing" (buying or selling stocks at the end of a reporting period to include desired stocks or eliminate undesired stocks from the reports in order to improve the appeared composition of the portfolio) and "portfolio pumping" (buying shares of stocks already held at the end of a reporting period to improve performance during the period).
6. Various rules to increase the effectiveness of independent fund boards.

Key Points That You Should Understand Before Proceeding

1. The '33 Act, the '34 Act, the '40 Act, and the Investment Advisors Act of 1940.
2. The relevance of these acts to a mutual fund.
3. Important aspects of being a regulated investment company (RIC).
4. Recent SEC priorities impacting mutual funds.

STRUCTURE OF A FUND

A mutual fund organization is structured as follows:

1. a *board of directors* (also called the *fund trustees*), which represents the *shareholders* who are the owners of the mutual fund
2. the mutual fund, which is an entity based on the Investment Company Act of 1940
3. an *investment advisor*, who manages the fund's portfolios and is a registered investment advisor (RIA) according to the Investment Advisor's Act of 1940
4. a *distributor* or broker-dealer, who is registered under the Securities Act of 1934
5. other service providers, both external to the fund (the independent public accountant, custodian, and transfer agent) and internal to the fund (marketing, legal, reporting, etc.)

The structure is illustrated in Figure 1.

The role of the **board of directors** is to represent the fund shareholders. The board is composed of both "interested" (or "inside") directors who are affiliated with the investment

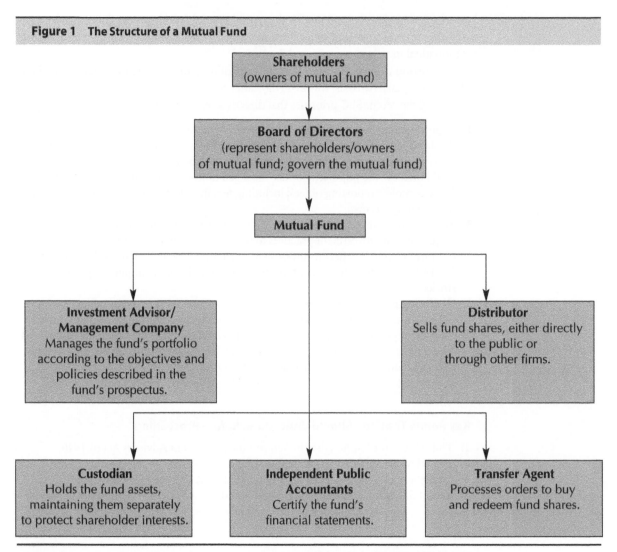

Figure 1   The Structure of a Mutual Fund

Shareholders
(owners of mutual fund)

Board of Directors
(represent shareholders/owners
of mutual fund; govern the mutual fund)

Mutual Fund

**Investment Advisor/
Management Company**
Manages the fund's portfolio
according to the objectives and
policies described in the
fund's prospectus.

Distributor
Sells fund shares, either directly
to the public or
through other firms.

Custodian
Holds the fund assets,
maintaining them separately
to protect shareholder interests.

**Independent Public
Accountants**
Certify the fund's
financial statements.

Transfer Agent
Processes orders to buy
and redeem fund shares.

Source: *Mutual Fund Fact Book, 40th ed. (Washington, D.C.: Investment Company Institute, 2000), p. 34.*

company (current or previous management) and "independent" (or "outside") directors who have no affiliation with the investment company. A majority of the board must be outside directors.

The mutual fund enters into a contract with an investment advisor to manage the fund's portfolios. The *investment advisor* can be an affiliate of a brokerage firm, an insurance company, a bank, an investment management firm, or an unrelated company. The distributor, which may or may not be affiliated with the mutual fund or investment advisor, is a broker-dealer. The role of the custodian is to hold the fund assets, segregating them from other accounts to protect the shareholders' interests. The transfer agent processes orders to buy and redeem fund shares, transfers the securities and cash, collects dividends and coupons, and makes distributions. The independent public accountant audits the fund's financial statements.

Some fund families manage all their funds internally. Other fund families use external managers to manage all or a portion of their internal funds. As explained earlier in this chapter, these external advisers are called *subadvisors*. There are several reasons why a family of funds would use subadvisors. Among them are

- developing a fund in an area in which the fund family has no expertise such as international stocks or bonds or alternative assets
- improving performance
- increased assets under management
- obtaining an attractive manager at a reasonable cost

Subadvised assets have grown faster than assets managed internally: From 2003 to 2006, subadvised assets grew at an annual rate of 27% compared to 23% for internally managed funds. Over this period, the market share of subadvised assets grew to 14% from 10%.[9]

Key Points That You Should Understand Before Proceeding

1. The duties of the investment advisor of a fund.
2. The role of the board of directors.

RECENT CHANGES IN THE MUTUAL FUND INDUSTRY

There have been several significant recent changes in the mutual fund industry in addition to those discussed previously in this chapter.

Distribution Channels

As explained earlier in this chapter, at the beginning of the 1990s, there were two primary distribution channels, direct sales to investors and sales through brokers. Since then, fund companies and fund distributors developed and expanded sales channels in the 1990s beyond the two traditional channels. Fund companies' use of multiple distribution channels has resulted in a blurring of the distinction between direct and sales-force funds that had characterized funds at the beginning of the 1990s.

Fund companies and distribution companies have developed new outlets for selling mutual funds and expanded their traditional sales channels. The changes that occurred are evident in the rising share of sales through third parties and intermediaries.

Significant market trends account for these changes. In particular, many funds that had previously marketed only directly turned increasingly toward third parties and intermediaries for distribution (thereby changing from no-load fund to a load fund, called "loading the fund). The nontraditional, third-party distribution channels used by direct-market funds were mutual fund supermarkets; mutual fund wrap-account programs; fee-based advisors; variable annuities; employer-sponsored pension plans; and bank trust departments.

Like direct-market funds, funds that were traditionally sold through a sales force have moved increasingly to nontraditional sources of sales such as employer-sponsored pension plans, banks, and life insurance companies. In the following text, we describe the various nontraditional distribution channels.

---

[9] Sue Asci, "Subadvisers are Grabbing a Larger Piece of the Market," *Investment News*, November 12, 2007.

Supermarkets

The introduction of the first mutual fund supermarket in 1992 marked the beginning of a significant change in the distribution of direct market funds. Specifically, during 1992, Charles Schwab & Company introduced its One Source service. With this and other supermarket programs, the organizer of the supermarket offers funds from a number of different mutual fund companies. These supermarkets allow investors to purchase funds from participating companies without investors having to contact each fund company. The organizer of the supermarket also provides the investor with consolidated record keeping and a simple account statement.

These services provide a program to provide access to multiple fund families under one roof and to help service the back-office needs of financial advisors. Through this service, investors can access many mutual fund families through one source.

On the one hand, these services make a mutual fund family more accessible to many more investors; on the other hand, they break the direct link between the mutual fund and the investor. According to these services, the mutual fund company does not know the identity of its investors through the supermarkets; only the supermarket, which distributes the funds directly to the investor, knows their identity. These supermarkets fit the needs of fee-based financial planners very well. For individual investors and planners as well, supermarkets can offer one-stop shopping, including the current "best of the breed." Currently, in addition to Schwab, there are other major mutual fund supermarkets. The investor pays the standard charge for the underlying funds plus the asset-based fee for the adviser in which the funds are wrapped, usually 1%.

While the method of charging by these supermarkets varies, a common method is as follows. The supermarket fund (call it SM) through its brokerage arm distributes mutual funds of other fund families (call them FF), both no-load and load funds. Consider first a no-load in an FF. The FF may either impose a transaction fee on the SM's customers or not, depending on an agreement between the SM with the specific FF. If the fund family chooses to impose no transaction fee, the SM conducts the transaction for its clients for the fund in the FF with no transaction fee. If the FF imposes a transaction fee, the SM will impose the transaction fee on its client and pass it through to the FF. The material provided by the FF in the SM will indicate whether or not there is a transaction fee. Load funds of other FF may also be distributed by a SM. In this case, there is no transaction fee, but the SM will impose the load depending on the share class (e.g., class A, B, C, or other) and pass it through to the FF.

Wrap Programs

Wrap accounts are managed accounts, typically mutual funds or ETFs "wrapped" in a service package. The service provided is often asset allocation counsel, that is, advice on the mix of managed funds or ETFs. Thus, wrap programs provide investors with advice and assistance for an asset-based fee rather than the traditional front-end load. Wrap products are currently offered by many fund and nonfund companies. Wrap accounts are not necessarily alternatives to mutual funds but represent a different way to package the funds.

Traditional direct-market funds as well as sales-force funds are marketed through this channel.

Fee-Based Financial Advisors

Fee-based financial advisors are independent financial planners who charge investors a fee rather than a transaction charge (a load) for investment services. These fees are typically a percentage of assets under management or alternatively an hourly fee, or a fixed retainer.

In return, they provide investment advice to their clients by selecting portfolios of mutual funds and securities. While most planners recommend mutual funds or ETFs to their clients, some recommend portfolios of planner-selected securities.

Variable Annuities

Variable annuities represent another distribution channel. Variable annuities are described as "mutual funds in an insurance wrapper." Among their insurance features are the tax deferral of investment earnings until they are withdrawn and higher charges (there is a mortality charge for the insurance provided). Variable annuities are sold through insurance agents and other distributors as well as directly through some fund companies.

Changes in the Costs of Purchasing Mutual Funds

The purchase cost of mutual funds has declined significantly. Purchase cost is measured by total shareholder costs, which includes both costs from annual fund expenses and from transaction-based sales loads. The decline in total shareholder costs occurred across all major types of funds.

In general, load funds responded to the competition of no-load funds by lowering distribution costs. Distribution cost is defined as the sum of the annualized sales load and 12b-1 fees. The distribution cost is the component of total shareholder cost that reflects the cost of advice and assistance provided by brokers and sales professionals to buyers of mutual funds.

Load funds lowered distribution costs, in part, by reducing front-end sales loads. In addition, load funds introduced alternatives to front-end loads that, depending on the investor's circumstances, could be less costly than front-end loads as a means of compensating sales professionals. One common distribution cost structure combined a 12b-1 fee with a contingent deferred sales load that would be paid by the investor when the shares were redeemed and, depending on the time the fund was held, could be zero.

The reduction in and reallocation of distribution costs since 1990 has been significant. For both equity and bond funds, the lowering of front-end loads along with the growth of alternatives to front-end loads together with more funds adopting 12b-1 fees resulted in 12b-1 fees becoming a much larger portion of distribution costs. A final element in the decline of total shareholder cost was the achievement of economies of scale by many individual costs. Some of the annual fund expenses, mainly those included in "other expenses" and those affected by breakpoints, have declined with the increase in size of some of the larger funds.

Mix and Match

Until recently, fund manufacturers distributed only their own funds; fund distributors distributed only one manufacturer's funds; and typically, employee-defined contribution plans, such as 401(k)s, offered funds from only one distributor. However, the investors' demands for choice and convenience, and also the distributors' need to appear objective, have motivated essentially all institutional users of funds and distribution organizations to offer funds from other fund families in addition to their own (that is, if they also manufacture their own funds). In addition, mutual fund supermarkets distribute funds of many fund families with considerable facility and low costs. This is called "open architecture."

The balance of power between fund manufacturers and distributors currently significantly favors distribution. That is, in general there are more funds available than distributors to sell them. Currently, in the mutual fund business, "distribution is king."

Domestic Acquisitions in the U.S. Funds Market

The merger and acquisition (M&A) business in the U.S. asset management business has been active. Just as there has been much M&A activity with fund families being both the acquirer and the acquired, there have also been many "deals" where a U.S. fund family was on one side of the deal and a nonfund U.S. asset manager was on the other. The former type of combination represents the increase in the scale of the mutual fund business, as previously discussed. The latter represents the continued homogenization of asset management in the United States; that is, there has been a consolidation among the following types of asset management:

mutual funds/variable annuities
institutional
• defined benefit
• foundation/endowment
individual/Separate Account/High Net Worth Individual

The U.S. asset management business continues to grow and consolidate across the various types of asset management.

Internationalization of the U.S. Funds Business

The combination of a U.S. fund company and an international asset manager could occur in either of two directions, that is, with either being the acquirer. But the dominant direction recently has been in the direction of an international asset manager acquiring a U.S. fund company. The reasons U.S. and international asset managers have aggressively acquired U.S. funds include the rapidly growing U.S. mutual fund business; continuing deregulation of the U.S. asset management business; and the general regulatory framework in the United States.

Key Points You Should Understand Before Proceeding

1. During the past decade, indirect sales of mutual funds through intermediaries have grown relative to direct sales.
2. The meaning of the following terms in the context of mutual funds: supermarket, wrap program, variable annuity.
3. The total shareholder costs of owning a mutual fund have decreased in recent years due to a reduction in distribution costs, and due to economies of scale in other fund expenses.

| ALTERNATIVES TO MUTUAL FUNDS

Due to the success of mutual funds, investment companies have developed several alternatives to mutual funds. The major alternatives to mutual funds are exchange-traded funds and segregated accounts.

EXCHANGE-TRADED FUNDS

As discussed in this chapter, mutual funds have become very popular with individual investors since the 1980s. However, they are often criticized for two reasons. First, mutual funds shares are priced at, and can be transacted only at, end-of-the-day (closing) prices. Specifically, transactions (i.e., purchases and sales) cannot be made at intraday prices, but only at the end-of-the-day closing prices. The second issue relates to taxes and investors' control over taxes. As noted earlier in this chapter, withdrawals by some fund shareholders can cause taxable realized capital gains (or losses) for other shareholders even though they maintain their positions.

Closed-end funds, in contrast, trade all during the day on a stock exchange. However, there is often a difference, in many cases a large difference, between the NAV of the underlying portfolios and (the value of the assets in the portfolios less its liabilities) and the price of the closed-end funds that are bought and sold—this difference is called a premium (the price of the closed-end fund is greater than the NAV), or a discount in the opposite case.

Thus, both mutual funds and closed-end funds are similar in that they are instruments based on the portfolios of their securities, which have a market value, the NAV. But closed-end funds are transacted continuously throughout the day because they are traded on an exchange. For this reason, they can be shorted and traded on margin. However, because the quantity of closed-end funds is fixed, the price at which the closed-end fund instrument trades throughout the day can be greater than or less than the NAV of the underlying portfolios; that is, closed-end funds can trade at a premium or discount to the NAV of the underlying portfolios.

Mutual fund shares, on the other hand, are always exchanged at a price equal to their NAV because the mutual fund sponsor will always issue new fund shares or redeem outstanding fund shares at NAV on a daily basis. Thus, the quantity of fund shares outstanding can increase or decrease (this is why a mutual fund is called an "open-end fund"). But because the mutual fund company cannot quickly and accurately value the portfolios of most mutual fund shares, they can redeem the shares of mutual funds only once a day, at the closing price for the day, and even then for many portfolios, with a significant delay after 4:00 P.M. The 4:00 P.M. EST closing time of the New York Stock Exchange is used as the time for the closing prices of most mutual funds. All mutual fund orders received after the previous 24 hours are settled at this single closing price (for illiquid portfolios, this closing price may not be available until the evening).

Would it not be ideal, the question is often posed, if there were an investment that embodied a combination of the desirable aspects of mutual funds (open-end-funds) and also closed-end funds? The resolution to this dichotomy would require portfolios to be traded like stocks throughout the day at a price equal to the continuously known NAV (that is, the price is not at a premium or discount to its NAV). Such an investment vehicle would be, in effect, a portfolio or fund traded on an exchange, hence called an **exchange-traded portfolio** or more commonly an ETF. At a very basic level, ETFs are easily understood. Most are essentially index funds. ETFs are different than conventional index funds in the way they are bought and sold. An ETF is traded throughout the day over an exchange, just like a stock. That means you can execute the types of orders (market, limit, and stop-loss orders) for ETFs, just as with individual stocks. ETFs can also be sold short or bought on margin (i.e., with borrowed money), and it is even possible to trade options on many ETFs. Since they trade on exchanges, they all have a ticker symbol.

ETFs are like open-end funds because their number of shares outstanding can change, as discussed below.

To assure that the price of the ETF would be very close to the continuously known NAV of the portfolio, an agent could be commissioned to arbitrage between the ETF and the underlying portfolio and keep their values equal. This agent could be commissioned to conduct a profitable arbitrage whereby it would buy the cheap ETF and sell the expensive underlying portfolio (at NAV) when the price of the ETF was less than the NAV of the underlying portfolio, and vice versa. This would be a profitable arbitrage for the agent since it buys the cheap ETF and sells the expensive portfolios or vice versa. This arbitrage would tend to maintain the price of the ETF to be very close (or equal) to that of the NAV. The agent who keeps the price of the ETF equal to (or close to) the portfolio's underlying NAV is, thus, called an *arbitrageur*.

The requirement for making this arbitrage process feasible would be that the composition and the NAV of the underlying portfolio be known accurately and continuously traded throughout the trading day. An example of such a portfolio would be the S&P 500 Index portfolio. The 500 stocks in the index are very liquid and their prices and the value of the index are quoted continuously throughout the trading day.

Thus, it is no coincidence that the first ETF was based on the S&P 500 Index. It began on January 1, 1993, at the American Stock Exchange with State Street Global Advisers (SSgA) as its adviser. Its ticker symbol was SPY and it quickly became known as the "Spider." However, this process would not be feasible for the typical actively managed mutual fund because the composition of its portfolios is not known throughout the trading day. Specifically mutual funds are required to make the composition of their funds public only four times a year and then only 45 days after the date of portfolio report.

So ETFs are feasible for indexes on broad liquid security indexes but not on typical actively managed mutual funds. Sustained efforts have been made, however, to develop ETFs on actively managed funds. The status of these efforts will be developed below.

Since their advent in 1993, ETFs have grown rapidly. At the end of 2007, there were 629 ETFs with assets of $608.4 billion versus 8,031 mutual funds with assets of $12,020.1 billion and 668 closed-end funds with assets of $314.9 billion. ETFs require SEC approval. The original ETFs were based on well-known stock and bond indexes, both U.S. and international. These included the following indexes that we will discuss in later chapters in this book: the S&P 500, Dow Jones Industrial Average, Russell 2000, Lehman Aggregate Bond Index, MSCI EAFE, and MSCI Emerging Markets. These were followed by ETFs based on narrower sector indexes covering financial, health care, industrial, natural resources, precious metals, technology, utilities, real estate, and others. These were, in turn, followed by ETFs based on new and often narrow indexes, specifically designed for ETFs.

Since ETFs are essentially stocks that trade on a stock exchange, they have ticker symbols. The five largest ETFs as of April 1, 2008, (with their ticker symbol shown in parentheses) were SPDR S&P 500 ETF (SPY), iShares MSCI EAFE (EFA), iShares MSCI Emerging Market Index Fund (EEM), street TRACKS Gold Shares ETF (GLD), and PowerShares QQQ Nasdaq 100 (QQQQ). The size of an ETF portfolio is most likely related to its liquidity; bigger ETFs are more liquid. The change in the size of the portfolio as measured by the number of ETF units outstanding demonstrates that ETFs are an "open-end" investment structure. "Open-end" means the fund can create new shares or redeem existing shares to meet market demand. Thus, ETFs are like mutual funds and unlike closed-end funds in this regard.

On March 25, 2008, the first active ETF was launched at the American Stock Exchange: the Bear Stearns Current Yield ETF (ticker symbol: YYY). According to the fund's statement: "The fund differs from an index fund since it is actively managed by its portfolio manager who has the discretion to choose securities for the fund's portfolio consistent with its investment objective." It remains to be seen how successful active ETFs will be in attracting investors and in providing returns.

Exchange-Traded Fund Creation/Redemption Process

When investors invest in a mutual fund, they (or their advisor) purchase shares directly from the fund company at a price equal to the fund's NAV, which is calculated at the end of each trading day based on the market prices of the securities held by the fund. However, the process of buying and selling ETFs works quite differently. Rather than dealing directly with the fund company, investors buy ETF shares from another individual investor via an exchange at a price determined by supply and demand for the ETF, not the ETF's underlying NAV as is the case for mutual funds. The NAV of the underlying portfolios, however, remains calculable, and available, and is dependent on the forces in the underlying securities markets.

For ETFs, individuals do not deal directly with the provider of the ETF (such as Barclays Global Investors (BGI), State Street (SSgA), or Vanguard). That privilege is reserved for a few very large investors called **authorized participants (AP)** who are the arbitragers referred to above. When these authorized participants want to sell ETF shares, they deliver their shares to the provider and in return receive the underlying portfolio of stocks. No cash changes hands. The same process works in reverse for purchases. The authorized participant assembles a portfolio of the stocks (in the same proportion that they are held in the ETF) and delivers the portfolio to the ETF provider, who then delivers the new ETF shares to the authorized participant.

Authorized participants are mainly large institutional traders who have contractual agreements with ETF funds. Authorized participants are the only investors who may create or redeem shares of an ETF with the ETF sponsor and then only in large, specified quantities called **creation/redemption units.** These unit sizes range from approximately 50,000 to 100,000 ETF shares. The authorized participant may create new ETF shares by providing the fund with a specified basket of stocks (that is, a **creation unit [CU]**) and the fund responds by transferring the corresponding number of the ETF shares to the authorized participant. Similarly, an authorized participant can redeem ETF shares by providing the fund with a specific number of ETF shares (a **redemption unit [RU]**), and the fund will transfer to the authorized participant the specific basket of stocks. These transfers are considered "in-kind transfers" of assets and have no cost or tax impact. This tax treatment is the basis for one of the major advantages of ETFs relative to mutual funds. This "in-kind" redemption and creation process also helps keep an ETF's market price close to its NAV. If discrepancies arise between a fund's market price and NAV, this discrepancy opens up a profit-making opportunity for an authorized participant. The very act of exploiting that opportunity drives the market price and NAV closer together.

Consider the dynamics of the relationship between the authorized participants, on one hand, and either the markets for the individual stock, which determine the NAV of the underlying portfolio, or the ETF fund on the other. If there is a large demand for an ETF, the ETF price will move above the underlying portfolio's NAV. The authorized participants will then earn a small arbitrage profit by buying the basket of securities (which are cheap relative to the ETF), and then engaging in an in-kind transfer of the basket of securities for the ETF units. There are two outcomes of this transfer. First, there are fewer securities available on the market, making the NAV increase and more ETF units available on the market, both of which make the gap between the price of the ETF and the NAV disappear and make the price of the ETF equal to the NAV. The arbitrage by authorized participants has eliminated the gap and so the ETF tracks the underlying basket of securities. Second, the ETF market has grown. There are more ETF units outstanding; the authorized participant could sell the ETFs received on the open market. And the ETF fund has more securities in its portfolios.

The case discussed previously where the ETF's price exceeds the NAV, resulting in the creation of new ETF shares, is illustrated in the top part of Figure 2. The case where the

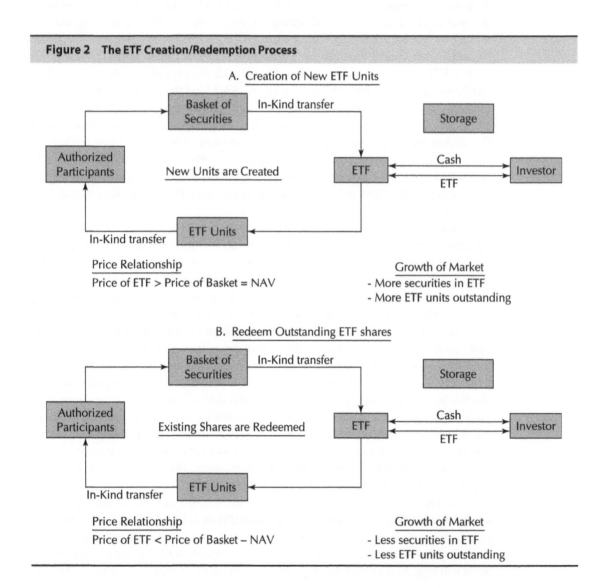

Figure 2 The ETF Creation/Redemption Process

ETF's price is less than the NAV, resulting in the redemption of ETF shares, is illustrated in the bottom panel of Figure 2. Both demonstrate the open-end nature of ETFs.

The role of the authorized participant is critical in meeting investor expectations. Since ETFs are based on passive indexes where value is represented by the NAV, investors in ETFs expect their return to be equal to that of the portfolio's NAV. This will be the case if the ETF price tracks the NAV perfectly, which is the authorized participant's function. However, if the ETF price does not track the NAV, the return on the ETF the investor actually experiences based on the NAV will be different, either higher or lower. This is called "tracking error." Tracking error is followed by ETF analysts and large tracking error is a negative for ETFs. The difficulty of tracking an active ETF may make such ETFs unattractive to investors.

The open-end aspect of mutual funds is direct; that is, investors invest funds directly in or withdraw funds from the mutual fund. The open-end aspect of ETFs is indirect in that the investors buy the ETF in a closed-end manner like closed-end funds and then the authorized participant arbitrages between the ETF and the underlying portfolio, providing the indirect open-end aspect of the ETF.

For this process to work effectively, the underlying securities need to be known and be liquid. If an authorized participant cannot trade the underlying securities in the exact proportions as they are in the NAV of the portfolios, the share price of an ETF and its NAV could diverge. If the composition of the underlying portfolio is not known exactly throughout the trading day, the arbitrage will be difficult. This issue is discussed below. In addition, this is also not an issue for liquid portfolios but it could be for ETFs based on less liquid portfolios. In either case, the tracking error could be significant.

Large investors are constantly monitoring the ETF market to take advantage of discounts and premiums when they develop. A high degree of transparency is required to make this process possible so that the authorized participants are always aware of what each ETF owns and what its shares are worth. Consequently, ETFs are required to publish their NAVs every 15 seconds throughout the trading day.

Exchange-Traded Fund Sponsors

Like mutual funds, ETFs require a company to sponsor them; these companies are referred to as sponsors for ETFs. The three largest ETF sponsors by size are BGI (their ETFs are called iShares), SSgA, and Vanguard. The ETF sponsor must (1) develop the index, (2) retain the authorized participants, (3) provide seed capital to initiate the ETF, (4) advertise and market the ETF to develop customer executions, and (5) engage in other activities. The authorized participants are typically large financial institutions. Retaining the authorized participants is essential because if the arbitrage between the ETF price and NAV of the portfolio is not effective, the ETF price will not track the portfolio's NAV and their returns may be different. The tracking error of an ETF depends on the liquidity of the underlying portfolios and the ability of the ETF's authorized participant.

Many ETFs employ an index previously developed by another company. The index providers are paid a commission by the sponsor for the use of their index. For example, BGI uses indexes supplied by Dow Jones, FTSE, Lehman Brothers, Morgan Stanley Capital International (MSCI), Morningstar, Russell, Standard & Poor's, and others.

Mutual Funds versus ETFs: Their Relative Advantages

ETFs have grown very rapidly since their introduction in 1993. Obviously ETFs have proved to be very attractive to investors. What are the relative advantages and disadvantages of ETFs?

First, mutual funds are priced only once a day by being redeemed or offered by the fund company at NAV. On the other hand, ETFs are traded on an exchange and so are priced continuously throughout the day. Moreover, because ETFs are traded on an exchange, their shares can be shorted and limit and stop orders can be used. ETFs can also be leveraged, while mutual fund shares cannot be.

Both passive mutual funds and ETFs (most are passive as of this writing) have low fees, but ETF fees tend to be somewhat lower. All ETFs trade on an exchange and, as a result, incur a commission ranging from a discount to a full-service commission. Mutual fund shares may be either no-load funds or load funds. For frequent, small investments (for example, monthly payroll deductions), mutual funds would most likely be better since no-load mutual funds cost nothing to trade and ETFs incur a commission cost. For infrequent, large investments, ETFs may be better because of their lower expenses.

With respect to taxes, as discussed earlier in this chapter, mutual funds may lead to capital gains taxes for investors who do not even liquidate their fund because the fund has to sell securities in their portfolio to fund the sales of shares of other investors. Because of the unique structure of ETFs, ETFs can fund redemptions by in-kind transfers without selling their holdings, which have no tax consequences. ETFs are, therefore, more tax efficient than mutual fund shares.

Mutual funds, however, may have some advantages. First, while ETFs have been exclusively passive or indexes, mutual fund families offer many types of active funds as well as passive funds. In addition, no-load mutual funds, both active and passive, permit transactions with no loads or commissions.

Table 6 provides an overall comparison of ETFs and mutuals. Table 7 compares the taxation of ETFs and mutual funds.

Key Points That You Should Understand Before Proceeding

1. ETFs overcome some of the drawbacks of investing in mutual funds.
2. Like mutual funds, ETFs have an open-end structure.
3. Like closed-end funds, ETFs are exchange traded and investors can place orders like any type of stock, short the shares, and create a leveraged position.
4. A key participant in an ETF is the authorized participant who functions to drive the ETF's price close to the NAV.
5. In an ETF, it is critical that the fund shares track the NAV; a large tracking error makes an ETF less attractive.

Separately Managed Accounts

Many high–net worth individuals object to using mutual funds because of the individual investor's lack of control over taxes, their lack of any input into investment decisions, and the absence of "high-touch" service. The use of **separately managed accounts (SMAs)** or segregated accounts responds to all these limitations of mutual funds. They are, however, more expensive. SMA are what the name indicates, managed accounts that are not

Table 6   Mutual Funds versus Exchange-Traded Funds

	Mutual Funds	ETFs
Variety	Wide choice.	Choices currently limited to stock indexes, but on many stock indexes.
Taxation	Subject to taxation on dividend and realized capital gains. *May have gains/losses when other investors redeem funds.* May have gains/losses when stocks in index are changed.	Subject to taxation on dividend and realized capital gain. *No gains/losses when other investors redeem funds.* May have gains/losses when stocks in index are changed.
Valuation	NAV, based on actual price.	Creations and redemptions at NAV. Secondary market price may be valued somewhat above or below NAV, but deviation typically small due to arbitrage.
Pricing	End-of-day.	Continuous.
Expenses	Low for index funds.	Low and, in some cases, even lower than for index mutual funds.
Transaction Cost	None (for no-load funds); Sales charge for load funds.	Commission or brokerage charge.
Management Fee	Depends on fund; even index funds have a range of management fees.	Depends on fund; tends to be very low on many stock index funds.

Table 7   Taxes: Mutual Funds versus Exchange-Traded Funds

	Mutual Funds	ETFs
HOLDING/MAINTAINING		
Taxes on Dividend, Income, and Realized Capital Gains	Fully taxable.	Fully taxable.
Turnover of Portfolio	Withdrawal by other investors may necessitate portfolio sales and realized capital gains for holder.	Withdrawal by others does not cause portfolio sales and, thus, no realized capital for holder.
DISPOSITION		
Withdrawal of Investment	Capital gains tax on difference between sales and purchase price.	Capital gains tax on difference between sales and purchase price.
Overall	Due to some portfolio turnover, will realize capital gains.	Due to very low portfolio turnover, will not realize significant capital gains.

commingled as are mutual funds, but are separately managed for the individual investor. As a result of having a separate portfolio, the investor can instruct the manager not to take capital gains, to avoid specific stocks or sectors (perhaps because they have these stocks in their 401(k)), or provide other specific inputs.

SMAs are all actively managed, as opposed to ETFs, which have been all passive. Some SMAs have specialities such as tax efficiency. SMAs have higher annual expenses than mutual funds. The choice for the investor, thus, is whether the higher level of service is worth the higher cost.

Previously, money managers offered SMAs only for only very large portfolios, typically $1 million and more. Currently, however, many money managers have significantly decreased the minimum size of their SMAs. As a result, many investors with mid-sized portfolios are utilizing segregated, individually managed accounts provided by many companies and other investment managers.

SUMMARY

Investment companies sell shares to the public and invest the proceeds in a diversified portfolio of securities, with each share representing a proportionate interest in the underlying portfolio of securities. There are three types of investment companies: open-end or mutual funds, closed-end funds, and unit trusts. A wide range of funds with many different investment objectives is available. Securities law requires that a fund clearly set forth its investment objective in its prospectus, and the objective identifies the type or types of assets the fund will purchase and hold.

Mutual funds and closed-end funds provide two crucial economic functions associated with financial intermediaries: risk reduction via diversification and lower costs of contracting and information processing. Money market funds allow shareholders to write checks against their shares, thus providing a payments mechanism, another economic function of financial intermediaries.

Mutual funds are extensively regulated, with most of that regulation occurring at the federal level. The key legislation is the Investment Company Act of 1940. An important feature regarding regulation is that the funds are exempt from taxation on their gains if the gains are distributed to investors within a relatively short period of time. Even allowing for that special tax-free status, it is necessary to recognize that regulations apply to many features of the funds' administration, including sales fees, asset management, degree of diversification, distributions, and advertising.

There has been widespread consumer-investor acceptance of the concept of family (or group or complex) funds. That is, an investment advisory company (such as American Funds, Fidelity Investments, or Vanguard Group) manages dozens of different funds, which span the spectrum of potential investment objectives, from aggressive growth to balanced income to international diversification. The success of these fund families has led to a considerable concentration of the mutual fund industry in a few large fund groups.

The assets in mutual funds have increased significantly since 1980, particularly in stock funds. The shift from stocks to stock funds was caused by the investor need for diversification, convenience, and expert portfolio management. The growth in mutual fund assets may, however, moderate as investor allocations to stock funds have matured and competitors to mutual funds have developed. Among these competitors are variable annuities, exchange traded funds, and separately managed accounts.

ETFs were initiated in 1993 and have grown significantly due both to individual and institutional investors. ETFs have some advantages over mutual funds, such as being traded intraday on an exchange and, thus, having continuous pricing and being able to short and be traded with stop and limit orders; tax advantages, including not being subject to capital gains tax when the investor does not liquidate a position; and slightly lower fees. ETFs are based on portfolios that track an index; that is, they are passive vehicles, although active ETFs are being developed.

KEY TERMS

- 12b-1 fee
- Authorized Participants (AP)
- Back-end load
- Board of directors
- Breakpoint
- Creation/redemption units
- Creation unit (CU)
- Closed-end fund
- Contingent deferred sales charge (CDSC)
- Exchange-traded funds (ETFs)
- Exchange-traded portfolio
- Investment advisor
- Investment advisory fee

- Investment Company Act of 1940
- Investment objective
- Level load
- Life-cycle funds
- Load
- Load funds
- Net asset value (NAV)
- No-load mutual fund
- Open-end (mutual) funds
- Redemption unit (RU)
- Separately managed accounts (SMAs)
- Target-date funds
- Unit trust

QUESTIONS

1. An investment company has $1.05 million of assets, $50,000 of liabilities, and 10,000 shares outstanding.
   a. What is its NAV?
   b. Suppose the fund pays off its liabilities while at the same time the value of its assets double. How many shares will a deposit of $5,000 receive?
2. "The NAV of an open-end fund is determined continuously throughout the trading day." Explain why you agree or disagree with this statement.
3. What are closed-end funds?
4. Why do some closed-end funds use leverage to raise more funds rather than issue new shares like mutual funds?
5. Why might the price of a share of a closed-end fund diverge from its NAV?
6. What is the difference between a unit trust and a closed-end fund?

7. **a.** Describe the following: front-end load, back-end load, level load, 12b-1 fee, management fee.
   b. Is there a limit on the fees that a mutual fund may charge?
8. Why do mutual funds have different classes of shares?
9. What is an index fund?
10. **a.** What is meant by a target-date fund?
    b. What is the motivation for the creation of such a fund?
11. What are the costs incurred by a mutual fund?
12. Why might the investor in a mutual fund be faced with a potential tax liability arising from capital gains even though the investor did not benefit from such a gain?
13. Does an investment company provide any economic function that individual investors cannot provide for themselves on their own? Explain your answer.

14. Why might a family of funds hire subadvisors for some of its funds?
15. **a.** How can a fund qualify as a regulated investment company?
    b. What is the benefit in gaming this status?
16. What is an ETF?
17. What are the advantages of an ETF relative to open-end and closed-end investment companies?
18. Explain the role of the authorized participant in an ETF.
19. Why is tracking error important for an ETF?
20. Comment on the following statement: "Exchange-traded funds are typically actively managed funds."
21. Briefly describe the following in the context of mutual funds:
    a. supermarket
    b. wrap program
    c. segregated managed accounts
    d. family of funds

Pension Funds

LEARNING OBJECTIVES

After reading this chapter, you will understand

- what a pension plan sponsor does

- the different types of pension plans, including defined-contribution plans, defined-benefit plans, and a hybrid plan, the cash balance plan

- what a 401(k) plan is

- what an insured plan is

- the principal provisions of the Employee Retirement Income Security Act (ERISA) of 1974

- what the Pension Benefit Guaranty Corporation does

- who the managers of pension funds are

- the various financial services provided to pension funds

- the role of mutual funds in contemporary pension plans

P ension funds, which exist in some form in all developed economies, are major institutional investors and participants in the financial markets. Pension funds have become important for several reasons. First, income and wealth have grown steadily over the post–World War II period, leaving households more money for long-term savings. Second, people are living longer and can expect more financial needs for longer retirement periods. Third, pensions represent compensation to employees that is free of tax liability to the employee until after the workers retire and their income from employment ceases, and employer contributions are tax deductible to the employer. This chapter discusses **pension plans** and provides an overview of pension fund management.

INTRODUCTION TO PENSION PLANS

A pension plan is a fund that is established for the eventual payment of retirement benefits. The entities that establish pension plans, called **pension plan sponsors**, may be private business entities acting for their employees (called *corporate* or *private plans*); federal, state, and local entities on behalf of their employees (called *public plans*); unions on behalf of their members (called *Taft Hartley plans*); and individuals for themselves (called *individually sponsored plans*). The 10 largest corporate, public, and union pension funds as of September 30, 2007 are shown in Table 1.

Table 1	Ten Largest Corporate, Public, and Union Defined-Benefit Plans as of September 30, 2007	
Ten Largest Corporate Pension Funds		**Total (in millions)**
1. General Motors		$133,835
2. AT&T		$117,537
3. General Electric		$88,237
4. IBM		$87,481
5. Boeing		$81,079
6. Verizon		$74,780
7. Ford Motor		$57,517
8. Lockheed Martin		$51,436
9. Alcatel—Lucent		$48,498
10. Northrop Grumman		$37,564
Total		**$777,964**
Ten Largest Public Pension Funds		**Total (in millions)**
1. California Public Employees		$254,627
2. California State Teachers		$176,270
3. New York State Common		$164,363
4. Florida State Board		$142,519
5. New York City Retirement		$127,945
6. Texas Teachers		$114,878
7. New York State Teachers		$106,042
8. Wisconsin Investment Board		$91,615
9. Ohio Public Employees		$84,349
10. New Jersey		$83,968
Total		**$777,964**
Ten Largest Union Funds		**Total (in millions)**
1. Teamsters, Western Conference		$32,600
2. Teamsters, Central States		$21,388
3. National Electric		$14,500
4. Operating Eng. International		$10,353
5. 1199SEIU National		$9,964
6. I.A.M. National		$9,302
7. Boilermaker—Blacksmith		$9,296
8. Electrical Ind., Joint Board		$7,484
9. UMWA Health and Retirement		$7,045
10. UFCW Industry		$6,941
Total		**$128,873**

Source: *Pensions & Investments, January 1, 2008.*

Pension funds are financed by contributions by the employer. In some plans, employer contributions are matched to some degree by employees. The great success of private pension plans is somewhat surprising because the system involves investing in an asset—the pension contract—that for the most part is very illiquid. It cannot be used, not even as collateral, until retirement. The key factor in explaining pension fund growth is that the employer's contributions and a specified amount of the employee's contributions, as well as the earnings of the fund's assets, are tax exempt. In essence, a pension is a form of employee remuneration for which the employee is *not taxed until funds are withdrawn*. This tax exemption results from meeting many federal requirements. Such plans are called *qualified pension plans*, which means that if the plan meets certain requirements, it qualifies for tax exemptions. Pension funds have also traditionally served to discourage employees from quitting, since the employee, until vested, could lose at least the accumulation resulting from the employer contribution.

Key Points That You Should Understand Before Proceeding

1. The role of the sponsor of a pension plan.
2. The importance of tax exemption to the structure and popularity of pension plans.

TYPES OF PENSION PLANS

There are two basic and widely used types of pension plans: defined-benefit plans and defined-contribution plans. In addition, a recently developed hybrid type of plan called a cash balance plan combines features of both these types.

Defined-Benefit Plan

In a **defined-benefit plan**, the plan sponsor agrees to make specified dollar payments annually to qualifying employees beginning at retirement (and some payments to beneficiaries in case of death before retirement). These payments typically occur monthly. The retirement payments are determined by a formula that usually takes into account the length of service of the employee and the employee's earnings. The pension obligations are effectively a debt obligation of the plan sponsor. The plan sponsor, thereby, assumes the risk of having insufficient funds in the plan to satisfy the regular contractual payments that must be made to retired employees.

A plan sponsor establishing a defined-benefit plan can use the payments made into the fund to purchase an annuity policy from a life insurance company. Defined-benefit plans that are guaranteed by life insurance products are called **insured benefit plans**. An insured plan is not necessarily safer than a noninsured plan, since it depends on the ability of the life insurance company to make the contractual payments, whereas the uninsured plan depends on the ability of the plan sponsor. Whether a private pension plan is insured or noninsured, a federal agency, the **Pension Benefit Guaranty Corporation (PBGC)**, which was established in 1974 by the ERISA legislation, insures the vested benefits of participants, as discussed in the following text.

Benefits become vested when employees reach a certain age and complete enough years of service so that they meet the minimum requirements for receiving benefits upon retirement.

The payment of benefits is not contingent upon a participant's continuation with the employer or union.

Firms in recent years have not adopted defined-benefit plans. Major firms that have them have been freezing their plans. For example, Verizon Communications froze its plan in 2005, and IBM froze its plan in 2006. One of the reasons for IBM's freezing of its plan, which is a fully funded plan, is that it is too costly and makes it difficult for IBM to compete with its competitors that do not offer a defined-benefit plan. Microsoft, for example, does not offer a defined-benefit plan. Verizon Communications competes with Internet firms that do not offer such plans. Beyond competitive reasons, there is the problem of managing the assets to be able to satisfy liabilities and the implications for financial reporting. We will discuss this later in this chapter when we look at the crisis in the pension fund area.

Defined-Contribution Plan

In a **defined-contribution plan**, the plan sponsor is responsible only for making specified contributions into the plan on behalf of qualifying participants, not specified payments to the employee after retirement. The amount contributed is typically either a percentage of the employee's salary and/or a percentage of the employer's profits. The plan sponsor does not guarantee any specific amount at retirement. The payments that will be made to qualifying participants upon retirement depend on the growth of the plan assets. That is, retirement benefit payments are determined by the investment performance of the funds in which the assets are invested and are not guaranteed by the plan sponsor. The plan sponsor gives the participants various options as to the investment vehicles in which they may invest. Defined-contribution pension plans come in several legal forms: 401(k) plans, money purchase pension plans, and employee stock ownership plans (ESOPs).

By far, the fastest-growing sector of the defined-contribution plan is the **401(k) plan,** or its equivalent in the nonprofit sector, the *403(b) plan,* and in the public sector, the *457 plan.* To the firm, this kind of plan offers the lowest costs and the least administrative problems. The employer makes a specified contribution to a specific plan/program, and the employee chooses how it is invested. To the employee, the plan is attractive because it offers some control over how the pension money is managed. In fact, plan sponsors frequently offer participants the opportunity to invest in one or more of a family of mutual funds. Over half of all defined-contribution plans (in public institutions such as state governments as well as private firms) use mutual funds, and the percentage of private corporations that use this approach is even higher.

Regulations issued by the U.S. Department of Labor require firms to offer their employees a set of distinctive choices, a development that has encouraged pension plans to select mutual funds as the investment vehicle of choice because families of mutual funds can readily provide investment vehicles offering different investment objectives.

There are several fundamental differences between defined-benefit plans and defined-contribution plans. In the defined-benefit plan, the plan sponsor: (1) guarantees the retirement benefits, (2) makes the investment choices, and (3) bears the investment risk if the investments do not earn enough to fund the guaranteed retirement benefits. In contrast, in a defined-contribution plan, the employer does not guarantee any retirement benefits. However, the employer may agree to make specified contributions to the employee's account. The employee selects the investment options, and the employee has for retirement only the return on the investment portfolio (plus, of course, the employee and employer contributions).

According to *Pension & Investments*, the largest public sponsor of a defined-contribution plan as of September 30, 2008, is the Federal Retirement Thrift ($233 billion). The Federal Retirement Thrift is an independent agency established by the Federal Employees' Retirement System Act of 1986 to provide federal employees the opportunity to save additional amounts in retirement and is similar to the 401(k) plan in the private sector. The four largest corporate sponsors of defined-contribution plans are AT&T ($41 billion), Boeing ($31 billion), IBM ($31 billion), and General Electric ($28 billion).

Hybrid Pensions Plans

Defined-benefit pension plans are cumbersome for the plan sponsor to administer and are not portable from one job to another by employees in an increasingly mobile workforce. Defined-contribution plans put the investment choices and investment risk on the employee. In response to these and other limitations, new forms of **hybrid pension plans**, that is, combinations of defined-benefit and defined-contribution plans, have been developed.

Although there are several types of hybrid plans, including pension equity, floor-offset, and others, the most common hybrid form is the cash balance plan. A **cash balance plan** is basically a defined benefit that has some of the features of a defined-contribution plan. A cash balance plan is a defined-benefit plan in that it defines future pension benefits, not employer contributions. Retirement benefits are based on a fixed-amount annual employer contribution and a guaranteed minimum annual investment return. Each participant in a cash balance plan has an account that is credited with a dollar amount that resembles an employer contribution and is generally determined as a percentage of pay. Each participant's account is also credited with interest linked to some fixed or variable index such as the consumer price index (CPI). The plan usually provides benefits in the form of a lump-sum distribution in an annuity. Interest is credited to the employee's account at a rate specified in the plan and is unrelated to the investment earnings of the employer's pension trust. The employee's benefit does not vary based on the interest credit. The promised benefits are fixed, and the investment gains or losses are borne by the employer. However, as in a defined-contribution plan, an individual employee can monitor his or her cash balance plan "account" in a regular statement.

Also like a defined-contribution plan and important to today's job-changing workforce, many cash balance plans allow the employee to take a lump-sum payment of vested benefits when terminating, which can be rolled over into an individual retirement plan (IRA) or to the new employer's plan. That is, cash balance plans are portable from one job to another. Table 2 summarizes the features of a cash balance plan that are similar to defined-benefit and defined-contribution plans.

Table 2 Features of Cash Balance Plans	
Defined-Benefit Like Features	Defined-Contributions Like Features
Plan benefits are fixed based on a formula.	Assets accumulated in an "account" for each employee.
Investment responsibility is borne by the employer.	Vested assets may be taken as a lump sum and rolled into an IRA or another qualified plan when the employee terminates employment.
Employees are automatically included in the plan. Plans are protected by the PBGC.	

Figure 1   Plot of Defined Benefit and Cash Balance

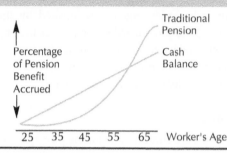

Source: *Cerulli Associates*

A cash balance plan is similar to some types of defined-contribution plans, particularly money purchase plans and profit sharing plans, according to which the employer contributes at a fixed rate but does not guarantee benefits. Since traditional defined-contribution plans are back-ended (i.e., most of the benefit is accrued during the past 10 years of a 20- to 30-year career with a company), younger workers often undervalue the benefit of a pension plan. Cash balance formulas provide for an earlier, more uniform accumulation of retirement pension benefits that can be enjoyed by employees who do not commit their entire careers to one company. Figure 1 shows the buildup of retirement benefits over time for defined-benefit and defined-contribution plans and cash balance plans. As shown, in a traditional plan benefits based on a combination of age and service build up sharply toward the end of the employee's career. In a cash balance plan, benefits build more uniformly each year.

Key Points That You Should Understand Before Proceeding

1. In a qualified pension plan, contributions (up to some extent) and earnings thereof are tax-exempt.
2. The difference between a defined-benefit pension plan and a defined-contribution pension plan.
3. The cash balance pension plan is a new hybrid plan that combines features of the defined-benefit plan and the defined-contribution plan.

INVESTMENTS

The aggregate asset mix of the 1,000 top defined-benefit and defined-contribution pension plans as of September 30, 2007, is summarized in Table 3 and Table 4. As indicated, the asset allocations for corporate and public defined-benefit plans are very similar, with approximately 65% of their assets in U.S. stocks and bonds. Corporate and public defined-benefit funds also have approximately 20% of their assets in international equity and fixed income.

The major difference between union plans and the other two types of plans is the small weight in union plans to international investments, only approximately 10% relative to 20% in corporate and public. There are no federal restrictions on investing in non–U.S. investments. The sponsors of a fund, however, are free to restrict the allocation of the

Table 3 Asset Allocation: Defined-Benefit and Defined-Contribution Pension Funds—Top 1,000 as of September 30, 2007

DEFINED-BENEFIT PENSION FUNDS

	Corporate	Public	Union
Domestic equity	39.4%	40.7%	46.3%
Domestic fixed income	25.6	23.3	23.9
International equity	17.3	19.8	8.6
International fixed income	2.4	1.3	0.8
Cash	1.6	1.5	2.3
Private equity	3.8	5.0	2.0
Real estate equity	2.9	5.1	6.4
Mortgage	0.1	0.5	0.4
Other	6.9	2.8	9.3
Total	100.0%	100.0%	100.0%

DEFINED-CONTRIBUTION PENSION FUNDS

	Corporate	Public	Union
Sponsoring company stock	20.5%	0%	0%
Other U.S. equity	31.1	47.3	30.4
International equity	7.4	8.7	6.2
Fixed income	5.2	21.1	22.2
Cash	2.8	2.2	3.9
Stable value	13.3	19.1	10.2
Other	19.8	5.2	27.1
Total*	100.0%	100.0%	100.0%

*Subject to rounding errors

Source: *Pensions & Investments, January 21, 2008.*

Table 4 Asset Mix of Top 1,000 Defined-Benefit Plans: 2005

Asset Class	Corporate	Public	Union
Domestic equity	45.00%	46.10%	45.60%
Domestic fixed income	25.90	25.20	34.60
International equity	16.10	16.40	5.00
International fixed income	1.50	1.60	0.70
Cash	1.10	1.40	2.20
Private equity	3.90	3.70	1.00
Real estate equity	3.30	3.80	4.60
Mortgages	0.30	0.70	1.00
Other	2.90	1.10	5.30
Total	100.00%	100.00%	100.00%

Source: *Pensions & Investments, http://www.pionline.com*

fund's assets to domestic investments. It is not uncommon for union-sponsored pension funds, however, to prohibit non–U.S. investments in their portfolios. Most corporate and public funds invest in international assets.

Qualified pension funds are exempt from federal income taxes. Thus, fund assets can accumulate tax free. Consequently, pension funds do not invest in assets that have the advantage of being largely or completely tax exempt.

Key Points That You Should Understand Before Proceeding

1. The largest share of both defined-benefit and defined-contribution pension fund assets is invested in common stocks, often a U.S. stock index.
2. Qualified pension plans rarely invest in tax-exempt assets.

REGULATION

Because pension plans are so important for U.S. workers, Congress passed comprehensive legislation in 1974 to regulate pension plans. This legislation, the **Employee Retirement Income Security Act of 1974 (ERISA)**, is fairly technical in its details. For our purposes, it is necessary only to understand its major provisions.

First, ERISA established *funding standards* for the minimum contributions that a plan sponsor must make to the pension plan to satisfy the actuarially projected benefit payments. Prior to the enactment of ERISA, many corporate plan sponsors followed a "pay-as-you-go" funding policy. That is, when an employee retired, the corporate plan sponsor paid for the necessary retirement benefits out of current cash flow. Under ERISA, such a practice is no longer allowed; rather, the program must be funded. That is, regular contributions to an investment pool along with investment earnings are sufficient to pay the employee retirement benefits.

Second, ERISA established fiduciary standards for pension fund trustees, managers, and advisors. Specifically, all parties responsible for the management of a pension fund are guided by the judgment of what is called a "prudent man" in seeking to determine which investments are proper. Because a trustee is responsible for other people's money, it is necessary to make sure that the trustee takes the role seriously. To fulfill their responsibilities, trustees must act as reasonably prudent people to acquire and use the information that is pertinent to making investment decisions.

Third, ERISA establishes minimum vesting standards. For example, the law specifies that, after five years of employment, a plan participant is entitled to 25% of accrued pension benefits. The percentage of entitlement increases to 100% after 10 years. There are also other vesting requirements.

Finally, ERISA created the Pension Benefit Guaranty Corporation (PBGC) to insure vested pension benefits. The insurance program is funded from annual premiums that must be paid by pension plans.

Responsibility for administering ERISA is delegated to the Department of Labor and the Internal Revenue Service. To ensure that a pension plan is in compliance with ERISA, periodic reporting and disclosure statements must be filed with these government agencies. It is important to recognize that ERISA does not require that a corporation establish a pension plan. If a corporation does establish a defined-benefit plan, however, it must comply with the numerous and complex regulations set forth in ERISA.

MANAGERS OF PENSION FUNDS

A plan sponsor chooses one of the following to manage the defined-benefit pension assets under its control: (1) use in-house staff to manage all the pension assets itself, (2) distribute the pension assets to one or more money management firms to manage, or (3) combine alternatives (1) and (2). Public pension funds typically manage a good portion of their assets internally.

In the case of a defined-contribution pension plan, the plan sponsor typically allows participants to select how to allocate their contributions among funds managed by one or more fund groups.[1]

Insurance companies have been involved in the pension business through their issuance of GICs and annuities. Insurance companies also have subsidiaries that manage pension funds. The trust departments of commercial banks, affiliates of investment banks and broker/dealers, and independent money management firms (that is, firms that are not affiliated with an insurance company, bank, investment bank, or broker-dealer) also manage pension funds. Foreign entities are also permitted to participate in the management of pension funds. In fact, several foreign financial institutions have acquired interests in U.S. money management firms in order to enter the pension fund money management business.

Managers of pension fund money obtain their income from managing the assets by charging a fee. The annual fee can range from 0.75% of assets under management to as little as 0.01%. Some plan sponsors have entered into management fee contracts based on performance rather than according to a fixed percentage of assets under management.

In addition to money managers, advisors called plan sponsor *consultants* provide other advisory services to pension plan sponsors. Among the functions that consultants provide to plan sponsors are

- developing plan investment policy and asset allocation among the major asset classes
- providing actuarial advice (liability modeling and forecasting)
- designing benchmarks against which the fund's money managers will be measured
- measuring and monitoring the performance of the fund's money managers
- searching for and recommending money managers to pension plans
- providing specialized research

---

[1] Keith Ambachtsheer, Ronald Capelle, and Tom Scheibelhut, "Improving Pension Fund Performance," *Financial Analysts Journal* (November/December 1998), pp. 15 ff. Francis Gupta, Eric Stubbs, and Yogi Thambiah, "U.S. Corporate Pension Plans," *The Journal of Portfolio Management* (Summer 2000), pp. 65 ff.

Defined-Benefit Plan Crisis[2]

Today, the crisis facing defined-benefit pension plans threatens the solvency of corporations, cities, states, and even the U.S. government. The magnitude of pension underfunding suggests that it poses the greatest financial danger since the S&L crisis. At the end of 2003, corporations' pension underfunding or deficit (i.e., the amount by which the fair value of the liabilities exceeds the value of the assets) was close to $250 billion, officially. Other commentators estimate that if pension liabilities were assigned market values, as they properly should be, then the U.S. corporate pension deficit would probably be double that.[3] Nor does the pension crisis exist only for corporate defined-benefit plans. According to Wilshire Associates, the "official" deficit for state pension funds amounts to $94 billion. But here, too, if the liabilities were properly valued, the deficit would swell—to more than $1 trillion in the case of all state and local funds, according to estimates by Morgan Stanley.

In essence, corporate and public plan sponsors, abetted by regulators and accountants, have systematically underestimated pension liabilities, producing the crisis we find ourselves in today. At the root of the problem is the accounting and actuarial treatment of pensions, which can inspire perverse behavior by sponsors of corporate defined-benefit plans. In making pension-funding decisions, corporations have often failed to take into consideration the liability structure of the plan. (The liability structure is the amount and timing of the projected payments to be made to the plan beneficiaries.) Their primary concern, naturally, is with the impact on the earnings, and because pension contributions show up as an expense on the income statement, corporations seek to minimize or even eliminate them. Offsetting the pension cost is the assumed **return on pension assets** (**ROA**). And that is where the problem begins.

Generally accepted accounting principles (GAAP) allow corporations to forecast pension ROA a year in advance. If a corporation knows what its pension expense will be a year out, they can perform a simple calculation to determine what ROA it will need to forecast to wash out this troublesome expense. Even better, if management predicts an ROA that exceeds this pension-cost breakeven point, they could create pension "income" rather than expenses, resulting in enhanced earnings. Consequently, forecast ROA can lead to a distortion of economic value.

A 2002 study by Zion and Carcache of Credit Suisse First Boston estimated that if the companies included in the Standard & Poor's 500 index had replaced the ROA projections for their pension plans with the plans' actual performance, the companies' aggregate reported earnings would have declined 69% in 2001 and 10% in 2000.[4] That's amazing! Basically, if pension expenses were properly accounted for in 2001, aggregate reported earnings would have been only 31% of what was reported. In addition, Zion and Carcache found that for 14 industry groups and for 82 S&P 500 companies, 2001 earnings would have been halved; for nine of the 14 industry groups and 41 of those companies, earnings would have gone from a profit to a loss! Thirty of the S&P 500 companies would have seen their 2001 earnings reduced by more than $1 billion and seven would have experienced a drop of more than $5 billion.

---

[2] This section draws from Frank J. Fabozzi and Ronald J. Ryan, "Redefining Pension Plans," *Institutional Investor* (January 2005), pp. 84–89.

[3] Fabozzi and Ryan, "Redefining Pension Plans," p. 84.

[4] A 2002 study by Zion and Carcache of Credit Suisse First Boston, "The Magic of Pension Accounting," by Credit Suisse First Boston analysts David Zion and Bill Carcache.

Zion and Carcache further estimated that the aggregate return on equity for S&P 500 companies in 2001 would have been only 2%, rather than the 8% figure arrived at using GAAP. For 40 of the 360 S&P 500 companies with defined-benefit plans, 2001 return on equity would have gone from positive to zero or negative.

But there is a check on ROA-forecast abuses. Pension-accounting rules permit corporations to make rosy ROA predictions for stocks and most other assets, provided that external auditors validate those estimates on the basis of historical returns for those asset classes. The only exception is bonds, for which the forecast ROA is based on current yields to maturity, not historical returns. This begets further complications. Modest bond yields can undercut a pension's overall forecast ROA, threatening pension income and thus placing a potential drag on corporate earnings. No wonder companies continually reduced their bond allocations in the late 1990s and early 2000s as interest rates declined to historical lows. Concurrently, according to *Pension & Investments'* annual asset allocation survey, companies were allocating a bigger proportion of their pension portfolios to equities as well as to hedge funds and other alternative investments, whose historical returns, or subjective market values (in the case of private equity and real estate), justified higher ROA forecasts.

Starting in about 1990, the yield of 10-year Treasuries fell below 8%. Yet according to a 2003 study by Zion and Carcache, the median forecast ROA for the S&P 500 companies exceeded 9% for every year from the early 1990s until 2001, falling 8.75% in 2002 alone.[5] Hence, the assumed return on bonds was less than that of most companies' forecast ROA.

Pension funds that increased their bond allocations would just subject their other assets to more stress to rationalize their forecast ROA, giving them less wiggle room for earnings enhancement. Consultants soon ceased to promote bonds to pension funds in their asset allocation models. If anything, the gap between bond yields and forecast ROA has grown wider since 1990. The yield on 10-year Treasuries has ranged from 3.11% to 5.52% since 2000. By contrast, Zion and Carcache note that the median forecast ROA for the pension plans of S&P 500 companies was 8.75% for 2002, 9.20% for 2001, and 9.36% for 2000.

What happens if the actual ROA differs from the forecast one? The difference gets amortized, usually over the life of the pension plan—typically, 15 years. The accountants' label for this adjustment on the income statement is "actuarial gain/loss." An actuarial gain from pension income increases corporate earnings; an actuarial loss reduces corporate earnings. The accounting profession invented this smoothing exercise to accommodate companies worried about excessive earnings volatility, which alarms investors.

On the surface, this approach sounds perfectly reasonable. However, the actuarial gain/loss adjustment had been blown out of proportion by the gulf that developed between companies' forecast and actual ROAs. The declining stock market from 2000 to 2002 deserves much of the blame, but corporate sponsors' inclination to forecast overly optimistic ROAs is an important contributing factor.

Ryan and Fabozzi estimate, based on the typical asset allocation, that the average actual ROA for S&P 500 companies was −2.50% in 2000, −5.40% in 2001, and −1.41% in 2002.[6] This is quite a contrast to the forecast ROAs used by corporate sponsors. The impact of this

---

[5] Zion and Carcache, "The Magic of Pension Accounting, Part II."

[6] Ronald J. Ryan and Frank J. Fabozzi, "Pension Fund Crisis Revealed," *Journal of Investing* (Fall 2003), pp. 43–48 and Ronald J. Ryan and Frank J. Fabozzi, "Rethinking Pension Liabilities and Asset Allocation," *Journal of Portfolio Management* (Summer 2002), pp. 7–15.

gap has been dramatic. In their 2003 study, Zion and Carcache showed that S&P 500 companies' cumulative unrecognized actuarial gains of $144 billion as of the end of 2000 had been transformed into a cumulative actuarial loss of $357 billion by the end of 2002. General Motors Corp. announced in the summer of 2003 that its cumulative actuarial loss amortization would cost the automaker $1.7 billion per year out of earnings for the next 20 years.

In selecting the discount rates, corporate sponsors of defined-benefit plans are concerned not only with the accounting implications but with Internal Revenue Service (IRS) regulations. Regulations by the IRS determine the actual amount of funding required (i.e., cash that must be paid into the fund). Corporate plan sponsors are inclined to employ as their discount rate for pension liabilities the highest interest rate that will pass muster with the IRS (for funding purposes) and also with their external accounting GAAP (for accounting purposes). (As explained in the next chapter, the higher the discount rate, the lower the present value.) Traditionally, GAAP accounting has relied on a corporate bond index that has numerous limitations.[7] Since the corporate bond index rate used is higher than the rate on U.S. Treasury securities, this means using a higher discount rate, resulting in a lower present value for the projected liabilities of the fund.

The bottom line is that the failure to properly value pension liabilities because of the use of an inappropriate discount rate and the impact it had on the allocation decision among major asset classes to justify a high forecast ROA were the two major contributing factors to this financial crisis.

The accounting profession has proposed a solution to rectify the accounting issue. With respect to funding, in April 2004, the Pension Funding Equity Act was passed. The purpose of the act was to give U.S. companies some "relief" from burdensome pension contributions and, as the act's summary stated, "protect the retirement benefits of millions of American workers and help ensure that their pension benefits will be there when they retire." The relief came in the form of a higher permissible discount rate, the critical number for valuing pension liabilities and therefore funding requirements. Under the applicable formula, a higher rate was permitted by the act. This permitted lower pension contributions. The formula for determining the appropriate discount rate under the act made little economic sense, although it was touted by high-level officials in the Treasury Department, as well as industry groups representing corporate sponsors of defined-benefit plans. The result is that the act was a short-term boon to companies, but, unfortunately, it solves none of the serious problems plaguing pension funding—and it may have created new ones. Corporations with defined-benefit plans will not be required to provide adequate information about the financial health of their pension plans. And critically, the act promotes reliance on the wrong standard for determining liabilities, guaranteeing that for private pension plans they will continue to be understated. Many companies no doubt felt that they needed relief from onerous pension contributions. But by permitting the incorrect valuation of pension liabilities to persist, Congress avoided the real issue.

---

[7] These limitations are explained in Fabozzi and Ryan, "Redefining Pension Plans."

PENSION PROTECTION ACT OF 2006

The **Pension Protection Act of 2006 (PPA)** contains two major parts. It provides significant changes in the operations of private pension plans and also extends some tax incentives for retirement savings.

The first part modifies ERISA, which provided the foundation of the current defined-benefit retirement system. The changes of this type in the PPA deal with the underfunding of these traditional retirement plans. The major changes, in general, were as follows:

* It required underfunded plans to pay additional premiums to the PBGC.
* It extended the requirement for companies terminating their pension plans to provide extra funding to the pension system.
* It closed loopholes that allowed underfunded plans to skip pension payments.
* It raised the caps on the amount that companies can contribute to their pension plans (which provide a tax shield) so they can contribute more during prosperous times.
* It required that companies measure their pension plan obligations more accurately.
* It prevented companies with underfunded pension plans from providing extra benefits to their workers without paying for these benefits up front.

While the protections for the employee provided by the PPA are obvious, some claim that the resulting restrictions and costs imposed on the plan sponsors may accelerate the decline in defined-benefit plans.

The second part of the PPA relates primarily to individuals' use of defined-contribution plans. Prior to the PPA, individuals did not optimize their retirement savings either because they did not enroll in their employers' 401(k) plan or they did not have a prudent asset allocation. According to the PPA, employers can automatically enroll their employees in a defined-contribution plan. In addition, before the PPA if the employee did not make an election on how to invest their funds, their funds were often invested in a money market account by the employer. The PPA permits employers to choose default options on behalf of the plan participants who do not make an election on how to invest their funds. The most common default option has been target-date funds. Of course, employees can still choose to opt out of the plan or choose their own investment options.

In addition, the PPA enables employees to obtain more investment advice for their employers by removing the fiduciary liability based on the perceived conflict of interest of self-interested investment advice provided by the employer. In doing so, the PPA provided employers with a safe harbor from certain parts of ERISA. According to the PPA, these employees can receive personalized investment advice from their employers, although with a few limitations.

The PPA also requires that defined-contribution plans must meet some diversification requirements with regard to employer stocks, thus addressing the common problem of employees being overconcentrated in their own company's stock.

There are also several other significant, but more narrow, elements of the PPA that are not covered in this chapter.

SUMMARY

A pension plan is a fund that is established by private employers, governments, or unions for the payment of retirement benefits. Pension plans have grown rapidly, largely because of favorable tax treatment. Qualified pension funds are exempt from federal income taxes, as are employer contributions. The two types of pension funds are defined-benefit plans and defined-contribution plans. In a defined-benefit plan, the sponsor agrees to make specified (or defined) payments to qualifying employees at retirement. In a defined-contribution plan, the sponsor is responsible only for making specified (or defined) contributions into the plan on behalf of qualifying employees but does not guarantee any specific amount at retirement. Recently, some hybrid plans blending features of both basic types of plans have appeared, the most prominent of which is the cash balance plan.

There is federal regulation of pension funds, as embodied in the ERISA. ERISA sets minimum standards for employer contributions, establishes rules of prudent management, and requires vesting in a specified period of time. Also, ERISA provides for insurance of vested benefits.

Pension funds are managed by the plan sponsor and/or by management firms hired by the sponsor. Management fees may reflect the amount of money being managed or the performance of the managers in achieving suitable rates of return for the funds. In addition, consulting firms provide assistance in the planning, administration, and evaluation of the funds.

KEY TERMS

- 401(k) plan
- Cash balance plan
- Defined-benefit plan
- Defined-contribution plan
- Employee Retirement Income Security Act of 1974 (ERISA)
- Hybrid pension plan
- Insured benefit plan
- Pension Benefit Guaranty Corporation (PBGC)
- Pension plan
- Pension plan sponsor
- Pension Protection Act of 2006 (PPA)
- Return on pension assets (ROA)

QUESTIONS

1. What is a plan sponsor?
2. How does a defined-benefit plan differ from a defined-contribution plan?
3. Why have some corporations frozen their defined-benefit plans?
4. **a.** What is a cash balance plan?
   b. Discuss the resemblance of a cash balance plan to a defined-benefit and a defined-contribution plan.
5. **a.** What is an insured pension plan?
   b. What is the function of PBGC?
6. What role do mutual funds play in 401(k) plans?
7. Can and do pension plans invest in foreign securities or tax-exempt securities?
8. **a.** What is the major legislation regulating pension funds?
   b. Does the legislation require every corporation to establish a pension fund?
9. Discuss ERISA's "prudent man" rule.
10. Who are plan sponsor consultants and what is their role?

11. In 2001, investor Warren Buffett had this to say about pension accounting:

> Unfortunately, the subject of pension [return] assumptions, critically important though it is, almost never comes up in corporate board meetings. . . . And now, of course, the need for discussion is paramount because these assumptions that are being made, with all eyes looking backward at the glories of the 1990s, are so extreme.

a. What does Mr. Buffett mean by the "pension return assumption"?

b. Why is the pension return assumption important in pension accounting in accordance with generally accepted accounting principles?

c. Why is the pension return assumption important in pension accounting in accordance with Internal Revenue rules?

d. Mr. Buffet went on to warn that too high an assumed return on pension assets risks litigation for a company's chief financial officer, its board, and its auditors. Why?

Properties and Pricing
of Financial Assets

From Chapter 9 of *Foundations of Financial Markets and Institutions*, 4/e. Frank J. Fabozzi. Franco Modigliani. Frank J. Jones.

Properties and Pricing of Financial Assets

LEARNING OBJECTIVES

After reading this chapter, you will understand

- the many key properties of financial assets: moneyness; divisibility and denomination; reversibility; cash flow and return; term to maturity; convertibility; currency; liquidity; return predictability or risk; complexity; and tax status

- the components of an asset's discount rate or required rate of return

- what is meant by a basis point

- how the discount rate is structured to encompass the components of an asset's risk

- the principles of valuing complex financial assets

- the inverse relationship between an asset's price and its discount rate

- the principles that reveal how the properties of an asset affect its value, either through the discount rate or through its expected cash flow

- what factors affect the price sensitivity of a financial asset to changes in interest rates

- what duration means, and how it is related to the price sensitivity of an asset to a change in interest rates

Financial assets have certain properties that determine or influence their attractiveness to different classes of investors and issuers. The chapter provides the basic principles of the valuation or pricing of financial assets and illustrates how several of the properties of financial assets affect their value. Because the valuation of financial assets requires an understanding of present value, this concept is explained in the appendix to this chapter available online at www.pearsonhighered.com/fabozzi.

PROPERTIES OF FINANCIAL ASSETS

The 11 properties of financial assets are (1) **moneyness**, (2) *divisibility and denomination*, (3) *reversibility*, (4) *cash flow*, (5) *term to maturity*, (6) *convertibility*, (7) *currency*, (8) *liquidity*, (9) *return predictability*, (10) *complexity*, and (11) *tax status.*[1]

Moneyness

Some financial assets are used as a medium of exchange or in settlement of transactions. These assets are called *money*. In the United States, money consists of currency and all forms of deposits that permit check writing. Other assets, although not money, are very close to money in that they can be transformed into money at little cost, delay, or risk. They are referred to as *near money*. In the case of the United States, these include time and savings deposits and a security issued by the U.S. government called a Treasury bill. Moneyness is clearly a desirable property for investors.

Divisibility and Denomination

Divisibility relates to the minimum size in which a financial asset can be liquidated and exchanged for money. The smaller the size, the more the financial asset is divisible. A financial asset such as a deposit is typically infinitely divisible (down to the penny), but other financial assets have varying degrees of divisibility depending on their denomination, which is the dollar value of the amount that each unit of the asset will pay at maturity. Thus, many bonds come in $1,000 denominations, commercial paper in $25,000 units, and certain types of certificates of deposit in $100,000 or more. In general, divisibility is desirable for investors but not for borrowers.

Reversibility

Reversibility refers to the cost of investing in a financial asset and then getting out of it and back into cash again. Consequently, reversibility is also referred to as **turnaround cost** or *round-trip cost.*

A financial asset such as a deposit at a bank is obviously highly reversible because usually there is no charge for adding to or withdrawing from it. Other transactions costs may be unavoidable, but these are small. For financial assets traded in organized markets or with **market makers**, the most relevant component of round-trip cost is the so-called **bid–ask spread**, to which might be added commissions and the time and cost, if any, of delivering the asset. The spread charged by a market maker varies sharply from one financial asset to another, reflecting primarily the amount of risk the market maker is assuming by "making" a market.

This market-making risk can be related to two main forces. One is the variability of the price as measured, say, by some measure of dispersion of the relative price over time. The greater the variability, the greater the probability of the market maker incurring a loss in excess of a stated bound between the time of buying and reselling the financial asset. The variability of prices differs widely across financial assets. Treasury bills, for example,

---

[1] Some of these properties are taken from James Tobin, "Properties of Assets," undated manuscript, Yale University, New Haven.

have a very stable price, for the reason explained at the end of this chapter, while a speculative stock will exhibit much larger short-run variations.

The second determining factor of the bid–ask spread charged by a market maker is what is commonly referred to as the **thickness of the market**: by this is meant essentially the prevailing rate at which buying and selling orders reach the market maker (that is, the frequency of transactions). A **thin market** is one that has few trades on a regular or continuing basis. Clearly, the greater the frequency of order flows, the shorter the time that the security will have to be held in the market maker's inventory, and hence the smaller the probability of an unfavorable price movement while held.

Thickness, too, varies from market to market. A three-month U.S. Treasury bill is easily the thickest market in the world. In contrast, trading in stock of small companies is not thick but thin. Because Treasury bills dominate other instruments both in price stability and thickness, their bid–ask spread tends to be the smallest in the market. A low turn-around cost is clearly a desirable property of a financial asset, and as a result thickness itself is a valuable property. This explains the potential advantage of larger over smaller markets (economies of scale), along with a market's tendency to standardize the instruments offered to the public.

Cash Flow

The return that an investor will realize by holding a financial asset depends on all the cash distributions that the financial asset will pay its owners; this includes dividends on shares and coupon payments on bonds. The return also considers the repayment of principal for a debt security and the expected sale price of a stock. In computing the expected return, noncash payments, such as stock dividends and options to purchase additional stock, or the distribution of other securities must also be accounted for.

In a world of nonnegligible inflation, it is also important to distinguish between **nominal expected return** and **real expected return**. The expected return that we described above is the nominal expected return. That is, it considers the dollars that are expected to be received, but does not adjust those dollars to take into consideration changes in their purchasing power. The net real expected return is the nominal expected return after adjustment for the loss of purchasing power of the financial asset as a result of anticipated inflation. For example, if the nominal expected return for a one-year investment of $1,000 is 6%, then at the end of one year the investor expects to realize $1,060, consisting of interest of $60 and the repayment of the $1,000 investment. However, if the inflation rate over the same period of time is 4%, then the purchasing power of $1,060 is only $1,019.23 ($1,060 divided by 1.04). Thus, the return in terms of purchasing power, or the real return, is 1.923%. In general, the expected real return can be approximated by subtracting the expected inflation rate from the expected nominal return. In our example, it is approximately 2% (6% to 4%).

Term to Maturity

Term to maturity is the length of the period until the date at which the instrument is scheduled to make its final payment, or the owner is entitled to demand liquidation. Instruments for which the creditor can ask for repayment at any time, such as checking accounts and many savings accounts, are called *demand instruments*. Maturity is an important characteristic of financial assets such as bonds, and can range from one day to a few decades. In the United Kingdom, there is one well-known type of bond that promises to pay a fixed amount per year indefinitely and not to repay the principal at any time; such an instrument is called a **perpetual**, or a *consul*. Many other instruments, including equities, have no maturity and are thus a form of perpetual.

It should be understood that even a financial asset with a stated maturity may terminate before its stated maturity. This may occur for several reasons, including bankruptcy or reorganization, or because of **call provisions** entitling the debtor to repay in advance, usually at some penalty and only after a number of years from the time of issuance. Sometimes the investor may have the privilege of asking for early repayment. This feature is called a **put option**. Some assets have maturities that may be increased or extended at the discretion of the issuer or the investor. For example, the French government issues a six-year *obligation renouvelable du Trésor*, which allows the investor, after the end of the third year, to switch into a new six-year debt. Similar bonds are issued by the British government. All these features regarding maturity are discussed in later chapters.

Convertibility

As the preceding discussion shows, an important property of some assets is that they are **convertible** into other assets. In some cases, the conversion takes place within one class of assets, as when a bond is converted into another bond. In other situations, the conversion spans classes. For example, a corporate *convertible bond* is a bond that the bondholder can change into equity shares. Preferred stock may be convertible into common stock. It is important to note that the timing, costs, and conditions for conversion are clearly spelled out in the legal descriptions of the convertible security at the time it is issued.

Currency

We have noted throughout our discussion that the global financial system has become increasingly integrated. In light of the freely floating and often volatile exchange rates among the major currencies, this fact gives added importance to the currency in which the financial asset will make cash flow payments. Most financial assets are denominated in one currency, such as U.S. dollars or yen or euros, and investors must choose them with that feature in mind.

Some issuers, responding to investors' wishes to reduce **currency** risk, have issued *dual-currency securities*. For example, some Eurobonds pay interest in one currency but principal or redemption value in a second. U.S. dollars and yen are commonly paired in these cases. Furthermore, some Eurobonds carry a currency option that allows the investor to specify that payments of either interest or principal be made in either one of two major currencies.

Liquidity

This is an important and widely used notion, although there is at present no uniformly accepted definition of liquidity. A useful way to think of liquidity and illiquidity, proposed by Professor James Tobin,[2] is in terms of how much sellers stand to lose if they wish to sell immediately as against engaging in a costly and time-consuming search.

An example of a quite illiquid financial asset is the stock of a small corporation or the bond issued by a small school district. The market for such a security is extremely thin, and one must search for one of a very few suitable buyers. Less suitable buyers, including speculators and market makers, may be located more promptly, but they will have to be enticed to invest in the illiquid financial asset by an appropriate discount in price.

For many other financial assets, liquidity is determined by contractual arrangements. Ordinary deposits, for example, are perfectly liquid because the bank has a contractual obligation to convert them at par on demand. Financial contracts representing a claim on a private pension fund may be regarded on the other hand as totally illiquid because these can be cashed only at retirement.

Liquidity may depend not only on the financial asset but also on the quantity one wishes to sell (or buy). Although a small quantity may be quite liquid, a large lot may run into illiquidity problems. Note that liquidity is again closely related to whether a market is thick or thin. Thinness always has the effect of increasing the turnaround cost, even of a liquid financial asset. But beyond some point, thinness becomes an obstacle to the formation of a market, and it has a direct effect on the illiquidity of the financial asset.

Return Predictability

Return **predictability** is a basic property of financial assets, in that it is a major determinant of their value. Assuming investors are risk averse, the riskiness of an asset can be equated with the uncertainty or unpredictability of its return. But whatever measure of volatility is used,[3] it is obvious that volatility varies greatly across financial assets. There are several reasons for this.

First, as illustrated later in this chapter, the value of a financial asset depends on the cash flow expected and on the interest rate used to discount this cash flow. Hence, volatility will be a consequence of the uncertainty about future interest rates and future cash flow. Now the future cash flow may be contractual, in which case the sole source of its uncertainty is the reliability of the debtor with regard to fulfilling the obligation. The cash flow may be in the nature of a residual equity claim, as is the case for the payments generated by the equity of a corporation. The cash flows from U.S. government securities are the only cash flows generally regarded as altogether riskless. Corporate debt and corporate stock cash flows are generally riskier than cash flows of U.S. government securities. Corporate equities represent a wide range of risk, from public utilities to highly speculative issues.

---

[2] Tobin, "Properties of Assets."

[3] Proxy measures for volatility include the standard deviation of expected returns or the range within which the outcome can be expected to fall with some stated probability.

As for a change in interest rates, it will in principle affect all prices in the opposite direction, but the effect is much larger in the case of the price of a financial asset with a long maturity than one with a short remaining life, as illustrated later in this chapter. Thus, on this account also, short-term U.S. government securities such as Treasury bills tend to be the safest assets, except for cash (if properly insured). For individual stocks the interest effect is generally swamped by cash flow uncertainty, although movements in interest rates have the characteristic of affecting all stocks in the same direction, while change in expected cash flow is largely dependent on a firm's particular financial situation. In general, uncertainty about returns and future prices can be expected to increase as the investment horizon lengthens.

What has been said so far relates to the predictability of nominal returns, although the relevant measure, of course, is real returns—returns corrected for gains or losses of purchasing power attributable to inflation. Of course, if inflation is absent or small, the determinants of real and nominal uncertainty and risk coincide. But in the presence of highly unpredictable inflation (which is usually the case with high inflation), real returns may be drastically harder to predict than nominal returns.

Complexity

Some financial assets are complex in the sense that they are actually combinations of two or more simpler assets. To find the true value of such an asset, one must break it down into its component parts and price each separately. The sum of those prices is the value of the complex asset. A good example of a complex asset is the **callable bond,** that is, a bond whose issuer is entitled to repay the debt prior to the maturity date. When investors buy such a bond, they in effect buy a bond and sell to the issuer an option that allows the issuer to redeem the bond at a set price prior to the issue's scheduled maturity. The correct or true price of a callable bond, therefore, is equal to the price of a similar noncallable bond less the value of the issuer's right to retire the bond early.

A complex asset may be viewed as a bundle or package of cash flows and options belonging to either the issuer or the holder, or both. Other examples of a complex asset include a convertible bond, a bond that has payments that can be made in a different currency at the option of the bondholder, and a bond that can be sold back to the issuer at a fixed price (that is, a **putable bond**).

In some cases, the degree of complexity is large: Many convertible bonds are also callable, and some bonds give their issuers the right either to extend the asset's maturity or to redeem it early. Also, some Japanese firms have issued bonds that are convertible into Japanese stock (denominated in yen, of course) but that are sold for, and make coupon and principal payments in, another currency, such as U.S. dollars.

Tax Status

An important feature of any asset is its **tax status**. Governmental regulations for taxing the income from the ownership or sale of financial assets vary widely, if not wildly. Tax rates differ from year to year, from country to country, and even among municipal units within a country (as with state and local taxes in the United States). Moreover, tax rates may differ from financial asset to financial asset, depending on the type of issuer, the length of time the asset is held, the nature of the owner, and so on. For example, in the United States, pension funds are exempt from income taxes, and coupon payments on municipal bonds are generally free of taxation by the federal government.

Key Points That You Should Understand Before Proceeding

1. A financial asset has many properties, and each affects the asset's value in a distinctive and important way.
2. Some properties are intrinsic to the asset, such as its maturity or promised cash flow.
3. Other properties are features of the market for the asset, such as the costs of trading the asset.
4. Still other properties reflect decisions by government about the asset's tax status.
5. A complex asset is one that provides options for the issuer or the investor, or both, and so represents a combination of simpler assets.

PRINCIPLES OF PRICING OF FINANCIAL ASSETS

The fundamental principle of finance is that the true or correct price of an asset equals the **present value** of all cash flows that the owner of the asset expects to receive during its life. In general, the correct price for a financial asset can be expressed as follows:

$$P = \frac{CF_1}{(1 + r)^1} + \frac{CF_2}{(1 + r)^2} + \frac{CF_3}{(1 + r)^3} + \ldots + \frac{CF_N}{(1 + r)^N}$$

where

$P =$ the price of the financial asset
$CF_t =$ the cash flow in year t $(t = 1, \ldots, N)$
$N =$ maturity of the financial asset
$r =$ appropriate discount rate

The Appropriate Discount Rate

The appropriate **discount rate**, r, is the return that the market or the consensus of investors requires on the asset. A convenient (but approximate) expression for the appropriate discount rate is this:

$$r = RR + IP + DP + MP + LP + EP$$

where

RR = the real rate of interest, which is the reward for not consuming and for lending to other users
IP = the inflation premium, which is the compensation for the expected decline in the purchasing power of the money lent to borrowers
DP = the default risk premium, which is the reward for taking on the risk of default in the case of a loan or bond or the risk of loss of principal for other assets
MP = the maturity premium, which is the compensation for lending money for long periods of time
LP = the liquidity premium, which is the reward for investing in an asset that may not be readily converted to cash at a fair market value

EP = the **exchange-rate risk premium**, which is the reward for investing in an asset that is not denominated in the investor's home currency.

Obviously, the price of an asset is inversely related to its discount rate: If the discount rate rises, the price falls; and if the rate declines, the price increases.

Illustration

Let us construct a simple example to illustrate the pricing of a financial asset. We can then use the hypothetical financial asset to illustrate some of the properties explained earlier in this chapter.

Suppose a bond has a maturity of four years and pays annual interest of $50 at the end of each year plus a principal of $1,000 at the conclusion of the fourth year. Since this bond pays $50 per $1,000 of principal, the periodic coupon rate is 5%. This rate is commonly and simply referred to as the **coupon rate**. Thus, using the previous notation,

$$N = 4 \quad CF_1 = \$50 \quad CF_2 = \$50 \quad CF_3 = \$50 \quad CF_N = \$1,050$$

Furthermore, assume that the market thinks the real rate is 2.5%, the inflation premium is 3%, the bond's default risk justifies a premium of 2%, the maturity premium is 0.5%, and the liquidity premium is 1%. Since the cash flows are denominated in U.S. dollars, the foreign-exchange rate premium is zero. That is,

$$RR = 2.5\% \quad IP = 3.0\% \quad DP = 2.0\% \quad MP = 0.5\% \quad LP = 1.0\% \quad EP = 0\%$$

Thus, we have this value for the discount rate:

$$r = 2.5\% + 3.0\% + 2.0\% + 0.5\% + 1.0\% + 0\% = 9.0\% \text{ or } 0.09$$

Using the formula for price, the price of this bond is

$$P = \frac{\$50}{(1.09)^1} + \frac{\$50}{(1.09)^2} + \frac{\$50}{(1.09)^3} + \frac{\$1,050}{(1.09)^4}$$
$$= \$870.41$$

Price and Asset Properties

We can use this hypothetical financial asset to illustrate the effect of some of the properties of financial assets on price or asset value. First, it should be clear that the price of a financial asset changes as the appropriate discount rate, r, changes. More specifically, the price changes in the opposite direction to the change in the appropriate discount rate. An illustration of this principle appears in Table 1, which shows the price of our hypothetical financial asset for various discount rates.

Let's look at how reversibility affects an asset's value. Suppose a **broker's commission** of $35 is imposed by brokers to buy or sell the bond. The price of the four-year bond is then

$$P = -\$35 + \frac{\$50}{(1.09)^1} + \frac{\$50}{(1.09)^2} + \frac{\$50}{(1.09)^3} + \frac{\$1,050 - \$35}{(1.09)^4}$$
$$= \$810.62$$

Notice that the initial commission of $35 is subtracted on an undiscounted basis because that payment is made at the time of purchase.

Table 1	**Price of a Four-Year Bond for Various Discount Rates**		
	Cash flow:		
$CF_1 = \$50$	$CF_2 = \$50$	$CF_3 = \$50$	$CF_4 = \$1,050$
Appropriate Discount Rate (%)			Price ($)
4			1,036.30
5			1,000.00
6			965.35
7			932.26
8			900.64
9			870.41
10			841.51
11			813.85
12			787.39
13			762.04
14			737.77

Suppose also a government entity imposes a transfer tax of $20 on each transaction. Because this rise in the cost of reversing an investment diminishes its reversibility to some extent, the present value of all cash flows associated with owning the bond now looks like this:

$$P = -\$35 - \$20 + \frac{\$50}{(1.09)^1} + \frac{\$50}{(1.09)^2} + \frac{\$50}{(1.09)^3} + \frac{\$1,050 - \$35 - \$20}{(1.09)^4}$$

$$= \$776.45$$

The change in price is significant and demonstrates why financial markets adjust so sharply (and rapidly) when governments impose restrictions on, or raise the cost of, capital market transactions.

To see how default risk affects the price of an asset, assume that, right before you bought the bond, a news story convinced investors that this bond is less risky than they had thought. So, the *default risk premium* falls from 2% to 1%, and the appropriate discount rate thus declines from 9% to 8%. Ignoring commissions and transfer fees, Table 1 shows that the price would increase from $870.41 to $900.64.

What about liquidity? Suppose immediately after the purchase of this bond, factors in the market for this bond cause its liquidity to decline. An investor buying this asset would plan for such a possibility by raising the liquidity premium. Assume that the liquidity premium increases from 1% to 3%. The appropriate discount rate then increases from 9% to 11%. Ignoring the commission and the transfer fee, Table 1 shows that the price would be $813.85. The fall in price, from the original $870.41 to $813.85, shows how important liquidity can be.

Now, let's tackle the notion of complexity by assuming that the bond is convertible into a fixed number of shares of common stock of the company that issued the bond. The price of our four-year bond would then be greater than $870.41 by an amount equal to the value that the market assigns to the right to convert the bond into common stock. For example, suppose we observe that the price of our hypothetical bond with the conversion privilege is $1,000.41. This means that the conversion privilege is valued by the market at $130.

The unresolved question is whether or not the $130 is a fair value for this conversion privilege. Valuation techniques to determine the fair value of any type of option such as a conversion privilege are available. For now, it is sufficient to understand why a knowledge of how to value an option is important. Because many financial assets have options embedded in them, failure to assess the options properly may lead to the mispricing of financial assets.

Now, let's turn our attention to currency. Suppose that this bond was issued by a German firm and that all payments are in euros. The cash flow in U.S. dollars that a U.S. investor will receive is uncertain because the dollar-euro exchange rate will fluctuate over the four years. Suppose that the market assigns an exchange premium of 3%. This means that the appropriate discount rate increases from 9% to 12% and the price would be $787.39 (see Table 1). To continue with the effect of currency risk, suppose that immediately after the purchase of this bond the market expects that the exchange rate between the U.S. dollar and the euro will become more volatile. The market will adjust for this by increasing the foreign currency risk premium, which, in turn, increases the appropriate discount rate and decreases the price.

It is easy to illustrate the impact of taxes. Suppose that our bond is granted a favorable tax treatment such that the interest and any capital gain from this bond would not be taxed. Suppose that the marginal tax rate on otherwise equivalent taxable bonds is 33.33% and the appropriate discount rate is 9%. This means that the after-tax discount rate would be approximately 6%, as shown below:

$$\text{Pretax discount rate} \times (1 - \text{marginal tax rate})$$
$$0.09 \times (1 - 0.3333) = 6\%$$

Since our hypothetical bond is free of taxes, the appropriate discount rate would be adjusted to compensate for this feature. The discount rate that would be used is 6%, because it is the equivalent of a 9% discount rate and a 33.33% marginal tax rate. From Table 1, we see that the price of the bond would be $965.35.

Continuing with the importance of tax features to the price of a financial asset, suppose that immediately after the purchase of this bond, the market comes to expect that the U.S. Congress will raise the marginal tax rate. This expectation would increase the value of the tax-exempt feature by decreasing the discount rate based on the anticipated rise in the marginal tax rate. The opposite would occur if the market came to expect that the U.S. Congress would lower the marginal tax rate.

Although we have used a single discount rate to discount each cash flow, there are theoretical reasons that suggest this is inappropriate. Specifically, we will look at the relationship between a bond's maturity and yield. In addition, we will see that a financial asset should be viewed as a package of cash flows. Each cash flow should be treated as if it is an individual asset with only one cash flow and that cash flow has its own discount rate that depends upon when it will be received. Consequently, a more general formula for pricing a financial asset would be

$$P = \frac{CF_1}{(1 + r_1)^1} + \frac{CF_2}{(1 + r_2)^2} + \frac{CF_3}{(1 + r_3)^3} + \cdots + \frac{CF_N}{(1 + r_N)^N}$$

where r_t is the discount rate appropriate for period t.

Key Points That You Should Understand Before Proceeding

1. An asset's price is the present value of its expected cash flows, discounted at an appropriate rate.
2. The appropriate discount rate for an asset's cash flows depends upon the properties of the asset.
3. The appropriate discount rate can often be approximated as the sum of rewards for the various risks an asset poses to its buyer.
4. The price of an asset moves in the opposite direction of a change in its discount rate.
5. The price of a complex asset is the sum of the prices of its component parts.

PRICE VOLATILITY OF FINANCIAL ASSETS

As Table 1 makes clear, a fundamental principle is that a financial asset's price changes in the opposite direction of the change in the required rate of return. We refer to the required rate of return as the *required* **yield**. This principle follows from the fact that the price of a financial asset is equal to the present value of its cash flow. An increase (decrease) in the yield required by investors decreases (increases) the present value of the cash flow and, therefore, the financial asset's price.

The price sensitivity of a financial asset to a change in the required yield will not be the same for all assets. For example, an increase in the required yield of one percentage point may result in a decline in one asset's price of 20%, but only 3% for another. In this section, we will see how the characteristics of a financial asset and the level of interest rates affect the price responsiveness of a financial asset to a change in the required yield. We also present a measure that can be used to gauge the approximate price sensitivity of a financial asset to changes in the required yield.

It is important to note that the analysis in this section applies fully and directly to bonds and other financial assets that have known expected cash flows and known expected maturities. An analysis of the price sensitivity of other major financial assets, such as preferred stock and common stock (which are perpetuals and have uncertain cash flows), must be postponed to a later chapter.

In our discussion, we will refer to changes in the required yield. It is convenient to measure a change in yield in terms of what market participants refer to as a **basis point** rather than in terms of a percentage change. One basis point is defined as 0.0001, or equivalently, 0.01%. Therefore, 100 basis points is equal to one percentage point, and a yield change from 9% to 10% represents a 100 basis point change in yield. A yield change from 7% to 7.5% is a 50 basis point change, and a yield change from 6% to 8.35% is a 235 basis point change in yield.

The Effect of Maturity

An asset's maturity is a factor that affects its price sensitivity to a change in yield. In fact, a bond's price sensitivity to a change in the discount rate is positively related to the bond's maturity. Consider the case of two bonds that have the same coupon rate and the same required yield but different maturities. If the required rate were to change, the price sensitivity of the bond with the longer maturity would be greater than that of the bond with the shorter maturity.

An illustration of this link between maturity and price change appears in Table 2, which shows the price of a bond that pays $50 annually and $1,000 at maturity—a 5% coupon rate—for various maturities and discount rates. Table 3, which is based on Table 2, shows the differences across maturities in a bond's dollar price decline and percentage price decline for an increase in the discount rate of 100 basis points. For example, if the discount rate rises from 9% to 10%, the price of a four-year bond falls from $870.41 to $841.51, which represents a price decline of $28.90 and a percentage price decline of 3.32%. In contrast, a similar rise in the discount rate causes the price of a 20-year bond to fall considerably more, from $634.86 to $574.32, which represents a price decline of $60.54 and a percentage price decline of 9.54%.

The Effect of the Coupon Rate

A bond's coupon rate also affects its price sensitivity. More specifically, for two bonds with the same maturity and with the same required yield, the lower the coupon rate, the greater the price responsiveness for a given change in the required yield.

To illustrate this, consider a 5% coupon bond and a 10% coupon bond, each of which has a maturity of 15 years and a principal of $1,000. If the required yield for both bonds is 9%, the price of the 5% coupon bond would be $677.57, and the price of the 10% coupon bond would be $1,080.61. If the required yield increases by 100 basis points, from 9% to 10%, the price of the 5% coupon bond will fall to $619.70, while the price of the 10% coupon bond would fall to $1,000. Thus, the 5% coupon bond's price declines by $57.87 or 8.5% ($57.87/$677.57), while the 10% coupon bond's price declines by $80.61 or by 7.5% ($80.61/$1,080.61). Although the dollar price change is greater for the higher-coupon bond, the percentage price change is less.

A special type of bond, one with no coupon rate, is called a **zero-coupon bond**. The investor who purchases a zero-coupon bond receives no periodic interest payment. Instead, the investor purchases the bond at a price below its principal and receives the principal at the maturity date. The difference between the principal and the price at

Table 2 **Price of a Bond Paying $50 Annually and $1,000 at Maturity for Various Discount Rates and Maturities**

Discount Rate (%)	Number of years to maturity			
	4	10	15	20
4%	$1,036.30	$1,081.11	$1,111.18	$1,135.90
5	1,000.00	1,000.00	1,000.00	1,000.00
6	965.35	926.40	902.88	885.30
7	932.26	859.53	817.84	788.12
8	900.64	798.70	743.22	705.46
9	870.41	743.29	677.57	634.86
10	841.51	692.77	619.70	574.32
11	813.85	646.65	568.55	522.20
12	787.39	604.48	523.24	477.14
13	762.04	565.90	483.01	438.02
14	737.77	530.55	447.20	403.92

Table 3   Price Decline if the Discount Rate Increases 100 Basis Points for a Bond Paying $50 Annually and $1,000 at Maturity for Various Discount Rates and Maturities

Price Change				
	Number of years to maturity			
Discount Rate Changes from	4	10	15	20
4% to 5%	−$36.30	−$81.11	−$111.18	−$135.91
5 to 6	−34.65	−73.60	−97.20	−114.70
6 to 7	−33.09	−66.87	−85.04	−97.18
7 to 8	−31.62	−60.83	−74.62	−82.66
8 to 9	−30.23	−55.41	−65.65	−70.60
9 to 10	−28.90	−50.52	−57.87	−60.54
10 to 11	−27.66	−46.12	−51.15	−52.12
11 to 12	−26.40	−42.17	−45.13	−45.06
12 to 13	−25.35	−38.58	−40.23	−39.12
13 to 14	−24.27	−35.35	−35.81	−34.12

Percentage Price Change				
	Number of years to maturity			
Discount Rate Changes from	4	10	15	20
4% to 5%	−3.50%	−7.50%	−10.01%	−11.96%
5 to 6	−3.47	−7.36	−9.71	−11.47
6 to 7	−3.43	−7.22	−9.42	−10.98
7 to 8	−3.39	−7.08	−9.12	−10.49
8 to 9	−3.36	−6.94	−8.83	−10.01
9 to 10	−3.32	−6.80	−8.54	−9.54
10 to 11	−3.29	−6.66	−8.25	−9.08
11 to 12	−3.25	−6.52	−7.97	−8.63
12 to 13	−3.22	−6.38	−7.69	−8.20
13 to 14	−3.18	−6.25	−7.41	−7.79

which the zero-coupon bond is purchased represents interest earned by the investor over the bond's life. For example, consider a zero-coupon bond with a principal of $1,000 and a maturity of 15 years. If the required yield is 9%, the price of this bond would be $274.54.[4] The difference between the principal of $1,000 and the price of $274.54 is the interest that the investor realizes at the maturity date.

A zero-coupon bond will have greater price sensitivity than a bond with a coupon rate selling at the same required yield and with the same maturity. For example, consider once again the 15-year zero-coupon bond. If the required yield increases from 9% to 10%, the price of this bond would fall to $239.39, a percentage price decline of 12.8% ($35.15/$274.54). This percentage change is greater than the declines in price for the 15-year maturity 5% coupon and 15-year 10% coupon bonds.

---

[4] The price is the present value of $1,000 15 years from now discounted at 9%.

The Effect of the Level of Yields

Tables 2 and 3 also bring out another interesting property about asset prices. Notice that, for a given maturity, the dollar price change and the percentage price change are higher for the lower initial discount rates than at the higher initial discount rates. For example, consider the 15-year bond when the discount rate is 5%. The price of the bond falls from $1,000 to $902.88 when the discount rate increases from 5% to 6%, a price decline of $97.20 and a percentage price decline of 9.72%. In contrast, a rise in the discount rate of 100 basis points from 13% to 14% reduces the same bond's price by $35.81 (from $483.01 to $447.20) and by the percentage of 7.41%.

The implication is that the lower the level of yields, the greater the effect a change in interest rates will have on the price of a financial asset.

Measuring Price Sensitivity to Interest Rate Changes: Duration

From our discussion thus far, we see that three factors affect the price sensitivity of an asset to changes in interest rates: the maturity, the coupon rate, and the level of interest rates. In managing the price sensitivity of a portfolio, market participants seek a measure of the sensitivity of assets to interest rate changes that encompasses all three factors.

A useful way to approximate an asset's price sensitivity to interest rate changes is to examine how the price changes if the yield changes by a small number of basis points. To do this, we will use the following notation:

$\Delta y =$ change in yield (in decimal)
$P_0 =$ initial price of the asset
$P_- =$ asset's price if the yield is decreased by Δy
$P_+ =$ asset's price if the yield is increased by Δy

Then, for a small decrease in yield, the percentage price change is

$$\frac{P_- - P_0}{P_0}$$

The percentage price change per basis point change is found by dividing the percentage price change by the number of basis points (Δy times 100). That is,

$$\frac{P_- - P_0}{P_0(\Delta y)100}$$

Similarly, the percentage price change per basis point increase in yield is

$$\frac{P_0 - P_+}{P_0(\Delta y)100}$$

The percentage price change for an increase and decrease in interest rates will not be the same. Consequently, the average percentage price change per basis point change in yield can be calculated. This is done as follows:

$$\frac{1}{2}\left[\frac{P_- - P_0}{P_0(\Delta y)100} + \frac{P_0 - P_+}{P_0(\Delta y)100}\right]$$

or equivalently,

$$\frac{P_- - P_+}{2P_0(\Delta y)100}$$

The approximate percentage price change for a 100 basis point change in yield is found by multiplying the previous formula by 100:

$$\frac{P_- - P_+}{2P_0(\Delta y)}$$

For example, the price of a 5% coupon bond with a principal of $1,000 and a maturity of 15 years is $677.57. If the yield is increased by 50 basis points from 9% to 9.5%, the price would be $647.73. If the yield is decreased by 50 basis points from 9% to 8.5%, the price would be $709.35. Then, we have these values:

$\Delta y = 0.005$
$P_0 = \$677.57$
$P_- = \$709.35$
$P_+ = \$647.73$

The application of the foregoing formula provides this number:

$$\frac{\$709.35 - \$647.73}{2(\$677.57)(0.005)} = 9.09$$

This measure of price sensitivity is popularly referred to as **duration**. Table 4 shows how the duration is determined for a 5% coupon bond with different maturities when the interest rate is initially at 9%.

Table 5 shows the duration for three coupon bonds with different maturities, under the assumption of different initial yields. As can be seen from this table, the relative magnitude of duration is consistent with the properties we described earlier. Specifically, (1) for bonds with the same coupon rate and the same yield, the longer the maturity the greater the duration; (2) for bonds with the same maturity and at the same yield, the lower the coupon rate the greater the duration; and (3) the lower the initial yield, the greater the duration for a given bond. Thus, duration picks up the effect of all three factors: maturity, coupon rate, and initial level of yield.

Duration is related to the price sensitivity as follows:

Approximate percentage change in a financial asset's price =
$-$ Duration $\times$ (Yield change in decimal form) $\times$ 100

Table 4   Determination of Duration for a 5% Coupon Bond with a Principal of $1,000 and an Initial Required Yield of 9%

	Number of years to maturity			
	4	10	15	20
Price at 9% (P_0)	870.41	743.29	677.57	634.86
Price at 9.5% (P_+)	855.80	717.45	647.73	603.44
Price at 8.5% (P_-)	885.35	770.35	709.35	668.78
Duration	3.40	7.12	9.09	10.29

$$\text{Duration} = \frac{P_- - P_+}{2(P_0)(0.005)}$$

Properties and Pricing of Financial Assets

Table 5 Duration for Various Bonds by Maturity, Coupon Rate, and Yield Level

Coupon Rate	Yield	Number of years to maturity			
		4	10	15	20
5%	5%	3.55	7.73	10.39	12.48
5	9	3.40	7.12	9.09	10.29
5	12	3.29	6.67	8.16	8.79
10	5	3.36	6.93	9.15	10.95
10	9	3.21	6.30	7.91	8.97
10	12	3.10	5.85	7.05	7.69
0	5	3.81	9.53	14.30	19.08
0	9	3.67	9.18	13.77	18.38
0	12	3.57	8.93	13.40	17.88

For example, suppose that the required yield on the 5% coupon, 15-year bond increases from 9% to 10% (0.01 in decimal form). Then, since this bond's duration is 9.09:

Approximate percentage change in price $= -9.09 \times (0.01) \times 100 = -9.09\%$

We showed earlier that the actual percentage change in price if the required yield increases from 9% to 10% would be a fall of 8.5%. Thus, duration is a close approximation of the percentage price change. The approximation is better for smaller changes in the required yield. For example, if the required yield changes by 20 basis points (0.002 in decimal form) from 9% to 9.20% rather than 100 basis points, then based on duration the approximate percentage change in price would be –1.82%. The actual price if the required yield increased by 20 basis points is $665.41, a decline of $12.16 from the price of $677.57 at 9%. The actual price change is therefore –1.79%(–$12.16/$677.57). Duration did an excellent job of approximating the percentage price change in this case.

In general, one can interpret duration as follows: *the approximate percentage change in price for a 100 basis point change in interest rates around the prevailing yield.* Duration does a good job of approximating the price change for a small change in yield on the order of 50 basis points in either direction. The larger the yield change, the poorer the approximation that duration provides.

Although we have developed duration in the context of bonds, we want to note that the basic principle applies equally to other financial assets. For example, consider a financial asset whose cash flow is as follows:

Year	Cash Flow
1	$ 30
2	75
3	120
4	140
5	200
6	250
7	300

Suppose that the appropriate discount rate is 7%. Then the price of this financial asset would be $794.31. If the yield is decreased by 50 basis points to 6.5%, the price would be $812.82. If the yield is increased by 50 basis points to 7.5%, the price would be $776.36. Thus, for this financial asset we know

$$\Delta y = 0.005$$
$$P_0 = \$794.31$$
$$P_- = \$812.82$$
$$P_+ = \$776.36$$

The duration is then 4.59, as follows:

$$\frac{\$812.82 - \$776.36}{2(\$794.31)(0.005)} = 4.59$$

Although we have focused on the price sensitivity of individual financial assets to changes in interest rates, we can extend the principle to a portfolio of financial assets. The duration of a portfolio of assets is simply the weighted average of the duration of the individual assets. The weight used for each asset is its market value in the portfolio.

Moreover, the principle can be extended to a liability stream. A liability can be viewed as a financial asset with a negative cash flow. The present value of the cash outlays is equal to the value or price of the liability stream. When interest rates change, the value of the liability stream changes. A duration for a liability stream can be calculated in the same way as the duration of a financial asset.

Importance of Measuring Price Sensitivity to Interest Rate Changes

The importance of being able to measure the sensitivity of an individual asset, a portfolio of assets, and a liability cannot be overemphasized. To control interest rate risk, it is necessary to be able to measure it. An investor with a portfolio of assets wants to be able to measure her exposure to interest rate changes in order to assess whether or not the exposure is acceptable. If it is not, she can alter the exposure. Various instruments that we describe later in this book provide a means for doing so. Financial institutions manage assets against liabilities. The interest rate risk exposure of a financial institution is the difference between the duration of its assets and the duration of its liabilities.

From our discussion, it may seem simple to calculate the duration of an asset. Unfortunately, this is not the case. The reason is that for most assets, the cash flow can change when interest rates change. In our illustrations, we have assumed that when interest rates change, the cash flows are unchanged. However, as we describe the various financial instruments in later chapters, we will see that as interest rates change either the issuer or the investor can alter the cash flow. Consequently, if a change in the cash flow is not considered when interest rates change, the duration calculation can be misleading.

When a duration is calculated under the assumption that the cash flows do not change when interest rates change, the resulting duration is called **modified duration**. In contrast, a duration calculated assuming that the cash flow changes when interest rates change is called **effective duration**. The difference between modified duration and effective duration for some assets can be quite dramatic. For example, with some of the more complex financial instruments discussed later in this book, the modified duration could be four while the effective duration could be 25! This means that an investor might believe that the price of the asset will change by approximately 4% for a 100 basis point change in interest rates (modified duration) when, in fact, it would change by approximately 25% for a 100 basis point change in interest rates (effective duration).

Macaulay Duration

The term *duration* was first used in 1938 by Frederick Macaulay as a measure of the weighted average time to maturity of a bond.[5] It can be shown that the measure Macaulay developed is related to the price sensitivity of a bond to interest rate changes. Unfortunately, too many market participants interpret duration as some measure of average life instead of a measure of price sensitivity to interest rate changes. This misinterpretation has been a key factor in several financial blunders. For example, for some complex financial assets, the effective duration is greater than the **Macaulay duration**. Market participants who interpret duration as a measure of the average life of an asset find this difficult to believe.

Consequently, when you hear the term *duration* used, interpret it as a measure of price sensitivity to rate changes, not some measure of the asset's average life. In addition, understand what type of duration measure is being used, effective duration or modified duration. Effective duration is the appropriate measure. Finally, if someone thinks that Macaulay duration means something for managing a portfolio or the asset/liability position of a financial institution, photocopy this page and tell them to review this discussion!

Key Points That You Should Understand Before Proceeding

1. Assets have different degrees of price sensitivity to a change in the discount rate or required yield.
2. Factors that influence an asset's price sensitivity include its maturity, its coupon rate, and the initial level of the required yield.
3. The longer an asset's maturity, the greater its price sensitivity to a change in the discount rate, other things being constant.
4. The larger an asset's coupon rate, the lower its price sensitivity to a change in the discount rate, if all else is the same.
5. The lower the initial discount rate, the greater the price sensitivity of most assets to a change in that rate.
6. Duration is a measure of price sensitivity that incorporates maturity, coupon, and level of yield; it provides an approximation of the percentage price change for small changes in yield.
7. It is important to be able to measure the price sensitivity of an asset or liability to interest rate changes, and the appropriate measure is the effective duration.

SUMMARY

In this chapter, we have introduced some key properties of financial assets: moneyness, divisibility and denomination, reversibility, cash flow, term to maturity, convertibility, currency, liquidity, return predictability or risk, complexity, and tax status. These properties,

---

[5] Frederick R. Macaulay, *Some Theoretical Problems Suggested by the Movements of Interest Rates, Bond Yields, and Stock Prices in the United States Since 1865* (New York: National Bureau of Economic Research, 1938).

which determine much of an asset's appeal and value to different classes of investors, are discussed in greater detail in later chapters. Furthermore, we have illustrated how various properties fit into the theory and practice of pricing assets. We presented a number of illustrations of the way to compute the prices of assets. The illustrations rely on the basic financial principle that price is the present value of expected future cash flows and that the discount rate contains rewards for accepting various features of the asset. Many properties, such as risk of default or term to maturity, influence prices through the required rate of return, which is inversely related to price. Other properties, such as reversibility and tax status, may affect the price of an asset through its expected cash flow.

Because it is so important to contemporary finance and to much of the material in this book, we decided that this first chapter on prices was the right place to introduce the concept of complexity in financial assets. Many assets contain rights, which are, in fact, options for issuers or investors to do something important with the assets. Options are valuable, and they affect the price of the assets that carry them. Later chapters provide extensive and detailed developments of the theme and notion of complexity.

The price of a financial asset will change in the opposite direction of the change in the discount rate or required yield. There are two characteristics of a financial asset that affect its price sensitivity: maturity and coupon rate (in the case of a bond). All other factors constant, the longer the maturity of a financial asset, the greater its price sensitivity to a change in the required yield. All other factors constant, the lower the coupon rate, the greater the price sensitivity to a change in the required yield. The level of interest rates or yields is another factor that affects price sensitivity to interest rate changes: the lower the yield level, the greater the price sensitivity.

Duration is a measure of the approximate price sensitivity of a financial asset to interest rate changes. In general, duration is the approximate percentage price sensitivity of a financial asset to a 100 basis point change in interest rates around some initial level of required yield.

KEY TERMS

- Basis point
- Bid–ask spread
- Broker's commission
- Call provision
- Callable bond
- Convertible
- Coupon rate
- Currency
- Default risk premium
- Discount rate
- Divisibility
- Duration
- Effective duration
- Exchange-rate risk premium
- Inflation premium
- Liquidity premium

- Macaulay duration
- Market maker
- Maturity premium
- Modified duration
- Moneyness
- Nominal expected return
- Perpetual
- Predictability
- Present value
- Put option
- Putable bond
- Real rate of interest
- Real expected return
- Reversibility
- Tax status
- Term to maturity

- Thickness of the market
- Thin market
- Turnaround cost

- Yield
- Zero-coupon bond

QUESTIONS

1. Your broker is recommending that you purchase U.S. government bonds. Here is the explanation: Listen, in these times of uncertainty, with many companies going bankrupt, it makes sense to play it safe and purchase long-term government bonds. They are issued by the U.S. government, so they are risk free.
How would you respond to the broker?

2. You just inherited 30,000 shares of a company you have never heard of, ABD Corporation. You call your broker to find out if you have finally struck it rich. After several minutes, she comes back on the telephone and says: "I don't have a clue about these shares. It's too bad they are not traded in a financial market. That would make life a lot easier for you." What does she mean by this?

3. Suppose you own a bond that pays $75 yearly in coupon interest and that is likely to be called in two years (because the firm has already announced that it will redeem the issue early). The call price will be $1,050. What is the price of your bond now, in the market, if the appropriate discount rate for this asset is 9%?

4. Your broker has advised you to buy shares of Hungry Boy Fast Foods, which has paid a dividend of $1.00 per year for 10 years and will (according to the broker) continue to do so for many years. The broker believes that the stock, which now has a price of $12, will be worth $25 per share in five years. You have good reason to think that the discount rate for this firm's stock is 22% per year, because that rate compensates the buyer for all pertinent risks. Is the stock's present price a good approximation of its true financial value?

5. You have been considering a zero-coupon bond, which pays no interest but will pay a principal of $1,000 at the end of five years. The price of the bond is now $712.99, and its required rate of

return is 7.0%. This morning's news contained a surprising development. The government announced that the rate of inflation appears to be 5.5% instead of the 4% that most people had been expecting. (Suppose most people had thought the real rate of interest was 3%.) What would be the price of the bond, once the market began to absorb this new information about inflation?

6. State the difference in basis points between each of the following:
   a. 5.5% and 6.5%
   b. 7% and 9%
   c. 6.4% and 7.8%
   d. 9.1% and 11.9%

7. a. Does a rise of 100 basis points in the discount rate change the price of a 20-year bond as much as it changes the price of a four-year bond, assuming that both bonds have the same coupon rate and offer the same yield?
   b. Does a rise of 100 basis points in the discount rate change the price of a 4% coupon bond as much as it changes the price of a 10% coupon bond, assuming that both bonds have the same maturity and offer the same yield?
   c. Does a rise of 100 basis points in the discount rate change the price of a 10-year bond to the same extent if the discount rate is 4% as it does if the discount rate is 12%?

8. During the early 1980s, interest rates for many long-term bonds were above 14%. In the early 1990s, rates on similar bonds were far lower. What do you think this dramatic decline in market interest rates means for the price volatility of bonds in response to a change in interest rates?

9. a. What is the cash flow of a 6% coupon bond that pays interest annually, matures in seven years, and has a principal of $1,000?

b. Assuming a discount rate of 8%, what is the price of this bond?

c. Assuming a discount rate of 8.5%, what is the price of this bond?

d. Assuming a discount rate of 7.5%, what is the price of this bond?

e. What is the duration of this bond, assuming that the price is the one you calculated in part (b)?

f. If the yield changes by 100 basis points, from 8% to 7%, by how much would you approximate the percentage price change to be using your estimate of duration in part (e)?

g. What is the actual percentage price change if the yield changes by 100 basis points?

10. Why is it important to be able to estimate the duration of a bond or bond portfolio?

11. Explain why you agree or disagree with the following statement: "Determining the duration of a financial asset is a simple process."

12. Explain why the effective duration is a more appropriate measure of a complex financial instrument's price sensitivity to interest rate changes than is modified duration.

The Level and Structure of Interest Rates

LEARNING OBJECTIVES

After reading this chapter, you will understand

- Fisher's classical approach to explaining the level of the interest rate

- the role in Fisher's theory of the saver's time preference and the borrowing firm's productivity of capital

- the meaning of equilibrium and how changes in the demand and supply function affect the equilibrium level of the interest rate

- the structure of Fisher's Law, which states that the nominal and observable interest rate is composed of two unobservable variables: the real rate of interest and the premium for expected inflation

- the loanable funds theory, which is an expansion of Fisher's theory

- the meaning of liquidity preference in Keynes's theory of the determination of interest rates

- how an increase in the money supply can affect the level of the interest rate through an impact on liquidity, income, and price expectations

- the features of a bond issue

- how the yield to maturity of a bond is calculated

- why historically the yields on securities issued by the U.S. Department of the Treasury have been used as the benchmark interest rates throughout the world

- the reason why the yields on U.S. Treasury securities are no longer as popular as benchmark interest rates and what alternative benchmarks are being considered by market participants

From Chapter 10 of *Foundations of Financial Markets and Institutions*, 4/e. Frank J. Fabozzi. Franco Modigliani. Frank J. Jones. Copyright © 2010 by Pearson Prentice Hall. All rights reserved.

- the different types of bonds

- what factors affect the yield spread between two bonds

- what the swap curve is and why it is used as an interest rate benchmark

In this chapter, we deal with two issues. The first is the theory of interest rate determination, and our discussion focuses on the general level of the interest rate in an economy. Second, we explain how interest rates function in the pricing of bonds. That explanation leads to consideration of the many different interest rates that an economy presents a borrower or an investor. We show how the rates are related to one another and to key features of bonds and economic conditions.

THE THEORY OF INTEREST RATES

An interest rate is the price paid by a borrower (or debtor) to a lender (or creditor) for the use of resources during some interval. The amount of the loan is the *principal*, and the price paid is typically expressed as a percentage of the principal per unit of time (generally, a year). In this section, we present the two most influential theories of the determination of the interest rate: **Fisher's theory of interest**, which underlies the loanable funds theory, and Keynes's **liquidity preference theory of interest**.

We focus first on the interest rate that provides the anchor for other rates, namely, the short-term, risk-free, real rate. By the *real rate*, we mean the rate that would prevail in the economy if the average prices for goods and services were expected to remain constant during the loan's life. By the *risk-free rate*, we mean the rate on a loan whose borrower will not default on any obligation. By *short-term*, we mean the rate on a loan that has one year to maturity. All other interest rates differ from this rate according to particular aspects of the loan, such as its maturity or risk of default, or because of the presence of inflation.

Fisher's Classical Approach

Irving Fisher analyzed the determination of the level of the interest rate in an economy by inquiring why people save (that is, why they do not consume all their resources) and why others borrow.[1] Here, we outline his theory in the context of a very simplified economy. That economy contains only individuals who consume and save with their current income, firms that borrow unconsumed income in loans and invest, a market where savers make loans of resources to borrowers, and projects in which firms invest. The interest rate on loans embodies no premium for default risk because borrowing firms are assumed to meet all obligations. (The prospect of inflation and its impact on the interest rate will be discussed in short order.)

Decisions on Saving and Borrowing

Saving is the choice between current and future consumption of goods and services. Individuals save some of their current income in order to be able to consume more in the future. A chief influence on the saving decision is the individual's **marginal rate of time preference**, which is the willingness to trade some consumption now for more future consumption. Individuals differ in their time preferences. Some people may have a rate of time preference

---

[1] Irving Fisher, *The Theory of Interest Rates* (New York: Macmillan, 1930).

that leads them to forgo current consumption for an increase of 10% in their future consumption, while others might save only if their future consumption possibilities rise by 20%.

Another influence on the saving decision is *income*. Generally, higher current income means the person will save more, although people with the same income may have different time preferences. The third variable affecting savings is the *reward for saving*, or the rate of interest on loans that savers make with their unconsumed income. Interest is what borrowers pay for the loans, and it makes greater future consumption possible. As the interest rate rises, each person becomes willing to save more, given that person's rate of time preference.

This description of the savings decision applies to all the people in the economy. The total savings (or the total supply of loans) available at any time is the sum of everybody's savings and a positive function of the interest rate. The relationship between total savings and the interest rate is graphed as the upward sloping supply function, *S*, in Figure 1, which relates the amount of savings/investment on the horizontal axis to the interest rate on the vertical axis.[2]

There can be no reward for savings if there is no demand for borrowed resources because someone must pay the interest. In our simple economy, firms do all the borrowing, and they borrow from savers in order to invest. Investment means directing resources to assets that will increase the firms' future capacity to produce. An important influence on the borrowing decision is the *gain from investment*, which is the positive difference between the resources used by a process and the total resources it will produce in the future. The gain is not constant, at any one time, across all possible projects and levels of total investment. The reason is that, at any time, only a certain number of projects are available, some offering high gains, others promising moderate gains, and still others yielding low gains. Firms will direct borrowed resources to projects in order of their profitability, starting with

Figure 1 Equilibrium in the Market for Savings

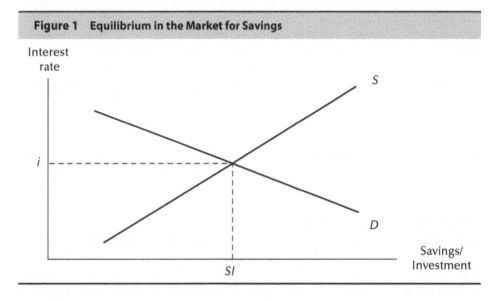

---

[2] For a more extensive analysis of the supply of savings, including the reason why the supply can reach negative levels and the reason why the supply curve can itself turn negative, see Frank J. Fabozzi and Franco Modigliani, *Capital Markets: Institutions and Instruments* (Englewood Cliffs, N.J.: Prentice Hall, 1992), pp. 338ff.

the most profitable and proceeding to those with lower gains. The gain from additional projects, as investment increases, is the **marginal productivity of capital**, which is negatively related to the amount of investment. In other words, as the amount of investment grows, additional gains necessarily fall, as more of the less profitable projects are accepted.

The maximum that a firm will invest depends on the *rate of interest*, which is the cost of loans. The firm will invest only as long as the marginal productivity of capital exceeds or equals the rate of interest. In other words, firms will accept only projects whose gain is not less than their cost of financing. Thus, the firm's demand for borrowing is negatively related to the interest rate. If the rate is high, only limited borrowing and investment make sense. At a low rate, more projects offer a profit, and the firm wants to borrow more. This negative relationship exists for each and all firms in the economy. The economy's total demand for borrowed resources (or loans of unconsumed income), as a function of the interest rate, appears as the downward-sloping line labeled D in Figure 1.

Equilibrium in the Market

The equilibrium rate of interest is determined by the interaction of the supply and demand functions. As a cost of borrowing and a reward for lending, the rate must reach the point where total supply of savings equals total demand for borrowing and investment. Figure 1 shows that this equilibrium rate of interest, labeled i, occurs at the intersection of the demand and supply curves, D and S. The equilibrium level of savings (which is the same as the equilibrium level of borrowing and investment) is given as SI. Clearly, Fisher's theory emphasizes that the long-run level of the interest rate and the amount of investment depend on a society's propensity to save and on technological development.

Let us now consider the effects of a sudden increase in technological capability, which makes production cheaper. With no change in any other relevant variable, lower production costs mean more gain on investments and a higher marginal productivity of capital. The resulting increase in firms' desired investment and borrowing through loans, at any level of the interest rate, is actually an upward shift in the demand function, as shown in Figure 2. That shift (from D to D^*) prompts a rise in the equilibrium interest rate, from i to i^*, and an increase in equilibrium borrowing and investment from SI to SI^*.

Now consider circumstances where individuals suddenly grow more willing to save, which amounts to a fall in the marginal rate of time preference. (All other economic considerations stay the same.) As Figure 3 depicts this change, the supply of loans function would shift downward (from S to S^*), and savings would be higher at every level of the interest rate. The equilibrium interest rate would also fall, from i to i^*. Total investment would rise, from SI to SI^*, as firms would get more funds and more projects would be profitable, at any interest rate.

The Real Rate and the Nominal Rate

It is useful here to consider the distinction between the **nominal rate of interest** and the **real rate of interest**. The real rate is the growth in the power to consume over the life of a loan. The nominal rate of interest, by contrast, is the number of monetary units to be paid per unit borrowed, and is, in fact, the observable market rate on a loan. In the absence of inflation, the nominal rate equals the real rate. Because we assume in our discussion that the purchasing power of the monetary units in a loan stays the same over the loan's life, the equilibrium interest rate we have discussed is both the nominal and the real rate of interest.

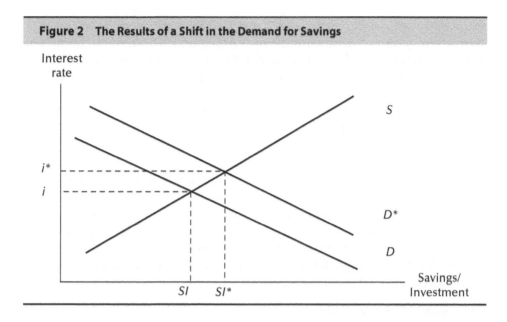

Figure 2 The Results of a Shift in the Demand for Savings

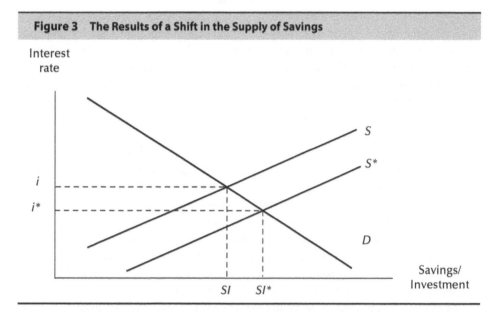

Figure 3 The Results of a Shift in the Supply of Savings

In the presence of inflation, however, the nominal rate is different from, and must exceed, the real rate. The reason is that savers demand a premium above the real rate as compensation for the expected loss in the purchasing power of their interest and principal. The relationship between inflation and interest rates is the well-known **Fisher's Law**, which can be expressed this way:

$$(1 + i) = (1 + r) \times (1 + p), \tag{1}$$

where i is the nominal rate, r is the real rate, and p is the expected percentage change in the price level of goods and services over the loan's life. Equation (1) shows that the nominal rate, i, reflects both the real rate and expected inflation. Also, the compensation demanded by savers applies to both the interest payment and the principal because the left-hand side variable is 100% plus the interest rate, or the full loan plus its interest.

Equation (1) can be simplified to a formula and, in most circumstances, approximates equation (1) closely enough:

$$i = r + p \qquad (2)$$

The only quantities from equation (1) not present in equation (2) are the values of 1, which cancel one another out, and the product of r and p, which is usually small enough to be ignored. For example, if the real rate is 3% or 0.03, and the expected inflation rate is 5% or 0.05, their product equals only 0.0015, or 0.15 of 1%. It is important to realize that the expected rate of inflation and the real rate are not observable. With fairly good estimates of expected inflation, p, it is possible to get a reasonable estimate of r from the nominal rate, but the precise value of the real rate must remain elusive.

The Loanable Funds Theory

Fisher's theory is a general one and obviously neglects certain practical matters, such as the power of the government (in concert with depository institutions) to create money and the government's often large demand for borrowed funds, which is frequently immune to the level of the interest rate. Also, Fisher's theory does not consider the possibility that individuals and firms might invest in cash balances. Expanding Fisher's theory to encompass these situations produces the **loanable funds theory of interest rates**.

This theory proposes that the general level of interest rates is determined by the complex interaction of two forces. The first is the total demand for funds by firms, governments, and households (or individuals), which carry out a variety of economic activities with those funds. This demand is negatively related to the interest rate (except for the government's demand, which may frequently not depend on the level of the interest rate). If income and other variables do not change, then an increase in the interest rate will reduce the demand for borrowing on the part of many firms and individuals, as projects become less profitable, and consumption and holding cash grow more costly. The second force affecting the level of the interest rate is the total supply of funds by firms, governments, banks, and individuals. Supply is positively related to the level of interest rates, if all other economic factors remain the same. With rising rates, firms and individuals save and lend more, and banks are more eager to extend more loans. (A rising interest rate probably does not significantly affect the government's supply of savings.)

In an equilibrium situation much like that depicted in Figure 1, the intersection of the supply and demand functions sets the interest rate level and the level of loans. In equilibrium, the demand for funds equals the supply of funds. This means that all agents are borrowing what they want, investing to the desired extent, and holding all the money they wish to hold. In other words, equilibrium extends through the money market, the bond market, and the market for investment assets.

As in Fisher's theory, shifts in the demand and supply curves may occur for many reasons: changes in the money supply, government deficits, changed preferences by individuals, new investment opportunities, and so on. These shifts affect the equilibrium level of the interest rate and of investment in predictable ways. Finally, the expectation of inflation can affect the equilibrium rate through the supply of funds curve, as savers demand higher rates (because of inflation) for any level of savings. Note that this analysis has excluded the question of default on loans: The rate discussed is the risk-free rate, either in its real or nominal form.

The Liquidity Preference Theory

The liquidity preference theory, originally developed by John Maynard Keynes,[3] analyzes the equilibrium level of the interest rate through the interaction of the supply of money and the public's aggregate demand for holding money. Keynes assumed that most people hold wealth in only two forms: "money" and "bonds." For Keynes, money is equivalent to currency and demand deposits, which pay little or no interest but are liquid and may be used for immediate transactions. Bonds represent a broad Keynesian category and include long-term, interest-paying financial assets that are not liquid and that pose some risk because their prices vary inversely with the interest rate level. Bonds may be liabilities of governments or firms. (Default risk is not considered here, and the rate is the risk-free rate, in real or nominal form.)

Demand, Supply, and Equilibrium

The public (consisting of individuals and firms) holds money for several reasons: ease of transactions, precaution against unexpected events, and speculation about possible rises in the interest rate. Although money pays no interest, the demand for money is a negative function of the interest rate. At a low rate, people hold a lot of money because they do not lose much interest by doing so and because the risk of a rise in rates (and a fall in the value of bonds) may be large. With a high interest rate, people desire to hold bonds rather than money, because the cost of liquidity is substantial in terms of lost interest payments and because a decline in the interest rate would lead to gains in the bonds' values. The negative linkage between the interest rate and the demand for money appears as curve *D* in Figure 4, which relates the interest rate to the amount of money in the economy, given the level of income and expected price inflation.

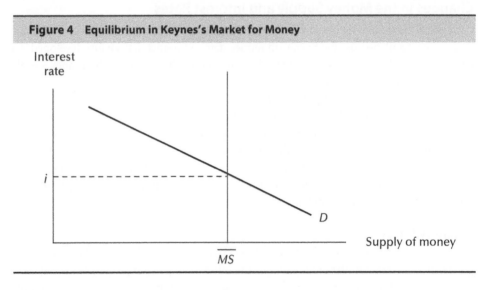

Figure 4   Equilibrium in Keynes's Market for Money

[3] John Maynard Keynes, *The General Theory of Employment, Interest and Money* (New York: Harcourt, Brace & World, 1936).

For Keynes, the supply of money is fully under the control of the central bank (which is the Fed in the United States). Moreover, the money supply is not affected by the level of the interest rate. (There is a positive link between the interest rate and the growth in the money supply.) Thus, the supply of money appears, in Figure 4, as the vertical line, $\overline{MS}$, and the line above the *MS* indicates a quantity not varying with the interest rate. Equilibrium in the money market requires, of course, that the total demand for money equals total supply. In Figure 4, equilibrium implies an interest rate of *i*. Furthermore, equilibrium in the money market implies the equilibrium of the bond market.

Shifts in the Rate of Interest

The equilibrium rate of interest can change if there is a change in any variable affecting the demand or supply curves. On the demand side, Keynes recognized the importance of two such variables: the level of income and the level of prices for goods and services. A rise in income (with no other variable changing) raises the value of money's liquidity and shifts the demand curve to the right, increasing the equilibrium interest rate. Because people want to hold amounts of "real money," or monetary units of specific purchasing power, a change in expected inflation would also shift the demand curve to the right and raise the level of interest.

The money supply curve can shift, in Keynes's view, only by actions of the central bank. The central bank's power over interest rates arises because of its ability to buy and sell securities (open market operations), which can alter the amount of money available in the economy. Generally, Keynes thought that an increase in the money supply would, by shifting the supply curve to the right, bring about a decline in the equilibrium interest rate. Similarly, he reasoned that a reduction in the money supply would raise rates. However, there is now widespread recognition that the question of linkage between the money supply and the level of the interest rate is rather more complex than that.

Changes in the Money Supply and Interest Rates

Changes in the money supply affect the level of interest rates. Now, we can discuss the matter in more detail, because the Keynesian money demand model that we just developed is a particularly useful framework for analyzing the relationship between the money supply and the level of the interest rate.

A change in the money supply has three different effects upon the level of the interest rate: the **liquidity effect**, the **income effect**, and the **price expectations effect**. These effects do not usually occur in a simultaneous manner but rather tend to be spread out over some time period following the change in the money supply. These effects move rates in different ways and to different extents. One effect may even cancel or overwhelm an earlier effect. The final magnitude and direction of the impact of a change in the money supply depends on the economy's level of output and employment.

Liquidity Effect

This effect represents the initial reaction of the interest rate to a change in the money supply. With an increase in the money supply, the initial reaction should be a fall in the rate. The reason for the fall is that a rise in the money supply represents a shift in the supply

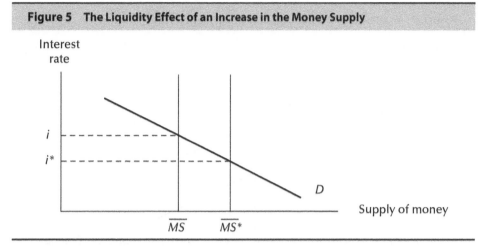

Figure 5 The Liquidity Effect of an Increase in the Money Supply

curve. For example, let us suppose that (in the United States) the Fed increases the supply of money by buying bonds, raising excess reserves, and allowing banks to offer more loans. With demand unchanging, the increase in the money supply amounts to a rightward shift of the supply and causes a fall in the equilibrium interest rate, from i to i^*. Figure 5 depicts the rise in the money supply (from $\overline{MS}$ to $\overline{MS^*}$) and the decline in the interest rate from i to i^*. (A decrease in the money supply would cause the supply of money function to shift to the left and the liquidity effect of an initial rise in the interest rate.)

Income Effect

It is well known that changes in the money supply affect the economy. A decline in the supply would tend to cause a contraction. An increase in the money supply, generally speaking, is economically expansionary: More loans are available and extended, more people are hired or work longer, and consumers and producers purchase more goods and services. Thus, money supply changes can cause income in the system to vary. Let us focus on an increase in the money supply, which raises income. Because the demand for money is a function of income, a rise in income shifts the demand function and increases the amount of money that the public will want to hold at any level of the interest rate. Figure 6 depicts the income effect by indicating that the shift of the demand function to the right, brought on by the increase in the money supply, causes a rise in the equilibrium interest rate.

No empirical data or economic theory can predict whether the income effect of a money supply increase will override its liquidity effect, or if so, after what interval of time. Under most circumstances, the income effect is likely to reverse some of the liquidity effect. But the relative magnitude of these two effects depends greatly on the state of the economy at the time the money supply changes.

Price Expectations Effect

Although an increase in the money supply is an economically expansionary policy, the resultant increase in income depends substantially on the amount of slack in the economy at the time of the Fed's action. If the economy is operating at less than full strength, an increase in the money supply can stimulate production, employment, and output; if the

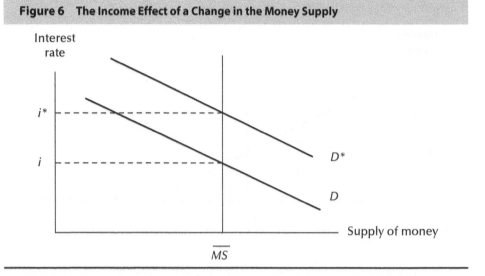

Figure 6   The Income Effect of a Change in the Money Supply

economy is producing all or almost all of the goods and services it can (given the size of the population and the amount of capital goods), then an increase in the money supply will largely stimulate expectations of a rising level of prices for goods and services. Thus, the price expectations effect usually occurs only if the money supply grows in a time of high output.

Because the price level (and expectations regarding its changes) affects the money demand function, the price expectations effect is an increase in the interest rate. That increase occurs because the demand for money balances shifts upward. This positive effect moves the interest rate in the same direction as the income effect, and in the opposite direction of the liquidity effect. (Of course, in a time of inflation, a reduction in the rate of growth in the money supply might dampen inflationary expectations and shift the demand curve to the left, leading to declines in the interest rate.)

There is no general guide to the relative size of the price expectations effect: It may be great enough to overwhelm the liquidity effect, or it may cancel only part of it. The magnitude of the income effect depends upon how much of the economy's productive capacity it is utilizing when the money supply rises.

Key Points That You Should Understand Before Proceeding

1. Interest is the price paid for the temporary use of resources, and the amount of a loan is its principal.
2. Fisher's theory of interest analyzes the equilibrium level of the interest rate as the result of the interaction of savers' willingness to save and borrowers' demand for investment funds.
3. In Fisher's terms, the interest rate reflects the interaction of the savers' marginal rate of time preference and borrowers' marginal productivity of capital.

4. Fisher's Law states that the observable nominal rate of interest is composed of two unobservable variables: the real rate of interest and the premium for expected inflation.

5. The loanable funds theory is an extension of Fisher's theory and proposes that the equilibrium rate of interest reflects the demand and supply of funds, which depend on savers' willingness to save, borrowers' expectations regarding the profitability of investing, and the government's action regarding money supply.

6. The liquidity preference theory is Keynes's view that the rate of interest is set in the market for money balances.

7. The demand for money, in this theory, reflects the liquidity of money by comparison with long-term financial instruments and depends on the interest rate, income, and the price level.

8. Changes in the money supply can affect the level of interest rates through the liquidity effect, the income effect, and the price expectations effect; their relative magnitudes depend upon the level of economic activity at the time of the change in the money supply.

THE DETERMINANTS OF THE STRUCTURE OF INTEREST RATES

There is not one interest rate in any economy. Rather, there is a structure of interest rates. The interest rate that a borrower will have to pay will depend on a myriad of factors. Although we describe these various factors in the process, we provide an overview of the fixed-income instruments. We begin with a basic description of a bond.

Features of a Bond

A bond is an instrument in which the issuer (debtor/borrower) promises to repay to the lender/investor the amount borrowed plus interest over some specified period of time. The **term to maturity** of a bond is the number of years during which the issuer has promised to meet the conditions of the obligation. The **maturity** of a bond refers to the day the debt will cease to exist and the day the issuer will redeem the bond by paying the amount owed. The practice in the bond market, however, is to refer to the *term to maturity* of a bond as simply its *maturity* or *term*. As we explain in the following text, there may be provisions that allow either the issuer or bondholder to alter a bond's term to maturity.

The **principal value** (or simply **principal**) of a bond is the amount that the issuer agrees to repay the bondholder at the maturity date. This amount is also referred to as the **par value, maturity value, redemption value**, or **face value**.

The *coupon rate* is the interest rate that the issuer agrees to pay each year. The annual amount of the interest payment made to owners during the term of the bond is called the *coupon*. The coupon rate when multiplied by the principal of the bond provides the dollar amount of the coupon. For example, a bond with an 8% coupon rate and a principal of $1,000 will pay annual interest of $80. In the United States and Japan, the usual practice is for the issuer to pay the coupon in two equal semiannual installments. In contrast, bonds issued in most European bond markets and the Eurobond market make coupon payments only once per year.

Yield on a Bond

The yield on a bond investment should reflect the coupon interest that will be earned plus either (1) any capital gain that will be realized from holding the bond to maturity, or (2) any capital loss that will be realized from holding the bond to maturity. For example, if a four-year bond with a coupon rate of 5% and a par value of $1,000 is selling for $900.64, the yield should reflect the coupon interest of $50 (5% times $1,000) every year plus the capital gain of $99.36 ($1,000 − $900.64) when the bond is redeemed at maturity. Moreover, the yield should also reflect the time value of money by considering the timing of the various payments associated with the bond.

The **yield to maturity** is a formal, widely accepted measure of the rate of return on a bond. As typically defined, the yield to maturity of a bond takes into account the coupon interest and any capital gain or loss, if the bond were to be held to maturity. The yield to maturity is defined as the interest rate that makes the present value of the cash flow of a bond equal to the bond's market price. In mathematical notation, the yield to maturity, y, is found by solving the following equation for y:

$$P = \frac{C}{(1 + y)^1} + \frac{C}{(1 + y)^2} + \frac{C}{(1 + y)^3} + \cdots + \frac{C + M}{(1 + y)^n}$$

where

P = market price of bond
C = coupon interest
M = maturity value
n = time to maturity

The yield to maturity is determined by a trial-and-error process. Even the algorithm in a calculator or computer program, which computes the yield to maturity (or internal rate of return) in an apparently direct way, uses a trial-and-error process. The steps in that process are as follows:

Step 1: Select an interest rate.
Step 2: Compute the present value of each cash flow using the interest rate selected in Step 1.
Step 3: Total the present value of the cash flows found in Step 2.
Step 4: Compare the total present value found in Step 3 with the market price of the bond and, if the total present value of the cash flows found in Step 3 is

- equal to the market price, then the interest rate used in Step 1 is the yield to maturity
- greater than the market price, then the interest rate is not the yield to maturity. Therefore, go back to Step 1 and use a higher interest rate
- less than the market price, then the interest rate is not the yield to maturity. Therefore, go back to Step 1 and use a lower interest rate

For example, suppose that a four-year bond that pays interest annually has a par value of $1,000, a coupon rate of 5%, and is selling in the market for $900.64. Table 1 shows the procedure for calculating the yield to maturity. When a 2% interest rate is tried, the total present value is equal to $1,136.52. As this value is greater than the market price of $900.64, it is not the yield to maturity and, therefore, a higher interest rate must be tried.

Table 1	Yield to Maturity of an Annual Pay Four-Year Bond with a Coupon Rate of 5% and a Market Price of $900.64

$C = \$50$ $\quad$ $M = \$1,000$ $\quad$ $P = \$900.64$ $\quad$ $n = 4$	
Interest Rate Tried	Total Present Value
2%	$1,136.52
3	1,106.57
4	1,036.30
5	1,000.00
6	965.35
7	932.26
8	900.64
9	870.41
10	841.51
11	813.85
12	787.39

Suppose a 12% interest rate is tried. Now the total present value of $787.39 is smaller than the market price, so a lower interest rate must be tried. When an 8% interest rate is tried, the total present value is equal to the market price, so the yield to maturity is 8%.

Had the market price of this bond been $813.85 rather than $900.64, the yield to maturity would be 11%. Notice that the lower the market price, the higher the yield to maturity.

There are several interesting points about the relationship among the coupon rate, market price, and yield to maturity that can be seen in Table 1.

1. If the market price is equal to the par value, then the yield to maturity is equal to the coupon rate.
2. If the market price is less than the par value, then the yield to maturity is greater than the coupon rate.
3. If the market price is greater than the par value, then the yield to maturity is less than the coupon rate.

In our illustration, we assumed that coupon payments are made once per year. As noted earlier, however, the practice in the U.S. bond market is to pay coupon interest every six months. This does not affect the procedure for calculating the yield to maturity; that is, it is still the interest rate that will make the present value of the cash flow equal to the market price. The cash flow, however, is not annual. Instead, the coupon payment is every six months and is equal to one-half the annual coupon payment. The resulting yield to maturity is then a semiannual yield to maturity. To annualize the semiannual yield, the *convention* adopted in the bond market is to double the semiannual yield. The resulting yield to maturity is said to be calculated on a **bond-equivalent yield basis**.

For example, consider an 18-year bond with a coupon rate of 6% and a par value of $1,000. Suppose that the bond pays interest semiannually and is selling for $700.89. The cash flow for this bond is $30 every six months for 35 six-month periods and $1,030 36 six-month periods from now. That is,

$$C = \$30 \; M = \$1,000 \text{ and } n = 36 \text{ (double the number of years to maturity)}$$

Table 2 shows the calculation of the yield to maturity for this bond. Notice that the interest rate that makes the total present value equal to the market price of $700.89 is 4.75%. This is the semiannual yield to maturity. Doubling this semiannual yield gives 9.5%, which is the yield to maturity on a bond-equivalent yield basis.

In the discussion to follow, we will refer to the yield to maturity of a bond as simply its yield. The difference between the yield on any two bond issues is called a **yield spread**, or simply **spread**. The spread is typically measured in basis points. For example, if the yield on bond A is 9%, and the yield on bond B is 8.5%, the yield spread is 50 basis points.

The Base Interest Rate

Now that we have examined the characteristics of a bond and how to measure the yield on a bond, we will look at the structure of interest rates. In our discussion, we use the terms *interest rate* and *yield* interchangeably.

The securities issued by the U.S. Department of the Treasury, popularly referred to as **Treasury securities**, or simply **Treasuries**, are backed by the full faith and credit of the U.S. government. Consequently, market participants throughout the world view them as having no credit risk. As a result, historically the interest rates on Treasury securities have served as the benchmark interest rates throughout the U.S. economy, as well as in international capital markets. Other important benchmarks have developed in international capital markets, and we discuss these later in this chapter.

Treasury securities are used to develop the benchmark interest rates. There are two categories of U.S. Treasury securities, discount and coupon securities. The fundamental difference between the two types is in the form of the stream of payments that the holder receives, which, in turn, is reflected in the prices at which the securities are issued. Coupon securities pay interest every six months, plus principal at maturity. Discount securities pay only a contractually fixed amount at maturity. Treasury securities are typically issued on an auction basis according to regular cycles for securities of specific maturities. Current Treasury practice is to issue all securities with maturities of one year or less as discount securities. These securities are called *Treasury bills*. All securities with maturities of two years or longer are issued as Treasury *coupon securities*.

Table 2 Yield to Maturity of a Semiannual Pay 18-Year Bond with a Coupon Rate of 6% and a Market Price of $700.89

$C = \$30$	$M = \$1,000$	$P = \$700.89$	$n = 36$
Interest Rate Tried			**Total Present Value**
3.25%			$947.40
3.50			898.54
3.75			853.14
4.00			810.92
4.25			771.61
4.50			735.01
4.75[*]			700.89

[*]Semiannual yield to maturity. Therefore, the yield to maturity on a bond-equivalent yield basis is 9.5% (2 times 4.75%).

The most recently auctioned Treasury issues for each maturity are referred to as **on-the-run Treasury issues** or **current coupon issues.** On May 20, 2008, the yield for four on-the-run issues as reported by the U.S. Department of the Treasury was

two-year Treasury 2.34%
five-year Treasury 3.02%
10-year Treasury 3.78%
30-year Treasury 4.53%

Issues auctioned prior to the current coupon issues are typically referred to as **off-the-run Treasury issues;** they are not as liquid as on-the-run issues, and, therefore, offer a higher yield than the corresponding on-the-run Treasury issue. Note that every day, the U.S. Department of the Treasury estimates the yield for Treasury securities based on the yield for on-the-run and off-the-run issues.[4]

The minimum interest rate or **base interest rate** that investors will demand for investing in a non-Treasury security is the yield offered on a comparable maturity on-the-run Treasury security. So, for example, if an investor wanted to purchase a 10-year bond on May 20, 2008, the minimum yield the investor would seek is 3.78%, the on-the-run Treasury yield reported above. The base interest rate is also referred to as the **benchmark interest rate.**

The Risk Premium

Market participants talk of interest rates on non-Treasury securities as "trading at a spread" to a particular on-the-run Treasury security (or a spread to any particular benchmark interest rate selected). For example, if the yield on a 10-year non-Treasury security on May 20, 2008, is 4.78%, then the spread is 100 basis points over the 3.78% Treasury yield. This spread reflects the additional risks the investor faces by acquiring a security that is not issued by the U.S. government and, therefore, can be called a **risk premium.** Thus, we can express the interest rate offered on a non-Treasury security as

$$\text{Base interest rate } + \text{ Spread}$$

or equivalently,

$$\text{Base interest rate } + \text{ Risk premium}$$

We have discussed the factors that affect the base interest rate. One of the factors is the expected rate of inflation. That is, the base interest rate can be expressed as

$$\text{Base interest rate } = \text{ Real rate of interest } + \text{ Expected rate of inflation}$$

How can the real rate of inflation required by market participants be estimated? Since 1997, the U.S. Department of the Treasury has issued securities indexed to the Consumer Price Index. These securities are called *Treasury Inflation Protection Securities* (TIPS).

Turning to the spread, the factors that affect it are (1) the type of issuer, (2) the issuer's perceived creditworthiness, (3) the term or maturity of the instrument, (4) provisions that grant either the issuer or the investor the option to do something, (5) the taxability of the interest received by investors, and (6) the expected liquidity of the issue. Notice that these factors are the ones that we discussed in the previous chapter as affecting the price of a security.

---

[4] http://www.treas.gov/offices/domestic-finance/debt-management/interest-rate/yield.shtml.

It is important to note that yield spreads must be interpreted relative to the benchmark interest rate used. This is particularly important to keep in mind for the second and last factors that affect the spread when the benchmark interest rate is other than the yield on U.S. Treasury securities.

Types of Issuers

A key feature of a debt obligation is the nature of the issuer. In addition to the U.S. government, there are agencies of the U.S. government, municipal governments, corporations (domestic and foreign), and foreign governments that issue bonds.

The bond market is classified by the type of issuer, and groups of securities of the various kinds of issuers are referred to as **market sectors.** The spread between the interest rates offered in two sectors of the bond market on obligations with the same maturity is referred to as an **intermarket sector spread.**

Excluding the Treasury market sector, the other market sectors include a wide range of issuers, each with different abilities to satisfy their contractual obligations. For example, within the corporate market sector, issuers are classified as follows: (1) utilities, (2) industrials, (3) finance, and (4) banks. The spread between two issues within a market sector is called an **intramarket sector spread.**

Perceived Creditworthiness of Issuer

Default risk or **credit risk** refers to the risk that the issuer of a bond may be unable to make timely principal or interest payments. Most market participants rely primarily on commercial rating companies to assess the default risk of an issuer. These companies perform credit analyses and express their conclusions by a system of ratings. The three commercial rating companies in the United States are (1) Moody's Investors Service (Moody's), (2) Standard & Poor's Corporation (S&P), and (3) FitchRatings (Fitch).

In all systems, the term **high grade** means low credit risk, or conversely, high probability of future payments. The highest-grade bonds are designated by Moody's by the symbol Aaa, and by S&P and Fitch by the symbol AAA. The next highest grade is denoted by the symbol Aa (Moody's) or AA (S&P and Fitch); for the third grade, all rating systems use A. The next three grades are Baa or BBB, Ba or BB, and B, respectively. There are also C grades. Moody's uses 1, 2, or 3 to provide a narrower credit quality breakdown within each class, and S&P and Fitch use plus and minus signs for the same purpose.

Bonds rated triple A (AAA or Aaa) are said to be *prime*; double A (AA or Aa) are of *high quality*; single A issues are called *upper medium grade*, and triple B are *medium grade*. Lower-rated bonds are said to have speculative elements or be distinctly speculative.

Bond issues that are assigned a rating in the top four categories are referred to as *investment-grade bonds*. Issues that carry a rating below the top four categories are referred to as *noninvestment-grade bonds*, or more popularly as *high-yield bonds* or *junk bonds*. Thus, the bond market can be divided into two sectors: the investment-grade and noninvestment-grade markets.

The spread between Treasury securities and non-Treasury securities that are identical in all respects except for credit quality is referred to as a **credit spread.** For example, Yahoo.com reported that the yield for corporate bonds with 10 years to maturity on May 20, 2008, was 5.14% for AAA rated bonds and 5.95% for AA rated bonds. The 10-year on-the-run Treasury rate was 3.78%. Hence, the yield spread for 10-year AAA corporate bonds was 136 basis points (5.14% − 3.78%) and 217 basis points (5.95% − 3.78%) for AA rated corporate bonds. As can be seen, the lower the credit rating, the larger the yield spread.

Let us return to the interpretation if the yield spread on a non–U.S. Treasury security is used as the benchmark interest rate. Since the U.S. Treasury securities are viewed by market participants as free of credit risk, the yield spread to U.S. Treasury securities is reflecting credit risk, as well as the other risks to be discussed. In the search for a new benchmark interest rate, it is desirable to use a benchmark that has minimal credit risk. There are three possible candidates for the benchmark. The first is the yield on securities offered by government-sponsored enterprises. They are currently viewed as having a triple A rating (AAA or Aaa) and, therefore, have minimal credit risk. The second alternative is corporate bond issuers that have triple A ratings. As we will see in our discussion of liquidity, corporate bond issuers may not be a viable candidate to replace Treasury securities as the benchmark. The third candidate is one that comes from a market, the interest rate swap market. A measure that comes out of the swap market is called the **swap rate**, which many market participants use as a benchmark. We will discuss this later in this chapter.

Term to Maturity

The price of a financial asset will fluctuate over its life as yields in the market change. As we demonstrated, the volatility of a bond's price is dependent on its maturity. More specifically, with all other factors constant the longer the maturity of a bond, the greater the price volatility resulting from a change in market yields. The spread between any two maturity sectors of the market is called a **maturity spread** or **yield curve spread.**

Although this spread can be calculated for any sector of the market, it is most commonly calculated for the Treasury sector. For example, this spread on May 20, 2008, for the four on-the-run Treasury issues whose yields were given above are

two-year/five-year maturity spread	3.02% − 2.34%	= 0.0068%	= 68 basis points
two-year/10-year maturity spread	3.78% − 2.34%	= 0.0144%	= 144 basis points
two-year/30-year maturity spread	4.53% − 2.34%	= 0.0219%	= 219 basis points
five-year/10-year maturity spread	3.78% − 3.02%	= 0.0066%	= 66 basis points
five-year/30-year maturity spread	4.53% − 3.02%	= 0.0151%	= 151 basis points
10-year/30-year maturity spread	4.53% − 3.78%	= 0.0075%	= 75 basis points

Note that although the maturity spread is the difference between the yield on the longer maturity and the yield on the shorter maturity, the market convention is to refer to the maturity spread as the "shorter maturity/longer maturity."

There are other market conventions when referring to maturity spreads. For example, some market participants refer to the two-year/10-year maturity spread as the "short-end of the yield curve" and the 10-year/30-year maturity spread as the "long-end of the yield curve."

In the corporate bond market, a maturity spread can be similarly calculated but the issues must have the same credit quality. For example, on May 20, 2009, Yahoo.com reported the following for A rated corporate bonds:[5]

---

[5] Yahoo.com did not report any yield for 30-year A rated corporate bonds. This is because there are not many issues with this maturity outstanding.

two-year A corporate bonds 3.82%
five-year A corporate bonds 4.87%
10-year A corporate bonds   5.39%

The maturity spreads are then

two-year/five-year maturity spread 4.87% − 3.82% = 0.0105% = 105 basis points
two-year/10-year maturity spread   5.39% − 3.82% = 0.0157% = 157 basis points
five-year/10-year maturity spread 5.39% − 4.87% = 0.0052% = 52 basis points

The relationship between the yields on comparable securities but different maturities is called the **term structure of interest rates**. The term-to-maturity topic is of such importance that we devote the entire next chapter to it.

Inclusion of Options

It is not uncommon for a bond issue to include a provision that gives either the bondholder and/or the issuer an option to take some action against the other party. An option that is included in a bond issue is referred to as an **embedded option**.

The most common type of option in a bond issue is a **call provision**. This provision grants the issuer the right to retire the debt, fully or partially, before the scheduled maturity date. The inclusion of a call feature benefits issuers by allowing them to replace an old bond issue with a lower interest cost issue should interest rates in the market decline. Effectively, a call provision allows the issuer to alter the maturity of a bond. A call provision is detrimental to the bondholder because the bondholder will be uncertain about maturity and might have to reinvest the proceeds received at a lower interest rate if the bond is called and the bondholder wants to keep his or her funds in issues of similar risk of default.

An issue may also include a provision that allows the bondholder to change the maturity of a bond. An issue with a **put provision** grants the bondholder the right to sell the issue back to the issuer at par value on designated dates. Here, the advantage to the investor is that, if interest rates rise after the issue date and result in a price that is less than the par value, the investor can force the issuer to redeem the bond at par value.

A **convertible bond** is an issue giving the bondholder the right to exchange the bond for a specified number of shares of common stock. This feature allows the bondholder to take advantage of favorable movements in the price of the issuer's common stock.

The presence of these embedded options has an effect on the spread of an issue relative to a Treasury security and the spread relative to otherwise comparable issues that do not have an embedded option. In general, market participants will require a larger spread over a comparable Treasury security for an issue with an embedded option that is favorable to the issuer (e.g., a call option) than for an issue without such an option. In contrast, market participants will require a smaller spread over a comparable Treasury security for an issue with an embedded option that is favorable to the investor (for example, put option and conversion option). In fact, for a bond with an option that is favorable to an investor, the interest rate on an issue may be less than that on a comparable Treasury security!

A major part of the bond market is the mortgage market. There is a wide range of mortgage-backed securities. But these securities expose an investor to a form of call risk called "prepayment risk." Consequently, a yield spread between a mortgage-backed security and a comparable on-the-run Treasury security reflects this call risk. To see this, consider a basic mortgage-backed security called a Ginnie Mae passthrough security. This security is backed by the full faith and credit of the U.S. government. Consequently, the yield spread between a Ginnie Mae passthrough security and a comparable Treasury security is not due to credit risk. Rather, it is primarily due to call risk.

Taxability of Interest

Unless exempted under the federal income tax code, interest income is taxable at the federal level. In addition to federal income taxes, there may be state and local taxes on interest income.

The federal tax code specifically exempts the interest income from qualified municipal bond issues from taxation at the federal level. **Municipal bonds** are securities issued by state and local governments and by their creations, such as "authorities" and special districts. The large majority of outstanding municipal bonds are tax-exempt securities. Because of the tax-exempt feature of municipal bonds, the yield on municipal bonds is less than that on Treasuries with the same maturity. The difference in yield between tax-exempt securities and Treasury securities is typically measured not in basis points but in percentage terms. More specifically, it is measured as the percentage of the yield on a tax-exempt security relative to a comparable Treasury security.

The yield on a taxable bond issue after federal income taxes are paid is equal to

$$\text{After-tax yield} = \text{Pretax yield} \times (1 - \text{Marginal tax rate})$$

For example, suppose a taxable bond issue offers a yield of 4% and is acquired by an investor facing a marginal tax rate of 35%. The after-tax yield would then be

$$\text{After-tax yield} = 0.04 \times (1 - 0.35) = 0.026 = 2.6\%$$

Alternatively, we can determine the yield that must be offered on a taxable bond issue to give the same after-tax yield as a tax-exempt issue. This yield is called the **equivalent taxable yield** and is determined as follows:

$$\text{Equivalent taxable yield} = \frac{\text{Tax-exempt yield}}{(1 - \text{Marginal tax rate})}$$

For example, consider an investor facing a 35% marginal tax rate who purchases a tax-exempt issue with a yield of 2.6%. The equivalent taxable yield is then

$$\text{Equivalent taxable yield} = \frac{0.026}{(1 - 0.35)} = 0.04 = 4\%$$

Notice that the lower the marginal tax rate, the lower the equivalent taxable yield. Thus, in our previous example, if the marginal tax rate is 25% rather than 35%, the equivalent taxable yield would be 3.47% rather than 4%, as shown below:

$$\text{Equivalent taxable yield} = \frac{0.026}{(1 - 0.25)} = 0.0347 = 3.47\%$$

State and local governments may tax interest income on bond issues that are exempt from federal income taxes. Some municipalities exempt interest income paid on all municipal issues from taxation; others do not. Some states exempt interest income from bonds issued by municipalities within the state but tax the interest income from bonds issued by municipalities outside of the state. The implication is that two municipal securities of the same quality rating and the same maturity may trade at some spread because of different tax policies and, hence, the relative demand for bonds of municipalities in different states. For example, in a high income tax state such as New York, the demand for bonds of municipalities will drive down their yield relative to municipalities in a low or zero income tax state such as Florida.

Municipalities are not permitted to tax the interest income from securities issued by the U.S. Treasury. Thus, part of the spread between Treasury securities and taxable non-Treasury securities of the same maturity reflects the value of the exemption from state and local taxes.

Expected Liquidity of an Issue

Bonds trade with different degrees of liquidity. The greater the expected liquidity with which an issue will trade, the lower the yield that investors would require. As noted earlier, Treasury securities are the most liquid securities in the world. The lower yield offered on Treasury securities relative to non-Treasury securities reflects, to a significant extent, the difference in liquidity. Even within the Treasury market, some differences in liquidity occur, because on-the-run issues have greater liquidity than off-the-run issues.

An important factor that affects the liquidity of an issue is the size of the issue. One of the reasons that U.S. Treasury securities are highly liquid is the large size of each individual issue. Government-sponsored enterprises in recent years have dramatically increased their issuance size. They have done this in their attempt to have the yield on their securities become the benchmark interest rates in the U.S. economy. As we noted earlier, the triple A credit rating of government-sponsored enterprises makes the yield on their securities an attractive candidate to replace the yield on Treasury securities as the benchmark interest rates. The large size and therefore liquidity of the securities issued by government-sponsored enterprises increase their attractiveness as an alternative benchmark. We also noted earlier that the yield on corporate bond issues rated triple A may make them a potential alternative benchmark. However, the size of each issue for the various triple A corporate bond issuers is considerably smaller than that of the securities issued by government-sponsored enterprises. For this reason, triple A corporate bond issuers may not be received by market participants as a benchmark alternative.

Swap Rate Yield Curve

The information that is obtained from the interest rate swap market is also used as an interest rate benchmark. We will briefly explain how and why here.

In a generic interest rate swap, the parties exchange interest rate payments on specified dates: One party pays a fixed rate and the other party a floating rate over the life of the swap. In a typical swap, the floating rate is based on a reference rate and the reference rate is typically the London Interbank Offered Rate (LIBOR). LIBOR is the interest rate at which prime banks in London pay other prime banks on U.S. dollar certificates of deposit.

The fixed interest rate that is paid by the fixed-rate counterparty is called the swap rate. Dealers in the swap market quote swap rates for different maturities. The relationship between the swap rate and maturity of a swap is called the **swap rate yield curve**, more commonly referred to as the **swap curve**. Because the reference rate is typically LIBOR, the swap curve is also called the **LIBOR curve.**

There is a swap curve for most countries. Table 3 shows the U.S. swap curve, Euro swap curve, and U.K. swap curve on October 16, 2007. For Euro interest rate swaps, the reference rate is the Euro Interbank Offered Rate (Euribor), which is the rate at which bank

Table 3 U.S., Euro, and U.K. Swap Rate Curve on October 16, 2007

Years to Maturity	Swap rate (%) for		
	U.S.	Euro	U.K.
1	4.96	4.72	6.19
2	4.85	4.65	5.97
3	4.90	4.64	5.91
5	5.12	4.65	5.80
7	5.18	4.69	5.70
10	5.33	4.77	5.56
12	5.39	4.82	5.50
15	5.46	4.88	5.40
20	5.52	4.92	5.27
15	5.54	4.92	5.14
30	5.54	4.90	5.04

Note: *The rates in this table were obtained from CLP Structured Finance's website, http://www.swap-rates.com.*

deposits in countries that have adopted the euro currency and are member states of the European Union[6] are offered by one prime bank to another prime bank.

The swap curve is used as a benchmark in many countries outside the United States. Unlike a country's government bond yield curve, however, the swap curve is not a default-free yield curve. Instead, it reflects the credit risk of the counterparty to an interest rate swap. Since the counterparty to an interest rate swap is typically a bank-related entity, the swap curve reflects the average credit risk of representative banks that provide interest rate swaps. More specifically, a swap curve is viewed as the *interbank yield curve*. It is also referred to as the *AA rated yield curve* because the banks that borrow money from each other at LIBOR have credit ratings of Aa/AA or above. In addition, the swap curve reflects liquidity risk. However, in recent years the liquidity of the interest rate swap has increased to the point where it is now a more liquid market than the market for some government bonds.

One would expect that if a country has a government bond market, the yields in that market would be the best benchmark. That is not necessarily the case. There are several advantages of using a swap curve over a country's government securities yield curve.[7]

First, there may be technical reasons why within a government bond market some of the interest rates may not be representative of the true interest rate but instead be biased by some technical or regulatory factor unique to that market. For example, market participants may need to cover a short position in a particular government bond and the actions to cover a short position would push up the demand for that particular government bond and drive down its yield. In the swap market, there is nothing that has to be delivered so technical market factors have less of an impact. Also, there may be government bonds selling above or below their par value. Moreover, as explained earlier, government tax authorities might tax such bonds differently if they are purchased and held to maturity. As a

---

[6] The euro is the official currency of many European Union member states. Countries where the euro is adopted as the official currency are commonly referred to as part of the Eurozone, Euroland, or Euro area.

[7] For a further discussion, see Uri Ron, "A Practical Guide to Swap Curve Construction," Chapter 6 in Frank J. Fabozzi (ed.), *Interest Rate, Term Structure, and Valuation Modeling* (New York: John Wiley & Sons, 2002).

result, the yields at which these bonds trade in the marketplace will reflect any tax advantage or disadvantage. Although it may be difficult to appreciate these factors at this point in your study of financial markets, the key is that the observed interest rate on government securities may not reflect the true interest rate due to these factors. This is not the case for swap rates. There is no regulation of this market and hence swap rates represent true interest rates. However, remember that swap rates do reflect credit risk and liquidity risk.

Second, to create a representative government bond yield curve, a large number of maturities must be available. However, in most government bond markets, securities with only a few maturities are issued. For example, the U.S. government issues only four securities with a maturity of two years or more (two, five, 10, and 30 years). While there are a good number of off-the-run issues available from which to construct a government bond yield curve, the yields on such issues may not be true interest rates for the reasons noted previously. In contrast, in the swap market, a wide range of maturities are quoted, as can be seen in Table 1. In fact, in the United States, there was a suspension in the issuance of 30-year bonds, and as a result, 30-year Treasury rates were unavailable. Yet, swap dealers quoted 30-year swap rates.

Finally, the ability to compare government yields across countries is difficult because there are differences in the credit risk for every country. In contrast, as explained earlier, the swap curve is an interbank yield curve and thereby makes cross-country comparisons of benchmark interest rates easier.

Key Points That You Should Understand Before Proceeding

1. Historically, the on-the-run Treasury security of a given maturity is the base or benchmark interest rate.
2. With the decline in the issuance of Treasury securities by the U.S. Department of the Treasury, there is now a search for an alternative interest rate benchmark.
3. Non-Treasury securities will trade at a spread (measured in basis points) relative to an on-the-run Treasury security.
4. The factors that affect yield spreads in the bond market are the type of issuer, credit risk, term to maturity, the presence of embedded options, the tax treatment of interest income, and liquidity.
5. The credit risk of an issuer is gauged by ratings assigned by commercial rating companies (Moody's, S&P, and Fitch).
6. Embedded options can either reduce the spread to Treasuries, if the option benefits the bondholder, or increase the spread to Treasuries, if the option benefits the issuer.
7. The interest income from municipal securities is generally exempt from federal income taxation, and as a result municipals offer a lower yield than Treasury securities.

SUMMARY

Two important theories of the determination of the level of the interest rate are Fisher's theory, adapted to the loanable funds model, and Keynes's liquidity preference theory. Fisher considers the reasons for saving to be the marginal rate of time preference, which is the willingness to forgo current consumption for enhanced future consumption, the level of income, and the rate of interest. The demand for borrowing arises because of firms' investment opportunities. The marginal productivity of capital is the gain from additional investment and it is negatively related to the interest rate. The equilibrium rate of interest is determined by the interaction of the demand for and supply of savings. In the presence of inflation, the equilibrium rate is composed of both the real rate of interest and a premium for expected inflation.

Keynes's theory emphasizes the role of liquid balances or money in transaction and states that the interest rate is determined in the money market. Demand for money reflects income and the level of prices for goods and services, and it is negatively related to the level of interest rates. The supply of money, in this theory, is controlled by the central bank, which can, by changing the money supply, affect the rate of interest. In fact, changes in the money supply can have three possibly conflicting effects on the level of the interest rate, depending on the economy's level of output and employment. Those effects are the liquidity effect, the income effect, and the price expectations effect.

The basic features of a bond include the coupon rate, the term to maturity, and the principal or par value. The yield to maturity of a bond is the interest rate that makes the total present value of the bond's cash flow equal to its market price.

Every economy operates with not just one interest rate but rather with a structure of interest rates. The yield spread is the difference between the yield on any two bonds and reflects the difference in their risks. A country's government bond market can be used as the base interest rate for that country. The base interest rate is equal to the real rate of interest plus the expected rate of inflation. The risk premium is the yield spread between a non-government security and a comparable government security. The factors that affect the yield spread include: (1) the type of issuer (agency, corporation, municipality), (2) the issuer's perceived creditworthiness as measured by the rating system of commercial rating companies, (3) the term or maturity of the instrument, (4) the embedded options in a bond issue (e.g., call, put, or conversion provisions), (5) the taxability of interest income at the federal and municipal levels, and (6) the expected liquidity of the issue.

The swap rate yield curve also provides information about interest rates in a country. The swap rate yield curve or simply swap curve is not a default-free yield curve but rather reflects interbank credit risk. In many countries, market participants use the country's swap curve as the benchmark interest rates rather than the country's government bond yield curve.

KEY TERMS

- Base interest rate (benchmark interest rate)
- Bond-equivalent yield basis
- Call provision
- Convertible bond
- Credit risk
- Credit spread
- Default risk
- Embedded option
- Equivalent taxable yield
- Fisher's Law
- Fisher's theory of interest

- High-grade
- Income effect
- Intermarket sector spread
- Intramarket sector spread
- LIBOR curve
- Liquidity effect
- Liquidity preference theory of interest
- Loanable funds theory of interest rates
- Marginal productivity of capital
- Marginal rate of time preference
- Market sectors
- Maturity

- Maturity spread
- Municipal bonds
- Nominal rate of interest
- Off-the-run Treasury issue
- On-the-run Treasury issue (current coupon issue)
- Price expectations effect
- Principal value (principal, par value, maturity value, redemption value, face value)
- Put provision

- Real rate of interest
- Risk premium
- Swap curve
- Swap rate
- Swap rate yield curve
- Term to maturity
- Term structure of interest rates
- Treasury security (Treasuries)
- Yield curve spread
- Yield spread (spread)
- Yield to maturity

QUESTIONS

1. Explain what these terms mean in Fisher's theory of interest rates:
   a. *marginal rate of time preference*
   b. *marginal productivity of capital*
   c. *equilibrium interest rate*

2. a. How does the loanable funds theory expand Fisher's theory of interest rate determination?
   b. How does a change in the government's deficit affect the equilibrium rate in the loanable funds theory?

3. a. How do the assets, money, and bonds differ in Keynes's liquidity preference theory?
   b. How does a change in income affect the equilibrium level of the interest rate in Keynes's theory?
   c. How does a change in the money supply affect that rate?

4. a. Explain these terms: the *liquidity effect*; the *income effect*; and the *price expectations effect*.
   b. How is it determined which of these three effects on interest rates an increase in the money supply will have?

5. Consider three bonds, all with a par value of $1,000:

Bond	Coupon Rate	Market Price
A	8%	$1,100
B	7	900
C	9	1,000

   a. What is the yield to maturity of bond C?
   b. Is the yield to maturity of bond A greater than or less than 8%?
   c. Is the yield to maturity of bond B greater than or less than 9%?

6. Consider the following bond: 19 years to maturity, 11% coupon rate, pays interest semiannually, $1,000 par value. Suppose that the market price of this bond is $1,233.64. Given the information below, determine the yield to maturity for this bond on a bond-equivalent yield basis.

Interest Rate Tried	Total Present Value of Cash Flow
3.00%	$1,562.32
3.25	1,486.96
3.50	1,416.82
3.75	1,351.46
4.00	1,290.52
4.25	1,233.64

7. a. Show the cash flows for the two bonds below, each of which has a par value of $1,000 and pays interest semiannually:

Bond	Coupon Rate	Years to Maturity	Price
W	7%	5	$884.20
Y	9	4	967.70

   b. Calculate the yield to maturity for the two bonds.

8. a. What is the credit risk associated with a U.S. Treasury security?
   b. Why is the Treasury yield considered the base interest rate?
   c. What is meant by *on-the-run Treasuries*?
   d. What is meant by *off-the-run Treasuries*?

9. What does the yield spread between the off-the-run Treasury issue and the on-the-run Treasury issue reflect?

10. On October 19, 2007, the yield for three on-the-run issues as reported by Yahoo.com was

    two-year Treasury 3.90%
    five-year Treasury 4.14%
    10-year Treasury 4.49%

    Compute all of the maturity spreads.

11. Yahoo.com reported that the yield for corporate bonds with 10 years to maturity on October 19, 2007, was 5.39% for AAA rated bonds and 5.66% for AA rated bonds. At the time, the 10-year on-the-run Treasury rate was 4.49%. Compute the two credit spreads.

12. In the May 29, 1992, *Weekly Market Update*, published by Goldman Sachs & Co., the following information was reported in various exhibits for certain corporate bonds as of the close of business Thursday, May 28, 1992:

Issuer	Rating	Yield	Spread	Treasury Benchmark
General Electric Capital Co.	Triple A	7.87%	50	10
Mobil Corp.	Double A	7.77	40	10
Southern Bell Tel & Teleg	Triple A	8.60	72	30
Bell Tel Co Pa	Double A	8.66	78	30
AMR Corp	Triple B	9.43	155	30

    a. What is meant by *rating*?
    b. Which of the five bonds has the greatest credit risk?
    c. What is meant by *spread*?
    d. What is meant by *Treasury benchmark*?
    e. Explain how each of the spreads reported above was determined.
    f. Why does each spread reported above reflect a risk premium?

13. For the corporate bond issues reported in the previous question, answer the following questions:

    a. Should a triple A rated bond issue offer a higher or lower yield than a double A rated bond issue of the same maturity?
    b. What is the spread between the General Electric Capital Company issue and the Mobil Corporation issue?
    c. Is the spread reported in (b) consistent with your answer to (a)?
    d. The yield spread between these two bond issues reflects more than just credit risk. What other factors would the spread reflect?
    e. The Mobil Corporation issue is not callable. However, the General Electric Capital Company issue is callable. How does this information help you in understanding the spread between these two issues?

14. For the corporate bond issues reported in question 12, answer the following questions:

    a. What is the yield spread between the Southern Bell Telephone and Telegraph bond issue and the Bell Telephone Company (Pennsylvania) bond issue?
    b. The Southern Bell Telephone and Telegraph bond issue is not callable but the Bell Telephone Company (Pennsylvania) bond issue is callable. What does the yield spread in (a) reflect?
    c. AMR Corporation is the parent company of American Airlines and is therefore classified in the transportation industry. The bond issue cited is not callable. What is the yield spread between the AMR Corporation and Southern Bell Telephone and Telegraph bond issue, and what does this spread reflect?

15. In the May 29, 1992, *Weekly Market Update*, published by Goldman Sachs & Co., the following information was reported in an exhibit for high-grade, tax-exempt securities as of the close of business Thursday, May 28, 1992:

Maturity	Yield	Yield as a Percent of Treasury Yield
1-year	3.20%	76.5%
3-year	4.65	80.4
5-year	5.10	76.4
10-year	5.80	78.7
30-year	6.50	82.5

a. What is meant by a *tax-exempt security*?

b. What is meant by a *high-grade* issue?

c. Why is the yield on a tax-exempt security less than the yield on a Treasury security of the same maturity?

d. What is meant by the *equivalent taxable yield*?

e. Also reported in the same issue of the Goldman Sachs report is information on "Intra-market Yield Spreads." What is an intra-market yield spread?

16. **a.** What is meant by an *embedded option* in a bond?

b. Give three examples of an embedded option that might be included in a bond issue.

c. Does an embedded option increase or decrease the risk premium relative to the base interest rate?

17. **a.** What is meant by the swap rate?

b. What is meant by the swap curve?

c. Explain whether you agree or disagree with the following statement: "A country's swap curve is default-free yield curve."

18. Why do market participants in some countries prefer to use the swap curve rather than the government bond yield curve?

The Term Structure of Interest Rates

LEARNING OBJECTIVES

After reading this chapter, you will understand

- what is meant by the term structure of interest rates

- what the yield curve is

- the different shapes that the term structure can take

- what is meant by a spot rate and a spot rate curve

- how a theoretical spot rate curve can be determined from the Treasury yield curve

- what is meant by an implicit forward rate and how it can be calculated

- how long-term rates are related to the current short-term rate and short-term forward rates

- the different theories about the determinants of the shape of the term structure: pure expectations theory, the liquidity theory, the preferred habitat theory, and the market segmentation theory

- the risks associated with investing in bonds when interest rates change—price risk and reinvestment

- the main economic influences on the shape of the Treasury yield curve

In this chapter, we extend the theories and principles of the last chapter to the relationship between the yield on a bond and its maturity. Since the maturity of a bond is referred to as its *term to maturity* or simply *term*, the relationship between yield and maturity is referred to as the **term structure of interest rates.** We also explain the various theories about the determinants of the term structure of interest rates.

From Chapter 11 of *Foundations of Financial Markets and Institutions*, 4/e. Frank J. Fabozzi. Franco Modigliani. Frank J. Jones.

THE YIELD CURVE AND THE TERM STRUCTURE

The graphic that depicts the relationship between the yield on bonds of the same credit quality but different maturities is known as the **yield curve**. Market participants have tended to construct yield curves from observations of prices and yields in the Treasury market. Two reasons account for this tendency. First, Treasury securities are free of default risk, and differences in creditworthiness do not affect yield estimates. Second, as the largest and most active bond market, the Treasury market offers the fewest problems of illiquidity or infrequent trading. Figure 1 shows the general shape of three hypothetical Treasury yield curves that have been observed from time to time in the United States. Daily yield curve information is available from a variety of sources on a real-time basis. Historical information about daily yield curves from 1990 is obtained from the U.S. Department of the Treasury's website.[1]

From a practical viewpoint, as we explained in the previous chapter, the Treasury yield curve functions mainly as a benchmark for pricing bonds and setting yields in many other sectors of the debt market—bank loans, mortgages, corporate debt, and international bonds. More recently market participants have come to realize that the traditionally constructed Treasury yield curve is an unsatisfactory measure of the relation between required yield and maturity. The key reason is that securities with the same maturity may actually provide different yields. As we will explain below, this phenomenon reflects the role and impact of differences in the bonds' coupon rates. Hence, it is necessary to develop more accurate and reliable estimates of the Treasury yield curve. In what follows, we will show the problems posed by traditional approaches to the Treasury yield curve and offer an innovative and increasingly popular approach to building a yield curve. The approach consists of identifying yields that apply to zero-coupon bonds and, therefore, eliminates the problem of nonuniqueness in the yield–maturity relationship.

Figure 1   Three Hypothetical Yield Curves

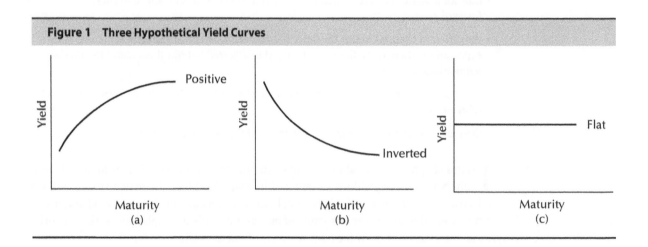

[1] http://www.ustreas.gov/offices/domestic-finance/debt-management/interest-rate/yield_historical_main.shtml.

Using the Yield Curve to Price a Bond

The price of any financial asset is the present value of its cash flow. However, in our illustrations and our discussion to this point, we have assumed that one interest rate should be used to discount all the cash flows from a financial asset. The appropriate interest rate is the yield on a Treasury security with the same maturity as the financial asset, plus an appropriate yield premium or spread.

As noted previously, however, there is a problem with using the Treasury yield curve to determine the appropriate yield at which to discount the cash flow of a bond. To illustrate this problem, consider the following two hypothetical five-year Treasury bonds, A and B. The difference between these two Treasury bonds is the coupon rate, which is 12% for A and 3% for B. The cash flow for these two bonds per $100 of par value for the 10 six-month periods to maturity would be:

Period	Cash Flow for A	Cash Flow for B
1–9	$ 6.00	$ 1.50
10	106.00	101.50

Because of the different cash flow patterns, it is not appropriate to use the same interest rate to discount all cash flows. Instead, each cash flow should be discounted at a unique interest rate that is appropriate for the time period in which the cash flow will be received. But what should be the interest rate for each period?

The correct way to think about bonds A and B is not as bonds but as packages of cash flows. More specifically, they are packages of zero-coupon instruments. A **zero-coupon instrument** is one that is purchased at an amount below its maturity value and that pays no interest periodically. Instead, the interest is earned at the maturity date when the investor receives the maturity or principal value. Thus, the interest earned is the difference between the maturity value and the price paid. For example, bond A can be viewed as 10 zero-coupon instruments: one with a maturity value of $6 maturing six months from now; a second with a maturity value of $6 maturing one year from now; a third with a maturity value of $6 maturing 1.5 years from now, and so on. The final zero-coupon instrument matures 10 six-month periods from now and has a maturity value of $106.

Likewise, bond B can be viewed as 10 zero-coupon instruments: one with a maturity value of $1.50 maturing six months from now; one with a maturity value of $1.50 maturing one year from now; one with a maturity value of $1.50 maturing 1.5 years from now, and so on. The final zero-coupon instrument matures 10 six-month periods from now and has a maturity value of $101.50. Obviously, in the case of each coupon bond, the value or price of the bond is equal to the total value of its component zero-coupon instruments.

In general, any bond can be viewed as a package of zero-coupon instruments. That is, each zero-coupon instrument in the package has a maturity equal to its coupon payment date or, in the case of the principal, the maturity date. The value of the bond should equal the value of all the component zero-coupon instruments. If this does not hold, it is possible for a market participant to generate riskless profits. Because no one can pass up riskless and certain profits, the market must drive these two prices to equality, and our discussion here assumes that equality.

To determine the value of each zero-coupon instrument, it is necessary to know the yield on a zero-coupon Treasury with that same maturity. This yield is called the **spot rate**, and the graphical depiction of the relationship between the spot rate and its maturity is called the **spot rate curve**. Below we will see how to derive this curve from theoretical considerations of the yields of the actually traded Treasury securities. Such a curve is called a *theoretical spot rate curve*.

Constructing the Theoretical Spot Rate Curve

In this section, we explain how the theoretical spot rate curve is constructed from the yield curve that is based on the observed yields of Treasury bills and Treasury coupon securities. The process of creating a theoretical spot rate curve in this way is called **bootstrapping**.[2] To explain this process, we will use the data for the hypothetical price, annualized yield (yield to maturity), and maturity of the 20 Treasury securities shown in Table 1. (In practice, all the coupon rates are estimated so that the price of each bond is par.)

Table 1	Maturity and Yield to Maturity for 20 Hypothetical Treasury Securities		
Maturity (years)	**Coupon Rate**	**Yield to Maturity**	**Price**
0.50	0.0000	0.0800	$ 96.15
1.00	0.0000	0.0830	92.19
1.50	0.0850	0.0890	99.45
2.00	0.0900	0.0920	99.64
4.00	0.1000	0.1040	98.72
4.50	0.1150	0.1060	103.16
5.00	0.0875	0.1080	92.24
5.50	0.1050	0.1090	98.38
6.00	0.1100	0.1120	99.14
2.50	0.1100	0.0940	103.49
3.00	0.0950	0.0970	99.49
3.50	0.1000	0.1000	100.00
6.50	0.0850	0.1140	86.94
7.00	0.0825	0.1160	84.24
7.50	0.1100	0.1180	96.09
8.00	0.0650	0.1190	72.62
8.50	0.0875	0.1200	82.97
9.00	0.1300	0.1220	104.30
9.50	0.1150	0.1240	95.06
10.00	0.1250	0.1250	100.00

---

[2] In practice, the Treasury securities that are used to construct the theoretical spot rate curve are the most recently auctioned Treasury securities of a given maturity. Such issues are referred to as the *on-the-run Treasury issues*. There are actual zero-coupon Treasury securities with a maturity greater than one year that are outstanding in the market. These securities are not issued by the U.S. Treasury but are created by certain market participants from actual coupon Treasury securities. It would seem logical that the observed yield on zero-coupon Treasury securities can be used to construct an actual spot rate curve, but there are problems with this approach. First, the liquidity of these securities is not as great as that of the coupon Treasury market. Second, there are maturity sectors of the zero-coupon Treasury market that attract specific investors who may be willing to trade off yield in exchange for an attractive feature associated with that particular maturity sector, thereby distorting the term structure relationship.

Throughout the analysis and illustrations to come, it is important to remember that the basic principle underlying bootstrapping is that the value of the Treasury coupon security should be equal to the value of the package of zero-coupon Treasury securities that duplicates the coupon bond's cash flow.

Consider the six-month Treasury bill in Table 1. As we explained in the previous chapter, a Treasury bill is a zero-coupon instrument. Therefore, its annualized yield of 8% is equal to the spot rate. Similarly, for the one-year Treasury, the cited yield of 8.3% is the one-year spot rate.[3] Given these two spot rates, we can compute the spot rate for a theoretical 1.5-year zero-coupon Treasury. The price of a theoretical 1.5-year zero-coupon Treasury should equal the present value of the three cash flows from an actual 1.5-year coupon Treasury, where the yield used for discounting is the spot rate corresponding to the cash flow. Using $100 as par, the cash flow for the 1.5-year Treasury with the 8.5% coupon rate is

$$
\begin{array}{lll}
0.5 \text{ years} & 0.085 \times \$100 \times 0.5 & = \$4.25 \\
1.0 \text{ years} & 0.085 \times \$100 \times 0.5 & = \$4.25 \\
1.5 \text{ years} & 0.085 \times \$100 \times 0.5 + 100 & = \$104.25
\end{array}
$$

The present value of the cash flow is then

$$
\frac{4.25}{(1 + z_1)^1} + \frac{4.25}{(1 + z_2)^2} + \frac{104.25}{(1 + z_3)^3}
$$

where

z_1 = one-half the annualized six-month theoretical spot rate
z_2 = one-half the one-year theoretical spot rate
z_3 = one-half the 1.5-year theoretical spot rate

Since the six-month spot rate and one-year spot rate are 8.0% and 8.3%, respectively, we know these facts:

$$
z_1 = 0.04 \text{ and } z_2 = 0.0415
$$

We can compute the present value of the 1.5-year coupon Treasury security as

$$
\frac{4.25}{(1.0400)^1} + \frac{4.25}{(1.0415)^2} + \frac{104.25}{(1 + z_3)^3}
$$

Since the price of the 1.5-year coupon Treasury security (from Table 1) is $99.45, the following relationship between market price and the present value of the cash flow must hold:

$$
99.45 = \frac{4.25}{(1.0400)^1} + \frac{4.25}{(1.0415)^2} + \frac{104.25}{(1 + z_3)^3}
$$

We can solve for the theoretical 1.5-year spot rate as follows:

$$
99.45 = 4.08654 + 3.91805 + \frac{104.25}{(1 + z_3)^3}
$$

$$
91.44541 = \frac{104.25}{(1 + z_3)^3}
$$

---

[3] For zero-coupon securities such as Treasury bills, the price is less than par value.

$$(1 + z_3)^3 = 1.140024$$
$$z_3 = 0.04465$$

Doubling this yield, we obtain the bond equivalent yield of 0.0893 or 8.93%, which is the theoretical 1.5-year spot rate. That rate is the rate that the market would apply to a 1.5-year zero-coupon Treasury security if, in fact, such a security existed.

Given the theoretical 1.5-year spot rate, we can obtain the theoretical two-year spot rate. The cash flow for the two-year coupon Treasury in Table 1 is

0.5 years	$0.090 \times \$100 \times 0.5$	$= \$4.50$
1.0 years	$0.090 \times \$100 \times 0.5$	$= \$4.50$
1.5 years	$0.090 \times \$100 \times 0.5$	$= \$4.50$
2.0 years	$0.090 \times \$100 \times 0.5 + 100$	$= \$104.50$

The present value of the cash flow is then

$$\frac{4.50}{(1 + z_1)^1} + \frac{4.50}{(1 + z_2)^2} + \frac{4.50}{(1 + z_3)^3} + \frac{104.50}{(1 + z_4)^4}$$

where z_4 is one-half the two-year theoretical spot rate. Since the six-month spot rate, one-year spot rate, and 1.5-year spot rate are 8.0%, 8.3%, and 8.93%, respectively, then

$$z_1 = 0.04, z_2 = 0.0415, \text{ and } z_3 = 0.04465$$

Therefore, the present value of the two-year coupon Treasury security is

$$\frac{4.50}{(1.0400)^1} + \frac{4.50}{(1.0415)^2} + \frac{4.50}{(1.04465)^3} + \frac{104.50}{(1 + z_4)^4}$$

Since the price of the two-year coupon Treasury security is $99.64, the following relationship must hold:

$$99.64 = \frac{4.50}{(1.0400)^1} + \frac{4.50}{(1.0415)^2} + \frac{4.50}{(1.04465)^3} + \frac{104.50}{(1 + z_4)^4}$$

We can solve for the theoretical two-year spot rate as follows:

$$99.64 = 4.32692 + 4.14853 + 3.94730 + \frac{104.25}{(1 + z_4)^4}$$

$$87.21725 = \frac{104.25}{(1 + z_4)^4}$$

$$(1 + z_4)^4 = 1.198158$$

$$z_4 = 0.046235$$

Doubling this yield, we obtain the theoretical two-year spot rate bond-equivalent yield of 9.247%.

One can follow this approach sequentially to derive the theoretical 2.5-year spot rate from the calculated values of z_1, z_2, z_3, and z_4 (the six-month, one-year, 1.5-year, and two-year rates), and the price and coupon of the bond with a maturity of 2.5 years. Furthermore, one could derive theoretical spot rates for the remaining 15 half-yearly rates. The spot rates thus obtained are shown in Table 2. They represent the term structure of interest rates for maturities up to 10 years, at the particular time to which the bond price quotations refer.

Table 2   Theoretical Spot Rates

Maturity (years)	Yield to Maturity	Theoretical Spot Rate
0.50	0.0800	0.08000
1.00	0.0830	0.08300
1.50	0.0890	0.08930
2.00	0.0920	0.09247
2.50	0.0940	0.09468
3.00	0.0970	0.09787
3.50	0.1000	0.10129
4.00	0.1040	0.10592
4.50	0.1060	0.10850
5.00	0.1080	0.11021
5.50	0.1090	0.11175
6.00	0.1120	0.11584
6.50	0.1140	0.11744
7.00	0.1160	0.11991
7.50	0.1180	0.12405
8.00	0.1190	0.12278
8.50	0.1200	0.12546
9.00	0.1220	0.13152
9.50	0.1240	0.13377
10.00	0.1250	0.13623

Column 2 of Table 2 reproduces the calculated yield to maturity for the coupon issue listed in Table 1. A comparison of this column with the last column giving the yield to maturity of a zero-coupon bond is instructive, for it confirms that bonds of the same maturity may have different yields to maturity. That is, the yield of bonds of the same credit quality does not depend on their maturity alone. While the two columns do not change much at the beginning, they diverge more after the third year, and by the ninth year the zero-coupon yield is nearly 100 basis points higher than that of the same maturity with a coupon of 13% and selling at a premium.

Using Spot Rates to Value a Bond

Given the spot rates, the theoretical value of a bond can be calculated. This is done by discounting a cash flow for a given period by the corresponding spot rate for that period. This is illustrated in Table 3.

The bond in our illustration is a 10-year, 10% coupon Treasury bond. The second column of Table 3 shows the cash flow per $100 of par value for a 10% coupon bond. The third column shows the theoretical spot rates. The fourth column is simply one half of the annual spot rate of the previous column. The last column shows the present value of the cash flow in the second column when discounted at the semiannual spot rate. The value of this bond is the total present value, $85.35477.

Table 3 Illustration of How to Value a 10-Year, 10% Treasury Bond Using Spot Rates

Maturity (years)	Case Flow	Spot Rate	Semiannual Spot Rate	Present Value
0.5	5	0.08000	0.04000	4.8077
1.0	5	0.08300	0.04150	4.6095
1.5	5	0.08930	0.04465	4.3859
2.0	5	0.09247	0.04624	4.1730
2.5	5	0.09468	0.04734	3.9676
3.0	5	0.09787	0.04894	3.7539
3.5	5	0.10129	0.05065	3.5382
4.0	5	0.10592	0.05296	3.3088
4.5	5	0.10850	0.05425	3.1080
5.0	5	0.11021	0.05511	2.9242
5.5	5	0.11175	0.05588	2.7494
6.0	5	0.11584	0.05792	2.5441
6.5	5	0.11744	0.05872	2.3813
7.0	5	0.11991	0.05996	2.2128
7.5	5	0.12405	0.06203	2.0274
8.0	5	0.12278	0.06139	1.9274
8.5	5	0.12546	0.06273	1.7774
9.0	5	0.13152	0.06576	1.5889
9.5	5	0.13377	0.06689	1.4613
10.0	105	0.13623	0.06812	28.1079
Total				85.35477

Key Points That You Should Understand Before Proceeding

1. What the yield curve represents.
2. Why any financial asset can be viewed as a package of zero-coupon instruments.
3. What is meant by spot rates and how the theoretical spot rates can be constructed from a Treasury yield curve.
4. How to value a bond using spot rates.

FORWARD RATES

Thus far, we have seen that from the Treasury yield curve we can extrapolate the theoretical spot rates. In addition, we can extrapolate what some market participants refer to as the *market's consensus of future interest rates*. To see the importance of knowing the market's consensus for future interest rates, consider the following two investment alternatives for an investor who has a one-year investment horizon:

Alternative 1: Investor buys a one-year instrument.
Alternative 2: Investor buys a six-month instrument and when it matures in six months, the investor buys another six-month instrument.

Figure 2   Two Alternative One-Year Investments

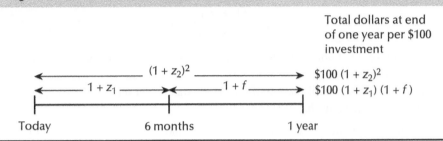

With Alternative 1, the investor will realize the one-year spot rate and that rate is known with certainty. In contrast, with Alternative 2, the investor will realize the six-month spot rate, but the six-month rate six months from now is unknown. Therefore, for Alternative 2, the rate that will be earned over one year is not known with certainty. This is illustrated in Figure 2.

Suppose that this investor expected that six months from now the six-month rate will be higher than it is today. The investor might then feel Alternative 2 would be the better investment. However, this is not necessarily true. To understand why and to appreciate the need to understand why it is necessary to know what the market's consensus of future interest rates is, let's continue with our illustration.

The investor will be indifferent to the two alternatives if they produce the same total dollars over the one-year investment horizon. Given the one-year spot rate, there is some rate on a six-month instrument six months from now that will make the investor indifferent between the two alternatives. We will denote that rate by f.

The value of f can be readily determined given the one-year spot rate and the six-month spot rate. If an investor placed $100 in a one-year instrument (Alternative 1), the total dollars that will be generated at the end of one year is

$$\text{Total dollars at the end of year for Alternative 1} = \$100(1 + z_2)^2$$

where z_2 is the one-year spot rate. (Remember we are working in six-month periods, so the subscript 2 represents two six-month periods, or one year.)

The proceeds from investing at the six-month spot rate will generate the following total dollars at the end of six months:

$$\text{Total dollars at the end of six months for Alternative 2} = \$100(1 + z_1)$$

where z_1 is the six-month spot rate. If this amount is reinvested at the six-month rate six months from now, which we denoted f, then the total dollars at the end of one year would be

$$\text{Total dollars at the end of year for Alternative 2} = \$100(1 + z_1)(1 + f)$$

The investor will be indifferent between the two alternatives if the total dollars are the same. Setting the two equations for the total dollars at end of one year for the two alternatives equal we get

$$\$100 = (1 + z_2)^2 = \$100(1 + z_1)(1 + f)$$

Solving the preceding equation for f, we get

$$f = \frac{(1 + z_2)^2}{(1 + z_1)} - 1$$

Doubling f gives the bond-equivalent yield for the six-month rate six months from now that we are interested in.

We can illustrate the calculation of f using the theoretical spot rates shown in Table 2. From that table, we know that

Six-month spot rate = 0.080, therefore z_1 = 0.0400
One-year spot rate = 0.083, therefore z_2 = 0.0415

Substituting into the formula, we have

$$f = \frac{(1.0415)^2}{(1.0400)} - 1$$
$$= 0.043$$

Therefore, the forward rate on a six-month security, quoted on a bond-equivalent basis, is 8.6% (0.043 × 2).

Here is how we use this rate of 8.6%. If the six-month rate six months from now is less than 8.6%, then the total dollars at the end of one year would be higher by investing in the one-year instrument (Alternative 1). If the six-month rate six months from now is greater than 8.6%, then the total dollars at the end of one year would be higher by investing in the six-month instrument and reinvesting the proceeds six months from now at the six-month rate at the time (Alternative 2). Of course, if the six-month rate six months from now is 8.6%, the two alternatives give the same total dollars at the end of one year.

Now that we have the rate f in which we are interested and we know how that rate can be used, let's return to the question we posed at the outset. From Table 2, the six-month spot rate is 8%. Suppose that the investor expects that six months from now, the six month rate will be 8.2%. That is, the investor expects that the six-month rate will be higher than its current level. Should the investor select Alternative 2 because the six-month rate six months from now is expected to be higher? The answer is no. As we explained in the previous paragraph, if the rate is less than 8.6%, then Alternative 1 is the better alternative. Since this investor expects a rate of 8.2%, then he or she should select Alternative 1 despite the fact that he or she expects the six-month rate to be higher than it is today.

This is a somewhat surprising result for some investors. But the reason for this is that the market prices its expectations of future interest rates into the rates offered on investments with different maturities. This is why knowing the market's consensus of future interest rates is critical. The rate that we determined for f is the market's consensus for the six-month rate six months from now. A future interest rate calculated from either the spot rates or the yield curve is called a **forward rate** or an **implied forward rate**.

Similarly, borrowers need to understand what a forward rate is. For example, suppose a borrower must choose between a one-year loan and a series of two six-month loans. If the forward rate is less than the borrower's expectations of six-month rates six months from now, then the borrower will be better off with a one-year loan. If, instead, the borrower's expectations are that six-month rates six months from now will be less than the forward rate, the borrower will be better off by choosing a series of two six-month loans.

There are two elements to the forward rate. The first is when in the future the rate begins. The second is the length of time for the rate. For example, the two-year forward rate three years from now means a rate three years from now for a length of two years. The notation used for a forward rate, f, will have two subscripts—one before f and one after f as shown below:

$$_tf_m$$

The subscript before f is t and is the length of time that the rate applies. The subscript after f is m and is when the forward rate begins. That is,

the length of time of the forward rate f when the forward rate begins

Remember our time periods are still six-month periods. Given the above notation, here is what the following mean:

Notation	Interpretation for the Forward Rate
$_1f_{12}$	six-month (one-period) forward rate beginning six years (12 periods) from now
$_2f_8$	one-year (two-period) forward rate beginning four years (8 periods) from now
$_6f_4$	three-year (six-period) forward rate beginning two years (4 periods) from now
$_8f_{10}$	four-year (eight-period) forward rate beginning five years (10 periods) from now

It can be demonstrated that the formula to compute any forward rate is

$$_tf_m = \left[\frac{(1 + z_{m+t})^{m+t}}{(1 + z_m)^m} \right]^{1/t} - 1$$

Notice that if t is equal to 1, the formula reduces to the one-period (six-month) forward rate.

To illustrate, for the spot rates shown in Table 2, suppose that an investor wants to know the two-year forward rate three years from now. In terms of the notation, t is equal to 4 and m is equal to 6. Substituting for t and m into the equation for the forward rate we have

$$_4f_6 = \left[\frac{(1 + z_{6+4})^{6+4}}{(1 + z_6)^6} \right]^{1/4} - 1$$

This means that the following two spot rates are needed: z_6 (the three-year spot rate) and z_{10} (the five-year spot rate). From Table 3, we know

z_6(the three-year spot rate) $= 9.9787\%/2 = 4.894\% = 0.04894$

z_{10}(the five-year spot rate) $= 13.623\%/2 = 6.812\% = 0.06812$

then

$$_4f_6 = \left[\frac{(1.06812)^{10}}{(1.04894)^6} \right]^{1/4} - 1 = 0.09755 = 9.755\%$$

Therefore, $_4f_6$ is equal to 9.755%, and doubling this rate gives 19.510%, the forward rate on a bond-equivalent basis.

We can verify this result. Investing $100 for 10 periods at the semiannual spot rate of 6.812% will produce the following value:

$$\$100(1.06812)^{10} = \$193.286.$$

By investing $100 for six periods at 4.894% and reinvesting the proceeds for four periods at the forward rate of 9.755%, it gives the same value

$$\$100(1.04894)^6(1.09755)^4 = \$193.286.$$

Relationship between Spot Rates and Short-Term Forward Rates

Suppose an investor purchases a five-year, zero-coupon Treasury security for $58.48 with a maturity value of $100. The investor could instead buy a six-month Treasury bill and reinvest the proceeds every six months for five years. The number of dollars that will be realized will depend on the six-month forward rates. Suppose that the investor can actually reinvest the proceeds maturing every six months at the implied six-month forward rates. Let us see how many dollars would accumulate at the end of five years. The implied six-month forward rates were calculated for the yield curve given in Table 2. Letting f_t denote the six-month forward rate beginning t six-month periods from now, then the semiannual implied forward rates using the spot rates shown in Table 2 are

$$f_1 = 0.043000 \quad f_2 = 0.050980 \quad f_3 = 0.051005 \quad f_4 = 0.051770$$
$$f_5 = 0.056945 \quad f_6 = 0.060965 \quad f_7 = 0.069310 \quad f_8 = 0.064625$$
$$f_9 = 0.062830$$

By investing the $58.48 at the six-month spot rate of 4% (8% on a bond-equivalent basis) and reinvesting at the foregoing forward rates, the number of dollars accumulated at the end of five years would be

$$\$58.48(1.04)(1.043)(1.05098)(1.051005)(1.05177)(1.056945)$$
$$(1.060965)(1.069310)(1.064625)(1.06283) = \$100$$

Therefore, we see that if the implied forward rates are realized, the $58.48 investment will produce the same number of dollars as an investment in a five-year, zero-coupon Treasury security at the five-year spot rate. From this illustration, we can see that the five-year spot rate is related to the current six-month spot rate and the implied six-month forward rates.

In general, the relationship between a t-period spot rate, the current six-month spot rate, and the implied six-month forward rates is as follows:

$$z_t = [(1 + z_1)(1 + f_1)(1 + f_2)(1 + f_3) \cdots (1 + f_{t-1})]^{1/t} - 1$$

To illustrate how to use this equation, look at how the five-year (10-period) spot rate is related to the six-month forward rates. Substituting into the preceding equation the relevant forward rates just given and the one-period spot rate of 4% (one-half the 8% annual spot rate), we obtain

$$z_{10} = [(1.04)(1.043)(1.05098)(1.051005)(1.05177)(1.056945)$$
$$(1.060965)(1.069310)(1.064625)(1.06283))]^{1/10} - 1$$
$$= 5.51\%$$

Doubling 5.51% gives an annual spot rate of 11.02%, which agrees with the spot rate given in Table 2.

Forward Rate as a Hedgeable Rate

A natural question about forward rates is how well they do at predicting future interest rates. Studies have demonstrated that forward rates do not do a good job in predicting future interest rates.[4] Then, why the big deal about understanding forward rates? The reason, as we demonstrated in our illustration of how to select between two alternative investments, is that the forward rates indicate how an investor's expectations must differ from the market consensus in order to make the correct decision.

In our illustration, the six-month forward rate may not be realized. That is irrelevant. The fact is that the six-month forward rate indicated to the investor that if expectations about the six-month rate six months from now are less than 8.6%, the investor would be better off with Alternative 1.

For this reason, as well as others explained later, some market participants prefer not to talk about forward rates as being market consensus rates. Instead, they refer to forward rates as being *hedgeable rates*. For example, by buying the one-year security, the investor was able to hedge the six-month rate six months from now.

HISTORICAL SHAPES OBSERVED FOR THE TREASURY YIELD CURVE

If we plot the term structure—the yield to maturity, or the spot rate, at successive maturities against maturity—what is it likely to look like? Figure 1 shows three *generic* shapes that have appeared for the U.S. Treasury yield curve with some frequency over time. Table 4 shows five selective daily Treasury yield curves in tabular form.

Panel A of Figure 1 shows an upward-sloping yield curve; that is, yield rises steadily as maturity increases. This shape is commonly referred to as a **positively sloped yield curve.** Market participants differentiate positively sloped yield curves based on the steepness or slope of the curve. The slope is commonly measured in terms of the maturity spread, where the maturity spread is the difference between long-term and short-term yields. While there are many maturity candidates to proxy for long-term and short-term yields, we will just use the maturity spread between the six-month and 30-year yield in our example.

The first two daily yield curves shown in Table 4 are positively sloped yield curves. Notice that the three-month and six-month yields are roughly the same for both dates.

Table 4   U.S. Treasury Yield Curve for Five Selected Dates

Day	3 months	6 months	1 year	2 years	3 years	5 years	7 years	10 years	20 years	30 years	Shape
4/23/2001	3.75	3.78	3.75	3.77	4.15	4.38	4.78	5.06	5.84	5.73	Normal
4/10/1992	3.74	3.88	4.12	5.16	5.72	6.62	7.03	7.37	N/A	7.89	Steep
8/14/1981	N/A	N/A	16.71	16.91	15.88	15.34	15.04	NA	14.74	13.95	Inverted
1/3/1990	7.89	7.94	7.85	7.94	7.96	7.92	8.04	7.99	N/A	8.04	Flat
1/4/2001	5.37	5.20	4.82	4.77	4.78	4.82	5.07	5/03	5.56	5.44	Humped

Note: *The data for 4/23/2001, 4/10/1992, 1/3/90, and 1/4/2001 were obtained from the daily yield curves provided by the U.S. Treasury. The data for 8/14/81 were obtained from various Treasury yield tables published by the U.S. Treasury.*

---

[4] Eugene F. Fama, "Forward Rates as Predictors of Future Spot Rates," *Journal of Financial Economics*, 3, no. 4 (1976), pp. 361–377.

However, the steepness of the slope is different. The maturity spread between the 30-year and six-month yield (i.e., the three-month/six-month spread) was 195 basis points (5.73% to 3.78%) on 4/23/2001 and 401 basis points (7.89% to 3.88%) on 4/10/1992. The convention in the marketplace is to refer to a positively sloped yield curve as a **normal yield curve** when the spread between the six-month and 30-year yield is 300 basis points or less; when the maturity spread is more than 300 basis points, the yield curve is said to be a **steep yield curve**.

When a yield curve's maturity spread increases (or in the parlance of the market, it "widens"), the yield curve is said to *steepen*; when the maturity spread decreases (i.e., "narrows"), the yield curve is said to *flatten*.

Panel B of Figure 1 shows a downward-sloping or **inverted yield curve**, where yields are in general decline as maturity increases. There have not been many instances in the recent history of the U.S. Treasury market where the yield curve exhibited this characteristic. The most notable example is in August 1981. Table 4 shows the daily yield curve for one day in that month, August 14th. Treasury yields at the time were at a historic high. The yield on the two-year was 16.91% and declined for each subsequent maturity until it reached 13.95% for the 30-year maturity.

Finally, panel C of Figure 1 shows a **flat yield curve**. While the figure suggests that in a flat yield curve the yields are identical for each maturity, that is not what is observed in the maturity. Rather, the yields for all maturities are similar. See the yield curve on 1/3/1990. Notice the very small six-month/30-year maturity spread: 10 basis points. A variant of the flat yield is one in which the yields on short-term and long-term Treasuries are similar but the yield on intermediate-term Treasuries is lower.

DETERMINANTS OF THE SHAPE OF THE TERM STRUCTURE

Two major theories have evolved to account for these observed shapes of the yield curve: the **expectations theory** and the **market segmentation theory**.

There are several forms of the expectations theory—the **pure expectations theory**, the **liquidity theory**, and the **preferred habitat theory**. All share a hypothesis about the behavior of short-term forward rates and also assume that the forward rates in current long-term contracts are closely related to the market's expectations about future short-term rates. These three theories differ, however, on whether or not other factors also affect forward rates, and how. The pure expectations theory postulates that no systematic factors other than expected future short-term rates affect forward rates; the liquidity theory and the preferred habitat theory assert that there are other factors. Accordingly, the last two forms of the expectations theory are sometimes referred to as **biased expectations theories**. Figure 3 depicts the relationship between these three theories.

The Pure Expectations Theory

According to the pure expectations theory, the forward rates exclusively represent the expected future rates. Thus, the entire term structure at a given time reflects the market's current expectations of the family of future short-term rates. Under this view, a rising term structure, as in panel A of Figure 1, must indicate that the market expects short-term rates to rise throughout the relevant future. Similarly, a flat term structure reflects an expectation that future short-term rates will be mostly constant, while a falling term structure must reflect an expectation that future short rates will decline steadily.

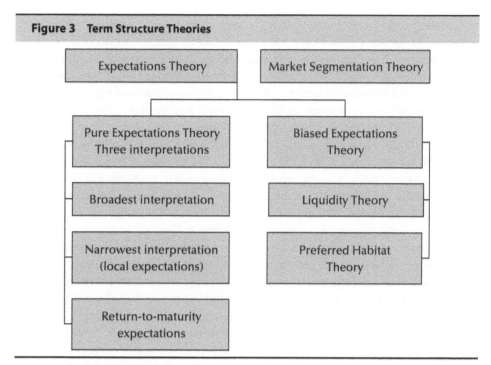

Figure 3   Term Structure Theories

Source: *Frank J. Fabozzi, Valuation of Fixed Income Securities and Derivatives (New Hope, PA: Frank J. Fabozzi Associates, 1995), p. 49.*

We can illustrate this theory by considering how an expectation of a rising short-term future rate would affect the behavior of various market participants, so as to result in a rising yield curve. Assume an initially flat term structure, and suppose that economic news subsequently leads market participants to expect interest rates to rise.

1. Those market participants interested in a long-term investment would not want to buy long-term bonds because they would expect the yield structure to rise sooner or later, resulting in a price decline for the bonds and a capital loss on the long-term bonds purchased. Instead, they would want to invest in short-term debt obligations until the rise in yield had occurred, permitting them to reinvest their funds at the higher yield.

2. Speculators expecting rising rates would anticipate a decline in the price of long-term bonds and, therefore, would want to sell any long-term bonds they own and possibly to "short sell" some they do not now own.[5] (Should interest rates rise as expected, the price of longer-term bonds will fall. Since the speculator sold these bonds short and can then purchase them at a lower price to cover the short sale, a profit will be earned.) The proceeds received from the selling of long-term debt issues the speculators now hold or the shorting of longer-term bonds will be invested in short-term debt obligations.

3. Borrowers wishing to acquire long-term funds would be pulled toward borrowing now, in the long end of the market, by the expectation that borrowing at a later time would be more expensive.

---

[5] Short selling means selling a security that is not owned but borrowed.

All these responses would tend either to lower the net demand for, or to increase the supply of, long-maturity bonds, and two responses would increase demand for short-term debt obligations. Clearing of the market would require a rise in long-term yields in relation to short-term yields; that is, these actions by investors, speculators, and borrowers would tilt the term structure upward until it is consistent with expectations of higher future interest rates. By analogous reasoning, an unexpected event leading to the expectation of lower future rates will result in the yield curve sloping down.

Unfortunately, the pure expectations theory suffers from one shortcoming, which, qualitatively, is quite serious. It neglects the risks inherent in investing in bonds and like instruments. If forward rates were perfect predictors of future interest rates, then the future prices of bonds would be known with certainty. The return over any investment period would be certain and independent of the maturity of the instrument initially acquired and of the time at which the investor needed to liquidate the instrument. However, with uncertainty about future interest rates and hence about future prices of bonds, these instruments become risky investments in the sense that the return over some investment horizon is unknown.

Similarly, from a borrower or issuer's perspective, the cost of borrowing for any required period of financing would be certain and independent of the maturity of the instrument initially sold if the rate at which the borrower must refinance debt in the future is known. But with uncertainty about future interest rates, the cost of borrowing is uncertain if the borrower must refinance at some time over the periods in which the funds are initially needed.

In the following section, we examine more closely the sources and types of risk that the pure expectations theory ignores.

Risks Associated with Bond Investment

There are two risks that cause uncertainty about the return over some investment horizon. The first is the uncertainty about the price of the bond at the end of the investment horizon. For example, an investor who plans to invest for five years might consider the following three investment alternatives: (1) invest in a five-year bond and hold it for five years, (2) invest in a 12-year bond and sell it at the end of five years, and (3) invest in a 30-year bond and sell it at the end of five years. The return that will be realized for the second and third alternatives is not known because the price of each long-term bond at the end of five years is not known. In the case of the 12-year bond, the price will depend on the yield on seven-year debt securities five years from now; and the price of the 30-year bond will depend on the yield on 25-year bonds five years from now. Since forward rates implicit in the current term structure for a future 12-year bond and a future 25-year bond are not perfect predictors of the actual future rates, there is uncertainty about the price for both bonds five years from now.

The risk that the price of the bond will be lower than currently expected at the end of the investment horizon is called **price risk**. An important feature of price risk is that it is greater the longer the maturity of the bond. The reason is that the longer the maturity, the greater the price volatility of a bond when yields rise. Thus, investors are exposed to price risk when they invest in a bond that will be sold prior to the bond's maturity date.

The second risk has to do with uncertainty about the rate at which the proceeds from a bond that matures prior to the maturity date can be reinvested until the maturity date. For example, an investor who plans to invest for five years might consider the following three alternative investments: (1) invest in a five-year bond and hold it for five years; (2) invest in a six-month instrument and, when it matures, reinvest the proceeds in six-month instruments over the entire five-year investment horizon; and (3) invest in a two-year bond and, when it matures, reinvest the proceeds in a three-year bond. The risk in the second and third alternatives is that the return over the five-year investment horizon is unknown because rates at which the proceeds can be reinvested until maturity are unknown. This risk is referred to as **reinvestment risk**.

Interpretations of the Pure Expectations Theory

There are several interpretations of the pure expectations theory that have been put forth by economists. These interpretations are not exact equivalents, nor are they consistent with each other, in large part because they offer different treatments of the two risks associated with realizing a return that we have just explained.[6]

The broadest interpretation of the pure expectations theory suggests that investors expect the return for any investment horizon to be the same, regardless of the maturity strategy selected.[7] For example, consider an investor who has a five-year investment horizon. According to this theory, it makes no difference if a five-year, 12-year, or 30-year bond is purchased and held for five years because the investor expects the return from all three bonds to be the same over five years. A major criticism of this very broad interpretation of the theory is that, because of price risk associated with investing in bonds with a maturity greater than the investment horizon, the expected returns from these three very different bond investments should differ in significant ways.[8]

A second interpretation, referred to as the *local expectations* form of the pure expectations theory, suggests that the return will be the same over a short-term investment horizon starting today. For example, if an investor has a six-month investment horizon, buying a five-year, 10-year, or 20-year bond will produce the same six-month return. It has been demonstrated that the local expectations formulation, which is narrow in scope, is the only one of the interpretations of the pure expectations theory that can be sustained in equilibrium.[9]

The third and final interpretation of the pure expectations theory suggests that the return that an investor will realize by rolling over short-term bonds to some investment horizon will be the same as holding a zero-coupon bond with a maturity that is the same as that investment horizon. (A zero-coupon bond has no reinvestment risk, so future interest rates over the investment horizon do not affect the return.) This variant is called the *return-to-maturity expectations* interpretation.

For example, let's once again assume that an investor has a five-year investment horizon. By buying a five-year zero-coupon bond and holding it to maturity, the investor's return is the difference between the maturity value and the price of the bond, all divided by the price of the bond. According to return-to-maturity expectations, the same return will be realized by buying a six-month instrument and rolling it over for five years. At this time, the validity of this interpretation is subject to considerable doubt.

---

[6] These formulations are summarized by John Cox, Jonathan Ingersoll, Jr., and Stephen Ross, "A Re-examination of Traditional Hypotheses About the Term Structure of Interest Rates," *Journal of Finance* (September 1981), pp. 769–799.

[7] F. Lutz, "The Structure of Interest Rates," *Quarterly Journal of Economics* (1940–41), pp. 36–63.

[8] Cox, Ingersoll, and Ross, "A Re-examination of Traditional Hypotheses," pp. 774–775.

[9] Cox, Ingersoll, and Ross, "A Re-examination of Traditional Hypotheses," pp. 774–775.

The Liquidity Theory

We have explained that the drawback of the pure expectations theory is that it does not consider the risks associated with investing in bonds. Nonetheless, we have just shown that there is indeed risk in holding a long-term bond for one period, and that risk increases with the bond's maturity because maturity and price volatility are directly related.

Given this uncertainty, and the reasonable consideration that investors typically do not like uncertainty, some economists and financial analysts have suggested a different theory. This theory states that investors will hold longer-term maturities if they are offered a long-term rate higher than the average of expected future rates by a risk premium that is positively related to the term to maturity.[10] Put differently, the forward rates should reflect both interest rate expectations and a "liquidity" premium (really a risk premium), and the premium should be higher for longer maturities.

According to this theory, which is called the **liquidity theory of the term structure**, the implicit forward rates will not be an unbiased estimate of the market's expectations of future interest rates because they embody a liquidity premium. Thus, an upward-sloping yield curve may reflect expectations that future interest rates either (1) will rise, or (2) will be flat or even fall, but with a liquidity premium increasing fast enough with maturity so as to produce an upward-sloping yield curve.

The Preferred Habitat Theory

Another theory, known as the preferred habitat theory, also adopts the view that the term structure reflects the expectation of the future path of interest rates as well as a risk premium. However, the habitat theory rejects the assertion that the risk premium must rise uniformly with maturity.[11] Proponents of the habitat theory say that the latter conclusion could be accepted if all investors intend to liquidate their investment at the first possible date, while all borrowers are eager to borrow long, but that this is an assumption that can be rejected for a number of reasons.

In the first place, it is obvious that many investors wish to carry resources forward for appreciable periods of time—to buy a house, for example, or to provide for retirement. Such investors are concerned with the amount available at the appropriate time, and not the path by which that goal is reached. Hence, risk aversion dictates that they should prefer an instrument with a maturity matching the period for which they wish to invest over shorter-term investment vehicles. If these investors buy a shorter instrument, they will bear reinvestment risk—the risk of a fall in the interest rates available for reinvesting proceeds of the shorter instrument. Investors can avoid that risk only by locking in the current long rate through a long-term contract. Similarly, if they buy an instrument with maturity longer than the time they wish to invest for, they will bear the risk of a loss in the price of the asset (price risk) when liquidating it before its maturity, because of a rise in interest rates. Entirely analogous considerations apply to borrowers; prudence and safety call for borrowing for a maturity by matching the length of time for which funds are required.

---

[10] John R. Hicks, *Value and Capital*, 2nd ed. (London: Oxford University Press, 1946), pp. 141–145.

[11] Franco Modigliani and Richard Sutch, "Innovations in Interest Rate Policy," *American Economic Review* (May 1966), pp. 178–197.

In the second place, a lot of the demand for and supply of securities these days comes from financial intermediaries, which have liabilities with specified maturities. These institutions seek to match as closely as possible the maturity of their liabilities with the cash flow of a portfolio of assets. In constructing such a portfolio, a financial institution will restrict its investments to certain maturity sectors.

To illustrate this preference for maturity sectors, consider a life insurance company that has issued a five-year guaranteed investment contract. The insurance company will not want to invest in six-month instruments because of the associated reinvestment risk. As another example, assume a thrift has borrowed funds at a fixed rate for one year with the proceeds from the issuance of a one-year certificate of deposit. The thrift is exposed to price (or interest rate) risk if the borrowed funds are invested in a bond with 20 years to maturity. Clearly, then, either of these institutions faces some kind of risk if it invests outside its preferred maturity sector.

The preferred habitat theory asserts that, to the extent that the demand and supply of funds in a given maturity range does not match, some lenders and borrowers will be induced to shift to maturities showing the opposite imbalances. However, they will need to be compensated by an appropriate risk premium whose magnitude will reflect the extent of aversion to either price or reinvestment risk.

Thus, this theory proposes that the shape of the yield curve is determined by both expectations of future interest rates and a risk premium, positive or negative, to induce market participants to shift out of their preferred habitat. Clearly, according to this theory, yield curves sloping up, down, flat, or humped are all possible.

Market Segmentation Theory

The market segmentation theory also recognizes that investors have preferred habitats dictated by saving and investment flows. This theory also proposes that the major reason for the shape of the yield curve lies in asset/liability management constraints (either regulatory or self-imposed) and/or creditors (borrowers) restricting their lending (financing) to specific maturity sectors.[12] However, the market segmentation theory differs from the preferred habitat theory in that it assumes that neither investors nor borrowers are willing to shift from one maturity sector to another to take advantage of opportunities arising from differences between expectations and forward rates.

Thus, for the segmentation theory, the shape of the yield curve is determined by supply of and demand for securities within each maturity sector. This formulation seems untenable because it presupposes the prevalence of absolute risk aversion, while the evidence does not support that proposition. Thus, market participants must be expected to shift away from their habitat when there are sufficiently large discrepancies between market and expected rates. This potential shifting ensures that the differences between market and expected rates will not grow too large, and this consideration leads back to the preferred habitat theory.

---

[12] This theory was suggested in J.M. Culbertson, "The Term Structure of Interest Rates," *Quarterly Journal of Economics* (November 1957), pp. 489–504.

THE MAIN INFLUENCES ON THE SHAPE OF THE YIELD CURVE

Comprehensive research on the main influences of the shape of the Treasury yield curve was done by Antti Ilmanen in a series of papers.[13] He finds that there are three main influences. The first is the market's expectations of future rate changes as explained earlier when we discussed the pure expectations theory. The other two are bond risk premiums and **convexity bias.**

Bond risk premiums are the expected return differentials across Treasury securities of different maturities. As explained in the previous section, there are theories of the term structure of interest rates that hypothesize why expected returns will vary by maturity. However, the theories disagree with respect to whether the risk premium is positive or negative. For example, the liquidity theory of the term structure would argue that the risk premium should increase with maturity; the market segmentation theory says that the bond risk premium can be positive or negative.

Ilmanen investigated the effect of the behavior of the bond risk premium using historical average *returns* on U.S. Treasury securities. Figure 4 shows the empirical average return curve as a function of average duration (not maturity) for the period 1972 to 2001. (Duration is a measure of the price sensitivity of a bond to changes in interest rates.) Also shown in the figure is the theoretical expected return curve based on expectations only (the first influence listed previously). Notice that this curve is linear (i.e., it increases linearly with duration). In contrast, notice that the empirical evidence suggests that the bond risk

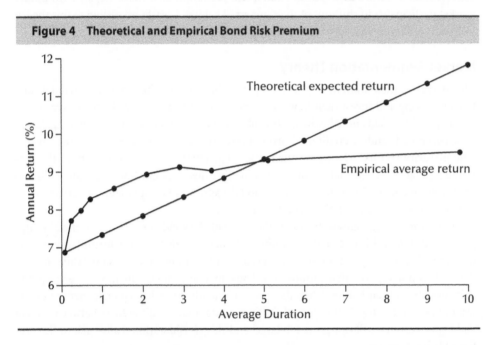

Figure 4   Theoretical and Empirical Bond Risk Premium

---

[13] The research first appeared as a report published by Salomon Brothers. Different parts of the research report were then published. See Antti Ilmanen, "Market's Rate Expectations and Forward Rates," *Journal of Fixed Income* (September 1996), pp. 8–22; Antti Ilmanen, "Does Duration Extension Enhance Long-Term Expected Returns?" *Journal of Fixed Income* (September 1996), pp. 23–36; Antti Ilmanen, "Convexity Bias in the Yield Curve," Chapter 3 in Narasimgan Jegadeesh and Bruce Tuckman (eds.), *Advanced Fixed-Income Valuation Tools* (New York: Wiley, 2000); and Antti Ilmanen, "Overview of Forward Rate Analysis," Chapter 8 in Frank J. Fabozzi (ed.), *The Handbook of Fixed Income Securities* (New York: McGraw Hill, 2005).

premiums are not linear in duration. Instead, the empirical evidence suggests that at the front end of the yield curve (i.e., up to a duration of 3), bond risk premiums increase steeply with duration. However, after a duration of 3, the bond risk premiums increase slowly. Ilmanen suggests that the shape shown in Figure 4 "may reflect the demand for long-term bonds from pension funds and other long-duration liability holders."[14] Pension funds seek long-term bonds to lock in rates to satisfy their liability obligation.

Now let's look to the convexity bias influence, an influence that Ilmanen argues is the least well known of the three influences. When interest rates change by a large number of basis points, a Treasury security's price change will not be the same for an increase and decrease in interest rates. More specifically, the price appreciation when interest rates fall will be greater than the price decline when interest rates rise by the same number of basis points. For example, if interest rates decline by 100 basis points, the price of a Treasury security might appreciate by 20%, but if interest rates increase by 100 basis points, the price of the same Treasury security might decline by only 15%. This attractive property of a bond is due to the shape of the relationship between price and yield and is referred to as the bond's convexity. The longer the maturity, the more convexity the security has. That is, longer-term Treasury securities have a more attractive feature due to convexity than shorter-term Treasury securities. As a result, investors are willing to pay more for longer-term Treasury securities and therefore accept lower returns. This influence on the shape of the Treasury yield curve is what is referred to as the *convexity bias*.

Key Points That You Should Understand Before Proceeding

1. The different shapes that have been observed for the yield curve.
2. The common hypothesis about the behavior of short-term forward rates shared by the various forms of the expectations theory.
3. The implications of the shape of the yield curve for future interest rates based on the pure expectations theory.
4. The two types of risks associated with investing in bonds and how these two risks affect the pure expectations theory.
5. How the two biased expectations theories differ from the pure expectations theory.
6. The three main influences on the shape of the Treasury yield curve are (1) the market's expectations of future rate changes, (2) bond risk premiums, and (3) convexity bias.

SUMMARY

The relationship between yield and maturity is referred to as the term structure of interest rates. The graphical depiction of the relationship between the yield on bonds of the same credit quality but different maturities is known as the yield curve. Since historically the yield on Treasury securities is the base rate off which a nongovernment bond's yield often is benchmarked, the most commonly constructed yield curve is the Treasury yield curve.

There is a problem with using the Treasury yield curve to determine the one yield at which to discount all the cash payments of any bond. Each cash flow within a bond's total

---

[14] Ilmanen, "Overview of Forward Rate Analysis," p. 167.

pattern of cash flows should be discounted at a unique interest rate that is applicable to the time period when the cash flow is to be received. Since any bond can be viewed as a package of zero-coupon instruments, its value should equal the value of all the component zero-coupon instruments. The rate on a zero-coupon bond is called the spot rate. The theoretical spot rate curve for Treasury securities can be estimated from the Treasury yield curve using a methodology known as bootstrapping.

Under certain assumptions, the market's expectation of future interest rates can be extrapolated from the theoretical Treasury spot rate curve. The resulting forward rate is called the implicit forward rate. The spot rate is related to the current six-month spot rate and the implicit six-month forward rates. A knowledge of the forward rates implicit in the current long-term rate is relevant in formulating both investment strategies and borrowing policies.

Several theories have been proposed about the determination of the term structure. The pure expectations theory hypothesizes that the one-period forward rates simply represent the market's expectations of future actual rates. Thus, the long-term spot rate would itself be explained fully by the market expectations of future short rates. The term structure might then be rising, falling, or flat, according to whether the market expects rising, falling, or unchanged short-term rates. This formulation fails to recognize the risks associated with investing in bonds—price risk and reinvestment risk—when investors buy bonds whose maturity is different from the time for which they plan to hold the bond.

The fact that there is price risk in investing in long-term bonds, and that it seems to increase with maturity, has given rise to an alternative liquidity theory of the term structure. According to this theory, forward rates are the sum of expected future rates and a risk premium that increases for more and more distant future rates and, hence, rises with the maturity of a bond. This formulation has shortcomings because it presupposes that all lenders want to lend short and all borrowers want to borrow long. If so, long borrowers would have to offer lenders a premium, rising with maturity, to accept the risk of going long. But in reality both lenders and borrowers have quite varied maturity preferences. Each market participant can eliminate risk, not by borrowing or lending short, but by lending (or borrowing) for a period coinciding with their preferred habitat. But, at the same time, agents would presumably be willing to depart from their preferred habitat by the inducement of a risk premium.

Accordingly, the third version of the expectations theory—namely, the preferred habitat theory—suggests, like the liquidity theory, that forward rates are the sum of a component reflecting expected future rates and a risk premium. However, the premium will not rise continuously with maturity but will materialize in any maturity neighborhood where supply exceeds demand. A negative premium or discount would be expected if supply exceeds demand.

One final theory explains the shape of the term structure by the concept of market segmentation. In common with the preferred habitat theory, it recognizes that participants in the bond market have maturity preferences. However, it postulates that these preferences are absolute and cannot be overcome by the expectation of a higher return from a different maturity, no matter how large. Each maturity is therefore a separate market, and the interest rate in every such market is determined by the given demand and supply. Thus, the interest rate at any maturity is totally unrelated to expectations of future rates. This formulation is of doubtful use because it implies highly irrational, implausible, and counterfactual behavior.

Empirical evidence suggests that the three main influences on the shape of the Treasury yield curve are (1) the market's expectations of future rate changes, (2) bond risk premiums, and (3) convexity bias.

KEY TERMS

- Biased expectations theories
- Bootstrapping
- Convexity bias
- Expectations theory
- Flat yield curve
- Forward rate (implied forward rate)
- Inverted yield curve
- Liquidity theory
- Liquidity theory of the term structure
- Market segmentation theory
- Normal yield curve

- Positively sloped yield curve
- Preferred habitat theory
- Price risk
- Pure expectations theory
- Reinvestment risk
- Steep yield curve
- Spot rate
- Spot rate curve
- Term structure of interest rates
- Yield curve
- Zero-coupon instrument

QUESTIONS

1. **a.** What is a yield curve?
   b. Historically, why has the Treasury yield curve been the one that is most closely watched by market participants?
2. What is meant by a spot rate?
3. Explain why it is inappropriate to use one yield to discount all the cash flows of a financial asset.
4. Explain why a financial asset can be viewed as a package of zero-coupon instruments.
5. Why is it important for lenders and borrowers to have a knowledge of forward rates?
6. How are spot rates related to forward rates?
7. You are a financial consultant. At various times, you have heard the following comments on interest rates from one of your clients. How would you respond to each comment?

   a. "The yield curve is upward sloping today. This suggests that the market consensus is that interest rates are expected to increase in the future."

   b. "I can't make any sense out of today's term structure. For short-term yields (up to three years), the spot rates increase with maturity; for maturities greater than three years but less than eight years, the spot rates decline with maturity; and for maturities greater than eight years the spot rates are virtually the same for each maturity. There is simply no theory that explains a term structure with this shape."

   c. "When I want to determine the market's consensus of future interest rates, I calculate the implicit forward rates."

8. You observe the Treasury yield curve below (all yields are shown on a bond-equivalent basis):

Year	Yield to Maturity	Spot Rate
0.5	5.25%	5.25%
1.0	5.50	5.50
1.5	5.75	5.76
2.0	6.00	?
2.5	6.25	?
3.0	6.50	?
3.5	6.75	?
4.0	7.00	?
4.5	7.25	?
5.0	7.50	?
5.5	7.75	7.97
6.0	8.00	8.27
6.5	8.25	8.59
7.0	8.50	8.92
7.5	8.75	9.25
8.0	9.00	9.61
8.5	9.25	9.97
9.0	9.50	10.36
9.5	9.75	10.77
10.0	10.00	11.20

All the securities maturing from 1.5 years on are selling at par. The 0.5-year and one-year securities are zero-coupon instruments.

a. Calculate the missing spot rates.

b. What should the price of the six-year Treasury security be?

c. What is the implicit six-month forward rate starting in the sixth year?

9. You observe the following Treasury yield curve (all yields are shown on a bond-equivalent basis):

Year	Yield to Maturity	Spot Rate
0.5	10.00%	10.00%
1.0	9.75	9.75
1.5	9.50	9.48
2.0	9.25	9.22
2.5	9.00	8.95
3.0	8.75	8.68
3.5	8.50	8.41
4.0	8.25	8.14
4.5	8.00	7.86
5.0	7.75	7.58
5.5	7.50	7.30
6.0	7.25	7.02
6.5	7.00	6.74
7.0	6.75	6.46
7.5	6.50	6.18
8.0	6.25	5.90
8.5	6.00	5.62
9.0	5.75	5.35
9.5	5.50	?
10.0	5.25	?

All the securities maturing from 1.5 years on are selling at par. The 0.5-year and one-year securities are zero-coupon instruments.

a. Calculate the missing spot rates.

b. What should the price of the four-year Treasury security be?

10. Using the theoretical spot rates in Table 2, calculate the theoretical value of a 7%, six-year Treasury bond.

11. **a.** Using the theoretical spot rates in Table 2, calculate the two-year forward rate four years from now.

b. Verify the answer by assuming an investment of $100 is invested for six years.

12. Explain the role that forward rates play in making investment decisions.

13. "Forward rates are poor predictors of the actual future rates that are realized. Consequently, they are of little value to an investor." Explain why you agree or disagree with this statement.

14. An investor is considering two alternative investments. The first alternative is to invest in an instrument that matures in two years. The second alternative is to invest in an instrument that matures in one year and at the end of one year, reinvest the proceeds in a one-year instrument. The investor believes that one-year interest rates one year from now will be higher than they are today and, therefore, is leaning in favor of the second alternative. What would you recommend to this investor?

15. **a.** What is the difference between a normal yield curve and steep yield curve?

b. What is meant by a humped yield curve?

16. What is the common hypothesis about the behavior of short-term forward rates shared by the various forms of the expectations theory?

17. What are the types of risks associated with investing in bonds and how do these two risks affect the pure expectations theory?

18. Give three interpretations of the pure expectations theory.

19. What are the two biased expectations theories about the term structure of interest rates?

20. What are the underlying hypotheses of the two biased expectations theories of interest rates?

21. **a.** "Empirical evidence suggests that with respect to bond risk premiums that influence the shape of the Treasury yield curve, there is a linear relationship between Treasury average returns and duration." Explain whether you agree or disagree with this statement. If you disagree, explain the type of relationship that has been observed.

b. What is meant by the "convexity bias" influence on the shape of the Treasury yield curve?

Risk/Return and Asset Pricing Models

LEARNING OBJECTIVES

After reading this chapter, you will understand

- the fundamental principles of portfolio theory

- how to calculate the historical single-period investment return for a security or portfolio of securities

- how to calculate the expected return and variability of expected return of a portfolio

- the components of a portfolio's total risk: systematic risk and unsystematic risk

- what the beta of a stock measures

- why diversification eliminates unsystematic risk

- the capital asset pricing model, the relevant measure of risk in this model, and the limitations of the model

- the development of the multifactor capital asset pricing model

- the empirical difficulties of testing the capital asset pricing model

- the fundamental principles underlying the arbitrage pricing theory model

- the empirical difficulties of testing the arbitrage pricing theory model

- the importance of the return distribution of financial assets in finance theory

- what behavioral finance is and how it differs from standard finance theory

Portfolio theory deals with the selection of optimal portfolios by rational risk-averse investors—that is, by investors who attempt to maximize their expected portfolio returns consistent with individually acceptable levels of portfolio risk. Capital markets theory deals with the implications for security prices of the decisions made by these investors—that is, the

From Chapter 12 of *Foundations of Financial Markets and Institutions*, 4/e. Frank J. Fabozzi. Franco Modigliani. Frank J. Jones.

relationship that should exist between security returns and risk if investors behave in this optimal fashion. Together, portfolio and capital markets theories provide a framework to specify and measure investment risk and to develop relationships between expected security return and risk (and hence between risk and required return on investment).

The purpose of this chapter is to introduce portfolio and capital markets theories. We begin with the basic concepts of portfolio theory and then build upon these concepts to develop the theoretical relationship between the expected return on a security and risk. Because the risk and return relationship indicates how much expected return a security should generate, given its relevant risks, it also tells us how assets should be priced. Hence, the risk and return relationship is also referred to as an asset pricing model.

The three asset pricing models that we present in this chapter are those that dominate financial thinking today: the capital asset pricing model, the multifactor capital asset pricing model, and the arbitrage pricing theory model. Our focus is on the key elements underlying portfolio theory and asset pricing theory. We do not attempt to provide a rigorous mathematical presentation of these theories.

Although the theories explained in this chapter are the cornerstone of much of finance, they have been under constant attack. The first attack has been on whether current financial theory is telling us the proper way to measure risk. The second is whether the way investors behave as assumed by standard finance theory is correct because it fails to take into account the behavior of investors in making investment decisions as suggested by the literature in the field of psychology. This has led to the development of a branch in finance called behavioral finance, which draws from the work of several well-known psychologists, one of whom, Daniel Kahneman, was the corecipient of the Alfred Nobel Memorial Prize in Economic Sciences in 2002. We provide a brief description of this behavioral approach to finance at the end of this chapter.

PORTFOLIO THEORY

In designing a portfolio, investors seek to maximize the expected return from their investment, given some level of risk they are willing to accept.[1] Portfolios that satisfy this requirement are called **efficient (or optimal) portfolios**.[2] To construct an efficient portfolio, it is necessary to understand what is meant by **expected return** and risk. The latter concept, risk, could mean any one of the many types of risk. We shall be more specific about its meaning as we proceed in the development of portfolio theory. We begin our exploration of portfolio theory with the concept of investment return.

Investment Return

The return on an investor's portfolio during a given interval is equal to the change in value of the portfolio plus any distributions received from the portfolio, expressed as a fraction of the initial portfolio value. It is important that any capital or income distributions made to the investor be included, or the measure of return will be deficient. Another way to look at

---

[1] Alternatively stated, investors seek to minimize the risk to which they are exposed, given some target expected return.

[2] The theoretical framework for selecting efficient portfolios was developed in Harry M. Markowitz, "Portfolio Selection," *Journal of Finance* (March 1952), pp. 71–91, and *Portfolio Selection: Efficient Diversification of Investments* (New York: John Wiley & Sons, Inc., 1959).

return is as the amount (expressed as a fraction of the initial portfolio value) that can be withdrawn at the end of the interval while maintaining the principal intact. The return on the investor's portfolio, designated R_p, is given by

$$R_p = \frac{V_1 - V_0 + D_1}{V_0} \tag{1}$$

where

V_1 = the portfolio market value at the end of the interval
V_0 = the portfolio market value at the beginning of the interval
D_1 = the cash distributions to the investor during the interval

The calculation assumes that any interest or dividend income received on the portfolio of securities and not distributed to the investor is reinvested in the portfolio (and thus reflected in V_1). Furthermore, the calculation assumes that any distributions occur at the end of the interval, or are held in the form of cash until the end of the interval. If the distributions were reinvested prior to the end of the interval, the calculation would have to be modified to consider the gains or losses on the amount reinvested. The formula also assumes no capital inflows during the interval. Otherwise, the calculation would have to be modified to reflect the increased investment base. Capital inflows at the end of the interval (or held in cash until the end), however, can be treated as just the reverse of distributions in the return calculation.

Thus, given the beginning and ending portfolio values, plus any contributions from or distributions to the investor (assumed to occur at the end of an interval), equation (1) lets us compute the investor's return. For example, if the XYZ pension fund had a market value of $100,000 at the end of June, a distribution of $5,000 made at the end of July, and an end-of-July market value of $103,000, the return for the month would be 8%:

$$R_p = \frac{103,000 - 100,000 + 5,000}{100,000} = 0.08$$

In principle, this sort of calculation of returns could be carried out for any interval of time, say, for one month or 10 years. Yet, there are several problems with this approach. First, it is apparent that a calculation made over a long period of time, say, more than a few months, would not be very reliable because of the underlying assumption that all cash payments and inflows are made and received at the end of the period. Clearly, if two investments have the same return as calculated from the formula above, but one investment makes a cash payment early and the other late, the one with early payment will be understated. Second, we cannot rely on the formula to compare return on a one-month investment with that on a 10-year return portfolio. For purposes of comparison, the return must be expressed per unit of time—say, per year.

In practice, we handle these two problems by first computing the return over a reasonably short unit of time, perhaps a quarter of a year or less. The return over the relevant horizon, consisting of several unit periods, is computed by averaging the return over the unit intervals.[3]

---

[3] There are three generally used methods of averaging: (1) the arithmetic average return, (2) the time-weighted rate of return (also referred to as the geometric rate of return), and (3) the dollar-weighted return. The averaging yields a measure of return per unit of time period. The measure can be converted to an annual or other period yield by standard procedures. For an explanation of these three methods of averaging, see Franco Modigliani and Gerald A. Pogue, "Risk, Return, and CAPM: Concepts and Evidence," Chapter 37 in Summer N. Levine (ed.), *The Financial Analysts Handbook* (Homewood, IL: Dow Jones-Irwin, 1988).

Portfolio Risk

The definition of investment risk leads us into less explored territory. Not everyone agrees on how to define risk, let alone measure it. Nevertheless, there are some attributes of risk that are reasonably well accepted.

An investor holding a portfolio of Treasury bills until the maturity date faces no uncertainty about monetary outcome. The value of the portfolio at maturity of the securities will be identical with the predicted value; the investor bears no monetary risk. In the case of a portfolio composed of common stocks, however, it will be impossible to predict the value of the portfolio at any future date. The best an investor can do is to make a best-guess or most-likely estimate, qualified by statements about the range and likelihood of other values. In this case, the investor does bear risk.

One measure of risk is the extent to which possible future portfolio values are likely to diverge from the expected or predicted value. More specifically, risk for most investors is related to the chance that future portfolio values will be less than expected. That is, if the investor's portfolio has a current value of $100,000, and an expected value of $110,000 at the end of the next year, what matters is the probability of values less than $110,000.

Before proceeding to the quantification of risk, it is convenient to shift our attention from the terminal value of the portfolio to the portfolio rate of return, R_p, because the increase in portfolio value is related directly to R_p.

Expected Portfolio Return

A particularly useful way to quantify the uncertainty about the portfolio return is to specify the probability associated with each of the possible future returns. Assume, for example, that an investor has identified five possible outcomes for the portfolio return during the next year. Associated with each return is a subjectively determined probability, or relative chance of occurrence. The five possible outcomes are

Outcome	Possible Return	Subjective Probability
1	50%	0.1
2	30	0.2
3	10	0.4
4	−10	0.2
5	−30	0.1

Note that the probabilities sum to 1 so that the actual portfolio return is confined to one of the five possible values. Given this **probability distribution**, we can measure the expected return and risk for the portfolio.

The expected return is simply the weighted average of possible outcomes, where the weights are the relative chances of occurrence. In general, the expected return on the portfolio, denoted $E(R_p)$, is given by

$$E(R_p) = P_1R_1 + P_2R_2 + \cdots + R_nP_n \qquad (2)$$

or

$$E(R_p) = \sum_{j=1}^{n} P_jR_j$$

where the R_js are the possible returns, the P_js the associated probabilities, and n is the number of possible outcomes.

The expected return of the portfolio in our illustration is:

$$E(R_p) = 0.1(50.0) + 0.2(30.0) + 0.4(10.0) + 0.2(-10.0) + 0.1(-30.0)$$
$$= 10\%$$

Variability of Expected Return

If risk is defined as the chance of achieving returns lower than expected, it would seem logical to measure risk by the dispersion of the possible returns below the expected value. Risk measures based on below-the-mean variability are difficult to work with, however, and moreover are unnecessary as long as the distribution of future return is reasonably symmetric about the expected value. Figure 1 shows three probability distributions: the first

---

Figure 1   Possible Shapes for Probability Distributions

Symmetric probability distribution

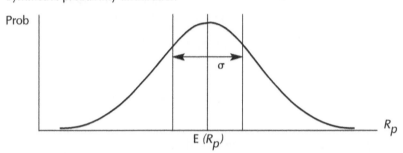

Probability distribution skewed to left

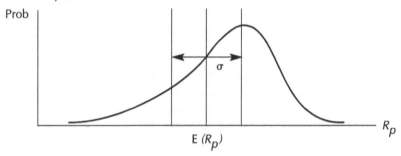

Probability distribution skewed to right

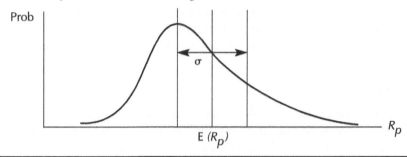

---

symmetric, the second skewed to the left, and the third skewed to the right. For a **symmetrical distribution**, the dispersion of returns on one side of the expected return is the same as the dispersion on the other side of the expected return.

If the probability distribution is symmetric, measures of the total variability of return will be twice as large as measures of the portfolio's variability below the expected return. Thus, if total variability is used as a risk surrogate, the risk ranking for a group of portfolios will be the same as when variability below the expected return is used. It is for this reason that total variability of returns has been used so widely as a surrogate for risk. While much of financial theory has been developed assuming the distribution is symmetric, at the end of this chapter, we discuss this assumption, its relevance, and its implications.

It now remains to choose a specific measure of total variability of returns. The most commonly used measures are the **variance** and **standard deviation** of returns.

The variance of return is a weighted sum of the squared deviations from the expected return. Squaring the deviations ensures that deviations above and below the expected value contribute equally to the measure of variability regardless of sign. The variance for the portfolio, designated σ_p^2, is given by

$$\sigma_p^2 = P_1[R_1 - E(R_p)]^2 + P_2[R_2 - E(R_p)]^2$$
$$+ \cdots + P_n[R_n - E(R_p)]^2$$

or

$$\sigma_p^2 = \sum_{j=1}^{n} P_j[R_j - E(R_p)]^2 \tag{3}$$

In the previous example, the variance for the portfolio is

$$\sigma_p^2 = 0.1(50.0 - 10.0)^2 + 0.2(30.0 - 10.0)^2$$
$$+ 0.4(10.0 - 10.0)^2 + 0.2(-10.0 - 10.0)^2$$
$$+ 0.1(-30.0 - 10.0)^2$$
$$= 480$$

The standard deviation (σ_p) is defined as the square root of the variance. It is equal to 22% in our example. The larger the variance or standard deviation, the greater the possible dispersion of future realized values around the expected value, and the larger the investor's uncertainty. As a rule of thumb for symmetric distributions, it is often suggested that roughly two-thirds of the possible returns will lie within one standard deviation on either side of the expected value, and that 95% will be within two standard deviations of the expected value.

A final remark before leaving portfolio risk measures. We have assumed implicitly that investors are *risk averse*; that is, they seek to minimize risk for a given level of return. This assumption appears to be valid for most investors in most situations. The entire theory of portfolio selection and capital asset pricing rests on the assumption that investors on the average are risk averse.

Diversification

Empirically, a comparison of the distribution of historical returns for a large portfolio of randomly selected stocks (say, 50 stocks) with the distribution of historical returns for an individual stock in the portfolio has indicated a curious relationship. It is not uncommon to find that (1) the standard deviation of return for the individual stocks in the portfolio is considerably larger than that of the portfolio, and (2) the average return of an individual stock is less than the portfolio return. Is the market so imperfect that it tends to reward substantially higher risk with lower stock return?

Not so. The answer lies in the fact that not all of an individual stock's risk is relevant. Much of the **total risk** (which equals standard deviation of return) is **diversifiable**. That is, if an investment in an individual stock is combined with other securities, a portion of the variation in its returns could be smoothed or canceled by complementary variation in the other securities. The same portfolio diversification effect accounts for the low standard deviation of return for a large stock portfolio. In fact, the portfolio standard deviation is lower than that of the typical security in the portfolio. Much of the total risk of the component securities has been eliminated by diversification. As long as much of the total risk can be eliminated simply by holding a stock in a portfolio, there is no economic requirement for the anticipated return to be in line with the total risk. Instead, we should expect realized returns to be related to that portion of security risk that cannot be eliminated by portfolio combination—so-called **systematic risk**. (We will have more to say on risk/return relationships later in this chapter.)

Diversification results from combining securities whose returns are less than perfectly correlated in order to reduce portfolio risk. The portfolio return is simply a weighted average of the individual security returns, no matter the number of securities in the portfolio. Therefore, diversification will not systematically affect the portfolio return, but it will reduce the variability (standard deviation) of return. In general, the less the **correlation** among security returns, the greater the impact of diversification on reducing variability. This is true no matter how risky the securities of the portfolio are when considered in isolation.

Theoretically, if we could find sufficient securities with uncorrelated returns, we could eliminate portfolio risk completely. Unfortunately, this situation is not typical in real financial markets, where returns are positively correlated to a considerable degree because they tend to respond to the same set of influences (for example, to business cycles and interest rates). Thus, while portfolio risk can be reduced substantially by diversification, it cannot be eliminated entirely.

This has been demonstrated very clearly by Wayne Wagner and Sheila Lau, who measured the standard deviations of randomly selected portfolios including various numbers of New York Stock Exchange (NYSE) securities.[4] Their study shows that the average return and the standard deviation for portfolios from the average return is unrelated to the number of issues in the portfolio. Yet, the standard deviation of return declines as the number of holdings increases. On the average, Wagner and Lau find that approximately 40% of the risk of an individual common stock is eliminated by forming randomly selected portfolios of 20 stocks. They also find (1) additional diversification yields rapidly diminishing reduction in risk, with the improvement only slight when the number of securities held is increased beyond, say, 10, and (2) a rapid decline in total portfolio risk as the portfolios were expanded from one to 10 securities.

---

[4] Wayne H. Wagner and Sheila Lau, "The Effect of Diversification on Risk," *Financial Analysts Journal* (November–December 1971), pp. 2–7.

Another key finding of the Wagner-Lau study was that the return on a diversified portfolio follows the market very closely. The degree of association is measured by the correlation coefficient of each portfolio with an unweighted index of NYSE stocks. Two securities with perfectly correlated patterns will have a correlation coefficient of 1.0. Conversely, if the return patterns are perfectly negatively correlated, the correlation coefficient will equal −1.0. Two securities with uncorrelated (that is, statistically unrelated) returns will have a correlation coefficient of zero. The 20-security portfolio in the Wagner-Lau study had a correlation of 0.89 with the market. The implication is that the risk remaining in the 20-stock portfolio is predominantly a reflection of uncertainty about the performance of the stock market in general.

These results of the Wagner-Lau study show that, while some risks can be eliminated through diversification, others cannot. Thus, we are led to distinguish between a security's **unsystematic risk**, which can be washed away by mixing the security with other securities in a diversified portfolio, and its *systematic risk*, which cannot be eliminated by diversification. As the Wagner-Lau study shows, total portfolio risk declines as the number of holdings increases. Increasing diversification gradually tends to eliminate the unsystematic risk, leaving only systematic, that is, market-related risk. The remaining variability results from the fact that the return on nearly every security depends to some degree on the overall performance of the market. This is illustrated in Figure 2. Consequently, the return on a well-diversified portfolio is highly correlated with the market, and its variability or uncertainty is basically the uncertainty of the market as a whole. Investors are exposed to market uncertainty no matter how many stocks they hold.

Figure 2 Systematic and Unsystematic Risk

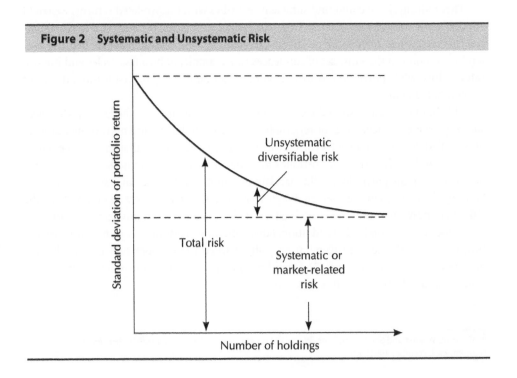

The Risk of Individual Securities

From the empirical evidence we have cited, we can conclude that the systematic risk of an individual security is that portion of its total risk (which, again, is the same as standard deviation of return) that cannot be eliminated by combining it with other securities in a well-diversified portfolio. We now need a way of quantifying the systematic risk of a security and relating the systematic risk of a portfolio to that of its component securities. This can be accomplished by dividing a security's return into two parts: one perfectly correlated with and proportionate to the market return, and a second independent from (uncorrelated with) the market. The first component of return is usually referred to as *systematic*, the second as *unsystematic*. Thus, we have

$$\text{Security return} = \text{Systematic return} + \text{Unsystematic return} \qquad (4)$$

Because the systematic return is proportional to the market return, it can be expressed as the symbol **beta** (β) times the market return, R_m. The proportionality factor of beta is a market sensitivity index, indicating how sensitive the security return is to changes in the market level. (How to estimate beta for a security or portfolio is discussed later.) The unsystematic return, which is independent of market returns, is usually represented by the symbol *epsilon prime* (ϵ'). Thus, the security return, R, may be expressed

$$R = \beta R_m + \epsilon' \qquad (5)$$

For example, if a security has a β factor of 2.0, then a 10% market return will generate a 20% systematic return for the stock. The security return for the period would be the 20% plus the unsystematic component.

The unsystematic component in equation (5) depends on factors that are unique or specific to the company that issued the security, such as labor difficulties, unexpectedly high or low sales, managerial issues, and so on. Thus, the unsystematic component is not linked to the overall market or economic system. It is important to note that a security's return variability that is due to this unsystematic component is diversifiable precisely because that variability represents events or situations that are specific (or unique) to the firm that issued the security. If a portfolio contains many securities issued by many companies, then events that are specific to any firm and affect that firm's returns can readily be offset by contrary or opposite developments that are unique to other firms and that influence their returns in different ways.

The security returns model given by equation (5) is usually written in such a way that the average value of the residual term, ϵ', is zero. This is accomplished by adding a factor, **alpha** (α), to the model to represent the average value of the unsystematic returns over time. That is, we set $\epsilon' = \alpha + \epsilon$ so that

$$R = \alpha + \beta R_m + \epsilon \qquad (6)$$

where the average ϵ over time should tend to zero. The reason the average value of the term is zero is that the term represents the eventual impact of unexpected events that are particular to the firm. If those events are random and unpredictable, their overall impact should be zero.

The model for security returns given by equation (6) is usually referred to as the **market model**.[5] Graphically, the model can be depicted as a line fitted to a plot of security returns against rates of return on the market index. This kind of line fitting is shown for a hypothetical security in Figure 3.

The beta factor can be thought of as the slope of the line. It gives the expected increase in security return for a 1% increase in market return. In Figure 3, the security has a beta of 1.0. Thus, a 10% market return will result, on the average, in a 10% security return.

The alpha factor is represented by the intercept of the line on the vertical security return axis. It is equal to the average value over time of the unsystematic returns (ϵ') on the stock. For most stocks, the alpha factor tends to be small and unstable.

Using this definition of security return given by the market model, the specification of systematic and unsystematic risk is simply the standard deviations of the two return components.

The systematic risk of a security is equal to β times the standard deviation of the market return:

$$\text{Systematic risk} = \beta\sigma_m \qquad (7)$$

The unsystematic risk equals the standard deviation of the residual return factor ϵ, or

$$\text{Unsystematic risk} = \sigma_\epsilon \qquad (8)$$

Figure 3   The Market Model for Security Returns

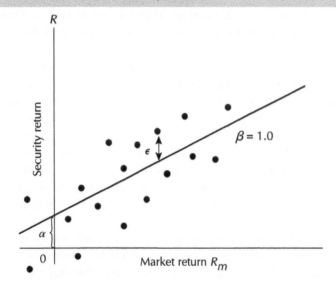

Beta (β), the market sensitivity index, is the slope of the line.
Alpha (α), the average of the residual return, is the intercept of the line on the security axis.
Epsilon (ϵ), the residual returns, are the perpendicular distances of the points from the line.

---

[5] It is also referred to as the *single-index market model* and the *characteristic line*.

Given measures of individual-security systematic risk, we can now compute the systematic risk of the portfolio. It is equal to the beta factor for the portfolio, β_p, times the risk of the market index, σ_m:

$$\text{Portfolio systematic risk} = \beta_p \sigma_m \qquad (9)$$

The portfolio beta factor in turn can be shown to be simply an average of the individual security betas, weighted by the proportion of each security in the portfolio, or

$$\beta_p = X_1\beta_1 + X_2\beta_2 + \cdots + X_n\beta_n$$

or more concisely as

$$\beta_p = \sum_{i=1}^{n} X_i\beta_i \qquad (10)$$

where

X_i = the proportion of portfolio market value represented by security i

n = the number of securities

Thus, the systematic risk of a portfolio is simply the market value-weighted average of the systematic risk of the individual securities. It follows that the β for a portfolio consisting of all stocks is 1. If a stock's β exceeds 1, it is above the average; if its beta is below 1, it is below the average. If the portfolio is composed of an equal dollar investment in each stock, the β_p is simply an unweighted average of the component security betas.

The unsystematic risk of the portfolio is also a function of the unsystematic security risks, but the form is more complex. The important point is that, with increasing diversification, this risk approaches zero.

To summarize these results, first, roughly 40% to 50% of total security risk can be eliminated by diversification. Second, the remaining systematic risk is equal to the security β times market risk. Third, portfolio systematic risk is a weighted average of security systematic risks.

The implications of these results are substantial. First, we would expect realized rates of return over substantial periods of time to be related to the systematic as opposed to the total risk of securities. As the unsystematic risk is relatively easily eliminated, we should not expect the market to offer investors a risk premium for bearing such risk. Second, because security systematic risk is equal to the security beta times σ_m (which is common to all securities), beta is useful as a *relative* risk measure. The β gives the systematic risk of a security (or portfolio) relative to the risk of the market index. Thus, it is often convenient to speak of systematic risk in relative terms, that is, in terms of beta rather than beta times σ_m.

Estimating Beta

The beta of a security or portfolio can be estimated using statistical analysis. More specifically, we use regression analysis on historical data to estimate the market model given by equation (6). The estimated slope for the market model is the estimate of beta. A series of returns is computed according to equation (1) over some time interval for some broad market index (such as the S&P 500 stock market index) and for the stock (or portfolio). For example, monthly returns can be calculated for the past five years; thus, there would be 60 return observations for both the market index and the stock or portfolio. Or weekly returns can be calculated for the past year.

There is nothing in portfolio theory that indicates whether weekly, monthly, or even daily returns should be used. Nor does theory indicate any specific number of observations, except that statistical methodology entails that more observations will give a more reliable measure of beta.[6] Our purpose here is not to provide an explanation of the mechanics of calculating beta but to point out the practical problems in obtaining beta. (There are many statistical issues also, but we do not focus on these.)

There will be a difference in the calculated beta depending on: (1) the length of time over which a return is calculated (e.g., daily, weekly, monthly), (2) the number of observations used (e.g., three years of monthly returns or five years of monthly returns), (3) the specific time period used (January 1, 1996, to December 31, 2000, for example, or January 1, 1995, to December 31, 1999); and (4) the market index selected (for instance, the S&P 500 stock market index or an index consisting of all stocks traded on exchanges weighted by their relative market value). Moreover, there is the question of the stability of beta over different time intervals—that is, does the beta of a stock or portfolio remain relatively unchanged over time, or does it change?

A very interesting question has to do with the economic determinants of the beta of a stock. The risk characteristics of a company should be reflected in its beta. Several empirical studies have attempted to identify these macroeconomic and microeconomic factors.

Key Points That You Should Understand Before Proceeding

1. Risk aversion means that investors want to minimize risk for any given level of expected return, or want to maximize return, for any given level of risk.
2. Risk is the likelihood that an actual return will deviate from the expected return.
3. Investors hold diversified portfolios rather than individual securities because portfolios eliminate some of the risk of most securities.
4. The relevant risk of any individual security is not total variability in returns but rather systematic variability, which is that portion of total variability that cannot be eliminated by combining it with other securities in a diversified portfolio.
5. The market model is the hypothesis that a security's return may be attributed to two forces, the returns on securities in general or the market, and events related to the firm itself.
6. The index of the sensitivity of a security's returns to movement in the market is the security's beta, which can be estimated with regression techniques from historical data.

THE CAPITAL ASSET PRICING MODEL

We have now developed two measures of risk: one is a measure of total risk (standard deviation), the other a relative index of systematic or nondiversifiable risk (beta). The beta measure would appear to be the more relevant for the pricing of securities. Returns expected by investors logically should be related to systematic as opposed to total risk. Securities with higher systematic risk should have higher expected returns.

---

[6] This assumes that the economic determinants that affect the beta of a stock do not change over the measurement period.

The question of interest now is the form of the relationship between risk and return. In this section we describe a relationship called the **capital asset pricing model (CAPM)**, which is based on elementary logic and simple economic principles.[7] The basic postulate underlying this finance theory is that assets with the same systematic risk should have the same expected rate of return; that is, the prices of assets in the capital markets should adjust until equivalent risk assets have identical expected returns. This principle is called the "law of one price."

To see the implications of this postulate, consider an investor who holds a risky portfolio that has the same risk as the market portfolio (beta equal to 1.0).[8] What return should she expect? Logically, she should expect the same return as that of the market portfolio. Consider another investor who holds a riskless protfolio, or one with a beta equal to zero. In this case, the investor should expect to earn the rate of return on riskless assets, such as Treasury bills. In other words, the investor who takes no risk earns only the riskless rate of return.

Now, consider the case of an investor who holds a mixture of these two portfolios. Assume he invests a proportion X of his money in the risky portfolio and the rest, or $(1 - X)$, in the riskless portfolio. What systematic risk does he bear, and what return should he expect? The risk of the composite portfolio is easily computed. Recall that the beta of a portfolio is simply a weighted average of the component security betas, where the weights are the portfolio proportions. Thus, the portfolio beta, β_p, is a weighted average of the beta of the market portfolio and that of the riskless portfolio. The market beta is 1.0, and the beta of the risk-free asset is 0. Thus,

$$\beta_p = (1 - X) \times 0 + X \times 1 \qquad (11)$$
$$= X$$

Thus, β_p is equal to the fraction of the money invested in the risky portfolio. If 100% or less of the investor's funds are invested in the risky portfolio, the portfolio beta will be between 0 and 1. If the investor borrows at the risk-free rate and invests the proceeds in the risky portfolio, so that X is larger than 1 and $(1 - X)$ is negative, the portfolio beta will be greater than 1.

The expected return of the composite portfolio is also a weighted average of the expected returns on the two portfolios; that is,

$$E(R_p) = (1 - X) \times R_f + X \times E(R_m) \qquad (12)$$

where $E(R_p)$ and $E(R_m)$ are the expected returns on the portfolio and the market index, and R_f is the risk-free rate. Now, from equation (11) we know that X is equal to β_p. Substituting into equation (12), we have

$$E(R_p) = (1 - \beta_p) \times R_f + \beta_p \times E(R_m) \qquad (13)$$

or

$$E(R_p) = R_f + \beta_p[E(R_m) - R_f]$$

---

[7] CAPM theory was developed by William F. Sharpe, "Capital Asset Prices: A Theory of Market Equilibrium Under Conditions of Risk," *Journal of Finance* (September 1964), pp. 425–442.

[8] We use the term *portfolio* in a general sense, including the case where the investor holds only one security. Because portfolio return and (systematic) risk are simply weighted averages of security values, risk/return relationships that hold for securities must also be true for portfolios, and vice versa.

Equation (13) is the capital asset pricing model. This extremely important theoretical result says that the expected return on a portfolio should exceed the riskless rate of return by an amount that is proportional to the portfolio beta. That is, the relationship between expected return and risk should be linear.

The CAPM is often stated in risk premium form. Risk premiums or excess returns are obtained by subtracting the risk-free rate from the rate of return. The expected portfolio and market risk premiums—designated $E(r_p)$ and $E(r_m)$, respectively—are given by

$$E(r_p) = E(R_p) - R_f$$

and

$$E(r_m) = E(R_m) - R_f$$

Substituting these risk premiums into equation (13), we obtain

$$E(r_p) = \beta_p E(r_m) \tag{14}$$

In this form, the CAPM states that the expected risk premium for the investor's portfolio is equal to its beta value times the expected market risk premium. Or, equivalently stated, the expected risk premium should be equal to the *quantity of risk* (as measured by beta) and the *market price of risk* (as measured by the expected market risk premium).

We can illustrate the model by assuming that the short-term (risk-free) interest rate is 6% and the expected return on the market is 10%. The expected risk premium for holding the market portfolio is simply the difference between the 10% and the short-term interest rate of 6%, or 4%. Investors who hold the market portfolio expect to earn 10%, which is 4% greater than they could earn on a short-term market instrument for certain. In order to satisfy equation (13), the expected return on securities or portfolios with different levels of risk must be as follows:

Beta	Expected Return
0.0	6%
0.5	8
1.0	10
1.5	12
2.0	14

The predictions of the model are inherently sensible. For safe investments ($\beta = 0$), the model predicts that investors would expect to earn the risk-free rate of interest. For a risky investment, ($\beta > 0$), investors would expect a rate of excess return proportional to the market sensitivity (or β) of the investment. Thus, stocks with lower-than-average market sensitivities would offer expected returns less than the expected market return. Stocks with above-average values of beta would offer expected returns in excess of the market.

Underlying Assumptions

In our development of the CAPM, we have implicitly made a number of assumptions that are required if the model is to be established on a rigorous basis. These assumptions involve investor behavior and conditions in the capital markets. The following assumptions are sufficient to allow a single derivation of the model:

1. The market is made up of risk-averse investors who measure risk in terms of standard deviation of portfolio return. This assumption provides a basis for the use of risk measures such as beta.
2. All investors have a common time horizon for investment decision making (for example, one month, one year, and so on). This assumption allows us to measure investor expectations over some common interval, thus making comparisons meaningful.
3. All investors are assumed to have the same expectations about future security returns and risks. The only reason why they choose different portfolios is differences in systematic risk and in risk preferences. Without this assumption, the analysis would become much more complicated.
4. Capital markets are perfect in the sense that all assets are completely divisible, there are no transactions costs or differential taxes, and borrowing and lending rates are equal to each other and the same for all investors. Without these conditions, there would exist frictional barriers to the equilibrium conditions on which the model is based.

Although these assumptions are sufficient to derive the model, it is not clear that all are necessary in this exact form. It may well be that several of the assumptions can be relaxed substantially without major change in the form of the model. A good deal of research has been conducted toward this end. As explained later in this chapter, the assumptions above dealing with investor behavior have been criticized precisely by proponents of behavioral finance.

Tests of the Capital Asset Pricing Model

The CAPM is indeed a simple and elegant model, but these qualities do not in and of themselves guarantee that it will be useful in explaining observed risk/return patterns. Here we briefly review the empirical literature on attempts to verify the model.

The major difficulty in testing the CAPM is that the model is stated in terms of investors' expectations and not in terms of realized returns. To test the CAPM, it is necessary to convert the theoretical CAPM given by equation (14) into a form that can be tested empirically. We will not go through this exercise here, but will simply provide a general statement of the model that is typically tested.[9] Nor will we delve into the statistical problems associated with testing the CAPM, although we will discuss later an important theoretical issue that raises serious questions about the testability of the CAPM and, therefore, the empirical findings of researchers.

The empirical analogue of equation (14) asserts that, over the period of time analyzed, (1) there is a linear relationship between the average risk premium return on the market and the average risk premium return on a stock or portfolio, and its slope is β, and (2) the linear relationship should pass through the origin. Moreover, according to the CAPM, beta is a complete relative measure of a stock's risk. Consequently, various alternative risk measures that might be proposed, the most common being the standard deviation of return, should not be significant contributors to the explanation of a stock's return. Recall that the standard deviation measures a stock's total risk and includes both systematic and unsystematic components.

---

[9] The interested reader can find the procedure for developing the empirical model tested in Franco Modigliani and Gerald A. Pogue, "Introduction to Risk and Return: Concepts and Evidence: Part II," *Financial Analysts Journal* (May–June 1974), pp. 69–86.

The CAPM theoretically applies to both individual securities and portfolios. Therefore, the empirical tests can be based on either. However, there are statistical problems associated with estimating the magnitude of the risk/return trade-off using individual securities. By grouping securities into portfolios, we can eliminate most of the statistical problems encountered for individual stocks and thereby get a much clearer view of the relationship between return and systematic risk.

The major results of the empirical tests conducted are summarized below:[10]

1. The evidence shows a significant positive relationship between realized returns and systematic risk as measured by beta. The average market risk premium estimated is usually less than that predicted by the CAPM, however.
2. The relationship between risk and return appears to be linear. The studies give no evidence of significant curvature in the risk/return relationship.
3. Tests that attempt to discriminate between the effects of systematic and unsystematic risk do not yield definitive results. Both kinds of risk appear to be positively related to security returns, but there is substantial support for the proposition that the relationship between return and unsystematic risk is at least partly spurious—that is, partly a reflection of statistical problems rather than the true nature of capital markets.

Obviously, we cannot claim that the CAPM is absolutely right. On the other hand, the early empirical tests do support the view that beta is a useful relative risk measure and that high-beta stocks tend to be priced so as to yield correspondingly high rates of return.

In 1977, however, Richard Roll wrote a paper criticizing previously published tests of the CAPM.[11] Roll argued that while the CAPM is testable in principle, no correct test of the theory had yet been presented. He also argued that there was practically no possibility that a correct test would ever be accomplished in the future.

The reasoning behind Roll's assertions is based on his observation that there is only one potentially testable hypothesis associated with the CAPM, namely, that the true market portfolio is mean-variance efficient. (This means that the market portfolio must have minimum risk for its level of return.) Furthermore, because the true market portfolio must contain all worldwide assets, the value of most of which cannot be observed (for example, human capital), the hypothesis is in all probability untestable.

Since 1977, there have been a number of studies that purport either to support or reject the CAPM. These tests have attempted to examine implications of the CAPM other than the linearity of the risk/return relation as the basis of their methodology. Unfortunately, none provides a definitive test, and most are subject to substantial criticism, suffering from the same problem of identifying the "true" market portfolio.

---

[10] Some of the earlier studies are Nancy Jacob, "The Measurement of Systematic Risk for Securities and Portfolios: Some Empirical Results," *Journal of Financial and Quantitative Analysis* (March 1971), pp. 815–834; Merton H. Miller and Myron S. Scholes, "Rates of Returns in Relation to Risk: A Reexamination of Recent Findings," and Fischer Black, Michael C. Jensen, and Myron S. Scholes, "The Capital Asset Pricing Model: Some Empirical Evidence," in Michael C. Jensen (ed.), *Studies in the Theory of Capital Markets* (New York: Praeger Books, 1972); Marshall E. Blume and Irwin Friend, "A New Look at the Capital Asset Pricing Model," *Journal of Finance* (March 1973), pp. 19–33; and Eugene F. Fama and James D. MacBeth, "Risk, Return and Equilibrium: Empirical Tests," Working Paper No. 7237, University of Chicago, Graduate School of Business, August 1972.

[11] Richard Roll, "A Critique of the Asset Pricing Theory: Part I. On the Past and Potential Testability of the Theory," *Journal of Financial Economics* (March 1977), pp. 129–176.

> **Key Points That You Should Understand Before Proceeding**
>
> 1. The CAPM hypothesizes that assets with the same level of systematic risk should experience the same level of returns.
> 2. The level of returns expected from any asset (which may be an individual security or a portfolio of securities) is a linear function of the risk-free rate, the asset's beta, and the returns expected on the market portfolio of risky assets.
> 3. Some reservations about the CAPM are inevitable because it makes many assumptions about investors' behavior and the structure of the market where assets are traded.
> 4. A major criticism of the CAPM is that it is basically untestable because the true or relevant market portfolio is an unobservable or unattainable portfolio diversified across all risky assets in the world.

THE MULTIFACTOR CAPITAL ASSET PRICING MODEL

The CAPM described above assumes that the only risk that an investor is concerned with is uncertainty about the future price of a security. Investors, however, usually are concerned with other risks that will affect their ability to consume goods and services in the future. Three examples would be the risks associated with future labor income, the future relative prices of consumer goods, and future investment opportunities.

Recognizing these other risks that investors face, Robert Merton has extended the CAPM to describe consumers deriving their optimal lifetime consumption when they face these "**extra-market**" sources of risk.[12] These extra-market sources of risk are also referred to as *factors*, so the model derived by Merton is called a *multifactor CAPM* and is given below in risk premium form:

$$E(r_p) = \beta_{pm}E(r_m) + \beta_{pF1}E(r_{F1}) + \beta_{pF2}E(r_{F2}) + \cdots + \beta_{pFk}E(r_{Fk}) \qquad (15)$$

where

K = number of factors or extra-market sources of risk
β_{pFk} = the sensitivity of the portfolio to the kth factor
$E(r_{Fk})$ = the expected return of factor k minus the risk-free rate

The total extra-market sources of risk are equal to

$$\beta_{pF1}E(r_{F1}) + \beta_{pF2}E(r_{F2}) + \cdots + \beta_{pFk}E(r_{Fk}) \qquad (16)$$

Equation (15) says that investors want to be compensated for the risk associated with each source of extra-market risk, in addition to market risk. Note that, if there are no extra-market sources of risk, equation (15) reduces to the CAPM as given by equation (14). In the case of the CAPM, investors hedge the uncertainty associated with future security prices through diversification by holding the market portfolio, which can be thought of as a

---

[12] Robert C. Merton, "An Intertemporal Capital Asset Pricing Model," *Econometrica* (September 1973), pp. 867–888.

mutual fund that invests in all securities based on their relative capitalizations. In the multifactor CAPM, besides investing in the market portfolio, investors will also allocate funds to something equivalent to a mutual fund that hedges a particular extra-market risk. While not all investors are concerned with the same sources of extra-market risk, those that are concerned with a specific extra-market risk will basically hedge them in the same way.

As individual securities are nothing more than portfolios consisting of only one security, equation (15) must hold for each security, i. That is,

$$E(r_i) = \beta_{im}E(r_m) + \beta_{iF1}E(r_{F1}) + \beta_{iF2}E(r_{F2}) + \cdots + \beta_{iFK}E(r_{FK}) \qquad (17)$$

From an empirical perspective, it may be difficult to identify the relevant extra-market risks. Moreover, it is difficult to distinguish the multifactor CAPM empirically from the next risk and return model described.

Key Points That You Should Understand Before Proceeding

1. The multifactor CAPM posits that extra-market factors influence expected returns on securities or portfolios.
2. This approach entails that a security's return has a beta-like sensitivity to each factor.

ARBITRAGE PRICING THEORY MODEL

An alternative model to the CAPM and the multifactor CAPM was developed by Stephen Ross in 1976.[13] This model is based purely on arbitrage arguments, and hence is called the **arbitrage pricing theory (APT) model**. It postulates that a security's expected return is influenced by a variety of factors, as opposed to just the single market index of the CAPM.

The APT model assumes that there are several factors that determine the rate of return on a security, not just one as in the case of the CAPM. To understand this, look back at equation (5), which states that the return on a security is dependent on its market sensitivity index and an unsystematic return. The APT in contrast states that the return on a security is linearly related to H factors. The APT does not specify what these factors are, but it is assumed that the relationship between security returns and the factors is linear.

For now, to illustrate the APT model, let's assume a simple world with a portfolio consisting of three securities in the presence of two factors. The notation is as follows:

$\overline{R}_i$ = the random rate of return on security i ($i = 1, 2, 3$)
$E(R_i)$ = the expected return on security i ($i = 1, 2, 3$)
F_h = the hth factor that is common to the returns of all three assets ($h = 1, 2$)
β_{ih} = the sensitivity of the ith security to the hth factor
e_i = the unsystematic return for security i ($i = 1, 2, 3$)

The APT model asserts that the random rate of return on security i is given by the relationship

$$\overline{R}_i = E(R_i) + \beta_{i1}\overline{F}_1 + \beta_{i2}\overline{F}_2 + \overline{e}_i \qquad (18)$$

---

[13] Stephen A. Ross, "The Arbitrage Theory of Capital Asset Pricing," *Journal of Economic Theory* (December 1976), pp. 343–362.

For equilibrium to exist among these three assets, an arbitrage condition must be satisfied: Using no additional funds (wealth) and without increasing risk, it should not be possible, on average, to create a portfolio to increase return. In essence, this condition states that there is no "money machine" available in the market. Ross has shown that the following risk and return relationship, in risk premium form, will result for each security i:

$$E(r_i) = \beta_{iF1}E(r_{F1}) + \beta_{iF2}E(r_{F2}) \tag{19}$$

where

$r_i = $ the excess return of security i over the risk-free rate
$\beta_{iFj} = $ the sensitivity of security i to the jth factor
$r_{Fj} = $ the excess return of the jth systematic factor over the risk-free rate, which can be thought of as the price (or risk premium) for the ith systematic risk

Equation (19) can be generalized to the case where there are H factors as follows:

$$E(r_i) = \beta_{iF1}E(r_{F1}) + \beta_{iF2}E(r_{F2}) + \cdots + \beta_{iFH}E(r_{FH}) \tag{20}$$

Equation (20) is the APT model. It states that investors want to be compensated for all the factors that systematically affect the return of a security. The compensation is the sum of the product of the quantity of systematic risk accepted for factor i, which is measured by the beta of the security with respect to the factor, and how the financial market prices that factor's risk, which is measured by the difference between the expected return for the factor and the risk-free rate. As in the case of the two other risk and return models described earlier, an investor is not compensated for accepting unsystematic risk.

Contrast equation (20) with the CAPM. If there is only one factor, equation (20) reduces to equation (14), and the one factor would be market risk. The CAPM is, therefore, a special case of the APT model. Now, contrast equation (20) with the multifactor CAPM given by equation (15). They look similar. Both say that investors are compensated for accepting all systematic risk and no unsystematic risk. The multifactor CAPM states that one of these systematic risks is market risk, while the APT model does not.

Supporters of the APT model argue that it has several major advantages over the CAPM or the multifactor CAPM. First, it makes less restrictive assumptions about investor preferences toward risk and return. The CAPM theory assumes investors trade off between risk and return solely on the basis of the expected returns and standard deviations of prospective investments. The APT, on the other hand, simply requires that some rather unobtrusive bounds be placed on potential investor utility functions. Second, no assumptions are made about the distribution of security returns. Finally, as the APT does not rely on identifying the true market index, the theory is potentially testable.

Empirical Evidence

To date, attempts to test the APT model empirically in the stock market have been inconclusive. Indeed, because of an inability to find a set of factors that consistently explains security returns, some question whether or not the APT is testable at all. The APT gives no direction as to the choice of the factors themselves or even how many factors might be required. Thus, the APT replaces the problem of the market portfolio in the CAPM with uncertainty over the choice and measurement of the underlying factors.

One study by Nai-fu Chen, Richard Roll, and Stephen Ross suggests four plausible economic factors:[14]

1. unanticipated changes in industrial production
2. unanticipated changes in the spread between the yield on low-grade and high-grade bonds
3. unanticipated changes in interest rates and the shape of the yield curve
4. unanticipated changes in inflation

It is interesting to note that one study expands that list to five factors, some similar to the previous group and some new.[15] The factors whose unexpected changes are said to have systematic impact on stock returns are these:

1. the business cycle, as measured by the Index of Industrial Production
2. interest rates, as given by the yields on long-term government bonds
3. investor confidence, as proxied by the spread between yields on high-grade and yields on low-grade bonds that are similar with regard to call provisions, maturity, and other features
4. short-term inflation, as measured by month-to-month changes in the Consumer Price Index
5. inflationary expectations, as represented in the changes in the short-term risk-free interest rate

As this study points out, some stocks are responsive to some factors, while other stocks are closely linked to different factors. Portfolio building involves identifying the pertinent factors and finding the price/risk reward for them. In its consideration of differing sensitivities to various systematic variables, the APT departs significantly from the CAPM.

Key Points That You Should Understand Before Proceeding

1. The APT model postulates that a security's return is a function of several factors and the security's sensitivity to changes in each of them.
2. If a security's market price were to deviate from the level justified by these factors and the security's price sensitivity to them, investors would engage in arbitrage and drive the market price to an appropriate level.
3. An appealing feature of the APT model is that it makes few assumptions about investors and the structure of the market.

ATTACKS ON THE THEORY

In this chapter, we have presented standard portfolio theory about how investors make investment decisions in order to construct an efficient portfolio. This theory is a **normative theory**—a theory that describes a norm of behavior that investors should pursue in constructing a portfolio. It does not mean that it is a theory that is actually followed. That is, standard portfolio theories should make decisions based on expected return and variance of return, but there is no assurance that they do. Also, the use of variance of returns depends

---

[14] Nai-fu Chen, Richard Roll, and Stephen A. Ross, "Economic Forces and the Stock Market: Testing the APT and Alternative Asset Pricing Theories," *Journal of Business* (July 1980), pp. 383–403.

[15] Roll and Ross Asset Management Corporation, *APT: Balancing Risk and Return* (undated), p. 14.

on whether the return distribution is symmetric and further, whether the return distribution is normally distributed. In this section, we review two attacks on standard portfolio theory. The first is an attack on the nature of the return distribution based on what has been empirically observed for financial assets. The second is the attack by the behavioral finance camp as to how investors make decisions.

Asset Return Distribution and Risk Measures

As explained in the chapter, the selection of a risk measure when investing in a financial asset is linked to the probability distribution for the return. If the distribution is symmetric, then the standard deviation can be and is used as a measure of risk.

Despite its use in finance, the preponderance of empirical evidence does not support the assumption that asset returns follow a normal distribution.[16] The evidence suggests that not only may observed probability distributions not be symmetric (i.e, they may be skewed) but that they unquestionably exhibit **fat tails** or **heavy tails**. The "tails" of the distribution are where the extreme values occur. If a probability distribution exhibits fat tails, this means that extreme values are more likely than would be predicted by the normal distribution. This means that between periods when the market exhibits relatively modest changes in returns, there will be periods when there are changes that are much higher (i.e., crashes and booms) than the normal distribution predicts.

To illustrate this, look at Figure 4. This figure shows the daily returns on a popular stock market index, the Standard & Poor's 500 (S&P 500), from 1928 to April 2006. Shown in the figure is the normal distribution. As noted earlier in this chapter, if stock returns do follow a normal distribution, returns that are three standard deviations from the mean (the mean is zero) are highly unlikely to occur. As can be seen from the figure, a considerable number of outliers (i.e., extreme values) have occurred. Four noteworthy events are the market crashes of October 19, 1987; October 28, 1929; and October 29, 1929; and the market boom on March 15, 1933. The number of standard deviations from the mean is reported. The likelihood of an event with the number of standard deviations shown for these four events if daily returns follow a normal distribution is zero. This is just one form of empirical evidence that asset returns do not follow a normal distribution.

The initial assault on the assumption that return distributions are not normally distributed was in the 1960s by Benoit Mandelbrot.[17] Empirically investigating various time series on commodity returns and interest rates, he not only rejected the assumption that returns (and prices) followed a normal distribution, but he conjectured that they are better described by a non-normal "stable" distribution. A discussion of a stable distribution, more specifically what Mandelbrot labeled a "stable Paretian distribution," is beyond the scope of this book.[18] His early investigations on asset returns were carried out further by Eugene Fama,[19] among others, and led to a consolidation of the hypothesis that asset returns can be better described as a stable Paretian distribution.

---

[16] See Chapter 11 in Svetlozar T. Rachev, Christian Menn, and Frank J. Fabozzi, *Fat-Tailed and Skewed Asset Return Distributions: Implications for Risk Management, Portfolio Selection, and Option Pricing* (John Wiley & Sons, 2005).

[17] Benoit B. Mandelbrot, "The Variation of Certain Speculative Prices," *Journal of Business*, 36 (1963), pp. 394–419.

[18] See Chapter 7 in Rachev, Menn, and Fabozzi, *Fat-Tailed and Skewed Asset Return Distributions: Implications for Risk Management, Portfolio Selection, and Option Pricing.*

[19] Eugene F. Fama, "Mandelbrot and the Stable Paretian Hypothesis," *Journal of Business*, 36 (1963), pp. 420–429.

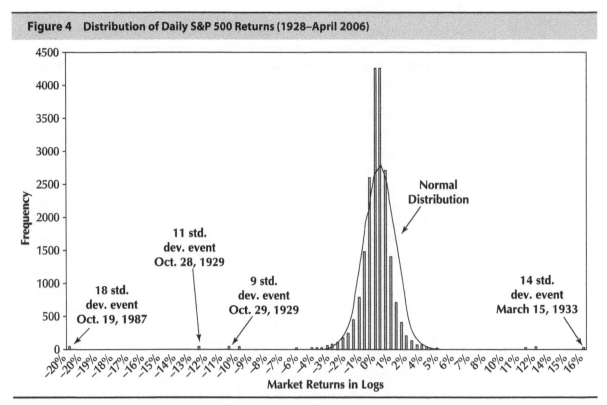

Figure 4   Distribution of Daily S&P 500 Returns (1928–April 2006)

Source: *Exhibit 4 in Jeremy Grantham, "Risk Management in Investing (Part Two): Risk and the Passage of Time," Letters to the Investment Committee VII (April 2006). © 2006 GMO LLC.*

An important implication of asset returns following a stable Paretian distribution is that the standard deviation is infinite. As we have seen, the standard deviation plays a key role in portfolio theory as well as capital market theory, discussed in the next chapter. If the standard deviation is infinite, then how could the standard deviation be used as a measure of risk?

As a result, some researchers have suggested other probability distributions that have a finance variance to get around the infinite variance problem. For example, one alternative type of distribution is the Student's *t* distribution, a distribution that under certain conditions not only has a finite variance but also allows for tails with more observations than the normal distribution.[20] Another distribution that has been proposed is a finite mixture of normal distributions.[21] Despite these proposals, there are strong theoretical reasons in favor of the stable Paretian distribution.[22]

---

[20] Empirical evidence supporting this distribution was provided by Robert C. Blattberg and Nicholas J. Gonedes, "A Comparison of the Stable and Student Distributions as Statistical Models for Stock Prices," *Journal of Business,* 47 (1974), pp. 244–280.

[21] Kon found that this distribution explains daily returns for stocks better than the Student's *t* distribution. See Stanley Kon, "Models of Stock Returns—A Comparison," *Journal of Finance,* 39 (1984), pp. 147–165.

[22] The reason is that a major drawback of all these alternative models is their lack of stability. This property is highly desirable for asset returns in the context of portfolio analysis and risk management. Only for stable (which includes the normal as a special case) distributed returns of independent assets does one obtain the property that the linear combination of the returns (portfolio returns) again follow a stable distribution. For the technical arguments, see Svetlozar T. Rachev and Stefan Mittnik, *Stable Paretian Models in Finance* (Chichester, UK: John Wiley & Sons, 2000).

Support for return distributions not being well characterized by a normal distribution comes from the collaborative efforts of economists and physicists who have developed mathematical models of the stock market.[23] In modeling the stock market, the interactions of investors are modeled. Although it is well recognized that such mathematical models are by their nature gross simplifications of real-world financial markets, they provide sufficient structure to analyze return distributions. The computer simulations of these models have been found to generate fat tails and other statistical characteristics that have been observed in real-world financial markets.

The issue of the return distribution also leads to competitors for how risk should be measured. There is a growing literature in finance in two areas. The first has been the development of the theory for assessing risk measures.[24] The second is alternative risk measures.[25] These two areas are beyond the scope of this chapter.

At this time, there is considerable research seeking to modify much of the finance theory described in this and the next chapter assuming that return distributions follow a distribution other than a normal distribution.

Assault by the Behavioral Finance Theory Camp

One of the earliest attacks on the foundations of economic principles that financial economists draw upon in formulating financial theories was in the late 1970s by Daniel Kahneman and Amos Tversky.[26] Based on numerous experiments, these two psychologists demonstrated that the actions of decision makers are inconsistent with the assumptions made by economists. Basically, they formulated a theory, known as "prospect theory," that attacks expected utility theory.[27] While we have not presented a full-blown derivation of capital market theory in this chapter, if we had, we would have seen the importance of expected utility theory.

Other attacks on the assumptions of standard financial theory drawing from the field of psychology led to the specialized field in finance known as behavioral finance.[28] **Behavioral finance** looks at how psychology affects investor decisions and the implications

---

[23] Probably the most well-known model is the Santa Fe Stock Market Model. See W. Brian Arthur, John H. Holland, Blake LeBaron, Richard Palmer, and Paul Tayler, "Asset Pricing under Endogenous Expectations in an Artificial Stock Market," in W. Brian Arthur, Steven N. Durlauf, and David A. Lane (eds.), *The Economy as an Evolving Complex System II* (Reading, MA: Addison-Wesley, 1997), pp. 15–44.

[24] See Philippe Artzner, Freddy Delbaen, Jean-Marc Heath, and David Eber, "Coherent Measures of Risk," *Mathematical Finance*, 9 (2000), pp. 203–228.

[25] See Sergio Ortobelli, Svetlozar T. Rachev, Stoyan Stoyanov, Frank J. Fabozzi, and Almira Biglova, "The Proper Use of Risk Measures in Portfolio Theory," *International Journal of Theoretical and Applied Finance*, 8 (December 2005), pp. 1–27, and Svetlozar T. Rachev, Sergio Ortobelli, Stoyan Stoyanov, Frank J. Fabozzi, and Almira Biglova, "Desirable Properties of an Ideal Risk Measure in Portfolio Theory," *International Journal of Theoretical and Applied Finance*, 11 (February 2008), pp. 19–54.

[26] It should be noted that the economists Adam Smith and John Maynard Keynes thought that investor psychology affected security prices.

[27] Daniel Kahneman and Amos Tversky, "Prospect Theory: An Analysis of Decision under Risk," *Econometrica* (March 1979), pp. 236–291. See also Daniel Kahneman and Amos Tversky, "Advances in Prospect Theory: Cumulative Representation of Uncertainty," *Journal of Risk and Uncertainty*, 5 (1992), pp. 297–323.

[28] For an extensive discussion of behavioral finance, see the following chapters in Frank J. Fabozzi (ed.), *The Handbook of Finance: Volume II* (Hoboken, N.J.: John Wiley & Sons, 2008): Meir Statman, "What Is Behavioral Finance"; Jarrod W. Wilcox, "Behavioral Finance"; Victor Ricciardi "The Psychology of Risk: The Behavioral Finance Perspective"; and Victor Ricciardi, "Risk: Traditional Finance versus Behavioral Finance."

not only for portfolio theory that we described in this chapter but also asset pricing theory and market efficiency. The foundations of behavioral finance draw from the research by Kahneman, Slovic, and Tversky.[29]

Shefrin notes the following three themes in the behavioral finance literature:[30]

Behavioral Finance Theme 1: Investors err in making investment decisions because they rely on rules of thumb.

Behavioral Finance Theme 2: Investors are influenced by form as well as substance in making investment decisions.

Behavioral Finance Theme 3: Prices in the financial market are affected by errors and decision frames.

The first behavioral finance theme involves the concept of **heuristics**. This term means a rule-of-thumb strategy or good guide to follow in order to shorten the time it takes to make a decision. For example, here are three rules of thumb provided on *MSN Money*'s website for increasing the likelihood of success when investing in common stock: (1) ignore guru predictions, (2) avoid cheap stocks, (3) follow the big players.[31] In planning for retirement, a rule of thumb that has been suggested for having enough to retire is to invest 10% of annual pretax income. As for what to invest in to reach that retirement goal (that is, the allocation among asset classes), a rule of thumb that has been suggested is that the percentage that an investor should allocate to bonds should be determined by subtracting from 100 the investor's age. So, for example, a 45-year-old individual should invest 55% of his or her retirement funds in bonds.

There are circumstances where heuristics can work fairly well. However, the psychology literature tells us that heuristics can lead to systematic biases in decision making, what psychologists refer to as **cognitive biases**. In the context of finance, these biases lead to errors in making investment decisions. Shefrin refers to these biases as **heuristic-driven biases**.

Now recall how investment decisions were assumed to be made in the standard finance theory that we described earlier in this chapter. The assumption is that an investor computes the mean and variance of the return of financial assets and constructs an optimal portfolio based on that statistical information.

The second behavioral finance theme involves the concept of framing. The term **framing** means the way in which a situation or choice is presented to an investor. Behavioral finance asserts that the framing of investment choices can result in significantly different assessments by an investor as to the risk and return of each choice and therefore the ultimate decision made.[32] Shefrin and Statman provide an example of faulty framing coupled with a cognitive bias.[33] Individual investors often fail to treat the value of their stock portfolio at market value. Instead, investors have a "mental account" where they continue to market the

---

[29] Daniel Kahneman, Paul Slovic, and Amos Tversky, *Judgment under Uncertainty: Heuristics and Biases* (New York: Cambridge University Press, 1982).

[30] Hersh Shefrin, *Beyond Greed and Fear: Understanding Behavioral Finance and the Psychology of Investing* (New York: Oxford Universtity Press, 2002), pp. 4–5.

[31] Harry Domash, "10 Rules for Picking Stock Winners," *MSN Money*, September 27, 1997.

[32] See Amos Tversky and Daniel Kahneman, "The Framing of Decisions and the Psychology of Choice," *Science*, 211 (1961), pp. 453–458, and Amos Tversky and Daniel Kahneman, "Rational Choice and the Framing of Decisions," *Journal of Business*, 59 (October 1986), Part 2, pp. 251–278.

[33] Hersh Shefrin and Meir Statman, "The Disposition to Sell Winners Too Early and Ride Losers Too Long: Theory and Evidence," *Journal of Finance*, 40 (July 1985), pp. 777–790.

value of each stock in their portfolio at the purchase price despite the change in the market value. The reason why they are reluctant to acknowledge any losses on stocks that they own is that it keeps alive the hope that those stocks that have realized losses will turn around so as to realize a gain. When they finally sell their stocks, they close the mental account and only at that time acknowledge a loss that had occurred on paper. Hence, investment decisions are affected by this mental accounting treatment rather than being based on the true economic impact that an investment decision would have on the investor. Behavioral finance assumes that there is "frame dependence" when it comes to making investment decisions and hence the second theme of behavioral finance carries that name. In contrast, standard finance theory assumes "frame independence." This means that investors "view all decisions through the transparent, objective lens of risk and return."[34]

Finally, the third theme of behavioral finance involves how errors caused by heuristics and framing dependence affect the pricing of assets. According to behavioral finance, asset prices will not reflect their fundamental value because of the way investors make decisions. That is, markets will be price inefficient. Hence, Shefrin labels the third behavioral finance theme "inefficient markets."

That leaves us with two theories. Who is right, supporters of standard finance theory or supporters of behavioral finance theory? In fairness, we have not provided the responses of the supporters of standard finance theory to the criticisms of those who support behavioral finance. Nor have we presented the attacks on behavioral finance. Fortunately, David Hirshleifer provided that analysis. He describes the common objections to both approaches. He refers to the standard finance theory as the "fully rational approach" and behavioral finance as the "psychological approach."[35] A criticism of both approaches is that they can go "theory fishing" to find theories in market data to support their position. Objections to the fully rational approach are (1) that the calculations needed to implement this approach are extremely difficult to do, and (2) that the empirical evidence in the finance literature does not support rational behavior by investors. Objections to the psychological approach according to Hirshleifer are (1) that "alleged psychology biases are arbitrary," and (2) that the experiments performed by research that find alleged psychological biases are arbitrary.

SUMMARY

This chapter explains the principles of portfolio theory, a theory that deals with the construction of optimal portfolios by rational risk-averse investors, and its implications for the returns on different assets and, hence, security prices. One way to evaluate the risk of a portfolio is by estimating the extent to which future portfolio values are likely to deviate from expected portfolio return. This is measured by the variance of the portfolio's return and is called the total portfolio risk. Total portfolio risk can be broken down into two types of risk: systematic risk and unsystematic risk.

Systematic risk, also called *market risk*, is the risk that affects all securities. The beta of any security or portfolio is the relative systematic risk of the asset and is measured statistically

---

[34] Shefrin, *Beyond Greed and Fear: Understanding Behavioral Finance and the Psychology of Investing*, p. 4.

[35] See Table 1 in David Hirshleifer, "Investor Psychology and Asset Pricing," *Journal of Finance*, 56 (September 2001), pp. 1533–1597.

(using historical return data) by the slope of the regression between the asset's and the market's returns. The regression line estimated is called the market model. Unsystematic risk is the risk that is unique to a company, and it can be eliminated by diversifying the portfolio. Thus, systematic risk and unsystematic risk are referred to as nondiversifiable and diversifiable risk, respectively.

The CAPM is an economic theory that attempts to provide a relationship between risk and return, or, equivalently, it is a model for the pricing of risky securities. The CAPM asserts that the only relevant risk that investors will require compensation for assuming is systematic risk because that risk cannot be eliminated by diversification. Basically, CAPM says that the expected return of a security or a portfolio is equal to the rate on a risk-free security plus a risk premium. The risk premium in the CAPM is proportional to the security or the portfolio beta. More specifically, the risk premium is the product of the quantity of risk and the market price of risk, measured by beta, and the difference between the expected market return and risk-free rate, respectively.

The CAPM assumes that investors are concerned with only one risk: the risk having to do with the future price of a security. However, there are other risks, such as the capacity of investors to consume goods and services in the future. The multifactor CAPM assumes investors face such extra-market sources of risk called factors. The expected return in the multifactor CAPM is the market risk, as in the case of the basic CAPM, plus a package of risk premiums. Each risk premium is the product of the beta of the security or portfolio with respect to the particular factor and the difference between the expected return for the factor and the risk-free rate.

The APT model is developed purely on arbitrage arguments. It postulates that the expected return on a security or a portfolio is influenced by several factors. Proponents of the APT model cite its use of less restrictive assumptions as a feature that makes it more appealing than the CAPM or the multifactor CAPM. Moreover, testing the APT model does not require identification of the true market portfolio. It does, however, require empirical determination of the factors because they are not specified by the theory. Consequently, the APT model replaces the problem of identifying the market portfolio in the CAPM with the problem of choosing and measuring the underlying factors.

All things considered, the CAPM, the multifactor CAPM, and the APT model all provide interesting conceptual insights into the issues of the pricing of risk and portfolio selection in securities markets. None can be said to dominate the others in terms of theoretical content or the simplicity of empirical testing. Only the future will decide which has the best claim to the ultimate truth. Indeed, on this question, all three pricing theories will probably make valuable contributions to the development of the next generation of equilibrium models.

Challenges to the standard theory of portfolio selection in terms of selecting portfolios based on expected value and variance of returns have been twofold. The first is a challenge to the notion that the return distribution for financial assets is symmetric and follows a normal distribution. If that is not the case, the standard deviation may be a poor measure of risk. Alternative risk measures have been proposed. The second attack is from a branch of finance known as behavioral finance. This branch of finance, which draws from the field of psychology, asserts that investor behavior is far different from that postulated in standard finance theory.

KEY TERMS

- Alpha
- Arbitrage pricing theory (APT) model
- Behavioral finance
- Beta
- Capital asset pricing model (CAPM)
- Cognitive biases
- Correlation
- Diversifiable risk
- Efficient (optimal) portfolio
- Expected return
- "Extra-market" source of risk
- Framing
- Fat tails
- Heavy tails
- Heuristic-driven biases
- Heuristics
- Market model
- Normative theory
- Probability distribution
- Standard deviation
- Symmetrical distribution
- Systematic risk
- Total risk
- Unsystematic risk
- Variance

QUESTIONS

1. A friend has asked you to help him figure out a statement he received from his broker. It seems that, at the start of last year, your friend paid $900 for a bond, and sold it at the end of the year for $890. During the year, he received a single coupon payment of $110. The statement claims that his return (not including commissions and taxes) is 11.11% for the year. Is this claim correct?

2. Suppose the probability distribution for the one-period return of some asset is as follows:

Return	Probability
0.20	0.10
0.15	0.20
0.10	0.30
0.03	0.25
−0.06	0.15

   a. What is this asset's expected one-period return?
   b. What is this asset's variance and standard deviation for the one-period return?

3. "A portfolio's expected return and variance of return are simply the weighted average of the expected return and variance of the individual assets." Do you agree with this statement?

4. In the January 25, 1991, issue of *The Value Line Investment Survey*, you note the following:

Company	Beta (β)
IBM	0.95
Bally Manufacturing	1.40
Cigna Corporation	1.00
British Telecom	0.60

   a. How do you interpret these betas?
   b. Is it reasonable to assume that the expected return on British Telecom is less than that on IBM shares?
   c. "Given that Cigna Corporation has a β of 1.00, one can mimic the performance of the stock market as a whole by buying only these shares." Do you agree with this statement?

5. Assume the following:

   Expected market return = 15%

   Risk-free rate = 5.7%

   If a security's beta is 1.3, what is its expected return according to the CAPM?

6. Professor Harry Markowitz, corecipient of the 1990 Nobel Prize in Economics, wrote the following:

   A portfolio with sixty different railway securities, for example, would not be as well diversified as the same size portfolio with some railroad, some public utility, mining, various sorts of manufacturing, etc.

Why is this true?

7. Following is an excerpt from an article, "Risk and Reward," in *The Economist* of October 20, 1990:

> Next question: is the CAPM supported by the facts? That is controversial, to put it mildly. It is a tribute to Mr. Sharpe [cowinner of the 1990 Nobel Prize in Economics] that his work, which dates from the early 1960s, is still argued over so heatedly. Attention has lately turned away from beta to more complicated ways of carving up risk. But the significance of CAPM for financial economics would be hard to exaggerate.

a. Summarize Roll's argument on the problems inherent in empirically verifying the CAPM.
b. What are some of the other "more complicated ways of carving up risk"?

8. **a.** What are the difficulties in practice of applying the arbitrage pricing theory model?
b. Does Roll's criticism also apply to this pricing model?
c. "In the CAPM investors should be compensated for accepting systematic risk: for the APT model, investors are rewarded for accepting both systematic risk and unsystematic risk." Do you agree with this statement?

9. **a.** What does it mean that a return distribution has a fat tail?
b. What is the implication if a return distribution is assumed to be normally distributed but is in fact a fat-tailed distribution?

10. How does the behavioral finance approach differ from the standard finance theory approach?

Primary Markets and the Underwriting of Securities

LEARNING OBJECTIVES

After reading this chapter, you will understand

- the role investment bankers play in the distribution of newly issued securities
- the risk associated with the underwriting of a security
- the different types of underwriting arrangements
- how the SEC regulates the distribution of newly issued securities
- what a registration statement is
- the impact of the SEC Rule 415 (shelf registration)
- what is a bought deal underwriting for a bond issue, and why it is used
- what a competitive bidding underwriting is
- what a rights offering for the sale of common stock is
- the advantages and disadvantages from an issuer's perspective of a private placement
- the reason for Rule 144A and its potential impact on the private placement market

Financial markets can be categorized as those dealing with financial claims that are newly issued, called the **primary market**, and those for exchanging financial claims previously issued, called the *secondary market*, or the market for seasoned securities. In this chapter, we focus on the primary market for securities; the next chapter covers the secondary market.

The primary market involves the distribution to investors of newly issued securities by central governments, their agencies, municipal governments, and corporations.[1] The participants in

---

[1] This also includes the offering of securities of government-owned companies to private investors. This process is referred to as *privatization*. An example in the United States is the initial public offering of the U.S. government-owned railroad company Conrail in March 1987. Non–U.S. examples include Great Britain's British Telecom, Chile's Pacifica, and France's Paribas.

the marketplace that work with issuers to distribute newly issued securities are called **investment bankers**. Investment banking is performed by two groups: commercial banks and securities houses. Prior to 1999, the Glass-Steagall Act separated the activities of commercial banks and securities house, restricting the types of securities that commercial banks in the United States could underwrite. This act had been on the books since the Great Depression. The Gramm-Leach-Bliley Financial Services Modernization Act of 1999 (the "GLB Act") supplanted the Glass-Steagall Act and eliminated the restrictions on the activities conducted by companies in each financial sector.

In this chapter, we explain the various ways that investment banking firms are involved in the issuance of new securities, the regulation of the primary market, and the private placement market.

THE TRADITIONAL PROCESS FOR ISSUING NEW SECURITIES

The traditional process in the United States for issuing new securities involves investment bankers performing one or more of the following three functions: (1) advising the issuer on the terms and the timing of the offering, (2) buying the securities from the issuer, and (3) distributing the issue to the public.[2] The advisor role may require investment bankers to design a security structure that is more palatable to investors than a particular traditional instrument. For example, the high interest rates in the United States in the late 1970s and early 1980s increased the cost of borrowing for issuers of even the highest-quality rating. To reduce the cost of borrowing for their clients, investment bankers designed securities with characteristics that were more attractive to investors but not onerous to issuers. They also designed security structures for low-quality bond issues, so-called high-yield or junk bond structures. We will give several examples of these financial innovations in later chapters.

In the sale of new securities, investment bankers need not undertake the second function—buying the securities from the issuer. An investment banker may merely act as an advisor and/or distributor of the new security. The function of buying the securities from the issuer is called **underwriting**. When an investment banking firm buys the securities from the issuer and accepts the risk of selling the securities to investors at a lower price, it is referred to as an *underwriter*. When the investment banking firm agrees to buy the securities from the issuer at a set price, the underwriting arrangement is referred to as a **firm commitment**. In contrast, in a **best efforts** arrangement, the investment banking firm agrees only to use its expertise to sell the securities—it does not buy the entire issue from the issuer.

The fee earned from underwriting a security is the difference between the price paid to the issuer and the price at which the investment bank reoffers the security to the public. This difference is called the **gross spread**, or the **underwriter discount**. Numerous factors affect the size of the gross spread. Two important factors are the type of security and the size of the offering. The major types of offerings can be classified as initial public offering, secondary common stock offering, and bond offering.

An **initial public offering (IPO)** is a common stock offering issued by companies that had not previously issued common stock to the public. For example, on September 22, 2006,

---

[2] When an investment banking firm commits its own funds on a long-term basis by either taking an equity interest or creditor position in companies, this activity is referred to as merchant banking.

DivX, Inc. conducted an IPO for 9,100,000 shares of common stock at a price to the public of $16.00 per share. The total amount raised was therefore $145,600,000. The underwriting discount (and commissions) was $1.12 per share or $10,192,000. As a percentage of proceeds raised, the underwriting discount was 7%. The range for a public offering is typically between 4.5% and 7.5% of the amount issued, with the lower end of the range being for large IPOs.

A **secondary common stock offering** is an offering of common stock that had been issued in the past by the corporation. The range for the gross spread as a percentage of the amount raised is between 3% and 6%. Because of the risk associated with pricing and then selling an IPO to investors, the gross spread is higher than for a secondary common stock offering. For traditional bond offerings, the gross spread as a percentage of the principal is around 50 basis points. This lower gross spread compared to common stock offerings reflects the lower risk associated with such underwritings.

The typical underwritten transaction involves so much risk of capital loss that a single investment banking firm undertaking it alone would be exposed to the danger of losing a significant portion of its capital. To share this risk, an investment banking firm forms a **syndicate** of firms to underwrite the issue. The gross spread is then divided among the lead underwriter(s) and the other firms in the underwriting syndicate. The lead underwriter manages the deal (or "runs the books" for the deal). In many cases, there may be more than one lead underwriter, so that the lead underwriters are said to colead or comanage the deal.

To realize the gross spread, the entire securities issue must be sold to the public at the planned reoffering price. This usually requires a great deal of marketing muscle. Investment banking firms have an investor client base (retail and institutional) to which they attempt to sell the securities. To increase the potential investor base, the lead underwriter will put together a **selling group**. This group includes the underwriting syndicate plus other firms that are not in the syndicate. Members of the selling group can buy the security at a concession price—a price less than the reoffering price. The gross spread is thereby divided among the lead underwriter, members of the underwriting syndicate, and members of the selling group.

A successful underwriting of a security requires that the underwriter have a strong sales force. The sales force provides feedback on advance interest in the security, and the traders (also called market makers) provide input in pricing the security as well. It would be a mistake to think that once the securities are all sold the investment banking firm's ties with the deal are ended. In the case of bonds, those who bought the securities will look to the investment banking firm to make a market in the issue. This means that the investment banking firm must be willing to take a principal position in secondary market transactions.

Key Points That You Should Understand Before Proceeding

1. There are three functions performed by investment bankers in the offering of new securities.
2. Depending on the type of underwriting agreement, the underwriting function may expose the investment banking firm to the risk of selling the securities to the public at a price less than the price paid to the issuer.
3. The gross spread earned by the underwriter depends on numerous factors.
4. Because of the risks associated with the underwriting of securities, an underwriting syndicate and a selling group are typically formed.

REGULATION OF THE PRIMARY MARKET

Underwriting activities are regulated by the Securities and Exchange Commission (SEC). The Securities Act of 1933 governs the issuance of securities. The act requires that a **registration statement** be filed with the SEC by the issuer of a security. The type of information contained in the registration statement is the nature of the business of the issuer, key provisions or features of the security, the nature of the investment risks associated with the security, and the background of management.[3] Financial statements must be included in the registration statement, and they must be certified by an independent public accountant.[4]

The registration is actually divided into two parts. Part I is the **prospectus**. It is this part that is typically distributed to the public as an offering of the securities. Part II contains supplemental information, which is not distributed to the public as part of the offering but is available from the SEC upon request.

The act provides for penalties in the form of fines and/or imprisonment if the information provided is inaccurate or material information is omitted. Moreover, investors who purchase the security are entitled to sue the issuer to recover damages if they incur a loss as a result of the misleading information. The underwriter may also be sued if it can be demonstrated that the underwriter did not conduct a reasonable investigation of the information reported by the issuer. One of the most important duties of an underwriter is to perform **due diligence**. The following quotation comes from a court decision that explains the obligation of an underwriter to perform due diligence:

> An underwriter by participating in an offering constructively represents that statements made in the registration materials are complete and accurate. The investing public properly relies upon the underwriter to check the accuracy of the statements and the soundness of the offer; when the underwriter does not speak out, the investor reasonably assumes that there are no undisclosed material deficiencies. The representations in the registration statement are those of the underwriter as much as they are those of the issuer.[5]

The filing of a registration statement with the SEC does not mean that the security can be offered to the public. The registration statement must be reviewed and approved by the SEC's Division of Corporate Finance before a public offering can be made. Typically, the staff of this division will find a problem with the registration statement. The staff then sends a "letter of comments" or "deficiency letter" to the issuer explaining the problem it has encountered. The issuer must remedy any problem by filing an amendment to the registration statement. If the staff is satisfied, the SEC will issue an order declaring that the registration statement is "effective," and the underwriter can solicit sales. The approval of the SEC, however, does not mean that the securities have investment merit or are properly priced or that the information is accurate. It merely means that the appropriate information appears to have been disclosed.

The time interval between the initial filing of the registration statement and the time the registration statement becomes effective is referred to as the **waiting period** (also called

---

[3] SEC Regulation S-K and the Industry Guidelines (SEC Securities Act Release No. 6384, March 3, 1982) specify the information that must be included in the registration statement.

[4] SEC Regulation S-X specifies the financial statements that must be disclosed.

[5] *Chris-Craft Industries, Inc. v. Piper Aircraft Corp,* 1973.

the "cooling-off period"). During the waiting period, the SEC does allow the underwriters to distribute a preliminary prospectus. Because the prospectus has not become effective, its cover page states this in red ink and, as a result, the preliminary prospectus is commonly called a **red herring**. During the waiting period, the underwriter cannot sell the security, nor may it accept written offers from investors to buy the security.

In 1982, the SEC approved Rule 415, which permits certain issuers to file a single registration document indicating that they intend to sell a certain amount of a certain class of securities at one or more times within the next two years.[6] Rule 415 is popularly referred to as the **shelf registration rule** because the securities can be viewed as sitting on a "shelf," and can be taken off that shelf and sold to the public without obtaining additional SEC approval. In essence, the filing of a single registration document allows the issuer to come to market quickly because the sale of the security has been preapproved by the SEC. Prior to establishment of Rule 415, there was a lengthy period required before a security could be sold to the public. As a result, in a fast-moving market, issuers could not come to market quickly with an offering to take advantage of what they perceived to be attractive financing opportunities. For example, if a corporation felt that interest rates were low and wanted to issue a bond, it had to file a registration statement and could not issue the bond until the registration statement became effective. The corporation was then taking the chance that during the waiting period interest rates would rise, making the bond offering more costly.

Key Points That You Should Understand Before Proceeding

1. The SEC regulates underwriting activities.
2. An issuer must file a registration statement, one part of which is the prospectus.
3. The underwriter must exercise due diligence to assure that there are no misstatements or omissions of fact in the registration statement or prospectus.
4. SEC Rule 415 (the shelf registration rule) gives greater flexibility to certain issuers by permitting them to file a single registration document for the offering of certain securities at one or more times within the next two years.

VARIATIONS IN THE UNDERWRITING PROCESS

Not all deals are underwritten using the traditional syndicate process we have described. Variations in the United States, the Euromarkets, and foreign markets include the **bought deal** for the underwriting of bonds, the auction process for both stocks and bonds, and a rights offering for underwriting common stock.

Bought Deal

The bought deal was introduced in the Eurobond market in 1981 when Credit Suisse First Boston purchased from General Motors Acceptance Corporation a $100 million issue without lining up an underwriting syndicate prior to the purchase. Thus, Credit Suisse

---

[6] The issuer qualifies for Rule 415 registration if the securities are investment-grade securities and/or the securities of companies that have historically filed registration statements and whose securities comply with minimum flotation requirements.

First Boston did not use the traditional syndication process to diversify the capital risk exposure associated with an underwriting that we described earlier.

The mechanics of a bought deal are as follows. The lead manager or a group of managers offers a potential issuer of debt securities a firm bid to purchase a specified amount of the securities with a certain interest (coupon) rate and maturity. The issuer is given a day or so (maybe even only a few hours) to accept or reject the bid. If the bid is accepted, the underwriting firm has bought the deal. It can, in turn, sell the securities to other investment banking firms for distribution to their clients and/or distribute the securities to its clients. Typically, the underwriting firm that buys the deal will have presold most of the issue to its institutional clients.

The bought deal found its way into the United States in mid-1985 when Merrill Lynch underwrote a bond issue for which it was the only underwriter. The gross spread on the bond, a $50 million issue of Norwest Financial, was 0.268%. This is far less than the gross spread typical of that time. Merrill Lynch offered a portion of the securities to investors and the balance to other investment banking firms.

There are several reasons why some underwriting firms find the bought deal attractive. While Rule 415 gives certain issuers timing flexibility to take advantage of windows of opportunities in the global marketplace, it requires that underwriting firms be prepared to respond on short notice to commit funds to a deal. This fact favors the bought deal because it gives the underwriting firm very little time to line up a syndicate. A consequence of accepting bought deals, however, is that underwriting firms need to expand their capital so that they can commit greater amounts of funds to such deals.

The risk of capital loss in a bought deal may not be as great as it first appears. Some deals are so straightforward that a large underwriting firm may have enough institutional investor interest to keep the risks of distributing the issue at the reoffering price quite small. Moreover, in the case of bonds, hedging strategies using the interest rate risk control tools that we discuss later in this book can reduce or eliminate the risk of realizing a loss of selling the bonds at a price below the reoffering price.

Auction Process

Another variation for underwriting securities is the auction process. In this method, the issuer announces the terms of the issue, and interested parties submit bids for the entire issue. The auction form is mandated for certain securities of regulated public utilities and many municipal debt obligations. It is more commonly referred to as a **competitive bidding underwriting**. For example, suppose that a public utility wishes to issue $100 million of bonds. Various underwriters will form syndicates and bid on the issue. The syndicate that bids the lowest yield (i.e., the lowest cost to the issuer) wins the entire $100 million bond issue and then reoffers it to the public.

In a variant of the process, the bidders indicate the price they are willing to pay and the amount they are willing to buy. The security is then allocated to bidders from the highest bid price (lowest yield in the case of a bond) to the lower ones (higher yield in the case of a bond) until the entire issue is allocated. For example, suppose that an issuer is offering $500 million of a bond issue, and nine bidders submit the following yield bids:

Bidder	Amount (in millions)	Bid
A	$150	5.1%
B	110	5.2
C	90	5.2
D	100	5.3
E	75	5.4
F	25	5.4
G	80	5.5
H	70	5.6
I	85	5.7

The first four bidders—A, B, C, and D—will be allocated the amount for which they bid because they submitted the lowest-yield bids. In total, they will receive $450 million of the $500 million to be issued. That leaves $50 million to be allocated to the next-lowest bidders. Both E and F submitted the next lowest yield bid, 5.4%. In total, they bid for $100 million. Since the total they bid for exceeds the remaining $50 million, they will receive an amount proportionate to the amount for which they bid. Specifically, E will be allocated three-quarters ($75 million divided by $100 million) of the $50 million or $37.5 million, and F will be allocated one-quarter ($25 million divided by $100 million) of the $50 million or $12.5 million.

The next question concerns the yield that all of the six winning bidders—A, B, C, D, E, and F—will have to pay for the amount of the issue allocated to them. One way in which a competitive bidding can occur is all bidders pay the highest winning yield bid (or, equivalently, the lowest winning price). In our example, all bidders would buy the amount allocated to them at 5.4%. This type of auction is referred to as a *single-price auction* or a **Dutch auction**. Another way is for each bidder to pay whatever each one bid. This type of auction is called a *multiple-price auction*. Historically both procedures have been used in the auctioning of U.S. Treasury securities.

Using an auction allows corporate issuers to place newly issued debt obligations directly with institutional investors rather than follow the indirect path of using an underwriting firm. Internet auctions of municipal originations to underwriters began during 1997. One method of issuing municipal securities (i.e., securities issued by state and local governments and their authorities) is via a competitive bidding process. During November 1997, MuniAuction auctioned over the Internet $70 million City of Pittsburgh municipal bonds despite the opposition of some major Wall Street traditional, competitive bond underwriters. In 1999, the City of Pittsburgh used MuniAuction to offer bonds directly to institutional investors, allowing them to bypass traditional underwriters. By late 2000, MuniAuction reported it had conducted more than 250 municipal auctions totaling $13.4 billion. As of late November 2000, 14% of all competitive municipal bond underwritings were conducted over the MuniAuction system. By contrast, with the exception of two corporate bonds sales (Dow Chemical and Deutsche Bank), the corporate bond market had not adopted electronic bidding for new issues.

Investment bankers' response to the practice of direct purchase of publicly registered securities is that, as intermediaries, they add value by searching their institutional client base, which increases the likelihood that the issuer will incur the lowest cost, after adjusting for the underwriting fees. By dealing with just a few institutional investors, investment bankers argue, issuers cannot be sure of obtaining funds at the lowest cost. In addition, investment bankers say that they often play another important role: They make a secondary market in the securities they issue. This market improves the perceived liquidity of the issue and, as a result, reduces the cost to issuers. The question whether or not investment bankers can obtain lower-cost funding (after accounting for underwriting fees) to issuers, by comparison to the cost of funding from a direct offering, is an interesting empirical question.

Preemptive Rights Offering

A corporation can issue new common stock directly to existing shareholders via a **preemptive rights offering**. A preemptive right grants existing shareholders the right to buy some proportion of the new shares issued at a price below market value. The price at which the new shares can be purchased is called the *subscription price*. A rights offering ensures that current shareholders may maintain their proportionate equity interest in the corporation. In the United States, the practice of issuing common stock via a preemptive rights offering is uncommon. In other countries, it is much more common; in some countries, it is the only means by which a new offering of common stock may be sold.

For the shares sold via a preemptive rights offering, the underwriting services of an investment banker are not needed. However, the issuing corporation may use the services of an investment banker for the distribution of common stock that is not subscribed to. A **standby underwriting arrangement** will be used in such instances. This arrangement calls for the underwriter to buy the unsubscribed shares. The issuing corporation pays a **standby fee** to the investment banking firm.

To demonstrate how a rights offering works, the effect on the economic wealth of shareholders, and how the terms set forth in a rights offering affect whether or not the issuer will need an underwriter, we will use an illustration. Suppose that the market price of the stock of XYZ Corporation is $20 per share and that there are 30,000 shares outstanding. Thus, the capitalization of this firm is $600,000. Suppose that the management of XYZ Corporation is considering a rights offering in connection with the issuance of 10,000 new shares. Each current shareholder would receive one right for every three shares owned. The terms of the rights offering are as follows: For three rights and $17 (the subscription price) a new share can be acquired. The subscription price must always be less than the market price or the rights will not be exercised. In our illustration, the subscription price is 15% ($3/20) below the market price.[7]

In addition to the number of rights and the subscription price, there are two other elements of a rights offering that are important. First is the choice to transfer the rights. This is done by selling the right in the open market. This is critical since, as we will see, the right has a value and that value can be captured by selling the right. The second element is the time when the right expires (that is, when it can no longer be used to acquire the stock). Typically, the time period before a right expires is short.

---

[7] Note that the same results can be achieved by issuing one right per share but requiring three rights plus the subscription price for a new share (except for rounding-off problems and implications for the value of one right discussed in the following text).

The value of a right can be found by calculating the difference between the price of a share before the rights offering and the price of a share after the rights offering.[8] That is,

Value of a right = Price before rights offering − Price after rights offering

Or, equivalently,

Value of a right = Share price rights on − Share price ex rights

Table 1 shows the impact of the rights offering on the price of a share. The price after the rights offering will be $19.25. Therefore, the value of a right is $0.75($20−$19.25).

The difference between the price before the rights offering and after the rights offering expressed as a percentage of the original price is called the *dilution effect of the rights issue*. In the present case, the dilution effect is $0.75/$20, or 3.75%. The larger the dilution is, the larger the ratio of old and new shares is, and the larger the discount is.[9]

The last section of Table 1 shows the net gain or loss to the initial shareholder as a result of the rights offering. The loss per share due to dilution is $0.75, but that is exactly equal to the value of a right which, if the shareholder desires, can be sold in the market. This result is important because it shows that the rights offering as such will not affect the sum of the value of the share without rights (referred to as ex rights) plus the value of the rights the

Table 1 Analysis of Rights Offering on the Market Price of XYZ Corporation

I. *Before rights issue*	
1. Capitalization	$600,000
2. Number of shares	30,000
3. Share price (rights on)	$20.00
II. *After issuance of shares via rights offering*	
4. Number of shares	40,000 (= 30,000 + 10,000)
5. Capitalization	$770,000 (= $600,000 + 10,000 × $17)
6. Share price (ex rights)	$19.25 (= $770,000/40,000)
7. Value of one right	$0.75 (= $20.00 − $19.25)
III. *Net gain or loss to initial stockholder*	
8. Loss per share due to dilution	$0.75 (= 3.75% × $20)
9. Gain per share from selling or exercising a right	$0.75
10. Net gain or loss	$ 0

---

[8] Alternatively, the value of a right can be found as follows:

$$\frac{\text{Price after rights offering} - \text{Subscription price}}{\text{Number of rights required to buy a share}}$$

[9] Specifically,

$$\text{Dilution effect} = \frac{\text{Discount \%}}{1 + (\text{Ratio of old to new shares})}$$

In our illustration, the discount is 15% and the ratio of old to new shares is 30,000/10,000 or 3, so the dilution effect is 15%/4, or 3.75%.

shareholder receives, no matter how much the dilution or the initial discount offered is. This is because a larger dilution is exactly compensated by the increase in the value of the rights.[10]

Key Points That You Should Understand Before Proceeding

1. There are variations in the traditional underwriting process.
2. In a bought deal, a lead manager or a group of managers offers a potential issuer of debt securities a firm bid to purchase a specified amount of a security.
3. An offering of a new security can be made by means of an auction process.
4. A corporation can offer existing shareholders new shares in a preemptive rights offering, and using a standby underwriting arrangement, the corporation can have an investment banking firm agree to distribute any shares not subscribed to.

PRIVATE PLACEMENT OF SECURITIES

In addition to underwriting securities for distribution to the public, securities may be placed with a limited number of institutional investors such as insurance companies, investment companies, and pension funds. **Private placement**, as this process is known, differs from the public offering of securities that we have described so far. Life insurance companies are the major investors in private placements.

Public and private offerings of securities differ in terms of the regulatory requirements that the issuer must satisfy. The Securities Act of 1933 and the Securities Exchange Act of 1934 require that all securities offered to the general public must be registered with the SEC, unless there is a specific exemption.

The Securities Acts allow three exemptions from federal registration. First, intrastate offerings—that is, securities sold only within a state—are exempt. Second, there is a small-offering exemption (Regulation A). Specifically, if the offering is for $1 million or less, the securities need not be registered. Finally, Section 4(2) of the 1933 act exempts from registration "transactions by an issuer not involving any public offering." At the same time, the 1933 act does not provide specific guidelines to identify what is a private offering or placement.

In 1982, the SEC adopted Regulation D, which sets forth the guidelines that determine if an issue is qualified for exemption from registration. The guidelines require that, in general, the securities cannot be offered through any form of general advertising or general solicitation that would prevail for public offerings. Most importantly, the guidelines restrict the sale of securities to "sophisticated" investors. Such "accredited" investors are defined as those who (1) have the capability to evaluate (or who can afford to employ an advisor to evaluate) the risk and return characteristics of the securities, and (2) have the resources to bear the economic risks.[11]

The exemption of an offering does not mean that the issuer need not disclose information to potential investors. In fact, the issuer must still furnish the same information deemed

---

[10] For a further discussion of why the size of the discount and dilution is relevant for the welfare of the stockholders and the factors that will affect the success of a rights offering, see Frank J. Fabozzi and Franco Modigliani, *Capital Markets: Institutions and Instruments* (Englewood Cliffs, N.J.: Prentice Hall, 1996), pp. 133–136.

[11] Under the current law, an accredited investor is one who satisfies either a net worth test (at least $1 million excluding automobiles, home, and home furnishings) or an annual income test (at least $200,000 for a single individual, $300,000 for a couple for the past two years, with expectations of such income to continue for the current year).

material by the SEC. The issuer supplies this information in a private placement memorandum, as opposed to a prospectus for a public offering. The distinction between the private placement memorandum and the prospectus is that the former does not include information deemed by the SEC "nonmaterial," if such information is required in a prospectus. Moreover, unlike a prospectus, the private placement memorandum is not subject to SEC review.

Investment banking firms assist in the private placement of securities in several ways. They work with the issuer and potential investors on the design and pricing of the security. Often, it has been in the private placement market that investment bankers first design new security structures. Field testing of many of the innovative securities that we describe in this book occurred in the private placement market.

The investment bankers may be involved with lining up the investors as well as designing the issue. Or, if the issuer has already identified the investors, the investment banker may serve only in an advisory capacity. An investment banker can also participate in the transaction on a best efforts underwriting arrangement.

Rule 144A

In the United States, one restriction imposed on buyers of privately placed securities is that they may not be resold for two years after acquisition. Thus, there is no liquidity in the market for that time period. Buyers of privately placed securities must be compensated for the lack of liquidity, which raises the cost to the issuer of the securities.

In April 1990, however, SEC **Rule 144A** became effective. This rule eliminates the two-year holding period by permitting large institutions to trade securities acquired in a private placement among themselves without having to register these securities with the SEC.

Private placements are now classified as Rule 144A offerings or non–Rule 144A offerings. The latter are more commonly referred to as traditional private placements. Rule 144A offerings are underwritten by investment bankers.

Rule 144A encourages non–U.S. corporations to issue securities in the U.S. private placement market for two reasons. First, it will attract new large institutional investors into the market that were unwilling previously to buy private placements because of the requirement to hold the securities for two years. Such an increase in the number of institutional investors may encourage non–U.S. entities to issue securities. Second, foreign entities were unwilling to raise funds in the United States prior to establishment of Rule 144A because they had to register their securities and furnish the necessary disclosure set forth by U.S. securities laws. Private placement requires less disclosure. Rule 144A also improves liquidity, reducing the cost of raising funds.

Key Points That You Should Understand Before Proceeding

1. A private placement is the distribution of shares to a limited number of institutional investors rather than through a public offering.
2. The SEC specifies the conditions that must be satisfied to qualify for a private placement.
3. Investment bankers will typically work with issuers in the design of a security for a private placement and line up the potential investors.
4. SEC Rule 144A improves the liquidity of securities acquired by certain institutional investors in a private placement.

SUMMARY

The primary market involves the distribution to investors of newly issued securities. Investment bankers perform one or more of three functions: (1) advising the issuer on the terms and the timing of the offering, (2) buying the securities from the issuer, and (3) distributing the issue to investors. The second function is referred to as the underwriting function. Investment banking activities are performed by commercial banks and securities houses.

The SEC is responsible for regulating the issuance of new securities, with the major provisions set forth in the Securities Act of 1933. The act requires that the issuer file a registration statement for approval by the SEC. Rule 415, the shelf registration rule, permits certain issuers to file a single registration document indicating that they intend to sell a certain amount of a certain class of securities at one or more times within the next two years.

Variations in the underwriting process include the bought deal for the underwriting of bonds, the auction process for both stocks and bonds, and a rights offering coupled with a standby arrangement for underwriting common stock.

A private placement is different from the public offering of securities in terms of the regulatory requirements that must be satisfied by the issuer. If an issue qualifies as a private placement, it is exempt from the more complex registration requirements imposed on public offerings. Rule 144A has contributed to the growth of the private placement market by improving the liquidity of securities issued in this market.

KEY TERMS

- Best efforts
- Bought deal
- Competitive bidding underwriting
- Due diligence
- Dutch auction
- Firm commitment
- Gross spread (underwriter discount)
- Initial public offering (IPO)
- Investment bankers
- Preemptive rights offering
- Primary market
- Private placement
- Prospectus

- Red herring
- Registration statement
- Rule 144A
- Secondary common stock offering
- Selling group
- Shelf registration rule
- Standby fee
- Standby underwriting arrangement
- Syndicate
- Underwriting
- Underwriter discount
- Waiting period

QUESTIONS

1. **a.** What are the three ways in which an investment banking firm may be involved in the issuance of a new security?
   b. What is meant by the underwriting function?

2. What is the difference between a firm commitment underwriting arrangement and a best efforts arrangement?

3. **a.** What is meant by a bought deal?
   b. Why do bought deals expose investment banking firms to greater capital risk than traditional underwriting?

4. A corporation is issuing a bond on a competitive bidding basis. The corporation has indicated that it will issue $200 million of an issue. The following

yield bids and the corresponding amounts were submitted:

Bidder	Amount (in millions)	Bid
A	$20	7.4%
B	40	7.5
C	10	7.5
D	50	7.5
E	40	7.6
F	20	7.6
G	10	7.7
H	10	7.7
I	20	7.8
J	25	7.9
K	28	7.9
L	20	8.0
M	18	8.1

a. Who are the winning bidders?

b. How much of the security will be allocated to each winning bidder?

c. If this auction is a single-price auction, at what yield will each winning bidder be awarded the security?

d. If this auction is a multiple-price auction, at what yield will each winning bidder be awarded the security?

5. **a.** What is a preemptive right?

b. What is a preemptive rights offering?

c. Is a preemptive rights offering common in the United States?

6. The market price of the stock of the Bernstein Corporation is $50 per share and there are one million shares outstanding. Suppose that the management of this corporation is considering a rights offering in connection with the issuance of 500,000 new shares. Each current shareholder would receive one right for every two shares owned. The terms of the rights offering are as follows: For two rights and $30 (the subscription price), a new share can be acquired.

a. What would the share price be after the rights offering?

b. What is the value of one right?

c. Demonstrate the effect on the economic well-being of the initial shareholders as a result of the rights offering.

7. What is a registration statement?

8. What is meant by the waiting period?

9. An underwriter is responsible for performing due diligence before offering a security to investors. What does due diligence mean?

10. The following statements come from the December 24, 1990, issue of *Corporate Financing Week*:

> As in the public market, growth in the private placement market was slowed this year by a rise in interest rates that pushed many issuers to the sidelines, by the Mideast crisis and by a flight to quality by investors. . . . Foreign private placements saw a marked increase due to Rule 144A.

a. What are the key distinctions between a private placement and a public offering?

b. What is Rule 144A?

c. Why do you think Rule 144A has increased foreign private placements?

Secondary Markets

From Chapter 14 of *Foundations of Financial Markets and Institutions*, 4/e. Frank J. Fabozzi. Franco Modigliani. Frank J. Jones.
Copyright © 2010 by Pearson Prentice Hall. All rights reserved.

Secondary Markets

LEARNING OBJECTIVES

After reading this chapter, you will understand

- the definition of a secondary market

- the need for secondary markets for financial assets

- the difference between a continuous and a call market

- the requirements of a perfect market

- frictions that cause actual financial markets to differ from a perfect market

- why brokers are necessary

- the role of a dealer as a market maker and the costs associated with market making

- what is meant by the operational efficiency of a market

- what is meant by the pricing efficiency of a market

- the implications of pricing efficiency

- the different forms of pricing efficiency

- the implications of pricing efficiency for market participants

Financial markets can be divided into primary and secondary markets. It is in the secondary market where already issued financial assets are traded. The key distinction between a primary market and a secondary market is that, in the secondary market, the issuer of the asset does not receive funds from the buyer. Rather, the existing issue changes hands in the secondary market, and funds flow from the buyer of the asset to the seller.

In this chapter, we explain the various features of secondary markets. These features are common to the trading of any type of financial instrument. We take a closer look at individual markets in later chapters.

FUNCTION OF SECONDARY MARKETS

It is worthwhile to review once again the function of secondary markets. In the secondary market, an issuer of securities—whether it is a corporation or a governmental unit—may obtain regular information about the value of the asset. The periodic trading of the asset reveals to the issuer the consensus price that the asset commands in an open market. Thus, firms can discover what value investors attach to their stocks, and firms or noncorporate issuers can observe the prices of their bonds and the implied interest rates investors expect and demand from them. Such information helps issuers assess how well they are using the funds acquired from earlier primary market activities, and it also indicates how receptive investors would be to new offerings. The other service that a secondary market offers issuers is the opportunity for the original buyer of an asset to reverse the investment by selling it for cash. Unless investors are confident that they can shift from one financial asset to another as they may feel necessary, they would naturally be reluctant to buy any financial asset. Such reluctance would harm potential issuers in one of two ways: Either issuers would be unable to sell new securities at all, or they would have to pay a higher rate of return, as investors would increase the discount rate in compensation for expected illiquidity in the securities.

Investors in financial assets receive several benefits from a secondary market. Such a market obviously offers them liquidity for their assets as well as information about the assets' fair or consensus values. Furthermore, secondary markets bring together many interested parties and, thereby, reduce the costs of searching for likely buyers and sellers of assets. Moreover, by accommodating many trades, secondary markets keep the cost of transactions low. By keeping the costs of both searching and transacting low, secondary markets encourage investors to purchase financial assets.

> **Key Points That You Should Understand Before Proceeding**
>
> 1. Secondary markets help the issuer of securities to track their values and required returns.
> 2. Secondary markets benefit investors by providing liquidity.

TRADING LOCATIONS

One indication of the usefulness of secondary markets is that they exist throughout the world. Here, we give just a few examples of these markets.

In the United States, secondary trading of common stock occurs in a number of trading locations. Many shares are traded on major national **stock exchanges** (the largest of which is the New York Stock Exchange) and regional stock exchanges, which are organized and somewhat regulated markets in specific geographical locations. Additional significant trading in stock takes place on the so-called **over-the-counter (OTC) market**, which is a geographically dispersed group of traders linked to one another via telecommunication systems. The dominant OTC market for stocks in the United States is Nasdaq. Some bonds are traded on exchanges, but most trading in bonds in the United States and throughout the world occurs in the OTC market.

MARKET STRUCTURES

Many secondary markets are **continuous markets**, which means that prices are determined continuously throughout the trading day as buyers and sellers submit orders. For example, given the order flow at 10:00 A.M., the market clearing price of a stock on some organized stock exchange may be $70; at 11:00 A.M. of the same trading day, the market-clearing price of the same stock, but with different order flows, may be $70.75. Thus, in a continuous market, prices may vary with the pattern of orders reaching the market and not because of any change in the basic situation of supply and demand. We will return to this point later.

A contrasting market structure is the **call market**, in which orders are batched or grouped together for simultaneous execution at the same price. That is, at certain times in the trading day (or possibly more than once in a day), a market maker holds an auction for a stock. The auction may be oral or written. In either case, the auction will determine or **fix**[1] the market clearing price at a particular time of the trading day.

Key Points That You Should Understand Before Proceeding

1. The basic features of the call method of trading.
2. What a continuous market is.
3. Some markets conduct the day's initial trades with a call method and most other trades in a continuous way.

PERFECT MARKETS

In order to explain the characteristics of secondary markets, we first describe a **perfect market** for a financial asset. Then, we can show how common occurrences in real markets keep them from being theoretically perfect.

In general, a perfect market results when the number of buyers and sellers is sufficiently large, and all participants are small enough relative to the market so that no individual market agent can influence the commodity's price. Consequently, all buyers and sellers are price-takers, and the market price is determined where there is equality of supply and demand. This condition is more likely to be satisfied if the commodity traded is fairly homogeneous (for example, corn or wheat). But a market is not perfect only because market agents are price-takers. A perfect market is also free of transactions costs and any impediment to the interaction of supply and demand for the commodity. Economists refer to these various costs and impediments as **frictions**. The costs associated with frictions generally result in buyers paying more than in the absence of frictions and/or in sellers receiving less.

---

[1] This use of the word fix is traditional, and not pejorative or suggestive of illegal activity. For example, the *Financial Times* reports on the activities of the London gold bullion market, which is a call market, and records prices set at the "morning fix" and the "afternoon fix." These fixes take place at the two call auctions, which are held daily.

In the case of financial markets, frictions would include:

- commissions charged by brokers
- bid–ask spreads charged by dealers
- order handling and clearance charges
- taxes (notably on capital gains) and government-imposed transfer fees
- costs of acquiring information about the financial asset
- trading restrictions, such as exchange-imposed restrictions on the size of a position in the financial asset that a buyer or seller may take
- restrictions on market makers
- halts to trading that may be imposed by regulators where the financial asset is traded

An investor who expects that the price of a security will increase can benefit from buying that security. However, suppose that an investor expects that the price of a security will decline and wants to benefit should the price actually decline. What can the investor do? The investor may be able to sell the security without owning it. How can this happen? There are various institutional arrangements that allow an investor to borrow securities so that the borrowed security can be delivered to satisfy the sale.

This practice of selling securities that are not owned at the time of sale is referred to as *selling short*. The security is purchased subsequently by the investor and returned to the party that lent it. In this way, the investor covers a short position. A profit will be realized if the purchase price is less than the price at which the issuer sold short the security.

The ability of investors to sell short is an important mechanism in financial markets. In the absence of an effective short-selling mechanism, security prices will tend to be biased toward the view of more optimistic investors, causing a market to depart from the standards of a perfect price-setting situation. In fact, many large and developed securities markets allow short selling, although regulatory bodies tend to monitor this practice more closely than other features of markets. Nonetheless, the prevalence of short selling is clear evidence of its usefulness to the price-setting function of securities markets.

Key Points That You Should Understand Before Proceeding

1. A market can be perfect, in a theoretical sense, only if it meets many conditions regarding number of participants, flow of information, freedom from regulation, and freedom from costs that hinder trading.
2. Market imperfections are called frictions.
3. A perfect market must also permit short selling, which is the sale of borrowed securities.

ROLE OF BROKERS AND DEALERS IN REAL MARKETS

Common occurrences in real markets keep them from meeting the theoretical standards of being perfect. Because of these occurrences, **brokers** and dealers are necessary to the smooth functioning of a secondary market.

Brokers

One way in which a real market might not meet all the exacting standards of a theoretically perfect market is that many investors may not be present at all times in the marketplace. Furthermore, a typical investor may not be skilled in the art of the deal or completely informed about every facet of trading in the asset. Clearly, most investors in even smoothly functioning markets need professional assistance. Investors need someone to receive and keep track of their orders for buying or selling, to find other parties wishing to sell or buy, to negotiate for good prices, to serve as a focal point for trading, and to execute the orders. The broker performs all these functions. Obviously, these functions are more important for the complicated trades, such as the small or large trades, than for simple transactions or those of typical size.

A broker is an entity that acts on behalf of an investor who wishes to execute orders. In economic and legal terms, a broker is said to be an *agent* of the investor. It is important to realize that the brokerage activity does not require the broker to buy and sell or hold in inventory the financial asset that is the subject of the trade. (Such activity is termed *taking a position* in the asset, and it is the role of the dealer, another important financial market participant discussed in the following text.) Rather, the broker receives, transmits, and executes investors' orders with other investors. The broker receives an explicit commission for these services, and the commission is a *transactions cost* of the securities markets. If the broker also provides other services, such as research, recordkeeping, or advising, investors may pay additional charges.

Dealers as Market Makers

A real market might also differ from the perfect market because of the possibly frequent event of a temporary imbalance in the number of buy and sell orders that investors may place for any security at any one time. Such unmatched or unbalanced flow causes two problems. One is that the security's price may change abruptly, even if there has been no shift in either supply or demand for the security. Another problem is that buyers may have to pay higher than market-clearing prices (or sellers accept lower ones) if they want to make their trade immediately.

An example can illustrate these points. Suppose that the consensus price for ABC security is $50, which was determined in several recent trades. Now, suppose that a flow of buy orders from investors who suddenly have cash arrives in the market, but there is no accompanying supply of sell orders. This temporary imbalance could be sufficient to push the price of ABC security to, say, $55. Thus, the price has changed sharply even though there has been no change in any fundamental financial aspect of the issuer. Buyers who want to buy immediately must pay $55 rather than $50, and this difference can be viewed as the price of **immediacy**. By immediacy, we mean that buyers and sellers do not want to wait for the arrival of sufficient orders on the other side of the trade, which would bring the price closer to the level of recent transactions.

The fact of imbalances explains the need for the **dealer** or market maker, who stands ready and willing to buy a financial asset for its own account (to add to an inventory of the financial asset) or sell from its own account (to reduce the inventory of the financial asset). At a given time, dealers are willing to buy a financial asset at a price (the bid price) that is less than what they are willing to sell the same financial asset for (the ask price).

In the 1960s, two economists, George Stigler[2] and Harold Demsetz,[3] analyzed the role of dealers in securities markets. They viewed dealers as the suppliers of immediacy—the

[2] George Stigler, "Public Regulation of Securities Markets," *Journal of Business* (April 1964), pp. 117–134.

[3] Harold Demsetz, "The Cost of Transacting," *Quarterly Journal of Economics* (October 1968), pp. 35–36.

ability to trade promptly—to the market. The bid–ask spread can be viewed in turn as the price charged by dealers for supplying immediacy together with short-run price stability (continuity or smoothness) in the presence of short-term order imbalances. There are two other roles that dealers play: providing reliable price information to market participants, and, in certain market structures, providing the services of an auctioneer in bringing order and fairness to a market.[4]

The price stabilization role follows from our earlier example of what may happen to the price of a particular transaction in the absence of any intervention when there is a temporary imbalance of orders. By taking the opposite side of a trade when there are no other orders, the dealer prevents the price from materially diverging from the price at which a recent trade was consummated.

Investors are concerned not only with immediacy, but also with being able to trade at prices that are reasonable, given prevailing conditions in the market. While dealers do not know with certainty the true price of a security, they do have a privileged position in some market structures with respect not just to the flow of market orders but also to **limit orders**, which are special orders that can be executed only if the market price of the asset changes in a specified way. For example, the dealers of the organized markets, called *specialists*, have just such a privileged position from which they get special information about the flow of market orders.

Finally, the dealer acts as an **auctioneer** in some market structures, thereby providing order and fairness in the operations of the market. For example, the market maker on organized stock exchanges in the United States performs this function by organizing trading to make sure that the exchange rules for the priority of trading are followed. The role of a market maker in a call market structure is that of an auctioneer. The market maker does not take a position in the traded asset, as a dealer does in a continuous market.

What factors determine the price dealers should charge for the services they provide? Or equivalently, what factors determine the *bid–ask spread*? One of the most important is the order processing costs incurred by dealers. The costs of equipment necessary to do business and a dealer's administrative and operations staff are examples. The lower these costs, the narrower the bid–ask spread. With the reduced cost of computing and better-trained personnel, these costs have declined since the 1960s.

Dealers also have to be compensated for bearing risk. A **dealer's position** may involve carrying inventory of a security (a *long position*) or selling a security that is not in inventory (a *short position*). There are three types of risks associated with maintaining a long or short position in a given security. First, there is the uncertainty about the future price of the security. A dealer who has a net long position in the security is concerned that the price will decline in the future; a dealer who is in a net short position is concerned that the price will rise.

The second type of risk has to do with the expected time it will take the dealer to unwind a position and its uncertainty. And this, in turn, depends primarily on the thickness of the market for the security. Finally, while a dealer may have access to better information about order flows than the general public, there are some trades where the dealer takes the risk of trading with someone who has better information.[5] This results in the better-informed

---

[4] For a more detailed discussion, see Chapter 1 in Robert A. Schwartz, *Equity Markets: Structure, Trading, and Performance* (New York: Harper & Row Publishers, 1988), pp. 389–397.

[5] Walter Bagehot, "The Only Game in Town," *Financial Analysts Journal* (March–April 1971), pp. 12–14, 22.

trader obtaining a better price at the expense of the dealer. Consequently, a dealer in establishing the bid–ask spread for a trade will assess whether or not the trader might have better information.[6]

Key Points That You Should Understand Before Proceeding

1. The relationship between a broker and an investor.
2. How a dealer makes a profit when making a market.
3. The benefits that a market derives from the actions of dealers.

MARKET EFFICIENCY

The term *efficient* capital market has been used in several contexts to describe the operating characteristics of a capital market. There is a distinction, however, between an **operationally** (or **internally**) **efficient market** and a **pricing** (or **externally**) **efficient capital market**.[7]

Operational Efficiency

In an operationally efficient market, investors can obtain transaction services as cheaply as possible, given the costs associated with furnishing those services. For example, in national equity markets throughout the world the degree of operational efficiency varies. At one time, brokerage commissions in the United States were fixed, and the brokerage industry charged high fees and functioned poorly. But that began to change in May 1975, as the American exchanges adopted a system of competitive and negotiated commissions. Non–U.S. markets have been moving toward more competitive brokerage fees. France, for example, adopted a system of negotiated commissions for large trades in 1985. In its "Big Bang" of 1986, the London Stock Exchange abolished fixed commissions. The Japanese version of the Big Bang began during 1996. One of its many goals was the liberalization of commissions.

Commissions are only part of the cost of transacting, as we noted above. The other part is the dealer spread. The minimum bid–offer spreads in the stock market have declined significantly in recent years. The minimum spread was one-eighths ("eighths") until 1997, a vestige of the early days of stock trading. The NYSE and other markets began trading in one-sixteenths ("teenies") on June 24, 1997. Effective August 24, 2000, the minimum spread was reduced to one cent ("decimals"), with trades on all stocks in decimals beginning on August 9, 2001. Bid–offer spreads for bonds vary by type of bond. For example, the bid–ask spread on U.S. Treasury securities is much smaller than for other bonds such as mortgage-backed bonds and derivative mortgage-backed instruments, which are key topics in later chapters. Even within the U.S. Treasury securities market, certain issues have a narrower bid–ask spread than other issues.

---

[6] Some trades can be viewed as informationless trades. This means that the dealer knows or believes that a trade is being requested to accomplish an investment objective that is not motivated by the potential future price movement of the security.

[7] Richard R. West, "Two Kinds of Market Efficiency," *Financial Analysts Journal* (November–December 1975), pp. 30–34.

Pricing Efficiency

Pricing efficiency refers to a market where prices at all times fully reflect all available information that is relevant to the valuation of securities. That is, investors quickly adjust the demand and supply schedules for a security when new information about it becomes available, and those actions quickly impound the information into the price of the security.

A price efficient market has implications for the investment strategy that investors may wish to pursue. There are various active strategies employed by investors. In an **active strategy**, investors seek to capitalize on what they perceive to be the mispricing of a security or securities. In a market that is price efficient, active strategies will not consistently generate a return after taking into consideration transactions costs and the risks associated with a strategy of frequent trading. The other strategy, in a market which seems to be price efficient, is simply to buy and hold a broad cross section of securities in the market. Some investors pursue this strategy through **indexing**, which is a policy that has the goal of matching the performance of some financial index from the market. It is in this market where the greatest amount of empirical evidence exists.

Key Points That You Should Understand Before Proceeding

1. What makes a market operationally or internally efficient.
2. The key characteristic of a market that has pricing or external efficiency.

ELECTRONIC TRADING

Historically, financial markets had physical locations where buyers and sellers (or their agents) met and negotiated the price of a security. Today, information technology has removed the necessity for a physical location and allowed the creation of a virtual marketplace. Electronic trading of stocks, bonds, and derivatives continues to replace physical markets. Here, we describe electronic bond trading.

Electronic Bond Trading

Traditionally, bond trading has been based on broker-dealer trading desks, which take principal positions to fill customer buy and sell orders. In recent years, however, there has been an evolution away from traditional bond trading toward electronic trading. This evolution toward electronic trading is likely to continue.

There are several related reasons for the transition to the electronic trading of bonds. Because the bond business has been a principal rather than an agency business, the capital of the market makers is critical. Whereas the amount of capital of the broker-dealers has increased during the past several years, the amount of capital of U.S. institutional investors (pension funds, mutual funds, insurance companies, and commercial banks) and international customers has increased much more, and the size of the orders has increased significantly. As a result, making markets in bonds has become more risky for the market makers.

In addition, the increase in the volatility of bond markets has increased the capital required of bond broker-dealers. Finally, the profitability of bond market making has declined since many of the products have become more commodity-like and their bid–offer spreads have decreased.

The combination of the increased risk and the decreased profitability of bond market making has induced the major market markets to deemphasize this business in the allocation of capital. Broker-dealer firms have determined that it is more efficient to employ their capital in other activities such as underwriting, asset management, and other agency-type brokerage businesses than in principal-type market-making businesses. As a result, the liquidity of the traditionally principal-oriented bond markets has declined, and this decline in liquidity has opened the way for other market-making mechanisms.

This retreat by traditional market-making firms opened the door for electronic trading. In fact, as indicated below, the same Wall Street firms that have been the major market makers in bonds have also been the supporters of electronic trading in bonds.

Electronic trading in bonds has helped fill this developing vacuum and provided liquidity to the bond markets. The growth of electronic trading will necessarily continue. Among the overall advantages of electronic trading are (1) providing liquidity to the markets, (2) price discovery (particularly for less liquid markets), (3) utilization of new technologies, and (4) trading and portfolio management efficiencies. As an example of the last advantage, portfolio managers can load their buy/sell orders onto a website, trade from these orders, and then clear these orders.

There are a variety of types of electronic trading systems for bonds. The two major types of electronic trading systems are the *dealer-to-customer systems* and the *exchange systems.*

Dealer-to-customer systems can be a *single-dealer system* or *multiple-dealer system.* Single-dealer systems are based on a customer dealing with a single, identified dealer over the computer. The single-dealer system simply computerizes the traditional customer–dealer market making mechanism. Multi-dealer systems provide some advancement over the single-dealer method. A customer can select from any of several identified dealers whose bids and offers are provided on a computer screen. The customer knows the identity of the dealer and the transaction is cleared through the dealer's procedures.

The exchange system is quite different and has potentially significantly greater value added. According to the exchange system, dealer and customer bids and offers are entered into the system on an anonymous basis, and the clearing of the executed trades is done through a common process. As a result, a common clearinghouse and common membership criteria based on the credit acceptability of the members have to be developed. This mechanism requires a much more onerous structure than the dealer-to-customer systems. Although there is a common clearinghouse for common stocks (Depository Trust Company [DTC]), there is none for bonds. Thus, the development of an open architecture system for bonds will be more difficult than for stocks.

Two different major types of exchange systems are those based on continuous trading and call auctions, described previously in this chapter. Continuous trading permits trading at continuously changing market determined prices throughout the day and is appropriate for liquid bonds, such as Treasury and agency securities. Call auctions provide for fixed price auctions (that is, all the transactions or exchanges occur at the same "fixed" price) at specific times during the day and are appropriate for less liquid bonds such as corporate bonds and municipal bonds. Table 1 summarizes the major issues in electronic bond trading.

There are currently three active multiple-dealer-to-customer systems: TradeWeb, MarketAxess, and Bloomberg.

Table 1 Summary of Major Issues in Electronic Bond Trading

	Dealer to Customer—Multiple Dealer	Exchange Systems
Characteristics	Customer and dealer know the identity of the counterparty	Counterparties are anonymous
	Clearing through specific dealer's clearing system	Common clearing through same system
	Counterparty credit determined by individual broker-dealer and customer	Counterparty credit determined by common clearing organization
	Large trades done as block trades through individual dealers	Large trades done as block trades through individual dealers
Ideal products	Liquid, tradable type products: Treasuries, agencies, and MBS	Inventory-type products: CMOs, ABS, corporate bonds, municipal bonds, other less liquid products
Examples	TradeWeb (Sponsors: CSFB, Goldman Sachs, Salomon Smith Barney, Merrill Lynch, Morgan Stanley Dean Witter, Bloomberg, and MarketAxess)	None currently

SUMMARY

A secondary market in financial assets is one where existing or outstanding assets are traded among investors. A secondary market serves several needs of the firm or governmental unit that issues securities in the primary market. The secondary market provides the issuer with regular information about the value of its outstanding stocks or bonds, and it encourages investors to buy securities from issuers because it offers them an ongoing opportunity for liquidating their investments in securities.

Investors also get services from the secondary market: The market supplies them with liquidity and prices for the assets they are holding or want to buy, and the market brings interested investors together, thereby reducing the costs of searching for other parties and of making trades.

Secondary markets for financial securities exist around the world. Such markets may be continuous, where trading and price determination go on throughout the day as orders to buy and sell reach the market. Some markets are call markets: Prices are determined by executions of batched or grouped orders to buy and sell at a specific time (or times) within the trading day. Some secondary markets combine features of call and continuous trading.

Even the most developed and smoothly functioning secondary market falls short of being perfect in the economically theoretical meaning of the term. Actual markets tend to have numerous frictions that affect prices and investors' behavior. Some key frictions are transactions costs, which include commissions, fees, and execution costs.

Because of imperfections in actual markets, investors need the services of two types of market participants: dealers and brokers. Brokers aid investors by collecting and transmitting orders to the market, by bringing willing buyers and sellers together, by negotiating prices, and by executing orders. The fee for these services is the broker's commission.

Dealers perform three functions in markets: (1) They provide the opportunity for investors to trade immediately rather than waiting for the arrival of sufficient orders on the other side of the trade (immediacy), and they do this while maintaining short-run price stability (continuity); (2) they offer price information to market participants; and (3) in certain market structures, dealers serve as auctioneers in bringing order and fairness to a market. Dealers buy for their own account and maintain inventories of assets, and their profits come from selling assets at higher prices than the prices at which they purchased them.

A market is operationally efficient if it offers investors reasonably priced services related to buying and selling. A market is price efficient if at all times prices fully reflect all available information that is relevant to the valuation of securities. In such a market, active strategies pursued will not consistently produce superior returns after adjusting for risk and transactions costs.

Electronic bond trading has improved the liquidity of the bond market, as the commitment to bond trading by dealers has not kept pace with the liquidity needs of institutional investors. The two major types of electronic trading systems are the dealer-to-customer systems (single- and multiple-dealer systems) and the *exchange systems*. In exchange systems, dealer and customer bids and offers are entered into the system on an anonymous basis, and the clearing of the executed trades is done through a common process. There are continuous trading and call auction exchange-trading systems.

KEY TERMS

- Active strategy
- Auctioneer
- Broker
- Call market
- Continuous market
- Dealer
- Dealer's position
- Fix
- Frictions

- Immediacy
- Indexing
- Limit order
- Operational (internal) efficient market
- Over-the-counter (OTC) market
- Perfect market
- Pricing (external) efficient capital market
- Stock exchange

QUESTIONS

1. Consider two transactions. The Norwegian government sells bonds in the United States. The buyer of one of those bonds is an insurance company, which, after holding the bond for a year, sells it to a mutual fund. Which of these transactions occurs in the primary market and which in the secondary market? Does the Norwegian government get any proceeds from the sale between the insurance company and the mutual fund?

2. Some years ago, Japan's four largest brokerage firms (Yamaichi Securities Co., Nomura Securities Co., Daiwa Securities Co., and Nikko Securities Co.) formally asked their government to lift bans that restrict their freedom to invest in stocks. One of those bans prevents a brokerage firm from trading for its own account (that is, buying and selling for itself rather than for clients) during certain times of the trading day. The other ban restricts a brokerage firm participating in more than 30% of the trading of any one stock within a month. Consider these restrictions in terms of the role of dealers in financial markets and the requirements for operational and price efficiency in a market. Do you think that lifting the restrictions would help the

Tokyo Stock Exchange to be more efficient with regard to price and operations?

3. The residential real estate market boasts many brokers but very few dealers. What explains this situation?

4. Some years ago, legislators in a state claimed that speculation on land was driving prices to too high a level. They proposed to pass a law that would require the buyer of any piece of land in the state to hold the land for at least three years before he or she could resell it.

   a. Analyze this proposal in terms of perfect markets and possible frictions that have been described in this chapter.

   b. If that proposal had passed, do you think land prices would have risen or fallen?

5. What is meant by the statement that "dealers offer both immediacy and price continuity to investors"?

6. In 1990, a trader on the Paris *Bourse* claimed to one of the authors of this book that "now, we are just like New York; everything is continuous." Do you think that the *Bourse*'s change from a call market to a continuous market, which took place in the 1980s, could have improved either price or operational efficiency in that market enough to warrant this assertion?

7. If a security is highly liquid, explain whether it would be more advantageous to develop a trading system with continuous trading or call auction.

8. Outline the problems associated with fixed brokerage commissions.

9. Indicate whether or not you agree with the following statement: "The minimum bid-offer spread on common stock is in terms of one-eighths."

10. Assume that UND stock normally has a bid–offer spread of three-eighths, or $0.375. What do you think would happen to that spread on a day when the stock market begins to fall very sharply? Explain your answer. Also, what would happen to the spread if the company announced that it was buying back 20% of its outstanding shares and would complete that repurchase within three months? Explain your view.

11. Suppose the federal government imposed a tax of $0.10 on each stock-buying transaction. Would stock prices in general rise or fall on such news? Explain your answer.

12. What are the reasons for the development of electronic bond trading?

Treasury and Agency Securities Markets

Treasury and Agency Securities Markets

LEARNING OBJECTIVES

After reading this chapter, you will understand

- the importance of the Treasury market

- the different types of securities issued by the Treasury

- the operation of the primary market for Treasury securities

- the role of government dealers and government brokers

- the secondary market for Treasury securities

- how Treasury securities are quoted in the secondary market

- how government dealers use the repurchase agreement market

- the zero-coupon Treasury securities market

- the difference between government-owned corporations and government-sponsored enterprises

- the major issuers in the federal agency securities market

- non–U.S. government bond markets

Treasury securities are issued by the U.S. Department of the Treasury and are backed by the full faith and credit of the U.S. government. Consequently, market participants view them as having no credit risk. Historically, interest rates on Treasury securities have been the benchmark interest rates throughout the U.S. economy. At the end of this chapter, we discuss non–U.S. government bond markets.

MARKET FOR TREASURY SECURITIES[1]

Two factors account for the prominent role of U.S. Treasury securities: volume (in terms of dollars outstanding) and liquidity. The Department of the Treasury is the largest single issuer of debt in the world. The large volume of total debt and the large size of any single issue have contributed to making the Treasury market the most active and hence the most liquid market in the world. The spread between bid and ask prices is considerably narrower than in other sectors of the bond market, and most issues can be traded easily. Many issues in the corporate and municipal markets are illiquid by contrast and cannot be traded readily.

Treasury securities are available in book-entry form at the Federal Reserve Bank. This means that the investor receives only a receipt as evidence of ownership instead of an engraved certificate. An advantage of book-entry is ease in transferring ownership of the security. Interest income from Treasury securities is subject to federal income taxes but is exempt from state and local income taxes.

Types of Treasury Securities

There are two categories of government securities: **discount** and **coupon securities**. The fundamental difference between the two types lies in the form of the stream of payments that the holder receives, which is reflected in turn in the prices at which the securities are issued. Coupon securities pay interest every six months, plus principal at maturity. Discount securities pay only a contractually fixed amount at maturity, called maturity value or face value. Discount instruments are issued below maturity value, and return to the investor the difference between maturity value and issue price.

Current Treasury practice is to issue all securities with maturities of one year or less as discount securities. These securities are called **Treasury bills**. All securities with maturities of two years or longer are issued as coupon securities. Treasury coupon securities issued with original maturities between two and 10 years are called **Treasury notes**; those with original maturities greater than 10 years are called **Treasury bonds**. While there is therefore a distinction between Treasury notes and bonds, in this chapter we refer to both as simply Treasury bonds.

Treasury Inflation Protection Securities

On January 29, 1997, the U.S. Department of the Treasury issued for the first time Treasury securities that adjust for inflation. These securities are popularly referred to as **Treasury inflation protection securities** (TIPS). (The Treasury refers to these securities as Treasury inflation indexed securities [TIIS].) The Treasury has issued TIPS that are notes and bonds. TIPS work as follows. The coupon rate on an issue is set at a fixed rate. That rate is determined via the auction process described later in this section. The coupon rate is called the "real rate" since it is the rate that the investor ultimately earns above the inflation rate. The inflation index that the government has decided to use for the inflation adjustment is the nonseasonally adjusted U.S. City Average All Items Consumer Price Index for All Urban Consumers (CPI-U).

The adjustment for inflation is as follows. The principal on which the Treasury Department will base both the dollar amount of the coupon payment and the maturity value is adjusted semiannually. This is called the inflation-adjusted principal. For example, suppose that the coupon rate for a TIPS is 3.5% and the annual inflation rate is 3%. Suppose further

---

[1] Portions of this section are adapted from Chapter 3 in Frank J. Fabozzi, *Bond Portfolio Management* (New Hope, PA: Frank J. Fabozzi Associates, 2001) and in other published writings by Frank J. Fabozzi.

that an investor purchases on January 1 $100,000 of par value (principal) of this issue. The semiannual inflation rate is 1.5% (3% divided by 2). The inflation-adjusted principal at the end of the first six-month period is found by multiplying the original par value by the semi-annual inflation rate. In our example, the inflation-adjusted principal at the end of the first six-month period is $101,500. It is this inflation-adjusted principal that is the basis for computing the coupon interest for the first six-month period. The coupon payment is then 1.75% (one-half the real rate of 3.5%) multiplied by the inflation-adjusted principal at the coupon payment date ($101,500). The coupon payment is, therefore, $1,776.25.

Let us look at the next six months. The inflation-adjusted principal at the beginning of the period is $101,500. Suppose that the semiannual inflation rate for the second six-month period is 1%. Then, the inflation-adjusted principal at the end of the second six-month period is the inflation-adjusted principal at the beginning of the six-month period ($101,500) increased by the semiannual inflation rate (1%). The adjustment to the principal is $1,015 (1% times $101,500). So, the inflation-adjusted principal at the end of the second six-month period (December 31 in our example) is $102,515 ($101,500 + $1,015). The coupon interest that will be paid to the investor at the second coupon payment date is found by multiplying the inflation-adjusted principal on the coupon payment date ($102,515) by one-half the real rate (i.e., one-half of 3.5%). That is, the coupon payment will be $1,794.01.

As can be seen, part of the adjustment for inflation comes in the coupon payment since it is based on the inflation-adjusted principal. However, the U.S. government has decided to tax the adjustment each year. This feature reduces the attractiveness of TIPS as an investment in the accounts of tax-paying entities.

Because of the possibility of disinflation (i.e., price declines), the inflation-adjusted principal at maturity may turn out to be less than the initial par value. However, the Treasury has structured TIPS so that they are redeemed at the greater of the inflation-adjusted principal and the initial par value.

An inflation-adjusted principal must be calculated for a settlement date. The inflation-adjusted principal is defined in terms of an index ratio, which is the ratio of the reference CPI for the settlement date to the reference CPI for the issue date. The reference CPI is calculated with a three-month lag. For example, the reference CPI for May 1 is the CPI-U reported in February. The U.S. Department of the Treasury publishes and makes available on its website (http://www.publicdebt.treas.gov) a daily index ratio for an issue.

The Primary Market

The primary market is the market for the issuance of newly issued Treasury securities.

Auction Cycles

The U.S. Department of the Treasury makes the determination of the procedure for auctioning new Treasury securities, when to auction them, and what maturities to issue. There have been occasional changes in the auction cycles and the maturity of the issues auctioned. Currently, there are weekly three-month and six-month bill auctions, and one-year bill auctions every four weeks. For coupon securities, there are monthly two-year note and five-year note auctions, and quarterly auctions for the 10-year note and 30-year bond (the "refunding" auction).[2]

---

[2] At one time, the U.S. Department of the Treasury offered three-year, four-year, and seven-year Treasury notes and 15-year and 20-year Treasury bonds.

On the announcement day, the Treasury announces the amount of each issue to be auctioned, the auction date, and maturities to be issued. Occasionally, an outstanding issue is **reopened issue** (that is, the amount of an outstanding note is increased) at an auction instead of a new issue auctioned. In recent years, the Department of the Treasury has reopened the ten-year note several times.

Determination of the Results of an Auction

The auction for Treasury securities is conducted on a competitive bidding basis. Competitive bids must be submitted on a yield basis. Noncompetitive tenders may also be submitted for up to a $1 million face amount. Such tenders are based only on quantity, not yield.

The auction results are determined by first deducting the total noncompetitive tenders and nonpublic purchases (such as purchases by the Federal Reserve itself) from the total securities being auctioned. The remainder is the amount to be awarded to the competitive bidders. The bids are then arranged from the lowest-yield bid to the highest-yield bid. This is equivalent to arranging the bids from the highest price to the lowest price. Starting from the lowest-yield bid, all competitive bids are accepted until the amount to be distributed to the competitive bidders is completely allocated. The highest yield accepted by the Treasury is referred to as the **stop yield**, and bidders at that yield are awarded a percentage of their total tender. Bidders higher in yield than the stop yield are not distributed any of the new issue. Such bidders are said to have "missed" or were "shut out."

At what yield is a winning bidder awarded the security? All U.S. Treasury auctions are single-price auctions. In a single-price auction, all bidders are awarded securities at the highest yield of accepted competitive tenders (i.e., the stop yield). This type of auction is called a "Dutch auction." Historically, the Treasury auctioned securities through multiple-price auctions. With multiple-price auctions, the Treasury still accepted the lowest-yielding bids up to the yield required to sell the amount offered (less the amount of noncompetitive bids), but accepted bids were awarded at the particular yields bid, rather than at the stop-out yield. In September 1992, the Treasury started conducting single-price auctions for the two- and five-year notes. In November 1998, the Treasury adopted the single-price method for all auctions.

Competitive bids must typically be submitted by 1:00 P.M. eastern time on the day of the auction. Noncompetitive bids must typically be submitted by noon on the day of the auction. The results of the auction are announced within an hour following the 1:00 P.M. auction deadline. When the results of the auction are announced, the Treasury provides the following information: the stop yield, the associated price, the proportion of securities awarded to those investors who bid exactly the stop yield, the quantity of noncompetitive tenders, the median yield bid, and the bid-to-cover ratio. The **bid-to-cover ratio** is the ratio of the total par amount of competitive and noncompetitive bids by the public divided by the total par amount of the securities awarded to the public. Some market observers consider this ratio to be an indicator of the bidding interest and, consequently, some barometer of the success of the auction. The higher the bid-to-cover ratio, the greater is the success of the auction.

Figure 1 shows the August 1, 2007, announcement by the U.S. Treasury of the August 2007 quarterly financing. The announcement explains that the U.S. Treasury is going to

Figure 1   Treasury Offering Announcement

DEPARTMENT OF THE TREASURY

TREASURY ⚖ NEWS

OFFICE OF PUBLIC AFFAIRS ● 1500 PENNSYLVANIA AVENUE, N.W. ● WASHINGTON, D.C.● 20220 ● (202) 622-2960

EMBARGOED UNTIL 9:00 A.M.   CONTACT: Office of Financing
August 1, 2007   202/504-3550

TREASURY AUGUST QUARTERLY FINANCING

The Treasury will auction $13,000 million of 10-year notes and $9,000 million of 29-year 9-month bonds to refund $62,639 million of publicly held securities maturing on August 15, 2007, and to pay down approximately $40,639 million.

Tenders for 29-year 9-month Treasury bonds to be held on the book-entry records of Legacy Treasury Direct will <u>not</u> be accepted. However, tenders for 29-year 9-month Treasury bonds to be held on the book-entry records of TreasuryDirect will be accepted.

In addition to the public holdings, Federal Reserve Banks, for their own accounts, hold $13,082 million of the maturing securities, which may be refunded by issuing additional amounts of the new securities.

Up to $1,000 million in noncompetitive bids from Foreign and International Monetary Authority (FIMA) accounts bidding through the Federal Reserve Bank of New York will be included within the offering amount of each auction. These noncompetitive bids will have a limit of $100 million per account and will be accepted in the order of smallest to largest, up to the aggregate award limit of $1,000 million.

Treasury Direct customers have scheduled purchases of approximately $112 million into the 10-year note.

The auctions being announced today will be conducted in the single-price auction format. All competitive and noncompetitive awards will be at the highest yield of accepted competitive tenders. The allocation percentage applied to bids awarded at the highest yield will be rounded up to the next hundredth of a whole percentage point, e.g., 17.13%.

The securities being offered today are eligible for the STRIPS program.

This offering of Treasury securities is governed by the terms and conditions set forth in the Uniform Offering Circular for the Sale and Issue of Marketable Book-Entry Treasury Bills, Notes, and Bonds (31 CFR Part 356, as amended).

Details about the securities are given in the attached offering highlights.

oOo

Attachment

(Continued)

Figure 1   Treasury Offering Announcement (Continued)

```
                    HIGHLIGHTS OF TREASURY OFFERINGS TO THE PUBLIC
                          AUGUST 2007 QUARTERLY FINANCING

                                                                    August 1, 2007

Offering Amount............................. $13,000 million       $9,000 million
Maximum Award (35% of Offering Amount)........ $ 4,550 million      $3,150 million
Maximum Recognized Bid at a Single Yield...... $ 4,550 million      $3,150 million
NLP Reporting Threshold....................... $ 4,550 million      $3,150 million

Description of Offering:
 Term and type of security.................... 10-year notes        29-year 9-month bonds
 Series....................................... E-2017               Bonds of May 2037
 CUSIP number................................. 912828 HA 1          912810 PU 6
 Auction date................................. August 8, 2007       August 9, 2007
 Issue date................................... August 15, 2007      August 15, 2007
 Dated date................................... August 15, 2007      May 15, 2007
 Maturity date................................ August 15, 2017      May 15, 2037
 Interest rate................................ Determined based on the highest   Determined based on the highest
                                               accepted competitive bid          accepted competitive bid
 Yield........................................ Determined at auction  Determined at auction
 Interest payment dates....................... February 15 and August 15  November 15 and May 15
 Minimum bid amount and multiples............. $1,000               $1,000
 Accrued interest payable by investor ........ None                 Determined at auction
 Premium or discount.......................... Determined at auction  Determined at auction

STRIPS Information:
 Minimum amount required...................... $1,000               $1,000
 Corpus CUSIP number.......................... 912820 PX 9          912803 DA 8
 Due date(s) and CUSIP number(s)
  for additional TINT(s) ..................... Not applicable       See chart below
```

29-year 9-month bond due dates and CUSIP numbers for additional TINTS:

	May 15	November 15
2030	- - -	912833 7N 4
2031	912833 7P 9	912833 7Q 7
2032	912833 7R 5	912833 7S 3
2033	912833 7T 1	912833 7U 8
2034	912833 7V 6	912833 7W 4
2035	912833 X8 8	912833 X9 6
2036	912833 Y2 0	912833 Y3 8
2037	912833 Y4 6	- - -

The following rules apply to all securities mentioned above:

Submission of Bids:

 Noncompetitive bids: Accepted in full up to $5 million at the highest accepted yield.

 Foreign and International Monetary Authority (FIMA) bids: Noncompetitive bids submitted through the Federal Reserve Banks as agents for FIMA accounts. Accepted in order of size from smallest to largest with no more than $100 million awarded per account. The total noncompetitive amount awarded to Federal Reserve Banks as agents for FIMA accounts will not exceed $1,000 million. A single bid that would cause the limit to be exceeded will be partially accepted in the amount that brings the aggregate award total to the $1,000 million limit. However, if there are two or more bids of equal amounts that would cause the limit to be exceeded, each will be prorated to avoid exceeding the limit.

 Competitive bids:

   (1) Must be expressed as a yield with three decimals, e.g., 7.123%.
   (2) Net long position (NLP) for each bidder must be reported when the sum of the total bid amount, at all yields, and the net long position equals or exceeds the NLP reporting threshold stated above.
   (3) Net long position must be determined as of one-half hour prior to the closing time for receipt of competitive tenders.
   (4) Competitive bids from Treasury Direct customers are not allowed.

Receipt of Tenders:

 Noncompetitive tenders........ Prior to 12:00 noon eastern daylight saving time on auction day
 Competitive tenders........... Prior to 1:00 p.m. eastern daylight saving time on auction day

Figure 2   Result of a Treasury Auction

PUBLIC DEBT NEWS

Department of the Treasury • Bureau of the Public Debt • Washington, DC 20239

```
                TREASURY SECURITY AUCTION RESULTS
                BUREAU OF THE PUBLIC DEBT - WASHINGTON DC

FOR IMMEDIATE RELEASE                    CONTACT:     Office of Financing
August 08, 2007                                       202-504-3550

            RESULTS OF TREASURY'S AUCTION OF 10-YEAR NOTES

Interest Rate:   4 3/4%            Issue Date:     August 15, 2007
Series:          E-2017            Dated Date:     August 15, 2007
CUSIP No:        912828HA1         Maturity Date:  August 15, 2017


            High Yield:   4.855%    Price:  99.175936

    All noncompetitive and successful competitive bidders were awarded
securities at the high yield.  Tenders at the high yield were
allotted  53.43%.  All tenders at lower yields were accepted in full.

            AMOUNTS TENDERED AND ACCEPTED (in thousands)

Tender Type                    Tendered                Accepted
-----------                ----------------         ----------------
Competitive            $      29,740,500       $      12,844,723
Noncompetitive                   155,327                 155,327
FIMA (noncompetitive)                  0                       0
                           ----------------         ----------------
   SUBTOTAL                   29,895,827              13,000,050 1/

Federal Reserve               7,000,000               7,000,000
                           ----------------         ----------------
   TOTAL               $      36,895,827       $      20,000,050
```

```
    Median yield   4.829%:  50% of the amount of accepted competitive tenders
was tendered at or below that rate.  Low yield  4.740%:   5% of the amount
of accepted competitive tenders was tendered at or below that rate.

Bid-to-Cover Ratio = 29,895,827 / 13,000,050 = 2.30

1/ Awards to TREASURY DIRECT = $140,150,000
```

auction two Treasury coupon securities: a 10-year note and a 29-year nine-month bond. Figure 2 shows the results of the 10-year note auction. Note the following:

- The high yield or stop yield was 4.855%, the yield at which all winning bidders were awarded securities.
- The coupon rate on the issue was set at 4.75%.
- Given the yield of 4.855%, a coupon rate of 4.75%, and a maturity of 10 years, the price that all winning bidders paid was $99.175936 (per $100 par value).
- For those bidders who bid the high yield of 4.855, they were allocated 53.43% of the amount that they bid.
- Because the total amount of bids by both competitive and noncompetitive bidders was $29,895,827,000 and the total amount awarded was $13,000,050,000, the bid-to-cover ratio was 2.30 ($29,895,827,000/$13,000,050,000).

Primary Dealers

Any firm can deal in government securities, but in implementing its open market operations, the Federal Reserve will deal directly only with dealers that it designates as **primary dealers** or *recognized dealers*. Basically, the Federal Reserve wants to be sure that firms requesting status as primary dealers have adequate capital relative to positions assumed in Treasury securities and do a reasonable amount of volume in Treasury securities.

When a firm requests status as a primary dealer, the Federal Reserve requests first that the applying firm informally report its positions and trading volume. If these are acceptable to the Federal Reserve, it gives the firm status as a *reporting dealer*. This means that the firm will be put on the Federal Reserve's regular reporting list. After the firm serves for some time as a reporting dealer, the Federal Reserve will make it a primary dealer if it is convinced that the firm will continue to meet the criteria established.

Submission of Bids

Until 1991, primary dealers and large commercial banks that were not primary dealers would submit bids for their own account and for their customers. Others who wished to participate in the auction process could only submit competitive bids for their own account, not their customers. Consequently, a broker-dealer in government securities that was not a primary dealer could not submit a competitive bid on behalf of its customers. Moreover, unlike primary dealers, nonprimary dealers had to make large cash deposits or provide guarantees to ensure that they could fulfill their obligation to purchase the securities for which they bid.

Well-publicized violations of the auction process by Salomon Brothers in the summer of 1991 forced Treasury officials to more closely scrutinize the activities of primary dealers and also reconsider the procedure by which Treasury securities are auctioned.[3] Specifically, the Treasury announced that it would allow qualified broker-dealers to bid for their customers at Treasury auctions. If a qualified broker-dealer establishes a payment link with the Federal Reserve system, no deposit or guaranty is required. Moreover, the auction is no longer handled by the submission of hand-delivered sealed bids to the Federal Reserve. The new auction process is a computerized auction system, which can be electronically accessed by qualified broker-dealers.

The Secondary Market

The secondary market for Treasury securities is an over-the-counter market where a group of U.S. government securities dealers offer continuous bid and ask prices on outstanding Treasuries.[4] There is virtual 24-hour trading of Treasury securities. The three primary trading locations are New York, London, and Tokyo. The normal settlement period for Treasury securities is the business day after the transaction day ("next day" settlement).

The most recently auctioned issue of a given maturity is referred to as the *on-the-run issue* or the *current issue*. Securities that are replaced by the on-the-run issues are called *off-the-run issues*. Issues that have been replaced by several on-the-run issues are said to be "well off-the-run issues."

---

[3] Salomon Brothers admitted that it repeatedly violated a restriction that limited the amount that any one firm could purchase at the Treasury auction. The firm also admitted that it submitted unauthorized bids for some of its customers.

[4] Some trading of Treasury coupon securities does occur on the New York Stock Exchange, but the volume of these exchange-traded transactions is very small when compared to over-the-counter transactions.

When-Issued Market

Treasury securities are traded prior to the time they are issued by the Treasury. This component of the Treasury secondary market is called the **when-issued market**, or **wi market**. When-issued trading for both bills and coupon securities extends from the day the auction is announced until the issue day.

Government Brokers

Government dealers trade with the investing public and with other dealer firms. When they trade with each other, it is through intermediaries known as *interdealer brokers or* **government brokers**. Dealers leave firm bids and offers with interdealer brokers who display the highest bid and lowest offer in a computer network tied to each trading desk and displayed on a monitor. Dealers use interdealer brokers because of the speed and efficiency with which trades can be accomplished.

Bid and Offer Quotes on Treasury Bills

The convention for quoting bids and offers is different for Treasury bills and Treasury coupon securities. Bids and offers on Treasury bills are quoted in a special way. Unlike bonds that pay coupon interest, Treasury bill values are quoted on a bank discount basis, not on a price basis. The **yield on a bank discount basis** is computed as follows:

$$Y = \frac{D}{F} \times \frac{360}{t}$$

where

Y = annualized yield on a bank discount basis
    (expressed as a decimal)
D = dollar discount, which is equal to the difference
    between the face value and the price
F = face value
t = number of days remaining to maturity

As an example, a Treasury bill with 100 days to maturity, a face value of \$100,000, and selling for \$97,569 would be quoted at 8.75% on a bank discount basis:

$$D = \$100,000 - \$97,569$$
$$= \$2,431$$

Therefore,

$$Y = \frac{\$2,431}{\$100,000} \times \frac{360}{100}$$
$$= 8.75\%$$

Given the yield on a bank discount basis, the price of a Treasury bill is found by first solving the formula for Y for the dollar discount as follows:

$$D = Y \times F \times t/360$$

The price is then

$$\text{Price} = F - D$$

For the 100-day Treasury bill with a face value of $100,000, if the yield on a bank discount basis is quoted as 8.75%, D is equal to

$$D = 0.0875 \times \$100,000 \times 100/360$$
$$= \$2,431$$

Therefore,

$$\text{Price} = \$100,000 - \$2,431$$
$$= \$97,569$$

The quoted yield on a bank discount basis is not a meaningful measure of the return from holding a Treasury bill for two reasons. First, the measure is based on a face value investment rather than on the actual dollar amount invested. Second, the yield is annualized according to a 360-day rather than 365-day year, making it difficult to compare Treasury bill yields with Treasury notes and bonds, which pay interest on a 365-day basis. Despite its shortcomings as a measure of return, this is the method dealers have adopted to quote Treasury bills.

Regulation of the Secondary Market

In the stock market, congressional and SEC actions have resulted in movement toward a consolidated tape for reporting trades on exchanges and the over-the-counter market, with a composite quotation system for the collection and display of bid and ask quotations. In the Treasury market, however, despite the fact that trading activity is concentrated in the over-the-counter market, and that daily trading volume exceeds $100 billion, reporting of trades does not exist. Nor is there a display of bid and ask quotations that provides reliable price quotes at which the general public can transact. Such quotations do exist, as we explained earlier, in the interdealer market on government broker screens. While nonprimary dealers can subscribe to the government broker screens, the information that they can obtain on these screens is limited. In particular, the government dealers that permit access to their screens provide information on only the best bid and offer quotation but not the size of the transaction.

Moreover, the rules for the sale of U.S. government securities have been exempt from most SEC provisions and rules.[5] Thus, government broker-dealers are not required to disclose the bid–ask spread on the Treasury securities that they buy from or sell to customers. There are guidelines established by the National Association of Security Dealers for reasonable bid–ask spreads, but lack of disclosure to customers makes it difficult for customers to monitor the pricing practice of a broker-dealer.

Dealer Use of the Repurchase Agreement Market

Suppose a government securities dealer has purchased $10 million of a particular Treasury security. Where does the dealer obtain the funds to finance that position? Of course, the dealer can use its own funds or borrow from a bank. Typically, however, the dealer uses the *repo* market to obtain financing. In the repo market, the dealer can use the $10 million of Treasury security purchased as collateral for a loan. The term of the loan and the interest rate

---

[5] Broker-dealers who sell government securities are always subject to the general fraud provisions of the Securities Act of 1933.

that the dealer agrees to pay (called the *repo rate*) are specified. When the term of the loan is one day, it is called an **overnight repo**; a loan for more than one day is called a **term repo**.

The transaction is referred to as a repurchase agreement because it calls for the sale of the security and its repurchase at a future date. Both the sale price and the purchase price are specified in the agreement. The difference between the purchase (repurchase) price and the sale price is the dollar interest cost of the loan.

Now, let's return to the dealer who needs to finance $10 million of a Treasury security. Suppose that the dealer plans to hold the bonds overnight. Suppose also that a customer of the dealer has excess funds of $10 million. (The customer might be a municipality with tax receipts that it has just collected, and no immediate need to disburse the funds.) The dealer would agree to deliver ("sell") $10 million of the Treasury security to the customer for an amount determined by the repo rate and buy ("repurchase") the same Treasury security from the customer for $10 million the next day. Suppose that the overnight repo rate is 6.5%. Then, the dealer would agree to deliver the Treasury securities for $9,998,194 and repurchase the same securities for $10 million the next day. The $1,806 difference between the "sale" price of $9,998,194 and the repurchase price of $10 million is the dollar interest on the financing. From the customer's perspective, the agreement is called a *reverse repo*.

The advantage to the dealer of using the repo market for borrowing on a short-term basis is that the rate is less than the cost of bank financing. From the customer's perspective, the repo market offers an attractive yield on a short-term secured transaction that is highly liquid.

Although the example illustrates financing a dealer's long position in the repo market, dealers can also use the market to cover a short position. For example, suppose a government dealer sold $10 million of Treasury securities two weeks ago and must now cover the position—that is, deliver the securities. The dealer can do a reverse repo (agree to buy the securities and sell them back). Of course, the dealer eventually would have to buy the Treasury security in the market in order to cover its short position.

There is a good deal of Wall Street jargon describing repo transactions. To understand it, remember that one party is lending money and accepting the security as collateral for the loan;[6] the other party is borrowing money and giving collateral to borrow money. When someone lends securities in order to receive cash (that is, to borrow money), that party is said to be *reversing out* securities. A party that lends money with the security as collateral is said to be *reversing in* securities. The expressions *to repo securities* and *to do repo* are also used. The former means that someone is going to finance securities using the security as collateral; the latter means that the party is going to invest in a repo. Finally, the expressions *selling collateral* and *buying collateral* are used to describe a party financing a security with a repo on the one hand, and lending on the basis of collateral, on the other.

It is important to note that both parties to the transaction are exposed to credit risk. The failure of a few small government securities dealer firms involved in repo transactions in the 1980s has made market participants more cautious about the creditworthiness of the counterparty to a repo. Repos are now more carefully structured to reduce credit risk exposure.[7]

There is no one repo rate; rates vary from transaction to transaction depending on factors such as the term of the repo and the availability of collateral. The more difficult it is to

---

[6] The collateral in a repo is not limited to government securities. Money market instruments, federal agency securities, and mortgage-backed securities are also used.

[7] For a description of the procedures used to reduce credit risk, see Frank J. Fabozzi (ed.), *Securities Lending and Repurchase Agreements* (New Hope, PA: Frank J. Fabozzi Associates, 1997).

obtain the collateral, the lower the repo rate. To understand why this is so, remember that the borrower (or equivalently the seller of the collateral) has a security that is a **hot**, or **special, issue**. The party that needs the collateral will be willing to lend funds at a lower repo rate in order to obtain the collateral.

Although the factors given above determine the repo rate on a particular transaction, the federal funds rate determines the general level of repo rates. The repo rate will be slightly below the federal funds rate because a repo involves collateralized borrowing, while a federal funds transaction is unsecured borrowing.

Because it is used by dealer firms (investment banking firms and money center banks acting as dealers) to finance positions and cover short positions, the repo market has evolved into one of the largest sectors of the money market. Financial and nonfinancial firms participate in the market as both sellers and buyers, depending on the circumstances they face. Thrifts and commercial banks are typically net sellers of collateral (that is, net borrowers of funds); money market funds, bank trust departments, municipalities, and corporations are typically net buyers of collateral (that is, providers of funds).

Although a dealer firm uses the repo market as the primary means for financing its inventory and covering short positions, it will also use the repo market to run a matched book where it takes on repos and reverse repos with the same maturity. The firm will do so to capture the spread at which it enters into the repo and reverse repo agreements. For example, suppose that a dealer firm enters into a term repo of 10 days with a money market fund and a reverse repo rate with a thrift for 10 days in which the collateral is identical. This means that the dealer firm is borrowing funds from the money market fund and lending money to the thrift. If the rate on the repo is 7.5% and the rate on the reverse repo is 7.55%, the dealer firm is borrowing at 7.5% and lending at 7.55%, locking in a spread of 0.05% (five basis points).

A Note on Terminology in the Repo Market

The Federal Reserve conducts open market operations by the outright purchase or sale of government securities or, more often, by repurchase agreements. In these agreements, the Fed either purchases or sells collateral. By buying collateral (that is, lending funds), the Fed injects money into the financial markets, thereby exerting downward pressure on short-term interest rates. When the Fed buys collateral for its own account, this is called a *system repo*. The Fed also buys collateral on behalf of foreign central banks in repo transactions that are referred to as *customer repos*. It is primarily through system repos that the Fed attempts to influence short-term rates. By selling securities for its own account, the Fed drains money from the financial markets, thereby exerting upward pressure on short-term interest rates. This transaction is called a *matched sale*.

Note the language that is used to describe the transactions of the Fed in the repo market. When the Fed lends funds based on collateral, we call it a system or customer repo, not a reverse repo. Borrowing funds using collateral is called a matched sale, not a repo. The jargon is confusing, which is why we used the terms of *buying collateral* and *selling collateral* to describe what parties in the repo market are doing.

Stripped Treasury Securities

The Treasury does not issue zero-coupon notes or bonds. In August 1982, however, both Merrill Lynch and Salomon Brothers created synthetic zero-coupon Treasury receipts. Merrill Lynch marketed its Treasury receipts as Treasury Income Growth Receipts (TIGRs);

Salomon Brothers marketed its as Certificates of Accrual on Treasury Securities (CATS). The procedure was to purchase Treasury bonds and deposit them in a bank custody account. The firms then issued (that is, sold) receipts representing an ownership interest in each coupon payment on the underlying Treasury bond in the account and a receipt for ownership of the underlying Treasury bond's maturity value. This process of separating each coupon payment, as well as the principal (called the *corpus*), and selling securities against them is referred to as *coupon stripping*. Although the receipts created from the coupon-stripping process are not issued by the U.S. Treasury, the underlying bond deposited in the bank custody account is a debt obligation of the U.S. Treasury, so the cash flow from the underlying security is certain.

To illustrate the process, suppose $100 million of a Treasury bond with a 10-year maturity and a coupon rate of 10% is purchased to create zero-coupon Treasury securities. The cash flow from this Treasury bond is 20 semiannual payments of $5 million each ($100 million times 0.10 divided by 2) and the repayment of principal (corpus) of $100 million 10 years from now. This Treasury bond is deposited in a bank custody account. Receipts are then issued, each with a different single payment claim on the bank custody account. As there are 21 different payments to be made by the Treasury, a receipt representing a single payment claim on each payment is issued, which is effectively a zero-coupon bond. The amount of the maturity value for a receipt on a particular payment, whether coupon or corpus, depends on the amount of the payment to be made by the Treasury on the underlying Treasury bond. In our example, 20 coupon receipts each have a maturity value of $5 million, and one receipt, the corpus, has a maturity value of $100 million. The maturity dates for the receipts coincide with the corresponding payment dates by the Treasury. This is illustrated in Figure 3.

Figure 3   Coupon Stripping: Creating Zero-Coupon Treasury Securities

Dealer purchases $100 million par of a 10%, 10-year Treasury security

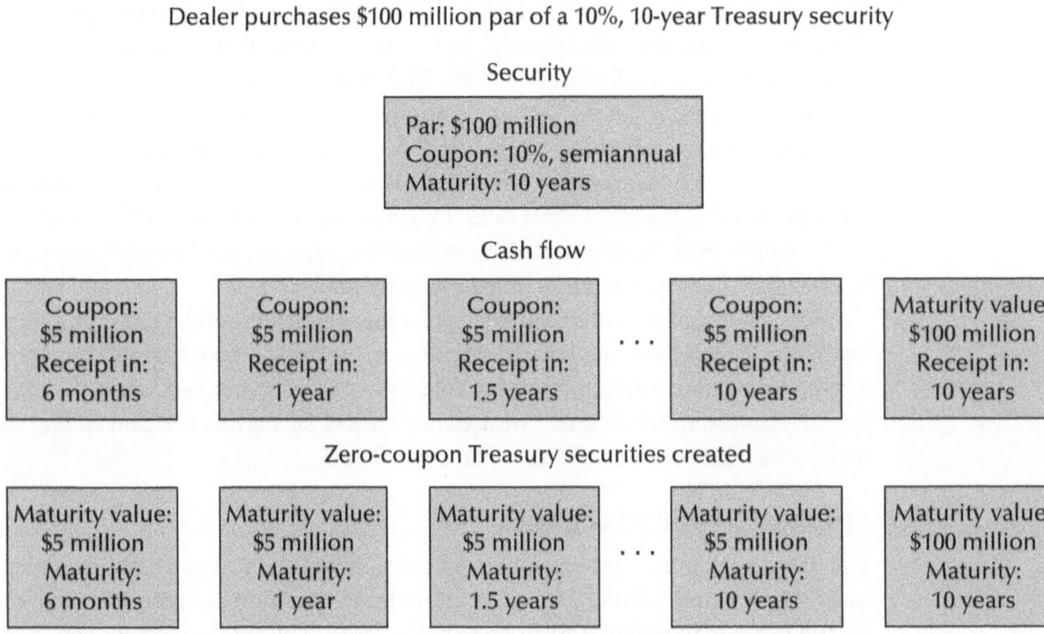

Other investment banking firms followed suit by creating their own receipts.[8] They all are referred to as **trademark zero-coupon Treasury securities** because they are associated with particular firms.[9] Receipts of one firm were rarely traded by competing dealers, so the secondary market was not liquid for any one trademark. Moreover, the investor was exposed to the risk—as small as it may be—that the custodian bank may go bankrupt.

To broaden the market and improve liquidity of these receipts, a group of primary dealers in the government market agreed to issue generic receipts that would not be directly associated with any of the participating dealers. These generic receipts are referred to as **Treasury receipts (TRs)**. Rather than representing a share of the trust as the trademarks do, TRs represent ownership of a Treasury security. A common problem with both trademark and generic receipts was that settlement required physical delivery, which is often cumbersome and inefficient.

In February 1985, the Treasury announced its **Separate Trading of Registered Interest and Principal of Securities (STRIPS)** program to facilitate the stripping of designated Treasury securities. Specifically, all new Treasury bonds and all new Treasury notes with maturities of ten years and longer are eligible. The zero-coupon Treasury securities created under the STRIPS program are direct obligations of the U.S. government. Moreover, the securities clear through the Federal Reserve's book-entry system.[10] Creation of the STRIPS program ended the origination of trademarks and generic receipts.

Today, **stripped Treasury securities** are simply referred to as *Treasury strips*. On dealer quote sheets and vendor screens, they are identified by whether the cash flow is created from the coupon (denoted "ci"), principal from a Treasury bond (denoted "bp"), or principal from a Treasury note (denoted "np"). Strips created from coupon payments are called *coupon strips* and those created from the principal are called *principal strips*. The reason why a distinction is made between coupon strips and the principal strips has to do with the tax treatment by non–U.S. entities, as discussed below.

A disadvantage of a taxable entity investing in Treasury strips is that accrued interest is taxed each year even though interest is not paid. Thus, these instruments are negative cash flow instruments until the maturity date. They have negative cash flow since tax payments on interest earned but not received in cash must be made. One reason for distinguishing between strips created from the principal and coupon is that some foreign buyers have a preference for the strips created from the principal (i.e., the principal strips). This preference is due to the tax treatment of the interest in their home country. Some country's tax laws treat the interest as a capital gain if the principal strip is purchased. The capital gain receives a preferential tax treatment (i.e., lower tax rate) compared to ordinary income.

Coupon Stripping and the Theoretical Value of Treasury Securities

Financial theory tells us that the theoretical value of a Treasury security should be equal to the present value of the cash flow where each cash flow is discounted at the appropriate theoretical spot rate. What we do not do in that chapter, however, is demonstrate what

---

[8] Lehman Brothers offered "Lehman Investment Opportunities Notes" (LIONs); E.F. Hutton offered "Treasury Bond Receipts" (TBRs); and Dean Witter Reynolds offered "Easy Growth Treasury Receipts" (ETRs). There were also GATORs, COUGARs, and—you will like this one—DOGS (Dibs on Government Securities).

[9] They are also called "animal products" for obvious reasons.

[10] In 1987, the Treasury permitted the conversion of stripped coupons into book-entry form under its Coupons Under Book-Entry Safekeeping (CUBES) program.

economic force will assure that the actual market price of a Treasury security will not depart significantly from its theoretical value. Given our discussion of these instruments, we can now demonstrate the economic force that will move the actual price of a Treasury security toward its theoretical value.

To demonstrate this, we will use the Treasury yield curve as represented by the 20 hypothetical Treasury securities. The longest-maturity bond given in that table is the 10-year, 12.5% coupon issue selling at par and, therefore, with a yield to maturity of 12.5%. Suppose that a government dealer buys a 14%, 10-year Treasury security. Since this is a 10-year security, using the yield for 10-year instruments of 12.5% would suggest that this issue should sell to offer a yield of 12.5%. Table 1 shows the price of a 14%, 10-year Treasury issue if it is selling in the market to yield 12.5%. The present value of the cash flows when discounted at 12.5% is $108.4305 per $100 of par value.

Suppose that this issue is selling at that price. A government dealer can purchase that issue and strip it. The stripped Treasury securities should offer approximately the theoretical spot rate. Table 2 shows the theoretical value of the 14% coupon issue if the cash flows are discounted at the theoretical spot rates. The theoretical value is

Table 1   Price of a 10-Year, 14% Coupon Treasury Based on the 10-Year Yield of 12.5%

Maturity	Cash Flow per $100 Par	Required Yield of 0.125	Semiannual Yield	Present Value
0.5	$ 7	0.125	0.0625	$ 6.5882
1.0	7	0.125	0.0625	6.2007
1.5	7	0.125	0.0625	5.8359
2.0	7	0.125	0.0625	5.4927
2.5	7	0.125	0.0625	5.1696
3.0	7	0.125	0.0625	4.8655
3.5	7	0.125	0.0625	4.5793
4.0	7	0.125	0.0625	4.3099
4.5	7	0.125	0.0625	4.0564
5.0	7	0.125	0.0625	3.8178
5.5	7	0.125	0.0625	3.5932
6.0	7	0.125	0.0625	3.3818
6.5	7	0.125	0.0625	3.1829
7.0	7	0.125	0.0625	2.9957
7.5	7	0.125	0.0625	2.8194
8.0	7	0.125	0.0625	2.6536
8.5	7	0.125	0.0625	2.4975
9.0	7	0.125	0.0625	2.3506
9.5	7	0.125	0.0625	2.2123
10.0	107	0.125	0.0625	31.8277
Total				$108.4305

Table 2 Theoretical Value of a 10-Year, 14% Coupon Treasury Based on the Theoretical Spot Rate

Maturity	Cash Flow per $100 Par	Required Yield of 0.125	Semiannual Yield	Present Value
0.5	$ 7	0.08000	0.04000	$ 6.7308
1.0	7	0.08300	0.04150	6.4533
1.5	7	0.08930	0.04465	6.1402
2.0	7	0.09247	0.04624	5.8423
2.5	7	0.09468	0.04734	5.5547
3.0	7	0.09787	0.04894	5.2554
3.5	7	0.10129	0.05065	4.9534
4.0	7	0.10592	0.05296	4.6324
4.5	7	0.10850	0.05425	4.3512
5.0	7	0.11021	0.05511	4.0939
5.5	7	0.11175	0.05588	3.8491
6.0	7	0.11584	0.05792	3.5618
6.5	7	0.11744	0.05872	3.3338
7.0	7	0.11991	0.05996	3.0979
7.5	7	0.12405	0.06203	2.8384
8.0	7	0.12278	0.06139	2.6983
8.5	7	0.12546	0.06273	2.4883
9.0	7	0.13152	0.06576	2.2245
9.5	7	0.13377	0.06689	2.0458
10.0	107	0.13623	0.06812	28.6433
Total				$108.7889

$108.7889 per $100 par value. Thus, if a dealer purchased this issue for $108.4305, stripped it, and subsequently resold the zero-coupon instruments created at about the theoretical spot rates, the dealer would generate $108.7889 per $100 par value. This would result in an arbitrage profit of $0.3584 per $100 of par value. The only way to eliminate this arbitrage profit is for this security to sell for approximately $108.7889—its theoretical value as determined by the theoretical spot rates.

In this instance, coupon stripping shows that the sum of the parts is greater than the whole. Consider instead of a 10-year, 14% coupon Treasury one in which the coupon rate is 10%. The theoretical value for that issue based on the spot rates would be $85.35477. If the cash flows are instead discounted at the 12.5% yield for 10-year Treasury securities, it can be shown that the price would be $85.9491. Thus, if the market price was $85.9491 when the theoretical value based on spot rates indicated a value of $85.35477, a dealer would not want to strip this issue. The proceeds received by selling the zero-coupon instruments created would be less than the cost of purchasing the issue.

In such cases, a dealer can purchase in the market a package of zero-coupon stripped Treasury securities such that the cash flow of the package of securities replicates the cash flow of the mispriced coupon Treasury security. By doing so, the dealer will realize a yield higher than the yield on the coupon Treasury security. By buying 20 zero-coupon bonds with maturity values identical to the cash flow for the 10%, 10-year Treasury, the dealer is effectively purchasing a 10-year Treasury coupon security at a cost of $85.35477 instead of $85.9491. This procedure to generate an arbitrage profit is referred to as **reconstitution**.

It is the process of coupon stripping and reconstituting that forces the price of a Treasury security to trade near its theoretical value based on spot rates.

Key Points That You Should Understand Before Proceeding

1. U.S. Treasury securities play a prominent role in global financial markets because they do not have credit risk.
2. Treasury securities are issued on an auction basis with regular cycles for securities of specific maturities.
3. In the secondary market, the most actively traded Treasury securities are the on-the-run issues, and government brokers are used as intermediaries for trading among primary dealers.
4. Securities dealers use the repo market to finance their position in Treasury securities.
5. Stripped Treasury securities are zero-coupon instruments that, while not issued by the U.S. government, are backed by Treasury securities from which they are created.
6. Why a Treasury security's price must reflect its theoretical value based on theoretical spot rates.

MARKET FOR FEDERAL AGENCY SECURITIES[11]

The U.S. Congress has chartered entities to provide funding support for the housing and agricultural sectors of the U.S. economy, as well as to provide funding for specific U.S. government projects. The market for the debt instruments issued by these government-chartered entities is called the federal **agency securities market**.

There are several types of government-chartered entities. One type is a **government-owned corporation**. Two examples are the Tennessee Valley Authority (TVA) and the U.S. Postal Service. However, the only government-owned corporation that is a frequent issuer of debt in the market is the TVA. Another type of government-chartered entity is a **government-sponsored enterprise (GSE)**. GSEs are divided into two types. The first is a publicly owned shareholder corporation. There are three such GSEs: Fannie Mae, Freddie Mac, and the Federal Agricultural Mortgage Corporation. In early September 2008, Fannie Mae and Freddie Mac were taken over by the U.S. government. The other type of GSE is a funding entity of a federally chartered bank lending system. These GSEs include the Federal Home Loan Banks and the Federal Farm Credit Banks.

The GSEs issue two types of securities: debentures and mortgage-backed securities. Our focus here is on the debentures. The debentures issued by the TVA and the GSEs make up about 97% of the federal agency market. These securities are *not* backed by the full faith and credit of the U.S. government. The GSEs use a traditional selling group, syndicate, and auctions for pricing and the initial distribution of new issues. Because of credit risk and liquidity,

---

[11] For a further discussion of the market for federal agency securities, see Frank J. Fabozzi and George P. Kegler, "Federal Agency Securities," in *The Handbook of Finance: Volume I* (Hoboken, NJ: John Wiley & Sons, 2008).

GSEs trade in the market at a yield premium (i.e., yield greater than) to comparable-maturity Treasury securities. The yield spread will differ for each issuing entity, the maturity, and structure of the security and the program through which it has been issued.

In the following paragraphs, we will describe the securities issued by the TVA and the GSEs, but it is important to know that there are smaller non–GSE federal agencies that were created by Congress to provide specific projects, and the debt of these entities carry either the full faith and credit of the U.S. government or a partial guarantee of the U.S. government. Examples of these entities are the Export-Import Bank, the Private Export Funding Corporation, Financing Corporation, and Small Business Administration. Many of these smaller entities have decided to limit or elected not to issue their own debt. Instead, they have utilized the Federal Financing Bank for their funding needs.

Tennessee Valley Authority

The TVA was established by Congress in 1933, primarily to provide flood control, navigation, and agricultural and industrial development, and to promote the use of electric power in the Tennessee Valley region. The TVA is the largest public power system in the United States. The TVA primarily finances its capital requirements through internally generated funds and by issuing debt.

The TVA issues a variety of debt securities in U.S. dollars and other currencies. The TVA issues securities that are issues targeted to individual investors (retail debt offerings) and institutional investors (nonretail offerings). The debt obligations issued by the TVA may be issued only to provide capital for its power program or to refund outstanding debt obligations. TVA debt obligations are not guaranteed by the U.S. government. However, the securities are rated AAA by Moody's and Standard & Poor's. The rating is based on the TVA's status as a wholly owned corporate agency of the U.S. government and the view of the rating agencies of the TVA's financial strengths. These strengths include (1) the requirements that bondholders of power bonds are given a first pledge of payment from net power proceeds, and (2) electricity rates charged by the TVA are sufficient to ensure both the full payment of annual debt service and operating and capital costs.

Fannie Mae

In the 1930s, Congress created a federally related institution, the Federal National Mortgage Association, popularly known as "Fannie Mae," which was charged with the responsibility to create a liquid secondary market for mortgages. Fannie Mae was to accomplish this objective by buying and selling mortgages. In 1968, Congress divided Fannie Mae into two entities: (1) the current Fannie Mae, and (2) the Government National Mortgage Association (popularly known as "Ginnie Mae"). Ginnie Mae's function is to use the "full faith and credit of the U.S. government" to support the market for government-insured mortgages. Although starting out as a federally related institution, today, Fannie Mae is a GSE and its official corporate name is Fannie Mae.

Fannie Mae issues Benchmark Bills, Benchmark Notes, Benchmark Bonds, Callable Benchmark Notes, Subordinated Benchmark Notes, Investment Notes, callable securities, and structured notes. Benchmark Notes and Benchmark Bonds are noncallable instruments. The minimum issue size is $4 billion for Benchmark Notes and $2 billion for Benchmark Bonds. Issued quarterly are two-, three-, five-, 10-, and 30-year maturities.

Fannie Mae, as well as Freddie Mac that we discuss next, issues bullet and callable medium-term notes (MTNs) and structured notes. There are securities denominated in U.S. dollars as well as issues denominated in a wide range of foreign currencies.

Freddie Mac

In 1970, Congress created the Federal Home Loan Mortgage Corporation (Freddie Mac). The reason for the creation of Freddie Mac was to provide support for conventional mortgages. These mortgages are not guaranteed by the U.S. government.

Freddie Mac issues Reference Bills, discount notes, medium-term notes, Reference Notes, Reference Bonds, Callable Reference Notes, Euro Reference Notes (debt denominated in euros), and global bonds. Reference Bills and discount notes are issued with maturities of one year or less. Reference Notes and Bonds have maturities of two to 30 years and Callable Reference Notes have maturities of two to 10 years. Freddie Mac will issue and/or reopen Reference Bills, Reference Notes, 30-year Reference Bonds, and Euro Reference Notes according to a published issuance calendar and within minimum issue size guidelines.

The Federal Agricultural Mortgage Corporation

The Federal Agricultural Mortgage Corporation (popularly known as "Farmer Mac") provides a secondary market for first mortgage agricultural real estate loans. It was created by Congress in 1998 to improve the availability of mortgage credit to farmers and ranchers as well as rural homeowners, businesses, and communities. It does so by purchasing qualified loans from lenders in the same way as Freddie Mac and Fannie Mae. Farmer Mac raises funds by selling debentures and mortgage-backed securities backed by the loans purchased. The latter securities are called **agricultural mortgage-backed securities**. The debentures that are issued include discount notes and medium-term notes.

Federal Home Loan Bank System

The Federal Home Loan Bank System (FHLBanks) consists of the 12 district Federal Home Loan Banks and their member banks.The Federal Home Loan Bank Board was originally responsible for regulating all federally chartered savings and loan associations and savings banks, as well as state-chartered institutions insured by the Federal Savings and Loan Insurance Corporation. These responsibilities have been curtailed since 1989.

The major source of debt funding for the Federal Home Loan Banks is the issuance of consolidated debt obligations, which are joint and several obligations of the 12 Federal Home Loan Banks. Consolidated FHLBank discount notes with maturities from one to 360 days are issued daily. The FHLBanks have several programs to facilitate the issuance of certain bond types. The TAP issue program aggregates FHLBank demand for six common (1.5-, two-, three-, five-, seven-, and 10-year) bullet maturities, and then offers them daily through competitive auctions. These issues feature standardized terms and are reopened via auction for three-month periods, enabling them to reach multibillion-dollar size. TAP issues can also be reopened as they roll down the curve. Callable bonds are issued daily, primarily as customized issues for institutional investors.

Federal Farm Credit Bank System

The purpose of the Federal Farm Credit Bank System (FFCBS) is to facilitate adequate, dependable credit and related services to the agricultural sector of the economy. The Farm Credit Bank System consists of three entities: the Federal Land Banks, Federal Intermediate Credit Banks, and Banks for Cooperatives. Prior to 1979, each entity issued securities in its own name. Starting in 1979, they began to issue debt on a consolidated basis as "joint and several obligations" of the FFCBS. All financing for the FFCBS is arranged through the Federal Farm Credit Banks Funding Corporation (FFCBFC), which issues consolidated obligations. The FFCBFC issues discount notes that are offered daily through posted rates. Calendar bonds of three- and six-month maturities are offered monthly. Designated bonds of typically two-year maturities can be offered twice monthly as either a new issue or reopening. Unscheduled Bonds are issued throughout the month in varying sizes and structures either by competitive bidding or based on requests from institutional investors. Master notes are issued as individually tailored daily investment agreements that are typically designed for a single investor.

Key Points That You Should Understand Before Proceeding

1. The federal agency securities market is the market for securities issued by U.S. government-chartered entities to provide funding support for the housing and agricultural sectors of the U.S. economy, as well as to provide funding for specific U.S. government projects.
2. A government-chartered entity is classified as either a government-owned corporation or a GSE.
3. The GSEs issue debentures and mortgage-backed securities and these securities are not backed by the full faith and credit of the U.S. government.
4. The major government-owned corporation that issues securities is the TVA.
5. GSEs include Fannie Mae, Freddie Mac, Federal Agricultural Mortgage Corporation, and Federal Home Loan Bank System.

NON–U.S. GOVERNMENT BOND MARKETS

Sovereign debt is the obligation of a country's central government. Earlier in this chapter, we discussed the debt obligations of the U.S. government. The largest government bond market outside of the United States is the Japanese government bond market, followed by the markets in Italy, Germany, and France.

It was not until the early 1990s that a liquid government bond market in Continental Europe developed. The market grew throughout the decade. However, the Euro government bond market (excludes the bonds issued by the U.K. government, gilts) was characterized as a fragmented market and, as a result, could not develop the type of liquidity that characterized the U.S. Treasury market. The difference in the currency used by each country hindered that integrated market and liquidity.

In January 1999, the structure of the market changed with the start of the European Monetary Union (EMU). The EMU, combined with the decline in the U.S. Treasury issuance of securities at that time, resulted in the Euro government bond market becoming the largest government bond market in the world in terms of size and number of issues.

By mid 2007, the European government market was the world's largest government bond market in terms of size (€3 trillion) and number of issues, representing about 40% of the world's outstanding government bonds. It is almost 50% larger than the Japanese government bond market and 65% larger than the U.S. Treasury market. The three largest government bond markets—those of Germany, Italy, and France—made up two-thirds of the European government bond market.[12]

Methods of Distribution of New Government Securities

We described the primary market for distribution of U.S. Treasury securities earlier in this chapter. There are four methods that have been used in distributing new securities of central governments:

- the regular calendar auction/Dutch-style system
- the regular calendar auction/minimum-price offering system
- the ad hoc auction system
- the tap system

In the **regular calendar auction/Dutch-style auction system**, there is a regular calendar auction and winning bidders are allocated securities at the yield (price) they bid.

In the **regular calendar auction/minimum-price offering system**, there is a regular calendar of offering. The price (yield) at which winning bidders are awarded the securities is different from the Dutch-style auction. Rather than awarding a winning bidder at the yield (price) they bid, all winning bidders are awarded securities at the highest yield accepted by the government (i.e., the stop-out yield). For example, if the highest yield or stop-out yield for a government issue at auction is 5.14% and someone bids 5.12%, that bidder would be awarded the securities at 5.12%. In contrast, with the minimum-price offering method, that bidder would be awarded securities at 5.14%, which means a lower price than at the bid price of 5.12%. We refer to this auction method as a single-price auction, and it is the auction method used in the U.S. government market. The regular calendar auction/minimum-price offering method is used in Germany and France.

In the **ad hoc auction system**, governments announce auctions when prevailing market conditions appear favorable. It is only at the time of the auction that the amount to be auctioned and the maturity of the security to be offered are announced. This is one of the methods used by the Bank of England in distributing British government bonds. From the issuing government's perspective, there are two advantages of an ad hoc auction system over a regular calendar auction. First, a regular calendar auction introduces greater market volatility than an ad hoc auction does because yields tend to rise as the announced auction date approaches and then fall afterward. Second, there is reduced flexibility in raising funds with a regular calendar auction.

In a **tap system**, additional bonds of a previously outstanding bond issue are auctioned. The government announces periodically that it is adding this new supply.

---

[12] Antonio Villarroya, "The Euro Government Bond Market," Chapter 25 in Frank J. Fabozzi (ed.), *The Handbook of Finance: Volume I* (Hoboken, NJ: John Wiley & Sons, 2008).

Inflation-Indexed Bonds

In the United States, the U.S. Treasury issues fixed-rate bonds and bonds whose coupon rate is indexed to the rate of inflation (Treasury Inflation Protection Securities). Outside the United States, bond coupon rates are linked to the rate of inflation and are referred to as **linkers**.[13]

Table 3 shows the size of the inflation-linked government market by the major issuers in terms of local face value and market value as of September 30, 2005. The market value is U.S. $809.9 billion. The number of issues for each country is also shown. As can be seen, the United States is by far the largest issuer of inflation-linked government securities, followed by the United Kingdom and then France.

The indexes are typically linked to a consumer price index (CPI); however, within a country the index may differ. For example, in France there are bonds indexed to the French CPI (excluding tobacco) and to the Eurozone's Harmonised Index of Consumer Prices (HICP; excluding tobacco).

Sovereign Bond Ratings

Sovereign debt is the obligation of a country's central government. Whereas U.S. government debt is not rated by any nationally recognized statistical rating organization, the debt of other national governments is rated. For the reasons discussed subsequently, there are two sovereign debt ratings assigned by rating agencies: a **local currency debt rating** and a **foreign currency debt rating**.

Table 3   Government Inflation-Linked Market as of September 30, 2005

Country	Face Value (local, millions)	Market Value (local, millions)	No. of Issues	Foreign Market Value (USD, millions)	Market Share (%)
Australia	6,020	8,978	3	6,856	0.85
Canada	19,725	34,292	4	29,547	3.65
Sweden	179,393	251,132	6	32,490	4.01
France	81,454	100,271	9	120,891	14.93
United Kingdom	46,899	105,047	9	185,839	22.95
United States	278,370	338,509	17	338,509	41.80
South Africa	39,116	61,442	4	9,664	1.19
Greece	5,200	6,788	1	8,184	1.01
Japan	1,971,400	1,958,621	5	17,281	2.13
Italy	45,549	50,273	4	60,612	7.48
Total			62	809,872	100.00

Source: *Prepared from data supplied by Robert Tzucker of Barclays Capital.*

---

[13] For comprehensive coverage of the use and analysis of linkers in the European bond market, see "European Inflation-Linked Bonds," Chapter 8 in Frank J. Fabozzi and Moorad Choudhry (eds.), *The Handbook of European Fixed Income Securities* (Hoboken, NJ: John Wiley & Sons, 2005).

Standard & Poor's, Moody's, and Fitch all assign ratings to sovereign bonds. The two general categories are economic risk and political risk. The former category is an assessment of the ability of a government to satisfy its obligations. Both quantitative and qualitative analyses are used in assessing economic risk. Political risk is an assessment of the willingness of a government to satisfy its obligations. A government may have the ability to pay but may be unwilling to pay. Political risk is assessed based on qualitative analysis of the economic and political factors that influence a government's economic policies.

The reason for distinguishing between local debt ratings and foreign currency debt ratings is that historically, the default frequency differs by the currency denomination of the debt. Specifically, defaults have been greater on foreign currency-denominated debt. The reason for the difference in default rates for local currency debt and foreign currency debt is that if a government is willing to raise taxes and control its domestic financial system, it can generate sufficient local currency to meet its local currency debt obligation. This is not the case with foreign currency-denominated debt. A national government must purchase foreign currency to meet a debt obligation in that foreign currency and therefore has less control with respect to its exchange rate. Thus, a significant depreciation of the local currency relative to a foreign currency in which a debt obligation is denominated will impair a national government's ability to satisfy such obligation.

The implication of this is that the factors S&P analyzes in assessing the creditworthiness of a national government's local currency debt and foreign currency debt will differ to some extent. In assessing the credit quality of local currency debt, for example, S&P emphasizes domestic government policies that foster or impede timely debt service. For foreign currency debt, credit analysis by S&P focuses on the interaction of domestic and foreign government policies. S&P analyzes a country's balance of payments and the structure of its external balance sheet. The areas of analysis with respect to its external balance sheet are the net public debt, total net external debt, and net external liabilities.

SUMMARY

The U.S. Treasury market is closely watched by all participants in the financial markets because interest rates on Treasury securities are the benchmark interest rates throughout the world. The Treasury issues three types of securities: bills, notes, and bonds. Treasury bills have a maturity of one year or less, are sold at a discount from par, and do not make periodic interest payments. Treasury notes and bonds are coupon securities. In 1997, the Treasury began issuing inflation protection securities.

Treasury securities are issued on a competitive bid auction basis, according to a regular auction cycle. The auction process relies on the participation of the primary government securities dealers, with which the Federal Reserve deals directly. The auction process has been revised to allow greater participation by eligible nonprimary dealers.

The secondary market for Treasury securities is an over-the-counter market, where dealers trade with the general investing public and with other dealers. In the secondary market, Treasury bills are quoted on a bank discount basis; Treasury coupon securities are quoted on a price basis.

Treasury dealers finance their position in the repo market. They also use the repo market to cover short positions.

Although the Treasury does not issue zero-coupon Treasury securities, government dealers have created these instruments synthetically by a process called coupon stripping. Zero-coupon Treasury securities include trademarks, Treasury receipts, and STRIPS. Creation of the first two types of zero-coupon Treasury securities has ceased; STRIPS now dominate the market. The ability to strip Treasury coupon securities and reconstitute stripped Treasury securities forces the market price of a Treasury security to sell at a price close to its theoretical value based on theoretical spot rates.

The federal agency securities market is the market for the debt instruments issued by government-chartered entities. They were created by Congress to provide assistance for certain borrowing sectors of the economy deemed to be important enough to warrant assistance. These sectors include housing and agriculture, as well as specific U.S. government projects. The primary issuers in this market are the TVA (a government-owned corporation) and five government-sponsored enterprises: Fannie Mae, Freddie Mac, the Federal Agricultural Mortgage Corporation, the Federal Home Loan Bank System, and the Federal Farm Credit Bank System. The securities issued by these entities are not guaranteed by the full faith and credit of the U.S. government.

Sovereign debt is the obligation of a country's central government. Ratings are assigned separately for local currency-denominated debt and foreign currency-denominated debt. The two general categories analyzed by rating companies in assigning ratings are economic risk and political risk.

KEY TERMS

- Ad hoc auction system
- Agency securities market
- Agricultural mortgage-backed securities
- Bid-to-cover ratio
- Coupon securities
- Discount securities
- Foreign currency debt rating
- Government-owned corporation
- Government-sponsored enterprise (GSE)
- Government brokers
- Hot (special) issue
- Linkers
- Local currency debt rating
- Overnight repo
- Primary dealers
- Regular calendar auction/Dutch-style auction system
- Regular calendar auction/minimum-price offering system
- Reconstitution
- Reopened issue
- Stop yield
- Stripped Treasury security
- Separate Trading of Registered Interest and Principle of Securities (STRIPS)
- Tap system
- Term repo
- Trademark zero-coupon Treasury securities
- Treasury bills
- Treasury bonds
- Treasury inflation protection security (TIPS)
- Treasury notes
- Treasury receipt (TR)
- When-issued (wi) market
- Yield on a bank discount basis

QUESTIONS

1. Why do government dealers use government brokers?

2. Consider the following Treasury auction and results:

   Total to be issued = $9.00 billion
   Noncompetitive bids = $3.44 billion

   Total competitive bids received:

Amount ($ billions)	Bid (yield %)
$0.20	7.55% (lowest yield/highest price)
0.26	7.56
0.33	7.57
0.57	7.58
0.79	7.59
0.96	7.60
1.25	7.61
1.52	7.62 (stop or largest yield/stop or lowest price)
2.00	7.63
1.12	7.64
1.10	7.65

   No bids above 7.65%

   a. How much is available to be awarded to competitive bidders?
   b. What is the stop yield?
   c. Which bidders will be awarded securities?
   d. At what yield will a winning bidder be awarded securities?
   e. If a bidder bid for $10 million at the stop yield, how much will be awarded to that bidder?
   f. What is the bid-to-cover ratio for this auction?

3. Suppose that the price of a Treasury bill with 90 days to maturity and a $1 million face value is $980,000. What is the yield on a bank discount basis?

4. Suppose a portfolio manager purchases $1 million of par value of a Treasury inflation protection security. The real rate (determined at the auction) is 3.2%.

   a. Assume that at the end of the first six months the CPI-U is 3.6% (annual rate). Compute (1) the inflation adjustment to principal at the end of the first six months, (2) the inflation-adjusted principal at the end of the first six months, and (3) the coupon payment made to the investor at the end of the first six months.

   b. Assume that at the end of the second six months the CPI-U is 4.0% (annual rate). Compute (1) the inflation adjustment to principal at the end of the second six months, (2) the inflation-adjusted principal at the end of the second six months, and (3) the coupon payment made to the investor at the end of the second six months.

5. **a.** What is the measure of the rate of inflation selected by the U.S. Treasury for determining the inflation adjustment for Treasury inflation protection securities?

   b. Suppose that there is deflation over the life of a Treasury inflation protection security resulting in an inflation-adjusted principal at the maturity date that is less than the initial par value. How much will the U.S. Treasury pay at the maturity date to redeem the principal?

   c. Why is it necessary for the U.S. Treasury to report a daily index ratio for each TIPS issue?

6. **a.** Does the U.S. Department of the Treasury use a single-price or multiple-price auction in the issuance of Treasury coupon securities?

   b. How is the yield of winning bidders determined in a Treasury auction?

7. **a.** What is the difference between a STRIP, a trademark Treasury zero-coupon security, and a Treasury receipt?

   b. What is the most common type of Treasury zero-coupon security?

8. **a.** How can a repurchase agreement be used by a dealer firm to finance a long position in a Treasury security?

   b. One party in a repo transaction is said to "buy collateral," the other party to "sell collateral." Why?

   c. When there is a shortage of a specific security for a repo transaction, will the repo rate increase or decrease?

9. Which rate should be higher: the overnight repo rate, or the overnight federal funds rate? Why?

10. What economic mechanism forces the actual market price of a Treasury security toward its theoretical value based on theoretical spot rates?

11. **a.** Based on a yield to maturity of 12.5% for 10-year Treasury securities, demonstrate that the price of a 13% coupon, 10-year Treasury would be $102.8102 per $100 par value if all cash flows are discounted at 12.5%.

    b. Based on the theoretical spot rates in Table 2, show that the theoretical value would be $102.9304 per $100 par value.

    c. Explain why the market price for this Treasury security would trade close to its theoretical value.

12. What is a government-sponsored enterprise?

13. Explain why you agree or disagree with the following statement: "The debt of government-owned corporations is guaranteed by the full faith and credit of the U.S. government, but that is not the case for the debt of government-sponsored enterprises."

14. Fannie Mae and Freddie Mac allow certain securities that they issue to be "stripped." What does that mean?

15. Fannie Mae and Freddie Mac issue both callable and noncallable debt. For comparable-maturity issues, which debt obligation would offer a higher yield, the callable or noncallable debt?

16. What are the different methods for the issuance of government securities?

17. Why do rating agencies assign both a local currency debt rating and a foreign currency debt rating?

Municipal Securities Markets

From Chapter 16 of *Foundations of Financial Markets and Institutions*, 4/e. Frank J. Fabozzi. Franco Modigliani. Frank J. Jones.

Municipal Securities Markets

LEARNING OBJECTIVES

After reading this chapter, you will understand

- who buys municipal securities and why the securities are attractive investments to these buyers

- the types of municipal securities and why they are issued

- the risks unique to investment in municipal securities

- the primary and secondary markets for municipal securities

- the yield relationship between municipal securities and taxable bonds

- the yield relationships among municipal securities within the municipal market

- the degree of regulation of the municipal securities market

In this chapter, we discuss municipal securities and the market in which they trade. Municipal securities are issued by state and local governments and by entities that they establish. All states issue municipal securities. Local governments include cities and counties. Political subdivisions of municipalities that issue securities include school districts and special districts for fire prevention, water, sewer, and other purposes. Public agencies or instrumentalities include authorities and commissions.

From an investor's perspective, the attractiveness of municipal securities is due to their tax treatment at the federal income tax level. Most municipal securities are tax exempt. This means that interest on municipal bonds is exempt from federal income taxation. The exemption applies to interest income, not capital gains. The exemption may or may not extend to the state and local levels. Each state has its own rule as to how interest on municipal securities is taxed.[1]

---

[1] The tax treatment at the state level will be one of the following: (1) exemption of interest from all municipal securities, (2) taxation of interest from all municipal securities, (3) exemption of interest from municipal securities where the issuer is in the state but taxation of interest where the issuer is out of the state.

While most municipal bonds outstanding are tax exempt, there are issues that are taxable at the federal level.

Municipal securities are issued for various purposes. Short-term notes typically are sold in anticipation of the receipt of funds from taxes or proceeds from the sale of a bond issue, for example. The proceeds from the sale of short-term notes permit the issuing municipality to cover seasonal and temporary imbalances between outlays for expenditures and tax inflows. Municipalities issue long-term bonds as the principal means for financing both (1) long-term capital projects such as the construction of schools, bridges, roads, and airports; and (2) long-term budget deficits that arise from current operations.

As the single most important advantage of municipal securities to investors is the exemption of interest income from federal taxation, the investor groups that have purchased these securities are those that benefit the most from this exemption. The three categories of investors dominating the municipal securities market are households (retail investors), commercial banks, and property and casualty insurance companies. Individual investors may purchase municipal securities directly or through investment companies.

TYPES AND FEATURES OF MUNICIPAL SECURITIES[2]

There are basically two types of municipal security structures: **tax-backed debt** and **revenue bonds**. There are also securities that share characteristics of tax-backed debt and revenue bonds.

Tax-Backed Debt

Tax-backed debt obligations are instruments issued by states, counties, special districts, cities, towns, and school districts that are secured by some form of tax revenue. Tax-backed debt includes general obligation debt, appropriation-backed obligations, and debt obligations supported by public credit enhancement programs.

General Obligation Debt

The broadest type of tax-backed debt is **general obligation debt**. There are two types of general obligation pledges: unlimited and limited. An unlimited tax general obligation debt is the stronger form of general obligation pledge because it is secured by the issuer's unlimited taxing power. The tax revenue sources include corporate and individual income taxes, sales taxes, and property taxes. Unlimited tax general obligation debt is said to be secured by the full faith and credit of the issuer. A limited tax general obligation debt is a limited tax pledge because for such debt there is a statutory limit on tax rates that the issuer may levy to service the debt.

Certain general obligation bonds are secured not only by the issuer's general taxing powers to create revenues accumulated in a general fund but also by certain identified fees, grants, and special charges, which provide additional revenues from outside the general fund. Such bonds are known as double-barreled in security because of the dual nature of the revenue sources. For example, the debt obligations issued by special-purpose service systems may be secured by a pledge of property taxes, a pledge of special fees/operating revenue from the service provided, or a pledge of both property taxes and special fees/operating revenues. In the last case, they are double-barreled.

---

[2] For a further discussion of these securities, see Chapter 5 in Frank J. Fabozzi, *Fixed Income Securities* (New Hope, PA: Frank J. Fabozzi Associates, 1998).

Appropriation-Backed Obligations

Agencies or authorities of several states have issued bonds that carry a potential state liability for making up shortfalls in the issuing entity's obligation. The appropriation of funds from the state's general tax revenue must be approved by the state legislature. However, the state's pledge is not binding. Debt obligations with this nonbinding pledge of tax revenue are called **moral obligation bonds**. Because a moral obligation bond requires legislative approval to appropriate the funds, it is classified as an **appropriation-backed obligation**. The purpose of the moral obligation pledge is to enhance the creditworthiness of the issuing entity. However, the investor must rely on the best efforts of the state to approve the appropriation. Another type of appropriation-backed obligation is lease-backed debt.

Debt Obligations Supported by Public Credit Enhancement Programs

While a moral obligation is a form of credit enhancement provided by a state, it is not a legally enforceable or legally binding obligation of the state. There are entities that have issued debt that carries some form of public credit enhancement that is legally enforceable. This occurs when there is a guarantee by the state or a federal agency or when there is an obligation to automatically withhold and deploy state aid to pay any defaulted debt service by the issuing entity. Typically, the latter form of public credit enhancement is used for debt obligations of a state's school systems.

Some examples of state credit enhancement programs include Virginia's bond guarantee program that authorizes the governor to withhold state aid payments to a municipality and divert those funds to pay principal and interest to a municipality's general obligation holders in the event of a default. South Carolina's constitution requires mandatory withholding of state aid by the state treasurer if a school district is not capable of meeting its general obligation debt. Texas created the Permanent School Fund to guarantee the timely payment of principal and interest of the debt obligations of qualified school districts. The fund's income is obtained from land and mineral rights owned by the state of Texas.

Revenue Bonds

The second basic type of security structure is found in a revenue bond. Such bonds are issued for either project or enterprise financings where the bond issuers pledge to the bondholders the revenues generated by the operating projects financed. A feasibility study is performed before the endeavor is undertaken to determine whether or not it will be self-supporting.

Following are examples of revenue bonds: airport revenue bonds, college and university revenue bonds, hospital revenue bonds, single-family mortgage revenue bonds, multifamily revenue bonds, public power revenue bonds, resource recovery revenue bonds, seaport revenue bonds, sports complex and convention center revenue bonds, student loan revenue bonds, toll road and gas tax revenue bonds, and water revenue bonds.

Hybrid and Special Bond Structures

Some municipal securities have special security structures that share characteristics of tax-backed debt and revenue bonds. These include **insured bonds**, prefunded bonds, and structured/asset-based bonds.

Insured Bonds

Insured bonds, in addition to being secured by the issuer's revenue, are also backed by insurance policies written by commercial insurance companies. Insurance on a municipal bond is an agreement by an insurance company to pay the bondholder any bond principal and/or coupon interest that is due on a stated maturity date but that has not been paid by the bond issuer. Once issued, this municipal bond insurance usually extends for the term of the bond issue, and it cannot be canceled by the insurance company.

Prerefunded Bonds

Although originally issued as either revenue or general obligation bonds, municipals are sometimes prerefunded and called **prerefunded municipal bonds**. (They are also called **refunded bonds**.) A prerefunding usually occurs when the original bonds are escrowed or collateralized by direct obligations guaranteed by the U.S. government.[3] By this, it is meant that a portfolio of securities guaranteed by the U.S. government is placed in a trust. The portfolio of securities is assembled such that the cash flows from the securities match the obligations that the issuer must pay. For example, suppose that a municipality has a 7% $100 million issue with 12 years remaining to maturity. The municipality's obligation is to make payments of $3.5 million every six months for the next 12 years and $100 million 12 years from now. If the issuer wants to prerefund this issue, a portfolio of U.S. government obligations can be purchased that has a cash flow of $3.5 million every six months for the next 12 years and $100 million 12 years from now.

Once this portfolio of securities whose cash flows match those of the municipality's obligation is in place, the prerefunded bonds are no longer secured as either general obligation or revenue bonds. The bonds are now supported by cash flows from the portfolio of securities held in an escrow fund. Such bonds, if escrowed with securities guaranteed by the U.S. government, have little, if any, credit risk. They are the safest municipal bonds available.

The escrow fund for a prerefunded municipal bond can be structured so that the bonds to be refunded are to be called at the first possible call date or a subsequent call date established in the original bond indenture. Although prerefunded bonds are usually retired at their first or subsequent call date, some are structured to match the debt obligation to the maturity date. Such bonds are known as *escrowed-to-maturity bonds*.

Asset-Backed Bonds

In recent years, states and local governments began issuing bonds where the debt service is to be paid from so-called "dedicated" revenues such as sales taxes, tobacco settlement payments, fees, and penalty payments. These structures, called **asset-backed bonds,** mimic asset-backed securities. Asset-backed bonds are also referred to as **dedicated revenue bonds** and **structured bonds**.

---

[3] Because the interest rate that a municipality must pay on borrowed funds is less than the interest rate paid by the U.S. government, in the absence of any restrictions in the tax code, a municipal issuer can realize a tax arbitrage. This can be done by issuing a bond and immediately investing the proceeds in a U.S. government security. Tax rules may prevent such arbitrage in some cases. Should a municipal issuer violate the tax arbitrage rules, the issue will be ruled to be taxable. If subsequent to the issuance of a bond, however, interest rates decline so that the issuer will find it advantageous to call the bond, the establishment of the escrow fund will not violate the tax arbitrage rules.

Municipal Notes

Municipal securities issued for periods up to three years are considered to be short term in nature. These include **tax anticipation notes (TANs)**, **revenue anticipation notes (RANs)**, **grant anticipation notes (GANs)**, and **bond anticipation notes (BANs)**.

TANs, RANs, GANs, and BANs are temporary borrowings by states, local governments, and special jurisdictions. Usually, notes are issued for a period of 12 months, although it is not uncommon for notes to be issued for periods as short as three months and for as long as three years. TANs and RANs (also known as TRANs) are issued in anticipation of the collection of taxes or other expected revenues. The purpose of these borrowings is to even out irregular flows into the treasuries of the issuing entity. BANs are issued in anticipation of the sale of long-term bonds.

Redemption Features

Municipal bonds are issued with one of two debt retirement structures or a combination of both. Either a bond has a **serial maturity structure** or a **term maturity structure**. A serial maturity structure requires a portion of the debt obligation to be retired each year. A term maturity structure provides for the debt obligation to be repaid at the end of the bond's planned life. Usually, term bonds have maturities ranging from 20 to 40 years. Such bonds often have sinking fund provisions that call for partial and systematic retirement of the debt on a set schedule that begins five or ten years before the time of maturity. Another provision that permits the early redemption of a term bond is the call privilege, which allows the issuer, under certain and well-specified circumstances, to pay off the debt prior to the scheduled maturity. Sinking fund and call provisions are noted features of corporate debt.

Key Points That You Should Understand Before Proceeding

1. There are two types of municipal securities: tax-backed debt and revenue bonds.
2. A general obligation bond is secured by the issuer's unlimited taxing power.
3. A revenue bond is issued for either project or enterprise financings where the bond issuer pledges the revenues generated by the project that is financed to the bondholders.
4. Municipal notes are issued for periods up to three years and represent temporary borrowings by states, local governments, and special jurisdictions.
5. The debt retirement structure for a municipal bond can be either a serial maturity structure or a term maturity structure.

MUNICIPAL BOND RATINGS

Although municipal bonds have long been considered second in safety only to U.S. Treasury securities, today there are new concerns about the credit risks of many municipal bonds.[4]

The first concern came out of the New York City billion-dollar financial crisis in 1975. On February 25, 1975, the state of New York's Urban Development Corporation defaulted on a $100 million note issue that was the obligation of New York City. Many market participants

---

[4] For a history of defaults of municipal bonds, see Chapter 2 in Sylvan G. Feldstein and Frank J. Fabozzi, *The Dow Jones-Irwin Guide to Municipal Bonds* (Homewood, IL: Dow Jones-Irwin, 1987).

had been convinced that the state of New York would not allow the issue to default. Although New York City was able later to obtain a $140 million revolving credit from banks to cure the default, lenders became concerned that the city would face difficulties in repaying its accumulated debt, which stood at $14 billion on March 31, 1975.[5] This financial crisis sent a loud and clear warning to market participants: Despite supposedly ironclad protection for the bondholder, when issuers such as large cities have severe financial difficulties, the financial stakes of public employee unions, vendors, and community groups may be dominant forces in balancing budgets. This reality was reinforced by the federal bankruptcy law taking effect in October 1979, which makes it easier for the issuer of a municipal security to go into bankruptcy.

The second reason for concern about the credit risk of municipal securities is the proliferation in this market of innovative financing techniques to secure new bond issues. In addition to the established general obligation bonds and revenue bonds, there are now more innovative, and legally untested, security mechanisms that do not require voters' approval of new debt. What distinguishes these newer bonds from the more traditional general obligation and revenue bonds is that there is no history of court decisions or other case law that firmly establishes the rights of the bondholders and the obligations of the issuers. It is not possible to determine in advance the probable legal outcome if the newer financing mechanisms were to be challenged in court. The importance of this uncertainty is illustrated most dramatically by the bonds of the Washington Public Power Supply System (WPPSS), where bondholder rights to certain revenues were not upheld by the highest court in the state of Washington.

More recently, municipal bond investors have been increasingly concerned with those who manage the investment funds of municipalities. This concern was the result of the collapse of the Orange County (California) Investment Pool, which lost $1.7 billion as a result of a poorly conceived investment strategy by Robert L. Citron, the county treasurer. Citron followed a strategy that resulted in a leveraged position in securities that benefited if interest rates declined. Basically, he used the repurchase agreement. Instead of using the repurchase agreement as a short-term investment vehicle, he used it to create leverage via a reverse repurchase agreement. The loss resulting from this strategy, as well as investments in structured notes, resulted in the bankruptcy of Orange County.[6]

Many institutional investors in the municipal bond market rely on their own in-house municipal credit analysts for determining the creditworthiness of a municipal issue; other investors rely on the three nationally recognized rating companies. The assigned rating system is the same as that used for corporate bonds.

To evaluate general obligation bonds, the commercial rating companies assess information in four basic categories. The first category includes information on the issuer's debt structure and overall debt burden. The second category relates to the issuer's ability and political discipline to maintain sound budgetary policy. The focus of attention here usually is on the issuer's general operating funds and whether it has maintained at least balanced budgets over three to five years. The third category involves determining the specific local

[5] Securities and Exchange Commission Staff Report on *Transactions in Securities of the City of New York* (Washington, DC: U.S. Government Printing Office, 1977), p. 2. The reasons for the New York City financial crisis are documented in Donna E. Shalala and Carol Bellamy, "A State Saves a City: The New York Case," *Duke Law Journal* (January 1976), pp. 1119–1126.

[6] For an excellent account of the Orange County bankruptcy, see Philipe Jorion, *Big Bets Gone Bad* (New York: Academic Press, 1995).

taxes and intergovernmental revenues available to the issuer, as well as obtaining historical information both on tax collection rates, which are important when looking at property tax levies, and on the dependence of local budgets on specific revenue sources. The fourth and last category of information necessary to the credit analysis is an assessment of the issuer's overall socioeconomic environment. The determinations that have to be made here include trends of local employment distribution and composition, population growth, real estate property valuation, and personal income, among other economic factors.

While there are numerous security structures for revenue bonds, the underlying principle in rating is whether or not the project being financed will generate sufficient cash flow to satisfy the obligations due bondholders.

Key Points That You Should Understand Before Proceeding

1. The investor in a municipal security is exposed to credit risk.
2. Commercial rating companies evaluate the credit risk associated with municipal securities and express the results of their analysis in the form of rating categories.
3. The factors used to determine a rating for a general obligation bond are different from those used for a revenue bond.

TAX RISKS ASSOCIATED WITH INVESTING IN MUNICIPAL SECURITIES

There are two types of tax risk to which tax-exempt municipal securities buyers are exposed. The first is the risk that the federal income tax rate will be reduced. The higher the marginal tax rate, the more valuable the tax-exemption feature. As the marginal tax rate declines, the price of a tax-exempt municipal security will decline. Proposals to reduce the marginal tax rate result in less demand for municipal securities and, as a result, a decline in their price. This occurred most recently in 1995 when there were proposals of a flat tax in which the tax rate would be less than the prevailing rate.

The second type of tax risk is that a municipal bond issued as a tax-exempt issue may be eventually declared by the Internal Revenue Service (IRS) to be taxable. This could happen because many municipal revenue bonds have elaborate security structures that could be subject to future adverse Congressional action and IRS interpretation. A loss of the tax-exemption feature will cause the municipal bond to decline in value in order to provide a yield comparable to similar taxable bonds. An example of this risk is the following situation: In June 1980, the Battery Park City Authority sold $97.315 million in notes, which at the time of issuance seemed to be exempt from federal income taxation. In November 1980, however, the IRS held that interest on these notes was not exempt. The legal question was not settled until September 1981, when the authority and the IRS signed a formal agreement resolving the matter so as to make the interest on the notes tax-exempt.

Key Points That You Should Understand Before Proceeding

1. A tax risk associated with investing in municipal bonds is that the highest marginal tax rate will be reduced, resulting in a decline in the value of municipal bonds.
2. Another tax risk associated with investing in municipal bonds is that a tax-exempt issue may be eventually declared by the IRS to be taxable.

THE PRIMARY MARKET

A substantial number of municipal obligations are brought to market each week. A state or local government can market its new issue by offering bonds publicly to the investing community or by placing them privately with a small group of investors. When a public offering is selected, the issue usually is underwritten by investment bankers and/or municipal bond departments of commercial banks. Public offerings may be marketed by either competitive bidding or direct negotiations with underwriters. In a competitive process, the bidder submitting the highest bid price for the security gets the right to market the debt to investors.

Most states mandate that general obligation issues be marketed through competitive bidding, but generally this is not necessary for revenue bonds. Usually, state and local governments require a competitive sale to be announced in a recognized financial publication, such as *The Bond Buyer*, which is a trade publication for the municipal bond industry. *The Bond Buyer* also provides information on upcoming competitive sales and most negotiated sales, as well as the results of previous weeks. However the debt is marketed, the municipal unit prepares an *official statement* describing its financial situation and the terms of the issue.[7] These terms include the call and sinking fund provisions previously mentioned.

THE SECONDARY MARKET

Municipal bonds are traded in the over-the-counter market supported by municipal bond dealers across the country. Markets for the debts of smaller issuers (referred to as *local credits*) are maintained by regional brokerage firms, local banks, and by some of the larger Wall Street firms. Markets for the bonds of larger issuers (referred to as *general names*) are supported by the larger brokerage firms and banks, many of whom have investment banking relationships with these issuers. There are brokers who serve as intermediaries in the sale of large blocks of municipal bonds among dealers and large institutional investors. Beginning in 2000, bonds in the secondary market as well as some new issue competitive and negotiated issues began to be auctioned and sold over the Internet by large and small broker-dealers to institutional and individual investors.

In the municipal bond market, an odd lot of bonds is $25,000 or less in par value for retail investors. For institutions, anything below $100,000 in par value is considered an odd lot. Dealer spreads depend on several factors. For the retail investor, the spread can range from as low as one-quarter of one point ($12.50 per $5,000 par value) on large blocks of actively traded bonds to four points ($200 per $5,000 of par value) for odd-lot sales of an inactive issue. For institutional investors, the dealer spread rarely exceeds one-half of one point ($25 per $5,000 of par value).

The convention for both corporate and Treasury bonds is to quote prices as a percentage of par value with 100 equal to par. Municipal bonds, however, generally are traded and quoted in terms of yield (yield to maturity or yield to call). The price of the bond in this case is called a *basis price*. The exception is certain long-maturity revenue bonds. A bond traded and quoted in dollar prices (actually, as a percentage of par value) is called a *dollar bond*.

---

[7] Nationally Recognized Municipal Securities Information Repositories (NRMSIRS) serve as the central collectors and disseminators of information about municipal securities.

Actual price and trade information for specific municipal bonds is available on a daily basis at no charge via the Internet at www.investinginbonds.com. It is the home page of the Bond Market Association. The trade information provided is from the Municipal Securities Rulemaking Board and Standard & Poor's J.J. Kenny. The original source of the trades reported is transactions between dealer to dealer and dealer to institutional customer and retail (individual investor).

THE TAXABLE MUNICIPAL BOND MARKET

Taxable municipal bonds are bonds whose interest is taxed at the federal income tax level. Because there is no tax advantage, an issuer must offer a higher yield than for another tax-exempt municipal bond. The yield must be higher than the yield on U.S. government bonds because an investor faces credit risk by investing in a taxable municipal bond. The investors in taxable municipal bonds are investors who view them as alternatives to corporate bonds.

Why would a municipality want to issue a taxable municipal bond and thereby have to pay a higher yield than if it issued a tax-exempt municipal bond? There are three reasons for this. First, prior to 1986, there were many more activities that municipalities could finance by issuing tax-exempt municipal bonds. The U.S. Congress felt that some of these activities should not be financed with tax-exempt municipal bonds because such activities do not benefit the public at large. As a result, Congress passed the Tax Reform Act of 1986, which imposed restrictions on what types of projects could be financed using tax-exempt municipal bonds. For example, within a particular project there is a maximum amount imposed on the issuance of tax-exempt municipal bonds for private activity bonds—the maximum amount is the greater of $150 million or $50 per state resident per year. As a result, municipalities had to finance these restricted activities in the taxable bond market.

The second reason is that the U.S. income tax code imposes restrictions on arbitrage opportunities that a municipality can realize from its financing activities. The third reason is that municipalities do not view their potential investor base as solely U.S. investors. Some issuers, for example, have been active issuers of bonds outside of the United States. When bonds are issued outside of the United States, the investor does not benefit from the tax-exempt feature. These last two reasons have to do with the flexibility afforded a municipality by using the taxable bond market rather than the tax-exempt bond market.

The most common types of activities for taxable municipal bonds used for financing are (1) local sports facilities, (2) investor-led housing projects, (3) advanced refunding of issues that are not permitted to be refunded because the tax law prohibits such activity, and (4) underfunded pension plan obligations of the municipality.

YIELDS ON MUNICIPAL BONDS

Because of the tax-exempt feature of municipal bonds, the yield on municipal bonds is usually less than that on Treasuries with the same maturity. The difference in yield between tax-exempt securities and Treasury securities is typically measured not in basis points but in percentage terms. More specifically, it is measured as the percentage of the yield on a municipal security relative to a comparable Treasury security and is called the **yield ratio**.

The yield ratio has changed over time. The higher the tax rate, the more attractive the tax-exempt feature and the lower the yield ratio. The yield ratio varies over time. This can be seen in Figure 1. The figure shows the yield ratio computed from the 20-year AAA general obligation bond and the 20-year Treasury bond from September 28, 2001, to August 31, 2006.

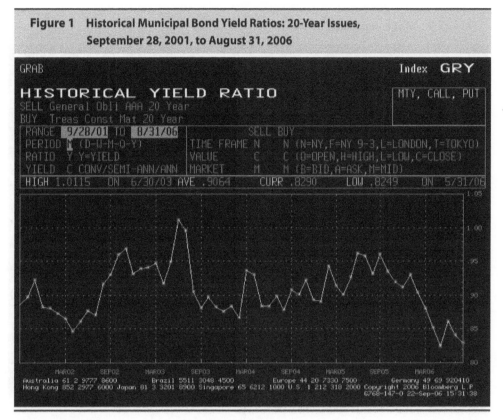

Figure 1   Historical Municipal Bond Yield Ratios: 20-Year Issues, September 28, 2001, to August 31, 2006

In the municipal bond market, several benchmark curves exist. In general, a benchmark yield curve is constructed for a AAA quality-rated state general obligation. In the Treasury and corporate bond markets, it is not unusual to find at different times shapes for the yield curve. In general, the municipal yield curve is positively sloped, as can be seen in Figure 2. There was a brief period where the municipal yield curve became inverted. However, during the period when the Treasury yield curve was inverted, the municipal yield curve maintained its upward-sloping shape. Prior to 1986, the municipal yield curve was consistently steeper than the Treasury yield curve as measured by the spread between the 30-year and one-year issues. Between 1986 and 1990, the steepness was comparable. In 1991, the municipal yield curve became steeper than the Treasury yield curve.

REGULATION OF THE MUNICIPAL SECURITIES MARKET[8]

Congress has specifically exempted municipal securities from both the registration requirements of the Securities Act of 1933 and the periodic reporting requirements of the Securities Exchange Act of 1934. When there was a significant expansion of the federal securities in

---

[8]Parts of this section are drawn from Thomas F. Mitchell, "Disclosure and the Municipal Bond Industry," Chapter 40, and Nancy H. Wojtas, "The SEC and Investor Safeguards," Chapter 42 in Frank J. Fabozzi, Sylvan G. Feldstein, Irving M. Pollack, and Frank Zarb (eds.), *The Municipal Bond Handbook: Volume I* (Homewood, IL: Dow Jones-Irwin, 1983). For a more recent discussion, see Paul S. Maco and Cristy C. Edwards, "The Role of the SEC," Chapter 23 in Sylvan Feldstein and Frank J. Fabozzi (eds.), *Handbook of Municipal Bonds* (Hoboken, NJ: John Wiley & Sons, 2008).

Figure 2   Municipal Yield Curves

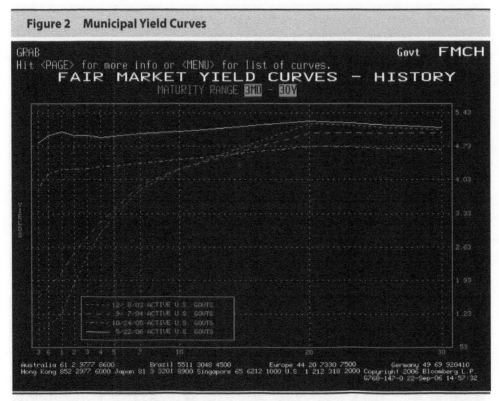

GRAB   Govt **FMCH**
Hit <PAGE> for more info or <MENU> for list of curves.
FAIR MARKET YIELD CURVES – HISTORY
MATURITY RANGE 3MO – 30Y

2002 with the passage of the Sarbanes-Oxley Act, Congress once again exempted issuers of municipal securities from the application from some of the important changes. However, antifraud provisions apply nevertheless to offerings of, or dealings in, municipal securities.

The reasons for the exemption afforded municipal securities appear to relate to (1) a desire for harmonious and cooperative relations among the various levels of government in the United States, (2) the absence of recurrent abuses in transactions involving municipal securities, (3) the greater level of sophistication of investors in this segment of the securities markets (the market was long dominated by institutional investors), and (4) the fact that there had been few defaults by municipal issuers. Consequently, between the enactment of federal securities acts in the early 1930s and early 1970s, the municipal securities market was relatively free from federal regulation.

In the early 1970s, however, circumstances changed. As incomes rose, individual investors began to participate in the municipal securities market to a much greater extent, and public concern over selling practices was expressed with greater frequency. Moreover, the financial problems of some municipal issuers, notably New York City, made market participants aware that municipal issuers have the potential to experience severe financial difficulties approaching bankruptcy levels.

Congress passed the Securities Act Amendment of 1975 to broaden federal regulation in the market for municipal debt. This legislation brought brokers and dealers in the municipal securities market, including banks that underwrite and trade municipal securities, under the regulatory umbrella of the Securities Exchange Act of 1934. The legislation mandated also that the SEC establish a 15-member Municipal Securities Rulemaking Board (MSRB) as an independent, self-regulatory agency whose primary responsibility is to develop rules governing the activities of banks, brokers, and dealers in municipal securities. Rules adopted by the MSRB must be approved by the SEC. The MSRB has no enforcement or inspection authority. That authority is vested with the SEC, the National Association of Securities Dealers, and certain regulatory banking agencies such as the Federal Reserve Bank.

The Securities Act Amendment of 1975 does not require municipal issuers to comply with the registration requirement of the 1933 act or the periodic reporting requirement of the 1934 act, despite several legislative proposals to mandate such financial disclosure. However, the SEC has been active in monitoring disclosure information for municipal securities. Even in the absence of federal legislation dealing with the regulation of financial disclosure, however, underwriters began insisting upon greater disclosure as it became apparent that the SEC was exercising stricter application of the antifraud provisions. Moreover, underwriters recognized the need for improved disclosure to sell municipal securities to an investing public that had become much more concerned about the credit risk of municipal issuers.

On June 28, 1989, the SEC formally approved the first bond disclosure rule, effective January 1, 1990. While the disclosure rule has several exemptions, in general it applies to new issue municipal securities offerings of $1 million or more.

SUMMARY

Municipal securities are issued by state and local governments and their authorities, with the interest on most issues being exempt from federal income taxes. The primary investors in these securities are households (which includes mutual funds), commercial banks, and property and casualty insurance companies.

There are both tax-exempt and taxable municipal securities, where "tax-exempt" means that interest on a municipal security is exempt from federal income taxation; most municipal securities that have been issued are tax-exempt.

There are basically two types of municipal security structures: tax-backed debt and revenue bonds. Tax-backed debt obligations are instruments issued by states, counties, special districts, cities, towns, and school districts that are secured by some form of tax revenue. Tax-backed debt includes general obligation debt (the broadest type of tax-backed debt), appropriation-backed obligations, and debt obligations supported by public credit enhancement programs. A general obligation bond is said to be double-barreled when it is secured not only by the issuer's general taxing powers to create revenues accumulated in a general fund but also by certain identified fees, grants, and special charges, which provide additional revenues from outside the general fund. Revenue bonds are issued for enterprise financings that are secured by the revenues generated by the completed projects themselves, or for general public-purpose financings in which the issuers pledge to the bondholders the tax and revenue resources that were previously part of the general fund.

Insured bonds, in addition to being secured by the issuer's revenue, are backed by insurance policies written by commercial insurance companies. Prerefunded bonds are no longer secured as either general obligation or revenue bonds but are supported by a portfolio of securities held in an escrow fund. If escrowed with securities guaranteed by the U.S. government, refunded bonds are the safest municipal bonds available. A prerefunded municipal bond is one in which the escrow fund is structured so that the bonds are to be called at the first possible call date or a subsequent call date established in the original bond indenture. There are municipal securities structured as asset-backed securities that are backed by "dedicated" revenues such as sales taxes, tobacco settlement payments, fees, and penalty payments.

Municipal notes are issued for shorter periods (one to three years) than municipal bonds. Municipal bonds may be retired with a serial maturity structure, a term maturity structure, or a combination of both. Investing in municipal securities exposes investors to credit risk and tax risk.

KEY TERMS

- Appropriation-backed obligation
- Asset-backed bond
- Bond anticipation note (BAN)
- Dedicated revenue bond
- General obligation debt
- Grant anticipation note (GAN)
- Insured bonds
- Moral obligation bond
- Prerefunded bonds (refunded bonds)

- Revenue bonds
- Revenue anticipation note (RAN)
- Serial maturity structure
- Structured bond
- Tax anticipation note (TAN)
- Tax-backed debt
- Taxable municipal bond
- Term maturity structure
- Yield ratio

QUESTIONS

1. Explain why you agree or disagree with the following statement: "All municipal bonds are exempt from federal income taxes."
2. **a.** Who are the three major investors in municipal securities?
   b. What aspect of their situation and what feature of these bonds attract these investors to this market?
3. If it is expected that the U.S. Congress will change the tax law so as to increase marginal tax rates, what do you think will happen to the price of municipal bonds?
4. What is the major difference between a tax-backed debt and a revenue bond?
5. What is the difference between a limited and unlimited general obligation bond?
6. **a.** Why are more municipal bonds insured today than in 1970?
   b. In your view, would the typical AAA rated municipal bond be insured?
7. "A moral obligation bond is a form of a limited general obligation bond." Explain why you agree or disagree with this statement.

8. **a.** What is a prerefunded bond?
   b. Identify two reasons why an issuing municipality would want to prerefund an outstanding bond.
9. Why does a properly structured prerefunded municipal bond have no credit risk?
10. In recent years, municipalities have begun to issue asset-backed securities. What are the revenues of these securities backed by?
11. For years, observers and analysts of the debt market believed that municipal securities were free of any risk of default. Why do most people now believe that municipal debt can carry a substantial amount of credit or default risk?
12. Because many people know that interest payments on municipal debt generally are exempt from taxation by the federal government, they would undoubtedly be surprised by the term tax risk of investing in municipal bonds. Can you explain this term and state why an astute investor should always be aware of this risk when buying municipal bonds?

13. How does the shape of the Treasury yield curve compare to that of the municipal yield curve?

14. Why isn't the Treasury yield curve used as a benchmark in measuring yield spreads between different sectors of the municipal bond market?

15. Are municipal securities exempt from regulation by the SEC?

16. The four largest tobacco companies in the United States reached a settlement with 46 state attorneys general to pay a total of $206 billion over the following 25 years.

   a. States and municipalities, New York City being the first, sold bonds backed by the future payments of the tobacco companies. What are these bonds called?

   b. What is the credit risk associated with these bonds?

Markets for Common Stock:
The Basic Characteristics

From Chapter 17 of *Foundations of Financial Markets and Institutions*, 4/e. Frank J. Fabozzi. Franco Modigliani. Frank J. Jones.

Markets for Common Stock: The Basic Characteristics[1]

LEARNING OBJECTIVES

After reading this chapter, you will understand

- trading mechanisms such as the types of orders, short selling, and margin transactions

- the types of transaction costs encountered when trading stocks

- trading arrangements to accommodate institutional traders such as block trades and program trades

- what the upstairs market is and its role in institutional trading

- price limits and collars imposed by exchanges

- the role played by stock market indicators and how those indicators are constructed

- various stock market indicators of interest to market participants

- evidence on the pricing efficiency of the stock market

- the implications of pricing efficiency for a common stock strategy

This chapter is devoted to common stock and the secondary markets where they trade. It is on the common stock market that investors express their opinions about the economic prospect of a company through the trades they make. The aggregate of these trades gives the market consensus opinion about the price of the stock. In turn, the company's cost of common stock is determined. Three interacting factors contributed to significant changes experienced by this market over the past 50 years: (1) the institutionalization of the stock market as a result

---

[1] This chapter draws from Frank J. Fabozzi, Frank J. Jones, Robert R. Johnson, and Bruce M. Collins, "Common Stock Markets, Trading Arrangements, and Trading Costs," Chapter 6 in Frank J. Fabozzi and Harry M. Markowitz (eds.), *The Theory and Practice of Investment Management* (Hoboken, NJ: John Wiley & Sons, 2002) and Frank J. Jones and Frank J. Fabozzi, "Common Stock Markets," Chapter 11 in Frank J. Fabozzi (ed.), *The Handbook of Finance: Volume I* (Hoboken, NJ: John Wiley & Sons, 2008).

of a shift away from traditional small investors to large institutional investors, (2) changes in government regulation of the market, and (3) innovation due largely to advances in computer technology. The institutionalization of this market imposes important implications for the design of trading systems, because the demands made by institutional investors differ from those made by traditional small investors.

Our focus in this chapter is on the basics of common stock trading, the costs associated with common stock trading, stock market indicators (indexes), and the efficiency of the stock market. Trading costs go well beyond the most obvious one of commissions and have important implications for the design of secondary markets. The most controversial aspect of the common stock market described in this chapter is the notion of market efficiency because of its impact on the design of common stock investment strategies. As we will see, there are two market structure designs: order driven and quote driven. The major controversy is which one is the best market structure for investors.

COMMON STOCK CHARACTERISTICS

Equity securities represent an ownership interest in a corporation. Holders of equity securities are entitled to the earnings of the corporation when those earnings are distributed in the form of dividends. They are also entitled to a pro rata share of the remaining equity in case of liquidation. The two types of equity securities are *common stock* and **preferred stock**. The key distinction between these two forms of equity securities lies in the degree to which they may participate in any distribution of earnings and the priority given to each in the distribution of earnings. Typically, preferred stockholders are entitled to a fixed dividend that they receive before common stockholders may receive dividends. We refer, therefore, to preferred stock as a senior corporate security.

For common stock, the total value is equal to the price per share multiplied by the number of common stock shares outstanding. The total value of a corporation's common stock is referred to as its **market capitalization** or simple market cap. For common stock investors, the return realized by holding this investment comes from two sources:

- dividend payments
- change in the price of the common stock

Dividends are distributions made by a corporation to its owners that represent a return on their investment. Dividends are typically in the form of cash. In addition to cash dividends, a corporation may provide shareholders with dividends in the form of additional shares of stock (referred to as stock dividends).[2] Dividends paid to common stockholders are not legal obligations of a corporation and some corporations do not pay cash dividends. But for those companies that pay dividends, changes in dividends are noticed by investors—increases in dividends are viewed favorably and are associated with increases in

---

[2] Historically, there have been instances where a corporation pays a dividend in the form of some type of property owned or product produced by the corporation.

the company's stock price, whereas decreases in dividends are viewed quite unfavorably and are associated with decreases in the company's stock price. It is observed that many corporations that do pay cash dividends only reluctantly lower or eliminate cash dividends. It is often the case, however, that relatively young, fast-growing companies do not pay dividends; as the companies mature they begin to pay dividends.[3]

At one time, dividend payments were taxed solely as ordinary income. Ordinary income means that the tax rate applicable is based on the investor's regular marginal tax bracket. However, to stimulate the stock market, the tax law was changed so that dividends are taxed as either ordinary income or as **qualified dividends**. The advantage of having dividends treated as qualified dividends is that they are subject to a preferential tax rate. More specifically, depending on the individual's income tax rate, qualified dividends are taxed at either 5% or 15%. If the individual has a regular income tax rate greater than or equal to 25%, then the qualified dividend tax rate is 15%. If the individual's regular income tax rate is less than 25%, then the qualified dividend tax rate is 5%. The Internal Revenue Code (IRC) sets forth the rule to determine whether dividends are qualified. Specifically, the IRC states that the investor "must have held the stock for more than 60 days during the 121-day period that begins 60 days before the ex-dividend date."

The change in the price of the common stock determines whether there is a gain or loss. If the price at a future date exceeds the purchase price, then there is a capital gain; if the price at a future date is less than the purchase price, then there is a capital loss. When an investor is calculating the return from holding common stock from the date of purchase to a given point in time but has not sold the common stock, the return reflects an unrealized capital gain or unrealized capital loss. The investor does not pay any tax on the capital gain or capital loss until the stock is sold. Once the stock is sold, the IRC specifies how the capital gain or capital loss is to be treated. The treatment depends on whether the investment is determined as "short term" or "long term." The IRC defines *short term* as a holding period of one year or less. If a capital gain is classified as a short-term capital gain, it is taxed as ordinary income at the investor's regular income tax rate. *Long term* is defined as holding an investment for more than one year. A long-term capital gain is taxed at a preferential tax rate in the same way as qualified dividends: either 5% or 15% depending on the individual investor's regular income tax rate.

Key Points That You Should Understand Before Proceeding

1. What an equity security is.
2. The difference between common stock and preferred stock.
3. The two potential sources of return from investing in common stock and their tax treatment.

TRADING MECHANICS

We begin with the key features involved in trading stocks. Later in the chapter, we discuss trading arrangements (block trades and program trades) that were developed specifically for coping with the trading needs of institutional investors.

---

[3] How much of a corporation's profit to pay out versus retain is called the corporation's "dividend policy," and the factors that influence that decision are covered in corporate finance courses.

Types of Orders

When an investor wants to buy or sell a share of common stock, the price and conditions under which the order is to be executed must be communicated to a broker. The simplest type of order is the **market order**, an order to be executed at the best price available in the market. The danger of a market order is that an adverse move may take place between the time the investor places the order and the time the order is executed. To avoid this danger, the investor can place a *limit order* that designates a price threshold for the execution of the trade. A *buy limit order* indicates that the stock may be purchased only at the designated price or lower. A *sell limit order* indicates that the stock may be sold at the designated price or higher. The key disadvantage of a limit order is that there is no guarantee that it will be executed at all; the designated price may simply not be obtainable. A limit order that is not executable at the time it reaches the market is recorded in a **limit order book**.

The limit order is a *conditional order*. It is executed only if the limit price or a better price can be obtained. Another type of conditional order is the **stop order**, which specifies that the order is not to be executed until the market moves to a designated price, at which time it becomes a market order. A *buy stop order* specifies that the order is not to be executed until the market rises to a designated price, that is, until it trades at or above, or is bid at or above, the designated price. A *sell stop order* specifies that the order is not to be executed until the market price falls below a designated price, that is, until it trades at or below, or is offered at or below, the designated price. A stop order is useful when an investor cannot watch the market constantly. Profits can be preserved or losses minimized on a stock position by allowing market movements to trigger a trade. In a sell (buy) stop order, the designated price is lower (higher) than the current market price of the stock. In a sell (buy) limit order, the designated price is higher (lower) than the current market price of the stock. The relationships between the two types of conditional orders, and the market movements that trigger them, appear in Table 1.

Two dangers are associated with stop orders. Stock prices sometimes exhibit abrupt price changes, so the direction of a change in a stock price may be quite temporary, resulting in the premature trading of a stock. Also, once the designated price is reached, the stop order becomes a market order and is subject to the uncertainty of the execution price noted earlier for market orders.

A stop-limit order, a hybrid of a stop order and a limit order, is a stop order that designates a price limit. In contrast to the stop order, which becomes a market order if the stop is reached, the stop-limit order becomes a limit order if the stop is reached. The stop-limit order can be used to cushion the market impact of a stop order. The investor can limit the possible execution price after the activation of the stop. As with a limit order, the limit price may never be reached after the order is activated, which therefore defeats one purpose of the stop order—to protect a profit or limit a loss.

An investor can also enter a **market if touched order**. This order becomes a market order if a designated price is reached. A market if touched order to buy becomes a market order if the market falls to a given price, whereas a stop order to buy becomes a market order if the market rises to a given price. Similarly, a market if touched order to sell becomes a market order if the market rises to a specified price, while the stop order to sell becomes a market order if the market falls to a given price. We can think of the stop order as an order

Price of Security	Limit Order	Market if Touched Order	Stop-Limit Order	Stop Order
Higher price	Price specified for a sell limit order	Price specified for a sell market if touched order	Price specified for a buy stop-limit order	Price specified for a buy stop order
Current price	—	—	—	—
Lower price	Price specified for a buy limit order	Price specified for a buy market if touched order	Price specified for a sell stop-limit order	Price specified for a sell stop order
Comment	Can be filled only at price or better; that is, does not become a market order when price is reached	Becomes market order when price is reached	Does not become a market order when price is reached; can be executed only at price or better	Becomes market order when price is reached

Table 1 Conditional Orders and the Direction of Triggering Security Price Movements

designed to get out of an existing position at an acceptable price (without specifying the exact price), and the market if touched order as an order designed to get into a position at an acceptable price (also without specifying the exact price).

Orders can be placed to buy or sell at the open or the close of trading for the day. An *opening order* indicates a trade to be executed only in the opening range for the day, and a *closing order* indicates a trade is to be executed only within the closing range for the day.

An investor may enter orders that contain order cancellation provisions. A **fill or kill order** must be executed as soon as it reaches the trading floor or it is immediately canceled. Orders may designate the time period for which the order is effective: a day, week, or month, or perhaps by a given time within the day. An **open order**, or *good till canceled order*, is good until the investor specifically terminates the order.

Orders are also classified by size. The normal unit of trading for common stock is typically a **round lot**, which is 100 shares of a stock. An **odd lot** is defined as less than a round lot. A **block trade** refers to a large dollar amount or number of shares of a given stock. For example, the New York Stock Exchange (NYSE) defines a block trade as an order of 10,000 shares of a given stock or a total market value of $200,000 or more.

Short Selling

Short selling involves the sale of a security not owned by the investor at the time of sale. Investors can arrange to have their broker borrow the stock from someone else, and the borrowed stock is delivered to implement the sale. To cover their short position, investors must subsequently purchase the stock and return it to the party that lent the stock.

Let us look at an example of how this is done in the stock market. Suppose that on March 17, 2008, Ms. Stokes believes that the common stock of General Motors Corporation (ticker symbol GM) is overpriced at $18.30 per share and wants to be in a position to benefit if her assessment is correct. Ms. Stokes calls her broker, Mr. Yats, indicating that she wants to sell 100 shares of GM. Mr. Yats will do two things: (1) sell 100 shares of GM on behalf of Ms. Stokes, and (2) arrange to borrow 100 shares of GM to deliver to the buyer. Suppose that Mr. Yats is able to sell the stock for $18.30 per share and borrows the stock from Mr. Jordan. The shares borrowed from Mr. Jordan will be delivered to the buyer of the 100 shares. The proceeds from the sale (ignoring commissions) will be $1,830. However, the proceeds do not go to Ms. Stokes because she has not given her broker the 100 shares of GM. Thus, Ms. Stokes is said to be "short 100 shares of GM."

Now, let's suppose one week later the price of GM stock declines to $15 per share. Ms. Stokes may instruct her broker to buy 100 shares of GM. The cost of buying the shares (once again ignoring commissions) is $1,500. The shares purchased are then delivered to Mr. Jordan, who lent 100 shares of GM to Ms. Stokes. At this point, Ms. Stokes has sold 100 shares and bought 100 shares of GM stock. So, she no longer has any obligation to her broker or to Mr. Jordan; she has "covered" her short position. She is entitled to the funds in her account that were generated by the selling and buying activity. She sold the stock for $1,830 and bought it for $1,500. Thus, she realizes a profit before commissions of $330. From this amount, commissions are subtracted.

Two more costs will reduce the profit further. First, a fee will be charged by the lender of the stock. We will discuss this fee shortly. Second, if there are any dividends paid by GM while the stock is borrowed, Ms. Stokes must compensate Mr. Jordan for the dividends to which he would have been entitled.

If instead of falling, the price of GM stock rises, Ms. Stokes will realize a loss when she is forced to cover her short position. For example, if the price rises to $24.30, Ms. Stokes will lose $500, to which must be added commissions and the cost of borrowing the stock (and possibly dividends).

Margin Transactions

Investors can borrow cash to buy securities and use the securities themselves as collateral. For example, suppose Mr. Huang has $10,000 to invest and is considering buying GM on March 17, 2008, at $18.30 per share. With his $18,300, Mr. Huang can buy 1,000 shares (ignoring commissions). Suppose Mr. Huang's broker can arrange for him to borrow an additional $18,300 so that he can buy an additional 1,000 shares. Thus, with a $36,600 investment, he can purchase a total of 2,000 shares. The 2,000 shares will be used as collateral for the $18,300 borrowed, and Mr. Huang will have to pay interest on the amount borrowed.

A transaction in which an investor borrows to buy shares using the shares themselves as collateral is called **buying on margin**. By borrowing funds, an investor creates financial leverage. Note that Mr. Huang, for an $18,300 investment, realizes the consequences associated with a price change of 2,000 shares rather than 1,000 shares. He will benefit if the price rises but be worse off if the price falls (compared to borrowing no funds).

To illustrate, we now look at what happens if the price subsequently changes. If the price of GM stock rises to $27.30 per share, ignoring commissions and the cost of borrowing, Mr. Huang will realize a profit of $9 per share on 2,000 shares, or $18,000. Had Mr. Huang not borrowed $18,300 to buy the additional 1,000 shares, his profit would be only $9,000. Suppose, instead, the price of GM stock decreases to $11.30 per share. Then, by borrowing to buy 500 additional shares, Mr. Huang lost $7 per share on 2,000 shares instead of $7 per share on just 1,000 shares.

The funds borrowed to buy the additional stock will be provided by the broker, and the broker gets the money from a bank. The interest rate that banks charge brokers for funds of this purpose is called the **broker call rate** or **call money rate**. For example, on March 17, 2008, the broker call rate was 4.75%. The broker charges the borrowing investor the call money rate plus a service charge.

Brokers are not free to lend as much as they wish to the investor to buy securities. The Securities Exchange Act of 1934 prohibits brokers from lending more than a specified percentage of the market value of the securities. The **initial margin requirement** is the proportion of the total market value of the securities that the investor must pay as an equity share, and the remainder is borrowed from the broker. The 1934 Act gives the Board of Governors of the Federal Reserve (the Fed) the responsibility to set initial margin requirements, which it does under Regulations T and U. The Fed changes margin requirements as an instrument of economic policy. The initial margin requirement for common stock has been below 40%; it was 50% as of March 2008. Initial margin requirements vary for stocks and bonds.

The Fed also establishes a **maintenance margin requirement**. This is the minimum proportion of (1) the equity in the investor's margin account to (2) the total market value. If the investor's margin account falls below the minimum maintenance margin (which would happen if the share's price fell), the investor is required to put up additional cash. The investor receives a margin call from the broker specifying the additional cash to be put into the investor's margin account. If the investor fails to put up the additional cash, the broker has the authority to sell the securities for the investor's account. As of March 2008, the maintenance margin requirement was 30%.

Let us illustrate the maintenance margin requirement. Assume an investor buys 100 shares of a stock at $60 per share for $6,000 of stock on 50% margin and the maintenance margin is 30%. By purchasing $6,000 of a stock on 50% margin, the investor must put up $3,000 of cash (or other equity) and, thus, borrows $3,000 (referred to as the "debit balance"). The investor, however, must maintain 30% margin. To what level must the stock price decline to hit the maintenance margin level? The price is $42.86. At this price, the stock position has a value of $4,286 ($42.86 × 100 shares). With a loan of $3,000, the equity in the account is $1,286 ($4,286 − $3,000), or 30% of the account value ($1,286/$4,286 = 30%). If the price of the stock decreases below $42.86, the investor must deposit more equity to bring the equity level up to 30%.

There are also margin practices for short selling. Consider a similar margin example for a short position. An investor shorts (borrows and sells) 100 shares of a stock at $60 for a total stock value of $6,000. With an initial margin of 50%, the investor must deposit $3,000 (in addition to leaving the $6,000 from the sale in the account). This leaves the investor with a credit balance of $9,000 (which does not change with the stock price since it is in cash). However, the investor owes 100 shares of the stock at the current market price. To what level must the stock price increase to hit the maintenance margin level, assumed to be 30% (which is the equity in the account as a percentage of the market value of the stock)? The answer is $69.23, for a total stock value of $6,923. If the stock is worth $6,923, there is $2,077 of equity in the account ($9,000 − $6,923), which represents 30% of the market value of the stock ($2,077/$6,923 = 30%). The value of the stock that triggered the maintenance level is calculated by multiplying the credit balance by 10/13 (10/13 × $9,000 = $6,923).

Key Points That You Should Understand Before Proceeding

1. The different types of orders that can be placed when purchasing common stock and the advantages and disadvantages of each type.
2. The mean of selling short and the mechanisms for doing so.
3. What margin transactions are and the mechanics of buying on margin.
4. The risks associated with short selling and margin transactions.

TRANSACTION COSTS

An important aspect of an investment strategy is controlling the transaction costs necessary to implement the strategy. **Transaction costs**, also referred to as **trading costs**, can be decomposed into two major components: explicit costs and implicit costs. *Explicit costs* are the direct costs of trading, such as broker commissions, fees, and taxes. *Implicit costs* represent such indirect costs as the price impact of the trade and the opportunity costs of failing to execute in a timely manner or at all. Whereas explicit costs are associated with identifiable accounting charges, no such reporting of implicit costs occurs.

Explicit Costs

The main explicit cost is the commission paid to the broker for execution. Commission costs are fully negotiable and vary systematically by broker type and market mechanism. The commission may depend on both the price per share and the number of shares in the transaction.[4] In addition to commissions, there may be other explicit costs. These explicit costs include *custodial fees* (the fees charged by an institution that holds securities in safekeeping for an investor) and *transfer fees* (the fees associated from transferring an asset from one owner to another).

Soft Dollars

Investors often choose their broker/dealer based on who will give them the best execution at the lowest transaction cost on a specific transaction, and also based on who will provide complementary services (such as research) over a period of time. Order flow can also be "purchased" by a broker/dealer from an investor with **soft dollars**. In this case, the broker/dealer provides the investor, without explicit charge, services such as research or electronic services, typically from a third party for which the investor would otherwise have had to pay "hard dollars" to the third party, in exchange for the investor's order flow. Of course, the investor pays the broker/dealer for the execution service.

According to such a relationship, the investor preferentially routes their order to the broker/dealer specified in the soft dollar relationship and does not have to pay "hard dollars," or real money, for the research or other services. This practice is called paying "soft dollars" (i.e., directing their order flow) for the ancillary research. For example, client A preferentially directs his order flow to broker/dealer B (often a specified amount of order flow over a specified period, such as a month or year) and pays the broker/dealer for these execution services. In turn, broker/dealer B pays for some research services provided to

---

[4] For more on this point, see Bruce M. Collins and Frank J. Fabozzi, "A Methodology for Measuring Transactions Costs," *Financial Analysts Journal* (March/April 1991), pp. 27–36.

client A. Very often the research provider is a separate firm, say, firm C. Thus, soft dollars refer to money paid by an investor to a broker/dealer or a third party through commission revenue rather than by direct payments.

The disadvantage to the broker/dealer is that they have to pay hard dollars (to the research provider) for the client's order flow. The disadvantage to the client is that they are not free to "shop around" for the best bid or best offer, net of commissions, for all their transactions, but have to do an agreed amount of transaction volume with the specific broker/dealer. In addition, the research provider may give a preferential price to the broker/dealer. Thus, each of these participants in the soft dollar relationship experiences some advantage, but also an offsetting disadvantage.

The SEC has imposed formal and informal limitations on the type and amount of soft dollar business institutional investors can conduct. For example, while an institutional investor can accept research in a soft dollar relationship, they cannot accept furniture or vacations. SEC disclosure rules, passed in 1995, require investment advisors to disclose, among other things, the details on any product or services received through soft dollars.[5]

Implicit Costs

Implicit trading costs include impact costs, timing costs, and opportunity costs.

Impact Costs

The **impact cost** of a transaction is the change in market price due to supply/demand imbalances caused by the presence of the trade. Bid–ask spread estimates, although informative, fail to capture the fact that large trades—those that exceed the number of shares the market maker is willing to trade at the quoted bid and ask prices—may move prices in the direction of the trade. That is, large trades can increase the price for buy orders and decrease the price for sell orders. The resulting *market impact* or *price impact* of the transaction can be thought of as the deviation of the transaction price from the "unperturbed price" that would have prevailed had the trade not occurred. As discussed previously, crossing networks are designed to minimize impact costs.

Timing Costs

The **timing cost** is measured as the price change between the time the parties to the implementation process assume responsibility for the trade and the time they complete the responsibility. Timing costs occur when orders are on the trading desk of a buy-side firm (e.g., an asset mangement firm) but have not been released to the broker because the trader fears that the trade may swamp the market.

Opportunity Costs

The *opportunity cost* is the "cost" of securities not traded. This cost results from missed or only partially completed trades. These costs are the natural consequence of the release delays. For example, if the price moves too much before the trade can be completed, the manager will not make the trade. In practice, this cost is measured on shares not traded based on the difference between the market price at the time of decision and the closing price 30 days later.

---

[5] The CFA Institute has published standards that provide guidance as to how investment professionals should utilize soft dollars in a manner that benefits clients.

Whereas commissions and impact costs are actual and visible out-of-pocket costs, opportunity costs and timing costs are the costs of foregone opportunities and are invisible. Opportunity costs can arise for two reasons. First, some orders are executed with a delay, during which the price moves against the investor. Second, some orders incur an opportunity cost because they are only partially filled or are not executed at all.

Key Points That You Should Understand Before Proceeding

1. There are two major components of transaction costs: explicit costs and implicit costs.
2. Explicit transaction costs are commissions, custodial fees, and transfer fees.
3. What a soft dollar arrangement is.
4. Implicit trading costs include impact costs, timing costs, and opportunity costs.

TRADING ARRANGEMENTS FOR RETAIL AND INSTITUTIONAL INVESTORS

Trades are executed by both individuals, called retail investors, and institutions. There are several differences in the way they trade. The first is size: Institutions typically transact much larger orders than individuals. The second is commissions: Consistent with their larger size, institutions typically pay lower commissions than individuals.

The third difference is the method of order execution. Although both an individual and an institution can trade through a broker-dealer, the ways in which their orders are entered and executed may be considerably different, even if the trades are through the same broker-dealer. An individual trading through a broker-dealer typically goes through a stockbroker. In the next chapter, we will see how these trades are executed.

Institutional investors typically give their order directly to the institutional broker-dealer execution desk, for both exchange and OTC orders. Exchange orders may be sent to the broker-dealer's floor broker, and OTC orders may be transacted with another broker-dealer or internalized (which we will explain in the next chapter) at a competitive bid or offer. Competing bids or offers are typically obtained in all cases.

Because of these differences in the execution of stock trades by individuals and institutions, the trends in common stock holdings is of consequence. During the past 50 years, common stock holdings in the United States have become increasingly institutionalized. The major institutional holders are pension funds (private [usually corporate], state and local government [called public], and labor union), asset management companies (investment companies and hedge funds), life insurance companies, bank trusts, endowments, and foundations.

Historically, there has been a decline in the direct household ownership of common stocks. This decline does not necessarily lead to the conclusion that households have decreased their common stock holdings. Rather, it means that households are holding more of their common stock through intermediaries such as mutual funds rather than directly in the form of common stock. Thus, households have "intermediated" their stock holdings. Although households hold more total common stock than before, they hold less common stock directly, and, thus, increasingly the stock executions are done by institutions, such as mutual funds, rather than by individuals.

Retail Stock Trading

Since May Day 1975, stock trading commissions have declined both for institutions and individuals. However, prior to about 1990, individuals traded stocks mainly through so-called "full-service brokers," where their commissions reflected not only the stock trade execution but also the counsel of a stockbroker and perhaps research. The largest full-service broker-dealers are also known as "wirehouses." These firms typically do institutional trading and investment banking as well as retail business. The commissions for these full-service brokers have declined since 1975.

A discount broker industry has also developed in which the stockbroker provides advice and no research. Individuals enter their orders via a telephone. More recently, individuals have been able to enter their orders via their computer: These are called online or Web-based brokerage firms. Consistent with the lower provision of service by discount brokers and online brokers, stock trading commissions decreased significantly. Thus, individuals could trade and own stocks more efficiently.

To remain competitive to a wide range of clients in this environment, the traditional full-service brokerage firms responded by offering their customers alternative means of transacting common stock. For example, many full-service brokerage firms offer the traditional services of a stockbroker and research at a high commission, and, in addition, offer direct order entry only at a lower commission. On the other hand, some discount brokers have begun to offer more service at a higher commission.

Institutional Trading

With the increase in trading by institutional investors, trading arrangements more suitable to these investors had to be developed. Their needs included trading in large size and trading groups of stocks, both at a low commission and with low market impact. This has resulted in the evolution of special arrangements for the execution of certain types of orders commonly sought by institutional investors: (1) orders requiring the execution of a trade of a large number of shares of a given stock, and (2) orders requiring the execution of trades in a large number of different stocks at as near the same time as possible. The former types of trades are called block trades; the latter are called program trades. An example of a block trade is a mutual fund that seeks to buy 15,000 shares of IBM stock. An example of a program trade is a pension fund that wants to buy shares of 200 names (companies) weighted by their market capitalization at the end of a trading day ("at the close").

The institutional arrangement that has evolved to accommodate these two types of institutional trades is the development of a network of trading desks of the major securities firms and other institutional investors who communicate with each other by means of electronic display systems and telephones. This network is referred to as the **upstairs market**. Participants in the upstairs market play a key role (1) by providing liquidity to the market so that such institutional trades can be executed, and (2) by arbitrage activities that help to integrate the fragmented stock market. We will have more to say about the upstairs market in the next chapter.

Block Trades

As noted previously in this chapter, the NYSE defines block trades as trades of either at least 10,000 shares of a given stock or trades of shares with a market value of at least $200,000, whichever is less. Since the execution of large numbers of block orders places strains on the

NYSE's specialist system (which is explained in the next chapter), special procedures have been developed to handle them. Typically, an institutional customer contacts its salesperson at a brokerage firm, indicating that it wishes to place a block order. The salesperson then gives the order to the brokerage firm's block execution department. Notice that the salesperson does not submit the order to be executed to an exchange. The sales traders in the block execution department then contact other institutions to attempt to find one or more institutions that would be willing to take the other side of the order. That is, they use the upstairs market in their search to fill the block trade order. If this can be accomplished, the execution of the order is completed.

If the sales traders cannot find enough institutions to take the entire block (for example, if the block trade order is for 40,000 shares of IBM, but only 25,000 can be "crossed" with other institutions), then the balance of the block trade order is given to the brokerage firm's market maker. There are two choices. First, the brokerage firm can take a position in the stock and buy the shares for its own account. Second, the unfilled order can be executed by using the services of competing market makers. In the former case, the brokerage firm is committing its own capital.

Program Trades

Program trades involve the buying and/or selling of a large number of names simultaneously. Such trades are also called **basket trades** because effectively a "basket" of stocks is being traded. The NYSE defines a program trade as any trade involving the purchase or sale of a basket of at least 15 stocks with a total value of $1 million or more.

The two major applications of program trades are asset allocation and index arbitrage. With respect to asset allocation trades, some examples of why an institutional investor may want to use a program trade are deployment of new cash into the stock market; implementation of a decision to move funds invested in the bond market to the stock market (or vice versa); and rebalancing the composition of a stock portfolio because of a change in investment strategy. A mutual fund money manager can, for example, move funds quickly into or out of the stock market for an entire portfolio of stocks through a single program trade. All these strategies are related to asset allocation.

The growth of mutual fund sales and massive equity investments by pension funds, hedge funds, and insurance companies during the 1990s have all given an impetus to such methods to trade baskets or bundles of stocks efficiently. Other reasons for which an institutional investor may have a need to execute a program trade should be apparent later when we discuss an investment strategy called indexing.

Program trading is also used for a strategy called index arbitrage. The price of a stock index futures contract is derived from the underlying cash product, namely the stocks included in the stock index. Specifically, there is a mathematical relationship between the price of the stock index futures contracts and the value of the stocks included in the index taking into account transaction costs and the cost of borrowing funds. This relationship establishes bounds for the price of the stock index futures contract. When the price of the stock index futures contract deviates from these bounds, there is an opportunity for a riskless profit by trading the two. For example, suppose that the price of the S&P 500 futures contract is higher than the upper bound established by the cash market price of the basket of 500 stocks and transaction costs and borrowing costs. Then, it would be profitable to sell the index in the futures market and buy the basket in the cash market. To the NYSE specialists, this would show up as a large simultaneous purchase of all stocks in the S&P 500 index. Index fund managers sometimes use program trades to choose between taking a position in the stock market by buying or selling stock or by buying or selling stock index futures contracts.

Several commission arrangements are available to an institution for a program trade, and each arrangement has numerous variants. Considerations in selecting one (in addition to commission costs) are the risks of failing to realize the best execution price and that the brokerage firms executing the program trade will use their knowledge of the program trade to benefit from the anticipated price movement that might result—in other words, that they will **frontrun** the transaction, for example, buying a stock for their own account before filling the customer buy order.

From a dealer's perspective, program trades can be conducted in two ways, namely, on an *agency basis* and on a *principal basis*. An intermediate type of program trade, the agency incentive arrangement, is also an alternative. A program trade executed on an agency basis involves the selection by the investor of a brokerage firm solely on the basis of commission bids (cents per share) submitted by various brokerage firms. The brokerage firm selected uses its best efforts as an agent of the institution to obtain the best price. Such trades have low explicit commissions. To the investor, the disadvantage of the agency program trade is that, while commissions may be the lowest, the execution price may not be the best because of impact costs and the potential frontrunning by the brokerage firms that were solicited to submit a commission bid. The investor knows in advance the commission paid but does not know the price at which its trades will be executed. Another disadvantage is that there is increased risk of adverse selection of the counterparty in the execution process.

Related to the agency basis is an *agency incentive arrangement*, in which a benchmark portfolio value is established for the group of stocks in the program trade. The price for each "name" (i.e., specific stock) in the program trade is determined as either the price at the end of the previous day or the average price of the previous day. If the brokerage firm can execute the trade on the next trading day such that a better-than-benchmark portfolio value results—a higher value in the case of a program trade involving selling, or a lower value in the case of a program trade involving buying—then the brokerage firm receives the specified commission plus some predetermined additional compensation. In this case, the investor does not know in advance the commission or the execution price precisely but has a reasonable expectation that the price will be better than a threshold level.

What if the brokerage firm does not achieve the benchmark portfolio value? It is in such a case that the variants come into play. One arrangement may call for the brokerage firm to receive just a previously agreed-upon commission. Other arrangements may involve sharing the risk of not realizing the benchmark portfolio value with the brokerage firm. That is, if the brokerage firm falls short of the benchmark portfolio value, it must absorb a portion of the shortfall. In these risk-sharing arrangements, the brokerage firm is risking its own capital. The greater the risk-sharing that the brokerage firm must accept, the higher the commission it will charge.

The brokerage firm can also choose to execute the trade on a principal basis. In this case, the dealer would commit its own capital to buy or sell the portfolio and complete the investor's transaction immediately. Since the dealer incurs market risk, it would also charge higher commissions. The key factors in pricing principal trades are liquidity characteristics, absolute dollar value, nature of trade, customer profile, and market volatility. In this case, the investor knows the trade execution price in advance but pays a higher commission.

To minimize frontrunning, institutions often use other types of program trade arrangements. They call for brokerage firms to receive aggregate statistical information about key portfolio parameters rather than specific names and quantities of stocks. Several brokerage firms then bid on a cents-per-share basis on the entire portfolio (also called blind baskets), guaranteeing execution at either closing price (termed market-at-close) or a particular intra-day price to the customer. Note that this is a principal trade. Since mutual fund net asset values are calculated using closing prices, a mutual fund that follows an indexing strategy (i.e., an index fund), for instance, would want guaranteed market-at-close execution to minimize its risk of not performing as well as the stock index. When the winning bidder has been selected, it receives the details of the portfolio. Although the commission in this type of transaction is higher, this procedure increases the risk to the brokerage firm of successfully executing the program trade. However, the brokerage firm can use stock index futures to protect itself from market-wide movements if the characteristics of the portfolio in the program trade are similar to the index underlying the stock index futures contract.

Brokerage firms can also execute the trade in the upstairs market or send orders electronically to an exchange. The counterparties in program trades are viewed as uninformed traders; that is, the entity asked to execute the order knows that the trade is being made for index-wide or portfolio-wide reasons and not stock-specific reasons. Such trades are called *informationless trades*.

Key Points That You Should Understand Before Proceeding

1. The reasons retail stock trading has become more attractive.
2. What block trading and program trading are and how they accommodate the trading needs of institutional investors.
3. The different types of commission arrangements for program trades.
4. The meaning of the term frontrunning and how institutional investors can avoid this problem.

BASIC FUNCTIONING OF STOCK MARKETS

In this section, we describe the basic functioning of stock markets, which includes:

- price reporting
- regulation
- clearance and settlement
- tick size
- block trade
- commissions
- price limits and collars

Price Reporting

Price reporting in the U.S. stock markets is conducted by the Consolidated Tape Association (CTA). The CTA oversees the dissemination of real-time trade and quote information (market data) from the NYSE and Amex listed securities (stocks and bonds).

The CTA is an independent, industry-wide organization. CTA manages two systems to govern the collection, processing, and dissemination of trade and quote data. The two systems are the Consolidated Tape System (CTS), which governs trades, and the Consolidated Quotation System (CQS), which governs quotes. Since the late 1970s, all SEC-registered exchanges and market centers that trade NYSE or Amex-listed securities send their trades and quotes to a central consolidator where the CTS and CQS data streams are produced and distributed worldwide.

The data collected by the CTA are provided on two networks, Network A (or Tape A) for NYSE-listed securities that is administered by the NYSE and Network B (or Tape B) for Amex and regional exchange-listed securities that is administered by the Amex. Nasdaq operates a similar tape for its listed securities, which is called Network C (or Tape C).

CTS is the electronic service that provides last sale and trade data for issues listed on the NYSE, Amex, and U.S. regional stock exchanges and was introduced in April 1976. CTS is the basis for the trade reports from the consolidated tape that runs across television screens on financial news programs or on the Internet sites. The "consolidated tape" is a high-speed, electronic system that constantly reports the latest price and volume data on sales of exchange-listed stocks.

CQS is the electronic service that provides quotation information for issues listed on the NYSE, Amex, and U.S. regional stock exchanges that are discussed in the next section. For every quote message received from a market center, CQS calculates a national best bid and offer (NBBO) based on a price, size, and time priority schema. We will explain the meaning of BBO in the next chapter. If the quote is a Nasdaq market maker quote, CQS also calculates a Nasdaq BBO. CQS disseminates the market center's root quote with an appendage that includes the National and Nasdaq BBOs.

In general, Tapes A and B are referred to as the "CTS Tapes" and Tape C as the "Nasdaq Tapes."

Regulation

The basis for the federal government regulation of the stock market resides with the SEC. The SEC's authority is primarily based on two important pieces of federal legislation. The first is the Securities Act of 1933 (the "Securities Act"), which covers the primary markets, that is, the new issues of securities. The second is the Securities Act of 1934 (the "Exchange Act"), which covers the secondary markets. The SEC was created by the Exchange Act.

In addition to the SEC regulations, the exchanges also play a role in their own regulation through self-regulating organizations (SROs). The SRO of the NYSE has been responsible for the member regulation, enforcement, and arbitration functions of the NYSE. In addition, the NASD has had the SEC authority to set standards for its member firms and standards of conduct for issuing securities and selling securities to the public. The NASD has also monitored the Nasdaq stock market. There have, however, been some overlapping responsibilities of these two SROs and, thus, some competition between them.

As a result, these two SROs merged and in July 2007 were replaced by a single organization, FINRA (the Financial Industry Regulation Authority), which consolidated the NASD and the member regulation, enforcement, and arbitration functions of NYSE. This consolidation resulted in all firms dealing with only one rulebook, one set of examiners, and one enforcement staff, thereby reducing costs and inconsistencies. Thus, FINRA is the single remaining SRO.

Clearance and Settlement

After a stock trade is completed, the delivery of the shares by the seller and the payment of cash by the buyer must occur quickly and efficiently. The efficiency of the trade settlement affects the total speed and the overall cost of the transaction. In the United States, there are several execution mechanisms (exchanges and other) for stocks. There is, however, only a single clearance and settlement mechanism for securities, the Depository Trust and Clearing Corporation (DTTC). In stock options, similarly, there is only one clearing mechanism, the Options Clearing Corporation (OCC).

In the futures markets, however, there are several clearing organizations, each typically associated with the related exchange. This control over clearing by futures exchanges makes it easier for them to preserve their monopolies in trading and also gives them a significant source of profitability. During February 2008, however, the U.S. Department of Justice questioned whether futures exchanges should be allowed to own or control clearing businesses that process their trades. The issue is whether futures clearing will become centralized like stock and options clearing.

All clearance and settlement services for the U.S. equities market (as well as corporate bonds, municipal bonds, exchange-traded funds, and unit investment trusts trades) are provided by the National Securities Clearance Corporation (NSCC). NSCC is a wholly owned subsidiary of the DTCC. NSCC generally clears and settles trades on a T+3 basis (that is, three business days after the trade date). DTCC is essentially a utility organization for the exchanges.

Other subsidiaries of DTCC provide clearance and settlement for other products and also trust services.

Tick Size

The minimum price variation for a security is referred to as its **tick size**. The U.S. stock market historically had a tick size of 1/8th of one point. The SEC wanted to reduce the bid–offer spread to increase the competition and lower costs. As a result, the NYSE and Nasdaq reduced the tick size first to 1/16th and then, in 2001, to pennies (1 cent).

This reduction in the tick size narrowed the bid–offer spread considerably, which reduced the costs to customers and the profits of the market makers. In addition, as an unintended consequence, it negatively affected the liquidity of the market. With pennies there are 100 pricing points per dollar, while with eights there are only eight. So with pennies, there is less liquidity at each pricing point and so there is less depth at the inside market (the best bid and best offer or the "top of the book"). (We will describe what is meant by the inside market in the next chapter.) Since only the top of the book is displayed, the advent of pennies reduced transparency and was one of the reasons for the development of dark pools, as discussed in the next chapter.

In addition, with pennies, quotes (bids or offers) are changed more frequently, and so the technology must have lower *latency*. Low latency, that is, a small amount of time necessary to complete an instruction, means high speed. Latency below 1 millisecond is now common. As indicated above, the advent of pennies is one reason for the development and growth of algorithmic trading, discussed in the next chapter. Sub-penny pricing is prohibited except for the stocks that trade for less than a dollar.

Block Trades

A *block* is a large holding or transaction of stock, generally 10,000 or more shares or any amount over $200,000. In a *block trade* (a "block facilitation trade") a broker-dealer commits capital to accommodate a large trade for an institutional customer. These trades are conducted "upstairs" (off the exchange) and "shown to" the market, for potential price improvement. Block trades are reported through the standard price reporting systems. With the growth in algorithmic trading, however, blocks that have traditionally been accomplished "upstairs" via internalization are now accomplished via algorithmic trading.

Commissions

Before 1975, stock exchanges were allowed to set minimum commissions on transactions. The fixed-commission structure did not allow the commission rate to decline as the number of shares in the order increased, thereby ignoring the economies of scale in executing transactions.

Pressure from institutional investors, who transacted large trades, led the SEC to eliminate fixed-commission rates in 1975. Since May 1, 1975, popularly referred to as Black Thursday (or May Day as previously indicated), commissions have been fully negotiable between investors and their brokers. Black Thursday began a period of severe price competition among brokers, with many firms failing, and a consolidation of firms taking place in the brokerage industry. This liberalization of commissions was the U.S. version of the "Big Bang," which was followed in the United Kingdom during 1986 and Japan during 1996.

Since the introduction of negotiated commissions, the opportunity has arisen for the development of discount brokers. These brokers charge commissions at rates much less than those charged by other brokers, but offer little or no advice or any other service apart from the execution of the transaction. Discount brokers have been particularly effective in inducing retail investors to participate in the market for individual stocks.

Price Limits and Collars

On Monday, October 19, 1987, popularly referred to as "Black Monday," the U.S. stock market experienced the largest single-day decline in its history at that time. (The largest decline occurred on September 29, 2008.) This event is often referred to simply as "the crash." On that day, a popular market index that we discuss later in this chapter, the Dow Jones Industrial Average (DJIA), declined by 23%, and other market indexes declined by roughly the same amount.

Afterward, the U.S. government and some exchanges commissioned several studies to assess the causes of the crash and to offer possible remedial measures to prevent any recurrence. Several government-sponsored studies and exchange-sponsored studies were conducted, including a study by a presidential task force that became known as the Brady Report.[6] These studies explained the crash as the result of (1) deficiencies in institutional arrangements in stock trading, (2) an overvaluation of stock prices, and (3) various forms of overreaction to economic news.

While several potential reasons for the crash were identified, no unambiguous conclusions resulted. One clear dynamic for the price decline, however, did exist. This dynamic

---

[6] Brady Report, *Presidential Task Force on Market Mechanisms*, 1988.

was that selling caused price declines, which caused further selling, and so on. (The opposite dynamic of "buying on dips" occurs when price declines cause buying rather than selling, which became more common after the crash.) Two potential reasons explain why price declines cause further selling. One is emotional; that is, price declines cause fear, which causes further selling. The second is a trading strategy, used by some institutional investors, that exacerbates any plunge in the market.[7] A stock market policy called *trading limits* or *price limits* resulted from Black Monday. Trading or price limits specify a minimum price limit, below which the market price index level may not decline due to an institutionally mandated termination of trading, at least at prices below the specified price (the price limit), for a specified period of time. For example, if the DJIA was trading at 11,000 and its price limit was 500 points below that, then no trades could occur below 10,500. This pause in trading is intended to "give the market a breather" to at least calm emotions. Previously, trading limits were used in the futures markets but not in the stock market.

Soon after the crash, the NYSE and other exchanges implemented these price limits, which they modified several times, bringing limits to their present design. Two different types of price limits are circuit breakers and trading collars. We discuss each below.

Circuit Breaker Rule

A **circuit breaker** is a temporary halting of trading during a severe market decline. The key to instituting circuit breakers is coordination and infrequency. As stated by the Working Group on Financial Markets, which included the high-level representatives of the SEC, U.S. Treasury, Federal Reserve Board, and Commodity Futures Trading Commision:

> [A] circuit breaker mechanism should be put in place that operates in a coordinated fashion across all markets, using pre-established limits broad enough to be tripped only on rare occasions, but which are sufficient to support the ability of payment and credit systems to keep pace with extraordinarily large market declines."[8]

Coordination across markets is important because of the interrelationship between the stock market, stock index futures market, and stock index options markets. The infrequency of temporarily suspending trading was emphasized by several studies following Black Monday. These studies note that too frequent halting of trading other than those in the case of extreme movements impedes price discovery and does not allow the efficient implementation of portfolio strategies by investors.

On April 15, 1998, the NYSE, following approval by the SEC, implemented new regulations to increase and widen thresholds at which trading is halted for single-day declines. The stock market indicator that was selected to measure the decline in the market was the DJIA. The point levels are set quarterly at 10% (Level One circuit breaker), 20% (Level Two circuit breaker), and 30% (Level Three circuit breaker) of the DJIA by using the DJIA average closing value of the previous month, rounded to the nearest 50 points. Point levels are adjusted on January 1, April 1, July 1, and October 1. The formulas for these thresholds are set forth in the NYSE Rule 80B.

---

[7] The strategy was called "portfolio insurance" or dynamic asset allocation.
[8] U.S. Senate hearing before the Committee on Banking, Housing, and Urban Affairs on May 24, 1988: "The Conclusions and Recommendations of the President's 'Working Group on Financial Markets.'"

For example, consider the circuit breakers established on April 1, 2007. The average value for the DJIA for March 2007 rounded to the nearest 50 points was used to calculate the three point levels. This resulted in the Level One (10%) circuit breaker set at 1,250 points, Level Two (20%) circuit breaker set at 2,450 points, and the Level Three (30%) circuit breaker set at 3,700 points. Each level then results in a different halting of activity. For example:

Level One: A 1,250-point drop in the DJIA halts trading for one hour if the decline occurs before 14:00; for 30 minutes if before 14:30; and has no effect between 14:30 and 16:00.

Level Two: A 2,450-point drop halts trading for two hours if the decline occurs before 13:00; for one hour if before 14:00; and for the rest of the day if after 14:00.

Level Three: A 3,700-point drop halts trading for the remainder of the day regardless of when the decline occurs.

Trading Collar Rule

Another type of trading restriction applies to index arbitrage trading whereby, for example, a basket of S&P 500 stocks is bought (sold) against the sale (purchase) of an S&P 500 futures contract. On February 16, 1999, following approval by the SEC, the NYSE implemented revisions to Rule 80A (the **trading collar rule**), which restricts index arbitrage trading. Under the revised rule, if the DJIA moves up or down 2% from the previous closing value, program trading orders to buy or sell the S&P 500 stocks as part of index arbitrage strategies must be entered with directions to have the order executions affected in a manner that stabilizes share prices. The collar restrictions are removed if the DJIA returns to or within 1% of its previous closing value. The trading collar rule's threshold of 2% is calculated at the beginning of each quarter. For example, on April 1, 2007, the average value for the DJIA for March 2007 was used to calculate a 2% collar trading rule threshold of 180 points.

STOCK MARKET INDICATORS

Stock market indicators have come to perform a variety of functions, from serving as benchmarks for evaluating the performance of professional money managers to answering the question "How did the market do today?" Thus, stock **market indicators** (**indexes** or averages) have become a part of everyday life. Even though many of the stock market indicators are used interchangeably, it is important to realize that each indicator applies to, and measures, a different facet of the stock market.

The most commonly quoted stock market indicator is the Dow Jones Industrial Average (DJIA). Other stock market indicators cited in the financial press are the Standard & Poor's 500 Composite (S&P 500), the New York Stock Exchange Composite Index (NYSE Composite), and the Nasdaq Composite Index. A myriad of other stock market indicators, such as the Wilshire, Russell, and Morgan Stanley stock indexes, are followed primarily by institutional money managers. Table 2 provides a list of the various stock indexes traded in the United States.

In general, stock market indexes rise and fall in fairly similar patterns. The indexes do not move in exactly the same ways at all times. The differences in movement reflect the different ways in which the indexes are constructed. Three factors enter into that construction: the universe of stocks represented by the sample underlying the index, the relative

Table 2   Stock Indexes Traded in the United States

Exchange Provided Indexes

NEW YORK STOCK EXCHANGE

NYSE Composite Index

NYSE U.S. 100 Index

NYSE World Leaders Index

NYSE TMT Index

THE AMERICAN STOCK EXCHANGE

Amex Composite

Amex 20 Stock Index

Amex Airline Index

Amex Basic Industries Sector Index

Amex Biotech Index

Amex Broker/Dealer Index

Amex Composite Index

Amex Computer Technology Index

Amex Consumer Service Sector Index

Amex Consumer Staples Sector Index

Amex CSFB Technology Index

Amex Cyclical/Transport Sector Index

Amex Defense Index I

Amex Disk Drive Index

Amex Drug Index

Amex Electric Power & Natural Gas

Amex Energy Sector Index

Amex Financial Sector Index

Amex Gold Bugs

Amex Industrial Sector Index

Amex LT 20 Index

Amex MS Consumer Index

Amex MS Cyclical Index

Amex MS Healthcare Payer Index

Amex MS Healthcare Products Index

Amex MS Healthcare Providers Index

Amex MS Hi-Tech 35 Index

Amex MS REIT Index

Amex Natural Gas Index

Amex Networking Index

Amex Oil & Gas Index

Amex Stockcar Stocks

Amex Technology Sector Index

(Continued)

Table 2   Stock Indexes Traded in the United States (Continued)

Amex Telecomm Index

Amex Utility Sector Index

Institutional Index

NASDAQ

NASDAQ Composite Index

NASDAQ National Market Composite Index

NASDAQ-100 Index

NASDAQ-100 Equal Weighted Index

NASDAQ-100 Technology Sector Index

NASDAQ-100 Ex-Tech Sector Index

NASDAQ Financial-100 Index

NASDAQ Biotechnology Index

NASDAQ Biotechnology Equal Weighted Index

NASDAQ Bank Index

NASDAQ Computer Index

NASDAQ Health Care Index

NASDAQ Industrial Index

NASDAQ National Market Industrial Index

NASDAQ Insurance Index

NASDAQ Other Finance Index

NASDAQ Telecommunications Index

NASDAQ Transportation Index

Non-Exchange Indexes

DOW JONES & CO.

Dow Jones Average—30 Industrial

Dow Jones Average—20 Transportation

Dow Jones Average—15 Utilities

DOW JONES & CO./WILSHIRE ASSOCIATES

Dow Jones Wilshire 5000 Total Market Index

The Dow Jones Wilshire 4500 Completion Index

Dow Jones Wilshire U.S. Large-Cap Index

Dow Jones Wilshire U.S. Mid-Cap Index

Dow Jones Wilshire U.S. Small-Cap Index

Dow Jones Wilshire U.S. Micro-Cap Index

Dow Jones Wilshire U.S. Large-Cap Value Index

Dow Jones Wilshire U.S. Large-Cap Growth Index

Dow Jones Wilshire U.S. Mid-Cap Value Index

Dow Jones Wilshire U.S. Mid-Cap Growth Index

Dow Jones Wilshire U.S. Small-Cap Value Index

(Continued)

Table 2   Stock Indexes Traded in the United States (Continued)

Dow Jones Wilshire U.S. Small-Cap Growth Index

Dow Jones Wilshire U.S. 2500 Index

The Wilshire Large Cap 750 Index

The Wilshire Mid-Cap 500 Index

The Wilshire Small Cap 1750 Index

The Wilshire Micro-Cap Index

The Wilshire Large Value Index

The Wilshire Large Growth Index

The Wilshire Mid-Cap Value Index

The Wilshire Mid-Cap Growth Index

The Wilshire Small Value Index

The Wilshire Small Growth Index

The Wilshire All Value Index

The Wilshire All Growth Index

The Wilshire Small Cap 250

STANDARD & POOR'S

S&P Composite 1500 Index

S&P 100 Index

S&P 500 Index

S&P Midcap 400 Index

S&P Smallcap 600 Index

FRANK RUSSELL

Russell—3000 Index

Russell—2000 Index

Russell—1000 Index

Russell 2000 Growth

Russell 2000 Value

Russell 1000 Growth

Russell 1000 Value

Frank Russell—Midcap Index

MSCI BARRA

MSCI US Broad Market Index

MSCI US Prime Market 750 Index

MSCI US Prime Market Value Index

MSCI US Prime Market Growth Index

MSCI US Mid Cap 450 Index

MSCI US Small Cap 1750 Index

MSCI US Small Cap Value Index

MSCI US Small Cap Growth Index

MSCI US Investable Market Consumer Discretionary Index

(Continued)

Table 2	Stock Indexes Traded in the United States (Continued)
	MSCI US Investable Market Consumer Staples Index
	MSCI US Investable Market Energy Index
	MSCI US Investable Market Financials Index
	MSCI US Investable Market Health Care Index
	MSCI US Investable Market Industrials Index
	MSCI US Investable Market Information Technology Index
	MSCI US Investable Market Materials Index
	MSCI US Investable Market Telecommunications Index
	MSCI US Investable Market Utilities Index

Source: *Compiled by the authors. The indexes listed in this table do not include indexes on non–U.S. stock markets nor non–U.S. companies.*

weights assigned to the stocks included in the index, and the method of averaging across all the stocks in the index.

Stock market indicators can be classified into three groups:

- those produced by stock exchanges based on all stocks traded on the exchanges
- those produced by organizations that subjectively select the stocks to be included in indexes
- those where stock selection is based on an objective measure, such as the market capitalization of the company

The first group includes the New York Stock Exchange Composite Index, which reflects the market value of all stocks traded on the exchange. The two most popular stock market indicators in the second group are the Dow Jones Industrial Average and the Standard & Poor's 500. The DJIA is constructed from 30 of the largest blue-chip industrial companies. The companies included in the average are those selected by Dow Jones & Company, publisher of the *Wall Street Journal*. The S&P 500 represents stocks chosen from the two major national stock exchanges and the over-the-counter market. The stocks in the index at any given time are determined by a committee of Standard & Poor's Corporation, which may occasionally add or delete individual stocks or the stocks of entire industry groups. The aim of the committee is to capture present overall stock market conditions as reflected in a very broad range of economic indicators.

Some indexes represent a broad segment of the stock market while others focus on a particular sector such as technology, oil and gas, and financial. In addition, because the notion of an equity investment style is widely accepted in the investment community, early acceptance of equity style investing in the form of growth versus value and small market capitalization versus large capitalization has led to the creation and proliferation of published *style and market cap indexes*. These indexes are shown in Table 2.

In the third group, we have the Wilshire indexes produced by Wilshire Associates (Santa Monica, California) and Russell indexes produced by the Frank Russell Company (Tacoma, Washington), a consultant to pension funds and other institutional investors. The criterion for inclusion in each of these indexes is solely a firm's market capitalization. The most comprehensive index is the Wilshire 5000, which currently includes more than 6,700 stocks, up from 5,000 at its inception. The Wilshire 4500 includes all stocks in the Wilshire 5000 except for those in the S&P 500. Thus, the shares in the Wilshire 4500 have smaller capitalization than those in the Wilshire 5000. The Russell 3000 encompasses the 3,000 largest companies in terms of their market capitalization. The Russell 1000 is limited to the largest 1,000 of those, and the Russell 2000 has the remaining smaller firms.

The stocks included in a stock market index must be combined in certain proportions, and each stock must be given a weight. The three main approaches to weighting are (1) weighting by the market capitalization of the stock's company, which is the value of the number of shares times the price per share; (2) weighting by the price of the stock; and (3) equal weighting for each stock, regardless of its price or its firm's market value. With the exception of the Dow Jones averages (such as the DJIA), all of the most widely used indexes are market-value weighted. The DJIA is a price-weighted average.

Key Points That You Should Understand Before Proceeding

1. What a market index is and what it is supposed to convey.
2. The key differences among the important stock market indexes in terms of the universe each index represents, the sample of stocks on which it is based, the method of weighting, the method of averaging, and the entity responsible for producing and publishing the index.

PRICING EFFICIENCY OF THE STOCK MARKET

A price-efficient market is one in which security prices at all times fully reflect all available information that is relevant to their valuation. When a market is price efficient, investment strategies pursued to outperform a broad-based stock market index will not consistently produce superior returns after adjusting for risk and transaction costs.

Numerous studies have examined the pricing efficiency of the stock market. While it is not our intent in this chapter to provide a comprehensive review of these studies, we can summarize their basic findings and their implications for investment strategies.

Forms of Efficiency

The three different **forms of pricing efficiency** are

- weak form
- semistrong form
- strong form

The distinctions among these forms lie in the relevant information that is believed to be taken into consideration in the price of the security at all times. *Weak-form efficiency* means that the price of the security reflects the past price and trading history of the security. *Semistrong-form efficiency* means that the price of the security fully reflects all public information (which, of course, includes, but is not limited to, historical price and trading patterns). *Strong-form efficiency* exists in a market where the price of a security reflects all information, whether it is publicly available or known only to insiders such as the firm's managers or directors.

The preponderance of empirical evidence supports the claim that the common stock market is efficient in the weak form. The evidence emerges from statistical tests that explore whether or not historical price movements can be used to project future prices in such a way as to produce returns above what one would expect from market movements and the risk class of the security. Such returns are known as **abnormal returns** and since they are positive they are referred "positive" abnormal returns. The implications are that investors who follow a strategy of selecting stocks solely on the basis of price patterns or trading volume—such investors are referred to as technical analysts or **chartists**—should not expect to do better than the market. In fact, they may fare worse because of higher transactions costs associated with frequent buying and selling of stocks.

Evidence on whether or not the stock market is price efficient in the semistrong form is mixed. Some studies support the proposition of efficiency when they suggest that investors who select stocks on the basis of fundamental security analysis—which consists of analyzing financial statements, the quality of management, and the economic environment of a company—will not outperform the market. This result is certainly reasonable: There are so many analysts using the same approach, with the same publicly available data, that the price of the stock remains in line with all the relevant factors that determine value. On the other hand, a sizable number of other studies have produced evidence indicating that there have been instances and patterns of pricing inefficiency in the stock market over long periods of time. Economists and financial analysts often label these examples of inefficient pricing as **anomalies in the market**, that is, phenomena that cannot be easily explained.

Empirical tests of strong-form pricing efficiency fall into two groups: (1) studies of the performance of professional money managers, and (2) studies of the activities of insiders (individuals who are either company directors, major officers, or major stockholders). Studying the performance of professional money managers to test the strong form of pricing efficiency has been based on the belief that professional managers have access to better information than the general public. Whether or not this is true is moot because the empirical evidence suggests professional managers have not been able to outperform the market consistently. In contrast, evidence based on the activities of insiders has generally revealed that this group often achieves higher returns than the stock market. Of course, insiders could not get those high abnormal returns if the stock prices fully reflected all relevant information about the values of the firms. Thus, the empirical evidence on insider trading argues against the notion that the market is efficient in the strong-form sense.

Implications for Investing in Common Stock

Common stock investment strategies can be classified into two general categories: active strategies and passive strategies. *Active strategies* are those that attempt to outperform the market by one or more of the following: timing the selection of transactions, such as in the case of technical analysis, identifying undervalued or overvalued stocks using **fundamental security analysis**, or selecting stocks according to one of the market anomalies. Obviously, the decision to pursue an active strategy must be based on the belief that there is some type of gain from such costly efforts, but gains are possible only if pricing inefficiencies exist. The particular strategy chosen depends on why the investor believes this is the case.

Investors who believe that the market prices stocks efficiently should accept the implication that any attempts to outperform the market cannot be systematically successful, except by luck. This implication does not mean that investors should shun the stock market, but rather that they should pursue a *passive strategy*, which is one that does not attempt to outperform the market. Is there an optimal investment strategy for someone who holds this belief in the pricing efficiency of the stock market? Indeed there is. Its theoretical basis is the modern portfolio theory and capital market theory. According to modern portfolio theory, the market portfolio offers the highest level of return per unit of risk in a market that is price efficient. A portfolio of financial assets with characteristics similar to those of a portfolio consisting of the entire market—the market portfolio—will capture the pricing efficiency of the market.

How can such a passive strategy be implemented? More specifically, what is meant by a market portfolio, and how should that portfolio be constructed? In theory, the market portfolio consists of all financial assets, not just common stock. The reason is that investors compare all investment opportunities, not just stock, when committing their capital. Thus, our principles of investing must be based on capital market theory, not just stock market theory. When the theory is applied to the stock market, the market portfolio has been defined as consisting of a large universe of common stocks. But how much of each common stock should be purchased when constructing the market portfolio? Theory states that the chosen portfolio should be an appropriate fraction of the market portfolio; hence, the weighting of each stock in the market portfolio should be based on its relative market capitalization. Thus, if the aggregate market capitalization of all stocks included in the market portfolio is $T and the market capitalization of one of these stocks is $A, then the fraction of this stock that should be held in the market portfolio is $A/$T.

The passive strategy that we have just described is called indexing. As pension fund sponsors have increasingly come to believe that money managers are unable to outperform the stock market, the amount of funds managed using an indexing strategy has grown substantially. Index funds, however, still account for a relatively small fraction of institutional stock investments.

Fundamental Indexing

Traditionally, as indicated, most indexes and, thus, index funds have been capitalization weighted. But beginning in 2004, the case began to be made for an alternative weighting methodology. The skeptics of capitalization weighting observed that during the technology bubble of the late 1990s, as the large capitalization growth stocks became what many observers believed was overvalued (based on recent returns, price-to-earnings ratios, and other metrics). Because of their rising prices, their market capitalization increased and, thus, their weights in a market capitalization-weighted index increased. Thus, a market capitalization-weighted index such as the S&P 500 index realized a progressively larger weighting to what were regarded as progressively overpriced stocks.

Some market participants argue that it would be preferable to use a weighting variable that does not reflect market capitalization. Fundamental variables such as dividends, earnings, or sales that reflect size have been suggested.

Consider some comments on this issue. Clearly, market capitalization-weighted indexes have a growth tilt and fundamental indexes have a value tilt. This difference introduces a discussion of the difference between an index and a strategy. Second, market capitalization-weighted indexes provide market clearing portfolios and require no rebalancing as stock prices change. Fundamentally weighted portfolios do not necessarily clear the market and require rebalancing as stock price change. Rebalancing also incurs costs.

The controversy between market capitalization weighting and funds market weighting continues. In practice, capitalization weighting continues to be the dominant practice, but fundamentally weighted mutual funds and ETFs have been introduced.

Overall, investors do not need to have a view on this debate to decide which type of weighting to employ, but simply a view on how they want their portfolios to behave.[9]

Key Points That You Should Understand Before Proceeding

1. The relevant information that is believed to be discounted in the price of a stock at all times for the three forms of pricing efficiency (weak form, semistrong form, and strong form).
2. The implications of the weak form of pricing efficiency for chartists or technical analysts.
3. The implications of the semistrong form of pricing efficiency for fundamental security analysts.
4. The general conclusion about pricing efficiency that empirical research into U.S. markets tends to support.
5. Why the price efficiency of a market influences the decision as to whether an investor will pursue an active strategy or passive strategy.

SUMMARY

Common stock represents an ownership interest in a corporation. The secondary market for common stock has undergone significant changes since the 1960s. The major participants are now institutional investors rather than retail investors, although the availability of discount brokers with their low commissions have induced some retail investors to become more active traders. Advances in computer technology have ushered in developments for linking the various market locations and systems for institution-to-institution direct trading.

Different types of orders may be submitted to the stock markets. The most common type is a market order, which means that the order must be filled immediately at the best price. Other types of orders, such as stop and limit orders, are filled only if the market price reaches a price specified in the order.

In buying and selling stock in the secondary market, the brokerage commission is the most obvious type of trading cost and object of competition among broker-dealers for both institutional and retail investors. However, other types of trading costs, such as impact costs and opportunity costs, may be larger than commissions. To accommodate the trading needs of institutional investors who tend to place orders of larger sizes and with a large number of names, special arrangements have evolved. Block trades are trades of 10,000 shares or more of a given stock or trades with a market value of $200,000 or more. Program

---

[9] For different views on fundamental indexing, see the following: Clifford Asness, "The Value of Fundamental Indexing," *Institutional Investor* (October 2006), pp. 95–99 and Robert Arnott, "An Overwrought Orthodoxy," *Institutional Investor* (December 2006), pp. 36–41.

trades, or basket trades, involve the buying and/or selling of a large number of names simultaneously. The institutional arrangement that has evolved to accommodate these needs is the upstairs market, which is a network of trading desks of the major securities firms and institutional investors that communicate with each other by means of electronic display systems and telephones.

Stock market indicators can be classified into three groups: (1) those produced by stock exchanges and that include all stocks to be traded on the exchange (such as the NYSE Composite Index), (2) those in which a committee subjectively selects the stocks to be included in the index (such as the S&P 500 Index), and (3) those in which the stocks selected are based solely on stocks' market capitalizations (such as the Wishire and Russell indexes).

There are three forms of pricing efficiency according to what is hypothesized to be the relevant information that is believed to be embodied in the price of a stock at all times: (1) weak form, (2) semistrong form, and (3) strong form. Most of the empirical evidence appears to suggest that markets are efficient in the weak form. The evidence on the semi-strong form is mixed, as pockets of inefficiency have been observed. Empirical tests of strong-form pricing efficiency have also produced conflicting results.

Active investment strategies, consisting of efforts to time purchases and select stocks, are pursued by investors who believe that securities are mispriced enough that it is possible to capitalize on strategies that are designed to exploit the perceived inefficiency. The optimal strategy to pursue when the stock market is perceived to be price efficient is indexing because it allows the investor to capture the efficiency of the market.

| KEY TERMS

- Abnormal returns
- Anomalies in the market
- Block trade
- Broker call rate
- Buying on margin
- Call money rate
- Chartist
- Circuit breaker
- Dividends
- Fill or kill order
- Forms of pricing efficiency
- Frontrun
- Fundamental security analysis
- Impact cost
- Initial margin requirement
- Limit order book
- Maintenance margin requirement
- Market capitalization

- Market if touched order
- Market indicator (index)
- Market order
- Odd lot
- Open order
- Preferred stock
- Program (basket) trade
- Qualified dividends
- Round lot
- Soft dollars
- Stop order
- Tick size
- Timing cost
- Trading collar rule
- Trading costs
- Transaction costs
- Upstairs marke

QUESTIONS

1. What are the three factors contributing to the significant changes in the common market over the past 50 years?

2. **a.** How does common stock differ from preferred stock?
   b. Why is preferred stock viewed as a senior corporate security?

3. What is the difference between ordinary dividends and qualified dividends and how is each treated for tax purposes?

4. What is meant by a long-term capital gain and how is it treated for tax purposes?

5. The following quote is taken from Wayne H. Wagner, "The Taxonomy of Trading Strategies," in Katrina F. Sherrerd (ed.), *Trading Strategies and Execution Costs* (Charlottesville, VA: The Institute of Chartered Financial Analysts, 1988).

   > When a trader decides how to bring an order to the market, he or she must deal with some very important issues; to me, the most important is: What kind of trade is this? It could be either an active or a passive trade. The type of trade will dictate whether speed of execution is more or less important than cost of execution. In other words, do I want immediate trading (a market order); or am I willing to forgo the immediate trade for the possibility of trading less expensively if I am willing to "give" on the timing of the trade (a limit order)?

   a. What is meant by a market order?
   b. Why would a market order be placed when an investor wants immediate trading?
   c. What is meant by a limit order?
   d. What are the risks associated with a limit order?

6. Suppose that Mr. Mancuso has purchased a stock for $45 and that he sets a maximum loss that he will accept on this stock of $6. What type of order can Mr. Mancuso place?

7. **a.** What is a program trade?
   b. What are the various types of commission arrangements for executing a program trade and the advantages and disadvantages of each?

8. **a.** Explain the mechanics and some key rules of a short sale.
   b. What restrictions are imposed on short selling activities?

9. What role does the broker call rate play in a margin purchase?

10. **a.** What is meant by maintenance margin when stocks are purchased on margin?
    b. What is meant by debit balance?
    c. What is meant by credit balance?

11. The following statements are taken from Greta E. Marshall's article "Execution Costs: The Plan Sponsor's View," which appears in *Trading Strategies and Execution Costs*, published by The Institute of Chartered Financial Analysts in 1988. (The publication is the product of a conference held in New York City on December 3, 1987):
    a. "There are three components of trading costs. First there are direct costs which may be measured—commissions. Second, there are indirect—or market impact—costs. Finally, there are the undefined costs of not trading." What are market impact costs, and what do you think the "undefined costs of not trading" represent?
    b. "Market impact, unlike broker commissions, is difficult to identify and measure." Why is market impact cost difficult to measure?

12. **a.** What is meant by "soft dollars"?
    b. What is the concern with soft dollars?

13. **a.** What is meant by tick size?
    b. What is the tick size for common stock?

14. Why were price limits and collars imposed on stock in the United States?

15. **a.** What is meant by the circuit breaker rule?
    b. What is meant by the trading collar rule?

16. What are the three general types of stock market indicators?

17. What is the difference between a market-value-weighted index and an equally weighted index?

18. What are the main features of the S&P 500 common stock index?

19. "The stocks selected for the S&P 500 are the largest 500 companies in the United States." Indicate whether you agree or disagree with this statement.

20. There are participants and analysts in the stock market that are called chartists or technical analysts. What does the theory that the market is weak-form efficient say about these investors' chances of beating the market?

21. The November 1985 prospectus of the Merrill Lynch Phoenix Fund, Inc., a mutual fund, stated the following investment objective:

> Based upon the belief that the pricing mechanism of the securities markets lacks perfect efficiency so that prices of securities of troubled issuers are often depressed to a greater extent than warranted by the condition of the issuer and that, while investment in such securities involves a high degree of risk, such investments offer the opportunity for significant capital gains.

What does this strategy assume about the pricing efficiency of the stock market?

22. Why should an investor who believes that the market is efficient pursue an indexing strategy?

Markets for Common Stock: Structure and Organization

From Chapter 18 of *Foundations of Financial Markets and Institutions*, 4/e. Frank J. Fabozzi. Franco Modigliani. Frank J. Jones.
Copyright © 2010 by Pearson Prentice Hall. All rights reserved.

Markets for Common Stock: Structure and Organization*

LEARNING OBJECTIVES

After reading this chapter, you will understand

- the different types of market structure: order-driven, quote-driven, and hybrid

- the natural buyers and natural sellers in a market

- the intermediaries in a quote-driven market

- what is meant by the national best bid and offer and the inside market

- the ownership and trading structure of exchanges

- the national exchanges and their basic features

- for the New York Stock Exchange: the specialist system, the role of the specialist, and the transactors on the exchange floor

- the difference between the New York Stock Exchange and the Nasdaq

- what off-exchange markets (alternative electronic markets) and the two categories of this market (electronic communication networks and alternative trading systems) are

- the different types of alternative trading systems: crossing networks and dark pools

- evolving stock market practices including order handling rules, small order routers, Securities Exchange Commission Regulation National Market Systems, internalization, alternative display facility, trade reporting facility, direct market access, and algorithmic trading

---

*A large part of this chapter, including all the tables and figures, draws from Frank J. Jones and Frank J. Fabozzi, "Common Stock Market," Chapter 11 in Frank J. Fabozzi (ed), *Handbook of Finance: Volume I* (Hoboken, NJ: John Wiley & Sons, 2008).

At the beginning of the twenty-first century, the world's stock exchanges were a complex of separate, independent, single-product exchanges. During the first part of this century, however, these exchanges have become interconnected within and across country lines and have become multiproduct exchanges. By multiproduct exchanges, we mean that not only is common stock traded on the exchange but other financial instruments such as bonds, options, and futures are also traded. Some of the world's stock exchanges have become international, multiproduct exchanges. The exchanges have and will continue to change rapidly, both diversifying and integrating. In addition to the sanctioned stock exchanges, there are so-called "off-exchange markets" that have become much more important in their size and diversity. The U.S. stock market has become a complex of interconnected exchanges and off-exchange markets.

This chapter offers a snapshot of the current but evolving U.S. stock markets. There are two fundamental differences among U.S. and international exchanges. The first is their method of trading, that is, their **market structure**.[1] The market structures of U.S. and international exchanges have evolved and even changed radically. One cannot appreciate current exchanges without understanding their market structure. The second fundamental difference is that the nature of the exchanges' business organizations have changed considerably, from membership floor-traded organizations to publicly owned electronic trading organizations. Figure 1 summarizes the structure of the mechanisms for equity transactions and

| Figure 1   Structure of Equity Transactions |

  I. *No Intermediary* (All "Naturals")
      A. Continuous
      B. Call Auction
         • Provides price discovery, i.e., priced at an internally determined price

  II. *Via Intermediaries*
      A. *Exchanges*
         1. *National*
            a. NYSE Hybrid—auction (specialist) and electronic (Direct+)
            b. NYSE-Area
            c. Nasdaq
            d. Amex

         2. *Regional*
            • CHX (Chicago)
            • PHLX (Philadelphia)
            • BSE (Boston)
            • National (NSX)
            • Pacific Exchange

      B. *Off-Exchange Systems/Alternative Electronic Markets*
         1. *Electronic Communication Networks*

         2. *Alternate Trading Systems*
            a. Crossing Networks
            b. Dark Pools
            c. Internalization

---

[1] For a more detailed discussion of some of the topics covered in this chapter, see Robert A. Schwartz and Reto Francioni, *Equity Markets in Action* (Hoboken, NJ: John Wiley and Sons, 2004).

Table 1   Key Dates

Dates	Events
1969	Instinet formed.
1971	Nasdaq formed, the world's first electronic stock market; began trading on 2/28/1971.
1978	Nasdaq and Amex merged to form the Nasdaq-Amex Group, Inc.
1987	Instinet acquired by Reuters.
12/9/1996	Archipelago founded.
1997	Order Handling Rules approved by SEC.
1997–2000	Proliferation of ECNs.
5/18/2001	Instinet conducts an IPO.
2001	Consolidation of ECNs.
7/2001	LSE IPO (ticker symbol: LSE).
10/20/2001	Archipelago granted exchange status by SEC.
2002	Advent of algorithmic trading.
07/01/2002	Nasdaq IPO (ticker symbol: NDAQ).
9/20/2002	Island acquired by Instinet.
12/06/2002	CME IPO (ticker symbol: CME).
1/2005	Archipelago announced plan to buy the Pacific Stock Exchange.
10/19/2005	CBOT Holdings IPO (ticker symbol: CBOT).
12/2005	Nasdaq buys Instinet Group (and its INET trading platform).
12/15/2005	NYSE launches its Hybrid Market, creating a blend of auction and electronic trading.
12/30/2005	The NYSE, in anticipation of its transformation into a publicly held company, ends member seat sales, which were replaced by the sale of annual trading licenses.
3/7/2006	NYSE buys electronic bourse operator Archipelago Holding (a for-profit, publicly owned company). NYSE Group Inc. formed out of a merger of the New York Stock Exchange and Archipelago Holdings, Inc.
3/8/2006	NYSE Group IPO (ticker symbol: NYX).
4/4/2007	NYSE Group completed merger with Euronext NV, creating the first trans-Atlantic exchange group, called NYSE Euronext.
7/2007	CME merged with CBOT.
7/2007	Reg. NMS implemented.

provides a useful guide for this chapter. Many of the key dates referred to in this chapter are summarized in Table 1.

There are two appendices to this chapter that are available online at www.prenhall.com/fabozzi/. Appendix 18-A describes the current state of the New York Stock Exchange. Appendix 18-B provides a summary of the current state of many of the major non–U.S. exchanges.

EXCHANGE MARKET STRUCTURES

An **exchange** is often defined as a market where intermediaries meet to deliver and execute customer orders. This description, however, also applies to many dealer networks. In the United States, an exchange is an institution that performs this function and is registered with the Securities and Exchange Commission (SEC) as an exchange. There are also some off-exchange markets that perform this function.

There are two overall market models for trading stocks. The first model is **order-driven**, in which buy and sell orders of public participants who are the holders of the securities establish the prices at which other public participants can trade. These orders can be either *market orders* or *limit orders*. An order-driven market is also referred to as an **auction market**. The second model is **quote-driven**, in which intermediaries, that is, market-makers or dealers, quote the prices at which the public participants trade. Market-makers provide a **bid quote** (to buy) and an **offer quote** (to sell) and realize revenues from the spread between these two quotes. Thus, market-makers derive a profit from the spread and the turnover of their stocks.

Order-Driven Markets

An order-driven market is also referred to as a **dealer market**. Participants in a *pure order-driven market* are referred to as "naturals" (the natural buyers and sellers). No intermediary participates as a trader in a pure order-driven market. Rather, the investors supply the liquidity themselves. That is, the **natural buyers** are the source of liquidity for the **natural sellers**, and vice versa. The naturals can be either buyers or sellers, each using market or limit orders.

Order-driven markets can be structured in two very different ways: a continuous market or a call auction at any point of time. In the **continuous market**, a trade can be made at any moment in continuous time during which a buy order and a sell order meet. In this case, trading is a series of bilateral matches. In the **call auction**, orders are batched together for a simultaneous execution in a multilateral trade at a specific point in time. At the time of the call, a market-clearing price is determined; buy orders at this price and higher and sell orders at this price and lower are executed.

Continuous trading is better for customers who need immediacy. On the other hand, for markets with very low trading volume, an intraday call may focus liquidity at one (or a few) times of the day and permit the trades to occur. In addition, very large orders—block trades that were described in the previous chapter—may be advantaged by the feasibility of continuous trading.

Non-intermediated markets involve only naturals; that is, such markets do not require a third party. A market may not, however, have sufficient liquidity to function without the participation of intermediaries, who are third parties in addition to the natural buyers and sellers. This leads to the need for intermediaries and quote-driven markets.

Quote-Driven Markets

Quote-driven markets permit intermediaries to provide liquidity. Intermediaries may be *brokers* (who are *agents* for the naturals); *dealers* or *market-makers* (who are *principals* in the trade); and **specialists**, as on the New York Stock Exchange (NYSE) (who act as both agents and principals). Dealers are independent, profit-making participants in the process.

Dealers operate as principals, not agents. Dealers continually provide bids and offer quotes to buy for or sell from their own accounts and profit from the spread between their bid and offer quotes. Dealers compete with each other in their bids and offers. Obviously, from the customer's perspective, the "best" market is the highest bid and lowest offer among the dealers. This highest bid/lowest offer combination is referred to as the "inside market" or the "top of the book." For example, assume that dealers A, B, and C have the bids and offers (also called *asking prices*) for stock Alpha as shown in the top panel in Figure 2.

Figure 2	Quote-Driven Dealer Market for Stock Alpha

a. *Bid-Offer by Three Dealers*

Dealer	Bid	Offer
A	40.50	41.20
B	40.35	41.10
C	40.20	41.00

b. *Top of the Book: Inside Market*

Dealer	Bid	Dealer	Offer	
A	40.50	C	41.00	top of the book: ⟵ 40.50/41.00
B	40.35	B	41.10	
C	40.20	A	41.20	

The best (highest) bid is by dealer A of 40.50; the best (lowest) offer is by dealer C of 41.00. Thus, the inside market is 40.50 bid (by A) and 41.00 offer (by C). Note that A's spread is 40.50 bid and 41.20 offer for a spread (or profit margin) of 0.70. A has the highest bid but not the lowest offer. C has the lowest offer but not the highest bid. B has neither the highest bid nor the lowest offer.

For a stock in the U.S. market, the highest bid and lowest offer across all markets is called the **national best bid and offer (NBBO)**.

Dealers provide value to the transaction process by providing capital for trading and facilitating order handling. With respect to providing capital for trading, they buy and sell for their own accounts at their bid and offer prices, respectively, thereby providing liquidity. With respect to order handling, they provide value in two ways. First, they assist in the price improvement of customer orders; that is, the order is executed within the bid–offer spread. Second, they facilitate the market timing of customer orders to achieve price discovery. Price discovery is a dynamic process that involves customer orders being translated into trades and transaction prices. Because price discovery is not instantaneous, individual participants have an incentive to "market-time" the placement of their orders. Intermediaries may understand the order flow and may assist the customer in this regard. The intermediary may be a person or an electronic system.

The over-the-counter (OTC) markets are quote-driven markets. The OTC markets began during a time when stocks were bought and sold in banks and the physical certificates were passed over the counter.

A customer may choose to buy or sell to a specific market-maker to whom they wish to direct an order. Directing an order to a specific market is referred to as **preferencing**.

Order-Driven versus Quote-Driven Markets

Overall, non-intermediated, order-driven markets may be less costly due to the absence of profit-seeking dealers. But the markets for many stocks are not inherently sufficiently liquid to operate in this way. For this reason, intermediated dealer markets are often necessary for inherently less liquid markets. The dealers provide dealer capital, participate in price discovery, and facilitate market timing, as discussed above.

Because of the different advantages of these two approaches, many equity markets are now **hybrid markets**. For example, the NYSE is primarily a continuous auction order-driven system based on customer orders, but the specialists enhance the liquidity by their market-making to maintain a fair and orderly market. In addition, the NYSE has other floor traders, call markets at the open and close, and upstairs dealers who provide proprietary capital to facilitate block transactions. Thus, the NYSE is a hybrid combination of these two models. Another hybrid aspect of the NYSE is that it opens and closes trading with a call auction. The continuous market and call auction market are combined. Thus, the NYSE is a continuous market during the trading day and a call auction market to open and close the market and to reopen after a stop in trading. Thus, the NYSE is a hybrid market.

Nasdaq (an acronym for the National Association of Securities Dealers Automated Quotations System), which will be discussed further later in this chapter, began as a descendant of the OTC dealer network, and is a dealer quote-driven market. It remains primarily a quote-driven market, but has added some order-driven aspects such as its limit order book called SuperMontage, discussed below, which made it a hybrid market.

An overview of the non-intermediated, auction, order-driven market and the intermediated, dealer, quote-driven markets is provided in Figure 3.

Another structural change that has occurred in exchanges is their evolution from membership-owned, floor-traded organizations to publicly owned electronically traded (that is, no trading floor) organizations. The nature of this evolution (or revolution) is discussed in the next section.

Key Points That You Should Understand Before Proceeding

1. The difference between an order-driven and quote-driven market.
2. What is meant by the natural buyers and natural sellers in the market.
3. Who the intermediaries are in a quote-driven market.
4. What is meant by the NBBO.
5. What is meant by a hybrid market structure.

Figure 3   Structure of Stock Markets

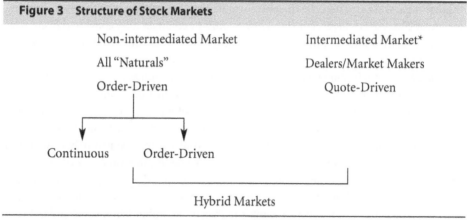

*Intermediaries include:
- Dealers/Market-Makers (principals)
- Brokers (agents)
- Specialists (operate as both principals and agents)

CHANGES IN EXCHANGE OWNERSHIP AND TRADING STRUCTURES

Exchanges have traditionally been organizations built around a physical trading floor. They have also usually been mutual organizations that are owned and operated on a nonprofit basis for the benefit of their members, those who operate on the trading floor. The ownership by the members is reflected in the memberships or "seats" that provide floor access or trading privileges as well as ownership rights. As the profits derived from these trading privileges increase, the price of the seats increase and the value of the members' equity in their exchange increases. Thus, a membership organization's goal is to increase the value of the access privileges, which increases the price of a seat. A mutual organization's primary objective, thus, is to increase the income of the individual members, not the profit of the overall organization, which is a nonprofit organization.

However, membership organizations may not find it beneficial to themselves to adopt some changes that are beneficial to the customers of the exchange, the buyers and sellers of the exchange's products, because such changes may not be beneficial to the owners of the exchange, the members. For example, adopting a new technology may benefit the customers by reducing the transaction costs but also decrease the value of access privileges and seats of a membership organization. Thus, the members/owners in a membership organization often resist technological innovations, which could benefit customers but reduce the value of their own trading income.

In contrast, a publicly owned equity-based organization is a corporation and operated for a profit. And the profit of the overall organization accrues to its shareholders via an increase in the value of its equity shares. Thus, an equity-based organization might adopt the above-mentioned technology if it benefited its customers, increased its profits, and increased its stock price. The equity-based organization is free of the conflicts of a member organization between trader income and organizational profits.

While an equity-based organization may be superior over time in serving its customers, the difficult issue is convincing the members/owners in a mutual organization to agree to a demutualization and public ownership. The demutualization occurs by giving the members shares or equity in the demutualized organization in exchange for their seats in the mutual organization. Thus, the members would receive wealth/equity shares in exchange for income/access privileges. For such reasons, many exchanges have converted from membership organizations to publicly owned equity-based demutualized organizations in recent years.

Such a demutualization will align the interests of the customers of the organization and the owners of the organization. After the demutualization from a mutual company to a stock company, however, one more step is necessary before equity capital can be raised for the exchange and alliances among exchanges can be easily made with stock. Immediately after the demutualization, the stock of the equity company may be privately held and the equity shares do not have a known market value. Knowing this value is necessary if the shares are going to be exchanged; new equity capital is raised; or mergers or acquisitions among such organizations are to be consummated. In order to give the stock a known market value, the newly equity-based organization has to "go public," that is, sell at least some of its stock on the public markets via an initial public offering (IPO), and then list its shares on a secondary stock market, such as the NYSE or Nasdaq. Once the IPO is complete, the resulting "corporation" knows its overall value ("market value," "market capitalization," or simply "market cap"), which is its share price multiplied by its number of shares. Corporations can then use their stock to acquire other corporations with their shares. Corporations can also use the value of their corporation as a basis for being acquired by another firm via its stock or cash. Equity or for-profit organizations have the flexibility to raise capital, make acquisitions, and acquire other organizations without resistance from their members, who would be considering their own income.

Overall, before demutualization, the market participants and market owners are the same via memberships, seats, or access privileges. This is ideal for a trading floor organization. The members derive their income from trading on the floor. As a result, floor trading organizations tend to be mutual organizations. After demutualization, the market participants and the market owners are not necessarily the same entities and, thus, may have different objectives, the traders motivated by trading income and the shareholders motivated by organizational (that is corporate) profits. Thus, after the demutualization and the subsequent IPO, a common change is that the corporation can take actions that benefit the corporation itself by providing better service to its customers, even though trader profits may be disadvantaged. The degree of electronic trading increases and trading may become exclusively electronic or remain a mix of floor trading and electronic, often called a hybrid. The owners are shareholders and they do not derive their income from trading on the floor. This sequence of actions is shown in Figure 4.

Traditionally, exchanges of most types have been based on floor trading and the ownership of the exchanges has been with the floor traders, both individuals and firms. Changes in

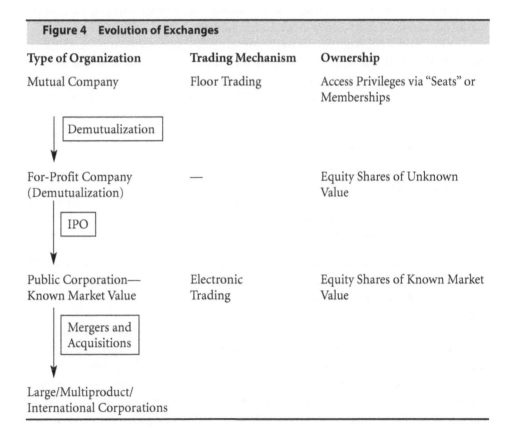

Figure 4   Evolution of Exchanges

Type of Organization	Trading Mechanism	Ownership
Mutual Company	Floor Trading	Access Privileges via "Seats" or Memberships
↓ Demutualization		
For-Profit Company (Demutualization)	—	Equity Shares of Unknown Value
↓ IPO		
Public Corporation— Known Market Value	Electronic Trading	Equity Shares of Known Market Value
↓ Mergers and Acquisitions		
Large/Multiproduct/ International Corporations		

exchange structure and ownership began in the 1980s. Most notable were the changes that related to the "Big Bang" in London during 1986. These reforms related to the London Stock Exchange (LSE) included the abolition of minimum commissions and the introduction of "dual capacity," whereby member firms could be both brokers (agents) and "jobbers" (the British term for dealers who are principals in a transaction). One outcome of these and other changes was that the LSE's trading floor was closed and replaced by "screen trading," that is, a dealer OTC market. The LSE became a public company in July 2001 (ticker symbol: LSE).

Since then, the major futures exchanges, including the Chicago Mercantile Exchange and the Chicago Board of Trade, have become electronic trading corporations and have merged. The International Securities Exchange, an electronic options exchange, began (in 2000) as a membership-owned exchange; subsequently demutualized; and then did an IPO (in 2005). The NYSE became a publicly owned mainly electronically traded stock exchange. There have been other such transformations.

THE U.S. STOCK MARKETS: EXCHANGES AND OVER-THE-COUNTER MARKETS

The view of the U.S. stock market "from 30,000 feet" is that of a large homogeneous market. But while it has been large, it has not been homogeneous since the 1970s. It has become even much more heterogeneous since the 1990s. The U.S. stock market is now composed of the stock exchanges and OTC markets and also, more recently, the off-exchange markets. This section provides the "big picture" of the current stock market—specific parts of the market are examined more closely in subsequent sections.

The U.S. stock market began over two centuries ago and has evolved considerably since then. The U.S. stock market has traditionally been the core of the world capital markets. Over the past few decades, there have been significant changes in the U.S. stock market and also international stock markets. But undoubtedly, the pace and extent of this change has accelerated.

The stock exchanges have been the primary component of the U.S. stock market. Among the types of changes in the U.S. stock exchanges are

- the market structures of the exchanges
- the trading mechanisms of the exchanges
- consolidation among different types of assets, for example, securities options and futures
- growth and diversity of the off-exchange markets
- consolidation internationally

While the exchanges have been the main component of the U.S. stock market, the OTC markets and the off-exchange markets have also become important parts of the U.S. stock market. The off-exchange markets have also grown and become much more diverse since 2005.

This section covers the exchanges and the OTC markets; the next section considers the off-exchange markets. Given the pace and extent of the recent changes, there is a high likelihood that the markets will be much different during the next decade than they are now.

The international stock exchanges have also changed and, in fact, in some cases, have become integrated with the U.S. exchanges. However, the international stock markets are not considered here except for their relationship with U.S. exchanges.

Figure 5 The "Big Picture" of the U.S. Stock Market

I. Stock Exchanges

A. *National Exchanges*

    1. NYSE Euronext
        a. NYSE Hybrid Market
        b. Archipelago ("Area")
    2. American Stock Exchange

B. *Regional Exchanges*

    1. Chicago Stock Exchange (CHX)
    2. Philadelphia Stock Exchange (PHLX)
    3. Boston Stock Exchange (BSE)
    4. National Stock Exchange (formerly the Cincinnati Stock Exchange) (NSX)
    5. Pacific Stock Exchange (owned by Archipelago; in turn owned by the NYSE)

C. *Nasdaq—the OTC Market* (technically became an exchange during June 2006)

    1. Nasdaq National Market (NNM)
    2. Small Cap Market

D. *Other OTC Markets*

    1. Bulletin Board ("Bullies")
    2. Pink Sheets

E. *Off-Exchange Markets/Alternative Electronic Markets*

    1. Electronic Communication Networks (ECNs)
    2. Alternative Trading Systems (ATS)
        a. Crossing Networks
        b. Dark Pools

Figure 5 provides a general overview, or the "big picture," of the current construct of the U.S. stock markets. The components of the current U.S. stock market are discussed individually in following sections. This section treats the components of the U.S. stock market, including the national exchanges, the NYSE and the American Stock Exchange (Amex); the regional stock exchanges; Nasdaq, technically an OTC market, not an exchange (until June 2006); other OTC markets; and other stock exchange markets.

National Exchanges

The U.S. stock markets are dominated by the NYSE and Nasdaq, the two largest exchanges (as discussed in the following text, until June 2006, Nasdaq was not technically an exchange).

New York Stock Exchange

The beginning of the NYSE is identified as May 17, 1792, when the Buttonwood Agreement was signed by 24 brokers outside of 68 Wall Street in New York under a buttonwood tree. The current NYSE building opened at 18 Broad Street on April 22, 1903 (the "main room"). In 1922, a new trading floor (the "garage") was opened at 11 Broad Street. Additional trading floor space was opened in 1969 and 1988 (the "blue room"). Finally, another trading floor was opened at 30 Broad Street in 2000. Notably, for reasons discussed below, during early 2006, the NYSE closed the trading room at 30 Broad Street with the beginning of the

NYSE Hybrid Market and a greater proportion of the trading being executed electronically. The NYSE is referred to as the "Big Board."

The NYSE trading mechanism has been based on the specialist system. This system, as discussed above, is a hybrid of primarily an order-driven market with some quote-driven features. According to this mechanism, each stock is assigned to an individual specialist. Each specialist "specializes" in many stocks but each stock is assigned to only one specialist. Each specialist is located at a "booth" or "post." All orders for a stock are received at this post and the specialist conducts an auction based on these orders to determine the execution price. The orders arrive at the specialists' posts either physically, delivered via firm brokers, or electronically via the Designated Order Turnaround (DOT) system or its successors, as discussed below. In conducting the auction, typically the specialist is an agent, simply matching orders. At times, however, the specialist becomes a principal and trades for itself in the interest of maintaining an "orderly market."

Limit orders, as opposed to market orders, are kept by the specialist in his or her "book," originally a physical paper book but now an electronic book. These limit orders are executed by the specialist when the market price moves to the limit. Until recently, the book could be seen only by the specialist, which was judged to be a significant advantage for the specialist, but now the book is open to all the traders on the exchange floor. Overall, the NYSE trading mechanism is an auction-based, order-driven market.

This type of mechanism is often judged to provide the best price but, on a time basis, often a less rapid execution. There is, thus, a trade-off between price and speed.

The need for "space" for trading floors for the NYSE derives from its trading mechanism, the floor-based specialist system. The amount of space necessary depends not only on overall trading volume, but also the fraction of this volume that is handled by the specialist.

The NYSE lists stocks throughout the United States (as well as some international stocks) and, thus, is a "national exchange."

Trading Mechanism—The Specialist System Fundamentally, the NYSE is an auction-type market based on orders (order-driven). As indicated above, the traditional trading mechanism for the NYSE is the specialist system. However, the volume of trading that has occurred electronically has increased continually. In 2006, with the advent of NYSE Hybrid, the degree of electronic trading that has occurred electronically increased significantly, as discussed in the following text.

Here, we discuss the traditional NYSE specialist system in more detail. Trading in stocks listed on the NYSE is conducted as a centralized continuous auction market at a designated physical location on the trading floor, called a post, with brokers representing their customers' buy and sell orders. A single specialist is the market-maker for each stock. A member firm may be designated as a specialist for the common stock of more than one company; that is, several stocks can trade at the same post. But only one specialist is designated for the common stock of each listed company.

The NYSE began its DOT system during 1976. This system, now called SuperDOT, is an electronic order routing and reporting system that links member firms worldwide electronically directly to the specialist's post on the trading floor of the NYSE. The NYSE SuperDOT system routes NYSE-listed stock orders electronically directly to a specialist on the exchange trading floor, rather than through a broker. The specialist then executes the orders. This system was initially introduced as the DOT system but is now referred to as the SuperDOT system. The SuperDOT system is used for small market orders, limit orders, and basket (or portfolio) trades and program trades. The SuperDOT system can be used for under 100,000 shares with priority given to orders of 2,100 shares or less. After the order has been executed, the report of the transaction is sent back through the SuperDOT system. According to the NYSE, as of 2007, over 99% of the orders executed through the NYSE were done through SuperDOT, which meets the continually increasing demand, which stood at 20 million quotes, 50 million orders, and 10 million reports daily.

In addition to the single specialist market-maker on the exchange, other firms that are members of an exchange can trade for themselves or on behalf of their customers. NYSE member firms, which are broker-dealer organizations that serve the investing public, are represented on the trading floor by brokers who serve as fiduciaries in the execution of customer orders.

The largest membership category on the NYSE is that of the **commission broker**. A commission broker is an employee of one of the securities houses (stock brokers or wire houses) devoted to handling business on the exchange. Commission brokers execute orders for their firm on behalf of their customers at agreed commission rates. These houses may deal for their own account as well as on behalf of their clients.

Other transactors on the exchange floor include the following categories. Independent **floor brokers** (nicknamed "$2 brokers") work on the exchange floor and execute orders for other exchange members who have more orders than they can handle alone or who require assistance in carrying out large orders. Floor brokers take a share in the commission received by the firm they are assisting. Registered traders, another category, are individual members who buy and sell for their own account. Alternatively, they may be trustees who maintain memberships for the convenience of dealing and to save fees.

The major type of exchange participant is the specialist.

NYSE Specialist As indicated, specialists are dealers or market-makers assigned by the NYSE to conduct the auction process and maintain an orderly market in one or more designated stocks. Specialists may act as both a broker (agent) and a dealer (principal). In their role as a broker or agent, specialists represent customer orders in their assigned stocks, which arrive at their post electronically or are entrusted to them by a floor broker to be executed if and when a stock reaches a price specified by a customer (limit or stop order). As a dealer or principal, specialists buy and sell shares in their assigned stocks for their own account as necessary to maintain an "orderly market." Specialists must always give precedence to public orders over trading for their own account.

In general, public orders for stocks traded on the NYSE, if they are not sent to the specialist's post via SuperDOT, are sent from the member firm's office to its representative on the exchange floor, who attempts to execute the order in the trading crowd. There are certain types of orders where the order will not be executed immediately on the trading floor. These are limit orders and stop orders. If the order is a limit order or a stop order and the member firm's floor broker cannot transact the order immediately, the floor broker can wait in the trading crowd or give the order to the specialist in the stock, who will enter the order in that specialist's **limit order book** (or simply, the *book*) for later execution based on the relationship between the market price and the price specified in the limit or stop order. The book is the list on which specialists keep the limit and stop orders that are given to them, arranged by size, from near the current market price to further away from it.

Whereas the book used to be an actual physical paper book, it is now electronic. While for many years only the specialist could see the orders in the limit order book, with the NYSE's introduction of OpenBook in January 2002, the book was made available electronically to the traders on the exchange floor.

A significant advantage of the NYSE market is its diversity of participants. At the exchange, public orders meet each other often with minimal dealer intervention, contributing to an efficient mechanism for achieving fair securities prices. The liquidity provided in the NYSE market stems from the active involvement of the following principal groups: the individual investor; the institutional investor; the member firm acting as both agent and dealer; the member-firm broker on the trading floor acting as agent, representing the firm's customer orders; the independent broker on the trading floor acting as agent and handling customer orders on behalf of other member firms; and the specialist, with assigned responsibility in individual securities on the trading floor. Together, these groups provide depth and diversity to the market.

NYSE-assigned specialists have four major roles:

1. As agents, they execute market orders entrusted to them by brokers, as well as orders awaiting a specific market price.
2. As catalysts, they help to bring buyers and sellers together.
3. As dealers, they trade for their own accounts when there is a temporary absence of public buyers or sellers, and only after the public orders in their possession have been satisfied at a specified price.
4. As auctioneers, they quote current bid–ask prices that reflect total supply and demand for each of the stocks assigned to them.

In carrying out their duties, specialists may, as indicated, act as either an agent or a principal. When acting as an agent, the specialists simply fill customer market orders or limit or stop orders (either new orders or orders from their book) by opposite orders (buy or sell). While acting as a principal, the specialists are charged with the responsibility of maintaining a "fair and orderly market." Specialists are prohibited from engaging in transactions in securities in which they are registered unless such transactions are necessary to maintain a fair and orderly market. Specialists profit only from those trades in which they are involved; that is, they realize no revenue for trades in which they are an agent.

The term *fair and orderly market* means a market in which there is price continuity and reasonable depth. Thus, specialists are required to maintain a reasonable spread between bids and offers and small changes in price between transactions. Specialists are expected to bid and offer for their own account if necessary to promote such a fair and orderly market. They cannot put their own interests ahead of public orders and are obliged to trade on their own accounts against the market trend to help maintain liquidity and continuity as the price of a stock goes up or down. They may purchase stock for their investment account only if such purchases are necessary to create a fair and orderly market.

Specialists are also responsible for balancing buy and sell orders at the opening of the trading day in order to arrange an equitable opening price for the stock. Specialists are expected to participate in the opening of the market only to the extent necessary to balance supply and demand for the security to affect a reasonable opening price. While trading throughout the day is via a continuous auction-based system, the opening is conducted via a single-priced call auction system. The specialists conduct the call and determine the single price.

If there is an imbalance between buy and sell orders either at the opening of or during the trading day and the specialists cannot maintain a fair and orderly market, then they may, under restricted conditions, close the market in that stock (that is, discontinue trading) until they are able to determine a price at which there is a balance of buy and sell orders. Such closes of trading can occur either during the trading day or at the opening, which is more common, and can last for minutes or days. Closings of a day or more may occur when, for example, there is an acquisition of one corporation by another or when there is an extreme announcement by the corporation. For this reason, many announcements are made after the close of trading or before the opening of trading.

NYSE trading officials oversee the activities of the specialists and trading-floor brokers. Approval from these officials must be sought for a delay in trading at the opening or to halt trading during the trading day when unusual trading situations or price disparities develop.

Because of their critical public role and the necessity of capital in performing their function as a market-maker, capital requirements are imposed by the exchanges for specialists.

American Stock Exchange

Amex dates from colonial times when brokers conducted outdoor markets to trade new government securities. Amex began trading at the curbstone on Broad Street near Exchange Place. Until 1929, it was called the New York Curb Exchange. In 1921, the Amex moved inside into the building where it still resides at 86 Trinity Place in New York City. In 1998, Amex merged with the National Association of Securities Dealers (NASD), which then operated Nasdaq, to create the Nasdaq-Amex Market Group wherein Amex was an independent member of the NASD parent. After conflicts between the NASD and Amex members, the Amex members bought Amex from NASD and acquired control in 2004. Amex continued to be owned by its members until its acquisition by the NYSE in early 2008.

Amex, like the NYSE, lists stocks from throughout the United States and also international stocks. Amex is therefore a national exchange. Amex is also an auction-type market based on orders. Its specialist system is similar to that of the NYSE.

Amex developed exchange traded funds (ETFs). The first ETF, the SPY ETF, based on the S&P 500 index, was listed on the Amex on January 29, 1993. Although ETFs have proved to be a very successful product and most of the listings remain on the Amex, most of the trading volume has migrated to other exchanges, including the NYSE and Nasdaq.

The number of listings on and the trading volume of stocks on the Amex have continued to decline in recent years, and as of early 2008, the Amex is regarded as a minor market in U.S. stocks, although it continues to trade some small to mid-sized stocks. Amex is now highly dependent on trading in stock options. In January 2008, the NYSE announced an agreement to purchase the Amex. When this transaction is completed, the Amex will most likely no longer exist.

Regional Exchanges

Regional exchanges developed to trade stocks of local firms that listed their shares on the regional exchanges and also to provide alternatives to the national stock exchanges for their listed stocks. Regional stock exchanges now exist in Chicago, Philadelphia, and Boston and have existed in many other U.S. cities. These exchanges have also been specialist-type, auction-based systems. Some of the regional stock exchanges, including Philadelphia and Boston, as well as the Amex have been driven by trading in stock options and index options rather than stocks in recent years.

Chicago Stock Exchange

The Chicago Stock Exchange (CHX) was founded on March 21, 1882. In 1949, it merged with the St. Louis, Cleveland, and Minneapolis/St. Paul Stock Exchanges and changed its name to the Midwest Stock Exchange. In 1993, it changed its name back to the CHX and is the most active regional exchange.

Philadelphia Stock Exchange

The Philadelphia Stock Exchange (PHLX) is the oldest stock exchange in the United States, founded in 1790. In 2005, a number of large financial firms purchased stakes in the PHLX as a hedge against growing consolidation of stock trading by the NYSE and Nasdaq. These firms—Morgan Stanley, Citigroup, Credit Suisse First Boston, UBS AG, Merrill Lynch, and Citadel Investment Group—collectively owned about 45% of the PHLX.

During October 2007, PHLX announced that it was for sale by a group of its shareholders. On November 7, 2007, Nasdaq announced a "definitive agreement" to purchase PHLX for $652 million and the transaction closed in early 2008. PHLX continues to operate as part of Nasdaq.

The PHLX handles trades for approximately 2,000 stocks, 1,700 equity options, 25 index options, and a number of currency options. As of 2007, it had a 14% U.S. market share in exchange-listed stock options trading.

Boston Stock Exchange

The Boston Stock Exchange (BSE) was founded in 1834 and is the third oldest stock exchange in the United States. The Boston Options Exchange (BCX), a facility of the BSE, is a fully automated options market. On October 2, 2007, Nasdaq agreed to acquire BSE for $61 million.

National Stock Exchange

The National Stock Exchange (NSX), now in Chicago, was founded in 1885 in Cincinnati, Ohio, as the Cincinnati Stock Exchange. In 1976, it closed its physical trading floor and became the first all-electronic stock market in the United States. The Cincinnati Stock Exchange moved its headquarters to Chicago in 1995 and changed its name to the National Stock Exchange during November 2003. The NSX handles a significant share, approximately 20%, of all Nasdaq-listed securities.

Pacific Exchange

The Pacific Exchange (PCX) began in 1957 when the San Francisco Stock and Bond Exchange (founded in 1882 with a trading floor in San Francisco) and the Los Angeles Oil Exchange (founded in 1889 with a trading floor in Los Angeles) merged to form the Pacific Coast Stock Exchange (the trading floors were kept in both places). The name was changed to the Pacific Stock Exchange in 1973 and options trading began in 1976. In 1997, its name was changed to the Pacific Exchange. In 1999, the PCX was the first U.S. stock exchange to demutualize. In 2001, the Los Angeles trading floor was closed, and the next year, the San Francisco trading floor was closed (the options trading floor still operates in San Francisco).

On September 27, 2005, the PCX was bought by the ECN Archipelago, which was in turn bought by the NYSE in 2006. No business is conducted under the name Pacific Exchange, thus ending its separate identity. All formerly PCX stock and options trading takes place through NYSE Arca.

Overall, as indicated by these brief descriptions of regional exchange, some of the regional exchanges have diversified into options trading to remain viable. Some have made the transformation from membership-owned, trading floor organizations to publicly owned electronic organizations, and others have remained in their original forms. Finally, the regional exchanges have become attractive acquisition targets for larger exchanges, with some having already been acquired and others remaining potential merger targets.

Nasdaq Stock Market: The Over-the-Counter Market

A significant change in the U.S. stock market occurred during 1971 when Nasdaq was founded. When it began trading on February 8, 1971, Nasdaq was the world's first electronic stock market. Nasdaq was founded by the NASD. Fundamentally, Nasdaq is a dealer-type system based on quotes (quote-driven).

NASD divested itself of Nasdaq in a series of sales in 2000 and 2001 to form a publicly traded company, the Nasdaq Stock Market, Inc. The Nasdaq Stock Market is a public corporation, the stock of which was listed on its own stock exchange during its IPO on July 1, 2002 (ticker: NDAQ).

Initially, the Nasdaq was simply a computer bulletin board system that did not connect buyers and sellers. The Nasdaq helped lower the spread (the difference between the bid price and the ask price of the stock) and so was unpopular among brokerage firms because they profited on the spread. Since then, the Nasdaq has become more of a stock market, adding automated trading systems and trade and volume reporting.

The Nasdaq, as an electronic exchange, has no physical trading floor, but makes all its trades through a computer and telecommunications system. Since there is no trading floor where the Nasdaq operates, the stock exchange built a site in New York City's Times Square to create a physical presence. The exchange is a dealers' market, meaning brokers buy and sell stocks through a market-maker rather than from each other. A market-maker deals in a particular stock and holds a certain number of stocks on its own books so that when a broker wants to purchase shares, the broker can purchase them directly from the market-maker.

Nasdaq is a dealer system or OTC system where multiple dealers provide quotes (bids and offers) and make trades. There is no specialist system and therefore there is no single place where an auction takes place. Nasdaq is essentially a telecommunication network that links thousands of geographically dispersed, market-making participants. Nasdaq is an electronic quotation system that provides price quotations to market participants on Nasdaq-listed stocks. Nasdaq is essentially an **electronic communication network (ECN)** structure that allows multiple market participants to trade through it. It allows multiple market participants to trade through its ECN structure, increasing competition.

Since Nasdaq dealers provide their quotes independently, the market has been called "fragmented, unlike the NYSE where the central auctions occur at a single place." So while the NYSE market is an auction/agency, order-based market, Nasdaq is a **competitive dealer, quote-based system**.

Until 1987, most trading occurred via telephone. During the October 9, 1987, crash, however, dealers did not respond to telephone calls. As a result, the Nasdaq developed the Small Order Execution System (SOES), which provides an electronic method for dealers to enter their trades. Nasdaq requires that the market-makers honor their trades over SOES.

The purpose of SOES is to ensure that during turbulent market conditions small market orders are not forgotten but are automatically processed.

Over the years, Nasdaq became more of a stock market by adding trade and volume reporting and automated trading systems. In October 2002, Nasdaq started a system, called SuperMontage, which has led to a change in Nasdaq from a quote-driven market to a market that provides both quote-driven and order-driven aspects; that is, it became a hybrid market. This system permits dealers to enter quotes and orders at multiple prices and then displays these aggregate submissions at five different prices on both the bid and offer sides of the market. SuperMontage also provides full anonymity, permits dealers to specify a reserve size (i.e., they do not have to display their full order), offers price and time priority, allows market-makers to internalize orders, and includes preferenced orders. In effect, SuperMontage is the Nasdaq's order display and execution system.

The advent of SuperMontage continues completing Nasdaq's transformation from a quote-driven market to a hybrid market that contains both quote- and order-driven features. Nasdaq added a third component to the hybrid, which is a call auction that both opens and closes the market. Currently, SuperMontage competes with the **Alternative Display Facility (ADF)**, which is operated by the Financial Industry Regulatory Authority (FINRA). SuperMontage is a key feature in Nasdaq's development.

There are two sections of the Nasdaq stock market, the Nasdaq National Market (NNM) and the Small Cap Market (also known as the Nasdaq Capital Market Issues). For a stock to be listed on the NNM, the company must meet certain strict financial criteria. For example, a company must maintain a stock price of at least $1, and the total value of outstanding stocks must be at least $1.1 million and must meet lower requirements for assets and capital. To qualify for listing on the exchange, a company must be registered with the SEC and have at least three market-makers. However, the Nasdaq also has a market for smaller companies unable to meet these and other requirements, called the Nasdaq Small Caps Market. Nasdaq will move companies from one market to the other as their eligibility changes.

During December 2005, Nasdaq acquired Instinet, the largest ECN and a large trader of Nasdaq-listed stocks.

On June 30, 2006, the SEC approved Nasdaq to begin operating as an exchange in Nasdaq-listed securities. Prior to this, as indicated above, Nasdaq had been an OTC stock market but not formally an exchange. This change is more technical than substantive.

Nasdaq was very acquisitive during 2007. During September 2007, Nasdaq agreed to buy the Middle East's Borse Dubai for approximately $4.9 billion. During August 2007, Nasdaq, after failing to acquire the LSE, partnered with Borse Dubai in the Middle East to gain control of Stockholm's OMX Nordic Exchange, which operates eight Nordic and Baltic exchanges. As part of the deal, Nasdaq sold its 28% position in the LSE to Borse Dubai, which ended up with nearly a 20% stake in Nasdaq, making Borse Dubai the largest stockholder of Nasdaq. This acquisition made the Middle East's Borse Dubai a minority owner of the combined Nasdaq/OMX. With the purchase of OMX following its agreement with Borse Dubai, Nasdaq captured 47% of the controlling stake in OMX. Nasdaq completed its acquisition of OMX in February 2008, becoming a trans-Atlantic exchange. The official name of Nasdaq is now Nasdaq OMX Group Inc.

In October 2007, Nasdaq announced plans to buy the BSE (for $61 million). In November 2007, the Nasdaq Stock Market announced that it would buy the PHLX for approximately $650 million, mainly to trade stock options. This deal, which closed in

August 2008, was Nasdaq's first effort in stock options. Nasdaq, a purely electronic exchange, is expected to maintain the Philadelphia trading floor.

NYSE versus Nasdaq

Fundamentally, the NYSE has been an auction-type market based on orders (order-driven) while Nasdaq has been a dealer-type market based on quotes (quote-driven).

For years and decades, debates continued about which system—the NYSE or Nasdaq system—was more competitive and efficient. Those who think the Nasdaq OTC market is superior to the specialist-based NYSE often cite the greater competition from numerous dealers and the greater amount of capital they bring to the trading system. They also argue that specialists are conflicted in balancing their obligation to conduct a fair and orderly market and their need to make a profit.

Proponents of the specialist NYSE market structure argue that the commitment of the dealers in the OTC market to provide a market for shares is weaker than the obligation of the specialists on the exchanges. On the NYSE, specialists are obligated to maintain fair and orderly markets. Failure to fulfill this obligation may result in a loss of specialist status. A dealer in the OTC market is under no such obligation to continue its market-making activity during volatile and uncertain market conditions. Supporters of the specialist system also assert that without a single location for an auction, the OTC markets are fragmented and do not achieve the best trade price.

Another difference of opinion comes from traders who say that the specialist system may arrive at the better price, but take a longer period of time, during which the market price may move against the trader, or at least expose the trader to the risk that it will do so. The OTC market may, on the other hand, lead to a faster execution but not arrive at a better, market-clearing price. Professional traders, in this case, often prefer higher speed over better pricing. Retail investors on the other hand may prefer a better price.

While the NYSE has been an auction-type, order-driven market, it has adopted many dealer-type features. Similarly, while Nasdaq has been a dealer-type, quote-driven market, it has adopted many auction-type features. Thus, while distinct differences continue between these two markets, they have converged considerably and are both currently hybrid markets, although with different mixes of order-driven and quote-driven features.

In general, the new electronic markets have greater latency (that is, greater speed), making rapid quotes feasible. However, these quotes are not persistent. Such markets also make the business scalable.

Exchange Volume Data

This section illustrates the fragmentation of the trading of the stocks listed on an exchange among different trading markets.

During the 1980s, an exchange actually traded all stocks listed by the exchange and only those stocks. Currently, however, stocks listed on one exchange can be traded by other exchanges, including regional exchanges, by non-exchange markets such as ECN, or via internalization, markets that are discussed below. For example, during the first week of January 2008, based on exchange data, of the 13,222,716 shares of NYSE-listed stocks traded during this week, 41.7% were traded by the NYSE Euronext and 12.3% by NYSE Arca. The remainder were traded by markets not related to the NYSE, including the regional markets, Nasdaq markets, and new stock markets such as the International Securities Exchange and Chicago Board Options Exchange, discussed in the following text.

To generalize this dispersion (or "fragmentation") of trading of an exchange's listed stocks across multiple trading venues on a day in January 2008, according to exchange data consider that of the

- 4,634,118,176 shares of NYSE-listed stocks traded, 39.7% were traded on the NYSE and 12.8% were traded on NYSE Arca, for a total of 52.5% on NYSE affiliated markets
- 2,573,601,692 shares of Nasdaq-listed stocks, 48.4% were traded on Nasdaq
- 1,245,043,387 shares of Amex-listed stocks, only 3.4% were traded on Amex

As indicated in the discussion on Regulation National Market Systems (NMS) later in this chapter, this increase in the fragmentation of trading among venues is likely to continue or even increase due to Regulation NMS.

Other Over-the-Counter Markets

The OTC market is often called a market for "unlisted" stocks. As described previously, there are listing requirements for exchanges. And while, technically, Nasdaq has not been an exchange—it was an OTC market—there are also listing requirements for the NNM and the Small Capitalization OTC markets. Nevertheless, exchange-traded stocks are called "listed," and stocks traded on the OTC markets, including Nasdaq, are called "unlisted."

There are three parts to the OTC market: two under Nasdaq and a third market for truly unlisted stocks, which is therefore a non-Nasdaq OTC market. The non-Nasdaq OTC market is composed of two parts, the OTC Bulletin Board (OTCBB) and the Pink Sheets.

Thus, technically, both exchanges and Nasdaq have listing requirements and only the non-Nasdaq OTC markets are non-listed. However, in common parlance, the exchanges are often called the "listed market," and Nasdaq, by default, is referred to as the "unlisted market." As a result, a more useful and practical categorization of the U.S. stock trading mechanisms is as follows:

1. Exchange-listed stocks
   a. National Exchanges
   b. Regional Exchanges
2. Nasdaq-listed OTC stocks
   a. NNM
   b. Nasdaq Small Cap Market (Capital Market Issues)
3. Non-Nasdaq OTC stocks—unlisted
   a. OTCBB
   b. Pink Sheets

There are two categories of non-Nasdaq stocks. The first is the OTCBB, also called simply the Bulletin Board or Bulletin (often just the "Bullies"). The OTCBB is a regulated electronic quotation service that displays real-time quotes, last sale prices, and volume information in the OTC equity securities. These equity securities are generally securities that are not listed or traded on the Nasdaq or the national stock exchanges. The OTCBB is not part of nor related to the Nasdaq stock market.

The OTCBB provides access to more than 3,300 securities and includes more than 230 participating market-makers. The traded companies do not have any filing or reporting requirements with Nasdaq or FINRA. However, issues of all securities quoted on the

OTCBB are subject to periodic filing requirements with the SEC or other regulatory authorities. Companies quoted on the OTCBB must be fully reporting (i.e., current with all required SEC fillings) but have no market capitalization, minimum share price, corporate governance, or other requirements. Companies that have been "de-listed" from stock exchanges for falling below minimum capitalization, minimum share price, or other requirements often end up being quoted on the OTCBB.

The second non-Nasdaq OTC market is the Pink Sheets. The Pink Sheets is an electronic quotation system that displays quotes from broker dealers for many OTC securities. Market-makers and other brokers who buy and sell OTC securities can use the Pink Sheets to publish their bid and ask quotation prices. The name "Pink Sheets" comes from the color of paper on which the quotes were historically printed prior to the electronic system. They are currently published today by Pink Sheets LLC, a privately owned company. Pink Sheets LLC is neither a NASD broker-dealer nor registered with the SEC; it is also not a stock exchange.

To be quoted in the Pink Sheets companies do not need to fulfill any requirements (e.g., filing statements with the SEC). With the exception of a few foreign issuers (mostly represented by American Depositary Receipts, or ADRs), the companies quoted in the Pink Sheets tend to be closely held, extremely small, and/or thinly traded. Most do not meet the minimum listing requirements for trading on a stock exchange such as the NYSE. Many of these companies do not file periodic reports or audited financial statements with the SEC, making it very difficult for investors to find reliable, unbiased information about those companies.

For these reasons, the SEC views companies listed on Pink Sheets as "among the most risky investments" and advises potential investors to heavily research the companies in which they plan to invest. Buying Pink Sheets stocks is intended to be difficult. Broker-dealers are enjoined to weed out unsophisticated investors who may get an e-mail or word-of-mouth tip about a small stock.

Most OTCBB companies are dually quoted, meaning they are quoted on both the OTCBB and Pink Sheets. Stocks traded on the OTCBB or Pink Sheets are usually thinly traded microcap or penny stocks and are avoided by many investors due to a well-founded fear that share prices are easily manipulated. The SEC issues stern warnings to investors to beware of common fraud and manipulation schemes.

Options Exchanges

In general, options trading is composed of two components: (1) options on individual stocks (stock options), and (2) options an indexes (index options).

Options exchanges are a combination of exchanges of two different origins. The first group began as options exchanges and, as discussed elsewhere, diversified into stock exchanges. They are the Chicago Board Options Exchange (CBOE) and the International Securities Exchange (ISE). The second group consists of stock exchanges that diversified into options exchanges. They are Amex, the PHLX, the BCX (a subsidiary of the BSE and now part of the Montreal Stock Exchange, which became part of the TSX Group), and the NYSE through its Archipelago holding, which had bought the Pacific Stock Exchange, which had added options to its original stock business. With the acquisition of the PHLX, Nasdaq has joined the NYSE as a newcomer in the options market.

A significant difference between stock and options trading is that stock trading is predominantly institutional but stock options trading has a larger retail component, as shown below:

	Institutional	Retail
Stock	85% to 90%	10% to 15%
Options	50%	50%

Other Stock Exchange Markets

Since options exchanges are registered with the SEC, they too can initiate and operate stock exchanges. During 2007, two options exchanges, the ISE and CBOE, began stock exchanges, called the ISE Stock Exchange and the Chicago Board Options Stock Exchange, respectively.

The ISE stock market has two components, the first of which began during September 2006. The first component, called the MidPoint Match, is a non-displayed market or "dark pool" (discussed below), where users can trade in a continuous, anonymous pool in which trades are executed at the midpoint of the NBBO. The second component is a fully displayed continuous and anonymous electronic market wherein quotes are integrated in an auction market. Thus, investors can benefit from the interaction between a non-displayed dark pool, the MidPoint Match, and the displayed liquidity pool. In this combination of systems, orders will have the opportunity for price improvement from the MidPoint Match system; or be executed or be displayed on the market's order book; or be routed out to other exchanges as required by the SEC's Regulation NMS.

Interestingly, the CBOE and ISE were options-only exchanges that subsequently developed stock exchanges. On the other hand, some of the regional stock exchanges, Philadelphia, Boston, and Pacific, later developed options exchanges. In addition, the NYSE is in the stock options business through its purchase of Archipelago, which previously bought the Pacific Stock Exchange. And Nasdaq entered the stock options business through its purchase of the PHLX.

Key Points That You Should Understand Before Proceeding

1. The types of changes that have occurred in the U.S. stock exchanges.
2. The national exchanges and their basic features.
3. The specialist system of the NYSE and the role of the specialist.
4. The transactors on the NYSE floor.
5. The difference between the NYSE and Nasdaq.

OFF-EXCHANGE MARKETS/ALTERNATIVE ELECTRONIC MARKETS

As explained earlier, the national and regional exchanges have continued to evolve and, in particular, have become much more electronically oriented. As of early 2008, however, a large volume of U.S. stock trading is done off any of the regulated stock exchanges. There has been significant growth and innovation in this sector of the U.S. stock markets in recent years. The **off-exchange markets** (also called **alternative electronic markets**) have continued to grow rapidly and become much more diverse.

Innovation in non-exchange (or off-exchange) trading began even before Nasdaq began. For example, Instinet (an acronym for Institutional Network) began trading in 1969 and was essentially the first electronic communication network (ECN) (although, as discussed below, it was not called an ECN until the late 1990s when the SEC introduced the term as part of the development of its order handling rules).

In general, these off-exchange markets are divided into two categories: ECNs and alternative trading systems.

Electronic Communication Networks

ECNs are essentially off-exchange exchanges. They are direct descendants of (and part of) Nasdaq, not the NYSE. ECNs are privately owned broker-dealers that operate as market participants, initially within the Nasdaq system. They display bids and offers; that is, they provide an open display. They provide institutions and market-makers with an anonymous way to enter orders. Essentially, an ECN is a limit order book that is widely disseminated and open for continuous trading to subscribers who may enter and access orders displayed on the ECN. ECNs offer transparency, anonymity, automated service, and reduced costs, and are therefore effective for handling small orders. ECNs may also be linked into the Nasdaq marketplace via a quotation representing the ECN's best buy and sell quote. In general, ECNs use the Internet to link buyers and sellers, bypassing brokers and trading floors. ECNs are informationally linked, even though they are distinct businesses. ECNs are subject to some of the best execution responsibilities including the SEC's Regulation NMS, which is discussed later in the text.

Consider the background of ECNs. Instinet, the first ECN, began operating in 1969 before Nasdaq was founded in 1971. Instinet was designed to be a trading system for institutional investors (and hence, the acronym for its name, which stands for "Institutional Network"). Instinet was viewed as an alternative to and competitor of the traditional Nasdaq dealer market. Instinet was intended to be a trading system for institutional investors, which allowed them to meet in an anonymous, disintermediated market.

Instinet seemed very similar to an exchange but was registered with the SEC, not as an exchange, but initially as a broker-dealer and subsequently as an ECN. Instinet took the position that they were just a broker-dealer that operated in the off-exchange ("upstairs") market as does any other broker-dealer that puts trades together for large customers. The only difference according to Instinet was that it operated electronically. This view emphasized the difficulty of distinguishing an exchange from a broker-dealer in a technological environment. The SEC acknowledged this difficulty by using a new category to apply to Instinet, that is, ECN, as discussed below when we explain order handling rules.

The number of ECNs increased considerably after the SEC imposed the order handling rules in 1997. As a result, ECNs significantly affected Nasdaq after 1997. ECNs such as Archipelago, Brut, Island, and Instinet captured a majority of Nasdaq volume in about two years. Instinet acquired Island in September 2002.

Archipelago, which began operating in 1997, handles both institutional and retail order flow. Another ECN, Island, was primarily retail. Prior to these developments, all the off-exchange systems were designed for institutional customers.

As many as a dozen ECNs existed by early 2000. Then, a wave of consolidations and acquisitions began that within only two years reduced that number down to a few. Some of the large ECNs were acquired: Instinet by Nasdaq during December 2005, and Archipelago by the NYSE during March 2006. Prior to its acquisition, Archipelago, an ECN at the time, acquired the Pacific Stock Exchange to form a fully electronic stock exchange.

As of early 2008, there were only a few ECNs operating; the largest is Better Alternative Trading System (BATS), which provides trades to Nasdaq, the NYSE, the ISE, and some regional exchanges. BATS began in January 2006 and applied to the SEC to become a fully licensed securities exchange during 2007. On August 25, 2008, Direct Edge, which had also applied to the SEC to become an exchange, announced that it would take control of the ISE Stock Exchange. This action allowed Direct Edge to operate as an exchange prior to the SEC approval of its own exchange.

Becoming an exchange permits BATS and Direct Edge to send out price quotes to customers more quickly and directly, as discussed in the following text. BATS handles approximately 10% of U.S. equities and Direct Edge handles 5%.

Among the other large ECNs are Bloomberg, LavaFlow, and Track Data.

Prior to 2000, ECNs could not penetrate the NYSE-listed stocks as they did the Nasdaq market. The main reason was the impediment imposed by the NYSE's Rule 390, also called the order consolidation or order concentration rule. According to Rule 390, dealers who traded NYSE-listed stocks in the OTC could not be members of the NYSE. For this reason, only a few dealers actively participated in the OTC market for NYSE-listed stocks and so NYSE-listed stocks were traded mainly on the NYSE.

All central markets have incentives to impose order consolidation rules on their members. However, the SEC, to open up the NYSE market, pressured the NYSE to eliminate Rule 390. The NYSE eliminated Rule 390 in December 1999. This elimination exposed the NYSE to the same type of fragmentation to which Nasdaq had been exposed. But in the years immediately after the elimination of Rule 390, the NYSE continued to conduct most of the trading in its stocks; that is, the NYSE market did not experience nearly as much fragmentation as the Nasdaq markets. Subsequently, however, the NYSE has lost considerable market share to ECNs and other exchanges.

Some of the key events for ECNs are summarized in Figure 6.

Alternative Trading Systems

In addition to ECNs, other **alternative trading systems (ATS)** developed as alternatives to exchanges. It is not necessary in order for two natural parties to conduct a transaction to use an intermediary. That is, the services of a broker or a dealer are not required to execute a trade. The direct trading of stocks between two customers without the use of a broker or an exchange is called an ATS.

A number of proprietary ATSs have been developed. These ATSs are for-profit "broker's brokers" that match investor orders and report trading activity to the marketplace via the Nasdaq or the NYSE. More recently, such trades have been reported through Trade Reporting Facilities, as discussed in the following text. In a sense, ATSs are similar to exchanges because they are designed to allow two participants to meet directly on the system and are maintained by a third party who also serves a limited regulatory function by imposing requirements on each subscriber.

Broadly, there are two types of ATS: (1) crossing networks, which have functioned since the 1980s; and (2) dark pools, which are much more recent.

Crossing Networks

Crossing networks are electronic venues that do not display quotes but anonymously match large orders. Crossing networks are systems developed to allow institutional

Figure 6	ECN Highlights
1969	Instinet (Institutional Network)—first ECN, formed in 1969, before Nasdaq • Electronic block-trading system for institutional investors
1997	OHRs (Order-Handling Rules) approved • ECNs grew quickly in number
1997	Archipelago formed in December 1996; began trading in 1997; granted exchange status by SEC in October 2001
1997	Island included in the Nasdaq Montage in January 1997
1999	NYSE Rule 390 eliminated
2000	Archipelago, an ECN, bought the Pacific Stock Exchange to form the first fully electronic stock exchange
2001	Instinet went public—IPO was a success
2002	Instinet acquired Island
2005	Instinet acquired by Nasdaq
2006	BATS ECN initiated
2006	Archipelago acquired by NYSE
2008	Only a few ECNs remain, including BATS, Direct Edge, and LavaFlow
2008	BATS ECN becomes a U.S. stock exchange
2008	Direct Edge ECN takes control of ISE Stock Exchange

investors to cross trades—that is, match buyers and sellers directly—typically via computer. These networks are batch processors that aggregate orders for execution at pre-specified times. Crossing networks provide anonymity and reduce costs, and are specifically designed to minimize market impact trading costs. They vary considerably in their approach, including the type of order information that can be entered by the subscriber and the amount of pre-trade transparency that is available to participants.

A crossing network matches buy and sell orders in a multinational trade at a price that is set elsewhere. The price used at the cross can be the midpoint of a bid–ask spread (such as the national bid and offer, as discussed below) or the last transaction price at a major market (such as the NYSE or Nasdaq) or linkage of markets. Thus, no price discovery results from a crossing network.

The major drawbacks of the crossing networks are that (1) their execution rates tend to be low, and (2) if they draw too much order flow away from the main market, they can, to their own detriment, undermine the quality of the very prices on which they are basing their trades. These limitations can be overcome in a call auction environment that includes price discovery.

ATSs began developing during October 1987 when Investment Technologies Group's (ITG) Posit began. Posit is a crossing network that matches customer buy and sell orders that meet or cross each other in price (this is the way crossing networks were named) at a price established by the NYSE or Nasdaq markets or the overall national market.

LiquidNet, a crossing network that started operation in 2001, is an ATS that enables institutional customers to meet anonymously, negotiate a price, and trade in large sizes (average trade size is nearly 50,000 shares). Part of LiquidNet's ability to attract order flow is attributable to its customers being able to negotiate their trades with reference to quotes prevailing in the major market centers. In other words, LiquidNet's customers do not have to participate in significant price discovery. Further, LiquidNet customers' anonymity and knowledge that counterparties in the system also wish to trade in size offers them some assurance that their orders will not have undue market impact. A key feature of the LiquidNet system is that customer matches are found electronically, and negotiations are also conducted electronically by the natural buyer and seller. LiquidNet has also developed in Europe.

Instinet, in addition to its continuous ECN, also developed an after-hours crossing, the Instinet Crossing Network. Instinet's after-hours cross was the first crossing network.

The Burlington Capital Markets, Burlington Large Order Cross (BLOX) also provides crossing systems. These systems enable institutions to trade with no price impact in a batched environment; the crosses are made at prices set in other stock market places. In addition, Harborside, which started operations in 2002, provides crossing services. These systems assist institutional customers to meet anonymously and negotiate their trades in an anonymous manner in an electronic environment using current quotes from external stock markets as benchmarks.

These crossing systems are designed exclusively for institutional order flow. Among the major current crossing networks and their area of specializations are

- *LiquidNet*: for the buy-side to buy-side only
- *Pipeline*: for buy-side to buy-side block business only
- *ITG Posit*: provides timed crossings five to 10 times per day for buy-side to buy-side only
- *BIDS*: unlike the first three is an agency broker; that is, it does not engage in proprietary trading and, thus, compete with its customers; launched in spring 2007

Crossing networks have provided attractive alternatives to institutions to trade without their orders having any impact on the prices. However, due to lack of liquidity, their execution rates tend to be low and if they draw too much order flow from the established markets, they could undermine the quality of the prices that are the bases for the trades. In effect, crossing networks, which use prices from the central stock markets to price their crosses, are "free riding" on the price discovery of the central markets. These limitations could be resolved in a call auction environment, which does provide price discovery.

In a call auction, sometimes called a period call, orders from customers are batched together for a simultaneous trade at a specific point in time. At the time of the call (in a "timed call"), a market clearing price is determined—that is, there is a price discovery—and buy orders at this price and higher and sell orders at this price and lower are executed.

But the two systems based on call auction methods have not developed liquidity. The two ATSs based on call auction principles were the Arizona Stock Exchange (which started operations in 1991 and has been inactive since 2001) and Optimark (which started in 1999 and has been inactive since 2000). Neither of these systems succeeded in attracting critical mass order flow. Their experiences point up the difficulty of implementing an innovative new trading system that has to compete with an established market center, especially when the new system provides independent price discovery. These call auction systems provided price discovery and, thus, competed with established market centers and had difficulty attracting order flow.

Crossing markets are offered by some of the major broker-dealers, who may also use such systems to "internalize" their order flow—match or cross bids and offers "upstairs"—that is, in their own organization. These orders may both be customer orders or one may be a customer order they cross with their own proprietary orders. Examples of firms involved in internalization are Citigroup, Credit Suisse, Goldman Sachs, Merrill Lynch, Morgan Stanley, and UBS.

Dark Pools

Another step in the evolution of non-exchange trading is the use of **dark pools.** Dark pools fulfill the need for a neutral gathering place and fulfill the traditional role of an exchange in the new paradigm. Dark pools are private crossing networks in which participants submit orders to cross trades at externally specified prices and, thus, provide anonymous sources of liquidity (hence, the name "dark"). No quotes are involved—only orders at the externally determined price—and, thus, there is no price discovery.

Dark pools are electronic execution systems that do not display quotes but provide transactions at externally provided prices. Both the buyer and seller must submit a willingness to transact at this externally provided price—often the midpoint of the NBBO—to complete a trade. Dark pools are designed to prevent information leakage and offer access to undisclosed liquidity. Unlike open or displayed quotes, dark pools are anonymous and leave no "footprints." The advent of pricing in pennies led to less transparent markets and was, thus, instrumental in the initiation of dark pools.

Dark pools, as well as crossing networks, are creating very fragmented markets for large trades and block trades. Customers also use algorithmic trading (discussed later) to respond to such hidden liquidity.

Among the advantages of dark pools are

- non-displayed liquidity
- prevention of information leakage (anonymous trading)
- volume discovery
- reduced market impact

Among the disadvantages are

- less or no visibility
- difficulty to interact with order flow
- no price discovery

The sponsors of dark pools can be

- exchanges (e.g., NYSE Euronext, the Nasdaq stock market, and the ISE)
- broker-dealers (e.g., Credit Suisse, Morgan Stanley, Goldman Sachs, Merrill Lynch, and others; can be used for brokerage internalization)
- independent organizations (e.g., Instinet, Liquidnet, Pipeline Trading Strategies and ITG Posit)
- consortia of other organizations

Key Points That You Should Understand Before Proceeding

1. What is meant by off-exchange markets (alternative electronic markets).
2. The two categories of off-exchange markets: ECNs and ATSs.
3. How a crossing network operates.
4. How dark pools work.

EVOLVING STOCK MARKET PRACTICES

In this section, we describe evolving stock market practices that include the following:

- order handling rules
- small order routers
- SEC Regulation NMS
- internalization
- ADF
- trade reporting facility
- direct market access
- algorithmic trading

Order Handling Rules

During the 1990s, the SEC continued its emphasis on greater quote and price transparency. In this regard, the SEC instituted new order handling rules in 1997. First, any market-maker who held a customer order had to display that order in their quote. Second, a market-maker could place a more aggressive quote in an ECN, if the ECN displayed the top of its book in the Nasdaq quote montage. Third, if the ECN's own best quote was not shown in the quote montage, then the market-maker had to update its own quote in Nasdaq to match the ECN quote.

While these rules may seem narrow and technical, their effect was significant. They were the basis for ECNs to become major participants in the stock market. Before these rules, Instinet was the only ECN. By 1999, there were nine ECNs.

All a new ECN needed to capture order flow was to be a gateway that attracted some customers to place limit orders on its electronic book. Connectivity with other markets (either directly or through one of Nasdaq's systems) would allow market orders from the customers of other firms to reach its books and become traders. ECNs did not have an impact on NYSE trades until Rule 390 was eliminated in 1999, as discussed above.

The Archipelago ECN began in December 1996. Archipelago stated on its website:

> In January 1997, the U.S Securities and Exchange Commission (SEC) implemented new Order Handling Rules that revolutionized trading in Nasdaq securities. The new rules created the opportunity for Electronic Communications Networks (ECNs), such as the Archipelago ECN, to interact directly with the Nasdaq National Market System. The Archipelago ECN was formed in December 1996 in response to these rules.

The SEC-enforced consolidation, transparency, and accessibility of price information caused by these SEC changes quickly caused the flow of limit orders to fragment onto multiple books and the ECNs' cheap, fast, and anonymous trading forced Nasdaq to alter its trading systems and organizational structure.

Then, with the passage of time, consolidation started taking place among the ECNs. Instinet acquired Island and Archipelago acquired the Pacific Stock Exchange (Archipelago and Instinet/Island accounted for most of the ECN volume). In May 2004, Nasdaq acquired the Brut ECN, previously owned by Sungard Data Systems.

Smart Order Routers

In concept, it might be expected that most of the trading volume of stocks listed on an exchange would be traded directly with the exchange. This has not, however, been the case.

The construct of Nasdaq as a dealer system has made it easy for ECNs and others to conduct the trades directly and report them to the exchange. And since NYSE Rule 390 was removed in 1999, it has been easier to trade NYSE listed stocks off the exchange. This trading of stock listed on an exchange off the exchange is called **fragmentation**. While the fragmentation of the NYSE has increased, the Nasdaq remains much more fragmented than the NYSE.

One of the many results of this fragmentation has been the need by customers for some new systems to provide order management, handling, and routing services. These services select a market often on the basis of recent trading activity, resulting in its user receiving the best executions across the markets by "consolidating" the information across the markets.

One outcome of these smart order routers (also called consolidators) is that customer order flow is "less sticky"; that is, the order flow will switch from one execution service to another quickly based on short-term, quantitative information.

Securities and Exchange Commission Regulation National Market System

The Securities Act amendments of 1975 mandated a U.S. national market system (NMS). The core of this national market was the Intermarket Trading System (ITS), which began operating in 1978. The ITS electronically linked eight markets (NYSE, Amex, Boston, Cincinnati, Chicago, Pacific, and Philadelphia Stock Exchanges, and the NASD OTC market) via ITS computers. The ITS permitted traders at any of these exchanges to go to the best available price at the other exchanges on which the security could trade. The NMS also included a consolidated electronic tape, as discussed elsewhere, which combined the last-sale prices from all the markets onto a single continuous tape. The use of the ITS, however, was voluntary.

Even though ITS evolved, by 2007, it was based on obsolete technology. During 2007, the ITS system was replaced by the new NMS. Regulation NMS was designed by the SEC for electronic exchanges. Regulation NMS requires that orders be executed at the market (exchanges or other execution venues), which offers the best price for the customers. Thus, exchanges must compete with each other on a level playing field. Regulation NMS's impact is attributable to two of its component rules.

The first rule is the Order Protection Rule (Trade-Through Rule). This rule requires that trades be executed at the best displayed prices provided by an electronic trading system and accessible under one second. This means that markets will have to "route out" their orders to other markets if the other markets have a better price (bids or offers). That is, a market cannot "trade through" a better price from another market and trade on their own market instead. As a result of NMS, each exchange has to send its orders to other exchanges if the other exchange has a better price.

The Trade-Through Rule provides price protection to top-of-book orders (best bids or best offers) placed on exchanges that are electronically accessible. Reserve and hidden orders are not protected. Only electronic quotes are protected. All exchanges are required to have capabilities to route orders to the market with the best bid or offer if they are not able to match the price to execute an order on their own exchange. Only the NBBO (or top-of-book) is displayed. In this environment, competitive pricing and low-latency systems are essential in attracting order flow.

The second rule is the Access Rule, which requires the use of private linkages among exchanges to facilitate access to quotes and sets a limit on the access fees by the markets. These private linkages replaced the ITS.

Exchanges had to go to electronic trading to offer protection under Regulation NMS. ECNs and broker-dealers are also covered by Regulation NMS.

A common view is that Regulation NMS will fundamentally change U.S. stock trading by creating a virtual centralized market in which all exchanges will be automated and interconnected. The NMS is expected to divert orders from the two major exchanges, NYSE Euronext and Nasdaq, to the regional exchanges and ECNs. Some regional exchanges view Regulation NMS as a great equalizer. The reason for this position is that the goal is that all investors will get the best price when transacting stocks, regardless of which exchange posts these prices.

Internalization

Internalization refers to off-exchange ("upstairs") trades, mainly of retail trades. As opposed to block trading, internalization involves keeping retail orders within the firm ("internalized") with the broker-dealer buying from its sell orders and selling from its buy orders, generally at the published best bid/offer or a penny better. This practice results in proprietary trading revenue for the broker-dealer. A broker-dealer with a large number of customer orders thereby has a trading opportunity to make a "dealer spread" (buying at the bid and selling at the offer) without interference and will lay off any unwanted positions in the primary market. Brokerage firms internalize through proprietary ATSs. Some believe that this practice reduces transparency, impairs price discovery, and harms investors.

The equity markets permit broker-dealers to internalize retail order flow upstairs. The trades are reported on the trade reporting facility (TRE), as discussed in the following text. While the SEC has approved such internalization in the stock markets, in the stock options markets, the orders must be shown to the public market before internalizing them upstairs. Internalization is, thus, treated differently in the stock and stock options markets.

Off-exchange (internalized) trades as of the end of 2007 account for about 30% of volume in Nasdaq's listed stocks and 16% of the consolidated volume in listed NYSE stocks. Brokers that internalize are reporting 500,000 trades a day in the Nasdaq world and about 350,000 trades a day in NYSE-listed stocks. This volume comes from broker-dealers interacting with their customers' order flow in their upstairs environment and then printing those trades on Nasdaq, as discussed next.[2]

The NYSE is opposed to internalization. It believes that orders are best represented when they interact with the broader marketplace.

Alternative Display Facility

An ADF is an entity independent of a registered securities exchange that collects and disseminates securities quotes and trades. It is a display-only facility. The ADF is an alternative to exchanges for publishing quotations and for comparing and reporting trades. This differs from a trading facility with execution capabilities (a stock exchange) in that the exchange would simply send back to the owner of the displayed order a notice of execution. The NASD operated an ADF since July 2002. It is now operated by FINRA.

The ADF provides members with a facility for the display of quotations, the reporting of trades, and the comparison of trades. As of March 2007, CTA-listed securities (NYSE,

---

[2] Ivy Schmerken, "Stock Exchanges Create Trade Reporting Facilities to Earn Market Data Fees From Internalized Trades," *Wall Street and Technology* (January 5, 2007).

Amex, and the regional exchanges), as well as Nasdaq-listed securities, are eligible for posting quotations through the ADF. ADF best bid and offer and trade reports are included in the consolidated data stream for CTA and Nasdaq-listed securities.

The ADF competes with Nasdaq's SuperMontage system. These organizations exist to capture some of the values of this information (which has been historically captured by exchanges) for the ADF's information suppliers, usually ECNs.

Trade Reporting Facility

As previously indicated, in the stock market trades can be internalized or arranged upstairs, that is, not traded on an exchange. But if they are traded via internalization, they are not reported on the exchange on which the stock is listed. Traditionally, NASD has had a TRF on which these off-exchange trades are printed—NASD's ADF. So, for example, if Merrill Lynch internalized a trade, it would be printed on NASDs TRF through its ADF.

Until recently, broker-dealers that internalized trades—as well as crossing networks and ECNs that matched trades among their subscribers—had to report these trades to their regulator, the NASD via the Nasdaq's Automated Confirmation Transaction System, known as ACT.

The SEC issued an order on June 30, 2006, approving Nasdaq to begin operating as an exchange in Nasdaq-listed securities. The order included approval of the TRF, a new limited liability company operated by Nasdaq and subject to NASD's oversight. In the wake of Nasdaq receiving SEC approval to become a national stock exchange, NASD and Nasdaq separated, and the SEC allowed Nasdaq to keep its TRF, but also opened this up to competition, thereby ending Nasdaq's and NASD's monopoly. Nasdaq's TRF went live August 1, 2006, the same day that it began operating as an exchange in Nasdaq-listed stocks. With the consolidation of the regulatory functions of NASD and NYSE, FINRA has taken over the reporting function. However, FINRA keeps the tape revenue. For this reason, exchanges can set up their own TRFs, report these trades, and keep some of the tape revenues.

The National Exchange (NSX) (the former Cincinnati Stock Exchange) has set up a TRF, so currently such trades can be reported through this exchange as well as the Nasdaq.

The NYSE integrated with the NASD to create a TRF, serving customers reporting off-exchange trades in all listed NMS stocks. Thus, stock brokers that internalize trades in NYSE-listed stocks would be able to report those trades to a jointly operated NYSE/NASD TRF. These trades are reported by NYSE's TRF as ADF(NYSE). The TRF for NYSE-listed stocks began in 2007.

While the NYSE remains opposed to the internalization of trades, the exchange is developing a TRF for competitive reasons. The NYSE believes that retail orders for individual investors are best represented when they interact with the broader marketplace.[3]

Regional exchanges, including the PHLX, the Boston Equity Exchange (BeX), and the CHX, are also proceeding with plans to create TRFs.

As of early 2008, approximately 30% of total stock volume was reported through a TRF.

Direct Market Access

In general, buy-side firms continued to take more control over the way their transactions were executed. **Direct market access (DMA)** refers to the use of electronic systems to access

---

[3] Schmerken, "Stock Exchanges Create Trade Reporting Facilities to Earn Market Data Fees From Internalized Trades."

various liquidity pools and execution venues directly, without the intervention of a sell-side firm trading desk or broker. There are several advantages of DMA to a buy-side firm:

- DMA is faster, allowing traders to benefit from short-term market opportunities.
- DMA has lower transactions costs.
- DMA provides anonymous transactions.
- DMA is not handled by brokers, so there is less chance for error.

With respect to cost, it is estimated that DMA commissions are about one cent per share; program trades are two cents per share; and block trades cost four to five cents per share. Hedge funds are aggressive users of DMA.[4]

Initially, the providers of DMA electronic services were independent firms. But increasingly, traditional sell-side firms have either acquired the independent firms or developed their own DMA systems to provide DMA services to sell-side firms. Among the major providers of this type are Goldman Sachs, Morgan Stanley, CSFB, Citigroup (which acquired Lava), and Bank of New York. Initially, DMA was used only for U.S. equities, but this focus has expanded to U.S. fixed-income and derivatives and into the international markets, Europe and the Asia/Pacific.

DMA has become commoditized and its providers now often provide a comprehensive set of services including program trading, block trading, and also the more sophisticated technique, algorithmic trading, which is discussed in the next section.

Algorithmic Trading

Traditionally, orders for stock executions have been conducted by traders who execute the trades on a trading desk for a portfolio manager or whomever determines what trades should be executed. Traders are judged to have "market information and savy," which permits them to conduct the trades at a lower cost and with less market impact than the portfolio manager conducting the trades on a less formal basis themselves.

The effectiveness of these traders is often measured by execution evaluation services and traders are often compensated partially on the basis of their effectiveness. But some observers believe that the traders, in the interest of maximizing their compensation, may have different incentives than the portfolio managers and do not optimize the portfolio manager's objectives—this is referred to as an agency effect. In addition, some think that trades could be conducted more efficiently by electronic systems than by human traders.

As a result, due to improved technology and quantitative techniques, and also regulatory changes, electronic trading systems have been developed to supplement or replace human traders and their trading desks. Such trading is called **algorithmic trading** or "algo." Algorithmic trading is a relatively recent type of trading technique whereby an overall trade (either buy or sell) is conducted electronically in a series of small transactions instead of one large transaction. Such trades are conducted via computers that make the decision to trade or not trade depending on whether recent price movements indicate whether the market will be receptive to the intended trade at the moment or, on the other hand, will cause the price to move significantly against the intended price. Algorithmic trading also permits the traders to hide their intentions. Trading may involve small trades on a continuous basis

---

[4] Ivy Schmerken, "Direct-Market-Access Trading," *Wall Street and Technology* (February 4, 2005).

rather than a large trade at a point in time. The algo is often said to leave no "footprint" and is a "soft touch" way of trading.

Algos, like dark pools, provide anonymity, which the "visible markets," like exchanges and ECNs, do not. Algos are often described as "hiding in plain view."

The advent and wide use of algos is due primarily to both technology and regulation. The technology element is based on faster and cheaper technological systems to execute via improved quantitative methods. The regulatory element is the adoption of pennies and the approval of the order handling rules, which provided for the growth of ECNs by the SEC. The adoption of "pennies," which provides for smaller pricing increments, and technological advancements which provide for low-latency trading have made algorithmic trading more necessary and feasible (low latency refers to a short period of time to execute an instruction, that is, high speed).

One important result of pennies in conjunction with algorithmic trading has been that the average trade size has been decreased significantly, again increasing the requirements for reporting and systems. There has been a significant reduction of the average trade size at the NYSE beginning in 2001. Order size on the NYSE declined significantly from over 2,000 shares in 1998 to slightly over 330 in 2007. The use of algorithmic trading is significant by large traders such as hedge funds and mutual funds. Some traders maintain their own algorithmic trading facilities and others use the systems provided by another organization. Overall, algorithmic trading has the advantages of being scalable, anonymous, transparent, and very fast.

SUMMARY

During the 1980s and 1990s, competition among equity transactions providers changed considerably and became much more intense. In the 1980s, the competition for equity transactions was mainly among the NYSE, the Amex, the regional exchanges, and Nasdaq. Gradually, the Amex and the regional exchanges lost ground and the competition became mainly between the two largest exchanges, the NYSE versus Nasdaq. This competition was significantly based on very different market structures: the order-driven, specialist, floor-based mechanism of the NYSE on the one hand; and the quote-driven, dealer-based, electronic mechanism of Nasdaq on the other. Debates on the merits of these competing market structures flourished. The advantage of the specialist system is the opportunity for price improvement and the advantage of the electronic system is speed of execution. The common view is that retail investors prefer better prices and professional traders prefer greater speed. This argument could be summarized, in the potential words of an advertising specialist, as "better pricing versus higher speed."

Gradually, however, these two market structures have converged significantly toward hybrid markets. Although both the NYSE and Nasdaq have converged toward hybrid markets from very different positions, their differences have remained significant. But as they became more similar in market structure and in other ways, the competition from other market venues became more intense. After the SEC approved new order handling rules in 1997, ECNs took larger shares first from Nasdaq and then, after 1999, when NYSE's Rule 390 was eliminated, from the NYSE. The NYSE and Nasdaq have also grown by acquiring other market venues. In addition, both the NYSE and Nasdaq have developed global relationships, Euronext for the NYSE and OMX Borse Dubai for the Nasdaq.

Meanwhile, some other forces have made it very difficult for either exchange or the ECNs to compete profitably for equity executions. Institutions, intermediaries, and increasingly hedge funds have become demanding with respect to three characteristics of execution services. The first is cost. Transactions costs in a very competitive, high turnover environment have become increasingly important. The second is speed. The volatility of the markets and the competition among market users have made "latency" a common concern. The third is anonymity. Hedge funds pursuing proprietary strategies and mutual funds whose buy and sell programs may endure over a long period require anonymous transactions.

As a result, ATSs have developed to satisfy these institutional market participant needs. Thus, while ECNs have been increasingly successful at competing with exchanges directly, crossing networks, dark pools, and internalization have competed with exchanges in very different ways based on their costs, speed, and anonymity. These mechanisms, however, fragment the central markets and depend on the central markets for price discovery. Thus, there are limits to their potential total activity or size.

Aggressive clients often consider the execution process in three levels. First, they try to cross orders internally where there would be no execution costs. If they do not have an internal match, they will then send their orders to a crossing network, which does not display quotes to avoid adverse price reactions. Finally, they send their orders to open markets or exchange only as a last resort. Some observers describe the orders that go to exchanges as "exhaust." In this regard, the data referred to herein indicate that the exchanges are trading a small share of their own listings.

In addition, Regulation NMS with its Trade-Through Rules levels the playing field among exchanges and ECNs. A common expectation is that Regulation NMS works to the advantage of the regional exchanges versus the NYSE and Nasdaq. There may, however, be few or no regional exchanges remaining.

But the competition is becoming more complex than simply the different execution venues competing with each other from different structures. Rather, they have begun competing against each other from similar structures. ECNs have and will become exchanges. While ATSs were the originators of dark pools and crosses, exchanges have also experimented with them (with the exception of buy-side to buy-side crosses). In addition, the importance of block trades diminishes as algorithmic trading reduces the trade size.

The upshot of these changes is that these execution venues all compete with each other and that the categories that formerly distinguished them are disappearing. The exchanges, ECNs, and ATSs will compete with each other for many of the same customers on the basis of the same functions and fees. Such competition may cause commoditization and a resulting low profitability for the providers of these services. Could equity transaction services follow the path of the U.S. inland water canals and the providers of some Internet services?

There may, however, be a limiting issue in such a development. The visible markets, the exchanges and ECNs, provide price discovery. Some of the other markets, crosses, dark pools, and internalization, do not provide price discovery, but rather have a free ride on the price discovery of the central and visible markets. But if the executions shift predominantly to the non-price discovery markets, how will prices be determined? This issue is similar to the issue in investments regarding active and passive investing and price discovery. That is, if all or most of the investors use a passive investment approach, there will be no active investors to provide the price discovery of the stocks. Opinions are not unanimous in either investments or stock execution.

KEY TERMS

- Algorithmic trading
- Alternative Display Facility (ADF)
- Alternative electronic markets
- Alternative trading systems (ATS)
- Auction market
- Bid quote
- Call auction
- Commission broker
- Competitive dealer, quote-based system
- Continuous market
- Crossing networks
- Dark pools
- Dealer market
- Direct market access (DMA)
- Electronic communication network (ECN)
- Exchange

- Floor brokers
- Fragmentation
- Hybrid market
- Internalization
- Limit order book
- Market structure
- National best bid and offer (NBBO)
- Natural buyers
- Natural sellers
- Offer quote
- Off-exchange markets
- Order-driven
- Preferencing
- Quote-driven
- Regional exchanges
- Specialist

QUESTIONS

1. How do order-driven and quote-driven market structures differ?
2. What is the role of natural buyers and natural sellers in order-driven markets?
3. Explain the two ways in which an order-driven market can be structured.
4. Who are the potential intermediaries in a quote-driven market?
5. Suppose the following quotes from three dealers:

Dealer	Bid	Offer
D	32.30	33.10
E	32.50	33.00
F	32.10	32.70
G	32.40	32.80

What is the NBBO?

6. This quotation is from an interview with William Donaldson, who at the time was the chairman of the NYSE, and appeared in the *New York Times* on January 30, 1990:

There's a need to understand the advantages of an auction market versus a dealer market. The auction market allows a buyer and a seller to get together and agree on a price and the dealer is not involved at all. That's opposed to a dealer market where the house is on both sides of the trade and the dealer makes the spread rather than having the spread shared by the buyer and the seller. One of the things we're coming to the forefront on now is the whole idea of what makes a good market. I think the best market is where you have the maximum number of people coming together in a single location and bidding against each other. . . . That is far superior to what we are getting now, which is a fractionalization of the market. Traders on machines, trades in the closet, trades in many areas where buyers and sellers don't have the opportunity to meet.

a. What is meant by an auction market?
b. What is meant by a dealer market?
c. Discuss Mr. Donaldson's opinion. In your answer, be sure to address the pros and cons of the different trading structures addressed in the chapter.

7. What is meant by a "fair and orderly market" on the NYSE?

8. Why is the Nasdaq referred to as a "fragmented market"?

9. What are the SuperDot and SuperMontage systems and what is their role?

10. What are the two sections of the Nasdaq stock market?

11. What are the three parts of the OTC market for stocks?

12. What is meant by off-exchange markets?

13. a. What is a crossing network?
    b. Name three crossing networks.
    c. What are the disadvantages of a crossing network?

14. a. What is a dark pool?
    b. What are the advantages of a dark pool?
    c. What are the disadvantages of a dark pool?

15. a. What is SEC Regulation NMS?
    b. What is the "Order Protection Rule" specified by Regulation NMS?
    c. What is the "Access Rule" specified by Regulation NMS?

16. a. What is meant by internalized trades?
    b. Why is the NYSE opposed to internalized trades?

17. a. What is meant by Direct Market Access?
    b. What are the advantages of DMA to buy-side firms?

18. a. What is algorithmic trading?
    b. Why is algorithmic trading used?

Markets for Corporate Senior Instruments: I

LEARNING OBJECTIVES

After reading this chapter, you will understand

- the various financing alternatives available to corporations

- the different forms of credit risk: default risk, credit spread risk, and downgrade risk

- the importance of credit ratings

- what commercial paper is

- the types of commercial paper: directly placed paper and dealer paper

- the differences between the U.S. commercial paper market and the Eurocommercial paper market

- what a medium-term note is

- what a syndicated loan is

- the two different ways a syndicated loan can be sold: assignment and participation

- the basic terms of a loan agreement

- what a lease financing transaction is

- the difference between a single-investor lease and a leveraged lease

Corporate senior instruments are financial obligations of a corporation that have priority over its common stock in the case of bankruptcy. They include debt obligations and preferred stock.

The market for corporate debt obligations can be classified into four sectors: (1) commercial paper market, (2) medium-term note market, (3) bank loan market, and (4) bond market. In this chapter, we look at the first four sectors. Unlike our discussion of common

From Chapter 19 of *Foundations of Financial Markets and Institutions*, 4/e. Frank J. Fabozzi. Franco Modigliani. Frank J. Jones.

stock, in which we focused first on the U.S. equity market and then the non–U.S. equity market, here we discuss both the U.S. markets and Euromarkets in which corporations can borrow funds.

Securities such as commercial paper, Euronotes, medium-term notes, and bonds represent alternatives to bank loans for companies needing to raise funds. The issuance of securities in the international market has increased substantially since the 1980s, in stark contrast to the bank borrowing trend. This phenomenon of borrower preference for issuing securities over borrowing directly from banks is referred to as the *securitization* of capital markets. The term *securitization* is actually used in two ways. It is in the broader sense that we use it here. In the more narrow sense, the term *securitization*, more specifically, *asset securitization*, is used to describe the process of pooling loans and issuing securities backed by these loans.

CREDIT RISK

Unlike investing in a U.S. Treasury security, an investor who lends funds to a corporation by purchasing its debt obligation is exposed to *credit risk*. But what is credit risk? Traditionally credit risk is defined as the risk that the borrower will fail to satisfy the terms of the obligation with respect to the timely payment of interest and repayment of the amount borrowed. This form of credit risk is called *default risk*.

In addition to default risk, there are other risks associated with the investment in debt securities that are also components of credit risk. Even in the absence of default, the investor is concerned that the market value of a debt instrument will decline in value and/or the relative price performance of that instrument will be worse than that of other debt obligations, which the investor is compared against. The yield on a corporate debt instrument is made up of two components: (1) the yield on a similar maturity Treasury issue, and (2) a premium to compensate for the risks associated with the debt instrument that do not exist in a Treasury issue, referred to as a *spread*. The part of the risk premium or spread attributable to credit risk is called the *credit spread*.

The price performance of a non-Treasury debt obligation and its return over some investment horizon will depend on how the credit spread changes. If the credit spread increases—investors say that the spread has "widened"—the market price of the debt obligation will decline. The risk that an issuer's debt obligation will decline due to an increase in the credit spread is called *credit spread risk*.

We explained credit risk first in our discussion of municipal securities. Professional money managers analyze an issuer's financial information and the specifications of the debt instrument itself in order to estimate the ability of the issuer to live up to its future contractual obligations. This activity is known as *credit analysis*. Some large institutional investors have their own credit analysis department, but most individual and institutional investors do not conduct such analytical studies. Instead, they rely primarily on commercial rating companies that perform credit analysis and express their conclusions by a system of ratings. There are three commercial rating companies: Standard & Poor's Corporation, Moody's Investors Service, Inc., and Fitch. In the next chapter, we will explain the factors that credit-rating companies consider in assigning a rating.

Once a rating is assigned to a corporate debt instrument, it can be changed based on subsequent economic and financial developments. An improvement in the credit quality of an issue or issuer is rewarded with a better credit rating, referred to as an *upgrade*; a deterioration in the credit quality of an issue or issuer is penalized by the assignment of an inferior credit rating, referred to as a *downgrade*. An unanticipated downgrading of an issue or issuer increases the credit spread sought by the market, resulting in a decline in the price of the issue or the issuer's debt obligation. This risk is referred to as *downgrade risk*.

The credit-rating companies play a key role in the functioning of debt markets. Investors take great comfort in knowing that the rating companies monitor the creditworthiness of issuers and keep the investing public informed of their findings. One would expect that other countries would have organizations that provide a similar function. This has not been the case. Only in recent years have credit-rating companies appeared in other countries. For example, in Japan, it was not until 1977 that a formal corporate bond-rating system was introduced. The original system for rating corporate bonds that was introduced in Japan in 1959 was based solely on the size of the issue.[1]

Key Points That You Should Understand Before Proceeding

1. Corporate debt obligations expose an investor to credit risk.
2. Credit risk consists of default risk, credit spread risk, and downgrade risk.
3. Credit risk is typically measured by the credit or quality ratings assigned by nationally recognized commercial rating companies.
4. Commercial rating companies play a key role in the functioning of debt markets in the United States, and their role in other countries is increasing.

COMMERCIAL PAPER

Commercial paper is a short-term unsecured promissory note issued in the open market that represents the obligation of the issuing corporation. The issuance of commercial paper is an alternative to bank borrowing for large corporations (nonfinancial and financial) with strong credit ratings.

While the original purpose of commercial paper was to provide short-term funds for seasonal and working capital needs, companies have used this instrument for other purposes in recent years. It has been used quite often for *bridge financing*. For example, suppose that a corporation needs long-term funds to build a plant or acquire equipment. Rather than raising long-term funds immediately, the corporation may elect to postpone the offering until more favorable capital market conditions prevail. The funds raised by issuing commercial paper are used until longer-term securities are sold.

In the United States, the maturity of commercial paper is typically less than 270 days, with the most common maturity range 30 to 50 days or less. There are reasons for this pattern of maturities. First, the Securities Act of 1933 requires that securities be registered with the Securities and Exchange Commission (SEC). Special provisions in the 1933 Act exempt commercial paper from registration so long as the maturity does not exceed 270 days. Hence, to avoid the costs associated with registering issues with the SEC, firms rarely issue commercial paper with maturities exceeding 270 days. Another consideration in

---

[1] Edwards W. Karp and Akira Koike, "The Japanese Corporate Bond Market," Chapter 11 in Frank J. Fabozzi (ed.), *The Japanese Bond Markets* (Chicago: Probus Publishing, 1990), p. 377.

determining the maturity is whether or not the commercial paper would be eligible collateral for a bank borrowing from the Federal Reserve Bank's discount window. In order to be eligible, the maturity of the paper may not exceed 90 days. Since eligible paper trades at a lower cost than paper that is not eligible, firms prefer to issue paper whose maturity does not exceed 90 days.

To pay off holders of maturing paper, issuers generally use the proceeds obtained by selling new commercial paper. This process is often described as rolling over short-term paper. The risk that the investor in commercial paper faces is that the issuer will be unable to sell new paper at maturity. As a safeguard against this rollover risk, commercial paper is typically backed by unused bank credit lines. The commitment fee the bank charges for providing a credit line increases the effective cost of issuing commercial paper.

Investors in commercial paper are institutional investors. Money market mutual funds purchase roughly one-third of all the commercial paper issued. Pension funds, commercial bank trust departments, state and local governments, and nonfinancial corporations seeking short-term investments purchase the balance. There are restrictions imposed on money market mutual funds by the SEC when investing in commercial paper. Rule 2a-7 of the Investment Company Act of 1940 limits the credit risk exposure of money market mutual funds by restricting their investments to "eligible" paper. Eligibility is defined in terms of the credit ratings. To be eligible paper, the issue must carry one of the two highest ratings ("1" or "2") from at least two of the credit rating companies. Tier-1 paper is defined as eligible paper that is rated "1" by at least two of the rating agencies; tier-2 paper security is defined as eligible paper that is not a tier-1 security. Money market funds may hold no more than 5% of their assets in the tier-1 paper of any individual issuer and no more than 1% of their assets in the tier-2 paper of any individual issuer. Furthermore, the holding of tier-2 paper may not represent more than 5% of the fund's assets.

There is very little secondary trading of commercial paper. Typically, an investor in commercial paper is an entity that plans to hold it until maturity. This is understandable because an investor can purchase commercial paper in a direct transaction with the issuer, which will sell paper with the specific maturity the investor desires.

Commercial paper is a discount instrument. That is, it is sold at a price that is less than its maturity value. The difference between the maturity value and the price paid is the interest earned by the investor, although there is some commercial paper that is issued as an interest-bearing instrument. For commercial paper, a year is treated as having 360 days.

The minimum round-lot transaction is $100,000, though some issuers will sell commercial paper in denominations of $25,000. The yield offered on commercial paper tracks that of other money market instruments. The commercial paper rate is higher than that on Treasury bills for the same maturity. There are three reasons for this. First, the investor in commercial paper is exposed to credit risk. Second, interest earned from investing in Treasury bills is exempt from state and local income taxes. As a result, commercial paper has to offer a higher yield to offset this tax advantage. Finally, commercial paper is less liquid than Treasury bills. The liquidity premium demanded is probably small, however, because investors typically follow a buy-and-hold strategy with commercial paper and so are less concerned with liquidity. The yield on commercial paper is higher by a few basis points than the yield on certificates of deposit for the same maturity. The higher yield available on commercial paper is attributable to the poorer liquidity relative to certificates of deposit.

Issuers of Commercial Paper

There are more than 1,700 issuers of commercial paper in the United States. Corporate issuers of commercial paper can be divided into fiancial companies and nonfinancial companies. There has been significantly greater use of commercial paper by financial companies.

There are three types of financial companies: **captive finance companies**, *bank-related finance companies*, and *independent finance companies*. Captive finance companies are subsidiaries of equipment manufacturing companies. Their primary purpose is to secure financing for the customers of the parent company. For example, the three major U.S. automobile manufacturers have captive finance companies: General Motors Acceptance Corporation (GMAC), Ford Credit, and Chrysler Financial. GMAC is by the far the largest issuer of commercial paper in the United States. Furthermore, a bank holding company may have a subsidiary that is a finance company, which provides loans to enable individuals and businesses to acquire a wide range of products. Independent finance companies are those that are not subsidiaries of equipment manufacturing firms or bank holding companies.

Although the issuers of commercial paper typically have high credit ratings, smaller and less well-known companies with lower credit ratings have been able to issue paper in recent years. They have been able to do so by means of credit support from a firm with a high credit rating (such paper is called *credit-supported commercial paper*) or by collateralizing the issue with high-quality assets (such paper is called *asset-backed commercial paper*). An example of credit-supported commercial paper is one supported by a *letter of credit* (LOC). The terms of a letter of credit specify that the bank issuing the letter guarantees that the bank will pay off the paper when it comes due, if the issuer fails to do so. The bank will charge a fee for the letter of credit. From the issuer's perspective the fee enables it to enter the commercial paper market and thereby obtain funding at a lower cost than that of bank borrowing. Commercial paper issued with this credit enhancement is referred to as **LOC paper**. The credit enhancement may also take the form of a surety bond from an insurance company.[2]

Both domestic and foreign corporations issue commercial paper in the United States. Commercial paper issued by foreign entities is called **Yankee commercial paper**.

The three rating companies assign ratings to commercial paper. These ratings are shown in Table 1.

Directly Placed versus Dealer-Placed Paper

Commercial paper is classified as either **direct paper** or **dealer-placed paper**. Directly placed paper is sold by the issuing firm directly to investors without the help of an agent or an intermediary. A large majority of the issuers of direct paper are financial companies. These entities require continuous funds in order to provide loans to customers. As a result, they find it cost-effective to establish a sales force to sell their commercial paper directly to investors. General Electric Capital Corporation (GE Capital) is an example of a direct issuer, having issued commercial paper for more than 50 years. GE Capital is the principal financial services arm of General Electric Company and is now the largest and most active direct issuer in the United States, with commercial paper outstanding of about $73 billion. The

---

[2] A surety bond is a policy written by an insurance company to protect another party against loss or violation of a contract.

Table 1   Commercial Paper Ratings*

| Category | Commercial Rating Company | | |
	Fitch	Moody's	S&P
Investment grade	F-1+		A-1+
	F-1	P-1	A-1
	F-2	P-2	A-2
	F-3	P-3	A-3
Noninvestment grade	F-S	NP (Not Prime)	B
			C
In default	D		D

*The definition of ratings varies by rating agency.
Source: Mitchell A. Post. "The Evolution of the U.S. Commercial Paper Market Since 1980," Federal Reserve Bulletin (December 1992), p. 882.

Corporate Treasury unit of GE Capital manages the commercial paper programs of General Electric Company, GE Capital Services, GE Capital, and other GE-related programs. The paper is marketed directly to institutional investors on a continuous basis by Corporate Treasury or through GECC Capital Markets Group, Inc.

Dealer-placed commercial paper requires the services of an agent to sell an issuer's paper. The agent distributes the paper on a best efforts underwriting basis.

Non–U.S. Commercial Paper Markets

Other countries have developed their own commercial paper markets. For example, in November 1987, the Japanese Ministry of Finance (MOF) approved the issuance of commercial paper by Japanese corporations in its domestic market. A few months later, the MOF approved the issuance of yen-denominated commercial paper in Japan by non-Japanese entities. Such paper is referred to as **Samurai commercial paper.**

Eurocommercial paper is issued and placed outside the jurisdiction of the currency of denomination. There are several differences between U.S. commercial paper and Eurocommercial paper with respect to the characteristics of the paper and the structure of the market. First, commercial paper issued in the United States usually has a maturity of less than 270 days, with the most common maturity range 30 to 50 days or less. The maturity of Eurocommercial paper can be considerably longer. Second, while an issuer in the United States must have unused bank credit lines, it is possible to issue commercial paper without such backing in the Eurocommercial paper market. Third, while in the United States, commercial paper can be directly placed or dealer placed, Eurocommercial paper is almost always dealer placed. The fourth distinction is that numerous dealers participate in the Eurocommercial paper market, while only a few dealers dominate the market in the United States. Finally, because of the longer maturity of Eurocommercial paper, that paper is traded more often in the secondary market than U.S. commercial paper. Investors in commercial paper in the United States typically buy and hold to maturity, and the secondary market is thin and illiquid.

> ### Key Points That You Should Understand Before Proceeding
>
> 1. Commercial paper is a short-term unsecured promissory note that is issued in the open market and represents the obligation of the issuing corporation. It is an alternative to bank borrowing for large corporations.
> 2. By using credit support, smaller and less well-known companies with lower credit ratings have been able to issue paper.
> 3. Commercial paper is rated by private rating companies.
> 4. Commercial paper can be directly placed by the issuer or issued by using the services of an agent or intermediary.
> 5. Other countries have developed their own commercial paper markets, and there is a Eurocommercial paper market.

MEDIUM-TERM NOTES

A **medium-term note (MTN)** is a corporate debt instrument, with the unique characteristic that notes are offered continuously to investors by an agent of the issuer. Investors can select from several maturity ranges: nine months to one year, more than one year to 18 months, more than 18 months to two years, and so on up to 30 years. Medium-term notes are registered with the SEC under Rule 415 (the shelf registration rule), which gives a corporation the maximum flexibility for issuing securities on a continuous basis.

The term *medium-term note* to describe this corporate debt instrument is misleading. Traditionally, the term *note* or *medium term* was used to refer to debt issues with a maturity greater than one year but less than 15 years. Certainly, this is not a characteristic of MTNs, since they have been sold with maturities from nine months to 30 years, and even longer. For example, in July 1993, Walt Disney Corporation issued a security with a 100-year maturity off its medium-term note shelf registration.

GMAC first used medium-term notes in 1972 to fund automobile loans with maturities of five years and less. The purpose of the MTN was to fill the funding gap between commercial paper and long-term bonds. It is for this reason that they are referred to as "medium term." The medium-term notes were issued directly to investors without the use of an agent. Only a few corporations issued MTNs in the 1970s. About $800 million of MTNs were outstanding by 1981.

The modern-day medium-term note was pioneered by Merrill Lynch in 1981. The first medium-term note issuer was Ford Motor Credit Company. By 1983, GMAC and Chrysler Financial used Merrill Lynch as an agent to issue medium-term notes. Merrill Lynch and other investment banking firms committed funds to make a secondary market for MTNs, thereby improving liquidity. In 1982, Rule 415 was adopted, making it easier for issuers to sell registered securities on a continuous basis.

Euro medium-term notes are those issued in the Euromarket. The market began in 1987. Euro medium-term notes are issued by sovereign issuers (i.e., governments and governmental agencies), nonfinancial corporations, and financial institutions. Euro medium-term notes have been issued in a variety of currencies. Most Euro medium-term notes were issued via the private placement market.

Size of Market and Issuers

The latest reported survey by the Federal Reserve for the amount of the MTNs outstanding is for 2004. In that year, there were $639 billion of MTNs outstanding issued by 132 firms using 440 programs. The importance of the MTN as a funding source is evidenced by the fact that MTN issuance exceeded the amount of corporate bond issuance in 2004.

The popularity of MTNs as a financing vehicle is due to the flexibility they provide borrowers in designing a structure that satisfies the needs of firms. They can issue fixed- or floating-rate debt. The coupon payments can be denominated in U.S. dollars or in a foreign currency. In the next chapter, we describe corporate bonds and the various security structures. These structures have been used by MTN issuers.

When the treasurer of a corporation is contemplating an offering of either MTNs or corporate bonds, there are two factors that affect the decision. The most obvious is the cost of the funds raised after consideration of registration and distribution costs. This cost is referred to as the *all-in-cost of funds*. The second is the flexibility afforded to the issuer in structuring the offering. The tremendous growth in the MTN market is evidence of the relative advantage of MTNs with respect to cost and flexibility for some offerings. However, the fact that there are corporations that raise funds by issuing both bonds and MTNs is evidence that there is no absolute advantage in all instances and market environments.

As with commercial paper, MTNs are rated by the nationally recognized rating companies. Most outstanding MTNs are rated investment grade.

The Primary Market

Medium-term notes differ from corporate bonds in the manner in which they are distributed to investors when they are initially sold. Although some investment-grade corporate bond issues are sold on a best efforts basis, they are typically underwritten by investment bankers. MTNs have been traditionally distributed on a best efforts basis by either an investment banking firm or other broker-dealers acting as agents. Another difference between corporate bonds and MTNs when they are offered is that MTNs are usually sold in relatively small amounts on a continuous or an intermittent basis, while corporate bonds are sold in large, discrete offerings.

A corporation that wants an MTN program will file a shelf registration with the SEC for the offering of securities. While the SEC registration for MTN offerings is between $100 and $1 billion, once the total is sold, the issuer can file another shelf registration.[3] The registration will include a list of the investment banking firms, usually two to four, that the corporation has arranged to act as agents to distribute the MTNs. The large New York–based investment banking firms dominate the distribution market for MTNs.

The issuer then posts rates over a range of maturities: for example, nine months to one year, one year to 18 months, 18 months to two years, and annually thereafter. Table 2 provides an example of an offering rate schedule for a medium-term note program. Usually, an issuer will post rates as a spread over a Treasury security of comparable maturity. For example, in the two- to three-year maturity range, the offering rate is 35 basis points over the two-year Treasury. Since the two-year Treasury is shown in the table at 4%,

---

[3] Leland E. Crabbe, "Medium-Term Notes," Chapter 12 in Frank J. Fabozzi (ed.), *The Handbook of Fixed Income Securities*, 6th ed. (New York: McGraw Hill, 2001).

Table 2 An Offering Rate Schedule for a Medium-Term Note Program

Medium-Term Notes			Treasury Securities	
Maturity Range	Yield (%)	Yield spread of MTN over Treasury Securities (basis points)	Maturity	Yield (%)
9 months to 12 months	(a)	(a)	9 months	3.35
12 months to 18 months	(a)	(a)	12 months	3.50
18 months to 2 years	(a)	(a)	18 months	3.80
2 years to 5 years	4.35	35	2 years	4.00
3 years to 4 years	5.05	55	3 years	4.50
4 years to 5 years	5.60	60	4 years	5.00
5 years to 6 years	6.05	60	5 years	5.45
6 years to 7 years	6.10	40	6 years	5.70
7 years to 8 years	6.30	40	7 years	5.90
8 years to 9 years	6.45	40	8 years	6.05
9 years to 10 years	6.60	40	10 years	6.20
10 years	6.70	40	10 years	6.30

ª No rate posted.

Source: *Leland E. Crabbe, "The Anatomy of the Medium-Term Note Market,"* Federal Reserve Bulletin *(August 1993), p. 753.*

the offering rate is 4.35%. Rates will not be posted for maturity ranges that the issuer does not desire to sell. For example, in Table 2, the issuer does not wish to sell MTNs with a maturity of less than two years.

The agents will then make the offering rate schedule available to their investor base interested in MTNs. An investor who is interested in the offering will contact the agent. In turn, the agent contacts the issuer to confirm the terms of the transaction. Since the maturity range in the offering rate schedule does not specify a specific maturity date, the investor can choose the final maturity subject to approval by the issuer. The minimum size that an investor can purchase of an MTN offering typically ranges from $1 million to $25 million.

The rate offering schedule can be changed at any time by the issuer either in response to changing market conditions or because the issuer has raised the desired amount of funds at a given maturity. In the latter case, the issuer can either not post a rate for that maturity range or lower the rate.

Structured Medium-Term Notes

It is common today for issuers of MTNs to couple their offerings with transactions in the derivative markets (options, futures/forwards, swaps, caps, and floors) so as to create debt obligations with more interesting risk/return features than are available in the corporate bond market. Specifically, an issue can be floating rate over all or part of the life of the security and the coupon reset formula can be based on a benchmark interest rate, equity index or individual stock price, a foreign exchange rate, or a commodity index. There are even MTNs with coupon reset formulas that vary inversely with a benchmark interest rate. That is, if the benchmark interest rate increases (decreases), the coupon rate decreases (increases). Debt instruments with this coupon characteristic are called *inverse floating-rate securities*.

MTNs created when the issuer simultaneously transacts in the derivative markets are called **structured notes**. It is estimated today that new-issue volume of structured notes is 20% to 30% of new-issuance volume. The most common derivative instrument used in creating structured notes is a swap.

Key Points That You Should Understand Before Proceeding

1. A unique characteristic of medium-term notes is that they are continuously offered to investors over a period of time by an agent of the issuer.
2. Medium-term notes are rated by the nationally recognized rating companies.
3. Investors can select issues from several maturity bands.
4. Unlike corporate bonds, medium-term notes are typically issued on a best efforts basis rather than underwritten by an investment banker.
5. A structured note is a medium-term note in which the issuer couples its offering with a position in a derivative instrument in order to create instruments with more interesting risk/return characteristics.

BANK LOANS

As an alternative to the issuance of securities, a corporation can raise funds by borrowing from a bank.[4] There are five sourcing alternatives for a corporation: (1) a domestic bank in the corporation's home country, (2) a subsidiary of a foreign bank that is established in the corporation's home country, (3) a foreign bank domiciled in a country where the corporation does business, (4) a subsidiary of a domestic bank that has been established in a country where the corporation does business, or (5) an offshore or Eurobank. Loans made by offshore banks are referred to as **Eurocurrency loans**.[5]

Secondary Market for Bank Loans

While at one time, a bank or banks who originated loans retained them in their loan portfolio, today those loans can be traded in the secondary market or securitized to create *collateralized loan obligations* (CLO) using the securitization technology.

The trade association that has been the main advocate of commercial loans as an asset class is the **Loan Syndications and Trading Association (LSTA)**, formed in 1995. The LSTA has helped foster the development of a liquid and transparent secondary market for bank loans by establishing market practices and settlement and operational procedures. The LSTA collects quotes on 2,500 U.S. loans on a daily basis. Quotes for three loans for

---

[4] Bank debt is widely used as the senior financing for a leveraged buyout, acquisition, or recapitalization. These are collectively referred to as *highly leveraged transactions* or HLTs.

[5] A loan can be denominated in a variety of currencies. Loans denominated in U.S. dollars are called *Eurodollar loans*. Similarly, there are *Euroyen loans*.

four companies as reported on the website of the LSTA for the week ending Friday, July 14, 2006, were as follows:

Name	Loan Rating Moody's/S&P	Coupon	Maturity	Average bid (pct. pts.)	Weekly change (pct. pts.)
Regal Cinemas, Inc.	N.R./BB-	L+225	Oct. 19, '10	99.43	−0.41
El Paso Corp.	B3/B+	L+275	Nov. 23, '09	100.21	−0.36
Lear Corp.	Baa3/B+	L+250	Mar. 29, '12	99.35	+0.31
Wynn Resorts	B2/B+	L+212.5	Dec. 14, '11	100.06	−0.15

The second column is the rating assigned by Moody's and S&P. An "N.R." means not rated. (The meaning of these ratings is explained in the next chapter.) The "L" in the second column means LIBOR. The next-to-the-last column shows the average bid price for the loan. The quote is the same as used for bonds (i.e., as a percentage of par). The last column shows the change in price.

The LSTA has also developed a loan index (the S&P/LSTA Leveraged Loan Index) to gauge the performance of the different sectors of the syndicated loan market.

Syndicated Bank Loans

A **syndicated bank loan** is one in which a group (or syndicate) of banks provides funds to the borrower. The need for a group of banks arises because the amount sought by a borrower may be too large for any one bank to be exposed to the credit risk of that borrower. Therefore, the syndicated bank loan market is used by borrowers who seek to raise a large amount of funds in the loan market rather than through the issuance of securities.

These bank loans are called **senior bank loans** because they have a priority position over subordinated lenders (bondholders) with respect to repayment of interest and principal. The interest rate on a syndicated bank loan is a rate that **floats**, which means that the loan rate is based on some reference rate. The loan rate is periodically reset at the reference rate plus a spread. The reference rate is typically the London Interbank Offered Rate (LIBOR), although it could be the prime rate (that is, the rate that a bank charges its most creditworthy customers) or the rate on certificates of deposit. The term of the loan is fixed. A syndicated loan is typically structured so that it is amortized according to a predetermined schedule, and repayment of principal begins after a specified number of years (typically not longer than five or six years). Structures in which no repayment of the principal is made until the maturity date can be arranged. Such loan structures are referred to as **bullet loans**.

A syndicated loan is arranged by either a bank or a securities house. The arranger then lines up the syndicate. Each bank in the syndicate provides the funds for which it has committed. The banks in the syndicate have the right to sell their parts of the loan subsequently to other banks.

Syndicated loans are distributed by two methods: assignment or participation. Each method has its relative advantages and disadvantages, with the method of assignment the more desirable of the two.

The holder of a loan who is interested in selling a portion can do so by passing the interest in the loan by the *method of assignment*. In this procedure, the seller transfers all rights completely to the holder of the assignment, now called the *assignee*. The assignee is said to have *privity of contract* with the borrower. Because of the clear path between the borrower and assignee, assignment is the more desirable choice of transfer and ownership.

A *participation* involves a holder of a loan "participating out" a portion of the holding in that particular loan. The holder of the participation does not become a party to the loan agreement, and has a relationship not with the borrower but with the seller of the participation. Unlike an assignment, a participation does not confer privity of contract on the holder of the participation, although the holder of the participation has the right to vote on certain legal matters concerning amendments to the loan agreement. These matters include changes regarding maturity, interest rate, and issues concerning the loan collateral. Because syndicated loans can be sold in this manner, they have become marketable.

In response to the large amount of bank loans issued in the 1980s and their strong credit protection, some commercial banks and securities houses have shown a willingness to commit capital and resources to facilitate trading as broker-dealers. Also, these senior bank loans have been securitized through the process for the securitization of mortgage loans. Further development of the senior bank loan market will no doubt eventually erode the once important distinction between a security and a loan: A security has long been seen as a marketable financial asset, while a loan has not been marketable. Interestingly, the trading of these loans is not limited to **performing loans**, which are loans whose borrowers are fulfilling contractual commitments. There is also a market in the trading of nonperforming loans—loans in which the borrowers have defaulted.

Lease Financing

The market for lease financing is a segment of the larger market for equipment financing. Any type of equipment that can be purchased with borrowed funds can also be leased. Our interest here is in the leasing of equipment that can be classified as a big-ticket item (that is, equipment costing more than $5 million). Included in this group are commercial aircraft, large ships, large quantities of production equipment, and energy facilities. A special type of leasing arrangement, known as a **leveraged lease**, is used in financing such equipment.

Leasing works as follows. The potential equipment user, called the **lessee,** first selects the equipment and the dealer or manufacturer from whom the equipment will be purchased. The lessee negotiates such aspects of the transaction as the purchase price, specifications, warranties, and delivery date. When the lessee accepts the terms of the deal, another party, such as a bank or finance company, buys the equipment from the dealer or manufacturer and leases it to the lessee. This party is called the **lessor.** The lease is so arranged that the lessor realizes the tax benefits associated with the ownership of the leased equipment.

Basically, leasing is a vehicle by which tax benefits can be transferred from the user of the equipment (the lessee), who may not have the capacity to take advantage of the tax benefits associated with equipment ownership (such as depreciation and any tax credits), to another entity who can utilize them (the lessor). In exchange for these tax benefits, a lessor provides lower-cost financing to the lessee than the lessee could get by purchasing the equipment with borrowed funds. Such leases are referred to as **tax-oriented leases**.

There are two possible ways for the lessor to finance the purchase of the equipment. One way is to provide all the financing from its own funds and therefore be at risk for 100% of the funds used to purchase the equipment. Such leasing arrangements are referred to as **single-investor** or **direct leases**. Essentially, such leases are two-party agreements (the lessee and the lessor). The second way is for the lessor to use only a portion of its own funds to purchase the equipment, and to borrow the balance from a bank or group of banks. This type of leasing arrangement is called a *leveraged lease*. There are three parties to a leveraged lease agreement: the lessee, the lessor, and the lender. The leveraged lease arrangement allows the lessor to realize all the tax benefits from owning the equipment and the tax benefits from borrowing funds—deductible interest payments—while putting up only a portion of its own funds to purchase the equipment. Because of this, leveraged leasing is commonly used in financing big-ticket items.

In a leveraged lease transaction, it is necessary for a party to arrange for the equity and the debt portions of the funding involved. The same party can arrange both. The equity portion is typically provided by one or more institutional investors. The debt portion is arranged with a bank. Since leveraged lease transactions are for large-ticket items, the bank debt is typically arranged as a syndicated bank loan.

The financing of aircraft is normally accomplished through leveraged lease financing. For example, between May and October 1991, Japanese banks arranged $1 billion in leveraged lease financing for airlines throughout the world.[6] One large Japanese bank, Mitsubishi Trust, arranged for a total of almost $250 million of equity and debt financing for British Airways to acquire four aircraft. Mitsubishi Trust also arranged for the equity financing in purchases by Quantas.[7]

Key Points That You Should Understand Before Proceeding

1. Bank loans are an alternative to the issuance of securities.
2. A syndicated bank loan is one in which a group of banks provides funds to the borrower, with the reference rate on the loan typically the London Interbank Offered Rate.
3. Senior loans can be distributed by either assignment or participation.
4. Any type of equipment that can be purchased with borrowed funds can also be leased.
5. A tax-oriented lease effectively allows the lessee to obtain financing at less cost than by bank borrowing.

| SUMMARY

Corporate senior instruments include debt obligations and preferred stock. Holders of these obligations have priority over holders of a corporation's common stock in the case of bankruptcy. In this chapter we discuss four sectors of this market: the commercial paper market, the medium-term note market, and the bank loan market.

Investors typically do not perform their own analysis of the issuer's creditworthiness. Instead, they rely on a system of credit ratings developed by commercial ratings companies. The three companies in the United States that rate corporate debt in terms of the likelihood of default are (1) Moody's Investors Service, (2) Standard & Poor's Corporation, and (3) Fitch.

---

[6] *International Financial Review*, Issue 902 (November 2, 1991), p. 12.
[7] *International Financial Review*, Issue 902 (November 2, 1991), p. 11.

Commercial paper is a short-term unsecured promissory note issued in the open market that represents the obligation of the issuing entity. Generally, commercial paper maturity is less than 90 days. Financial and nonfinancial corporations issue commercial paper, with the majority issued by the former. Directly placed paper is sold by the issuing firm directly to investors without using an agent as an intermediary; for dealer-placed commercial paper, the issuer uses the services of an agent to sell its paper. Commercial paper markets have been developed in other countries. Eurocommercial paper is paper issued and placed outside the jurisdiction of the currency of denomination.

Medium-term notes are corporate debt obligations offered on a continuous basis. The maturities range from nine months to 30 years and have provided a financing alternative with maturities between those of commercial paper and long-term bonds.

Bank loans represent an alternative to the issuance of securities. A syndicated bank loan is one in which a group of banks provides funds to the borrower. Senior bank loans have become marketable; they are now more actively traded and have been securitized.

Leasing is a form of bank borrowing. Basically leasing is a vehicle by which tax benefits can be transferred from the user of the equipment (the lessee), who may not have the capacity to utilize the tax benefits associated with equipment ownership, to another entity who can utilize them. A single-investor lease is a two-party agreement involving the lessee and the lessor. In a leveraged lease, the lessor uses only a portion of its own funds to purchase the equipment and borrows the balance from a bank or group of banks.

KEY TERMS

- Bullet loan
- Captive finance companies
- Commercial paper
- Dealer-placed paper
- Direct paper
- Eurocommercial paper
- Eurocurrency loans
- Euro medium-term notes
- Floats
- Lessee
- Lessor
- Leveraged lease
- Loan Syndications and Trading Association (LSTA)
- LOC paper
- Medium-term note (MTN)
- Performing loan
- Samurai commercial paper
- Senior bank loan
- Single-investor (direct) lease
- Structured note
- Syndicated bank loan
- Tax-oriented leases
- Yankee commercial paper

QUESTIONS

1. What are the different forms of credit risk?
2. What role do rating companies play in financial markets?
3. What is meant by a credit or quality spread?
4. **a.** Why is commercial paper an alternative to short-term bank borrowing for a corporation?
   b. What is the difference between directly placed paper and dealer-placed paper?
5. What does the yield spread between commercial paper and Treasury bills of the same maturity reflect?
6. **a.** What is Eurocommercial paper?
   b. How does it differ from U.S. commercial paper?

7. **a.** What is a medium-term note?
   b. What determines the yield that will be offered on a MTN?
   c. What is a Euro medium-term note?

8. Explain whether you agree or disagree with the following statements.
   a. MTNs are issued for maturities from one year to five years.
   b. MTNs are issued by low credit rated corporations.
   c. MTNs are much less frequently used as a funding source compared to corporate bonds.

9. What is a structured note?

10. What has The Loan Syndications and Trading Association done to enhance commercial loans secondary market trading?

11. **a.** What is a syndicated bank loan?
   b. What is the reference rate typically used for a syndicated bank loan?
   c. What is the difference between an amortized bank loan and a bullet bank loan?

12. Explain the two ways in which a bank can sell its position in a syndicated loan.

13. **a.** For a lease financing transaction, who is the lessee and the lessor?
   b. Who is entitled to the tax benefits, and what are those tax benefits?
   c. If a manufacturing corporation has no taxable income, is it likely to buy equipment or lease equipment? Why?

14. What is the difference between a single-investor lease and a leveraged lease?

Markets for Corporate Senior Instruments: II

From Chapter 20 of *Foundations of Financial Markets and Institutions*, 4/e. Frank J. Fabozzi. Franco Modigliani. Frank J. Jones.

Markets for Corporate Senior Instruments: II

LEARNING OBJECTIVES

After reading this chapter, you will understand

- the key provisions of a corporate bond issue

- the risks associated with investing in corporate bonds

- what a callable bond is

- bonds with special features and why they are issued

- factors considered by rating agencies in rating bonds

- the secondary bond market including the different types of electronic bond trading systems

- the high-yield or junk bond sector of the corporate bond market

- the different types of bond structures used in the junk bond market

- the Eurobond market and the different types of bond structures issued

- the difference between preferred stock, corporate debt, and common stock

- the difference between the various types of preferred stock: fixed-rate, adjustable-rate, and auction and remarketed preferred stock

- the basic provisions of the U.S. bankruptcy law

- the difference between a liquidation and a reorganization

- the principle of absolute priority in a bankruptcy

In this chapter, we focus on corporate bonds and preferred stock. Preferred stock is classified as a senior instrument in that holders of these securities have priority over common stockholders in the case of bankruptcy. We conclude this chapter with a discussion of corporate bankruptcy.

CORPORATE BONDS

Corporate bonds are classified by the type of issuer. The four general classifications used by bond information services are: (1) utilities, (2) transportations, (3) industrial, and (4) banks and finance companies. Finer breakdowns are often made to create more homogeneous groupings. For example, utilities are subdivided into electric power companies, gas distribution companies, water companies, and communication companies. Transportations are further divided into airlines, railroads, and trucking companies. Industrials are the catchall class, and the most heterogeneous of the groupings with respect to investment characteristics. Industrials include all kinds of manufacturing, merchandising, and service companies. In recent years, industrials have raised the largest amount in the corporate bond market, followed by financial institutions and then utilities.[1] The largest investor group is life insurance companies, followed by pension funds, public and private. Historically, these institutional investors hold more than half of outstanding corporate bonds. The balance is held by households, foreign investors, depository institutions, non-life insurance companies, and mutual funds and securities brokers and dealers.

Basic Features of a Corporate Bond Issue

The essential features of a corporate bond are relatively simple. The corporate issuer promises to pay a specified percentage of par value (known as the coupon payments) on designated dates, and to repay par or principal value of the bond at maturity. Failure to pay either principal or interest when due constitutes legal default, and court proceedings can be instituted to enforce the contract. Bondholders, as creditors, have a prior legal claim over common and preferred stockholders as to both income and assets of the corporation for the principal and interest due them.

The promises of corporate bond issuers and the rights of investors who buy them are set forth in great detail in contracts called **bond indentures**. If bondholders were handed the complete indenture, they would have trouble understanding its language, and even greater difficulty in determining at a particular time whether or not the corporate issuer were keeping all its promises. These problems are solved for the most part by bringing in a corporate trustee as a third party to the contract. The indenture is made out to the corporate trustee as a representative of the interests of bondholders; that is, the trustee acts in a fiduciary capacity for investors who own the bond issue. A corporate trustee is a bond or trust company with a corporate trust department and officers who are experts in performing the functions of a trustee.

A bond's indenture clearly outlines three important aspects: its maturity, its security, and its provisions for retirement.

Maturity of Bonds

Most corporate bonds are *term bonds*; that is, they run for a term of years, then become due and payable. Term bonds are often referred to as **bullet-maturity**, or, simply, **bullet bonds**. Any amount of the liability that has not been paid off prior to maturity must be paid off at

---

[1] *Moody's Bond Survey*, selected, year-end issues.

that time. The bond's term may be long or short. Generally, obligations due less than ten years from the date of issue are called *notes*.[2]

Most corporate borrowings take the form of *bonds* due in 20 to 30 years. Term bonds may be retired by payment at final maturity or retired prior to maturity if provided for in the indenture. Some corporate bond issues are so arranged that specified principal amounts become due on specified dates prior to maturity. Such issues are called **serial bonds**. Equipment trust certificates (discussed later) are structured as serial bonds.

Security for Bonds

Either real property (using a mortgage) or personal property may be pledged to offer security beyond that of the general credit standing of the issuer. A **mortgage bond** grants the bondholders a lien against the pledged assets. A *lien* is a legal right to sell mortgaged property to satisfy unpaid obligations to bondholders. In practice, foreclosure and sale of mortgaged property are unusual. If a default occurs, there is usually a financial reorganization of the issuer when provision is made for settlement of the debt to bondholders. The mortgage lien is important, though, because it gives the mortgage bondholders a very strong bargaining position relative to other creditors in determining the terms of a reorganization.

Some companies do not own fixed assets or other real property, and so have nothing on which they can give a mortgage lien to secure bondholders. Instead, these firms own securities of other companies and, thus, are *holding companies*. The firms whose shares are owned are *subsidiaries*. To satisfy the desire of bondholders for security, the holding companies pledge stocks, notes, bonds, or whatever other kind of financial instruments they own. These assets are termed *collateral* (or personal property), and bonds secured by such assets are called **collateral trust bonds**.

Many years ago, the railway companies developed a way of financing the purchase of cars and locomotives, called *rolling stock*, that enabled them to borrow at just about the lowest rates in the corporate bond market. Railway rolling stock has for a long time been regarded by investors as excellent security for debt. The equipment is sufficiently standardized that it can be used by one railway as well as another. And, of course, it can readily be moved from the tracks of one railroad to those of another. Therefore, there is generally a good market for lease or sale of cars and locomotives. The railroads have taken advantage of these characteristics of rolling stock by developing a legal arrangement for giving investors a legal claim on it that is different from, and generally superior to, a mortgage lien.

The legal arrangement in this situation is one that vests legal title to railway equipment in a trustee. When a railway company orders some cars and locomotives from a manufacturer, the manufacturer transfers legal title to the equipment to a trustee. The trustee, in turn, leases the equipment to the railroad, and at the same time sells **equipment trust certificates** to obtain the funds to pay the manufacturer. The trustee collects lease payments from the railroad and uses these receipts to pay interest and principal on the certificates. The principal is therefore paid off on specified dates, a provision that makes a certificate different from a term bond.

---

[2] It can be seen that the word *notes* is used to describe a variety of instruments—medium-term notes and Euronotes. The use of the term *notes* here is as a market convention distinguishing notes and bonds on the basis of the number of years to maturity at the time the security is issued.

The general idea of the equipment trust arrangement has also been used by companies engaged in providing other kinds of transportation. For example, trucking companies finance the purchase of huge fleets of trucks in the same manner; airlines use this kind of financing to purchase transport planes; and international oil companies use this financing method to buy huge tankers.

A **debenture bond** is not secured by a specific pledge of property, but that does not mean that this type of bond has no claim on property of issuers or on their earnings. Debenture bondholders have the claim of general creditors on all assets of the issuer not pledged specifically to secure other debt. Also, holders of debentures even have a claim on pledged assets to the extent that these assets have value greater than necessary to satisfy secured creditors. A **subordinated debenture bond** is an issue that ranks after secured debt, after debenture bonds, and often after some general creditors in its claim on assets and earnings.

The type of corporate security issued determines the cost to the issuer. For a given corporation, mortgage bonds will cost less than debenture bonds; debenture bonds will cost less than subordinated debenture bonds.

A **guaranteed bond** is an obligation guaranteed by another entity. The safety of a guaranteed bond depends upon the financial capability of the guarantor to satisfy the terms of the guarantee, as well as the financial capability of the issuer. The terms of the guarantee may call for the guarantor to guarantee the payment of interest and/or repayment of the principal.

It is important to recognize that a superior legal status will not prevent bondholders from suffering financial loss when the issuer's ability to generate cash flow adequate to pay its obligations is seriously eroded.

Provisions for Paying Off Bonds

Most corporate issues have a call provision allowing the issuer an option to buy back all or part of the issue prior to maturity. Some issues carry a sinking fund provision, which specifies that the issuer must retire a predetermined amount of the issue periodically.[3]

An important question in negotiating the terms of a new bond issue is whether or not the issuer shall have the right to redeem the *entire amount* of bonds outstanding on a date before maturity. Issuers generally want this right because they recognize that at some time in the future the general level of interest rates may fall sufficiently below the issue's coupon rate, so that redeeming the issue and replacing it with another issue carrying a lower coupon rate would be attractive. For reasons discussed later in this chapter, this right represents a disadvantage to the bondholder.

The usual practice is a provision that denies the issuer the right to redeem bonds during the first five to 10 years following the date of issue with proceeds received from the sale of lower-cost debt obligations that have an equal or superior rank to the debt to be redeemed. This type of redemption is called **refunding**. While most long-term issues have these refunding restrictions, they may be immediately callable, in whole or in part, if the source of funds is something other than money raised with debt of a lower interest. Under such a provision, acceptable sources include cash flow from operations, proceeds from a common stock sale, or funds from the sale of property.

---

[3] For a more detailed explanation of corporate call provisions, see Richard S. Wilson and Frank J. Fabozzi, *Corporate Bonds: Structures & Analysis* (New Hope, PA: Frank J. Fabozzi Associates, 1996).

Investors often confuse refunding protection with call protection. Call protection is much more comprehensive because it prohibits the early redemption of the bonds *for any reason*. Refunding restrictions, by contrast, provide protection only against the one type of redemption previously mentioned.

As a rule, corporate bonds are callable at a premium above par. Generally, the amount of the premium declines as the bond approaches maturity and often reaches zero after a number of years following issuance. The initial amount of the premium may be as much as one year's coupon interest, or as little as the coupon interest for half of a year.

If the issuer has the choice to retire all or part of an issue prior to maturity, the buyer of the bond takes the chance that the issue will be called away at a disadvantageous time. This risk is referred to as **call risk**, or **timing risk**. There are two disadvantages of call provisions from the investor's perspective. First, a decline in interest rates in the economy will increase the price of a debt instrument, although in the case of a callable bond, the price increase is somewhat limited. If and when interest rates decline far enough below the coupon rate to make call an immediate or prospective danger, the market value of the callable bond will not rise as much as that of noncallable issues that are similar in all other respects. Second, when a bond issue is called as a result of a decline in interest rates, the investor must reinvest the proceeds received at a lower interest rate (unless the investor chooses debt of greater risk).

Corporate bond indentures may require the issuer to retire a specified portion of an issue each year. This **sinking fund provision** for the repayment of the debt may be designed to liquidate all of a bond issue by the maturity date, or it may call for the liquidation of only a part of the total by the end of the term. If only a part of the outstanding bond is paid before retirement, the remainder is called a *balloon maturity*. The purpose of the sinking fund provision is to reduce credit risk. Generally, the issuer may satisfy the sinking fund requirement by either (1) making a cash payment of the face amount of the bonds to be retired to the corporate trustee, who then calls the bonds for redemption using a lottery, or (2) delivering to the trustee bonds with a total face value equal to the amount that must be retired from bonds purchased in the open market.

Bonds with Special Features

Prior to the 1970s, securities issued in the U.S. bond market had a simple structure. They had a fixed coupon rate and a fixed maturity date. The only option available to the issuer was the right to call all or part of the issue prior to the stated maturity date. The historically high interest rates that prevailed in the United States in the late 1970s and early 1980s, and the volatile interest rates since the 1970s, prompted introduction of new structures or the increased use of existing structures with special features that made issues more attractive to both borrowers and investors. Various bond structures are reviewed in the following text.

Convertible and Exchangeable Bonds

The conversion provision in a corporate bond issue grants the bondholder the right to convert the bond to a predetermined number of shares of common stock of the issuer. A **convertible bond** is, therefore, a corporate bond with a call option to buy the common stock of the issuer. An **exchangeable bond** grants the bondholder the right to exchange the bonds for the common stock of a firm *other* than the issuer of the bond. For example, Ford

Motor Credit exchangeable bonds are exchangeable for the common stock of its parent company, Ford Motor Company.

Issues of Debt with Warrants

Warrants may be attached as part of a bond issue. A **warrant** grants the holder the right to purchase a designated security at a specified price from the issuer of the bond. A warrant is simply a call option. It may permit the holder to purchase the common stock of the issuer of the debt or the common stock of a firm other than the issuer's. Or, the warrant may grant the holder the right to purchase a debt obligation of the issuer. Generally, warrants can be detached from the bond and sold separately. Typically, in exercising the warrant, an investor may choose either to pay cash or to offer the debt, to be valued at par, that was part of the offering. A major difference between warrants and either convertible or exchangeable bonds is that an investor exercising the option provided by the latter must turn the bond in to the issuer.

Putable Bonds

A **putable bond** grants the bondholder the right to sell the issue back to the issuer at par value on designated dates. The advantage to the bondholder is that if interest rates rise after the issue date, thereby reducing the market value of the bond, the bondholder can sell the bond back to the issuer for par.

Zero-Coupon Bonds

Zero-coupon bonds are, just as the name implies, bonds without coupon payments or a stated interest rate. In the Treasury market, the U.S. government does not issue zero-coupon bonds. Dealers strip issues and create these bonds from the cash flow of a coupon Treasury bond. Corporations, however, can and do issue zero-coupon bonds. The first such public offering was in the spring of 1981. The attractiveness of a zero-coupon bond from the investor's perspective is that the investor who holds the bond to the maturity date will realize a predetermined return on the bond, unlike a coupon bond where the actual return realized, if the bond is held to maturity, depends on the rate at which coupon payments can be reinvested.

Floating-Rate Securities

The coupon interest on **floating-rate securities** is reset periodically to follow changes in the level of some predetermined benchmark rate. For example, the coupon rate may be reset every six months to a rate equal to a spread of 100 basis points over the six-month Treasury bill rate.

Floating-rate securities are attractive to some institutional investors because they allow them to buy an asset with an income stream that closely matches the floating nature of the income of some of their liabilities. Certain floating-rate instruments are viewed by some investors as a passive substitute for short-term investments, particularly that part of a short-term portfolio that is more or less consistently maintained at certain minimum levels. Thus, floating-rate securities save on the costs of constantly rolling over short-term securities as they reach maturity.

Why do corporations issue floating-rate securities? Closer matching of their income flows from variable-rate assets with floating-rate liabilities is of major importance, especially with lenders such as banks, thrifts, and finance companies. Issuers can fix or lock in a spread between the cost of borrowed funds and the rate at which those funds are lent out. Another reason might be to avoid uncertainties associated with what could be an unreceptive market at some future date. The issuer can tap a new source for intermediate- to long-term funds at short-term rates, thereby making fewer trips to the marketplace and avoiding related issuance costs.

Also, in the presence of inflation, a floating-rate security (rolled over, if needed) may have a lower interest cost than a fixed-rate, long-term security. The reason is that, with inflation, the long rate may incorporate a substantial premium against the uncertainty of future inflation and interest rates. Finally, an issuer may find that it can issue a floating-rate security and convert its payments into a fixed-rate stream through an interest rate swap agreement. An issuer will elect this approach if the cost of issuing a floating-rate security and then using an interest rate swap will result in a lower cost than simply issuing a fixed-rate security.

There may be other features in a floating-rate issue. For example, many floating-rate issues include a put option. Some issues are exchangeable either automatically at a certain date (often five years after issuance) or at the option of the issuer into fixed-rate securities. A few issues are convertible into the common stock of the issuer. Some floating-rate issues have a ceiling or maximum interest rate for the coupon rate; some have a floor or minimum interest rate for the coupon rate.

Corporate Bond Credit Ratings

As we stated in the previous chapter, market participants typically do not do their own credit analysis of a debt obligation. Instead, they rely primarily on nationally recognized rating companies that perform credit analyses and issue their conclusions in the form of ratings. The three nationally recognized rating companies are (1) Moody's Investors Service, (2) Standard & Poor's Corporation, and (3) Fitch. The rating systems use similar symbols, as shown in Table 1.

In all systems, the term *high grade* means low credit risk, or conversely, high probability of future payments. The highest-grade bonds are designated by Moody's by the symbol Aaa, and by the other three rating systems by the symbol AAA. The next highest grade is denoted by the symbol Aa (Moody's) or AA (the other three rating systems); for the third grade all rating systems use A. The next three grades are Baa or BBB, Ba or BB, and B, respectively. There are also C grades. Moody's uses 1, 2, or 3 to provide a narrower credit quality breakdown within each class, and the other three rating companies use plus and minus signs for the same purpose.

Bonds rated triple A (AAA or Aaa) are said to be *prime*; double A (AA or Aa) are of high quality; single A issues are called *upper medium grade*, and triple B are *medium grade*. Lower-rated bonds are said to have speculative elements or be distinctly speculative.

Bond issues that are assigned a rating in the top four categories are referred to as **investment-grade bonds.** Issues that carry a rating below the top four categories are referred to as *noninvestment-grade bonds*, or more popularly as **high-yield bonds** or **junk bonds.** Thus, the corporate bond market can be divided into two sectors: the investment-grade and noninvestment-grade markets.

Table 1 Summary of Corporate Bond Rating Systems and Symbols

Moody's	S&P	Fitch	Brief Definition
INVESTMENT GRADE—HIGH CREDITWORTHINESS			
Aaa	AAA	AAA	Gilt edge, prime, maximum safety
Aa1	AA+	AA+	
Aa2	AA	AA	Very high grade, high quality
Aa3	AA−	AA−	
A1	A+	A+	
A2	A	A	Upper medium grade
A3	A−	A−	
Baa1	BBB+	BBB+	
Baa2	BBB	BBB	Lower medium grade
Baa3	BBB−	BBB−	
DISTINCTLY SPECULATIVE—LOW CREDITWORTHINESS			
Ba1	BB+	BB+	
Ba2	BB	BB	Low grade, speculative
Ba3	BB−	BB−	
B1	B+	B+	
B2	B	B	Highly speculative
B3	B−	B−	
PREDOMINANTLY SPECULATIVE—SUBSTANTIAL RISK OF DEFAULT			
	CCC+		
Caa	CCC	CCC	Substantial risk, in poor standing
	CCC−		
Ca	CC	CC	May be in default, extremely speculative
C	C	C	Even more speculative than those above
	C1		C1=Income bonds—no interest is being paid
		DDD	Default
		DD	
	D	D	

Source: *Richard S. Wilson and Frank J. Fabozzi, Corporate Bonds: Structures & Analysis (New Hope, PA: Frank J. Fabozzi Associates, 1996).*

Ratings of bonds change over time. Issuers are upgraded when their likelihood of default as assessed by the rating company improves and downgraded when their likelihood of default as assessed by the rating company deteriorates. The rating companies publish the issues that they are reviewing for possible rating change. These lists are called *credit watch lists*.

Each rating agency periodically publishes a table showing the upgrade and downgrade history of the issues that it rated. Such a table is called a *rating transition matrix*. The table shows the percentage of issues of each rating at the beginning of a time period that were downgraded, upgraded, or unchanged by the end of some time period. This information helps investors assess the prospects that an issue will be downgraded or upgraded over some time period.

Occasionally, the ability of an issuer to make interest and principal payments is seriously and unexpectedly changed by (1) a natural or industrial accident or some regulatory change, or (2) a takeover or corporate restructuring. These risks are referred to generically as *event risk*. Two examples of the first type of event risk are (1) a change in the accounting treatment of loan losses for commercial banks, and (2) the cancellation of nuclear plants by public utilities.

An example of the second type of event risk is the takeover in 1988 of RJR Nabisco for $25 billion through a financing technique known as a **leveraged buyout (LBO)**. The new company took on a substantial amount of debt to finance the acquisition of the firm.[4] In the case of RJR Nabisco, the debt and equity after the leveraged buyout were $29.9 and $1.2 billion, respectively. Because of the need to service a larger amount of debt, the company's quality rating was reduced. RJR Nabisco's quality rating as assigned by Moody's dropped from A1 to B3. As a result, investors demanded a higher credit spread because of this new capital structure with a greater proportion of debt. The yield spread to a benchmark Treasury rate increased from about 100 basis points to 350 basis points.

Factors Considered by Rating Agencies

In assessing the credit risk of a corporate issuer, corporate bond issue, or corporate loan, the rating agencies generally look at three factors:

- the protections afforded to debt holders that are provided by covenants limiting management's discretion
- the collateral available for the debt holder should the issuer fail to make the required payments
- the ability of an issuer to make the contractual payments to debt holders

The indenture includes the covenants imposed on management. Covenants establish rules for several important areas of operation for corporate management. These provisions are safeguards for the debt holder. Indenture provisions are analyzed carefully in assigning a rating to a bond or loan.

In assessing the ability of an issuer to service its debt (i.e., make timely payment of interest and principal), one immediately thinks about the crunching of numbers based on the financial statements of the issuing corporation. While that is extremely important, the ability of an issuer to generate cash flow goes considerably beyond the calculation and analysis of a myriad of financial ratios and cash flow measures that can be used as a basic assessment of a company's financial risk. Analysts also look at qualitative factors such as the issuer's business risk and corporate governance risk to assess the issuer's ability to pay. Thus, the rating agencies look at business risk, corporate governance risk, and financial risk.

---

[4] For a discussion of event risk associated with takeovers, see N.R. Vijayarghavan and Randy Snook, "Takeover Event Risk and Corporate Bond Portfolio Management," in Frank J. Fabozzi (ed.), *Advances and Innovations in Bond and Mortgage Markets* (Chicago: Probus Publishing, 1989).

Business risk is the risk associated with operating cash flows. Operating cash flows are not certain because the revenues and the expenditures comprising the cash flows are uncertain. Revenues depend on conditions in the economy as a whole and the industry in which the company operates, as well as the actions of management and its competitors. In assessing business risk, the three rating agencies look at the same general areas. S&P states that in analyzing business risk it considers country risk, industry characteristics, company position, product portfolio/marketing, technology, cost efficiency, strategic and operational management competence, and profitability/peer group comparisons.[5] Moody's investigates industry trends, national political and regulatory environment, management quality and attitude towards risk-taking, and basic operating and competitive position.[6] Fitch reviews industry trends, operating environment, market position, and management.[7]

Corporate governance issues involve (1) the ownership structure of the corporation, (2) the practices followed by management, and (3) policies for financial disclosure. The eagerness of corporate management to present favorable results to shareholders and the market has been a major factor in several of the corporate scandals in recent years and is what is referred to as **corporate governance risk**. Chief executive officers (CEOs), chief financial officers, and the board of directors are being held directly accountable for disclosures in financial statements and other corporate decisions. There are mechanisms that can mitigate the likelihood that management will act in its own self-interest. The mechanisms fall into two general categories. The first is to more strongly align the interests of management with those of shareholders. This can be accomplished by granting management an economically meaningful equity interest in the company. Also, manager compensation can be linked to the performance of the company's common stock. The second category of mechanism is by means of the company's internal corporate control systems, which can provide a way for effectively monitoring the performance and decision-making behavior of management.

In addition to corporate governance, rating agencies look at the quality of management in assessing a corporation's ability to pay. Moody's notes the following regarding the quality of management:

> Although difficult to quantify, management quality is one of the most important factors supporting an issuer's credit strength. When the unexpected occurs, it is a management's ability to react appropriately that will sustain the company's performance. Assessment of management's plans in comparison with those of their industry peers can also provide important insights into the company's ability to compete, how likely it is to use debt capacity, its treatment of its subsidiaries, its relationship with regulators, and its position vis-à-vis all fundamentals affecting the company's long-term credit strength.[8]

---

[5] Standard & Poor's Corporation, *Corporate Rating Criteria*, 2005, p. 20.

[6] Moody's Investors Service, *Industrial Company Rating Methodology*, July 1998, p. 3.

[7] FitchRatings, *Corporate Rating Methodology*, undated, pp. 1–2.

[8] Moody's Investors Service, *Industrial Company Rating Methodology*, p. 6.

In assessing management quality, Moody's tries to understand the business strategies and policies formulated by management. The factors Moody's considers are: (1) strategic direction, (2) financial philosophy, (3) conservatism, (4) track record, (5) succession planning, and (6) control systems.

Having achieved an understanding of a corporation's business risk and corporate governance risk, the rating agencies move on to assessing **financial risk**. This analysis involves traditional ratio analysis and other factors affecting the firm's financing. These measures, which are described in most books on investment management, involve interest coverage, leverage, cash flow, net assets, and working capital. Once these measures are calculated for the firm being analyzed, rating agencies compare them relative to other firms in the same industry.

Recovery Ratings

While credit ratings provide guidance for the probability of default and recovery given default, the market needed better recovery information for specific bond issues. In response to this need, two ratings agencies, Fitch and Standard & Poor's, developed **recovery rating systems** for corporate bonds. The recovery ratings were for secured debt. The S&P recovery ratings use an ordinal scale of one through five. Each recovery rating category corresponds to a specific range of recovery values.

Fitch introduced a recovery rating system for corporate bonds rated single B and below. The factors considered in assigning a recovery rating to an issue by Fitch are (1) the collateral, (2) the seniority relative to other obligations in the capital structure, and (3) the expected value of the issuer in distress. The recovery rating system does not attempt to precisely predict a given level of recovery. Rather, the ratings are in the form of an ordinal scale and referred to accordingly as a *recovery ratings scale*.

High-Yield Sector

As we have noted, high-yield bonds are issues with a credit rating below triple B. Bond issues in this sector of the market may have been rated investment grade at the time of issuance and have been downgraded subsequently to noninvestment grade, or they may have been rated noninvestment grade at the time of issuance, called *original-issue, high-yield bonds*. Bonds that have been downgraded fall into two groups: (1) issues that have been downgraded because the issuer voluntarily significantly increased their debt as a result of a leveraged buyout or a recapitalization, and (2) issues that have been downgraded for other reasons. The latter issues are commonly referred to as **fallen angels**.

The Role of High-Yield Bonds in Corporate Finance

The introduction of original-issue, high-yield bonds has been a very important financial innovation with wide impact throughout the financial system. There was a common view that high default risk bonds would not be attractive to the investing public, at least at interest rates that would be acceptable to the borrower. The view rested on the skewed nature of the outcomes offered by the instrument: The maximum return that an investor may obtain is capped by the coupon and face value, but the loss could be as large as the principal invested. It was the merit of Drexel Burnham Lambert, and particularly of Michael Milken of that firm, to disprove that view as evidenced by the explosive growth of that market.

Before development of the high-yield market, U.S. corporations that could not issue securities in the public debt market would borrow from commercial banks or finance companies on a short-term to intermediate-term basis or would be shut off from credit. With the advent of the high-yield bond structure, financing shifted from commercial banks to the public market. One study estimated that about two-thirds of the $90 billion to $100 billion of the high-yield bonds issued represent simply a replacement of commercial bank borrowing. The same study concluded that high-yield bonds are "no more a threat to the stability of the financial system than that bank debt itself was."[9]

In essence, the high-yield bond market shifts the risk from commercial banks to the investing public in general. There are several advantages to such a shift. First, when commercial banks lend to high credit risk borrowers, that risk is accepted indirectly by all U.S. citizens, who may not wish to accept the risk. The reason is that commercial bank liabilities are backed by the Federal Deposit Insurance Company (FDIC). If high credit risk corporations default on their loans, causing an FDIC bailout, all taxpayers eventually may have to pay. The liabilities of other investors (excluding thrifts that have invested in high-yield bonds) are not backed by the U.S. government (and, therefore, not by U.S. citizens). The risks of this investing are accepted by the specific investor group willing to accept them.

The second advantage is that commercial bank loans are typically short-term, floating-rate loans, which make debt financing less attractive to corporations. High-yield bond issues give corporations the opportunity to issue long-term, fixed-rate debt. Third, commercial banks set interest rates based on their credit analysis. When high-yield bonds are traded in a public market, the investing public establishes the interest rate. Finally, the high-yield market opens the possibility of funding for some firms that previously had no means to it.

Corporate bond issuers use the proceeds from a bond sale for a number of purposes. These include working capital, expansion of facilities, refinancing of outstanding debt, and financing takeovers (mergers and acquisitions). In the case of noninvestment-grade bonds, it is the use of the proceeds to finance takeovers (particularly hostile takeovers) that has aroused some public concern over the excessive use of debt by U.S. corporations.[10]

High-Yield Bond Structures

In the early years of the high-yield market, all the issues had a conventional structure; that is, the issues paid a fixed coupon rate and were term bonds. Today, however, there are more

---

[9] November 1986 speech by John Paulus, chief economist at Morgan Stanley, at a conference sponsored by Citizens for a Sound Economy.

[10] A hostile takeover is one in which the targeted firm's management resists the merger or acquisition.

complex bond structures in the junk bond area, particularly for bonds issued for LBO financing and recapitalizations producing higher debt.

In an LBO or a recapitalization, the heavy interest payment burden that the corporation assumes placed severe cash flow constraints on the firm. To reduce this burden, firms involved in LBOs and recapitalizations have issued bonds with deferred coupon structures that permit the issuer to avoid using cash to make interest payments for a period of three to seven years. There are three types of deferred coupon structures: (1) deferred-interest bonds, (2) step-up bonds, and (3) payment-in-kind bonds.

Deferred-interest bonds are the most common type of **deferred coupon structure**. These bonds sell at a deep discount and do not pay interest for an initial period, typically from three to seven years. (Because no interest is paid for the initial period, these bonds are sometimes referred to as zero-coupon bonds.) **Step-up bonds** do pay coupon interest, but the coupon rate is low for an initial period and then increases ("steps up") to a higher coupon rate. Finally, **payment-in-kind (PIK) bonds** give the issuer an option to pay cash at a coupon payment date or give the bondholder a similar bond (i.e., a bond with the same coupon rate and a par value equal to the amount of the coupon payment that would have been paid). The period during which the issuer can make this choice varies from five to 10 years.

Secondary Market

As with all bonds, the principal secondary market for corporate bonds is the over-the-counter market. The major concern is market transparency.

Trade Reporting and Compliance Engine

Efforts to increase price transparency in the U.S. corporate debt market resulted in the introduction in July 2002 by the National Association of Securities Dealers (NASD) of mandatory reporting of over-the-counter secondary market transactions for corporate bonds that met specific criteria. The reporting system, the **Trade Reporting and Compliance Engine (TRACE)**, requires that all broker-dealers who are NASD member firms report transactions in corporate bonds to TRACE.

When first introduced in July 2002, TRACE included only 500 U.S. investment-grade corporate bonds with an original issue size of $1 billion. Since then, the criteria for reporting transactions in TRACE resulted by October 2004 in 17,000 corporate bond issues being included, including most high-yield bonds. By February 2005, reporting criteria resulted in almost the entire corporate bond universe being included in TRACE (29,000 publicly traded issues).

At the end of each trading day, market aggregate statistics are published on corporate bond market activity. End-of-day recap information provided includes (1) the number of securities and total par amount traded; (2) advances, declines, and 52-week highs and lows; and (3) the 10 most active investment grade, high-yield, and convertible bonds for the day.

Electronic Bond Trading

Traditionally, corporate bond trading has been an OTC market conducted via telephone and based on broker-dealer trading desks, which take principal positions in corporate bonds in order to fulfill the buy and sell orders of their customers. There has been a transition away from this traditional form of bond trading and toward electronic trading.[11]

Electronic bond trading makes up about 30% of corporate bond trading. The major advantages of electronic trading over traditional corporate bond trading in the over-the-counter market are (1) providing liquidity to the markets, (2) price discovery (particularly for less liquid markets), (3) use of new technologies, and (4) trading and portfolio management efficiencies.[12] As an example of the last advantage, a portfolio manager can load buy–sell orders on a website, trade from these orders, and then clear these orders.

There are five types of electronic corporate bond trading systems. **Auction systems** allow market participants to conduct electronic auctions of securities offerings for both new issues in the primary markets and secondary market offerings. Auction systems are not typically used. **Cross-matching systems** bring dealers and institutional investors together in electronic trading networks that provide real-time or periodic cross-matching sessions. Buy and sell orders are executed automatically when matched. **Interdealer systems** allow dealers to execute transactions electronically with other dealers via the anonymous services of "brokers' brokers." The clients of dealers are not involved in interdealer systems. **Multidealer systems** allow customers with consolidated orders from two or more dealers the ability to execute from among multiple quotes. Multidealer systems, also called **client-to-dealer systems**, typically display to customers the best bid or offer price of those posted by all dealers. The participating dealer usually acts as the principal in the transaction. **Single-dealer systems** permit investors to execute transactions directly with the specific dealer desired; this dealer acts as a principal in the transaction with access to the dealer by the investor, which increasingly has been through the Internet. Single-dealer systems therefore simply replace telephone contact between a single dealer and a customer with Internet contact.

Eurobond Market

The **Eurobond** sector of the global bond market includes bonds with several distinguishing features: (1) they are underwritten by an international syndicate, (2) at issuance they are offered simultaneously to investors in a number of countries, (3) they are issued outside the jurisdiction of any single country, and (4) they are in unregistered form. Although Eurobonds are typically listed on a national stock exchange (the most common are the Luxembourg, London, or Zurich exchanges), the bulk of all trading is in the over-the-counter market. Firms list these bonds purely to circumvent restrictions imposed on some institutional investors that are prohibited from purchasing securities not listed on an exchange. Some of the stronger issuers privately place their debt with international institutional investors.

---

[11] For an explanation of the reasons for the transitions to electronic bond trading and why the trend is expected to continue, see Frank J. Jones and Frank J. Fabozzi, "The Primary and Secondary Bond Markets," *The Handbook of Fixed Income Securities*, 7th ed. (New York: McGraw Hill, 2005).

[12] Jones and Fabozzi, "The Primary and Secondary Bond Markets," p. 47.

Borrowers in the Eurobond market include nonfinancial corporations, banks, sovereign governments, entities whose debt is guaranteed by a sovereign government, provinces, municipalities, cities, and supranational entities such as the World Bank. The major issuer group is nonfinancial corporations, followed by banks. Traditionally, the main currency used in Eurobond offerings has been the U.S. dollar, although the share of Eurobond offerings denominated in U.S. dollars has been declining.

The Eurobond market has been characterized by new and innovative bond structures to accommodate particular needs of issuers and investors throughout the world. Some issues, of course, are the "plain vanilla," fixed-rate coupon bonds, referred to as **Euro straights**. Because they are issued on an unsecured basis, they are usually the debt of high-quality entities.

Coupon payments on Eurobonds are made annually, rather than semiannually. There are also zero-coupon bond issues, deferred-coupon issues, and step-up issues. Some of the innovative issues in this market are **dual-currency issues:** They pay coupon interest in one currency but the principal in a different currency. For example, the coupon interest payments can be made in Swiss francs, while the principal may be paid in U.S. dollars.

Some Eurobonds are convertible or exchangeable, and bonds with attached warrants represent a large part of the market. Most warrants on Eurobonds are detachable from the bond with which they originally came to market. That is, the bondholder may detach the warrant from the bond and sell it separately.

The warrants on Eurobonds are varied: Some are equity warrants, others are debt warrants, and still others may be currency warrants. An equity warrant permits the warrant owner to buy the common stock of the issuer at a specified price. A debt warrant entitles the warrant owner to buy additional bonds from the issuer at the same price and yield as the host bond. The debt warrant owner will benefit if interest rates decline because the warrant allows the owner to purchase a bond with a higher coupon than the same issuer would offer. A currency warrant permits the warrant owner to exchange one currency for another at a set price (that is, a fixed exchange rate). This feature protects the bondholder against a depreciation of the foreign currency in which the bond's cash flows are denominated. Finally, we also note that some warrants are gold warrants and allow the warrant holder to purchase gold from the bond issuer at a prespecified price.

Eurobonds make use of a wide variety of floating-rate structures. Almost all the floating-rate notes are denominated in U.S. dollars, and non–U.S. banks are the major issuers of these bonds. The coupon rate on a floating-rate note is some stated margin over the London Interbank Offered Rate (LIBOR), the bid on LIBOR (referred to as LIBID), or the arithmetic average of LIBOR and LIBID (referred to as LIMEAN). Many floating-rate issues have either a minimum rate (or floor) that the coupon rate cannot fall below or a maximum rate (or cap) that the coupon rate cannot exceed. An issue that has both a floor and a cap is said to be *collared*. Some floating-rate issues grant the borrower the right to convert the floating coupon rate into a fixed coupon rate at some time. Some issues, referred to as *drop-lock bonds*, automatically convert the floating coupon rate into a fixed coupon rate under certain circumstances.

> **Key Points That You Should Understand Before Proceeding**
>
> 1. The bond indenture sets forth the obligations of the issuer and the rights of the bondholders.
> 2. Either real property or personal property may be pledged to offer security beyond that of the general credit standing of the issuer.
> 3. Bonds typically carry provisions that allow for the principal to be repaid prior to the stated maturity date, with the most common provision being the right of the issuer to call the issue. This is an advantage to the issuer and a disadvantage to the bondholder.
> 4. There is a wide variety of bond structures with special features that make issues more attractive to both borrowers and investors.
> 5. In addition to credit risk, corporate bond investors are exposed to event risk.
> 6. High-yield bonds are issues whose quality rating is designated as noninvestment grade, and there are several unique bond structures in this sector of the market.
> 7. The Eurobond market has been characterized by new and innovative bond structures to accommodate particular needs of issuers and investors throughout the world.

PREFERRED STOCK

Preferred stock is a class of stock, not a debt instrument, but it shares characteristics of both common stock and debt. Like the holder of common stock, the preferred stockholder is entitled to dividends. Unlike those on common stock, however, preferred dividends are a specified percentage of par or face value.[13] The percentage is called the dividend rate; it need not be fixed, but may float over the life of the issue.

Failure to make preferred stock dividend payments cannot force the issuer into bankruptcy. Should the issuer not make the preferred stock dividend payment, usually paid quarterly, one of two things can happen, depending on the terms of the issue. First, the dividend payment can accrue until it is fully paid. Preferred stock with this feature is called **cumulative preferred stock**. If a dividend payment is missed and the securityholder must forgo the payment, the preferred stock is said to be **noncumulative preferred stock**. Second, the failure to make dividend payments may result in the imposition of certain restrictions on management. For example, if dividend payments are in arrears, preferred stockholders might be granted voting rights.

Preferred stock differs from debt in a major way: The current tax code for corporations treats payments made to preferred stockholders as a distribution of earnings and not as tax-deductible expenses, which is how the tax code views interest payments. While this difference in tax status raises the after-tax cost of funds for a corporation issuing preferred stock rather than borrowing, another factor in the tax code reduces the cost differential. A provision in the tax code exempts 70% of qualified dividends from federal income taxation, if the recipient is a qualified corporation.

For example, if Corporation A owns the preferred stock of Corporation B, then only $30 of each $100 that A receives in dividends from B will be taxed at A's marginal tax rate. The purpose of this provision is to mitigate the effect of the double taxation of corporate

---

[13] Almost all preferred stock limits the securityholder to the specified amount. Historically, there have been issues entitling the preferred stockholder to participate in earnings distribution beyond the specified amount (based on some formula). Preferred stock with this feature is referred to as participating preferred stock.

earnings. There are two implications of this tax treatment of preferred stock dividends. First, the major buyers of preferred stock are corporations seeking tax-advantaged investments. Second, the cost of preferred stock issuance is lower than it would be in the absence of the tax provision, because the tax benefits are passed through to the issuer by the willingness of buyers to accept a lower dividend rate.

Preferred stock, particularly cumulative preferred stock, has some important similarities with debt: (1) The issuer promises fixed cash payments to preferred stockholders, and (2) preferred stockholders have priority over common stockholders with respect to dividend payments and the distribution of assets in the case of bankruptcy. (The position of noncumulative preferred stock is considerably weaker.) It is because of this second feature that preferred stock is called a senior corporate instrument—it is senior to common stock. Note, however, that preferred stock is classified as equity on corporate balance sheets.

Almost all preferred stock has a sinking fund provision, and some preferred stock is convertible into common stock. Preferred stock may be issued without a maturity date. This is called **perpetual preferred stock**.

The preferred stock is a relatively small part of the financial system. Historically, utilities have been the major issuers of preferred stock, accounting for more than half of each year's issuance. Since 1985, major issuers have become financially oriented companies— finance companies, banks, thrifts, and insurance companies.

The same four commercial companies that assign ratings to corporate bond issues also rate preferred stock issues.

There are three types of preferred stock: (1) fixed-rate preferred stock, (2) adjustable-rate preferred stock, and (3) auction and remarketed preferred stock. Before 1982, all publicly issued preferred stock was fixed-rate preferred stock. In May 1982, the first adjustable-rate preferred stock issue was sold in the public market.[14]

Adjustable-Rate Preferred Stock

The dividend rate on an **adjustable-rate preferred stock (ARPS)** is fixed quarterly and based on a predetermined spread from the highest of three points on the Treasury yield curve.[15] The predetermined spread is called the *dividend reset spread*. The motivation for linking the dividend rate to the highest of the three points on the Treasury yield curve is to provide the investor with protection against unfavorable shifts in the yield curve.

Most ARPS is perpetual, with a floor and ceiling imposed on the dividend rate of most issues. Because an ARP is typically not putable, it can trade below par if, after issuance, the

---

[14] Private placement of ARPS occurred as early as 1978—illustrating how an innovation is first developed in this market. For historical background on the development of the ARPS market, see Richard S. Wilson, "Adjustable Rate Preferred Stocks," Chapter 3 in Frank J. Fabozzi (ed.), *Floating Rate Instruments: Characteristics, Valuation and Portfolio Strategies* (Chicago: Probus Publishing, 1986).

[15] The three points on the yield curve (called the benchmark rate) to which the dividend reset spread is either added or subtracted are the highest of: (1) the three-month Treasury bill rate, (2) the two-year constant maturity rate, or (3) a 10-year or 30-year constant maturity rate. The Treasury constant maturity rate is reported in the Federal Reserve Report H.15(519). It is based on the closing market bid yields on actively traded Treasury securities.

spread demanded by the market to reflect the issuer's credit risk is greater than the dividend reset spread.

The major issuers of ARPS have been bank holding companies. There are two reasons bank holding companies have become major issuers of ARPS. First, floating-rate obligations provide a better liability match, given the floating-rate nature of bank assets. Second, bank holding companies are seeking to strengthen their capital positions, and regulators permit bank holding companies to count perpetual preferred stock as part of their primary capital. Issuing ARPS provides not only a better asset/liability match, but also permits bank holding companies to improve primary capital without having to issue common stock.

Auction and Remarketed Preferred Stock

The popularity of ARPS declined when instruments began to trade below their par value—because the dividend reset rate is determined at the time of issuance, not by market forces. In 1984, a new type of preferred stock, **auction preferred stock (APS)**, was designed to overcome this problem, particularly for corporate treasurers who sought tax-advantaged short-term instruments to invest excess funds.[16] The dividend rate on APS is set periodically, as with ARPS, but it is established through an auction process.[17] Participants in the auction consist of current holders and potential buyers. The dividend rate that participants are willing to accept reflects current market conditions.

In the case of **remarketed preferred stock (RP)**, the dividend rate is determined periodically by a remarketing agent who resets the dividend rate so that any preferred stock can be tendered at par and be resold (remarketed) at the original offering price. An investor has the choice of dividend resets every seven days or every 49 days.

Since 1985, APS and RP have become the dominant types of preferred stock issued.

Key Points That You Should Understand Before Proceeding

1. Preferred stock is a class of stock in which the dividend rate is typically a fixed percentage of par or face value.
2. Payments made to preferred stockholders are treated as a distribution of earnings and therefore are not tax deductible to the issuing corporation.
3. Because the tax code exempts 70% of qualified dividends from federal income taxation if the recipient is a qualified corporation, the major buyers of preferred stock are corporations seeking tax-advantaged investments; these investors are willing to accept a lower dividend rate.
4. Preferred stock has some important similarities with debt.
5. There are various types of preferred stock: fixed-rate, adjustable-rate, auction, and remarketed preferred stock.

---

[16] Each investment bank developed its own trademark name for APS. The instrument developed by Shearson Lehman/American Express was called Money Market Preferred (MMP). Salomon Brothers called it Dutch Auction Rate Transferable Securities (DARTS).

[17] The auction process is described in Richard S. Wilson, "Money Market Preferred Stock," Chapter 4 in Frank J. Fabozzi (ed.), *Floating Rate Instruments*, pp. 85–88.

BANKRUPTCY AND CREDITOR RIGHTS

In this chapter, we refer to *senior* corporate securities. By senior, we mean that the holder of the security has priority over the equity owners in the case of the bankruptcy of a corporation. And, as we explain in this chapter, there are creditors who have priority over other creditors. In this section, we provide an overview of the bankruptcy process and then look at what actually happens to creditors in bankruptcies.

The U.S. bankruptcy law gives debtors who are unable to meet their debt obligations a mechanism for formulating a plan to resolve their debts through an allocation of their assets among their creditors.[18] One purpose of the bankruptcy law is to set forth the rules for a corporation to be liquidated or reorganized. *Liquidation* means that all the assets of the corporation will be distributed to holders of claims on the corporation, and no corporate entity will survive. In a *reorganization*, a new corporate entity will result. Some holders of claims on the bankrupt corporation will receive cash in exchange for their claims; others may receive new securities in the corporation that results from the reorganization; and still others may receive a combination of both cash and new securities in the resulting corporation.

Another purpose of the bankruptcy act is to give a corporation time to decide whether to reorganize or to liquidate, and then provide the necessary time to formulate a plan to accomplish either a reorganization or liquidation. This is achieved because a bankruptcy filing allows the corporation protection from creditors who seek to collect their claims.[19] A company that files for protection under the bankruptcy act generally becomes a **debtor-in-possession**, and continues to operate its business under the supervision of the court.

The bankruptcy act has 15 chapters, each covering a particular type of bankruptcy. Of particular interest to us are two of the chapters, **Chapter 7** and **Chapter 11**. Chapter 7 deals with the liquidation of a company; Chapter 11 covers reorganization.

When a company is liquidated, creditors receive distributions based on the **absolute priority rule** to the extent assets are available. The absolute priority rule is the principle that senior creditors are paid in full before junior creditors are paid anything. For secured creditors and unsecured creditors, the absolute priority rule guarantees their seniority to equity holders.

In liquidations, the absolute priority rule generally holds, but in reorganizations under Chapter 11, it is often violated. Studies of actual reorganizations under Chapter 11 have found that the violation of absolute priority is the rule rather than the exception.[20]

There are several reasons that have been suggested as to why, in a reorganization, the distribution made to claimholders will diverge from that required by the absolute priority principle.[21] One reason commonly cited has to do with the negotiation process that takes

---

[18] Congress passed the Bankruptcy Code under its Constitutional grant of authority to "establish . . . uniform laws on the subject of Bankruptcy throughout the United States." The U.S. Bankruptcy Courts are responsible for the supervising and litigating bankruptcy proceedings.

[19] The petition for bankruptcy can be filed either by the company itself, in which case it is called a *voluntary bankruptcy*, or be filed by its creditors, in which case it is called an *involuntary bankruptcy*.

[20] See Julian R. Franks and Walter N. Torous, "An Empirical Investigation of U.S. Firms in Reorganization," *Journal of Finance* (July 1989), pp. 747–769; Lawrence A. Weiss, "Bankruptcy Resolution: Direct Costs and Violation of Priority of Claims," *Journal of Financial Economics* (1990), pp. 285–314; and Frank J. Fabozzi, Jane Tripp Howe, Takashi Makabe, and Toshihide Sudo, "Recent Evidence on the Distribution Patterns in Chapter 11 Reorganizations," *Journal of Fixed Income* (Spring 1993), pp. 6–23.

[21] For a discussion of these reasons, see Fabozzi, et. al., "Recent Evidence on the Distribution Patterns in Chapter 11 Reorganizations," op. cit.

place among the various classes of claimholders in a reorganization. In a reorganization, a committee representing the various claimholders is appointed with the purpose of formulating a plan of reorganization. To be accepted, a plan of reorganization must be approved by at least two-thirds of the amount and a majority of the number of claims voting, and at least two-thirds of the outstanding shares of each class of interests. Consequently, a long-lasting bargaining process is expected. The longer the negotiation process among the parties, the more likely the company is to be operated in a manner that is not in the best interest of the creditors and, as a result, the smaller the amount to be distributed to all parties. Since all impaired classes including equityholders generally must approve the plan of reorganization, creditors often convince equityholders to accept the plan by offering to distribute some value to them.

Consequently, while investors in the debt of a corporation may feel that they have priority over the equity owners and priority over other classes of debtors, the actual outcome of a bankruptcy may be far different from what the terms of the debt agreement state.

Key Points That You Should Understand Before Proceeding

1. Bankruptcy law is a federal statutory law that provides for the development of a plan allowing debtors who are not able to pay their creditors to resolve their debts through the division of their assets among their creditors.
2. Chapter 7 of the act deals with the liquidation of a company, and Chapter 11 deals with the reorganization of a company.
3. When a company is liquidated, creditors receive distributions based on the absolute priority rule to the extent assets are available.
4. In liquidations, the absolute priority rule generally holds, but in reorganizations under Chapter 11, it is often violated.

SUMMARY

Corporate bonds are debt obligating a corporation to pay periodic interest with full repayment at maturity. The promises of the corporate bond issuer and the rights of the investors are set forth in the bond indenture. Provisions to be specified include call and sinking fund provisions.

Security for bonds may be real or personal property. Debenture bonds are not secured by a specific pledge of property. Subordinated debenture bonds are issues that rank after secured debt, after debenture bonds, and often after some general creditors in their claims on assets and earnings.

The credit risk of a corporate borrower can be gauged by the credit rating assigned by the three nationally recognized rating companies. Issues rated in the top ratings of the three raters are referred to as investment-grade bonds; those below the top four ratings are called noninvestment-grade bonds, high-yield bonds, or junk bonds. In assigning a credit rating, the credit rate companies assess the protections set forth in the bond indenture, the collateral available for the debt holders should the issuer fail to make the required payments, and the capacity of an issuer to fulfill its payment obligations. In assessing the ability of an issuer to service its debt, rating agencies assess the issuer's business risk, corporate governance risk, and financial risk. Business risk is the risk associated with operating cash flows. In assessing business risk, some of the main factors considered are industry characteristics and trends, the company's market and competitive positions, management characteristics, and the national political and regulatory environment. Corporate governance risk involves assessing (1) the ownership structure of the corporation, (2) the practices followed by management, and (3) policies for financial disclosure. Assessing financial risk involves traditional ratio analysis and other factors affecting the firm's financing. The more important financial ratios analyzed are interest coverage, leverage, cash flow, net assets, and working capital.

Secondary trading information for corporate bonds is provided by TRACE. There are the following five types of electronic corporate bond trading systems: auction systems, cross-matching systems, interdealer systems, multidealer systems, and single-dealer systems.

Special corporate bond features include convertible and exchangeable bonds, units of debt with warrants, putable bonds, zero-coupon bonds, and floating-rate securities. Junk bonds or high-yield bonds are issues with quality ratings below triple B. Recent years have seen the introduction of several complex bond structures in the junk bond area, particularly bonds issued for LBO financing and recapitalizations producing higher levels of debt to equity. These include deferred-coupon bonds (deferred-interest bonds, step-up bonds, and payment-in-kind bonds) and extendable reset bonds.

Many innovative bond structures have been introduced in the Eurobond market such as dual-currency issues and various types of convertible bonds and bonds with warrants. A warrant permits its owner to enter into another financial transaction with the issuer if the owner will benefit by doing so. The floating-rate sector of the Eurobond market is dominated by U.S. dollar-denominated issues.

Preferred stock as a class of stock has characteristics of both common stock and debt. Because a special provision in the tax code allows taxation of only a portion of dividends when they are received by a corporation, the major buyers of preferred stock are corporations. There are three types of preferred stock besides the traditional fixed-rate preferred stock: adjustable-rate preferred stock, auction preferred stock, and remarketed preferred stock.

The bankruptcy law governs the bankruptcy process in the United States. Chapter 7 of the bankruptcy act deals with the liquidation of a company. Chapter 11 deals with the reorganization of a company. Creditors receive distributions based on the absolute priority rule to the extent assets are available. This means that senior creditors are paid in full before junior creditors are paid anything. Generally, this rule holds in the case of liquidations. In contrast, the absolute priority rule is typically violated in a reorganization.

| KEY TERMS

- Absolute priority rule
- Adjustable-rate preferred stock (ARPS)
- Auction preferred stock (APS)
- Auction systems
- Bond indenture
- Bullet-maturity (bullet) bond
- Business risk
- Call risk (timing risk)
- Chapter 7

- Chapter 11
- Client-to-dealer system
- Collateral trust bond
- Convertible bond
- Corporate governance risk
- Cross-matching systems
- Cumulative preferred stock
- Debenture bond
- Debtor-in-possession

- Deferred coupon structure
- Deferred-interest bond
- Dual-currency issue
- Equipment trust certificate
- Euro straights
- Eurobond
- Exchangeable bond
- Fallen angel
- Financial risk
- Floating-rate security
- Guaranteed bond
- High-yield bond (junk bond)
- Interdealer systems
- Investment-grade bond
- Leveraged buyout (LBO)
- Mortgage bond
- Multidealer systems

- Noncumulative preferred stock
- Payment-in-kind (PIK) bond
- Perpetual preferred stock
- Preferred stock
- Putable bond
- Recovery rating systems
- Refunding
- Remarketed preferred stock (RP)
- Serial bond
- Single-dealer systems
- Sinking fund provision
- Step-up bond
- Subordinated debenture bond
- Trade Reporting and Compliance Engine (TRACE)
- Warrant

QUESTIONS

1. **a.** What are the disadvantages of investing in a callable bond?
   b. What is the advantage to the issuer of issuing a callable bond?
   c. What is the difference between a noncallable bond and a nonrefundable bond?
2. **a.** What is a sinking fund requirement in a bond issue?
   b. "A sinking fund provision in a bond issue benefits the investor." Do you agree with this statement?
3. What is a
   a. serial bond?
   b. mortgage bond?
   c. equipment trust certificate?
   d. collateral bond?
4. What is the difference between a convertible bond and an exchangeable bond?
5. Do you agree or disagree with this statement: "Zero-coupon corporate bonds are created in the same way as in the Treasury market—by stripping coupon bonds"?
6. **a.** What is event risk?
   b. Give two examples of event risk.

7. What is meant by a rating transition matrix?
8. In assigning a credit rating, the credit rating companies analyze a company's business risk. What is meant by business risk?
9. **a.** What is meant by corporate governance risk?
   b. What are two mechanisms for mitigating corporate governance risk?
10. How does a credit rating differ from a recovery rating?
11. What are the major advantages of electronic trading over traditional corporate bond trading in the over-the-counter market?
12. What is the difference between a fallen angel and an original-issue, high-yield bond?
13. Indicate why you agree or disagree with the following statement: "Today, the proceeds from most original-issue, high-yield bonds are used for leveraged buyouts and recapitalizations."
14. **a.** What is a Eurobond?
    b. How often is the coupon payment on a Eurobond made?
    c. Name the two currencies most often used to denominate Eurobonds.
15. What is a dual-currency bond?

16. **a.** Explain what an institutional investor will do to purchase or sell a corporate bond.

    b. What has happened to the commitment of capital of dealer firms to the high-yield corporate bond market in recent years?

17. **a.** Why are corporate treasurers the main buyers of preferred stock?

    b. What is the reason for the popularity of auction and remarketed preferred stock?

18. **a.** What is the difference between a liquidation and a reorganization?

    b. What is the difference between a Chapter 7 and Chapter 11 bankruptcy filing?

    c. What is meant by a debtor-in-possession?

19. **a.** What is meant by the principle of absolute priority?

    b. Comment on this statement: "An investor who purchases the mortgage bonds of a corporation knows that, should the corporation become bankrupt, mortgage bondholders will be paid in full before the common stockholders receive any proceeds."

The Markets for Bank Obligations

LEARNING OBJECTIVES

After reading this chapter, you will understand

- a categorization of banks that is useful for understanding the supply of bank obligations

- what a negotiable certificate of deposit or CD is, and the different types of certificates of deposit

- what a Euro CD is and how it differs from a Yankee CD

- what determines a CD's yield or rate of interest

- what federal funds are, and how banks use them to meet Federal Reserve requirements

- what the effective fed funds rate is

- the size of the fed funds market and the role brokers play in it

- what a bankers acceptance is, and how it is created

- what the bankers acceptance's credit risk is, and what an eligible bankers acceptance is

Commercial banks are special types of corporations. Larger banks will raise funds using the various debt markets described in the previous two chapters. In this chapter, we describe three other debt obligations: large-denomination certificates of deposit, federal funds, and **bankers acceptances.** All these instruments trade in what is collectively known as the *money market*, the market for short-term debt instruments. Typically, money market instruments have a maturity of one year or less. While our discussion focuses on commercial banks, other depository institutions may also issue the same types of obligations.

From Chapter 21 of *Foundations of Financial Markets and Institutions*, 4/e. Frank J. Fabozzi. Franco Modigliani. Frank J. Jones.

TYPES OF BANKS OPERATING IN THE UNITED STATES

Banks in the United States can be classified into four groups. First are the **money center banks**—banks that raise most of their funds from the domestic and international money markets and rely less on depositors for funds. The second group is **regional banks**, which rely primarily on deposits for funding and make less use of the money markets to obtain funds. **Japanese banks** are the third group of banks. The fourth group of banks are **Yankee banks**. These are foreign banks with U.S. branches. Included in this group are non-Japanese branches of foreign banks, such as Credit Lyonnais and Deutsche Bank.

LARGE-DENOMINATION NEGOTIABLE CERTIFICATES OF DEPOSIT

A **certificate of deposit (CD)** is a financial asset issued by a bank or thrift that indicates a specified sum of money has been deposited at the issuing depository institution. CDs are issued by banks and thrifts to raise funds for financing their business activities. A CD bears a maturity date and a specified interest rate, and can be issued in any denomination. CDs issued by banks are insured by the Federal Deposit Insurance Corporation but only for amounts up to $100,000 (for qualified retirement accounts the insured amount is $250,000). This was temporarily increased through December 29, 2009, to $250,000 for regular accounts and $500,000 for qualified retirement accounts. There is no limit on the maximum maturity, but by Federal Reserve regulations CDs cannot have a maturity of less than seven days.

A CD may be *nonnegotiable* or **negotiable**. In the former case, the initial depositor must wait until the maturity date of the CD to obtain the funds. If the depositor chooses to withdraw funds prior to the maturity date, an early withdrawal penalty is imposed. In contrast, a negotiable CD allows the initial depositor (or any subsequent owner of the CD) to sell the CD in the open market prior to the maturity date.

Negotiable CDs were introduced in the early sixties. At that time the interest rate banks could pay on various types of deposits was subject to ceilings administered by the Federal Reserve (except for demand deposits defined as deposits of less than one month that by law could pay no interest). For complex historical reasons, these ceiling rates started very low, rose with maturity, and remained below market rates up to some fairly long maturity. Before introduction of the negotiable CD, those with money to invest for, say, one month had no incentive to deposit it with a bank, for they would get a below-market rate unless they were prepared to tie up their capital for a much longer period of time. When negotiable CDs came along, they could buy a three-month or longer negotiable CD yielding a market interest rate, and recoup all or more than the investment (depending on market conditions) by selling it in the market.

This innovation was critical in helping banks to increase the amount of funds raised in the money market, a position that had languished in the earlier postwar period. It also motivated competition among banks, ushering in a new era. There are now two types of negotiable CDs. The first is the large-denomination CD, usually issued in denominations of $1 million or more. These are the negotiable CDs whose history we previously described.

In 1982, Merrill Lynch entered the retail CD business by opening up a primary and secondary market in small-denomination (less than $100,000) CDs. While it made the CDs of its numerous banking and savings institution clients available to retail customers, Merrill Lynch also began to give these customers the negotiability enjoyed by institutional investors by standing ready to buy back the CDs prior to maturity. Today, several retail-oriented brokerage firms offer CDs that are salable in a secondary market. These are the second type of negotiable CD. Our focus in this chapter, though, is on the large-denomination negotiable CD, and we refer to them simply as CDs throughout the chapter.

CD Issuers

CDs can be classified into four types, according to the issuing institution. First are CDs issued by domestic banks. Second are CDs that are denominated in U.S. dollars but are issued outside the United States. These CDs are called **Eurodollar CDs.** A third type of CD is the **Yankee CD**, which is a CD denominated in U.S. dollars and issued by a foreign bank with a branch in the United States. Finally, **thrift CDs** are those issued by savings and loan associations and savings banks.

Money center banks and large regional banks are the primary issuers of domestic CDs. Most CDs are issued with a maturity of less than one year. Those issued with a maturity greater than one year are called **term CDs.**

Unlike Treasury bills, commercial paper, and bankers acceptances, yields on domestic CDs are quoted on an interest-bearing basis. CDs with a maturity of one year or less pay interest at maturity. For purposes of calculating interest, a year is treated as having 360 days. Term CDs issued in the United States normally pay interest semiannually, again with a year taken as 360 days.

A floating-rate CD (FRCD) is one whose interest rate changes periodically in accordance with a predetermined formula that indicates the spread (or margin) above some index at which the rate will reset periodically. There are FRCDs that reset the coupon daily, weekly, monthly, quarterly, or semiannually. Typically FRCDs have maturities from 18 months to five years.

Eurodollar CDs are U.S. dollar–denominated CDs issued primarily in London by U.S., European, Canadian, and Japanese banks. The yields on Eurodollar CDs play an important role in the world financial markets because they are viewed globally as the cost of bank borrowing, since they are effectively the rates at which major international banks offer to pay each other to borrow money by issuing a Eurodollar (CD) with given maturities. The interest rate paid is called the **London interbank offered rate (LIBOR).**

Yields on Certificates of Deposit

The yields posted on CDs vary depending on three factors: (1) the credit rating of the issuing bank, (2) the maturity of the CD, and (3) the supply and demand for CDs. With respect to the third factor, banks and thrifts issue CDs as part of their liability management strategy, so the supply of CDs will be driven by the demand for bank loans and the cost of alternative sources of capital to fund these loans. Moreover, bank loan demand will depend on the cost of alternative funding sources such as commercial paper. When loan demand is weak, CD rates decline. When demand is strong, the rates rise. The effect of maturity depends on the shape of the yield curve.

Credit risk has become more of an issue. At one time, domestic CDs issued by money center banks traded on a *no-name basis*. Recent financial crises in the banking industry, however, have caused investors to take a closer look at issuing banks. **Prime CDs** (those issued by high-rated domestic banks) trade at a lower yield than **nonprime CDs** (those issued by lower-rated domestic banks). Because of the unfamiliarity investors have with foreign banks, generally Yankee CDs trade at a higher yield than domestic CDs.

As just noted, the rate or yield offered on Eurodollar CDs is LIBOR. This yield is higher than the yield on domestic CDs. There are three reasons for this. First, there are reserve requirements imposed by the Federal Reserve on CDs issued by U.S. banks in the United States that do not apply to issuers of Eurodollar CDs. The reserve requirement effectively raises the cost of funds to the issuing bank because it cannot invest all the proceeds it receives from the issuance of a CD, and the amount that must be kept as reserves will not earn a return for the bank. Because it will earn less on funds raised by selling domestic CDs, the domestic issuing bank will pay less on its domestic CD than a Eurodollar CD. Second, the bank issuing the CD must pay an insurance premium to the FDIC, which again raises the cost of funds. Finally, Eurodollar CDs are dollar obligations that are payable by an entity operating under a foreign jurisdiction, exposing the holders to a risk (referred to as sovereign risk) that their claim may not be enforced by the foreign jurisdiction. As a result, a portion of the spread between the yield offered on Eurodollar CDs and domestic CDs reflects what can be termed a sovereign risk premium. This premium varies with the degree of confidence in the international banking system.

The maturities for the Eurodollar CD range from overnight to five years. So, references to "three-month LIBOR" indicate the interest rate that major international banks are offering to pay to other such banks on a CD that matures in three months. During the 1990s, LIBOR increasingly became the reference rate of choice for borrowing arrangements—loans and floating-rate securities. When we discuss derivatives instruments used to control interest rate risk, we will see that the reference rate for many of them (particularly interest rate swaps) is LIBOR.

CD yields are higher than yields on Treasury securities of the same maturity. The spread is due mainly to the credit risk that a CD investor is exposed to and the fact that CDs offer less liquidity. The spread due to credit risk will vary with both economic conditions and confidence in the banking system, increasing when there is a "flight to quality" (which means investors shift their funds in significant amounts to debt of high quality or little risk), or when there is a crisis in the banking system.

At one time, there were more than 30 dealers who made markets in CDs. The presence of that many dealers provided good liquidity to the market. Today, fewer dealers are interested in making markets in CDs, and the market can be characterized as an illiquid one.

Key Points That You Should Understand Before Proceeding

1. A negotiable CD allows the initial depositor (or any subsequent owner of the CD) to sell the CD in the open market prior to the maturity date.
2. CDs can be classified into four types, based on the issuing entity: domestic CD, Eurodollar CD, Yankee CD, and thrift CD.
3. The yield offered on a CD depends on the credit rating of the issuing bank, the maturity of the CD, and the supply and demand for CDs.
4. CD yields are higher than yields on Treasury securities of the same maturity.
5. The important role played by the Eurodollar CD and the rate paid, LIBOR.

FEDERAL FUNDS

The rate determined in the federal funds market is the major factor that influences the rates paid on all the other money market instruments described in this chapter. Depository institutions (commercial banks and thrifts) are required to maintain reserves. The reserves are deposits at their district Federal Reserve Bank, which are called *federal funds*. The level of the reserves that a bank must maintain is based on its average daily deposits over the previous 14 days. Of all depository institutions, commercial banks are by far the largest holders of federal funds.

No interest is earned on federal funds. Consequently, a depository institution that maintains federal funds in excess of the amount required incurs an opportunity cost—the loss of interest income that could be earned on the excess reserves. At the same time, there are depository institutions whose federal funds are less than the amount required. Typically, smaller banks have excess reserves, while money center banks find themselves short of reserves and must make up the shortfall. Banks maintain federal funds desks whose managers are responsible for the bank's federal funds position.

Most transactions involving fed funds last for only one night; that is, a bank with insufficient reserves that borrows excess reserves from another financial institution will typically do so for the period of one full day. Because these loans last for such a short time, fed funds are often referred to as *overnight money*.

One way that banks with less than the required reserves can bring reserves to the required level is to enter into a repurchase agreement (or *repo*) with a nonbank customer. The repo, which consists of the sale of a security and an agreement by the bank to repurchase it later, will provide funds for a short period of time, after which the bank buys back the security, as previously agreed. An alternative to the repo is for the bank to borrow federal funds from a bank that has excess reserves. The market in which federal funds are bought (borrowed) by banks that need these funds and sold (lent) by banks that have excess federal funds is called the federal funds market. The equilibrium interest rate, which is determined by the supply and demand for federal funds, is the federal funds rate.

Federal Funds Rate

The federal funds rate and the repo rate are tied together because both are a means for a bank to borrow. The federal funds rate is higher because the lending of federal funds is done on an unsecured basis; this differs from the repo, where the lender has a security as collateral. The spread between the two rates varies depending on market conditions; typically the spread is around 25 basis points.

The rate most often cited for the fed funds market is known as the **effective fed funds rate**. The *Federal Reserve Bulletin* defines "the daily effective rate" as "a weighted average of rates on trades through N.Y. brokers." This weighting process, which takes the size of transactions into account, can be illustrated in an example. Suppose only two transactions took place on September 1, one for $50 million at 3.375% and another for $150 million at 3.625%. The simple arithmetic average of this day's rates would be (3.375% + 3.625%)/2, or 3.5%. By contrast, the transactions-weighted average for that day is (50/200)(3.375%) + (150/200) (3.625%), or 3.5625%. The weighted average exceeds the arithmetic average because the larger transaction occurred at the higher interest rate.

The fed funds rate is frequently a significant operating target of the Federal Reserve Board's monetary policy. Through its open market operations that lower or raise the level of excess reserves in the banking system, the Fed will often change the fed funds rate as part of its effort to change the rate of activity in the country's economy. For this reason, the fed funds rate often shows a high level of volatility over short periods of time. Although this rate does generally tend to move in the direction of other money market rates, the fed funds rate often is the first of these rates to change, and frequently it changes more substantially than the other money market rates.

Market for Federal Funds

Although the term of most federal funds transactions is overnight, there are longer-term transactions that range from one week to six months. Trading typically takes place directly between the buyer and seller—usually between a large bank and one of its correspondent banks. Some federal funds transactions require the use of a broker. The broker stays in constant touch with likely buyers and sellers of funds and arranges deals between them for a commission. Brokers provide another service to this market in (normally) unsecured loans because they often can give lenders credit analyses of borrowers if the lenders have not done business with them previously.[1]

Key Points That You Should Understand Before Proceeding

1. The rate determined in the federal funds market is the major factor that influences the rate paid on all other private money market instruments.
2. Commercial banks are by far the largest holders of federal funds, with most transactions involving fed funds lasting for only one night.
3. Borrowing in the federal funds market is an alternative to borrowing in the repo market.
4. The federal funds rate is higher than the repo rate because the lending of federal funds is done on an unsecured basis.
5. The effective fed funds rate is the rate most often cited for the fed funds market.

BANKERS ACCEPTANCES

Simply put, a bankers acceptance is a vehicle created to facilitate commercial trade transactions. The instrument is called a bankers acceptance because a bank accepts the ultimate responsibility to repay a loan to its holder. The use of bankers acceptances to finance a commercial transaction is referred to as **acceptance financing**.

The transactions in which bankers acceptances are created include (1) the importing of goods into the United States, (2) the exporting of goods from the United States to foreign entities, (3) the storing and shipping of goods between two foreign countries where neither the importer nor the exporter is a U.S. firm,[2] and (4) the storing and shipping of goods between two entities in the United States.

---

[1] Marvin Goodfriend, "Federal Funds," in *Instruments of the Money Market*, Federal Reserve Bank of Richmond, 1993.

[2] Bankers acceptances created from these transactions are called third-country acceptances.

All four groups of banks that we describe earlier in this chapter create bankers acceptances (that is, are **accepting banks**). They have their own sales forces to sell bankers acceptances rather than using the services of a dealer. The larger regional banks maintain their own sales forces to sell the bankers acceptances they create but will use dealers to distribute those they cannot sell.

Bankers acceptances are sold on a discounted basis just as Treasury bills and commercial paper. The major investors in bankers acceptances are money market mutual funds and municipal entities.

To calculate the rate to be charged the customer for issuing a bankers acceptance, the bank determines the rate for which it can sell its bankers acceptance in the open market. To this rate it adds a commission.

Illustration of the Creation of a Bankers Acceptance

The best way to explain the creation of a bankers acceptance is by an illustration.

Several entities are involved in our transaction:

- Car Imports Corporation of America (Car Imports), a firm in New Jersey that sells automobiles
- Germany Fast Autos Inc. (GFA), a manufacturer of automobiles in Germany
- First Hoboken Bank (Hoboken Bank), a commercial bank in Hoboken, New Jersey
- West Berlin National Bank (Berlin Bank), a bank in Germany
- High-Caliber Money Market Fund, a mutual fund in the United States that invests in money market instruments

Car Imports and GFA are considering a commercial transaction. Car Imports wants to import 15 cars manufactured by GFA. GFA is concerned with the ability of Car Imports to make payment on the 15 cars when they are received.

Acceptance financing is suggested as a means for facilitating the transaction. Car Imports offers $300,000 for the 15 cars. The terms of the sale stipulate payment to be made to GFA 60 days after it ships the 15 cars to Car Imports. GFA determines whether it is willing to accept the $300,000. In considering the offering price, GFA must calculate the present value of the $300,000, because it will not be receiving payment until 60 days after shipment. Suppose that GFA agrees to these terms.

Car Imports arranges with its bank, Hoboken Bank, to issue a letter of credit. The letter of credit indicates that Hoboken Bank will make good on the payment of $300,000 that Car Imports must make to GFA 60 days after shipment. The letter of credit, or time draft, will be sent by Hoboken Bank to GFA's bank, Berlin Bank. Upon receipt of the letter of credit, Berlin Bank will notify GFA, which will then ship the 15 cars. After the cars are shipped, GFA presents the shipping documents to Berlin Bank and receives the present value of $300,000. GFA is now out of the picture.

Berlin Bank presents the time draft and the shipping documents to Hoboken Bank. The latter will then stamp "accepted" on the time draft. By doing so, Hoboken Bank has created a bankers acceptance. This means that Hoboken Bank agrees to pay the holder of the bankers acceptance $300,000 at the maturity date. Car Imports will receive the shipping documents so that it can procure the 15 cars once it signs a note or some other type of financing arrangement with Hoboken Bank.

At this point, the holder of the bankers acceptance is the Berlin Bank. It has two choices. It can continue to hold the bankers acceptance as an investment in its loan portfolio, or it can request that Hoboken Bank make a payment of the present value of $300,000. Let's assume that Berlin Bank requests payment of the present value of $300,000.

Now the holder of the bankers acceptance is Hoboken Bank. It has two choices: retain the bankers acceptance as an investment as part of its loan portfolio, or sell it to an investor. Suppose that Hoboken Bank chooses the latter, and that High-Caliber Money Market Fund is seeking a high-quality investment with the same maturity as that of the bankers acceptance. Hoboken Bank sells the bankers acceptance to the money market fund at the present value of $300,000. Rather than sell the instrument directly to an investor, Hoboken Bank could sell it to a dealer, who would then resell it to an investor such as a money market fund. In either case, at the maturity date, the money market fund presents the bankers acceptance to Hoboken Bank, receiving $300,000, which the bank in turn recovers from Car Imports.

Eligible Bankers Acceptance

An accepting bank that has decided to retain a bankers acceptance in its portfolio may be able to use it as collateral for a loan at the discount window of the Federal Reserve. The reason we say "may" is that, to be used as collateral, bankers acceptances must meet certain eligibility requirements established by the Federal Reserve. One requirement for eligibility is maturity, which with a few exceptions cannot exceed six months. While the other requirements for eligibility are too detailed to review here, the basic principle is simple. The bankers acceptance should be financing a self-liquidating commercial transaction.

Eligibility is also important because the Federal Reserve imposes a reserve requirement on funds raised via bankers acceptances that are ineligible. Bankers acceptances sold by an accepting bank are potential liabilities of the bank, but no reserve requirements are imposed for eligible bankers acceptances. Consequently, most bankers acceptances satisfy the various eligibility criteria. Finally, the Federal Reserve also imposes a limit on the amount of eligible bankers acceptances that may be issued by a bank.[3]

Credit Risk

Investing in bankers acceptances exposes the investor to credit risk. This is the risk that neither the borrower nor the accepting bank will be able to pay the principal due at the maturity date. The market interest rates that acceptances offer investors reflect this risk because BAs have higher yields than risk-free Treasury bills. A yield may also include a premium for relative illiquidity. The BA yield has such a premium because its secondary market is far less developed than that of the Treasury. Hence, the spread between BA rates and Treasury rates represents a combined reward to investors for bearing the higher risk and relative illiquidity of the acceptance. That spread is not constant over time. The change in the spread reveals shifting investor valuation of the risk and illiquidity differences between the assets.

---

[3] It may not exceed 150% of a bank's capital and surplus.

> **Key Points That You Should Understand Before Proceeding**
>
> 1. A bankers acceptance is a vehicle created to facilitate commercial trade transactions wherein a bank accepts the ultimate responsibility to repay a loan to its holder.
> 2. Banks creating banker acceptances are money center banks, regional banks, Japanese banks, and Yankee banks.
> 3. Eligible bankers acceptances held in a bank's portfolio may be used as collateral for a loan at the discount window of the Federal Reserve.
> 4. A bank may sell its bankers acceptances directly to investors, or may sell all or part to dealers.
> 5. The investor in a bankers acceptance is exposed to credit risk.

SUMMARY

Commercial banks raise funds in the same equity and debt markets that we describe in earlier chapters of the book. In addition, they can issue special debt obligations: large-denomination CDs, federal funds, and bankers acceptances.

Certificates of deposit are issued by banks and thrifts to raise funds for financing their business activities. Unlike other bank deposits, these are negotiable in the secondary market. CDs can be classified into four types: domestic CDs, Eurodollar CDs, Yankee CDs, and thrift CDs. Unlike Treasury bills, commercial paper, and bankers acceptances, yields on domestic CDs are quoted on an interest-bearing basis. A floating-rate CD is one whose coupon interest rate changes periodically in accordance with a predetermined formula. The rate paid on Eurodollar CDs has become an important rate because it is viewed as the global cost of borrowing. The rate or yield paid on Eurodollar CDs is LIBOR.

The federal funds market is the market where depository institutions borrow (buy) and sell (lend) excess reserves held in the form of deposits in a Federal Reserve bank. The federal funds rate, which is the rate at which all money market interest rates are anchored, is determined in this market. The federal funds rate is higher than the repo rate because borrowing done in the federal funds market is unsecured borrowing. The fed funds rate is often a target of the Fed's monetary policy, so it can exhibit a considerable amount of volatility or change in level over time.

A bankers acceptance is a vehicle created to facilitate commercial trade transactions, particularly international transactions. The name, bankers acceptance, arises because a bank accepts the responsibility to repay a loan to the holder of the vehicle created in a commercial transaction in case the debtor fails to perform. Bankers acceptances are sold on a discounted basis, as are Treasury bills and commercial paper.

KEY TERMS

- Acceptance financing
- Accepting bank
- Bankers acceptance
- Certificate of deposit (CD)
- Effective fed funds rate

- Eurodollar CD
- Japanese bank
- London interbank offered rate (LIBOR)
- Money center bank
- Negotiable

- Nonprime CD
- Prime CD
- Regional bank
- Term CD

- Thrift CD
- Yankee bank
- Yankee CD

QUESTIONS

1. Explain the difference between a domestic U.S. bank and a Yankee bank.
2. Explain what a negotiable certificate of deposit is.
3. What are the four types of negotiable CDs?
4. **a.** What is the chief reason that the yield on a six-month CD exceeds that on a six-month Treasury bill?
   b. Explain why a Eurodollar CD should offer a higher yield than a domestic CD issued by the same bank for the same time to maturity.
5. **a.** What is the London interbank offered rate?
   b. Why has this rate become so important in financial markets?
6. Explain how federal funds are related to the reserve requirements that the Federal Reserve places on commercial banks.
7. How does a repurchase agreement that a bank might enter into with a securities dealer regarding a U.S. Treasury bill substitute for the borrowing of federal funds from another bank?
8. Why are fed funds called overnight money?
9. Explain whether or not the rate on an overnight repurchase agreement can be higher than the rate on overnight federal funds.
10. What is the chief reason that the fed funds rate is an unusually volatile short-term interest rate?
11. What are the four transactions whose financing can lead to the creation of bankers acceptances?
12. Why is a bank that creates a BA called an accepting bank?
13. Why is the eligibility of a bankers acceptance important?
14. How does a bank determine the rate it will charge its customer for issuing a bankers acceptance?

The Residential Mortgage Market

LEARNING OBJECTIVES

After reading this chapter, you will understand

- what a mortgage is

- who the major originators of residential mortgages are

- the mortgage origination process

- the borrower and property characteristics considered by a lender in evaluating the credit risk of an applicant for a mortgage loan

- the risks associated with the origination process for residential mortgage loans

- what the servicing of a residential mortgage loan involves

- the types of residential mortgage loans based on lien status, credit classification, interest-rate type, amortization type, credit guarantees, loan balances, and prepayments and prepayment penalties

- what a prepayment is

- the cash flow of a mortgage loan

- what a prepayment penalty mortgage is

- risks associated with investing in mortgages

- the significance of prepayment risk

The mortgage market is a collection of markets, which includes a primary (or origination) market and a secondary market where mortgages trade. A mortgage is a pledge of property to secure payment of a debt. Typically, property refers to real estate. If the property owner (the mortgagor) fails to pay the lender (the mortgagee), the lender has the right to foreclose the loan and seize the property in order to ensure that it is repaid. The types of real estate properties that can be mortgaged are divided into two broad categories: single-family (one-to four-family) residential and commercial properties. The former category includes houses, condominiums, cooperatives, and apartments. Commercial properties are income-producing properties: multifamily properties (i.e., apartment buildings), office buildings, industrial properties (including warehouses), shopping centers, hotels, and health care facilities (e.g., senior housing care facilities).

Our focus in this chapter is on residential mortgage loans.

ORIGINATION OF RESIDENTIAL MORTGAGE LOANS

The original lender is called the **mortgage originator**. The principal originators of residential mortgage loans are thrifts, commercial banks, and mortgage bankers.

Mortgage originators may generate income from mortgage activity in one or more ways. First, they typically charge an **origination fee**. This fee is expressed in terms of points, where each point represents 1% of the borrowed funds. For example, an origination fee of two points on a $200,000 mortgage loan is $4,000. Originators also may charge application fees and certain processing fees. The second source of revenue is the profit that might be generated from selling a mortgage at a higher price than it originally cost. This profit is called **secondary market profit**. If mortgage rates rise, an originator will realize a loss when the mortgages are sold in the secondary market.

Although the sources of revenue attributable to the origination function are technically origination fees and secondary marketing profits, there are two other potential sources. First, mortgage originators may service the mortgages they originate, for which they obtain a **servicing fee**. Servicing of the mortgage involves collecting monthly payments from mortgagors and forwarding proceeds to owners of the loan, sending payment notices to mortgagors, reminding mortgagors when payments are overdue, maintaining records of mortgage balances, furnishing tax information to mortgagors, administering an escrow account for real estate taxes and insurance purposes, and, if necessary, initiating foreclosure proceedings. The servicing fee is a fixed percentage of the outstanding mortgage balance, typically 25 basis points to 100 basis points per year. The mortgage originator may sell the servicing of the mortgage to another party, who would then receive the servicing fee. Second, the mortgage originator may hold the mortgage in its investment portfolio.

Mortgage banking refers to the activity of originating mortgages. Banks and thrifts undertake mortgage banking. However, there are companies not associated with a bank or thrift that are involved in mortgage banking. These mortgage bankers, unlike banks and thrifts, typically do not invest in the mortgages that they originate. Instead, they derive their income from the origination fees. Commercial banks derive their income from all three sources.

The Mortgage Origination Process

Someone who wants to borrow funds to purchase a home will apply for a loan from a mortgage originator. Most mortgage loans are originated with a 30-year original term, although some borrowers prefer shorter maturities such 20, 15, or 10 years. The potential homeowner completes an application form, which provides financial information about the applicant, and pays an application fee; then the mortgage originator performs a credit evaluation of the applicant. The requirements specified by the originator in order to grant the loan are referred to as **underwriting standards**.

The two primary quantitative underwriting standards are (1) the **payment-to-income ratio (PTI)**, and (2) the **loan-to-value ratio (LTV)**. The first is the ratio of monthly payments to monthly income, which measures the ability of the applicant to make monthly payments (both mortgage and real estate tax payments). The lower this ratio, the greater the likelihood that the applicant will be able to meet the required payments.

The difference between the purchase price of the property and the amount borrowed is the borrower's down payment. The LTV is the ratio of the amount of the loan to the market (or appraised) value of the property. The lower this ratio, the greater the protection for the lender if the applicant defaults on the payments and the lender must repossess and sell the property. For example, if an applicant wants to borrow $225,000 on property with an appraised value of $300,000, the LTV is 75%. Suppose the applicant subsequently defaults on the mortgage. The lender can then repossess the property and sell it to recover the amount owed. But the amount that will be received by the lender depends on the market value of the property. In our example, even if conditions in the housing market are weak, the lender will still be able to recover the proceeds lent, if the value of the property declines by $75,000. Suppose, instead, that the applicant wanted to borrow $270,000 for the same property. The LTV would then be 90%. If the lender had to foreclose on the property and then sell it because the applicant defaults, there is less protection for the lender.

If the lender decides to lend the funds, it sends a **commitment letter** to the applicant. This letter commits the lender to provide funds to the applicant. The length of time of the commitment varies between 30 and 60 days. At the time of the commitment letter, the lender will require that the applicant pay a commitment fee. It is important to understand that the commitment letter obligates the lender—not the applicant—to perform. The commitment fee that the applicant pays is lost if the applicant decides not to purchase the property or uses an alternative source of funds to purchase the property. Thus, the commitment letter states that, for a fee, the applicant has the right but not the obligation to require the lender to provide funds at a certain interest rate and on certain terms.

At the time the application is submitted, the mortgage originator will give the applicant a choice among various types of mortgages. Basically, the choice is between a fixed-rate mortgage, an adjustable-rate mortgage, or some type of "hybrid" mortgage. In the case of a fixed-rate mortgage, the lender typically gives the applicant a choice as to when the interest rate on the mortgage will be determined. The three choices may be (1) at the time the loan application is submitted, (2) at the time a commitment letter is issued to the borrower, or (3) at the closing date (the date that the property is purchased).

These choices granted the applicant—the right to decide whether or not to close on the property and the right to select when to set the interest rate—expose the mortgage originator to certain risks, against which the originator will protect itself.

Mortgage originators can either (1) hold the mortgage in their portfolio, (2) sell the mortgage to an investor that wishes to hold the mortgage in its portfolio or that will place the mortgage in a pool of mortgages to be used as collateral for the issuance of a security, or (3) use the mortgage themselves as collateral for the issuance of a security. When a mortgage is used as collateral for the issuance of a security, the mortgage is said to be securitized. In the next chapter, we will discuss the securitization of residential mortgage loans.

When a mortgage originator intends to sell the mortgage, it will obtain a commitment from the potential investor (buyer). Two government-sponsored enterprises (GSEs) and several private companies buy mortgages. Because these entities pool these mortgages and sell them to investors, they are called **conduits**. We will discuss conduits in the next chapter.

The interest rate that the originator will set on the loan, referred to as the **note rate**, will depend on the interest rate required by the investor who plans to purchase the mortgage. At any time, there are different mortgage rates for delivery at different future times (30 days, 60 days, or 90 days).

The Risks Associated with Mortgage Origination

The loan applications being processed and the commitments made by a mortgage originator together are called its **pipeline**. **Pipeline risk** refers to the risks associated with originating mortgages. This risk has two components: price risk and fallout risk.

Price risk refers to the adverse effects on the value of the pipeline if mortgage rates in the market rise. If mortgage rates rise, and the mortgage originator has made commitments at a lower mortgage rate, it will either have to sell the mortgages when they close at a value below the funds lent to homeowners, or retain the mortgages as a portfolio investment earning a below-market mortgage rate. The mortgage originator faces the same risk for mortgage applications in the pipeline where the applicant has elected to fix the rate at the time the application is submitted.

Fallout risk is the risk that applicants or those who were issued commitment letters will not close (i.e., complete the transaction by purchasing the property with funds borrowed from the mortgage originator). A major reason that potential borrowers may cancel their commitment or withdraw their mortgage application is that mortgage rates have declined sufficiently so that it is economic to seek an alternative lender. Fallout risk is the result of the mortgage originator giving the potential borrower the right but not the obligation to close (that is, the right to cancel the agreement). There are reasons other than a decline in mortgage rates that may cause a potential borrower to fall out of the pipeline. There may be an unfavorable property inspection report, or the purchase could have been predicated on a change in employment that does not occur.

Mortgage originators have several alternatives to protect themselves against pipeline risk. To protect against price risk, the originator could get a commitment from the GSE or the private conduit to whom the mortgage originator plans to sell the mortgage. This sort of commitment is effectively a forward contract. The mortgage originator agrees to deliver a mortgage at a future date, and another party (either one of the GSEs or a private conduit) agrees to buy the mortgage at that time at a predetermined price (or mortgage rate).

Consider what happens, however, if mortgage rates decline and potential borrowers elect to cancel the agreement. The mortgage originator has agreed to deliver a mortgage with a specified mortgage rate. If the potential borrower does not close and the mortgage originator has made a commitment to deliver the mortgage to a GSE or private conduit, the mortgage originator cannot back out of the transaction. As a result, the mortgage originator will realize a loss—it must deliver a mortgage at a higher mortgage rate in a lower mortgage rate environment. This is fallout risk.

Mortgage originators can protect themselves against fallout risk by entering into an agreement with a GSE or private conduit for optional rather than mandatory delivery of the mortgage. In such an agreement, the mortgage originator is effectively buying an option that gives it the right, but not the obligation, to deliver a mortgage. The agency or private conduit has sold that option to the mortgage originator and, therefore, charges a fee for allowing optional delivery.

Mortgage Servicers

Every mortgage loan must be serviced. As explained earlier, servicing of a mortgage loan involves collecting monthly payments and forwarding proceeds to owners of the loan, sending payment notices to mortgagors, reminding mortgagors when payments are overdue, maintaining records of principal balances, administering an escrow balance for real estate taxes and insurance purposes, initiating foreclosure proceedings if necessary, and furnishing tax information to mortgagors when applicable.

Mortgage servicers include bank-related entities, thrift-related entities, and mortgage bankers. There are five sources of revenue from mortgage servicing. The primary source is the servicing fee. This fee is a fixed percentage of the outstanding mortgage balance. Consequently, the revenue from servicing declines over time as the mortgage balance amortizes. The second source of servicing income arises from the interest that can be earned by the servicer from the escrow balance that the borrower often maintains with the servicer. The third source of revenue is the float earned on the monthly mortgage payment. This opportunity arises because of the delay permitted between the time the servicer receives the payment and the time that the payment must be sent to the investor. Fourth, there are three potential sources of ancillary income: (1) a late fee charged by the servicer if the payment is not made on time, (2) commissions from cross-selling their borrowers' life and other insurance products, and (3) fees generated from selling mailing lists. Finally, there are other benefits of servicing rights for servicers who are also lenders. Their portfolio of borrowers is a potential source for other loans, such as second mortgages, automobile loans, and credit cards.

Key Points That You Should Understand Before Proceeding

1. The mortgage originator is the original lender of mortgage funds, and the activity of originating mortgages is called mortgage banking.
2. The principal originators of residential mortgage loans are thrifts, commercial banks, and mortgage bankers.
3. Mortgage originators may generate income from origination fees, secondary market profit, servicing fees, and investment income from holding the mortgages.
4. The two primary factors in determining whether funds will be lent to a mortgage loan applicant are the PTI and LTV.
5. Two GSEs and several private companies buy mortgages for purposes of pooling them and selling them to investors.
6. Pipeline risk is the risk associated with mortgage origination; it is made up of price risk and fallout risk.

TYPES OF RESIDENTIAL MORTGAGE LOANS

There are different types of residential mortgage loans. They can be classified according to the following attributes:

- lien status
- credit classification
- interest rate type
- amortization type
- credit guarantees
- loan balances
- prepayments and prepayment penalties[1]

Lien Status

The **lien status** of a mortgage loan indicates the loan's seniority in the event of the forced liquidation of the property due to default by the obligor. For a mortgage loan that is a **first lien,** the lender would have first call on the proceeds of the liquidation of the property if it were to be repossessed. A mortgage loan could also be a **second lien** or **junior lien**, and the claims of the lender on the proceeds in the case of liquidation come after the holders of the first lien are paid in full.

Credit Classification

A loan that is originated where the borrower is viewed to have a high credit quality (i.e., where the borrower has strong employment and credit histories, income sufficient to pay the loan obligation without compromising the borrower's creditworthiness, and substantial equity in the underlying property) is classified as a **prime loan.** A loan originated where the borrow is of lower credit quality is classified as a **subprime loan.** Between the prime and subprime sector is a somewhat nebulous category referred to as an **alternative-A loan** or, more commonly, **alt-A loan.** These loans are considered to be prime loans (the "A" refers to the A grade assigned by underwriting systems), but they have some attributes that either increase their perceived credit riskiness or cause them to be difficult to categorize and evaluate.

In assessing the credit quality of a mortgage applicant, lenders look at various measures. The starting point is the applicant's *credit score.* Several firms collect data on the payment histories of individuals from lending institutions and, using statistical models, evaluate and quantify individual creditworthiness in terms of a credit score. Basically, a credit score is a numerical grade of the credit history of the borrower. The three most popular credit reporting companies that compute credit scores are Experian, Transunion, and Equifax. Although the credit scores have different underlying methodologies, the scores generically are referred to as **FICO scores.**[2] Typically, a lender will obtain more than one score in order to minimize the impact of variations in credit scores across providers. FICO scores range from 350 to 850. The higher the FICO score, the lower the credit risk.

---

[1] See Frank J. Fabozzi, Anand K. Bhattacharya, and William S. Berliner, *Mortgage-Backed Securities: Products, Structuring, and Analytical Techniques* (Hoboken, NJ: John Wiley & Sons, 2007).
[2] This is because credit scoring companies generally use a model developed by Fair, Isaacs & Company. The model uses 45 criteria to rank the creditworthiness of an individual.

The LTV has proven to be a good predictor of default: the higher the LTV, the greater the likelihood of default. By definition, the LTV of the loan in a purchase transaction is a function of both the down payment and the purchase price of the property. However, borrowers refinance their loans when rates decline. When a lender is evaluating an application from a borrower who is refinancing, the LTV is dependent upon the requested amount of the new loan and the market value of the property as determined by an appraisal. When the loan amount requested exceeds the original loan amount, the transaction is referred to as a **cash-out refinancing**. If, instead, the loan balance remains unchanged, the transaction is said to be a **rate-and-term refinancing** or **no-cash refinancing**. That is, the purpose of the loan is refinancing, to either obtain a better note rate or change the term of the loan.

Lenders calculate income ratios such as the PTI to assess the applicant's ability to pay. These ratios compare the monthly payment that the applicant would have to pay if the loan is granted to the applicant's monthly income. The most common measures are the front ratio and the back ratio. The **front ratio** is computed by dividing the total monthly payments (which includes interest and principal on the loan plus property taxes and homeowner insurance) by the applicant's pretax monthly income. The **back ratio** is computed in a similar manner. The modification is that it adds other debt payments such as auto loan and credit card payments to the total payments. In order for a loan to be classified as "prime," the front and back ratios should be no more than 28% and 36%, respectively.

The credit score is the primary attribute used to characterize loans as either prime or subprime. Prime (or A grade) loans generally have FICO scores of 660 or higher, front and back ratios with the above-noted maximum of 28% and 36%, and LTVs less than 95%. Alt-A loans may vary in a number of important ways. While subprime loans typically have FICO scores below 660, the loan programs and grades are highly lender-specific. One lender might consider a loan with a 620 FICO score to be a "B rated loan," while another lender would grade the same loan higher or lower, especially if the other attributes of the loan (such as the LTV) are higher or lower than average levels.

Interest Rate Type

The note rate on a mortgage loan, the interest rate that the borrower agrees to pay, can be fixed or change over the life of the loan. For a **fixed-rate mortgage (FRM)**, the interest rate is set at the closing of the loan and remains unchanged over the life of the loan.

For an **adjustable-rate mortgage (ARM)**, as the name implies, the note rate changes over the life of the loan. The note rate is based on both the movement of an underlying rate called the **index** or **reference rate**, and a spread over the index called the **margin**. Two categories of reference rates have been used in ARMs: (1) market-determined rates, and (2) calculated rates based on the cost of funds for thrifts. Market-determined rates include the London Interbank Offered Rate (LIBOR), the one-year Constant Maturity Treasury (CMT), and the 12-month Moving Treasury Average (MTA), a rate calculated from monthly averages of the one-year CMT. The two most popular calculated rates are the Eleventh Federal Home Loan Bank Board District Cost of Funds Index (COFI) and the National Cost of Funds Index. Depository institutions prefer to hold ARMs in their portfolios rather than FRMs because ARMs provide a better match with their liabilities.

The basic ARM is one that resets periodically and has no other terms that affect the monthly mortgage payment. Typically, the mortgage rate is affected by other terms. These include (1) **periodic caps** and (2) **lifetime rate caps** and floors. Periodic caps limit the amount that the interest rate may increase or decrease at the reset date. The periodic rate cap is expressed in percentage points. Most ARMs have an upper limit on the mortgage rate that can be charged over the life of the loan. This lifetime loan cap is expressed in terms of the initial rate; the most common lifetime cap is 5% to 6%. For example, if the initial mortgage rate is 7% and the lifetime cap is 5%, the maximum interest rate that the lender can charge over the life of the loan is 12%. Many ARMs also have a lower limit (floor) on the interest rate that can be charged over the life of the loan.

A popular form of an ARM is the **hybrid ARM**. For this loan type, for a specified number of years (three, five, seven, and 10 years), the note rate is fixed. At the end of the initial fixed-rate period, the loan resets in a fashion very similar to that of more traditional ARM loans.

Amortization Type

The amount of the monthly loan payment that represents the repayment of the principal borrowed is called the **amortization**. Traditionally, both FRMs and ARMs were **fully amortizing loans**. What this means is that the monthly mortgage payments made by the borrower not only provide the lender with the contractual interest but also are sufficient to completely repay the amount borrowed when the last monthly mortgage payment is made. Thus, for example, for a fully amortizing 30-year loan, at the end of the 360th month, the last mortgage payment is sufficient to pay off any loan balance so that after that last payment the amount owed is zero.

Fully amortizing fixed-rate loans have a payment that is constant over the life of the loan. For example, suppose a loan has an original balance of $200,000, a note rate of 7.5%, and a term of 30 years. Then the monthly mortgage payment would be $1,398.43. The formula for calculating the monthly mortgage payment is provided in Table 1, as well as the illustration showing how $1,398.43 is obtained. Assuming that the borrower has made all monthly payments on a timely basis, then after the last monthly mortgage payment is made, the outstanding balance is zero (i.e., the loan is paid off). This can be seen in the schedule shown in Table 2, which is referred to as an **amortization schedule**. (Not all 360 months are shown to conserve space.) The column labeled "Principal Repayment" is the monthly scheduled principal repayment or amortization of the loan. Notice that in the 360th month, the ending balance is zero. Also note that in each month the amount of the monthly mortgage payment applied to interest declines. This is because the amount of the outstanding balance declines each month.

In the case of an ARM, the monthly mortgage payment adjusts periodically. Thus, the monthly mortgage payments must be recalculated at each reset date. This process of resetting the mortgage loan payment is referred to as **recasting the loan**. For example, consider once again a $200,000 30-year loan. Assume that the loan adjusts annually and that the initial note rate (i.e., the note rate for the first 12 months) is 7.5%. How much of the loan will be outstanding at the end of one year? We can determine this from Table 2 by looking at the last column ("Ending Balance") for month 12. That amount is $198,156.33. (Alternatively, the formula in Table 1 can be used.) Now recasting the loan involves computing the monthly mortgage payment that will fully amortize a loan of $198,156.33 for 29 years (348 months) because after one year there are 29 years remaining on the loan. The note rate used is the reset rate. Suppose that the reset rate is 8.5%. Then the monthly

---

Table 1   Mortgage Calculation Formulas

1. *Monthly mortgage payment:*

$$MP = MB_o \left[\frac{i(1 + i)^n}{(1 + i)^n - 1} \right]$$

where

MP = monthly mortgage payment ($)

MB_o = original mortgage balance ($)

i = note rate divided by 12 (in decimal)

n = number of months of the mortgage loan

Illustration:

$MB_o = \$200,000; i = 0.075/12 = 0.00625; n = 360$

$$MP = \$200,000 \left[\frac{0.00625(1.00625)^{360}}{(1.00625)^{360} - 1} \right] = \$1,398.43.$$

2. *The remaining mortgage balance at the end of month* t:

$$MB_t = MB_o \left[\frac{(1 + i)^n - (1 + i)^t}{(1 + i)^n - 1} \right]$$

where

MB_t = mortgage balance after t months

Illustration:

$MB_o = \$200,000; i = 0.00625; n = 360; t = 12$

$$MB_t = \$200,000 \left[\frac{(1.00625)^{360} - (1.00625)^{12}}{(1.00625)^{360} - 1} \right] = \$198,156.33$$

3. *The scheduled principal repayment for month* t:

$$SP_t = MB_o \left[\frac{i(1 + i)^{t-1}}{(1 + i)^n - 1} \right]$$

where

SP_t = scheduled principal repayment for month t

Illustration:

$MB_o = \$200,000; i = 0.00625; n = 360; t = 12$

$$SP_{12} = \$200,000 \left[\frac{0.00625(1.00625)^{12-1}}{(1.00625)^{360} - 1} \right] = \$158.95$$

---

mortgage payment to fully amortize the loan is $1,535.26 and that is the monthly mortgage payment for the next 12 months.

In recent years, several types of nontraditional amortization schemes have become popular in the mortgage market. The most popular is the **interest-only product**. With this type of loan, only interest is paid for a predetermined period of time called the **lockout period**. Following the lockout period, the loan is recast such that the monthly

Table 2   Amortization Schedule

Original balance	$200,000.00
Note rate	7.50%
Term	30 years
Monthly payment	$1,398.43

Month	Beginning Balance	Interest	Principal Repayment	Ending Balance
1	$200,000.00	$1,250.00	$148.43	$199,851.57
2	199,851.57	1,249.07	149.36	199,702.21
3	199,702.21	1,248.14	150.29	199,551.92
4	199,551.92	1,247.20	151.23	199,400.69
5	199,400.69	1,246.25	152.17	199,248.52
6	199,248.52	1,245.30	153.13	199,095.39
7	199,095.39	1,244.35	154.08	198,941.31
8	198,941.31	1,243.38	155.05	198,786.27
9	198,786.27	1,242.41	156.01	198,630.25
10	198,630.25	1,241.44	156.99	198,473.26
11	198,473.26	1,240.46	157.97	198,315.29
12	198,315.29	1,239.47	158.96	198,156.33
13	198,156.33	1,238.48	159.95	197,996.38
14	197,996.38	1,237.48	160.95	197,835.43
...	...	...	...	...
89	182,656.63	1,141.60	256.83	182,399.81
90	182,399.81	1,140.00	258.43	182,141.37
91	182,141.37	1,138.38	260.05	181,881.33
...	...	...	...	...
145	165,499.78	1,034.37	364.06	165,135.73
146	165,135.73	1,032.10	366.33	164,769.40
147	164,769.40	1,029.81	368.62	164,400.77
...	...	...	...	...
173	154,397.69	964.99	433.44	153,964.24
174	153,964.24	962.28	436.15	153,528.09
175	153,528.09	959.55	438.88	153,089.21
...	...	...	...	...
210	136,417.23	852.61	545.82	135,871.40
211	135,871.40	849.20	549.23	135,322.17
212	135,322.17	845.76	552.67	134,769.51
...	...	...	...	...
290	79,987.35	499.92	898.51	79,088.84
291	79,088.84	494.31	904.12	78,184.71
292	78,184.71	488.65	909.77	77,274.94
...	...	...	...	...
358	4,143.39	25.90	1,372.53	2,770.85
359	2,770.85	17.32	1,381.11	1,389.74
360	1,389.74	8.69	1,389.74	0.00

mortgage payments will be sufficient to fully amortize the original amount of the loan over the remaining term of the loan. The interest-only product can be an FRM, ARM, or hybrid ARM.

For example, consider a $200,000 30-year interest-only loan with a lockout period of five years and a note rate of 7.5% (i.e., a FRM). For the first 60 months, the monthly mortgage payment is only the monthly interest, which is $1,250 (7.5% times $200,000 divided by 12). In the 61st month, the monthly mortgage payment must include both interest and amortization (principal repayment). The monthly mortgage payment for the remaining life of the mortgage loan is the payment necessary to fully amortize a $200,000 25-year loan with a note rate of 7.5%. That monthly mortgage payment is $1,477.98. Note the following. First, if the mortgage had been a 30-year fixed-rate loan at 7.5%, the monthly mortgage payment for the first five years would have been $1,398.43 instead of $1,250 for the interest-only loan. This is the appealing feature of the interest-only loan. The homeowner can purchase a more expensive home using an interest-only loan. The disadvantage for the homeowner is that for the remaining term of the loan, the interest-only loan requires a higher monthly mortgage payment ($1,477.98) compared to a 30-year fully amortizing loan ($1,398.43). However, if the homeowner anticipates a rise in income, this could more than offset the impact of the higher monthly mortgage payment. From the lender's perspective, however, there is greater credit risk. This is because at the end of five years, the lender's exposure remains at $200,000 rather than being reduced by the amortization over the lockout period.

Credit Guarantees

Mortgage loans can be classified based upon whether a credit guaranty associated with the loan is provided by the federal government, a GSE, or a private entity.

Loans that are backed by agencies of the federal government are referred to under the generic term of **government loans** and are guaranteed by the full faith and credit of the U.S. government. The Department of Housing and Urban Development (HUD) oversees two agencies that guarantee government loans. The first is the Federal Housing Administration (FHA), a governmental entity created by Congress in 1934 that became part of HUD in 1965. **FHA-insured loans** are for those borrowers who can afford only a low down payment and generally also have relatively low levels of income. The second is the Veterans Administration (VA), which is part of the U.S. Department of Veterans Affairs. The **VA-guaranteed loans** are made to eligible veterans and reservists, allowing them to receive favorable loan terms. Although there is no maximum amount for the loans that are guaranteed, typically the loans are limited to a statutorily determined amount because when the VA sells loans that it originates in the secondary market, these limits are important as explained later and in the next chapter.

In contrast to government loans, there are loans that have no *explicit* guaranty from the federal government. Such loans are said to obtained from "conventional financing" and therefore are referred to in the market as **conventional loans.** A conventional loan may not be insured when it is originated, but a loan may qualify to be insured when it is included in a pool of mortgage loans that backs a mortgage-backed security. More specifically, the mortgage-backed securities are those issued by two GSEs, Freddie Mac and Fannie Mae. Because the guarantees of Freddie Mac and Fannie Mae do not carry the full faith and credit of the U.S. government, they are not classified as government loans. We will discuss this further in the next chapter.

A conventional loan can be insured by a **private mortgage insurer**. Two examples of private mortgage insurers are MGIC Investment Corp. and the PMI Group, Inc. From an investor's perspective, the guaranty is only as good as the credit rating of the insurer.

Loan Balances

For government loans and the loans guaranteed by Freddie Mac and Fannie Mae, there are limits on the loan balance. The maximum loan size for one- to four-family homes changes every year, based on the percentage change in the average home price (for both new and existing homes) published by the Federal Housing Finance Board. The loan limits, referred to as **conforming limits**, for Freddie Mac and Fannie Mae are identical because they are specified by the same statute. Loans larger than the conforming limit are referred to as **jumbo loans**.

Prepayments and Prepayment Penalties

Homeowners often repay all or part of their mortgage balance prior to the scheduled maturity date. The amount of the payment made in excess of the monthly mortgage payment is called a **prepayment**. For example, consider the $200,000 30-year mortgage with a 7.5% note rate. The monthly mortgage payment is $1,398.43. Suppose the homeowner makes a payment of $5,398.43. This payment exceeds the monthly mortgage payment by $4,000. This amount represents a prepayment and reduces the outstanding mortgage balance by $4,000. For example, look at Table 2. Suppose that the prepayment is made in month 90. In the absence of the prepayment, the mortgage balance at the end of month 90 is $182,141.37. Because of the prepayment of $4,000, the mortgage balance at the end of month 90 is $178,141.37.

This type of prepayment in which the entire mortgage balance is not paid off is called a **partial prepayment** or **curtailment**. When a curtailment is made, the loan is not recast. Instead, the borrower continues to make the same monthly mortgage payment. The effect of the prepayment is that more of the subsequent monthly mortgage payment is applied to the principal. For example, once again assume that the prepayment of $4,000 is made in month 90. In the next month, month 91, the amount of interest to be paid is based on $178,141.37. The interest is $1,113.38 (7.5%/12 times $178,141.37), which is less than the amount shown in Table 2. Therefore, for month 91, the principal repayment is $1,398.43 minus the interest of $1,113.38, or $285.05 compared to the amount shown in Table 2 of $260.05. The net effect of the prepayment is that the loan is paid off faster than the scheduled maturity date. That is, the maturity of the loan is "curtailed."

The more common type of prepayment is one in which the entire mortgage balance is paid off. All mortgage loans have a "due on sale" clause, which means that the remaining balance of the loan must be paid when the house is sold. Existing mortgages can also be refinanced by the obligor if the prevailing level of mortgage rates declines, or if a more attractive financing vehicle is proposed to them.

Effectively, the borrower's right to prepay a loan in whole or in part without a penalty is a call option. A mortgage design that mitigates the borrower's right to prepay is the **prepayment penalty mortgage**. This mortgage design imposes penalties if the borrower prepays. The penalties are designed to discourage refinancing activity and require a fee to be paid if the loan is prepaid within a certain amount of time after funding. Penalties are typically structured to allow borrowers to partially prepay up to 20% of their loan each year the penalty is in effect, and charge the borrower six months of interest for prepayments on the remaining 80% of their balance. Some penalties are waived if the home is sold and are described as "soft" penalties; hard penalties require the penalty to be paid even if the prepayment occurs as the sale of the underlying property.[3]

CONFORMING LOANS

Freddie Mac and Fannie Mae are GSEs whose mission is to provide liquidity and support to the mortgage market. Although they are private corporations, they receive a charter from the federal government. This federal charter allows these GSEs to operate with certain benefits that are not available to other corporations. However, the federal charter imposes limits on their business activities.

One of the ways that they fulfill their mission is by buying and selling mortgages.[4] The loans they purchase can be held in a portfolio or packaged to create a mortgage-backed security. The securities they create are the subject of the next chapter. Fannie Mae and Freddie Mac can buy or sell any type of residential mortgage, but the mortgages that are packaged into securities are restricted to government loans and those that satisfy their underwriting guidelines. The conventional loans that qualify are referred to as **conforming loans**. Thus, a conforming loan is simply a conventional loan that meets the underwriting standard of Fannie Mae and Freddie Mac. Conventional loans in the market are referred to as **conforming conventional loans** and **nonconforming conventional loans**.

One of the underwriting standards is the loan balance at the time of origination. As noted in the previous section, conventional loans that meet the underwriting standards of the two GSEs are called conforming limits. But there are other important underwriting standards that must be satisfied. These include:[5]

* type of property (primary residence, vacation/second home, investment property)
* loan type (e.g., fixed rate, ARM)
* transaction type (rate and term refinances, equity buyouts, cash-out refinances)
* loan-to-value ratio by loan type
* loan-to-value ratio by loan type and transaction type
* borrower credit history
* documentation

Qualifying for a conforming loan is important for both the borrower and the mortgage originator. This is because the two GSEs are the largest buyers of mortgages in the United States. Hence, loans that qualify as conforming loans have a greater probability of being purchased by Fannie Mae and Freddie Mac to be packaged into a mortgage-backed security. As a result, they have lower interest rates than nonconforming conventional loans.

---

[3] The laws and regulations governing the imposition of prepayment penalties are established at the federal and state levels. Usually, the applicable laws for fixed-rate mortgages are specified at the state level. There are states that do not permit prepayment penalties on fixed-rate mortgages with a first lien. There are states that do permit prepayment penalties but restrict the type of penalty. For some mortgage designs, such as adjustable-rate and balloon mortgages, there are federal laws that override state laws.

[4] The two GSEs must allocate a specific percentage of the loans made for low- and moderate-income households or properties located in targeted geographic areas as designated by the Department of Housing and Urban Development. Such loans are classified as "affordable housing loans."

[5] See, for example, Fannie Mae's publication of January 2007, *Guide to Underwriting with DU*, which covers underwriting conventional loans. "DU" is Fannie Mae's automated underwriting system whose purpose is to assist mortgage lenders to make credit lending decisions.

Key Points That You Should Understand Before Proceeding

1. Lien status indicates the lender's seniority in the event of a forced liquidation of the property.
2. In terms of credit classification, loans are classified as prime loans and subprime loans.
3. The note rate can be fixed over the life of the loan (FRM), adjust periodically based on a reference rate plus a margin (ARM), or be fixed for a specified number of years and then adjust for the remaining life of the mortgage (hybrid ARM).
4. Mortgage loans can be guaranteed by the federal government, a GSE, or a private entity.
5. A borrower can make a payment in excess of the monthly mortgage payment; the excess is referred to as a prepayment.
6. There are prepayment penalty mortgages available to mitigate the adverse impact of prepayment.

INVESTMENT RISKS

The principal investors in mortgage loans include thrifts and commercial banks. Pension funds and life insurance companies also invest in these loans, but their ownership is small compared to that of the banks and thrifts. Investors face four main risks by investing in residential mortgage loans: (1) credit risk, (2) liquidity risk, (3) price risk, and (4) prepayment risk.

Credit Risk

Credit risk is the risk that the homeowner/borrower will default. For FHA- and VA-insured mortgages, this risk is minimal. For privately insured mortgages, the risk can be gauged by the credit rating of the private insurance company that has insured the mortgage. For conventional mortgages that are uninsured, the credit risk depends on the credit quality of the borrower. The LTV ratio provides a useful measure of the risk of loss of principal in case of default. When the LTV ratio is high, default is more likely because the borrower has little equity in the property.

Liquidity Risk

Although there is a secondary market for mortgage loans, which we discuss in the next chapter, the fact is that bid–ask spreads are large compared to other debt instruments. That is, mortgage loans tend to be rather illiquid because they are large and indivisible.

Price Risk

The price of a fixed-income instrument will move in an opposite direction from market interest rates. Thus, a rise in interest rates will decrease the price of a mortgage loan.

Prepayments and Cash Flow Uncertainty

The three components of the cash flow are

- interest
- principal repayment (scheduled principal repayment or amortization)
- prepayment

Prepayment risk is the risk associated with a mortgage's cash flow due to prepayments. More specifically, investors are concerned that borrowers will pay off a mortgage when prevailing mortgage rates fall below the loan's note rate. For example, if the note rate on a mortgage originated five years ago is 8% and the prevailing mortgage rate (i.e., rate at which a new loan can be obtained) is 5.5%, then there is an incentive for the borrower to refinance the loan. The decision to refinance will depend on several factors, but the single most important one is the prevailing mortgage rate compared to the note rate. The disadvantage to the investor is that the proceeds received from the repayment of the loan must be reinvested at a lower interest rate than the note rate.

This risk is the same as that faced by an investor in a callable corporate or municipal bond. However, unlike a callable bond, there is no premium that may have to be paid by the borrower in the case of a residential mortgage loan. Any principal repaid in advance of the scheduled due date is paid at par value. The exception, of course, is if the loan is a prepayment penalty mortgage.

Key Points That You Should Understand Before Proceeding

1. There are four main risks associated with investing in mortgages: credit risk, liquidity risk, price risk, and prepayment risk.
2. Credit risk can be reduced if the mortgage is insured by a government agency or a private insurance company.
3. Mortgages are not liquid assets—they tend to have a large bid–ask spread.
4. Because of prepayments, the investor is uncertain about the cash flows that will be realized from investing in a residential mortgage loan.

SUMMARY

A mortgage is a pledge of property to secure payment of a debt with the property typically a form of real estate. The two general types of real estate properties that can be mortgaged are single-family (one- to four-family) residential and commercial properties.

Mortgage originators (i.e., the original lenders) include thrifts, commercial banks, and mortgage bankers. Mortgage originators charge an origination fee and may generate additional income in other ways. Underwriting standards are the requirements specified by the originator in order to grant the loan. The two primary quantitative underwriting standards are the PTI and LIV.

A mortgage originator's pipeline consists of the loan applications being processed plus the commitments made. The risk associated with originating mortgages is pipeline risk, and this risk consists of price risk and fallout risk.

Every mortgage loan must be serviced. Mortgage servicers include bank-related entities, thrift-related entities, and mortgage bankers.

Residential mortgage loans can be classified according to lien status (first and second liens), credit classification (prime and subprime), interest rate type (fixed rate and adjustable rate), amortization type (fully amortizing and interest-only), credit guarantees (government loans and conventional loans), loan balances, and prepayments and prepayment penalties.

The two GSEs, Fannie Mae and Freddie Mac, can purchase any type of loan; however, the only conventional loans that they can securitize to create a mortgage-backed security are conforming loans, that is, conventional loans that satisfy their underwriting standards.

The cash flow of a mortgage loan consists of interest, scheduled principal repayment, and prepayments. The lender faces four main risks by investing in residential mortgage loans: (1) credit risk, (2) liquidity risk, (3) price risk, and (4) prepayment risk. Prepayment risk is the risk associated with a mortgage's cash flow due to prepayments.

KEY TERMS

- Adjustable-rate mortgage (ARM)
- Alt-A loan
- Alternative-A loan
- Amortization
- Amortization schedule
- Back ratio
- Cash-out refinancing
- Commitment letter
- Conduit
- Conforming conventional loans
- Conforming limits
- Conforming loans
- Conventional loans
- Curtailment
- Fallout risk
- FHA-insured loans
- FICO score
- First lien
- Fixed-rate mortgage (FRM)
- Front ratio
- Fully amortizing loan
- Government loans
- Hybrid ARM
- Index
- Interest-only product
- Jumbo loans
- Junior lien
- Lien status
- Lifetime rate caps
- Loan-to-value ratio (LTV)
- Lockout period
- Margin
- Mortgage banking
- Mortgage originator
- Mortgage servicers
- No-cash refinancing
- Nonconforming conventional loans
- Note rate
- Origination fee
- Partial prepayment
- Payment-to-income ratio (PTI)
- Periodic caps
- Pipeline
- Pipeline risk
- Prepayment
- Prepayment penalty mortgage
- Prepayment risk
- Price risk
- Prime loan
- Private mortgage insurer
- Rate-and-term refinancing
- Recasting the loan
- Reference rate
- Second lien
- Secondary market profit
- Servicing fee
- Subprime loan
- Underwriting standards
- VA-guaranteed loans

QUESTIONS

1. What type of property is security for a residential mortgage loan?

2. **a.** What are the sources of revenue arising from mortgage origination?

   b. What are the risks associated with the mortgage origination process?

   c. What can mortgage originators do with a loan after originating it?

3. **a.** In selling a mortgage loan for future delivery, what is the advantage of obtaining an optional rather than mandatory delivery agreement?

   b. What is the disadvantage of optional delivery?

4. What are the sources of revenue for mortgage servicers?

5. What are the two primary factors in determining whether or not funds will be lent to an applicant for a residential mortgage loan?

6. All other factors constant, explain why the higher the loan-to-value ratio, the greater the credit risk to which the lender is exposed.

7. What is the difference between a cash-out refinancing and a rate-and-term refinancing?

8. What is the front ratio and back ratio and how do they differ?

9. **a.** What is the difference between a prime loan and a subprime loan?

   b. How are FICO scores used in classifying loans?

   c. What is an alternative-A loan?

10. **a.** What is an FHA-insured loan?

    b. What is a conventional loan?

11. **a.** What is meant by conforming limits?

    b. What is a jumbo loan?

12. **a.** When a prepayment is made that is less than the full amount to completely pay off the loan, what happens to future monthly mortgage payments for a fixed-rate mortgage loan?

    b. What is the impact of a prepayment that is less than the amount required to completely pay off a loan?

13. Consider the following fixed-rate, level-payment mortgage:

Maturity = 360 months
Amount borrowed = $100,000
Annual mortgage rate = 10%

a. Construct an amortization schedule for the first 10 months.

b. What will the mortgage balance be at the end of the 360th month, assuming no prepayments?

c. Without constructing an amortization schedule, what is the mortgage balance at the end of month 270, assuming no prepayments?

d. Without constructing an amortization schedule, what is the scheduled principal payment at the end of month 270, assuming no prepayments?

14. Explain why in a fixed-rate mortgage the amount of the mortgage payment applied to interest declines over time, while the amount applied to the repayment of principal increases.

15. **a.** Why is the cash flow of a residential mortgage loan unknown?

    b. In what sense has the investor in a residential mortgage loan granted the borrower (homeowner) a call option?

16. Why do depository institutions prefer to invest in adjustable-rate mortgages rather than fixed-rate mortgages?

17. What is a hybrid ARM?

18. What is the advantage of a prepayment penalty mortgage from the perspective of the lender?

19. Explain whether you agree or disagree with the following statements:

    a. "Freddie Mac and Fannie Mae are only allowed to purchase conforming conventional loans."

    b. "In packaging loans to create a mortgage-backed security, Freddie Mac and Fannie Mae can only use government loans."

20. **a.** What features of an ARM will affect its cash flow?

    b. What are the two categories of benchmark indexes used in ARMs?

Residential Mortgage-Backed Securities Market

From Chapter 23 of *Foundations of Financial Markets and Institutions*, 4/e. Frank J. Fabozzi. Franco Modigliani. Frank J. Jones.

Residential Mortgage-Backed Securities Market

LEARNING OBJECTIVES

After reading this chapter, you will understand

- the development of the current residential mortgage market and the role of public and private conduits

- the process of securitizing residential loans

- the different sectors in the residential mortgage-backed securities market: agency and nonagency

- the different types of agency mortgage-backed securities and their investment characteristics: pass-through securities, collateralized mortgage obligations, and stripped mortgage-backed securities

- what is meant by prepayment risk and how prepayments are measured

- how tranches with different prepayment risk are created in a collateralized mortgage obligation

- the two sectors of the nonagency mortgage-backed securities market: private label and subprime

- how credit risk is redistributed in a nonagency collateralized mortgage obligation

- the different credit enhancement mechanisms for a nonagency collateralized mortgage obligation

- the subprime crisis in the summer of 2007

Our major focus in this chapter is on the market for securities created from residential mortgage loans. The basic mortgage-backed security is the mortgage pass-through security. From this security, derivative mortgage-backed securities are created: **collateralized mortgage obligations (CMOs)** and stripped mortgage-backed securities. We begin by describing how the process of securitizing mortgages resulted in the strong secondary mortgage market that exists today.

SECTORS OF THE RESIDENTIAL MORTGAGE-BACKED SECURITIES MARKET

The residential mortgage market can be divided into two subsectors based on the credit quality of the borrower: private label mort-gage market and subprime mortgage market. The former sector includes loans that (1) satisfy the underwriting standards of Ginnie Mae, Fannie Mae, and Freddie Mac (i.e., conforming loans); and (2) those that fail to conform for a reason other than credit quality or if the loan is not a first lien on the property. The subprime mortgage sector is the market for loans provided to borrowers with impaired credit rating or where the loan is a second lien.

All of these loans can be securitized in subsectors of the **residential mortgage-backed security (RMBS)** market. Loans that satisfy the underwriting standard of the agencies are typically used to create RMBS that are referred to as **agency mortgage-backed securities**. All other loans are included in what is referred to generically as **nonagency mortgage-backed securities**. In turn, this subsector is classified into **private label mortgage-backed securities**, where prime loans are the collateral, and **subprime mortgage-backed securities**, where subprime loans are the collateral. The names given to the nonagency mortgage-backed securities are arbitrarily assigned. Some market participants refer to private label mortgage-backed securities as "residential deals" or "prime deals." Subprime mortgage-backed securities are also referred to as "mortgage-related asset-backed securities."[1] In fact, market participants often classify agency mortgage-backed securities and private label mortgage-backed securities as part of the RMBS market and subprime mortgage-backed securities as part of the market for asset-backed securities. This classification is somewhat arbitrary. For purposes of this chapter, we will discuss all RMBS products and explain why a distinction is made between private label mortgage-backed securities and subprime mortgage-backed securities.

In terms of market size, the agency mortgage-backed security market is the largest sector of the U.S. investment-grade market. That is, of all securities that have an investment-grade rating (which includes U.S. Treasury securities), the agency mortgage-backed security market is the largest sector. In fact, as of 2008, it was roughly 45% of the investment-grade market. The agency mortgage-backed security market includes three types of securities: agency mortgage pass-through securities, agency CMOs, and agency stripped mortgage-backed securities. As will be explained in the following text, agency stripped mortgage-backed securities and agency CMOs are created from mortgage pass-through securities.

AGENCY PASS-THROUGH SECURITIES

Investing in mortgages exposes the investor to default risk, price risk, liquidity risk, and prepayment risk. A more efficient investment technique is to invest in a **mortgage pass-through security**. This is a security created when one or more holders of mortgages form

---

[1] See Frank J. Fabozzi, Anand K. Bhattacharya, and William S. Berliner, *Mortgage-Backed Securities: Products, Structuring, and Analytical Techniques* (Hoboken, NJ: John Wiley & Sons, 2007.)

a collection (pool) of mortgages and sell shares or participation certificates in the pool. A pool may consist of several thousand mortgages or only a few. The first mortgage pass-through security was created in 1968. Risk-averse investors prefer investing in a pool to investing in a single mortgage, partly because a mortgage pass-through security is considerably more liquid than an individual mortgage.

When a mortgage is included in a pool of mortgages that is used as collateral for a mortgage pass-through security, the mortgage is said to be **securitized**. Agency pass-through securities refer to mortgage pass-through securities issued by Ginnie Mae, Fannie Mae, or Freddie Mac. We describe these securities in this section.

Cash Flow Characteristics

The cash flow of a mortgage pass-through security depends on the cash flow of the underlying mortgages. As we explained in the previous chapter, the cash flow consists of monthly mortgage payments representing interest, the scheduled repayment of principal, and any prepayments.

Payments are made to securityholders each month. The amounts and the timing of the cash flow from the pool of mortgages and the cash flow passed through to investors, however, are not identical. The monthly cash flow for a pass-through security is less than the monthly cash flow of the underlying mortgages by an amount equal to servicing and other fees. The other fees are those charged by the issuer or guarantor of the pass-through security for guaranteeing the issue (discussed later).

The timing of the cash flow is also different. The monthly mortgage payment is due from each mortgagor on the first day of each month, but there is a delay in passing through the corresponding monthly cash flow to the securityholders. The length of the delay varies by the type of pass-through security.

Figure 1 illustrates the process of creating a mortgage pass-through security.

Issuers of Agency Pass-Through Securities

Agency pass-through securities are issued by the Government National Mortgage Association (Ginnie Mae), Fannie Mae, and Freddie Mac. These three entities were created by Congress to increase the supply of capital to the residential mortgage market and to provide support for an active secondary market.

Ginnie Mae is a federally related institution because it is part of the Department of Housing and Urban Development. As a result, the pass-through securities that it guarantees carry the full faith and credit of the U.S. government with respect to timely payment of both interest and principal. That is, the interest and principal are paid when due even if mortgagors fail to make their monthly mortgage payment. The security guaranteed by Ginnie Mae is actually called a **mortgage-backed security (MBS)**. The first MBS was issued in 1968.

Although Ginnie Mae provides the guarantee, it is not the issuer. Pass-through securities that carry its guarantee and bear its name are issued by lenders it approves, such as thrifts, commercial banks, and mortgage bankers. These lenders receive approval only if the underlying loans satisfy the underwriting standards established by Ginnie Mae. When it guarantees securities issued by approved lenders, Ginnie Mae permits these lenders to

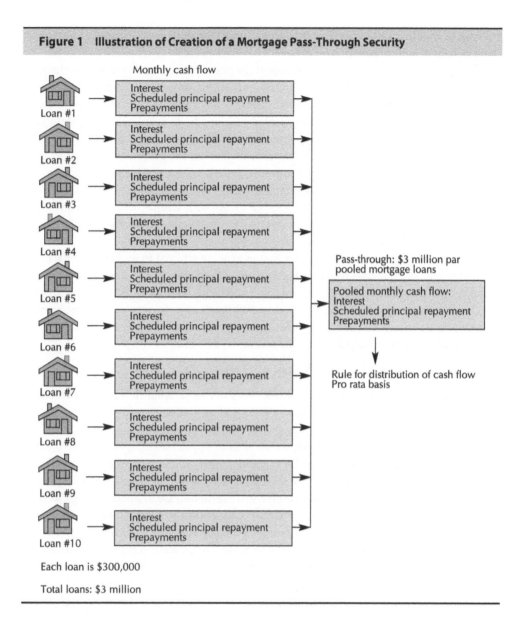

Figure 1   Illustration of Creation of a Mortgage Pass-Through Security

Monthly cash flow

Loan #1 — Interest / Scheduled principal repayment / Prepayments

Loan #2 — Interest / Scheduled principal repayment / Prepayments

Loan #3 — Interest / Scheduled principal repayment / Prepayments

Loan #4 — Interest / Scheduled principal repayment / Prepayments

Loan #5 — Interest / Scheduled principal repayment / Prepayments

Loan #6 — Interest / Scheduled principal repayment / Prepayments

Loan #7 — Interest / Scheduled principal repayment / Prepayments

Loan #8 — Interest / Scheduled principal repayment / Prepayments

Loan #9 — Interest / Scheduled principal repayment / Prepayments

Loan #10 — Interest / Scheduled principal repayment / Prepayments

Pass-through: $3 million par pooled mortgage loans

Pooled monthly cash flow:
Interest
Scheduled principal repayment
Prepayments

Rule for distribution of cash flow
Pro rata basis

Each loan is $300,000

Total loans: $3 million

convert illiquid individual loans into liquid securities backed by the U.S. government. In the process, Ginnie Mae accomplishes its goal to supply funds to the residential mortgage market and provide an active secondary market. For the guarantee, Ginnie Mae receives a fee, called the **guaranty fee**.

Although the MBS issued by Fannie Mae and Freddie Mac are commonly referred to as "agency MBS," both are in fact shareholder-owned corporations chartered by Congress to fulfill a public mission. Their stocks trade on the New York Stock Exchange. Fannie Mae and Freddie Mac are government-sponsored enterprises (GSEs). In early September 2008, Fannie Mae and Freddie Mac were taken over by the U.S. government because of the financial difficulties it faced as a result of the subprime mortgage crisis described later in this chapter.

The mission of these two GSEs is to support the liquidity and stability of the mortgage market. They accomplish this by (1) buying and selling mortgages, (2) creating pass-through securities and guaranteeing them, and (3) buying MBS. The mortgages purchased and held as investments by Fannie Mae and Freddie Mac are held in a portfolio referred to as the *retained portfolio*. However, the MBS that they issue are not guaranteed by the full faith and credit of the U.S. government. Rather, the payments to investors in MBS are secured first by the cash flow from the underlying pool of loans and then by a corporate guarantee. That corporate guarantee, however, is the same as the corporate guarantee to the other creditors of the two GSEs. As with Ginnie Mae, the two GSEs receive a guaranty fee for taking on the credit risk associated with borrowers failing to satisfy their loan obligations.

The pass-through securities issued by Fannie Mae are referred to as *Mortgage-Backed Securities*; Freddie Mac uses the term *Participation Certificate* (PC) to describe its pass-through security. All Fannie Mae MBS are guaranteed with respect to the timely payment of interest and principal. Although Freddie Mac PCs that it now issues carry the same guarantee, there are some outstanding PCs that guarantee the timely payment of interest but the eventual return of principal within one year of the due date.[2]

Prepayment Risks Associated with Pass-Through Securities

An investor who owns pass-through securities does not know what the cash flow will be because cash flow depends on prepayments. The risk associated with prepayments is called **prepayment risk.**

To understand prepayment risk, suppose an investor buys a 10% coupon Ginnie Mae at a time when mortgage rates are 10%. Let's consider what will happen to prepayments if mortgage rates decline to, say, 6%. There will be two adverse consequences. First, the price of an option-free bond such as a Treasury bond will rise. In the case of a pass-through security, the rise in price will not be as large as that of an option-free bond, because a fall in interest rates will increase the probability that the market rate will fall below the rate the borrower is paying. This fall in rates gives the borrower an incentive to prepay the loan and refinance the debt at a lower rate. To the extent that this happens, the securityholder will be repaid not at a price incorporating the premium but at par value. The holder risks capital loss, which reflects the fact that the anticipated reimbursements at par will not yield the initial cash flow.

The adverse consequences when mortgage rates decline are the same as those faced by holders of callable corporate and municipal bonds. As in the case of those instruments, the upside price potential of a pass-through security is truncated because of prepayments. This should not be surprising because a mortgage loan effectively grants the borrower the right to call the loan at par value. The adverse consequence when mortgage rates decline is referred to as **contraction risk.**

---

[2] The securities issued by Fannie Mae and Freddie Mac are sometimes referred to as "conventional pass-through securities." This is because the collateral is typically conventional loans that conform to the underwriting standards of these two GSEs.

Now let's look at what happens if mortgage rates rise to 15%. The price of the pass-through, like the price of any bond, will decline. But again it will decline more because the higher rates will tend to slow down the rate of prepayment, in effect increasing the amount invested at the coupon rate, which is lower than the market rate. Prepayments will slow down because homeowners will not refinance or partially prepay their mortgages when mortgage rates are higher than the contractual rate of 10%. Of course, this is just the time when investors want prepayments to speed up so that they can reinvest the prepayments at the higher market interest rate. This adverse consequence of rising mortgage rates is called **extension risk.**

Therefore, prepayment risk encompasses contraction risk and extension risk. Prepayment risk makes pass-throughs unattractive for certain financial institutions to hold from an asset/liability perspective. Let's look at why particular institutional investors may find pass-throughs unattractive:

1. Thrifts and commercial banks want to lock in a spread over their cost of funds. Their funds are raised on a short-term basis. If they invest in fixed-rate pass-through securities, they will be mismatched because a pass-through is a longer-term security. In particular, depository institutions are exposed to extension risk when they invest in pass-through securities.
2. To satisfy certain obligations of insurance companies, pass-through securities may be unattractive. More specifically, consider a life insurance company that has issued a four-year guaranteed investment contract. The uncertainty about the cash flow from a pass-through security, and the likelihood that slow prepayments will result in the instrument being long-term, make it an unappealing investment vehicle for such accounts. In such instances, a pass-through security exposes the insurance company to extension risk.
3. Consider a pension fund that wants to fund a 15-year liability. Buying a pass-through security exposes the pension fund to the risk that prepayments will speed up and that the maturity of the investment will shorten to considerably less than 15 years. Prepayments will speed up when interest rates decline, thereby forcing reinvestment of the prepaid amounts at a lower interest rate. In this case, the pension fund is open to contraction risk.

We can see that some institutional investors are concerned with extension risk and others with contraction risk when they purchase a pass-through security. Is it possible to alter the cash flow of a pass-through so as to reduce the contraction risk and extension risk for institutional investors? This is explained later in this chapter when we cover collateralized mortgage obligations.

Prepayment Conventions

The only way to project a cash flow is to make some assumption about the prepayment rate over the life of the underlying mortgage pool. The prepayment rate assumed is called the **prepayment speed** or, simply, *speed.*

Conditional Prepayment Rate

The **conditional prepayment rate** (CPR) assumes that some fraction of the remaining principal in the pool is prepaid each year for the remaining term of the mortgage. The prepayment rate assumed for a pool is based on the characteristics of the pool (including its historical prepayment experience) and the current and expected future economic environment. It is referred to as a *conditional* rate because it is conditional on the remaining mortgage balance.

The CPR is an annual prepayment rate. To estimate monthly prepayments, the CPR must be converted into a monthly prepayment rate, commonly referred to as the **single-monthly mortality rate (SMM)**. The following formula can be used to determine the SMM for a given CPR:

$$SMM = 1 - (1 - CPR)^{1/12} \tag{1}$$

Suppose that the CPR used to estimate prepayments is 6%. The corresponding SMM is

$$SMM = 1 - (1 - 0.06)^{1/12}$$
$$= 1 - (0.94)^{0.08333} = 0.005143$$

An SMM of $w\%$ means that approximately $w\%$ of the remaining mortgage balance at the beginning of the month, less the scheduled principal payment, will prepay that month. That is,

$$\text{Prepayment for month } t = SMM \times (\text{Beginning mortgage balance for month } t$$
$$- \text{ Scheduled principal payment for month } t) \tag{2}$$

For example, suppose that an investor owns a pass-through in which the remaining mortgage balance at the beginning of some month is $290 million. Assuming that the SMM is 0.5143% and the scheduled principal payment is $3 million, the estimated prepayment for the month is

$$0.005143 \times (\$290,000,000 - \$3,000,000) = \$1,476,041$$

Public Securities Association Benchmark

The **Public Securities Association (PSA) prepayment benchmark** is expressed as a monthly series of annual prepayment rates. The PSA benchmark assumes that prepayment rates are low for newly originated mortgages and then will speed up as the mortgages become seasoned.

The PSA benchmark assumes the following CPRs for 30-year mortgages:

1. a CPR of 0.2% for the first month, increased by 0.2% per month for the next 30 months when it reaches 6% per year, and
2. a 6% CPR for the remaining years.

This benchmark, referred to as *100% PSA* or simply *100 PSA*, is graphically depicted in Figure 2. Mathematically, 100 PSA can be expressed as follows:

If $t \leq 30$, then CPR $= 6\%(t/30)$
If $t > 30$, then CPR $= 6\%$

where t is the number of months since the mortgage originated.

Slower or faster speeds are then referred to as some percentage of PSA. For example, 50 PSA means one-half the CPR of the PSA benchmark prepayment rate; 150 PSA means one-and-a-half times the CPR of the PSA benchmark prepayment rate; 300 PSA means three

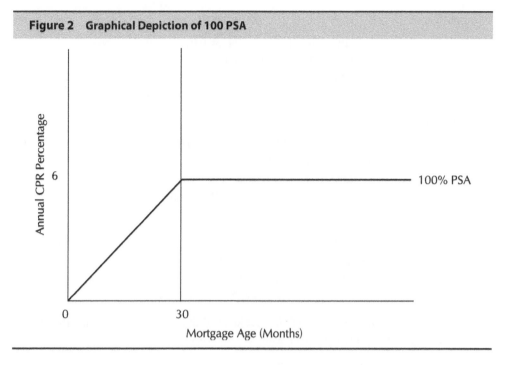

Figure 2 Graphical Depiction of 100 PSA

times the CPR of the benchmark prepayment rate. A prepayment rate of 0 PSA means that no prepayments are assumed.

The CPR is converted to an SMM using equation (1). For example, the SMMs for month 5, month 20, and months 31 through 360 assuming 100 PSA are calculated as follows:
For month 5,

$$CPR = 6\%(5/30) = 1\% = 0.01$$
$$SMM = 1 - (1 - 0.01)^{1/12}$$
$$= 1 - (0.99)^{0.083333} = 0.000837$$

For month 20,

$$CPR = 6\%(20/30) = 4\% = 0.04$$
$$SMM = 1 - (1 - 0.04)^{1/12}$$
$$= 1 - (0.96)^{0.083333} = 0.003396$$

For months 31 to 360,

$$CPR = 6\%$$
$$SMM = 1 - (1 - 0.06)^{1/12}$$
$$= 1 - (0.94)^{0.083333} = 0.005143$$

The SMMs for month 5, month 20, and months 31 through 360 assuming 165 PSA are computed as follows:

For month 5,

$$CPR = 6\%(5/30) = 1\% = 0.01$$
$$165\ PSA = 1.65(0.01) = 0.0165$$
$$SMM = 1 - (1 - 0.0165)^{1/12}$$
$$= 1 - (0.9835)^{0.083333} = 0.001386$$

For month 20,

$$CPR = 6\%(20/30) = 4\% = 0.04$$
$$165\ PSA = 1.65(0.04) = 0.066$$
$$SMM = 1 - (1 - 0.066)^{1/12}$$
$$= 1 - (0.934)^{0.083333} = 0.005674$$

For months 31 to 360,

$$CPR = 6\%$$
$$165\ PSA = 1.65(0.06) = 0.099$$
$$SMM = 1 - (1 - 0.099)^{1/12}$$
$$= 1 - (0.901)^{0.083333} = 0.007828$$

Notice that the SMM assuming 165 PSA is not just 1.65 times the SMM assuming 100 PSA. It is the CPR that is a multiple of the CPR assuming 100 PSA.

Illustration of Monthly Cash Flow Construction

We now show how to construct a monthly cash flow for a hypothetical pass-through given a PSA assumption. For the purpose of this illustration, the underlying mortgages for this hypothetical pass-through are assumed to be fixed-rate, level-payment mortgages and the pass-through rate is assumed to be 7.5%. Furthermore, it is assumed that the weighted average maturity (WAM) of the pool of mortgages is 357 months.[3]

Table 1 shows the cash flow for selected months assuming 100 PSA. The cash flow is broken down into three components: (1) interest (based on the pass-through rate), (2) the regularly scheduled principal repayment, and (3) prepayments based on 100 PSA.

Let's walk through Table 1 column by column.

Column 1: This column is the month.
Column 2: This column gives the outstanding mortgage balance at the beginning of the month. It is equal to the outstanding balance at the beginning of the previous month reduced by the total principal payment in the previous month.
Column 3: This column shows the SMM for 100 PSA. Two things should be noted in this column. First, for month 1, the SMM is for a pass-through that has been seasoned three months. That is, the CPR is 0.8%. This is because the WAM is 357. Second, from month 27 on, the SMM is 0.00514, which corresponds to a CPR of 6%.
Column 4: The total monthly mortgage payment is shown in this column. Notice that the total monthly mortgage payment declines over time as prepayments reduce the mortgage balance outstanding. There is a formula to determine what the monthly mortgage balance will be for each month given prepayments.[4]

---

[3] It is necessary to calculate a WAM for a pool of mortgages because not all the mortgages have the same number of months remaining to maturity.

[4] The formula is presented in Chapter 20 of Frank J. Fabozzi, *Fixed Income Mathematics: Analytical and Statistical Techniques* (Chicago: Probus Publishing, 1993).

Table 1 Monthly Cash Flow for a $400 Million, 7.5% Pass-Through Rate with a WAC of 8.125% and a WAM of 357 Months Assuming 100 PSA

(1)	(2)	(3)	(4)	(5)	(6)	(7)	(8)	(9)
Month	Outstanding Balance	SMM	Mortgage Payment	Net Interest	Scheduled Principal	Prepayment	Total Principal	Total Cash Flow
1	$400,000,000	0.00067	$2,975,868	$2,500,000	$267,535	$ 267,470	$ 535,005	$3,035,005
2	399,464,995	0.00084	2,973,877	2,496,656	269,166	334,198	603,364	3,100,020
3	398,861,631	0.00101	2,971,387	2,492,885	270,762	400,800	671,562	3,164,447
4	398,190,069	0.00117	2,968,399	2,488,688	272,321	467,243	739,564	3,228,252
5	397,450,505	0.00134	2,964,914	2,484,066	273,843	533,493	807,335	3,291,401
6	396,643,170	0.00151	2,960,931	2,479,020	275,327	599,514	874,841	3,353,860
7	395,768,329	0.00168	2,956,453	2,473,552	276,772	665,273	942,045	3,415,597
8	394,826,284	0.00185	2,951,480	2,467,664	278,177	730,736	1,008,913	3,476,577
9	393,817,371	0.00202	2,946,013	2,461,359	279,542	795,869	1,075,410	3,536,769
10	392,741,961	0.00219	2,940,056	2,454,637	280,865	860,637	1,141,502	3,596,140
11	391,600,459	0.00236	2,933,608	2,447,503	282,147	925,008	1,207,155	3,654,658
12	390,393,304	0.00254	2,926,674	2,439,958	283,386	988,948	1,272,333	3,712,291
13	389,120,971	0.00271	2,919,254	2,432,006	284,581	1,052,423	1,337,004	3,769,010
14	387,783,966	0.00288	2,911,353	2,423,650	285,733	1,115,402	1,401,134	3,824,784
15	386,382,832	0.00305	2,902,973	2,414,893	286,839	1,177,851	1,464,690	3,879,583
16	384,918,142	0.00322	2,894,117	2,405,738	287,900	1,239,739	1,527,639	3,933,378
17	383,390,502	0.00340	2,884,789	2,396,191	288,915	1,301,033	1,589,949	3,986,139
18	381,800,553	0.00357	2,874,992	2,386,253	289,884	1,361,703	1,651,587	4,037,840
19	380,148,966	0.00374	2,864,730	2,375,931	290,805	1,421,717	1,712,522	4,088,453
20	378,436,444	0.00392	2,854,008	2,365,228	291,678	1,481,046	1,772,724	4,137,952
21	376,663,720	0.00409	2,842,830	2,354,148	292,503	1,539,658	1,832,161	4,186,309
22	374,831,559	0.00427	2,831,201	2,342,697	293,279	1,597,525	1,890,804	4,233,501
23	372,940,755	0.00444	2,819,125	2,330,880	294,005	1,654,618	1,948,623	4,279,503
24	370,992,132	0.00462	2,806,607	2,318,701	294,681	1,710,908	2,005,589	4,324,290
25	368,986,543	0.00479	2,793,654	2,306,166	295,307	1,766,368	2,061,675	4,367,841
26	366,924,868	0.00497	2,780,270	2,293,280	295,883	1,820,970	2,116,852	4,410,133
27	364,808,016	0.00514	2,766,461	2,280,050	296,406	1,874,688	2,171,094	4,451,144
28	362,636,921	0.00514	2,752,233	2,266,481	296,879	1,863,519	2,160,398	4,426,879
29	360,476,523	0.00514	2,738,078	2,252,978	297,351	1,852,406	2,149,758	4,402,736
30	358,326,766	0.00514	2,723,996	2,239,542	297,825	1,841,347	2,139,173	4,378,715
...								
100	231,249,776	0.00514	1,898,682	1,445,311	332,928	1,187,608	1,520,537	2,965,848
101	229,729,239	0.00514	1,888,917	1,435,808	333,459	1,179,785	1,513,244	2,949,052
102	228,215,995	0.00514	1,879,202	1,426,350	333,990	1,172,000	1,505,990	2,932,340
103	226,710,004	0.00514	1,869,538	1,416,938	334,522	1,164,252	1,498,774	2,915,712
104	225,211,230	0.00514	1,859,923	1,407,570	335,055	1,156,541	1,491,596	2,899,166
105	223,719,634	0.00514	1,850,357	1,398,248	335,589	1,148,867	1,484,456	2,882,703
...								
200	109,791,339	0.00514	1,133,751	686,196	390,372	562,651	953,023	1,639,219
201	108,838,316	0.00514	1,127,920	680,239	390,994	557,746	948,740	1,628,980

(*Continued*)

Table 1 Monthly Cash Flow for a $400 Million, 7.5% Pass-Through Rate with a WAC of 8.125% and a WAM of 357 Months Assuming 100 PSA (Continued)

(1) Month	(2) Outstanding Balance	(3) SMM	(4) Mortgage Payment	(5) Net Interest	(6) Scheduled Principal	(7) Prepayment	(8) Total Principal	(9) Total Cash
202	107,889,576	0.00514	1,122,119	674,310	391,617	552,863	944,480	1,618,790
203	106,945,096	0.00514	1,116,348	668,407	392,241	548,003	940,243	1,608,650
204	106,004,852	0.00514	1,110,607	662,530	392,866	543,164	936,029	1,598,560
205	105,068,823	0.00514	1,104,895	656,680	393,491	538,347	931,838	1,588,518
...								
300	32,383,611	0.00514	676,991	202,398	457,727	164,195	621,923	824,320
301	31,761,689	0.00514	673,510	198,511	458,457	160,993	619,449	817,960
302	31,142,239	0.00514	670,046	194,639	459,187	157,803	616,990	811,629
303	30,525,249	0.00514	666,600	190,783	459,918	154,626	614,545	805,328
304	29,910,704	0.00514	663,171	186,942	460,651	151,462	612,113	799,055
305	29,298,591	0.00514	659,761	183,116	461,385	148,310	609,695	792,811
...								
350	4,060,411	0.00514	523,138	25,378	495,645	18,334	513,979	539,356
351	3,546,432	0.00514	520,447	22,165	496,435	15,686	512,121	534,286
352	3,034,311	0.00514	517,770	18,964	497,226	13,048	510,274	529,238
353	2,524,037	0.00514	515,107	15,775	498,018	10,420	508,437	524,213
354	2,015,600	0.00514	512,458	12,597	498,811	7,801	506,612	519,209
355	1,508,988	0.00514	509,823	9,431	499,606	5,191	504,797	514,228
356	1,004,191	0.00514	507,201	6,276	500,401	2,591	502,992	509,269
357	501,199	0.00514	504,592	3,132	501,199	0	501,199	504,331

Column 5: The monthly interest paid to the pass-through investor is found in this column. This value is determined by multiplying the outstanding mortgage balance at the beginning of the month by the pass-through rate of 7.5% and dividing by 12.

Column 6: This column gives the regularly scheduled principal repayment. This is the difference between the total monthly mortgage payment (the amount shown in column 4) and the gross coupon interest for the month. The gross coupon interest is 8.125% multiplied by the outstanding mortgage balance at the beginning of the month, then divided by 12.

Column 7: The prepayment for the month is reported in this column. The prepayment is found by using equation (2). So, for example, in month 100, the beginning mortgage balance is $231,249,776, the scheduled principal payment is $332,298, and the SMM at 100 PSA is 0.00514301 (only 0.00514 is shown in the table to save space), so the prepayment is

$$0.00514301 \times (\$231,249,776 - \$332,928) = \$1,187,608$$

Column 8: The total principal payment, which is the sum of columns 6 and 7, is shown in this column.

Column 9: The projected monthly cash flow for this pass-through is shown in this last column. The monthly cash flow is the sum of the interest paid to the pass-through investor (column 5) and the total principal payments for the month (column 8).

Table 2 shows selected monthly cash flows for the same pass-through assuming 165 PSA.

	Table 2		Monthly Cash Flow for a $400 Million, 7.5% Pass-Through Rate with a WAC of 8.125% and a WAM of 357 Months Assuming 165 PSA					
(1)	(2)	(3)	(4)	(5)	(6)	(7)	(8)	(9)
Month	Outstanding Balance	SMM	Mortgage Payment	Net Interest	Scheduled Principal	Prepayment	Total Principal	Total Cash Flow
1	$400,000,000	0.00111	$2,975,868	$2,500,000	$267,535	$ 442,389	$ 709,923	$3,209,923
2	399,290,077	0.00139	2,972,575	2,495,563	269,048	552,847	821,896	3,317,459
3	398,468,181	0.00167	2,968,456	2,490,426	270,495	663,065	933,560	3,423,986
4	397,534,621	0.00195	2,963,513	2,484,591	271,873	772,949	1,044,822	3,529,413
5	396,489,799	0.00223	2,957,747	2,478,061	273,181	882,405	1,155,586	3,633,647
6	395,334,213	0.00251	2,951,160	2,470,839	274,418	991,341	1,265,759	3,736,598
7	394,068,454	0.00279	2,943,755	2,462,928	275,583	1,099,664	1,375,246	3,838,174
8	392,693,208	0.00308	2,935,534	2,454,333	276,674	1,207,280	1,483,954	3,938,287
9	391,209,254	0.00336	2,926,503	2,445,058	277,690	1,314,099	1,591,789	4,036,847
10	389,617,464	0.00365	2,916,666	2,435,109	278,631	1,420,029	1,698,659	4,133,769
11	387,918,805	0.00393	2,906,028	2,424,493	279,494	1,524,979	1,804,473	4,228,965
12	386,114,332	0.00422	2,894,595	2,413,215	280,280	1,628,859	1,909,139	4,322,353
13	384,205,194	0.00451	2,882,375	2,401,282	280,986	1,731,581	2,012,567	4,413,850
14	382,192,626	0.00480	2,869,375	2,388,704	281,613	1,833,058	2,114,670	4,503,374
15	380,077,956	0.00509	2,855,603	2,375,487	282,159	1,933,203	2,215,361	4,590,848
16	377,862,595	0.00538	2,841,068	2,361,641	282,623	2,031,931	2,314,554	4,676,195
17	375,548,041	0.00567	2,825,779	2,347,175	283,006	2,129,159	2,412,164	4,759,339
18	373,135,877	0.00597	2,809,746	2,332,099	283,305	2,224,805	2,508,110	4,840,210
19	370,627,766	0.00626	2,792,980	2,316,424	283,521	2,318,790	2,602,312	4,918,735
20	368,025,455	0.00656	2,775,493	2,300,159	283,654	2,411,036	2,694,690	4,994,849
21	365,330,765	0.00685	2,757,296	2,283,317	283,702	2,501,466	2,785,169	5,068,486
22	362,545,596	0.00715	2,738,402	2,265,910	283,666	2,590,008	2,873,674	5,139,584
23	359,671,922	0.00745	2,718,823	2,247,950	283,545	2,676,588	2,960,133	5,208,083
24	356,711,789	0.00775	2,698,575	2,229,449	283,338	2,761,139	3,044,477	5,273,926
25	353,667,312	0.00805	2,677,670	2,210,421	283,047	2,843,593	3,126,640	5,337,061
26	350,540,672	0.00835	2,656,123	2,190,879	282,671	2,923,885	3,206,556	5,397,435
27	347,334,116	0.00865	2,633,950	2,170,838	282,209	3,001,955	3,284,164	5,455,002
28	344,049,952	0.00865	2,611,167	2,150,312	281,662	2,973,553	3,255,215	5,405,527
29	340,794,737	0.00865	2,588,581	2,129,967	281,116	2,945,400	3,226,516	5,356,483
30	337,568,221	0.00865	2,566,190	2,109,801	280,572	2,917,496	3,198,067	5,307,869
...								
100	170,142,350	0.00865	1,396,958	1,063,390	244,953	1,469,591	1,714,544	2,777,933
101	168,427,806	0.00865	1,384,875	1,052,674	244,478	1,454,765	1,699,243	2,751,916
102	166,728,563	0.00865	1,372,896	1,042,054	244,004	1,440,071	1,684,075	2,726,128
103	165,044,489	0.00865	1,361,020	1,031,528	243,531	1,425,508	1,669,039	2,700,567
104	163,375,450	0.00865	1,349,248	1,021,097	243,060	1,411,075	1,654,134	2,675,231
105	161,721,315	0.00865	1,337,577	1,010,758	242,589	1,396,771	1,639,359	2,650,118

(Continued)

Table 2	Monthly Cash Flow for a $400 Million, 7.5% Pass-Through Rate with a WAC of 8.125% and a WAM of 357 Months Assuming 165 PSA (Continued)							
(1)	(2)	(3)	(4)	(5)	(6)	(7)	(8)	(9)
Month	Outstanding Balance	SMM	Mortgage Payment	Net Interest	Scheduled Principal	Prepayment	Total Principal	Total Cash Flow
200	56,746,664	0.00865	585,990	354,667	201,767	489,106	690,874	1,045,540
201	56,055,790	0.00865	580,921	350,349	201,377	483,134	684,510	1,034,859
202	55,371,280	0.00865	575,896	346,070	200,986	477,216	678,202	1,024,273
203	54,693,077	0.00865	570,915	341,832	200,597	471,353	671,950	1,013,782
204	54,021,127	0.00865	565,976	337,632	200,208	465,544	665,752	1,003,384
205	53,355,375	0.00865	561,081	333,471	199,820	459,789	659,609	993,080
300	11,758,141	0.00865	245,808	73,488	166,196	100,269	266,465	339,953
301	11,491,677	0.00865	243,682	71,823	165,874	97,967	263,841	335,664
302	11,227,836	0.00865	241,574	70,174	165,552	95,687	261,240	331,414
303	10,966,596	0.00865	239,485	68,541	165,232	93,430	258,662	327,203
304	10,707,934	0.00865	237,413	66,925	164,912	91,196	256,107	323,032
305	10,451,827	0.00865	235,360	65,324	164,592	88,983	253,575	318,899
...								
350	1,235,674	0.00865	159,202	7,723	150,836	9,384	160,220	167,943
351	1,075,454	0.00865	157,825	6,722	150,544	8,000	158,544	165,266
352	916,910	0.00865	156,460	5,731	150,252	6,631	156,883	162,614
353	760,027	0.00865	155,107	4,750	149,961	5,277	155,238	159,988
354	604,789	0.00865	153,765	3,780	149,670	3,937	153,607	157,387
355	451,182	0.00865	152,435	2,820	149,380	2,611	151,991	154,811
356	299,191	0.00865	151,117	1,870	149,091	1,298	150,398	152,259
357	148,802	0.00865	149,809	930	148,802	0	148,802	149,732

Average Life

The stated maturity of a mortgage pass-through security is an inappropriate measure of the security's life because of prepayments. Instead, market participants commonly use the security's average life. The **average life** of a mortgage-backed security is the average time to receipt of principal payments (scheduled principal payments and projected prepayments), weighted by the amount of principal expected. Mathematically, the average life is expressed as follows:

$$\text{Average life} = \sum_{t=1}^{T} \frac{t \times \text{ Principal received at time } t}{12(\text{Total principal})}$$

where T is the number of months.

The average life of a pass-through depends on the PSA prepayment assumption. To see this, the average life follows for different prepayment speeds for the pass-through we used to illustrate the cash flow for 100 PSA and 165 PSA in Table 1 and Table 2:

PSA speed	50	100	165	200	300	400	500	600	700
Average life	15.11	11.66	8.76	7.68	5.63	4.44	3.68	3.16	2.78

> **Key Points That You Should Understand Before Proceeding**
>
> 1. A mortgage pass-through security is created when one or more holders of mortgages form a collection (pool) of mortgages and sell shares or PCs in the pool.
> 2. The cash flow of a mortgage pass-through security depends on the cash flow of the underlying mortgages, which consists of monthly mortgage payments representing interest, the scheduled repayment of principal, and any prepayments.
> 3. The three major types of pass-through securities are guaranteed by either Ginnie Mae (a federally related entity), Fannie Mae (a government-sponsored enterprise), or Freddie Mac (a government-sponsored enterprise), and are referred to as agency pass-through securities.
> 4. There are private issuers of mortgage pass-through securities that are not explicitly or implicitly guaranteed by the U.S. government; these securities are called nonagency pass-through securities.
> 5. Of the mortgage pass-through securities guaranteed by one of the three agencies, only those guaranteed by Ginnie Mae carry the full faith and credit of the U.S. government; nonagency pass-through securities are rated by a commercial rating company, and often they are supported by credit enhancements so that they can obtain a high rating.
> 6. An investor in a mortgage pass-through security is exposed to prepayment risk, which can be decomposed into two types of risk, contraction risk and extension risk.
> 7. The cash flow of a mortgage pass-through is projected based on an assumed PSA.

AGENCY COLLATERALIZED MORTGAGE OBLIGATIONS

Some institutional investors are concerned with extension risk and others with contraction risk when they invest in a pass-through. This problem can be mitigated by redirecting the cash flows of mortgage pass-through securities to different bond classes, called **tranches**, so as to create securities that have different exposure to prepayment risk and, therefore, different risk/return patterns than the pass-through securities from which the tranches were created.

When the cash flows of pools of mortgage pass-through securities are redistributed to different bond classes, the resulting securities are called **agency CMOs**. The creation of a CMO cannot eliminate prepayment risk; it can only distribute the various forms of this risk among different classes of bondholders. The CMO's major financial innovation is that the securities created more closely satisfy the asset/ liability needs of institutional investors and thus broaden the appeal of mortgage-backed products to traditional bond investors.

Rather than list the different types of tranches that can be created in a CMO structure, we will show how the tranches can be created. This will provide an excellent illustration of financial engineering. Although there are many different types of CMOs that have been created, we will only look at three of the key innovations in the CMO market: sequential-pay tranches, accrual tranches, and planned amortization class bonds. Two other important tranches that are not illustrated here are the *floating-rate tranche* and *inverse floating-rate tranche*.

Sequential-Pay Collateralized Mortgage Obligations

The first CMO was created in 1983 and was structured so that each class of bond would be retired sequentially. Such structures are referred to as **sequential-pay CMOs**. To illustrate a sequential-pay CMO, we discuss CMO-1, a hypothetical deal made up to illustrate the basic features of the structure. The collateral for this hypothetical CMO is a hypothetical pass-through with a total par value of $400 million and the following characteristics: (1) The pass-through coupon rate is 7.5%, (2) the weighted average coupon (WAC) is 8.125%, and (3) the WAM is 357 months. This is the same pass-through that we used earlier in this chapter to describe the cash flow of a pass-through based on some PSA assumption.

From this $400 million of collateral, four bond classes or tranches are created. Their characteristics are summarized in Table 3. The total par value of the four tranches is equal to the par value of the collateral (i.e., the pass-through security). In this simple structure, the coupon rate is the same for each tranche and also the same as the coupon rate on the collateral. There is no reason why this must be so, and, in fact, typically the coupon rate varies by tranche.

Now remember that a CMO is created by redistributing the cash flow—interest and principal—to the different tranches based on a set of payment rules. The payment rules at the bottom of Table 3 describe how the cash flow from the pass-through (i.e., collateral) is to be distributed to the four tranches. There are separate rules for the payment of the coupon interest and the payment of principal, the principal being the total of the regularly scheduled principal payment and any prepayments.

In CMO-1, each tranche receives periodic coupon interest payments based on the amount of the outstanding balance at the beginning of the month. The disbursement of the principal, however, is made in a special way. A tranche is not entitled to receive principal until the entire principal of the tranche has been paid off. More specifically, tranche A receives all the principal payments until the entire principal amount owed to that bond class, $194,500,000, is paid off; then tranche B begins to receive principal and continues to do so until it is paid the entire $36,000,000. Tranche C then receives principal, and when it is paid off, tranche D starts receiving principal payments.

Although the priority rules for the disbursement of the principal payments are known, the precise amount of the principal in each period is not. This will depend on the cash flow and, therefore, on the principal payments of the collateral, which will depend on the actual prepayment rate of the collateral. An assumed PSA speed allows the cash flow to be projected. Table 2 shows the cash flow (interest, regularly scheduled principal repayment, and prepayments)

Table 3 CMO-1: A Hypothetical Four-Tranche, Sequential-Pay Structure

Tranche	Par Amount	Coupon Rate
A	$194,500,000	7.5%
B	36,000,000	7.5
C	96,500,000	7.5
D	73,000,000	7.5
Total	$400,000,000	

Payment rules:

1. *For payment of periodic coupon interest:* Disburse periodic coupon interest to each tranche on the basis of the amount of principal outstanding at the beginning of the period.

2. *For disbursement of principal payments:* Disburse principal payments to tranche A until it is completely paid off. After tranche A is completely paid off, disburse principal payments to tranche B until it is completely paid off. After tranche B is completely paid off, disburse principal payments to tranche C until it is completely paid off. After tranche C is completely paid off, disburse principal payments to tranche D until it is completely paid off.

assuming 165 PSA. Assuming that the collateral does prepay at 165 PSA, the cash flow available to all four tranches of CMO-1 will be precisely the cash flow shown in Table 2.

To demonstrate how the priority rules for CMO-1 work, Table 4 shows the cash flow for selected months assuming the collateral prepays at 165 PSA. For each tranche, the table shows (1) the balance at the end of the month, (2) the principal paid down

Table 4 Monthly Cash Flow for Selected Months for CMO-1 Assuming 165 PSA

	Tranche A			Tranche B		
Month	Balance	Principal	Interest	Balance	Principal	Interest
1	$194,500,000	$ 709,923	$1,215,625	$36,000,000	$ 0	$225,000
2	193,790,077	821,896	1,211,188	36,000,000	0	255,000
3	192,968,181	933,560	1,206,051	36,000,000	0	225,000
4	192,034,621	1,044,822	1,200,216	36,000,000	0	225,000
5	190,989,799	1,155,586	1,193,686	36,000,000	0	225,000
6	189,834,213	1,265,759	1,186,464	36,000,000	0	225,000
7	188,568,454	1,375,246	1,178,553	36,000,000	0	225,000
8	187,193,208	1,483,954	1,169,958	36,000,000	0	225,000
9	185,709,254	1,591,789	1,160,683	36,000,000	0	225,000
10	184,117,464	1,698,659	1,150,734	36,000,000	0	225,000
11	182,418,805	1,804,473	1,140,118	36,000,000	0	225,000
12	180,614,332	1,909,139	1,128,840	36,000,000	0	225,000
...						
75	12,893,479	2,143,974	80,584	36,000,000	0	225,000
76	10,749,504	2,124,935	67,184	36,000,000	0	225,000
77	8,624,569	2,106,062	53,904	36,000,000	0	225,000
78	6,518,507	2,087,353	40,741	36,000,000	0	225,000
79	4,431,154	2,068,807	27,695	36,000,000	0	225,000
80	2,362,347	2,050,422	14,765	36,000,000	0	225,000
81	311,926	311,926	1,950	36,000,000	1,720,271	225,000
82	0	0	0	34,279,729	2,014,130	214,248
83	0	0	0	32,265,599	1,996,221	201,660
84	0	0	0	30,269,378	1,978,468	189,184
85	0	0	0	28,290,911	1,960,869	176,818
95	0	0	0	9,449,331	1,793,089	59,058
96	0	0	0	7,656,242	1,777,104	47,852
97	0	0	0	5,879,138	1,761,258	36,745
98	0	0	0	4,117,880	1,745,550	25,737
99	0	0	0	2,372,329	1,729,979	14,827
100	0	0	0	642,350	642,350	4,015
101	0	0	0	0	0	0
102	0	0	0	0	0	0
103	0	0	0	0	0	0
104	0	0	0	0	0	0
105	0	0	0	0	0	0

(Continued)

Month	Tranche C			Tranche D		
	Balance	Principal	Interest	Balance	Principal	Interest
1	$96,500,000	$ 0	$603,125	$73,000,000	$ 0	$456,250
2	96,500,000	0	603,125	73,000,000	0	456,250
3	96,500,000	0	603,125	73,000,000	0	456,250
4	96,500,000	0	603,125	73,000,000	0	456,250
5	96,500,000	0	603,125	73,000,000	0	456,250
6	96,500,000	0	603,125	73,000,000	0	456,250
7	96,500,000	0	603,125	73,000,000	0	456,250
8	96,500,000	0	603,125	73,000,000	0	456,250
9	96,500,000	0	603,125	73,000,000	0	456,250
10	96,500,000	0	603,125	73,000,000	0	456,250
11	96,500,000	0	603,125	73,000,000	0	456,250
12	96,500,000	0	603,125	73,000,000	0	456,250
...						
95	96,500,000	0	603,125	73,000,000	0	456,250
96	96,500,000	0	603,125	73,000,000	0	456,250
97	96,500,000	0	603,125	73,000,000	0	456,250
98	96,500,000	0	603,125	73,000,000	0	456,250
99	96,500,000	0	603,125	73,000,000	0	456,250
100	96,500,000	1,072,194	603,125	73,000,000	0	456,250
101	95,427,806	1,699,243	596,424	73,000,000	0	456,250
102	93,728,563	1,684,075	585,804	73,000,000	0	456,250
103	92,044,489	1,669,039	575,278	73,000,000	0	456,250
104	90,375,450	1,654,134	564,847	73,000,000	0	456,250
105	88,721,315	1,639,359	554,508	73,000,000	0	456,250
...						
175	3,260,287	869,602	20,377	73,000,000	0	456,250
176	2,390,685	861,673	14,942	73,000,000	0	456,250
177	1,529,013	853,813	9,556	73,000,000	0	456,250
178	675,199	675,199	4,220	73,000,000	170,824	456,250
179	0	0	0	72,829,176	838,300	455,182
180	0	0	0	71,990,876	830,646	449,943
181	0	0	0	71,160,230	823,058	444,751
182	0	0	0	70,337,173	815,536	439,607
183	0	0	0	69,521,637	808,081	434,510
184	0	0	0	68,713,556	800,690	429,460
185	0	0	0	67,912,866	793,365	424,455
...						
350	0	0	0	1,235,674	160,220	7,723
351	0	0	0	1,075,454	158,544	6,722
352	0	0	0	916,910	156,883	5,731
353	0	0	0	760,027	155,238	4,750
354	0	0	0	604,789	153,607	3,780
355	0	0	0	451,182	151,991	2,820
356	0	0	0	299,191	150,389	1,870
357	0	0	0	148,802	148,802	930

(regularly scheduled principal repayment plus prepayments), and (3) interest. In month 1, the cash flow for the collateral consists of principal payment of $709,923 and interest of $2.5 million (0.075 times $400 million divided by 12). The interest payment is distributed to the four tranches based on the amount of the par value outstanding. So, for example, tranche A receives $1,215,625 (0.075 times $194,500,000 divided by 12) of the $2.5 million. The principal, however, is all distributed to tranche A. Therefore, the cash flow for tranche A in month 1 is $1,925,548. The principal balance at the end of month 1 for tranche A is $193,790,076 (the original principal balance of $194,500,000 less the principal payment of $709,923). No principal payment is distributed to the three other tranches because there is still a principal balance outstanding for tranche A. This will be true for months 2 through 80.

After month 81, the principal balance will be zero for tranche A. For the collateral, the cash flow in month 81 is $3,318,521, consisting of a principal payment of $2,032,196 and interest of $1,286,325. At the beginning of month 81 (end of month 80), the principal balance for tranche A is $311,926. Therefore, $311,926 of the $2,032,196 of the principal payment from the collateral will be disbursed to tranche A. After this payment is made, no additional principal payments are made to this tranche as the principal balance is zero. The remaining principal payment from the collateral, $1,720,271, is disbursed to tranche B. According to the assumed prepayment speed of 165 PSA, tranche B then begins receiving principal payments in month 81.

Table 4 shows that tranche B is fully paid off by month 100, when tranche C now begins to receive principal payments. Tranche C is not fully paid off until month 178, at which time tranche D begins receiving the remaining principal payments. The maturity (i.e., the time until the principal is fully paid off) for these four tranches assuming 165 PSA would be 81 months for tranche A, 100 months for tranche B, 178 months for tranche C, and 357 months for tranche D.

Let's look at what has been accomplished by creating the CMO. First, as shown earlier in this chapter, the average life for the pass-through is 8.76 years, assuming a prepayment speed of 165 PSA. Table 5 reports the average life of the collateral and the four tranches assuming different prepayment speeds. Notice that the four tranches have average lives that

Table 5 Average Life for the Collateral and the Four Tranches of CMO-1					
	Average life for				
Prepayment Speed (PSA)	Collateral	Tranche A	Tranche B	Tranche C	Tranche D
50	15.11	7.48	15.98	21.02	27.24
100	11.66	4.90	10.86	15.78	24.58
165	8.76	3.48	7.49	11.19	20.27
200	7.68	3.05	6.42	9.60	18.11
300	5.63	2.32	4.64	6.81	13.36
400	4.44	1.94	3.70	5.31	10.34
500	3.68	1.69	3.12	4.38	8.35
600	3.16	1.51	2.74	3.75	6.96
700	2.78	1.38	2.47	3.30	5.95

are both shorter and longer than the collateral, thereby attracting investors who have a preference for an average life different from that of the collateral.

There is still a major problem: There is considerable variability of the average life for the tranches. We will see how this can be tackled later on. However, there is some protection provided for each tranche against prepayment risk. This is because prioritizing the distribution of principal (i.e., establishing the payment rules for principal) effectively protects the shorter-term tranche A in this structure against extension risk. This protection must come from somewhere, so it comes from the three other tranches. Similarly, tranches C and D provide protection against extension risk for tranches A and B. At the same time, tranches C and D benefit because they are provided protection against contraction risk, the protection coming from tranches A and B.

Accrual Bonds

In CMO-1, the payment rules for interest provide for all tranches to be paid interest each month. In many sequential-pay CMO structures, at least one tranche does not receive current interest. Instead, the interest for that tranche would accrue and be added to the principal balance. Such a bond class is commonly referred to as an **accrual tranche**, or a **Z bond** (because the bond is similar to a zero-coupon bond). The interest that would have been paid to the accrual bond class is then used to speed up paying down the principal balance of earlier bond classes.

To see this, consider CMO-2, a hypothetical CMO structure with the same collateral as CMO-1 and with four tranches, each with a coupon rate of 7.5%. The structure is shown in Table 6. The difference is in the last tranche, Z, which is an accrual bond.

Let's look at month 1 and compare it to month 1 in Table 4 based on 165 PSA. The principal payment from the collateral is $709,923. In CMO-1, this is the principal paydown for tranche A. In CMO-2, the interest for tranche Z, $456,250, is not paid to that tranche but instead is used to pay down the principal of tranche A. So, the principal payment to tranche A is $1,166,173, the collateral's principal payment of $709,923 plus the interest of $456,250 that was diverted from tranche Z.

Table 6   CMO-2: A Hypothetical Four-Tranche Sequential-Pay Structure with an Accrual Bond Class

Tranche	Par Amount	Coupon Rate
A	$194,500,000	7.5%
B	36,000,000	7.5
C	96,500,000	7.5
Z (Accrual)	73,000,000	7.5
Total	$400,000,000	

Payment rules:

1. *For payment of periodic coupon interest:* Disburse periodic coupon interest to tranches A, B, and C on the basis of the amount of principal outstanding at the beginning of the period. For tranche Z, accrue the interest based on the principal plus accrued interest in the previous period. The interest for tranche Z is to be paid to the earlier tranches as a principal paydown.

2. *For disbursement of principal payments:* Disburse principal payments to tranche A until it is completely paid off. After tranche A is completely paid off, disburse principal payments to tranche B until it is completely paid off. After tranche B is completely paid off, disburse principal payments to tranche C until it is completely paid off. After tranche C is completely paid off, disburse principal payments to tranche Z until the original principal balance plus accrued interest is completely paid off.

The inclusion of the accrual tranche results in a shortening of the expected final maturity for tranches A, B, and C. The final payout for tranche A is 64 months rather than 81 months, for tranche B it is 77 months rather than 100 months, and for tranche C it is 112 rather than 178 months.

The average lives for tranches A, B, and C are shorter in CMO-2 compared to CMO-1 because of the inclusion of the accrual bond. For example, at 165 PSA, the average lives are as follows:

Structure	Tranche A	Tranche B	Tranche C
CMO-2	2.90	5.86	7.87
CMO-1	3.48	7.49	11.19

The reason for the shortening of the nonaccrual tranches is that the interest that would be paid to the accrual bond is being allocated to the other tranches. Tranche Z in CMO-2 will have a longer average life than tranche D in CMO-1.

Thus, shorter-term tranches and a longer-term tranche are created by including an accrual bond. The accrual bond appeals to investors who are concerned with reinvestment risk. Since there are no coupon payments to reinvest, reinvestment risk is eliminated until all the other tranches are paid off.

Planned Amortization Class Tranches

Many investors were still concerned about investing in an instrument that they continued to perceive as posing significant prepayment risk because of the substantial average variability despite the innovations designed to reduce prepayment risk. Traditional corporate bond buyers sought a structure with both the characteristics of a corporate bond (either a bullet maturity or a sinking fund type of schedule for principal repayment) and high credit quality. While CMOs satisfied the second condition, they did not satisfy the first.

In 1987, CMO issuers began issuing bonds with the characteristic that if prepayments are within a specified range, the cash flow pattern is known. The greater predictability of the cash flow for these classes of bonds, referred to as **planned amortization class (PAC) bonds,** occurs because there is a principal repayment schedule that must be satisfied. PAC bondholders have priority over all other classes in the CMO issue in receiving principal payments from the underlying collateral. The greater certainty of the cash flow for the PAC bonds comes at the expense of the non-PAC classes, called the **support bonds** or **companion bonds.** It is these bonds that absorb the prepayment risk. Because PAC bonds have protection against both extension risk and contraction risk, they are said to provide *two-sided prepayment protection.*

To illustrate how to create a PAC bond, we will use as collateral the $400 million pass-through with a coupon rate of 7.5%, a WAC of 8.125%, and a WAM of 357 months. The second column of Table 7 shows the principal payment (regularly scheduled principal repayment plus prepayments) for selected months assuming a prepayment speed of 90 PSA, and the next column shows the principal payments for selected months assuming that the pass-through prepays at 300 PSA.

The last column of Table 7 gives the *minimum* principal payment if the collateral speed is 90 PSA or 300 PSA for months 1 to 349. (After month 346, the outstanding principal balance will be paid off if the prepayment speed is between 90 PSA and 300 PSA.) For

Table 7 Monthly Principal Payment for $400 Million, 7.5% Coupon Pass-Through with an 8.125% WAC and a 357 WAM Assuming Prepayment Rates of 90 PSA and 300 PSA

Month	At 90% PSA	At 300% PSA	Minimum Principal Payment—the PAC Schedule
1	$ 508,169.52	$1,075,931.20	$ 508,169.52
2	569,843.43	1,279,412.11	569,843.43
3	631,377.11	1,482,194.45	631,377.11
4	692,741.89	1,683,966.17	692,741.89
5	753,909.12	1,884,414.62	753,909.12
6	814,850.22	2,083,227.31	814,850.22
7	875,536.68	2,280,092.68	875,536.68
8	935,940.10	2,474,700.92	935,940.10
9	996,032.19	2,666,744.77	996,032.19
10	1,055,784.82	2,855,920.32	1,055,784.82
11	1,115,170.01	3,041,927.81	1,115,170.01
12	1,174,160.00	3,224,472.44	1,174,160.00
13	1,232,727.22	3,403,265.17	1,232,727.22
14	1,290,844.32	3,578,023.49	1,290,844.32
15	1,348,484.24	3,748,472.23	1,348,484.24
16	1,405,620.17	3,914,344.26	1,405,620.17
17	1,462,225.60	4,075,381.29	1,462,225.60
18	1,518,274.36	4,231,334.57	1,518,274.36
. . .			
101	1,458,719.34	1,510,072.17	1,458,719.34
102	1,452,725.55	1,484,126.59	1,452,725.55
103	1,446,761.00	1,458,618.04	1,446,761.00
104	1,440,825.55	1,433,539.23	1,433,539.23
105	1,434,919.07	1,408,883.01	1,408,883.01
. . .			
211	949,482.58	213,309.00	213,309.00
212	946,033.34	209,409.09	209,409.09
213	942,601.99	205,577.05	205,577.05
. . .			
346	618,684.59	13,269.17	13,269.17
347	617,071.58	12,944.51	12,944.51
348	615,468.65	12,626.21	12,626.21
349	613,875.77	12,314.16	3,432.32
350	612,292.88	12,008.25	0
351	610,719.96	11,708.38	0
352	609,156.96	11,414.42	0
353	607,603.84	11,126.28	0
354	606,060.57	10,843.85	0
355	604,527.09	10,567.02	0
356	603,003.38	10,295.70	0
357	601,489.39	10,029.78	0

example, in the first month, the principal payment would be $508,169.52 if the collateral prepays at 90 PSA and $1,075,931.20 if the collateral prepays at 300 PSA. Thus, the minimum principal payment is $508,169.52, as reported in the last column of Table 7. In month 103, the minimum principal payment is also the amount if the prepayment speed is 90 PSA, $1,446,761, compared to $1,458,618.04 for 300 PSA. In month 104, however, a prepayment speed of 300 PSA would produce a principal payment of $1,433,539.23, which is less than the principal payment of $1,440,825.55 assuming 90 PSA. So, $1,433,539.23 is reported in the last column of Table 7. In fact, from month 104 on, the minimum principal payment is the one that would result, assuming a prepayment speed of 300 PSA.

In fact, if the collateral prepays at *any* speed between 90 PSA and 300 PSA, the minimum principal payment would be the amount reported in the last column of Table 7. For example, if we had included principal payment figures assuming a prepayment speed of 200 PSA, the minimum principal payment would not change: From month 11 through month 103, the minimum principal payment is that generated from 90 PSA, but from month 104 on, the minimum principal payment is that generated from 300 PSA.

This characteristic of the collateral allows for the creation of a PAC bond, assuming that the collateral prepays over its life at a constant speed between 90 PSA and 300 PSA. A schedule of principal repayments that the PAC bondholders are entitled to receive before any other bond class in the CMO is specified. The monthly schedule of principal repayments is as specified in the last column of Table 7, which shows the minimum principal payment. Although there is no assurance that the collateral will prepay between these two speeds, a PAC bond can be structured to assume that it will.

Table 8 shows a CMO structure, CMO-3, created from the $400 million, 7.5% coupon pass-through with a WAC of 8.125% and a WAM of 357 months.

There are just two bond classes in this structure: a 7.5% coupon PAC bond created assuming 90 to 300 PSA with a par value of $243.8 million, and a support bond with a par value of $156.2 million.

Table 9 reports the average life for the PAC bond and the support bond in CMO-3 assuming various *actual* prepayment speeds. Notice that between 90 PSA and 300 PSA, the average life for the PAC bond is stable at 7.26 years. However, at slower or faster PSA speeds, the schedule is broken, and the average life changes, lengthening when the prepayment

Table 8   CMO-3 CMO Structure with One PAC Bond and One Support Bond

Tranche	Par Amount	Coupon Rate
P (PAC)	$243,800,000	7.5%
S (Support)	156,200,000	7.5%
Total	$400,000,000	

Payment rules:

1. *For payment of periodic coupon interest:* Disburse periodic coupon interest to each tranche on thebasis of the amount of principal outstanding at the beginning of the period.

2. *For disbursement of principal payments:* Disburse principal payments to tranche P based on its schedule of principal repayments. Tranche P has priority with respect to current and future principal payments to satisfy the schedule. Any excess principal payments in a month over the amount necessary to satisfy the schedule for tranche P are paid to tranche S. When tranche S is completely paid off, all principal payments are to be made to tranche P regardless of the schedule.

Table 9 Average Life for PAC Bond and Support Bond in CMO-3 Assuming Various Prepayment Speeds

Prepayment Rate (PSA)	PAC Bond (P)	Support Bond (S)
0	15.97	27.26
50	9.44	24.00
90	7.26	18.56
100	7.26	18.56
150	7.26	12.57
165	7.26	11.16
200	7.26	8.38
250	7.26	5.37
300	7.26	3.13
350	6.56	2.51
400	5.92	2.17
450	5.38	1.94
500	4.93	1.77
700	3.70	1.37

Key Points That You Should Understand Before Proceeding

1. A CMO is a security backed by a pool of mortgage pass-through securities or mortgages and is referred to as a derivative security.
2. In a CMO structure, there are several bond classes called tranches.
3. With the exception of support bonds, a CMO reduces the uncertainty concerning the maturity of a tranche, thereby providing a risk/return pattern not available with typical mortgage pass-through securities.
4. Tranche types that have been included in a CMO structure are sequential-pay bonds, accrual bonds (or Z-bonds), PAC bonds, and support bonds.
5. A PAC bond is a class of bonds designed to reduce prepayment risk by specifying a schedule for the amortization of the principal owed to the bondholder; the reduction in the prepayment risk comes at the expense of the support bonds.

---

speed is less than 90 PSA and shortening when it is greater than 300 PSA. Even so, there is much greater variability for the average life of the support bond. The average life for the support bond is substantial.

AGENCY STRIPPED MORTGAGE-BACKED SECURITIES

Agency stripped mortgage-backed securities, introduced by Fannie Mae in 1986, are another example of derivative mortgage securities. A mortgage pass-through security divides the cash flow from the underlying pool of mortgages on a pro rata basis to the securityholders. A stripped mortgage-backed security is created by altering that distribution of principal and interest from a pro rata distribution to an unequal distribution. The result is that some of the securities created will have a price/yield relationship that is different from the price/yield relationship of the underlying mortgage pool. Stripped mortgage-backed securities, if properly used, provide a means by which investors can hedge prepayment risk.

The first generation of stripped mortgage-backed securities were partially stripped. We can see this by looking at the stripped mortgage-backed securities issued by Fannie Mae in mid 1986. The Class B stripped mortgage-backed securities were backed by FNMA pass-through securities with a 9% coupon. The mortgage payments from the underlying mortgage pool were distributed to Class B-1 and Class B-2 so that both classes received an equal amount of the principal, but Class B-1 received one-third of the interest payments while Class B-2 received two-thirds.

In a subsequent issue, Fannie Mae distributed the cash flow from the underlying mortgage pool in a far different way. Using FNMA 11% coupon pools, Fannie Mae created Class A-1 and Class A-2. Class A-1 was given 4.95% of the 11% coupon interest, while Class A-2 received the other 6.05%. Class A-1 was given almost all of the principal payments, 99%, while Class A-2 was allotted only 1% of the principal payments.

In early 1987, stripped mortgage-backed securities began to be issued allocating all the interest to one class [called the **interest-only (IO) class**] and all the principal to the other class [called the **principal-only (PO) class**]. The IO class receives no principal payments. IO and PO securities are also referred to as **mortgage strips**.

The PO security is purchased at a substantial discount from par value. The yield an investor realizes depends on the speed at which prepayments are made. The faster the prepayments, the higher the investor's yield. For example, suppose there is a mortgage pool consisting of only 30-year mortgages, with $400 million in principal, and that investors can purchase POs backed by this mortgage pool for $175 million. The dollar return on this investment will be $225 million. How quickly that dollar return is recovered by PO investors determines the yield that will be realized. In the extreme case, if all homeowners in the underlying mortgage pool decide to prepay their mortgage loans immediately, PO investors will realize the $225 million immediately. At the other extreme, if all homeowners decide to remain in their homes for 30 years and make no prepayments, the $225 million will be spread out over 30 years, which would result in a lower yield for PO investors.

A PO is a security whose price would rise when interest rates decline and fall when interest rates rise. This is typical of all the bonds we have discussed thus far in this book. A characteristic of a PO is that its price is very sensitive to changes in interest rates.

An IO has no par value. In contrast to the PO investor, the IO investor wants prepayments to be slow. The reason is that the IO investor receives interest only on the amount of the principal outstanding. When prepayments are made, less dollar interest will be received as the outstanding principal declines. In fact, if prepayments are too fast, the *IO investor may not recover the amount paid for the IO*. The unique aspect of an IO is that its price changes in the *same* direction as the change in interest rates. Moreover, as in the case of the PO, its price is highly responsive to a change in interest rates.

Because of these price volatility characteristics of stripped mortgage-backed securities, institutional investors have used them to control the risk of a portfolio of mortgage-backed securities so as to create a risk/return pattern that better fits their needs.

Key Points That You Should Understand Before Proceeding

1. A stripped mortgage-backed security is created by distributing the principal and interest from a pool of underlying mortgages on an unequal basis to two classes of securityholders.
2. A stripped mortgage-backed security is another example of a derivative mortgage security.
3. Stripped mortgage-backed securities can be used to hedge a portfolio exposed to prepayment risk.
4. There are two types of stripped mortgage-backed securities: partially stripped and IO/PO securities.

NONAGENCY MORTGAGE-BACKED SECURITY

Nonagency MBS represent MBS issued by entities other than Ginnie Mae, Fannie Mae, and Freddie Mac. Nonagency MBS are issued by conduits of (1) commercial banks (e.g., Citigroup's CitiMortgage), (2) investment banking firms, and (3) entities not associated with either commercial banks or investment banking firms (e.g. Countrywide Financial Corp.

For an agency CMO, we said that there are pass-through, CMO, and stripped MBS. Typically, the structure that is used for a nonagency MBS is the CMO structure, referred to as a **nonagency CMO**. The creation of a nonagency CMO is different from that of an agency CMO. When we described agency CMOs, we said that the process first involves pooling loans to create an agency pass-through security. Then a pool of agency pass-through securities is pooled to create an agency CMO. In a nonagency CMO, the loans are pooled and used to create different bond classes, which we refer to as tranches.

Credit Enhancement

Unlike agency MBS, nonagency CMOs are rated by one or more of the credit rating agencies. Because there is no government guarantee or guarantee by a GSE, to receive an investment-grade rating these securities must be structured with additional credit support. The credit support is needed to absorb expected losses from the underlying loan pool due to defaults. This additional credit support is referred to as a **credit enhancement**. There are different forms of credit enhancement: (1) senior-subordinate structure, (2) excess spread, (3) overcollateralization, and (4) **monoline insurance**. We will describe them briefly here.

When rating agencies assign a rating to the tranches in a nonagency CMO, they look at the credit risk associated with a tranche. Basically, that analysis begins by looking at the credit quality of the underlying pool of loans. For example, a pool of loans can consist of prime borrowers or subprime borrowers. Obviously, one would expect that a pool consisting of prime borrowers would have fewer expected losses as a percentage of the dollar amount of the loan pool compared to a pool consisting of subprime borrowers. Given the credit quality of the borrowers in the pool and other factors such as the structure of the transaction, a rating agency will determine the dollar amount of the credit enhancement needed for a particular tranche to receive a specific credit rating. The process by which the rating agencies determine the amount of credit enhancement needed is referred to as *sizing the transaction*.

There are standard mechanisms for providing credit enhancement in nonagency CMOs. We will describe these mechanisms shortly. When prime loans are securitized, the credit enhancement mechanisms and therefore the structures are not complicated. In contrast, when subprime loans are securitized, the structures are more complex because of the need for greater credit enhancement. Since these more complex structures are found in certain types of ABS, market participants classify securitization involving subprime loans as part of the ABS market (recall that they are referred to as mortgage-related ABS).

Senior-Subordinate Structure

In a **senior-subordinate structure**, two general categories of tranches are created: a senior tranche and subordinate tranches. For example, consider the following hypothetical nonagency CMO structure consisting of $400 million of collateral:

Tranche	Principal Amount	Credit Rating
X1	$350 million	AAA
X2	$ 20 million	AA
X3	$ 10 million	A
X4	$ 5 million	BBB
X5	$ 5 million	BB
X6	$ 5 million	B
X7	$ 5 million	not rated

Notice that there are seven tranches in this transaction. The tranche with the highest rating is referred to as the *senior tranche*. The *subordinate tranches* are those below the senior tranche. The rules for the distribution of the cash flow (interest and principal) among the tranches as well as how losses are to be distributed are explained in the prospectus. These rules are referred to as the deal's *waterfall*. Basically, the losses are distributed based on the tranche's position in the structure. Losses start from the bottom (the lowest or unrated tranche) to the senior tranche. For example, if over the life of this nonagency CMO the losses are less than $5 million, only tranche X7 will realize a loss. If the loss is, say, $15 million, tranches X7, X6, X5, and X4 will realize total losses and the other tranches no losses.

Note a few points about this structure. First, the credit enhancement for tranches is being provided by other tranches within the structure. For example, the senior tranche, X1, is being protected against losses up to $50 million. This is because it is only until $50 million of losses are realized that tranche X1 will realize a loss. Tranche X4 has credit enhancement of $20 million because the collateral can realize $20 million in losses before tranche X4 realizes a loss.

Second, compare what is being done to distribute credit risk in this nonagency CMO compared to an agency CMO. In an agency CMO, there is no credit risk. What is being done in creating the different tranches is the redistribution of prepayment risk. In contrast, in a nonagency CMO, there is both credit risk and prepayment risk. By creating the senior-subordinate tranches, credit risk is being redistributed among the tranches in the structure. Hence, what is being done is *credit tranching*. Can prepayment risk also be redistributed? This is typically done in nonagency CMOs but only at the senior tranche level. That is, the $350 million of senior tranches in our hypothetical nonagency CMO structure can be carved up to create senior tranches with different exposure to prepayment risk.

Finally, when the tranches are sold in the market, they are sold at different yields. Obviously, the lower the credit rating of a tranche, the higher the yield at which it must be offered.

Excess Spread

Excess spread is basically the interest from the collateral that is not being used to satisfy the liabilities (i.e., the interest payments to the tranches in the structure) and the fees (such as mortgage servicing and administrative fees). The excess spread can be used to help offset any losses. If the excess spread is retained in the structure rather than paid out, it can be accumulated in a reserve account and used to pay not only current losses experienced by the collateral but future losses. Hence, excess spread is a form of credit enhancement.

Because the loan rate on subprime loans is greater than the loan rate on prime loans and because the expected losses are greater for subprime loans, excess spread is an important source of credit enhancement for subprime MBS.

Overcollateralization

In our hypothetical nonagency CMO, the liabilities are $400 million and are assumed to match the amount of the collateral. Suppose instead that the collateral has a par value of $405 million. This means that the assets exceed the liabilities by $5 million. This excess collateral is referred to as **overcollateralization** and can be used to absorb losses. Hence, it is a form of credit enhancement.

Overcollateralization is more commonly used as a form of credit enhancement in subprime deals than in prime deals. This is one of the aspects that makes subprime deals more complicated because there are a series of tests built into the structure as to when collateral can be released.

Monoline Insurance

Some insurance companies, by charter, provide only financial guarantees. These insurance companies are called *monoline insurance companies*. These are the same companies that provide the guaranty for insured municipal bonds. For RMBS, they provide the same function and therefore this is viewed as a form of credit enhancement.

Subprime Mortgage-Backed Security Meltdown

In the previous chapter, we discussed subprime loans. In this chapter, we discussed their securitization. In the summer of 2007, there was a crisis in the subprime MBS market and this crisis led to a credit and liquidity crisis that had a rippling impact on other sectors of the credit market and the equity market through 2008. This episode is referred to as the "subprime meltdown."

There is a good deal that will be written about this crisis in the future. As of this writing, there are widely differing viewpoints regarding the crisis. Some market observers saw it as the inevitable bursting of the "housing bubble" that had characterized the housing market in prior years. Others viewed it as the product of unsavory practices by mortgage lenders who deceived subprime borrowers into purchasing homes that they could not afford. Moreover, specific mortgage designs such as hybrid interest-only loans, which made it possible for a subprime borrower to obtain a loan that could have been expected to cause financial difficulties in the future when loan rates were adjusted upward in the case of a hybrid loan or higher mortgage payments after the lockout period in the case of an interest-only loan. Of course, mortgage lenders blamed borrowers for misleading them. Another contingent laid the blame at the feet of Wall Street bankers who packaged subprime loans into bonds and sold them to investors and the rating agencies that gave these bonds investment-grade ratings.

Whatever the precise cause, it's hard to deny that securitization—the financial framework that allowed Wall Street to package these loans into RMBS—is of enormous benefit to the economy. Securitization has increased the supply of credit to homeowners and reduced the cost of borrowing. It also spreads the risk among a larger pool of investors rather than concentrating it in a small group of banks and thrifts and makes credit available to a wider group of borrowers. Critics of securitization argue that such borrowers may not be suitable candidates for loans and the only reason why a lender would make such loans is because it does not hold them on its balance sheet but rather sells the loans into the market either to a conduit that will securitize the loans or will securitize them itself.

While it can be argued that not all those who were shut out from the market prior to securitization were in fact weak borrowers, there is no question that in the case of the securitization of subprime loans that the low credit standards of lenders was the major reason for the problem. However, that is an attack on underwriting standards for the mortgage sector and not a reason for attacking securitization in general. Securitization is an important and legitimate way for the financial markets to function more efficiently today than in the past. It is not smoke-and-mirror financial structures that fraudulent companies have used to hide the true nature of their operations. Real securitization, while sometimes complex, generally takes place in regulated debt markets with the participation of sophisticated parties such as underwriters, loan servicers, institutional investors, rating agencies, and monoline insurance companies that provide financial guarantees. Each of these has a unique role that helps to produce a balanced—but not a riskless—result.

As explained in this chapter, the securitization of subprime loans works by dividing pools of credit into classes, or tranches, separated by the amount of risk each class represents. Naturally, the classes with less risk offer lower potential returns while the classes with more risk offer higher potential returns. Investors in the riskier, or more junior, tranches are paid only after the investors in the senior classes are paid. Senior tranches, therefore, are well cushioned from defaults—reflected in typically high credit ratings, but relatively low returns. Similarly, rating agencies generally assign lower ratings to the more junior classes, but classes can earn relatively high returns as long as the pool of loans performs well.

The more junior, riskier classes are purchased by sophisticated institutional investors who understand that they will sometimes incur losses, but hope for high enough returns over a long period of time to offset possible losses. In fact, as we have stressed throughout this book, a financial product is not created randomly. Rather, the demand must come from investors. In the case of RMBS backed by subprime loans, it came ultimately from hedge fund managers. Basically, the major purchasers of subprime MBS were portfolio managers of collateralized debt obligations (CDOs). Managers of CDOs created tranches that were effectively leveraged positions in a portfolio of RMBS. Hedge fund managers bought the tranches that were necessary for a transaction to get done. Thus, in the absence of the demand by hedge fund managers for these tranches, it is likely that fewer CDOs that purchased subprime MBS would have been done. So, one question that must be asked is whether one should be concerned that this institutional investor group was hurt by the subprime meltdown. Hedge funds are in the business of taking large bets and if they do not work out, that's a normal business risk.

Rating agencies were also viewed by some market observers as being a major contributor to the crisis. Recall that to aid investors in comparing the relative credit risk of securities, issuers generally ask one or more rating agency to assign a credit rating to the securitization. Although no one, not even the rating agencies, can always accurately predict the performance of a bond over time, the agencies' long-term track record is solid. Their published research shows that AAA—the highest rated—securities have experienced extraordinarily low credit losses—the lowest among structured credits. AA rated securities have experienced the next lowest losses, and so forth. The research has also demonstrated that the credit loss experience of securitized products is quite similar to that of like-rated corporate securities, so that ratings are comparable across debt markets. However, this does not mean that in every instance, highly rated securities will perform well, or low-rated instruments will perform poorly. The accuracy of ratings, like any other indicator of credit risk, can only be assessed on a statistical basis over a long period of time. Nor does it mean that ratings will necessarily remain the same over time. Rating agencies continually monitor the securities they have rated and as performance and expectations of credit losses change, the agency may upgrade or downgrade a given rating. Unfortunately, it is only the anomalous episodes like the subprime market crisis that captures widespread market attention.

What is surprising is why the crisis occurred in July 2007. There was no new information in the market at the time. Investors knew well before that time all about the potential defaults. Moreover, since 2005, the rating agencies took action that was transparent to the market. Specifically, rating agencies adjusted their criteria and assumptions regarding how they were rating subprime MBS transactions, they downgraded some issues, and they publicly commented on their concerns about the subprime sector.

The impact of the suprime mortgage crisis on the financial markets has been devastating. But the suggestion that it was securitization that caused this would be wrong. In a speech by Robert Steel, Under Secretary of the U.S. Department of the Treasury, before the American Securitization forum in February 5, 2008, he stated:

> The securitization market is an example of how this incredible pace of innovation has changed financial markets. Secretary Paulson and I have been very clear—we believe that the benefits of securitization are significant. It enables investors to improve their risk management, achieve better risk adjusted returns and access more liquidity.
>
> While being an advocate for the benefits of your industry, it is also important for me to be straightforward. We must be honest and admit some degree of malfeasance. It is clear that in some instances market participants acted inappropriately. Secretary Paulson has indicated that certain adjustments to the mortgage process, such as licensing standards for mortgage originators, would help in weeding out the bad actors. Commonsense licensing standards would take into account prior fraudulent or criminal activity, and should require initial and ongoing education.[5]

---

[5] http://www.ustreas.gov/press/releases/hp808.htm

Mr. Steel further remarked

> Secretary Paulson is leading the President's Working Group to evaluate broad, long-term lessons-learned from current challenges, and where appropriate make recommendations.
>
> Securitization can remain a strong market in the future, but market participants must accept some degree of responsibility and commit to lessons-learned.

In a September 20, 2007, article in *The Economist*, "When it goes wrong . . .," the following comment was made regarding securitization

> But do not expect a rush back to the ways of the 1960s. Securitisation has become far too important for that. Indeed, it has not yet fulfilled its promise. Wall Street eggheads may be licking their wounds at present, but they will soon be coming up with even more products. And, given time, there will no doubt be another wave of buying. More importantly, the transformation of sticky debt into something more tradable, for all its imperfections, has forged hugely beneficial links between individual borrowers and vast capital markets that were previously out of reach. As it comes under scrutiny, the debate should be about how this system can be improved, not dismantled.

SUMMARY

In this chapter, we discussed the market for RMBS and the important role that securitization played in the development of the secondary mortgage market. The RMBS market is divided into two sectors: agency MBS and nonagency MBS.

MBS issued by Ginnie Mae, Fannie Mae, and Freddie Mac are included in the agency MBS sector. The loans that are used as collateral in these securities are conforming loans. Agency MBS include pass-through securities, CMOs, and stripped MBS. CMOs are created from pass-through securities to address the prepayment risk associated with investing in pass-through securities—contraction risk and extension risk. CMO tranches are created to meet the different needs of institutional investors. Like a CMO, a stripped MBS is created from a pass-through security. The purpose of creating a stripped MBS is to provide an instrument that can be used to control the risk of a portfolio of mortgage-related securities.

The nonagency MBS market is divided into the private label MBS market and subprime MBS market. Nonagency MBS require that credit enhancement be provided to protect against losses from the underlying pool of loans. Mechanisms for credit enhancement include senior-subordinate structures, excess spread, overcollateralization, and monoline insurance. The senior-subordinate structure allows for the redistribution of credit risk among the tranches in the structure. The difference in the creation of prime MBS and subprime MBS is the complexity of the structure for dealing with credit enhancement.

KEY TERMS

- Accrual tranche
- Agency CMO
- Agency mortgage-backed securities
- Agency pass-through securities
- Agency stripped mortgage-backed securities
- Average life
- Collateralized mortgage obligation (CMO)
- Companion bonds
- Conditional prepayment rate (CPR)
- Contraction risk

- Credit enhancement
- Excess spread
- Extension risk
- Guaranty fee
- Interest-only (IO) class
- Mortgage-backed security (MBS)
- Mortgage pass-through securities
- Mortgage strips
- Monoline insurance
- Nonagency CMO
- Nonagency mortgage-backed securities
- Overcollateralization
- Planned amortization class (PAC) bond
- Prepayment risk
- Prepayment speed
- Principal-only (PO) class
- Private label mortgage-backed securities
- Public Securities Association (PSA) prepayment benchmark
- Residential mortgage-backed security
- Securitize
- Senior-subordinate structure
- Sequential-pay CMOs
- Single-monthly mortality rate (SMM)
- Subprime mortgage-backed securities
- Support bond
- Tranches
- Z bond

QUESTIONS

1. What is a mortgage pass-through security?
2. Describe the cash flow of a mortgage pass-through security.
3. How has securitization enhanced the liquidity of mortgages?
4. What are the different types of agency pass-through securities?
5. How does the guaranty for a Ginnie Mae MBS differ from that of a MBS issued by Fannie Mae and Freddie Mac?
6. What is meant by prepayment risk, contraction risk, and extension risk?
7. Why would a pass-through be an unattractive investment for a savings and loan association?
8. What is meant by the average life of a pass-through?
9. Why is an assumed prepayment speed necessary to project the cash flow of a pass-through?
10. A cash flow for a pass-through typically is based on some prepayment benchmark. Describe the benchmark.
11. What does a conditional prepayment rate of 8% mean?
12. What does 150 PSA mean?
13. How does a CMO alter the cash flow from mortgages so as to shift the prepayment risk across various classes of bondholders?

14. "By creating a CMO, an issuer eliminates the prepayment risk associated with the underlying mortgages." Do you agree with this statement? Explain.
15. Explain the effect of including an accrual tranche in a CMO structure on the average lives of the sequential-pay structures.
16. What types of investors would be attracted to an accrual bond?
17. What was the motivation for the creation of PAC bonds?
18. Describe how the schedule for a PAC tranche is created.
19. a. Why is it necessary for a nonagency MBS to have credit enhancement?
    b. Who determines the amount of credit enhancement needed?
20. What is the difference between a prime and subprime MBS? Be sure to mention how they differ in terms of credit enhancement.
21. a. What is meant by a senior-subordinate structure?
    b. Why is the senior-subordinate structure a form of credit enhancement?
22. How can excess spread be a form of credit enhancement?

Market for Commercial Mortgage Loans and Commercial Morgage-Backed Securities

LEARNING OBJECTIVES

After reading this chapter, you will understand

- how commercial mortgage loans differ from residential mortgage loans

- the different property types for which commercial mortgage loans are obtained

- the two indicators of performance used for evaluating commercial mortgage loans—debt-to-service coverage ratio and loan-to-value ratio

- the different types of call protection provided for in commercial mortgage loans and in a commercial mortgage-backed security

- what balloon risk is for a commercial mortgage loan and a commercial mortgage-backed security

- differences in structuring a commercial mortgage-backed and residential mortgage-backed securities transaction

- the structural features of a commercial mortgage-backed securities deal

- the different types of servicers in a commercial mortgage-backed securities deal

- how commercial mortgage-backed securities trade in the market

The mortgage market consists of residential mortgages and commercial mortgages. Residential mortgage loans are for properties with one to four single-family units and are used to create residential mortgage-backed securities. In this chapter, we look at commercial mortgage loans and securities backed by commercial mortgages—commercial mortgage-backed securities.

COMMERCIAL MORTGAGE LOANS

Commercial mortgage loans are for mortgage loans for income-producing properties. A commercial mortgage loan is originated either to finance the purchase of a commercial property or to refinance a prior mortgage obligation on a commercial property. Commercial mortgage loans are **nonrecourse loans**, which means that if the borrower fails to make the contractual payments, the lender can only look to the income-producing property backing the loan for interest and principal repayment.

The major property types that have been securitized are

- multifamily properties
- apartment buildings
- office buildings
- industrial properties (including warehouses)
- shopping centers
- hotels
- health care facilities (e.g., senior housing care facilities)

Indicators of Potential Performance

Because commercial mortgage loans are nonrecourse loans, the lender looks only to the property to generate sufficient cash flow to repay principal and to pay interest. If there is a default, the lender looks to the proceeds from the sale of the property for repayment and has no recourse to the borrower for any unpaid balance. There are different risks associated with investing in each property type.

Regardless of the property type, the two measures that have been found to be key indicators of the potential credit performance are the debt-to-service coverage ratio and the loan-to-value ratio.

The **debt-to-service coverage (DSC) ratio** is the ratio of a property's **net operating income (NOI)** divided by the debt service. The NOI is defined as the rental income reduced by cash operating expenses (adjusted for a replacement reserve). A ratio greater than 1 means that the cash flow from the property is sufficient to cover debt servicing. The higher the ratio, the more likely it is that the borrower will be able to meet debt servicing from the property's cash flow.

The **loan-to-value (LTV) ratio** is a measure used in residential mortgage loans. For residential mortgage loans, "value" is either market value or appraised value. For income-producing properties, the value of the property is based on the fundamental principles of valuation: The value of an asset is the present value of its expected cash flow. Valuation requires projecting an asset's cash flow and discounting it at an appropriate interest rate(s). In valuing commercial property, the cash flow is the future NOI. A discount rate (a single rate), referred to as the "capitalization rate," reflecting the risks associated with the cash flow is then used to compute the present value of the future NOI. Consequently, there can be considerable variation in the estimates of NOI and the appropriate capitalization rate in estimating a property's value. Thus, investors are often skeptical about estimates of value and the resulting LTVs reported for properties.

Call Protection

For residential mortgage loans, only prepayment penalty mortgages provide some protection against prepayments. For commercial mortgage loans, call protection can take the following forms: (1) prepayment lockout, (2) defeasance, (3) prepayment penalty points, and (4) yield maintenance charges.

A **prepayment lockout** is a contractual agreement that prohibits any prepayments during a specified period of time, called the **lockout period**. The lockout period can be from two to 10 years. After the lockout period, call protection usually comes in the form of either prepayment penalty points or yield maintenance charges.

With **defeasance**, the borrower provides sufficient funds for the servicer to invest in a portfolio of Treasury securities that replicates the cash flows that would exist in the absence of prepayments. Defeasance is a method commonly used by municipal bond issuers for prerefunding a bond issue. For example, in May 2005, the Fountainbleau Hilton in Miami was defeased.

Prepayment penalty points are predetermined penalties that must be paid by the borrower if the borrower wishes to refinance. For example, 5-4-3-2-1 is a common prepayment penalty point structure. That is, if the borrower wishes to prepay during the first year, the borrower must pay a 5% penalty; in the second year, a 4% penalty would apply; and so on.

A **yield maintenance charge**, in its simplest terms, is designed to make the lender indifferent as to the timing of prepayments. The yield maintenance charge, also called the make whole charge, makes it uneconomical to refinance solely to get a lower mortgage rate. The simplest and most restrictive form of yield maintenance charge ("Treasury flat yield maintenance") penalizes the borrower based on the difference between the mortgage coupon rate and the prevailing Treasury rate.

Balloon Maturity Provisions

Commercial mortgage loans are typically balloon loans requiring substantial principal payment at the end of the balloon term. If the borrower fails to make the balloon payment, the borrower is in default. The lender may extend the loan and in so doing will typically modify the original loan terms. During the workout period for the loan, a higher interest rate will be charged, the **default interest rate**. The risk that a borrower will not be able to make the balloon payment because the borrower either cannot arrange for refinancing by the balloon payment date or cannot sell the property to generate sufficient funds to pay off the balloon balance is called **balloon risk**. Because the term of the loan will be extended by the lender during the workout period, balloon risk is also referred to as **extension risk**.

Key Points That You Should Understand Before Proceeding

1. Commercial mortgage loans are nonrecourse loans for the purchase of income-producing properties, the major ones being apartment buildings, office buildings, industrial properties, shopping centers, hotels, and health care facilities.
2. The two measures that have been found to be key indicators of the potential credit performance of a commercial mortgage loan are the DSC ratio and the LTV ratio.
3. Call protection for commercial mortgage loans includes prepayment lockout, defeasance, prepayment penalty points, and yield maintenance charges.
4. Balloon risk associated with a commercial mortgage loan is the risk that a borrower will not be able to make the balloon payment because either the borrower cannot arrange for refinancing at the balloon payment date or cannot sell the property to generate sufficient funds to pay off the balloon balance.

COMMERCIAL MORTGAGE-BACKED SECURITIES

Many types of commercial loans can be sold by the originator as a commercial whole loan or structured into a **commercial mortgage-backed security (CMBS)** transaction. A CMBS is a security backed by one or more commercial mortgage loans. The whole loan market, which is largely dominated by insurance companies and banks, is focused on loans between $10 and $50 million issued on traditional property types (multifamily, retail, office, and industrial). CMBS transactions, on the other hand, can involve loans of virtually any size (from as small as $1 million to single property transactions as large as $200 million) and/or property type. Worldwide, the four largest property types that have been securitized, representing more than 80% of market issuance, have been retail properties such as shopping centers, office buildings, hotels, and multifamily houses. In the first quarter of 2006, for example, the share of these four property types in CMBS was as follows: shopping centers (36%), office buildings (23%), hotels (14%), and multifamily houses (13%).[1]

Issuers of Commercial Mortgage-Backed Securities

As with residential mortgage-backed securities (RMBS), CMBS can be issued by Ginnie Mae, Fannie Mae, Freddie Mac, and private entities. All of the securities issued by Ginnie Mae, Fannie Mae, and Freddie Mac are consistent with their mission of providing funding for residential housing. This includes securities backed by nursing home projects and health care facilities.

Ginnie Mae–issued securities are backed by Federal Housing Administration–insured multifamily housing loans. These loans are called **project loans**. From these loans, Ginnie Mae creates project loan pass-through securities. The securities can be backed by a single project loan on a completed project or one or more project loans. Freddie Mac and Fannie Mae purchase multifamily loans from approved lenders and either retain them in their portfolio or use them as collateral for a security. This is no different from what these two government-sponsored enterprises do with single-family mortgage loans that they acquire.

Although securities backed by Ginnie Mae and issued by the two government-sponsored enterprises constitute the largest sector of the RMBS market, it is the securities issued by private entities that is by far the largest sector of the CMBS market. Typically, it is more than 97% of the market.

CMBS are backed by either newly originated or seasoned commercial mortgage loans. Most CMBS are backed by newly originated loans. CMBS can be classified by the type of loan pool. The first type of CMBS are those backed by a single borrower. Usually such CMBS are backed by large properties such as regional malls or office buildings. The investors in this type of CMBS are insurance companies. In the first quarter of 2006, single-borrower deals represented about 12% of market issuance in the U.S. market but 71% of deals outside the United States.

The second type of CMBS is that backed by loans to multiple borrowers. This is the most common type of CMBS and is backed by a variety of property types. The most prevalent form of deal backed by commercial mortgage loans to multiple borrowers is the **conduit deal**. These deals are created by investment banking firms that establish a conduit arrangement with

---

[1] As reported by *Commercial Mortgage Alert*.

mortgage bankers to originate commercial mortgage loans specifically for the purpose of securitizing them (i.e., creating CMBS). The mortgage bankers originate and underwrite the loans using the capital provided by the investment banking firm. There are multiple borrower CMBS deals that combine loans that are included in conduit deals with a large or "mega" loan. These CMBS deals are called **fusion deals** or **hybrid deals**. For the first quarter of 2006, fusion deals dominated the U.S. market—79% of market issuance—while outside the United States, conduit/fusion deals made up 23% of market issuance.

As noted earlier, a CMBS deal can be backed by seasoned commercial mortgage loans. A seasoned loan is one that is already residing on the balance sheet of a bank or insurance company. Typically, the reason why a bank or insurance company will securitize a seasoned commercial loan is to remove the loan from its balance sheet; that is, it uses securitization to restructure its balance sheet. CMBS deals in the United States that are backed by seasoned collateral usually represent less than 3% of market issuance.

Servicers

As with a nonagency RMBS, a servicer is required and plays an important role. The responsibilities of the servicer include collecting monthly loan payments, keeping records relating to payments, maintaining property escrow for taxes and insurance, monitoring the condition of underlying properties, preparing reports for the trustee, and transferring collected funds to the trustee for payment to bondholders.

In a CMBS transaction, there is usually a master servicer and special servicer. The **master servicer** is responsible for (1) overseeing the deal, (2) verifying that all servicing agreements are being maintained, and (3) facilitating the timely payment of interest and principal. This last function is critical for a CMBS transaction. If a loan is in default, it is the master servicer that must provide for servicing advances. To fulfill this role, the master servicer must have the financial capacity to provide advances.

A **special servicer** is responsible for delinquent loans and workout situations. Basically, the objective of the special service is to maximize the recovery of defaulted loans.

Illustration of a Commercial Mortgage-Backed Security Deal

In the previous chapter, we discussed how an agency CMO and a nonagency CMO are created. The structure of a CMBS deal is much the same. There are different bond classes or tranches and there are rules for the distribution of interest, principal, and losses.

Table 1 shows the bond classes of a CMBS deal, Banc of America Commercial Mortgage Trust 2006-1. Only the bond classes offered to the public are identified. The credit rating for each bond class is shown. For the bond classes offered, the senior certificates in this CMBS deal are Class A-1, Class A-2, Class A-3A, Class A-3B, Class A-4, Class A-1A, and Class XP Certificates. The junior certificates are Class A-M, Class A-J, Class B, Class C, and Class D. The subordination (credit support), priority of payment, and order of loss allocation as set forth in the prospectus supplement are reproduced in Figure 1.

The mortgage pool consists of 192 loans. A loan may be for more than one property. Table 2 shows the number of mortgage properties by type. The 10 largest loans in the mortgage pool are listed in Table 3, along with the LTV and DSC ratios at the time of issuance.

The master servicer for this deal is Capital Markets Servicing Group of Bank of America. The special servicer is Midland Loan Services, Inc.

Table 1	CMBS Deal Illustration: Banc of America Commercial Mortgage Trust 2006-1		
Class	Balance	Coupon Rate	Moody/S&P Rating
Class A-1	$ 81,500,000	5.219%	Aaa/AAA
Class A-2	84,400,000	5.334%	Aaa/AAA
Class A-3A	130,100,000	5.447%	Aaa/AAA
Class A-3B	25,000,000	5.447%	Aaa/AAA
Class A-4	616,500,000	5.372%[a]	Aaa/AAA
Class A-1A	355,399,000	5.378%[a]	Aaa/AAA
Class A-M	203,766,000	5.421%[a]	Aaa/AAA
Class A-J	142,637,000	5.46%[a]	Aaa/AAA
Class XP	1,989,427,000	0.3406%[b]	Aaa/AAA
Class B	20,377,000	5.49%[a]	Aa1/AA+
Class C	22,924,000	5.509%[a]	Aa2/AA
Class D	20,376,000	5.6424%[c]	Aa3/AA−

(a) The Class A-4, Class A-1A, Class A-M, Class A-J, Class B, and Class C Certificates will each accrue interest at a fixed rate subject to a cap at the weighted average net mortgage rate.
(b) The Class D Certificates will accrue interest at the weighted average net mortgage rate minus 0.134%.
(c) The Class XP Certificates will accrue interest on their related notional amount as described in the prospectus supplement.

Source: *Prospectus Supplement*

Differences Between CMBS and Nonagency RMBS Structuring

The structure of a transaction is the same as in a nonagency RMBS in that most structures have multiple bond classes (tranches) with different ratings, and there are rules for the distribution of interest and principal to the bond classes. However, there are three major differences due to the features of the underlying loans.[2]

First, as explained earlier, prepayment terms for commercial mortgages differ significantly from residential mortgages. The former impose prepayment penalties or restrictions on prepayments. Although there are residential mortgages with prepayment penalties, they are a small fraction of the market. In structuring a CMBS, there are rules for the allocation of any prepayment penalties among the bondholders. In addition, if there is a defeasance, the credit risk of a CMBS virtually disappears because it is then backed by U.S. Treasury securities.

The second difference in structuring is due to the significant difference between commercial and residential mortgages with respect to the role of the servicer when there is a default. With commercial mortgages, the loan can be transferred by the servicer to the *special* servicer when the borrower is in default, imminent default, or in violation of covenants. The key here is that it is transferred when there is an imminent default. The special servicer has the responsibility of modifying the loan terms in the case of an imminent default to reduce the likelihood of default. There is no equivalent feature for a residential mortgage in the case of an imminent default. The particular choice of action that may be taken by the special servicer for a commercial mortgage will generally have different effects on the various bond classes in a CMBS structure. Moreover, there can be a default due to

---

[2] David P. Jacob, James M. Manzi, and Frank J. Fabozzi, "The Impact of Structuring on CMBS Bond Class Performance," Chapter 51 in Frank J. Fabozzi (ed.), *The Handbook of Mortgage-Backed Securities*, 6th ed. (New York: McGraw-Hill, 2006).

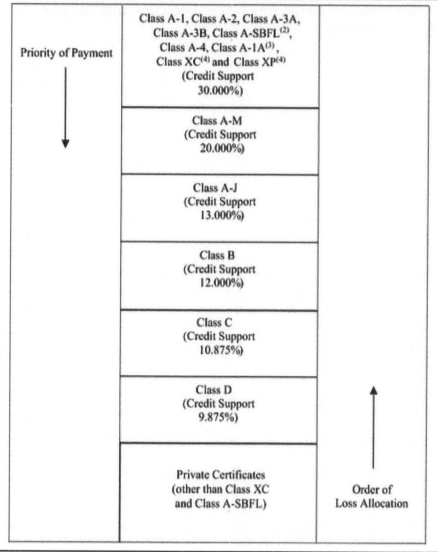

Figure 1 Subordination (Credit Support),[1] Priority of Payment, and Order of Loss Allocation for Banc of America Commercial Mortgage Trust 2006-1

Priority of Payment

Class A-1, Class A-2, Class A-3A, Class A-3B, Class A-SBFL[2], Class A-4, Class A-1A[3], Class XC[4] and Class XP[4] (Credit Support 30.000%)

Class A-M (Credit Support 20.000%)

Class A-J (Credit Support 13.000%)

Class B (Credit Support 12.000%)

Class C (Credit Support 10.875%)

Class D (Credit Support 9.875%)

Private Certificates (other than Class XC and Class A-SBFL)

Order of Loss Allocation

Notes:

[1] The credit support percentage set forth in this chart shows the aggregate initial class balance of the classes of certificates subordinate to a class or classes as a percentage of the initial aggregate principal balance of the mortgage loans.

[2] The Class A-SBFL regular interest has a certain priority with respect to being paid down to its planned principal balance on any distribution date as described in this prospectus supplement.

[3] The Class A-1A Certificates generally have a priority entitlement to principal payments received in respect of mortgage loans included in loan group 2. The Class A-1, Class A-2, Class A-3A, Class A-3B and Class A-4 Certificates and the Class A-SBFL regular interest generally have a priority entitlement to principal payments received in respect of mortgage loans included in loan group 1. See "Description of the Certificates—The Available Distribution Amount" in this prospectus supplement.

[4] The Class XC and Class XP Certificates will be senior only with respect to payments of interest and will not be entitled to receive any payments in respect of principal.

No other form of credit enhancement will be available for the benefit of the holders of the offered certificates.

In addition, while mortgage loan losses will not be directly allocated to the Class A-SBFL certificates, mortgage loan losses allocated to the Class A-SBFL regular interest will result in a corresponding decrease in the certificate balance of the Class A-SBFL certificates, and any interest shortfalls suffered by the Class A-SBFL regular interest will reduce the amount of interest distributed on the Class A-SBFL certificates.

Any allocation of a loss to the Class A-SBFL regular interest (and the corresponding Class A-SBFL certificates) will reduce the principal amount of the Class A-SBFL regular interest (and the corresponding Class A-SBFL certificates).

Source: Prospectus Supplement

Table 2   Property Types Included in Banc of America Commercial Mortgage Trust 2006-1

Property Type	Number of Mortgaged Properties	Balance	% of Initial Pool Balance
Office	34	$401,697,123	19.7%
Multifamily	45	320,198,140	15.7
Hotel	19	209,246,699	10.3
Other	713	149,625,000	7.3
Self Storage	38	123,898,067	6.1
Industrial	13	94,209,849	4.6
Manufactured Housing	6	63,940,000	3.1
Mixed Use	6	32,283,553	1.6

Source: *Prospectus Supplement*

Table 3   Ten Largest Loans in Banc of America Commercial Mortgage Trust 2006-1

Loan Name	Balance at Cutoff Date	% of Initial Pool Balance	Property Type	Cutoff Date LTV Ratio	DSCR	Mortage Rate
KinderCare Portfolio	$149,625,000	7.3%	Other	40.8%	3.21x	5.24%
Desert Passage	131,883,334	6.5	Retail	72.6	1.28	5.46
Waterfront at Port Chester	110,000,000	5.4	Retail	71.9	1.2	5.46
Fairmont Sonoma Mission Inn & Spa	55,000,000	2.7	Hotel	52.1	1.94	5.4
Torre Mayor	55,000,000	2.7	Office	38.3	1.8	7.55
Medical Mutual Headquarters	52,715,219	2.6	Office	73.2	1.2	5.65
Frandor Shopping Center	39,500,000	1.9	Retail	57	1.53	5.46
Metro Plaza at Jersey City	39,000,000	1.9	Retail	75	1.2	5.73
Plaza Antonio	39,000,000	1.9	Retail	65.7	1.2	6.08
Main Event Portfolio	35,512,892	1.7	Retail	68.6	1.45	5.62
Total/Wtd Avg	**$707,236,445**	**34.7%**		**60.2%**	**1.78x**	**5.64%**

Source: *Prospectus Supplement*

failure to make the balloon payment at the end of the loan term. There can be differences in loans as to how to deal with defaults due to a failure to meet the balloon payment. Thus, balloon risk must be taken into account in structuring a CMBS transaction, which because of the significant size of the payment can have a considerable impact on the cash flow of the structure. Balloon risk is not something that has to be dealt with in structuring an RMBS.

The third difference in structuring between CMBS and RMBS has to do with the role of the buyers when the structure is being created. More specifically, potential buyers of the junior bond classes are typically first sought by the issuer before the deal is structured. The potential buyers first review the proposed pool of mortgage loans, and in the review process, depending on market demand for CMBS products, may request the removal of some loans from the pool. This phase in the structuring process, which one does not find in RMBS transactions, provides an additional layer of security for the senior buyers, particularly because some of the buyers of the junior classes have tended to be knowledgeable real estate investors.

How Commercial Mortgage-Backed Securities Trade in the Market

One might think that because CMBS and RMBS are backed by mortgage loans, they would trade in a similar manner in the marketplace. That is not the case, and the primary reason has to do with the greater prepayment protection afforded investors in CMBS compared to RMBS. We described that protection at the loan level. At the structure level (i.e., when the commercial mortgage loans are pooled to create a CMBS), certain tranches can be created that give even greater prepayment protection. We described how this is done for certain RMBS tranches in collateralized mortgage obligations. As a result, CMBS trade much like corporate bonds.[3]

Key Points That You Should Understand Before Proceeding

1. A CMBS is a security backed by one or more commercial mortgage loans, the loans being either newly originated or seasoned loans.
2. A CMBS can be issued by Ginnie Mae, Fannie Mae, Freddie Mac, and private entities.
3. A CMBS can be classified by the type of loan pool: CMBS with loans from a single borrower and those with loans from multiple borrowers.
4. The most prevalent form of deal backed by commercial mortgage loans to multiple borrowers is the conduit deal.
5. Fusion or hybrid deals are multiple borrower CMBS deals that combine loans that are included in conduit deals with a large or "mega" loan.
6. In a CMBS transaction, there is usually a master servicer and special servicer, the former responsible for overseeing the deal, verifying that all servicing agreements are being maintained, and facilitating the timely payment of interest and principal.

SUMMARY

Commercial mortgage loans are for income-producing properties. Commercial mortgage loans are nonrecourse loans. Consequently, the lender looks only to the property to generate sufficient cash flow to repay principal and to pay interest and, if there is a default, the lender looks to the proceeds from the sale of the property for repayment.

Two measures that have been found to be important measures of potential credit performance for a commercial mortgage loan are the DSC ratio and the LTV ratio. For commercial mortgage loans, call protection can take one or more of the following forms: prepayment lockout, defeasance, prepayment penalty points, or yield maintenance charges. Commercial mortgage loans are typically balloon loans requiring substantial principal

---

[3] See Brian P. Lancaster, "Introduction to Commercial Mortgage-Backed Securities," Chapter 23 in Frank J. Fabozzi (ed.), *The Handbook of Nonagency Mortgage-Backed Securities* (Hoboken, NJ: John Wiley & Sons, 1999).

payment at the end of the balloon term. If the borrower fails to make the balloon payment, the borrower is in default. Balloon risk, also called extension risk, is the risk that a borrower will not be able to make the balloon payment because the borrower either cannot arrange for refinancing at the balloon payment date or cannot sell the property to generate sufficient funds to pay off the balloon balance.

CMBS are issued by Ginnie Mae, Fannie Mae, Freddie Mac, and private entities, with the latter representing the largest part of the market. The structure of a transaction is the same as in a nonagency residential mortgage-backed security, with the typical structure having multiple bond classes with different ratings. There are rules for the distribution of interest and principal to the bond classes and the distribution of losses. However, there are differences in structuring transactions due to prepayment features, the role of the special servicer in the case of imminent default, and the role of potential investors when the deal is being structured.

KEY TERMS

- Balloon risk
- Commercial mortgage-backed security (CMBS)
- Commercial mortgage loans
- Conduit deal
- Debt-to-service coverage (DSC) ratio
- Default interest rate
- Defeasance
- Extension risk
- Fusion deal
- Hybrid deal

- Loan-to-value (LTV) ratio
- Lockout period
- Master servicer
- Net operating income (NOI)
- Nonrecourse loans
- Prepayment lockout
- Prepayment penalty points
- Project loans
- Special servicer
- Yield maintenance charge

QUESTIONS

1. What is a commercial mortgage loan?
2. How is the NOI of a commercial property determined?
3. Why might an investor be skeptical about the LTV ratio for a commercial mortgage loan?
4. What is the underlying principle for a yield maintenance charge?
5. What types of prepayment protection provisions result in a prepayment premium being paid if a borrower prepays?
6. Why is balloon risk referred to as extension risk?
7. What are the major differences in structuring CMBS and RMBS transactions?
8. What are the typical duties of a special servicer?
9. The following statement was made in a special report, *Commercial Mortgage Special Report*

(September 19, 2005, p. 2) by Fitch Ratings: "Defeasance of a loan in a CMBS transaction is a positive credit event." Explain why.
10. Explain whether you agree or disagree with each of the following statements:
    a. "The largest sector of the CMBS market is securities issued by agencies and government-sponsored securities."
    b. "Most CMBS deals are backed by newly originated commercial mortgage loans."
    c. "A fusion CMBS deal has only one single large borrower."
11. Why do CMBS trade in the market more like corporate bonds than RMBS?

Asset-Backed Securities Markets

LEARNING OBJECTIVES

After reading this chapter, you will understand

- how asset-backed securities are created

- the basic structure of a securitization

- the parties to a securitization

- the primary motivation for a corporation to raise funds via a securitization

- the role of the special purpose vehicle

- the different types of structures: self-liquidating and revolving

- the various forms of credit enhancement

- the cash flow characteristics of the major types of asset-backed securities not backed by residential mortgage loans

- the credit risks associated with asset-backed securities

- the role of securitization in financial markets

A security created by pooling loans other than residential prime mortgage loans is referred to as an **asset-backed security (ABS)**. The market classifies securities backed by subprime mortgage loans as mortgage-related ABS. The two types of assets that can be used as collateral for an asset-backed securitization are existing assets/existing receivables or assets/receivables to arise in the future. Securitizations with the former type of collateral are referred to as **existing asset securitizations**. Securitizations of assets/receivables to arise in the future are referred to as **future flow securitizations**. The types of non–real estate–related assets that have been securitized include consumer and commercial loans/receivables. Consumer loans/receivables that have been securitized include auto loans and leases, credit card receivables, student loans, and home improvement loans. Commercial loans/receivables that have been securitized include trade receivables (e.g., health care receivables), equipment leases, operating assets (e.g., aircraft, marine cargo containers), entertainment assets (e.g., film rights, music publishing royalties), franchise loans, small business loans, and whole businesses.

In this chapter, we will discuss the basic features of ABS and the motivation for their issuance, and provide an overview of the five major non-mortgage-related ABS types.

CREATION OF AN ASSET-BACKED SECURITY

To explain how an ABS is created and to understand the parties to a securitization, we will use an illustration.

Suppose that Exception Dental Equipment Inc. manufactures high-quality dental equipment. Although the company has cash sales, a bulk of its sales are from installment sales contracts. An installment sale contract is a loan to the buyer of the dental equipment (e.g., a dental practice) wherein the buyer agrees to repay Exceptional Dental Equipment Inc. over a specified period of time for the amount borrowed plus interest. The dental equipment purchased is the collateral for the loan. We will assume that the loans are all for five years.

The credit department of Exceptional Dental Equipment Inc. makes the decision as to whether or not to extend credit to a customer. That is, the credit department will receive a credit application from a potential customer and, based on criteria established by the company, will decide whether to make a loan. The criteria for granting a loan are referred to as **underwriting standards**. Because Exceptional Dental Equipment Inc. is granting the loan, the company is referred to as the **originator** of the loan.

Moreover, Exceptional Dental Equipment Inc. may have a department that is responsible for servicing the loan. Servicing involves collecting payments from borrowers, notifying borrowers who may be delinquent, and, when necessary, recovering and disposing of the collateral (i.e., the dental equipment in our illustration) if the borrower fails to make the contractual loan payments. While the servicer of the loans need not be the originator of the loans, in our illustration we are assuming that Exceptional Dental Equipment Inc. is the servicer.

Now let's get to how these loans are used in a securitization transaction. We will assume that Exceptional Dental Equipment Inc. has more than $300 million of installment sales contracts. We will further assume that Exceptional Dental Equipment Inc. wants to raise $300 million. Rather than issuing corporate bonds for $300 million, the treasurer of the corporation decides to raise the funds via a securitization. To do so, Exceptional Dental Equipment Inc. will set up a legal entity referred to as a **special purpose vehicle (SPV)**. At this point, we will not explain the purpose of this legal entity, but it will be made clear later that the SPV is critical in a securitization transaction. In our illustration, the SPV that is set up is called DE Asset Trust (DEAT). Exceptional Dental Equipment Inc. will then sell to DEAT $300 million of the loans. Exceptional Dental Equipment Inc. will receive from DEAT $300 million in cash, the amount of funds it wanted to raise. DEAT obtains the $300 million by selling securities that are backed by the $300 million of loans. The securities are the ABS we referred to earlier. In the prospectus for a securitization, these securities are usually referred to as *certificates*.

The Parties to a Securitization

Let's make sure we understand the parties to a securitization. In our hypothetical securitization, Exceptional Dental Equipment Inc. is not the issuer of the ABS (although it is sometimes referred to as the issuer because it is the entity that ultimately raises the funds). Rather, it originated the loans. Hence, in this transaction, Exceptional Dental Equipment Inc. is called the "seller." The reason it is referred to as the "seller" is because it sold the receivables to DEAT. Exceptional Dental Equipment Inc. is also called the "originator" because it originated the loans. The SPV in a securitization is referred to as the "issuer" or "trust" in the prospectus.

In our simple transaction, Exceptional Dental Equipment Inc. manufactured the dental equipment and originated the loans. But there is another type of securitization transaction involving another company, called a **conduit**, that buys the loans and securitizes them. For example, consider a hypothetical company, Dental Equipment Financing Corporation, whose business is to provide financing to dental equipment manufacturers who want to sell their equipment on an installment basis. Dental Equipment Financing Corporation would then develop a relationship with manufacturers of dental equipment (such as Exceptional Dental Equipment Inc.) to purchase their installment contracts. Dental Equipment Financing Corporation would warehouse the installment contracts purchased until it had a sufficient amount to sell to an SPV, which would then issue the ABS.

There will be a trustee for the securities issued. The responsibilities of the trustee are to represent the interests of the bond classes by monitoring compliance with covenants and in the event of default to enforce remedies as specified in the governing documents.[1]

Transaction Structure

In creating the various bond classes (or tranches) in a securitization, there will be rules for distribution of principal and interest. As explained in the previous chapter, the creation of the different bond classes results in securities with different risk/return characteristics. The structure is designed to create bond classes with investment characteristics that are more attractive to institutional investors. By doing so, the entity seeking to raise funds can obtain the best price for the securities it sells (referred to as "best execution").

As explained in the previous chapter, nonagency mortgage-backed securities are credit enhanced. All asset-backed securities are credit enhanced. Credit enhancement levels are determined relative to a specific rating desired by the seller/servicer for a security by each rating agency. Typically in a securitization, there are at least two classes of bondholders: senior bond classes and subordinate bond classes. This structure is the senior/subordinate structure.

Role of the Special Purpose Vehicle

To understand the role of the SPV, we need to understand why a corporation would want to raise funds via securitization rather than simply issue corporate bonds. There are four

---

[1] For a further discussion of the role of the trustee in a securitization, see Karen Cook and F. Jim Della Sala, "The Role of the Trustee in Asset-Backed Securities," Chapter 7 in Frank J. Fabozzi (ed.), *Handbook of Structured Financial Products* (Hoboken, NJ: John Wiley & Sons, 1998).

principal reasons why a corporation may elect to raise funds via a securitization rather than a corporate bond:

1. the potential for reducing funding costs
2. to diversify funding sources
3. to accelerate earnings for financial reporting purposes
4. for regulated entities, potential relief from capital requirements

We will only focus on the first of these reasons in order to see the critical role of the SPV in a securitization.[2]

Let's suppose that Exceptional Dental Equipment Inc. has a double B credit rating (i.e., a below investment-grade credit rating). If it wants to raise funds equal to $300 million by issuing a corporate bond, its funding cost would be whatever the benchmark Treasury yield is plus a credit spread for double B issuers. Suppose, instead, that Exceptional Dental Equipment Inc. uses $300 million of its installment sales contracts (i.e., the loans it has made to customers) as collateral for a bond issue. What will be its funding cost? It probably will be the same as if it issued a corporate bond. The reason is that if Exceptional Dental Equipment Inc. defaults on any of its outstanding debt, the creditors will go after all its assets, including the loans to its customers.

Suppose that Exceptional Dental Equipment Inc. can create a legal entity and sell the loans to that entity. That entity is the SPV. In our illustration, the SPV is DEAT. If the sale of the loans by Exceptional Dental Equipment Inc. to DEAT is done properly,[3] DEAT then legally owns the receivables, not Exceptional Dental Equipment Inc. As a result, if Exceptional Dental Equipment Inc. is ever forced into bankruptcy while the loans sold to DEAT are still outstanding, the creditors of Exceptional Dental Equipment Inc. cannot recover the loans because they are legally owned by DEAT.

The legal implication is that when DEAT issues the ABS that are backed by the loans, investors contemplating the purchase of any bond class will evaluate the credit risk associated with collecting the payments due on the loans independent of the credit rating of Exceptional Dental Equipment Inc. The credit rating assigned to the different bond classes created in the securitization will depend on how the rating agencies will evaluate the credit risk based on the collateral (i.e., the loans). In turn, this will depend on the credit enhancement for each bond class. So, due to the SPV, quality of the collateral, and credit enhancement, a corporation can raise funds via a securitization where some of the bond classes have a credit rating better than the corporation seeking to raise funds and where in the aggregate the funding cost is less than issuing corporate bonds.

Credit Enhancement Mechanisms

The different forms of credit enhancement for nonagency mortgage-backed securities and commercial mortgage-backed securities include external credit enhancement and internal credit enhancement. The credit enhancement forms are used both individually and in combination, depending on the loan types that are backing the securities.

External credit enhancement involves a guarantee from a third party. The risk faced by an investor is the potential for the third party to be downgraded and, as a result, the bond

---

[2] For a discussion of the other reasons, see W. Alexander Roever and Frank J. Fabozzi, "Primer on Securitization," *Journal of Structured and Project Finance* (Summer 2003), pp. 5–19.
[3] More specifically, it has to be a sale of the loans at a fair market value.

classes guaranteed by the third party may be downgraded. The most common form of external credit enhancement is **bond insurance**, referred to as a **surety bond** or a **wrap**. Bond insurance is a financial guaranty from a monoline insurance company requiring that the insurer guarantee the timely payments of principal and interest if these payments cannot be satisfied from the cash flow from the underlying loan pool. The principal payments will be made without acceleration, except if the insurer elects to do so. However, the downgrading of the monoline insurers in 2008 makes it unlikely that this form of credit enhancement will be significant in the future.

Internal credit enhancements come in more complicated forms than external credit enhancements and may alter the cash flow characteristics of the loans even in the absence of default. Credit enhancement levels are determined by the rating agencies from which the issuer seeks a rating for the bond classes. This is referred to as "sizing" the transaction and is based on the rating agencies' expectations for the performance of the loans collateralizing the deal in question.

Most securitization transactions that employ internal credit enhancements follow a predetermined schedule that prioritizes the manner in which principal and interest generated by the underlying collateral must be used. This schedule, which is explained in the deal's prospectus, is known as the **cash flow waterfall**, or simply the **waterfall**. At the top of the waterfall would be cash flows due to senior bondholders (interest and principal, depending upon the principal repayment schedule) as well as some standard fees and expenses (e.g., administration and servicing fee). After the cash flow obligations at the top of the waterfall are met, cash flows down to lower priority classes (those AA, A, and BBB bond classes and so on). The cash flows that remain after all of the scheduled periodic payment obligations are met is the **excess spread**. The excess spread is the first line of defense against collateral losses, because deals that are structured to have a large amount of excess spread can absorb relatively large levels of collateral losses. If the excess spread is fully eaten away by losses, the next lowest-rated class will begin to be negatively affected by credit losses.

The most common forms of internal credit enhancement are senior/subordinate structures, overcollateralization, and reserve funds.

Example of an Actual Securitization

Let's look at an actual securitization—Caterpillar Financial Asset Trust 1997-A. For this securitization, Caterpillar Financial Asset Trust 1997-A is the SPV, the issuer, and the trust. The collateral (i.e., financial assets) for the transaction is a pool of retail installment sales contracts that are secured by new and used machinery manufactured primarily by Caterpillar Inc. The retail installment sales contracts carry a fixed interest rate and were originated by the Caterpillar Financial Funding Corporation, a wholly owned subsidiary of Caterpillar Financial Services Corporation. Caterpillar Financial Services Corporation is a wholly owned subsidiary of Caterpillar Inc., and because it sold the retail installment sales contracts to Caterpillar Financial Asset Trust 1997-A, Caterpillar Financial Funding Corporation is referred to in the prospectus as the "Seller."

The prospectus states that:

THE NOTES REPRESENT OBLIGATIONS OF THE ISSUER ONLY AND DO NOT REPRESENT OBLIGATIONS OF OR INTERESTS IN CATERPILLAR

FINANCIAL FUNDING CORPORATION, CATERPILLAR FINANCIAL SER-
VICES CORPORATION, CATERPILLAR INC. OR ANY OF THEIR RESPECTIVE
AFFILIATES.

As previously noted, this is the key feature in a securitization transaction—the separation of the collateral from the creditors of Caterpillar Inc. The servicer of the retail installment sales contracts is Caterpillar Financial Services Corporation, a wholly owned finance
subsidiary of Caterpillar Inc., referred to as the "Servicer" in the prospectus. For servicing
the collateral, Caterpillar Financial Services Corporation receives a servicing fee of 100
basis points of the outstanding loan balance.

The securities were issued on May 19, 1997, and had a par value of $337,970,000. In the
prospectus, the securities were referred to as "asset-backed notes." The structure was as follows. There were four rated bond classes:

Bond Class	Par Value
Class A-1	$ 88,000,000
Class A-2	$128,000,000
Class A-3	$108,100,000
Class B	$ 13,870,000

This is a senior-subordinate structure. The senior bond classes in this transaction are
Class A-1, Class A-2, and Class A-3. The subordinate class is Class B. The cash flow waterfall
is as follows. The senior classes are paid off in sequence—first Class A-1 is paid principal
until it has paid off its entire balance, then Class A-2 starts receiving principal payments
until it is paid off entirely, and then finally Class A-3 is paid off. Class B begins receiving
principal payments after Class A-3 is paid off. Any losses on the collateral are realized by
Class B. If the losses exceed $13,870,000 (the par value of Class B) less the losses that can be
absorbed by the reserve account, the senior classes absorb the loss on a pro rata basis.

Key Points That You Should Understand Before Proceeding

1. Securitization is an alternative funding source to issuing corporate bonds whereby
   ABS are issued.
2. In a securitization, the originator or conduit sells the loans or receivables to
   an SPV.
3. The SPV is the issuer of the ABS.
4. The different bond classes created have different risk/return characteristics from
   the collateral and are created so as to have appealing investment attributes to
   institutional investors.
5. The SPV plays a critical role in a securitization because it legally separates the loans
   and receivables sold to the SPV from the originator and therefore reduces funding
   costs because investors look to the credit risk of the collateral rather than the credit
   risk of the originator.
6. Securitizations require credit enhancement and the mechanisms for credit enhancing
   a structure are classified as internal and external.

COLLATERAL TYPE AND SECURITIZATION STRUCTURE

Structuring a securitization will depend on the characteristics of the underlying assets. Here we will discuss how two characteristics affect the structure: amortization and interest rate. Specifically, the structure depends on whether (1) the assets are amortizing or non-amortizing, and (2) the interest rate on the collateral is fixed or floating.

Amortizing versus Nonamortizing Assets

The collateral in a securitization can be classified as either amortizing or nonamortizing assets. **Amortizing assets** are loans in which the borrower's periodic payment consists of scheduled principal and interest payments over the life of the loan. The schedule for the repayment of the principal is called an **amortization schedule**. The standard residential mortgage loan falls into this category. Auto loans are amortizing assets. A prepayment is any excess payment over the scheduled principal payment. For an amortizing asset, projection of the cash flows requires projecting prepayments.

In contrast to amortizing assets, **nonamortizing assets** do not have a schedule for the periodic payments that the individual borrower must make. Instead, a nonamortizing asset is one in which the borrower must make a minimum periodic payment. If that payment is less than the interest on the outstanding loan balance, the shortfall is added to the outstanding loan balance. If the periodic payment is greater than the interest on the outstanding loan balance, then the difference is applied to the reduction of the outstanding loan balance. Because there is no schedule of principal payments (i.e., no amortization schedule) for a nonamortizing asset, the concept of a prepayment does not apply. Credit card receivables are examples of nonamortizing assets.

Typically, when amortizing assets are securitized, the collateral is fixed over the life of the structure. That is, no new assets are acquired. The collateral composition stays the same except for prepayments and defaults. Consequently, all principal received by the trust is paid out to the bond classes. The structure in this case is referred to as a **self-liquidating structure**. In the case of nonamortizing assets, for a period of time, referred to as the **lockout period** or **revolving period**, all principal received is used to purchase new collateral. Hence, new assets are being added to the collateral, and this structure is referred to as a **revolving structure**. After the lockout period, called the **amortization period**, principal received is distributed to the bond classes.

Fixed-Rate versus Floating-Rate Assets

The assets that are securitized can have a fixed rate or a floating rate. This impacts the structure in terms of the coupon rate for the bonds issued. For example, a structure with all floating-rate bond classes backed by collateral consisting of only fixed-rate contracts exposes bondholders to interest rate risk. If the reference rate for the floating-rate bond classes increases sufficiently, there could be a shortfall between the interest received from the collateral and the aggregate interest payment that must be made to the bond classes. If the collateral consists of only floating-rate contracts and the bond classes all have a fixed coupon rate, the exposure in this case is that the reference rate for the contracts will decline sufficiently so that the interest paid by the borrowers will be less than the total interest due to the bondholders.

To deal with situations where there may be a mismatch between the cash flow characteristics of the asset and the liabilities, interest rate derivative instruments are used in a securitization. The two common interest rate derivatives used are interest rate swaps and interest rate caps.

Key Points That You Should Understand Before Proceeding

1. The collateral in a securitization can be classified as either amortizing or nonamortizing assets.
2. When amortizing assets are securitized, the composition of the collateral is fixed over the life of the structure, all principal received by the trust is paid out to the bond classes, and the securitization is said to be a self-liquidating structure.
3. When nonamortizing assets are securitized, there is a lockout period or revolving period where all principal received is used to purchase new collateral. Hence, the securitization is said to be a revolving structure; following the lockout period, there is an amortization period where principal received is distributed to the bond classes.

REVIEW OF MAJOR NON-MORTGAGE-RELATED TYPES OF ABS

In this section, we briefly review five of the largest sectors within the ABS market that are not backed by real estate mortgage loans: (1) credit card receivable-backed securities, (2) auto loan-backed securities, (3) rate reduction bonds, (4) student loan-backed securities, and (5) Small Business Administration loan-backed securities.

Credit Card Receivable-Backed Securities

There are three general categories of credit card: general-purpose credit cards (Visa and MasterCard), independent networks (American Express and Discover), and private-label credit cards. The last category is the smallest, the largest issuer in this category by far being Sears, Roebuck & Co.

Credit card receivable-backed securities are backed by the cash flow of a pool of credit card receivables. The cash flow consists of finance charges collected, fees, and principal. Finance charges collected represent the periodic interest the credit card borrower is charged based on the unpaid balance after the grace period. Fees include late payment fees and any annual membership fees. Interest to the bond classes is paid periodically (e.g., monthly, quarterly, or semiannually). The interest rate may be fixed or floating.

A credit card receivable is a nonamortizing asset and therefore has a revolving structure. During the lockout period the principal payments made by credit card borrowers comprising the pool are retained by the trustee and reinvested in additional receivables to maintain the size of the pool. The lockout period can vary from 18 months to 10 years. So, during the lockout period, the cash flow that is paid out to the bond classes is based on finance charges collected and fees. The lockout period is followed by the principal amortization period, when the principal is no longer reinvested but paid to bondholders.

There are provisions in credit card receivable-backed securities that require early amortization of the principal if certain events occur. Such a provision, which is referred to as either an **early amortization provision** or a **rapid amortization provision**, is included to safeguard the credit quality of the structure. The only way that the principal cash flows can be altered is by triggering the early amortization provision. Typically, early amortization allows for the rapid return of principal in the event that the three-month average excess spread earned on the receivables falls to zero or less. When early amortization occurs, the bond classes are retired sequentially (i.e., first the AAA bond, then the AA rated bond, etc.). This is accomplished by distributing the principal payments to the specified bond class instead of using those payments to acquire more receivables.

Auto Loan-Backed Securities

Auto loan-backed securities are issued by the financial subsidiaries of auto manufacturers (domestic and foreign), commercial banks, and independent finance companies and small financial institutions specializing in auto loans. The cash flow for auto loan-backed securities consists of regularly scheduled monthly loan payments (interest and scheduled principal repayments) and any prepayments. For securities backed by auto loans, prepayments result from (1) sales and trade-ins requiring full payoff of the loan, (2) repossession and subsequent resale of the automobile, (3) loss or destruction of the vehicle, (4) payoff of the loan with cash to save on the interest cost, and (5) refinancing of the loan at a lower interest cost. Although refinancings may be a major reason for prepayments of residential mortgage loans, they are of minor importance for automobile loans.

Rate Reduction Bonds

Rate reduction bonds are backed by a special charge (tariff) included in the utility bills of utility customers. The charge, called the competitive transition charge (CTC), is effectively a legislated asset. It is the result of the movement to make the electric utility industry more competitive by deregulating the industry. Prior to deregulation, electric utilities were entitled to set utility rates so as to earn a competitive return on the assets on their balance sheet. After deregulation, the setting of utility rates to recover a competitive return was no longer permissible. As a result, many electric utilities had a substantial amount of assets that they acquired prior to deregulation that would likely become uneconomic, and utilities would no longer be assured that they could charge a high enough rate to recover the costs of these assets. These assets are referred to as "stranded assets" and the associated costs referred to as "stranded costs." For this reason, rate reduction bonds are also known as **stranded cost bonds** or **stranded asset bonds**. Some market participants refer to this sector of the ABS market as the "utilities" sector.

The CTC is collected by the utility over a specific period of time. Because the state legislature designates the CTC to be a statutory property right, it can be sold by a utility to an SPV and then securitized. It is the legislative designation of the CTC as an asset that makes rate reduction bonds different from the typical asset securitized.

The CTC is initially calculated based on projections of utility usage and the ability to collect revenues. However, actual collection experience may differ from initial projections. Because of this, there is a "true-up" mechanism in these securitizations. This mechanism permits the utility to recompute the CTC on a periodic basis over the term of the securitization based on actual collection experience. The advantage of the true-up mechanism to the bond classes is that it provides cash flow stability as well as a form of credit enhancement.

Student Loan-Backed Securities

Student loans are made to cover college costs (undergraduate, graduate, and professional programs such as medical and law school) and tuition for a wide range of vocational and trade schools. **Student loan-backed securities,** popularly referred to as SLABS, have similar structural features to other ABS already discussed.

The student loans most commonly securitized are those made under the Federal Family Education Loan Program (FFELP). Under this program, the government makes loans to a student via private lenders. The decision by private lenders to extend a loan to a student is not based on the applicant's ability to repay the loan. If a default of a loan occurs and the loan has been properly serviced, then the government will guarantee up to 98% of the principal plus accrued interest. By far, the leading issuer of SLABS is Sallie Mae.[4] In 2006, Sallie Mae issued $34 billion of SLABS, almost six times more than the second largest issuer, Nelnet Student Loan.

Loans that are not part of a government guarantee program are called **private student loans.** These loans are basically consumer loans, and the lender's decision to extend such a loan will be based on the ability of the applicant to repay the loan. The largest issuers of ABS backed by private student loans are Sallie Mae (SML Private Credit), First Marble, Access Group, and Keycorp.

The cash flow for the student loans themselves involve three periods with respect to the borrower's payments: deferment period, grace period, and loan repayment period. Typically, student loans work as follows. While a student is in school—the deferment period—no payments are made by the student on the loan. Upon leaving school, the student is extended a grace period of usually six months when no payments on the loan must be made. After this period, payments are made on the loan by the borrower.

Prepayments typically occur due to default recoveries or loan consolidation. Default recoveries are payments made by the insurer of the loan. Consolidation of a loan occurs when the student who has loans over several years combines them into a single loan. The proceeds from the consolidation are distributed to the original lender and, in turn, distributed to the bondholders.

Small Business Administration Loan-Backed Securities

The Small Business Association (SBA) is an agency of the U.S. government empowered to guarantee loans made by approved SBA lenders to qualified borrowers. The loans are backed by the full faith and credit of the government. Most SBA loans are variable-rate loans where the reference rate is the prime rate. SBA regulations specify the maximum coupon allowable in the secondary market. Newly originated loans have maturities between five and 25 years.

Most SBA loans make monthly payments consisting of interest and principal repayment. The amount of the monthly payment for an individual loan is determined as follows. Given the coupon formula of the prime rate plus the loan's quoted margin, the interest rate is determined for each loan. Given the interest rate, a level payment amortization schedule

---

[4] Sallie Mae was originally a government-sponsored enterprise created by Congress to purchase student loans in the secondary market and to securitize pools of student loans. In December 2004, Sallie Mae (whose original name was the Student Loan Marketing Association) was privatized and, hence, is no longer a government-sponsored enterprise.

is determined. It is this level payment that is paid for the next month until the coupon rate is reset. The monthly cash flow that the investor in an SBA-backed security receives consists of the coupon interest based on the coupon rate set for the period, the scheduled principal repayment (i.e., scheduled amortization), and prepayments. Voluntary prepayments can be made by the borrower without any penalty.

The Small Business Secondary Market Improvement Act, passed in 1984, permitted the pooling of SBA loans. Securities backed by SBA loans are called **SBA loan-backed securities**.

Key Points That You Should Understand Before Proceeding

1. Credit card receivable-backed securities are backed by the cash flow of a pool of credit card receivables and the cash flow consists of finance charges collected, fees, and principal.
2. The cash flow for auto loan-backed securities consists of regularly scheduled monthly loan payments (interest and scheduled principal repayments) and any prepayments.
3. Rate reduction bonds, also called stranded cost bonds or stranded asset bonds, are backed by a state-legislative approved special charge, referred to as the CTC, charged by utility companies.
4. Student loan-backed securities are backed by federally guaranteed and private student loans and involve three periods with respect to the borrower's payments: deferment period, grace period, and loan repayment period.
5. The SBA loan-backed securities are backed by loans made by SBA lenders to qualified businesses and backed by the full faith and credit of the government.

CREDIT RISKS ASSOCIATED WITH INVESTING IN ASSET-BACKED SECURITIES

Investors in ABS are exposed to credit risk and rely on rating agencies to evaluate that risk for the bond classes in a securitization. While the three rating agencies have different approaches in assigning credit ratings, they do focus on the same areas of analysis. Moody's, for example, investigates (1) asset risks, (2) structural risks, and (3) third parties to the structure.[5] We discuss each here. In addition, rating agencies analyze the legal structure (i.e., the SPV). We also discuss the legal issue regarding securitizations in general.

Asset Risks

Evaluating asset risks involves the analysis of the credit quality of the collateral. The rating agencies will look at the underlying borrower's ability to pay and the borrower's equity in the asset. The reason for looking at the latter is because it is a key determinant as to whether the underlying borrower will default or sell the asset and pay off a loan. The rating agencies will look at the experience of the originators of the underlying loans and will assess whether the loans underlying a specific transaction have the same characteristics as the experience reported by the seller.

---

[5]Andrew A. Silver, "Rating Structured Securities," Chapter 5 in Frank J. Fabozzi (ed.), *Issuer Perspectives on Securities* (Hoboken, NJ: John Wiley & Sons, 1998).

The concentration of loans is examined. The underlying principle of asset securitization is that a large number of borrowers in a pool will reduce the credit risk via diversification. If there are a few borrowers in the pool that are significant in size relative to the entire pool balance, this diversification benefit can be lost, resulting in a higher level of credit risk referred to as **concentration risk**. To reduce concentration risk, concentration limits on the amount or percentage of receivables from any one borrower, region of the country, or industry (in the case of commercial assets) will be established by rating agencies. If at issuance the concentration limit is exceeded, some or all of the bond classes will receive a lower credit rating than if the concentration limit were within the established range. Subsequent to issuance, bond classes may be downgraded if the concentration limit is exceeded.

Employing statistical analysis, the rating agencies assess the most likely loss to a bond class that would result from the performance of the collateral. This is done by analyzing various scenarios that the rating agencies specify. Based on the result of the analysis, the rating agencies compute both a weighted average loss and variability of loss for each bond class. To appreciate why the variability of loss is important, suppose that a bond class has protection against a 7% loss in the value of the collateral due to defaults. To simplify the illustration, suppose that a rating agency evaluates two equally likely scenarios and that in the first scenario the loss is 6% and in the second scenario 4%. The weighted average loss is 5%. This is less than the 7% loss against which a bond class has protection and therefore the rating agency would expect it to be unlikely that the bond class would realize a loss. Let's change the two outcomes now. Suppose that the outcome of the two scenarios is that the loss is 8% in the first scenario and 2% in the second scenario. While the expected value for the loss is still 5%, the variability of the loss is much greater than before. In fact, in the second scenario if an 8% loss occurs, the bond class would realize a loss of 1% (8% loss in the scenario minus the 7% protection).

Structural Risks

The decision on the structure is up to the seller. Once selected, the rating agencies examine the extent to which the cash flow from the collateral can satisfy all the obligations of the bond classes in the securitization. The cash flow of the underlying collateral is interest and principal repayment. The cash flow payments that must be made are interest and principal to investors, servicing fees, and any other expenses for which the issuer is liable. This is described by the structure's cash flow waterfall. The rating agencies analyze the structure to test whether the collateral's cash flows match the payments that must be made to satisfy the issuer's obligations. This risk is referred to as **structural risk**. In analyzing this risk, the rating agency must make assumptions about losses and delinquencies and consider various interest rate scenarios after taking into consideration credit enhancements.

In considering the structure, the rating agencies will consider (1) the loss allocation (how losses will be allocated among the bond classes in the structure), (2) the cash flow allocation (i.e., the cash flow waterfall), (3) the interest rate spread between the interest earned on the collateral and the interest paid to the bond classes plus the servicing fee, (4) the potential for a trigger event to occur that will cause the early amortization of a deal (discussed later), and (5) how credit enhancement may change over time.

Third-Party Providers

In a securitization, several third parties are involved. These include third-party credit guarantors (most commonly bond insurers), the servicer, a trustee, issuer's counsel, a guaranteed investment contract provider (this entity insures the reinvestment rate on investable funds), and accountants. The rating agency will investigate all third-party providers. For the third-party guarantors, the rating agencies will perform a credit analysis of their ability to pay.

All loans must be serviced. Servicing involves collecting payments from borrowers, notifying borrowers who may be delinquent, and, when necessary, recovering and disposing of the collateral if the borrower does not make loan repayments by a specified time. The servicer is responsible for these activities. Moreover, while still viewed as a "third party" in many securitizations, the servicer is likely to be the originator of the loans used as the collateral.

In addition to the administration of the loan portfolio as just described, the servicer is responsible for distributing the proceeds collected from the borrowers to the different bond classes in the structure according to the cash flow waterfall. Where there are floating-rate securities in the transaction, the servicer will determine the interest rate for the period. The servicer may also be responsible for advancing payments when there are delinquencies in payments (that are likely to be collected in the future), resulting in a temporary shortfall in the payments that must be made to the bondholders.

The role of the servicer is critical in a securitization. Therefore, rating agencies look at the ability of a servicer to perform all these activities before they assign a rating to the bonds in a transaction. For example, the following factors are reviewed when evaluating servicers: servicing history, experience, underwriting standard for loan originations, servicing capabilities, human resources, financial condition, and growth/competition/business environment. Transactions where there is a concern about the ability of a servicer to perform are either not rated or the rating agency may require a backup servicer.

Recent cases have made rating agencies pay even closer attention to the importance of the underlying business of the seller/originator, the strength of the servicer, and the economics that will produce the cash flows for the collateral. Primarily, this was as a result of the alleged fraud of National Century Financial Enterprises (NCFE), purchaser of health care receivables that were then securitized and serviced, and DVI, a securitizer of medical equipment leases. In addition, NCFE and DVI highlighted the need for a trustee to be more proactive if the performance of the servicer deterorates. That is, the trustee's role should be expanded beyond the traditional function of merely performing the ongoing tests on the collateral that are set forth in the deal documents. This is, in fact, happening in recent deals where the trustee under certain circumstances can take on an expanded role. This is referred to as a *trustee event trigger*.

Potential Legal Challenges

The long-standing view is that investors in ABS are protected from the creditors of the seller of the collateral. That is, when the seller of the collateral transfers it to the trust (the SPV), the transfer represents a "true sale" and therefore in the case of the seller's bankruptcy, the bankruptcy court cannot penetrate the trust to recover the collateral or cash flow from the collateral. However, this issue has never been fully tested. The closest challenge was the bankruptcy of LTV Steel Company. In the bankruptcy, LTV argued that its securitizations were not true sales and therefore it should be entitled to the cash flows that it transferred to the trust. Although the case was settled and the settlement included a summary finding that LTV's securitizations were a true sale, the court's decision to permit LTV to use the cash flows prior to the settlement is a major concern to investors.

There are also concerns regarding the outcome of a bankruptcy involving Conseco Finance Corp. The firm filed for bankruptcy in December 2002. Conseco Finance had been the largest originator of manufactured housing loans, as, well as the originator of other types of assets. At the time of filing, Conseco was the servicer for its prior securitizations, charging a servicing fee of 50 basis points. The bankruptcy court took the position that a 50 basis points servicing fee was not adequate compensation, ordering it to be increased (to 115 basis points). That increase in the servicing fee was obtained by reducing the excess spread in the securitization transactions that Conseco was servicing. As a result of a reduction in the excess spread, the credit enhancement levels for the transactions being serviced were reduced and several of the subordinate tranches in those transactions were downgraded.[6]

Key Points That You Should Understand Before Proceeding

1. In assessing the risk on ABS, rating agencies focus on asset risks, structural risks, third parties to the structure, and the legal structure.
2. Evaluating asset risks involves the analysis of the credit quality of the collateral and considers the underlying borrower's ability to pay and the borrower's equity in the asset, the experience of the originators of the underlying loans, the concentration of the loans, and statistically estimated likely loss to a bond class that would result from the performance of the collateral.
3. The rating agencies analyze the structure to test whether the collateral's cash flows match the payments that must be made to satisfy the issuer's obligations, and in doing so they must make assumptions about losses and delinquencies and consider various interest rate scenarios after taking into consideration credit enhancements.
4. Because there are several third parties involved in a securitization (e.g., bond insurer, servicer, a trustee, issuer's counsel) and they all play an important role, the rating agency will investigate all of them to determine their ability to perform.

SECURITIZATION AND THE IMPACT ON FINANCIAL MARKETS

The three economic functions of financial intermediaries are as follows: (1) providing maturity intermediation, (2) reducing risk via diversification, and (3) reducing the costs of contracting and information processing. However, securitization is a vehicle for raising funds directly in the public market without the need for a financial intermediary. That is, securitization is said to result in financial disintermediation.

---

[6] For a further discussion of the implications of the Conseco Finance bankruptcy, see Frank J. Fabozzi, "The Structured Finance Market: An Investor's Perspective," *Financial Analysts Journal* (May–June 2005), pp. 27–40.

Let's see how securitization can fulfill the three economic roles of financial intermediaries. First, a pool of loans can be used to create ABS with different maturity ranges. For example, a pool of 30-year residential mortgage loans can be used to create securities with maturities that are short, intermediate, and long term. Hence, securitization provides maturity intermediation. Second, diversification within an asset type is accomplished because of the large number of loans in a typical securitization. Hence, securitization reduces risk via diversification. Finally, the costs of contracting and information processing are provided in asset securitization. The contracting costs are provided by the originator of the loans. Information processing is provided at two levels. The first is when a loan is originated. The second is when a rating agency rates the individual ABS in the transaction.

The key benefit of securitization to financial markets is that it allows for the creation of tradable securities with better liquidity for financial claims that would otherwise have remained in the portfolio of financial intermediaries and, therefore, highly illiquid. For example, very few institutional investors or individual investors would be willing to invest in residential mortgage loans, automobile loans, or credit card receivables. Yet they would be willing to invest in a security backed by these loan types. By making financial assets tradable in this way, securitization (1) reduces agency costs, thereby making financial markets more efficient; and (2) improves liquidity for the underlying financial claims, thereby reducing liquidity risk in the financial system. The concerns with the financial disintermediating impact of securitization are that fewer assets will be held in the portfolio of banks and as a result this will make it more difficult for the Federal Reserve to implement monetary policy. Moreover, there is a concern that securitization of loans from bank portfolios will lead to a lower profitability for banks and the loans not securitized and held in bank portfolios will be of lower credit quality.[7]

SUMMARY

ABS are created by pooling loans and receivables through a process known as securitization. The main parties to a securitization are the seller/originator (party seeking to raise funds), SPV, and servicer. The motivation for issuing ABS rather than issuing a corporate bond is the potential reduction in funding cost. The key to this savings is the role of the SPV.

ABS are credit enhanced to provide greater protection to bond classes against defaults. There are two general types of credit enhancement mechanisms: external and internal. External credit enhancements come in the form of third-party guaranties, the most common being bond insurance. Internal credit enhancements include reserve funds (cash reserves and excess spread), overcollateralization, and senior/subordinate structures.

In analyzing credit risk, the rating agencies will examine asset risks, structural risks, and third parties to the structure. Based on this analysis, a rating agency will determine the amount of credit enhancement needed for a bond class to receive a specific credit rating.

Securitization has resulted in financial disintermediation. While there are benefits of securitization, there are also concerns about its impact.

---

[7] For a further discussion, see Stuart I. Greenbaum and Anjan V. Thakor, "Bank Funding Modes: Securitization versus Deposits," *Journal of Banking and Finance*, 11 (1987), pp. 379–392; and Richard Cantor and Stanislas Rouyer, "Another Perspective on Credit Risk Transfer and Assets Securitization," *Journal of Risk Finance* (Winter 2000), pp. 37–47.

KEY TERMS

- Amortization period
- Amortization schedule
- Amortizing assets
- Asset-backed security (ABS)
- Auto loan-backed securities
- Bond insurance
- Cash flow waterfall (waterfall)
- Concentration risk
- Conduit
- Credit card receivable-backed securities
- Early amortization provision
- Excess spread
- Existing asset securitizations
- Future flow securitizations
- Lockout period
- Nonamortizing assets
- Originator
- Private student loans
- Rapid amortization provision
- Rate reduction bonds
- Revolving period
- Revolving structure
- SBA loan-backed securities
- Self-liquidating structure
- Special purpose vehicle (SPV)
- Stranded cost bonds (stranded asset bonds)
- Structural risk
- Student loan-backed securities
- Surety bond
- Surety wrap
- Underwriting standards

QUESTIONS

1. A financial corporation with a BBB rating has a consumer loan portfolio. An investment banker suggested that this corporation consider issuing an ABS where the collateral for the security is the consumer loan portfolio. What would be the advantage of issuing an ABS rather than a straight offering of corporate bonds?

2. Why is the entity seeking to raise funds through a securitization referred to as the "seller" or the "originator"?

3. In achieving the benefits associated with a securitization, why is the SPV important to the transaction?

4. In a securitization, what is the difference between a servicer and an SPV?

5. What is meant by a cash flow waterfall?

6. Explain the difference in the treatment of principal received for a self-liquidating trust and a revolving trust.

7. In a securitization, what is (a) a lockout period, and (b) an early amortization provision?

8. a. Why is credit enhancement required in a securitization?

   b. What entity determines the amount of credit enhancement needed in a securitization?

9. What is the limitation of a third-party guaranty as a form of credit enhancement?

10. An ABS has been credit enhanced with a letter of credit from a bank with a single A credit rating. If this is the only form of credit enhancement, explain whether this issue can be assigned a triple credit rating at the time of issuance.

11. A corporation is considering a securitization and is considering two possible credit enhancement structures backed by a pool of automobile loans. Total principal value underlying the ABS is $300 million.

Principal Value for:	Structure I	Structure II
Pool of automobile loans	$304 million	$301 million
Senior class	$250 million	$270 million
Subordinate class	$50 million	$30 million

   a. Which structure would receive a higher credit rating and why?

   b. What forms of credit enhancement are being used in both structures?

12. **a.** What is meant by concentration risk?
    b. How do rating agencies seek to limit the exposure of a pool of loans to concentration risk?

13. What factors do the rating agencies consider in analyzing the structural risk in a securitization?

14. Why would an interest rate derivative be used in a securitization structure?

15. What is the cash flow for an auto loan–backed security?

16. The following questions relate to credit card receivable-backed securities.
    a. What happens to the principal repaid by borrowers in a credit card receivable–backed security during the lockout period?
    b. What is the role of the early amortization provision in a credit card receivable–backed security structure?
    c. How can the cash flow of a credit card receivable–backed security be altered prior to the principal-amortization period?

17. The following questions relate to rate reduction bonds:
    a. What asset is the collateral?
    b. Who is the servicer?
    c. What is a true-up provision in a securitization creating rate reduction bonds?

18. What are the components of the cash flow for an SBA-backed security?

19. **a.** What is the benefit of securitization to a financial market?
    b. What are the concerns with securitization?

Financial Futures Markets

From Chapter 26 of *Foundations of Financial Markets and Institutions*, 4/e. Frank J. Fabozzi. Franco Modigliani. Frank J. Jones.

Financial Futures Markets

LEARNING OBJECTIVES

After reading this chapter, you will understand

- what a futures contract is

- the basic economic function of a futures contract

- the differences between futures and forward contracts

- the role of the clearinghouse

- the mark-to-market and margin requirements of a futures contract

- the role of futures markets in the economy

- features of U.S. stock index futures contracts, single stock futures contracts, and narrow-based stock index futures contracts

- features of interest rate futures contracts

- findings of the General Accounting Office study on financial derivatives

In this chapter, we describe the financial futures market and the various contracts traded in it. The basic economic function of futures markets is to provide an opportunity for market participants to hedge against the risk of adverse price movements.

Futures contracts are products created by exchanges. To create a particular futures contract, an exchange must obtain approval from the Commodity Futures Trading Commission (CFTC), a government regulatory agency. In its application to the CFTC, the exchange must demonstrate that there is an economic purpose for the contract. While numerous futures contracts obtain approval for trading, only those contracts that spark investor interest and serve investor needs ultimately succeed.

Prior to 1972, only futures contracts involving traditional agricultural commodities (such as grain and livestock), imported foodstuffs (such as coffee, cocoa, and sugar), or industrial commodities were traded. Collectively, such futures contracts are known as *commodity futures*. Futures contracts based on a financial instrument or a financial index are known as *financial futures*. Financial futures can be classified as (1) stock index futures, (2) interest rate futures, and (3) currency futures.

As the value of a futures contract is derived from the value of the underlying instrument, futures contracts are commonly called *derivative instruments*. Options, discussed in the next chapter, are another example of derivative instruments.

In the United States, the development of the markets for futures and options on stock indexes and debt obligations was a response to the need for an efficient risk-transference mechanism as stock price and interest rate volatility in the United States increased. Other countries have shared the U.S. experience with volatility and, as a result, developed derivative markets.

Historically, the trading of futures contracts has been via an open outcry environment where traders and brokers shout out bids and offers in a trading pit or ring. Although open outcry has been the primary method of trading certain types of futures contract, since 2004, trading in many financial futures in the United States has moved towards an electronic trading platform wherein market participants post their bids and offers on a computerized trading system. The trading of futures contracts outside the United States takes place on an electronic platform.

FUTURES CONTRACTS

A **futures contract** is an agreement between a buyer and a seller, in which

1. the buyer agrees to take delivery of something at a specified price at the end of a designated period of time
2. the seller agrees to make delivery of something at a specified price at the end of a designated period of time

Of course, no one buys or sells anything when entering into a futures contract. Rather, the parties to the contract agree to buy or sell a specific amount of a specific item at a specified future date. When we speak of the "buyer" or the "seller" of a contract, we are simply adopting the jargon of the futures market, which refers to parties of the contract in terms of the future obligation they are committing themselves to.

Let's look closely at the key elements of this contract. The price at which the parties agree to transact in the future is called the **futures price**. The designated date at which the parties must transact is called the **settlement date** or **delivery date**. The "something" that the parties agree to exchange is called the **underlying**.

To illustrate, suppose there is a futures contract traded on an exchange where the underlying to be bought or sold is Asset XYZ, and the settlement is three months from now. Assume further that Bob buys this futures contract, and Sally sells this futures contract, and the price at which they agree to transact in the future is $100. Then $100 is the futures price. At the settlement date, Sally will deliver Asset XYZ to Bob. Bob will give Sally $100, the futures price.

When an investor takes a position in the market by buying a futures contract (or agreeing to buy at the future date), the investor is said to be in a **long position** or to be **long futures**. If, instead, the investor's opening position is the sale of a futures contract (which means the contractual obligation to sell something in the future), the investor is said to be in a **short position** or to be **short futures**.

The buyer of a futures contract will realize a profit if the futures price increases; the seller of a futures contract will realize a profit if the futures price decreases. For example, suppose that one month after Bob and Sally take their positions in the futures contract, the futures price of Asset XYZ increases to $120. Bob, the buyer of the futures contract, could then sell the futures contract and realize a profit of $20. Effectively, he has agreed to buy, at the settlement date, Asset XYZ for $100 and to sell Asset XYZ for $120. Sally, the seller of the futures contract, will realize a loss of $20.

If the futures price falls to $40 and Sally buys the contract, she realizes a profit of $60 because she agreed to sell Asset XYZ for $100 and now can buy it for $40. Bob would realize a loss of $60. Thus, if the futures price decreases, the buyer of the futures contract realizes a loss while the seller of the futures contract realizes a profit.

Liquidating a Position

Most financial futures contracts have settlement dates in the months of March, June, September, or December. This means that at a predetermined time in the contract settlement month the contract stops trading, and a price is determined by the exchange for settlement of the contract. The contract with the closest settlement date is called the **nearby futures contract**. The next futures contract is the one that settles just after the nearby contract. The contract farthest away in time from settlement is called the **most distant** (or **deferred**) **futures contract**.

A party to a futures contract has two choices on liquidation of the position. First, the position can be liquidated prior to the settlement date. For this purpose, the party must take an offsetting position in the same contract. For the buyer of a futures contract, this means selling the same number of identical futures contracts; for the seller of a futures contract, this means buying the same number of identical futures contracts.

The alternative is to wait until the settlement date. At that time, the party purchasing a futures contract accepts delivery of the underlying; the party that sells a futures contract liquidates the position by delivering the underlying at the agreed-upon price. For some futures contracts that we shall describe later in this chapter, settlement is made in cash only. Such contracts are referred to as **cash settlement contracts**.

A useful statistic measuring the liquidity of a contract is the number of contracts that have been entered into but not yet liquidated. This figure is called the contract's **open interest**. An open interest figure is reported by an exchange for all the futures contracts traded on the exchange.

The Role of the Clearinghouse

Associated with every futures exchange is a **clearinghouse**, which performs several functions. One of these functions is to guarantee that the two parties to the transaction will perform. To see the importance of this function, consider potential problems in the futures transaction described earlier from the perspective of the two parties—Bob the buyer and Sally the seller. Each must be concerned with the other's ability to fulfill the obligation at the settlement date. Suppose that at the settlement date the price of Asset XYZ in the cash market is $70. Sally can buy Asset XYZ for $70 and deliver it to Bob, who in turn must pay her $100. If Bob does not have the capacity to pay $100 or refuses to pay, however, Sally has lost the opportunity to realize a profit of $30. Suppose, instead, that the price of Asset XYZ in the cash market is $150 at the settlement date. In this case, Bob is ready and willing to accept delivery of Asset XYZ and pay the agreed-upon price of $100. If Sally cannot deliver or refuses to deliver Asset XYZ, Bob has lost the opportunity to realize a profit of $50.

The clearinghouse exists to eliminate this problem. When someone takes a position in the futures market, the clearinghouse takes the opposite position and agrees to satisfy the terms set forth in the contract. Because of the clearinghouse, the two parties need not worry about the financial strength and integrity of the party taking the opposite side of the contract. After initial execution of an order, the relationship between the two parties ends. The clearinghouse interposes itself as the buyer for every sale and the seller for every purchase. Thus, the two parties are then free to liquidate their positions without involving the other party in the original contract, and without worry that the other party may default. This function is referred to as the *guarantee function*.

Besides its guarantee function, the clearinghouse makes it simple for parties to a futures contract to unwind their positions prior to the settlement date. Suppose that Bob wants to get out of his futures position. He will not have to seek out Sally and work out an agreement with her to terminate the original contract. Instead, Bob can unwind his position by selling an identical futures contract. As far as the clearinghouse is concerned, its records will show that Bob has bought and sold an identical futures contract. At the settlement date, Sally will not deliver Asset XYZ to Bob but will be instructed by the clearinghouse to deliver to someone who bought and still has an open futures position. In the same way, if Sally wants to unwind her position prior to the settlement date, she can buy an identical futures contract.

Margin Requirements

When a position is first taken in a futures contract, the investor must deposit a minimum dollar amount per contract as specified by the exchange. This amount, called **initial margin**, is required as a deposit for the contract. Individual brokerage firms are free to set margin requirements above the minimum established by the exchange. The initial margin may be in the form of an interest-bearing security such as a Treasury bill. As the price of the futures contract fluctuates each trading day, the value of the investor's **equity** in the position changes. The equity in a futures account is the sum of all margins posted and all daily gains less all daily losses to the account. We develop this important concept throughout this section.

At the end of each trading day, the exchange determines the **settlement price** for the futures contract. The settlement price is different from the closing price, which many people know from the stock market and which is the price of the security in the final trade of the day (whenever that trade occurred during the day). The settlement price by contrast is that value that the exchange considers to be representative of trading at the end of the day. The representative price may in fact be the price in the day's last trade. But, if there is a flurry of trading at the end of the day, the exchange looks at all trades in the last few minutes and identifies a median or average price among those trades. The exchange uses the settlement price to mark to market the investor's position, so that any gain or loss from the position is quickly reflected in the investor's equity account.

Maintenance margin is the minimum level (specified by the exchange) to which an investor's equity position may fall as a result of an unfavorable price movement before the investor is required to deposit additional margin. The additional margin deposited is called **variation margin**, and it is an amount necessary to bring the equity in the account back to its initial margin level. Unlike initial margin, the variation margin must be in cash rather than interest-bearing instruments. Any excess margin in the account may be withdrawn by the investor. If a party to a futures contract who is required to deposit variation margin fails to do so within 24 hours, the exchange closes the futures position out.

Although there are initial and maintenance margin requirements for buying securities on margin, the concept of margin differs for securities and futures. When securities are acquired on margin, the difference between the price of the security and the initial margin is borrowed from the broker. The security purchased serves as collateral for the loan, and the investor pays interest. For futures contracts, the initial margin, in effect, serves as good faith money, an indication that the investor will satisfy the obligation of the contract. Normally, no money is borrowed by the investor who takes a futures position.

To illustrate the mark-to-market procedure, let's assume the following margin requirements for Asset XYZ:

Initial margin	$7 per contract
Maintenance margin	$4 per contract

Let's assume that Bob buys 500 contracts at a futures price of $100, and Sally sells the same number of contracts at the same futures price. The initial margin for both Bob and Sally is $3,500, which is determined by multiplying the initial margin of $7 by the number of contracts, which is 500. Bob and Sally must put up $3,500 in cash or Treasury bills or other acceptable collateral. At this time, $3,500 is also called the equity in the account. The maintenance margin for the two positions is $2,000 (the maintenance margin per contract of $4 multiplied by 500 contracts). The equity in the account may not fall below $2,000. If it does, the party whose equity falls below the maintenance margin must put up additional margin, which is the variation margin. There are two things to note here. First, the variation margin must be cash. Second, the amount of variation margin required is the amount to bring the equity up to the initial margin, not to the maintenance margin.

To illustrate the mark-to-market procedure, we assume the following settlement prices at the end of several trading days after the transaction was entered into. Those prices are

Trading Day	Settlement Price
1	$99
2	97
3	98
4	95

First, consider Bob's position. At the end of trading day 1, Bob realizes a loss of $1 per contract or $500 for the 500 contracts he bought. Bob's initial equity of $3,500 is reduced by $500 to $3,000. No action is taken by the clearinghouse because Bob's equity is still above the maintenance margin of $2,000. At the end of the second day, Bob realizes a further loss as the price of the futures contract has declined another $2 to $97, resulting in an additional reduction in his equity position by $1,000. Bob's equity is then $2,000: the equity at the end of trading day 1 of $3,000 minus the loss on trading day 2 of $1,000. Despite the loss, no action is taken by the clearinghouse, because the equity still meets the $2,000 maintenance requirement. At the end of trading day 3, Bob realizes a profit from the previous trading day of $1 per contract or $500. Bob's equity increases to $2,500. The drop in price from $98 to $95 at the end of trading day 4 results in a loss for the 500 contracts of $1,500 and consequent reduction of Bob's equity to $1,000. As Bob's equity is now below the $2,000 maintenance margin, Bob is required to put up additional margin of $2,500 (variation margin) to bring the equity up to the initial margin of $3,500. If Bob cannot put up the variation margin his position will be liquidated.

Now, let's look at Sally's position. Sally as the seller of the futures contract benefits if the price of the futures contract declines. As a result, her equity increases at the end of the first two trading days. In fact, at the end of trading day 1, she realizes a profit of $500, which increases her equity to $4,000. She is entitled to take out the $500 profit and use these funds elsewhere. Suppose she does, and her equity, therefore, remains at $3,500 at the end of trading day 1. At the end of trading day 2, she realizes an additional profit of $1,000 that she also withdraws. At the end of trading day 3, she realizes a loss of $500 with the increase of the price from $97 to $98. This results in a reduction of her equity to $3,000. Finally, on trading day 4, she realizes a profit of $1,000, making her equity $4,000. She can withdraw $500.

Leveraging Aspect of Futures

A party taking a position in a futures contract need not put up the entire amount of the investment. Instead, the exchange and/or clearinghouse requires only the initial margin to be put up. To see the crucial consequences of this fact, suppose Bob has $100 and wants to invest in Asset XYZ because he believes its price will appreciate. If Asset XYZ is selling for $100, he can buy one unit of the asset. His payoff will then be based on the price action of one unit of Asset XYZ.

Suppose further that the exchange where the futures contract for Asset XYZ is traded requires an initial margin of only 5%, which in this case, would be $5. This means Bob can purchase 20 contracts with his $100 investment. (We ignore the fact that Bob may need funds for variation margin.) His payoff will then depend on the price action of 20 units of Asset XYZ. Thus, he can leverage the use of his funds. (The degree of leverage equals 1/margin rate. In this case, the degree of leverage equals 1/0.05 or 20.) While the degree of leverage available in the futures market varies from contract to contract, as the initial margin requirement varies, the leverage attainable is considerably greater than in the cash market.

At first, the leverage available in the futures market may suggest that the market benefits mainly those who want to speculate on price movements. However, futures markets can also be used to reduce price risk. Without the leverage possible in futures transactions, the cost of reducing price risk using futures would be too high for many market participants.

Daily Price Limits

The exchange has the right to impose a limit on the daily price movement of a futures contract from the previous day's closing price. A **daily price limit** sets the minimum and maximum price at which the futures contract may trade that day.[1] When a daily price limit is reached, trading does not stop but rather continues at a price that does not violate the minimum or maximum price.

---

[1] For a discussion of price limits on equity index futures contracts on the Chicago Mercantile Exchange, go to *http://www.cme.com/market/riskman/pricelmt.html* and *http://www.cme.com/market/riskman/pricelmtfaq.html.*

The rationale offered for the imposition of daily price limits is that they provide stability to the market at times when new information may cause the futures price to exhibit extreme fluctuations. Those who support daily price limits argue that giving market participants time to digest or reassess such information if trading ceases when price limits would be violated gives them greater confidence in the market. Not all economists agree with this rationale. The question of the role of daily price limits and whether they are necessary remains the subject of extensive debate.

Key Points That You Should Understand Before Proceeding

1. A futures contract is an agreement between a buyer and a seller in which the buyer agrees to take delivery of something at the futures price at the settlement date and the seller agrees to make delivery.
2. A party to a futures contract can liquidate a position prior to the settlement date by taking an offsetting position in the same contract.
3. Associated with every futures exchange is a clearinghouse, which provides a guarantee function.
4. Parties to a futures contract must satisfy margin requirements (initial, maintenance, and variation), and futures contracts are marked to market at the end of each trading day.
5. Futures contracts are leveraged instruments that can be used to control risk.

FUTURES VERSUS FORWARD CONTRACTS

A **forward contract**, just like a futures contract, is an agreement for the future delivery of something at a specified price at the end of a designated period of time. Futures contracts are standardized agreements as to the delivery date (or month) and quality of the deliverable, and are traded on organized exchanges. A forward contract is usually nonstandardized because the terms of each contract are negotiated individually between buyer and seller. Also, there is no clearinghouse for trading forward contracts, and secondary markets are often nonexistent or extremely thin. Unlike a futures contract, which is an exchange-traded product, a forward contract is an over-the-counter instrument.

Although both futures and forward contracts set forth terms of delivery, futures contracts are not intended to be settled by delivery. In fact, generally fewer than 2% of outstanding contracts are settled by delivery. Forward contracts, in contrast, are intended for delivery.

Futures contracts are marked to market at the end of each trading day. Consequently, futures contracts are subject to interim cash flows as additional margin may be required in the case of adverse price movements, or as an investor who has experienced favorable price movements withdraws any cash that exceeds the account's margin requirement. A forward contract may or may not be marked to market, depending on the wishes of the two parties. For a forward contract that is not marked to market, there are no interim cash flow effects because no additional margin is required.

Finally, the parties in a forward contract are exposed to credit risk because either party may default on the obligation. Credit risk is minimal in the case of futures contracts because the clearinghouse associated with the exchange guarantees the other side of any transaction.

Other than these differences, which reflect the institutional arrangements in the two markets, most of what we say about futures contracts applies equally to forward contracts.

THE ROLE OF FUTURES IN FINANCIAL MARKETS

Without financial futures, investors would have only one trading location to alter portfolio positions when they get new information that is expected to influence the value of assets—the cash market. If they hear economic news that is expected to impact the value of an asset adversely, investors want to reduce their price risk exposure to that asset. The opposite would be true if the new information is expected to impact the value of an asset favorably: An investor would increase price risk exposure to that asset. There are, of course, transactions costs associated with altering exposure to an asset—explicit costs (commissions) and execution costs (bid–ask spreads and market impact costs).

The futures market is an alternative market that investors can use to alter their risk exposure to an asset when new information is acquired. But which market—cash or futures—should the investor employ to alter a position quickly on the receipt of new information? The answer is simple: the one that most efficiently achieves the objective. The factors to consider are liquidity, transactions costs, taxes, and leverage advantages of the futures contract.

The market that investors consider more efficient for their investment objective should be the one where prices will first be established that reflect the new economic information. That is, this will be the market where price discovery takes place. Price information is then transmitted to the other market. For many of the financial assets that we have discussed, it is in the futures market that it is easier and less costly to alter a portfolio position. Therefore, it is the futures market that will be the market of choice and will serve as the price discovery market. It is in the futures market that investors send a collective message about how any new information is expected to impact the cash market.

How is this message sent to the cash market? To understand how, it is necessary to understand that there is a relationship between the futures price and the cash price. More specifically, the futures price and the cash market price are tied together by the cost of carry. If the futures price deviates from the cash market price by more than the cost of carry, arbitrageurs (in attempting to obtain arbitrage profits) would pursue a strategy to bring them back into line. Arbitrage is the mechanism that assures that the cash market price will reflect the information that has been collected in the futures market.

Some investors and the popular press believe the introduction of a futures market for a financial asset will increase the price volatility of that financial asset in the cash market. That is, some market observers believe that, as a result of speculative trading of futures contracts, the cash market instrument does not reflect its fundamental economic value. The implication here is that the price of the financial asset would better reflect its true economic value in the absence of a futures market for that financial asset.

Whether or not the introduction of futures markets destabilizes prices of financial assets is an empirical question. Whether or not the introduction of futures contracts increases cash market price volatility, we might ask whether greater volatility has negative effects on financial markets. At first glance, it might seem that volatility has adverse effects from the points of view of allocative efficiency and participation in financial markets.

Actually, it has been pointed out that this inference may not be justified if, say, the introduction of futures markets lets prices respond more promptly to changes in factors that affect the economic value of a financial asset, and if these factors themselves are subject to large shocks.[2] Thus, the greater volatility resulting from an innovation may simply more faithfully reflect the actual variability of factors that affect the economic value of financial assets. In this case, "more" volatility of a financial asset's price need not be bad but, rather, may be a manifestation of a well-functioning market. Of course, to say that more volatility need not be bad does not mean that it is good.

For example, we describe in the following text one type of futures contract in which the underlying is a stock market index. Critics of these futures contracts assert that their introduction has created greater volatility for stock market prices. While the empirical evidence has not supported this view, the key point is that increased volatility of stock market prices may be due to the greater quantity and frequency of information released by the government about important economic indicators that affect the value of the common stock of all companies. That information itself is subject to a great deal of variability. Thus, if there is any observed increase in the volatility of stock prices, that volatility may be due to the substantial variability of economic information, not to the presence of a futures contract on a stock market index.

Clearly, price volatility greater than what can be justified by relevant new information is undesirable. By definition, it makes prices inefficient. This is referred to as "excess volatility."[3]

Key Points That You Should Understand Before Proceeding

1. The key role of futures contracts is that, in a well-functioning futures market, these contracts provide a more efficient means for investors to alter their risk exposure to an asset.
2. A futures market will be the price discovery market when market participants prefer to use this market rather than the cash market to change their risk exposure to an asset.
3. The futures market and the cash market for an asset are tied together by an arbitrage process.
4. The argument that futures markets destabilize the prices of the underlying financial assets is an empirical one, but greater price volatility by itself is not an undesirable attribute of a financial market.

U.S. FINANCIAL FUTURES MARKETS

In this section, we review the more important financial futures markets in the United States.

---

[2] Eugene F. Fama, "Perspectives on October 1987, or What Did We Learn from the Crash?" in Robert J. Barro, et al. (eds.), *Black Monday and the Future of Financial Markets* (Homewood, IL: Dow Jones-Irwin, 1989), p. 72.

[3] Franklin R. Edwards, "Futures Trading and Cash Market Volatility: Stock Index and Interest Rate Futures," *The Journal of Futures Markets*, Vol. 8, No. 4 (1988), p. 423.

Stock Index Futures Markets

In 1982, three futures contracts on broadly based common stock indexes made their debut: the Standard & Poor's 500 futures contract traded on the international Monetary Market of the Chicago Mercantile Exchange (CME), the New York Stock Exchange Composite futures contract traded on the New York Futures Exchange, and the Value Line Average traded on the Kansas City Board of Trade. Since then, broad-based and specialized **stock index futures contracts** have been introduced. In the United States, the exchange that offers the most popular stock index futures contracts is the CME. Table 1 lists the stock index futures

Table 1	List of Stock Index Futures Contracts Listed on the Chicago Mercantile Exchange*

Contract	Multiple
S&P 500	250
e-mini S&P 500	50
NASDAQ-100	100
e-mini NASDAQ-100	20
e-mini NASDAQ Composite	50
e-mini MSCI EAFE	50
S&P MidCap 400	500
e-mini S&P MidCap 400	100
S&P SmallCap 600	200
Russell 2000	500
e-mini Russell 2000	100
e-mini Russell 1000	100
S&P 500/Citigroup Growth	250
S&P 500/Citigroup Value	250
SPCTR Futures	125
Nikkei 225—Dollar based	5
Nikkei 225—Yen based	500
E-mini S&P Asia 50	25

*"E-mini" contracts are one-fifth the size of the corresponding regular ("big") contract.
Underlying/Index:
S&P 500: The stocks of the 500 large capitalization U.S. companies actively traded on the NYSE, the AMEX, and Nasdaq Stock Market.
NASDAQ-100: Modified, capitalization-weighted index of 100 of the largest and most active nonfinancial, domestic stocks traded on the Nasdaq Stock Market.
NASDAQ Composite: Market capitalization of all the stocks traded on the Nasdaq Stock Market.
MSCI EAFE: Non–U.S. stock index consisting of stocks from Europe, Australasia, and the Far East.
S&P MidCap 400: Index of mid capitalization stocks.
S&P SmallCap 600: Index of small capitalization stocks.
Russell 2000: Capitalization-weighted index of approximately 2,000 actively traded, small-capitalization U.S. stocks on the NYSE, the AMEX, and Nasdaq Stock Market.
Russell 1000: 1,000 largest companies in the U.S. based on total market capitalization.
S&P 500/Citigroup Growth: U.S. stocks in the S&P 500 that are classified as growth stocks.
S&P 500/Citigroup Value: U.S. stocks in the S&P 500 that are classified as value stocks.
SPCTR Futures: Industry-specific sector indexes comprising the benchmark CME S&P 500. There is a financial and a technology contract.
Nikkei 225: Price-weighted index comprised of the 225 top-tier Japanese companies listed in the First Section of the Tokyo Stock Exchange.
e-mini S&P Asia 50: Broad-based capitalization-weighted index of the 50 largest stocks traded in Hong Kong, Korea, Singapore, and Taiwan.

contracts traded on the CME. The most actively traded contract is the S&P 500 futures contract. On the Chicago Board of Trade (CBOT), stock index futures are traded on the Dow Jones Industrial Average.

The dollar value of a stock index futures contract is the product of the futures price and the contract's *multiple;* that is,

$$\text{Dollar value of a stock index futures contract} = \text{Futures price} \times \text{Multiple}$$

The multiple for each CME contract is shown in Table 1. For example, if the futures price for the S&P 500 is 1300, since the multiple is $250, the dollar value of a stock index futures contract is

$$1300 \times \$250 = \$325,000$$

For the S&P Nasdaq 100, suppose that the futures price is 1600. Since the multiple for this contract is $100, then the value of this futures contract is

$$1600 \times \$100 = \$160,000$$

Now that we know how the value of a stock index futures contract is determined, let's see how an investor gains or loses when the futures price changes. Once again, consider the S&P 500 futures contract. Suppose an investor buys (takes a long position in) an S&P 500 futures contract at 1300 and sells it at 1315; the investor realizes a profit of 15 times $250, or $3,750. If the futures contract is sold instead for 1280, the investor will realize a loss of 20 times $250, or $5,000.

Stock index futures contracts are cash settlement contracts. This means that, at the settlement date, cash will be exchanged to settle the contract. For example, if an investor buys an S&P 500 futures contract at 1300 and the settlement index is 1350, settlement would be as follows. The investor has agreed to buy the S&P 500 for 1300 times $250, or $325,000. The S&P 500 value at the settlement date is 1350 times $250, or $337,500. The seller of this futures contract must pay the investor $12,500 ($337,500 − $325,000). Had the index at the settlement date been 1280 instead of 1350, the value of the S&P 500 would be $320,000 (1280 × $250). The investor must pay the seller of the contract $5,000 ($325,000 − $320,000).

Single Stock Futures Contracts

Single stock futures are equity futures in which the underlying is the stock of an individual company. These contracts received approval for trading in the United States in 2001. Single stock futures are traded on two exchanges: OneChicago and Nasdaq Liffe Markets. OneChicago is a joint venture of the Chicago Board Options Exchange, CME Inc., and the CBOT. Nasdaq Liffe Market is a joint venture of the Nasdaq Stock Market and the London International Financial Futures and Options Exchange (an exchange that trades exchange-traded derivatives).

Single stock futures of only actively traded New York Stock Exchange and Nasdaq stocks are traded. The contracts are for 100 shares of the underlying stock. At the settlement date, physical delivery of the stock is required.

Narrow-Based Stock Indexes

Futures exchanges have found that there are investors who want to take long and short positions in the futures market for a group of stocks and do so by paying for only one trade. Hence, only one brokerage commission is paid to trade the group of stocks. These futures contracts are referred to as **narrow-based stock index futures.**

For example, as of August 31, 2006, OneChicago created "OneChicago Select Indexes." These indexes typically consist of the stock of from three to seven companies. The determination of the companies included is based on what large institutional investors who are customers of the exchange have identified as interesting for their trading strategies. The OneChicago Select Index F contains the following components and their initial share lots:

Underlying	Initial Share Lots
Bank of Montreal	400
Bank of Nova Scotia	500
Enbridge Inc Corp.	700
Sun Life Financial	500
Toronto-Dominion Bank	400
TransCanada Corp	700

The unit of trading for these indexes is the notional value of the index divided by 1,000. That is, the market value for each component of the index is multiplied by its number of shares specified in the contract. The sum of the market values of the components is then computed. The total market value is then divided by 1,000.

Interest Rate Futures Markets

In October 1975, the CBOT pioneered trading in a futures contract based on a fixed-income instrument—Government National Mortgage Association certificates. Three months later, the International Monetary Market of the CME began trading futures contracts based on 13-week Treasury bills. Other exchanges soon followed with their own interest rate futures contracts.

Interest rate futures contracts can be classified by the maturity of their underlying security. Short-term interest rate futures contracts have an underlying security that matures in less than one year. The maturity of the underlying security of long-term futures contracts exceeds one year. Examples of the former are the futures contracts in which the underlying is a three-month Treasury bill, three-month London Interbank Offered Rate (LIBOR), and 30-day federal funds. All of these contracts are traded on the CME. Examples of long-term futures are contracts in which the underlying is a Treasury bond and a Treasury note. The more actively traded contracts traded in the United States are described here. Most major financial markets outside the United States have similar futures contracts in which the underlying security is a fixed-income security issued by the central government.

Eurodollar Futures

A Eurodollar futures contract represents a commitment to pay/receive a quarterly interest payment determined by the level of three-month LIBOR. The dollar amount paid is based on a notional principal of $1 million on the settlement date. There are various quarterly settlement dates for Eurodollar futures contracts available—March, June, September, and December—that extend out 10 years. The Eurodollar futures contracts trade on the CME, as well as the London International Financial Futures Exchange.

The contract is is traded on an index-price basis. The index-price basis in which the contract is quoted is equal to 100 minus the annualized futures LIBOR. For example, a Eurodollar futures price of 94.00 means a futures three-month LIBOR of 6%.

The minimum price fluctuation (tick) for this contract is 0.01 (or 0.0001 in terms of LIBOR). It means that the price value of a basis point for this contract is $25, found as follows. The simple interest on $1 million for 90 days is equal to

$$\$1,000,000 \times (\text{LIBOR} \times 90/360)$$

If LIBOR changes by one basis point (0.0001), then

$$\$1,000,000 \times (0.0001 \times 90/360) = \$25$$

The Eurodollar futures contract is a cash settlement contract. That is, the parties settle in cash for the value of the contract based on LIBOR at the settlement date. The Eurodollar futures contract is one of the most heavily traded futures contracts in the world. It is frequently used to trade the short end of the yield curve, and many hedgers have found this contract to be the best hedging vehicle for a wide range of situations.

Treasury Bill Futures

The Treasury bill futures contract, which is traded on the International Monetary Market, is based on a 13-week (three-month) Treasury bill with a face value of $1 million. More specifically, the seller of a Treasury bill futures contract agrees to deliver to the buyer at the settlement date a Treasury bill with 13 weeks remaining to maturity and a face value of $1 million. The Treasury bill that would be delivered by the terms of this contract can be newly issued or seasoned. The futures price is the price at which the Treasury bill will be sold by the short and purchased by the buyer. For example, a nine-month Treasury bill futures contract requires that, nine months from now, the short deliver to the long $1 million face value of a Treasury bill with 13 weeks remaining to maturity. The Treasury bill could be a newly issued 13-week Treasury bill or a Treasury bill that was issued one year prior to the settlement date and that therefore, at the settlement, has only 13 weeks remaining to maturity.

Treasury bills are quoted in the cash market in terms of the annualized yield on a bank discount basis. The Treasury bill futures contract is not quoted directly in terms of yield but, just like the Eurodollar futures contract, is quoted on an index basis that is related to the yield on a bank discount basis as follows:

$$\text{Index price} = 100 - (\text{Yield on a bank discount basis} \times 100)$$

For example, if the yield on a bank discount basis is 8%, then

$$\text{Index price} = 100 - (0.08 \times 100) = 92$$

Federal Funds Futures Contract

Using its three tools of monetary policy—open market operations, reserve requirements, and discount rate—the Federal Reserve influences the demand for, and supply of, balances that banks hold at Federal Reserve banks. By doing so, this alters the federal funds rate, which ultimately influences other short-term and long-term interest rates.

The 30-day federal funds futures contract, traded on the CBOT, is designed for financial institutions and businesses who want to control their exposure to movements in the federal funds rate. These contracts have a notional amount of $5 million, and the contract can be written for the current month up to 24 months in the future. Underlying this contract is the simple average overnight federal funds rate (i.e., the effective rate) for the delivery month. As such, this contract is settled in cash on the last business day of the month. Just like the other short-term interest rate futures contracts discussed above, prices are quoted on the basis of 100 minus the overnight federal funds rate for the delivery month. These contracts are marked to market using the effective daily federal funds rate as reported by the Federal Reserve Bank of New York.

Treasury Bond Futures

The underlying for a Treasury bond futures contract is $100,000 par value of a hypothetical 20-year, 6% coupon bond. While prices and yields of the Treasury bond futures contract are quoted in terms of this hypothetical Treasury bond, the seller of the futures contract has the choice of several actual Treasury bonds that are acceptable to deliver. The CBOT (where the contract is traded) allows the seller to deliver any Treasury bond that has at least 15 years to maturity from the date of delivery if it is not callable; in the case of callable bonds, the issue must not be callable for at least 15 years from the first day of the delivery month. Settling a contract calls for an acceptable bond to be delivered. That is, the contract is not a cash settlement contract.

The delivery process for the Treasury bond futures contract makes the contract interesting. At the settlement date, the seller of a futures contract (the short) is required to deliver to the buyer (the long) $100,000 par value of a 6%, 20-year Treasury bond. Since no such bond exists, the seller must choose from the list of acceptable, deliverable bonds that the exchange has specified. But this choice raises a problem. Suppose the seller is entitled to deliver $100,000 of a 4%, 20-year Treasury bond to settle the futures contract. The value of this bond, of course, is less than the value of a 6%, 20-year bond. If the seller delivers the 4%, 20-year, this would be unfair to the buyer of the futures contract who contracted to receive $100,000 of a 6%, 20-year Treasury bond. Alternatively, suppose the seller delivers $100,000 of a 10%, 20-year Treasury bond. The value of a 10%, 20-year Treasury bond is greater than that of a 6%, 20-year bond, so this would be a disadvantage to the seller.

How can this problem be resolved? To make delivery equitable to both parties, and to tie cash prices to futures prices, the CBOT has introduced **conversion factors** for determining the invoice price of each acceptable deliverable Treasury issue against the Treasury bond futures contract. The conversion factor is determined by the CBOT before a contract with a specific settlement date begins trading. The conversion factor is based on the price that a deliverable bond would sell for, at the beginning of the delivery month, if it were to yield 6%. The conversion factor is constant throughout the trading period of the futures contract. The short must notify the long, one day before the delivery date, of the actual bond that will be delivered.

The invoice price paid by the buyer of the Treasury bonds that the seller delivers is determined using the formula:

Invoice price = Contract size × Future contract settlement price × Conversion factor

Suppose the Treasury bond futures contract settles at 96 (0.96 in decimal form) and that the short elects to deliver a Treasury bond issue with a conversion factor of 1.15. As the contract size is $100,000, the invoice price is

$$\$100,000 \times 0.96 \times 1.15 = \$110,400$$

The invoice price in the formula is just for the principal. The buyer of the futures contract must also pay the seller accrued interest on the bond delivered.

In selecting the issue to be delivered, the short will select from all the deliverable issues the bond that is cheapest to deliver. This issue is referred to as the **cheapest-to-deliver issue** and is found by determining the issue that will produce the largest rate of return in a cash-and-carry trade. That is, for each deliverable issue the rate of return is calculated by assuming the issue is purchased and held to the futures delivery date. The rate of return calculated is called the **implied repo rate**. The cheapest-to-deliver issue is the one that offers the largest implied repo rate from among all the deliverable issues. This issue may change over the life of the contract. The cheapest-to-deliver issue plays a key role in the pricing of this futures contract.

In addition to the option of which acceptable Treasury issue to deliver—sometimes referred to as the **quality** (or **swap**) **option**—the short position has two more options granted under CBOT delivery guidelines. First, the short position is permitted to decide when in the delivery month actually to make the delivery. This is called the **timing option**. The second option is the right of the short position to give notice of intent to deliver up to 8:00 P.M. Chicago time after the closing of the exchange (3:15 P.M. Chicago time) on the date when the futures settlement price has been fixed. This option is referred to as the **wild card option**. The quality option, the timing option, and the wild card option (in sum, referred to as the *delivery options*) mean that the long position can never be sure which Treasury bond will be delivered or when it will be delivered.

Treasury Note Futures

There are three Treasury note futures contracts: 10-year, five-year, and two-year. All three contracts are modeled after the Treasury bond futures contract and are traded on the CBOT. The underlying instrument for the 10-year Treasury note futures contract is $100,000 par value of a hypothetical 6%, 10-year Treasury note. There are several acceptable Treasury issues that may be delivered by the short. An issue is acceptable if the maturity is not less than 6.5 years and not greater than 10 years from the first day of the delivery month. The delivery options granted to the short position and the minimum price fluctuation are the same as for the Treasury bond futures contract.

For the five-year Treasury note futures contract, the underlying is $100,000 par value of a 6% notional coupon U.S. Treasury note that satisfies the following conditions: (1) an original maturity of not more than five years and three months, (2) a remaining maturity no greater than five years and three months, and (3) a remaining maturity not less than four years and two months.

The underlying for the two-year Treasury note futures contract is $200,000 par value of a 6% notional coupon U.S. Treasury note with a remaining maturity of not more than two years and not less than one year and nine months. Moreover, the *original maturity* of the note delivered to satisfy the two-year futures cannot be more than five years and three months.

Key Points That You Should Understand Before Proceeding

1. Equity futures contracts listed in the United States include stock index futures contracts, single stock futures contracts, and narrow-based stock index futures contracts.
2. Stock index futures contracts are cash settlement contracts whose underlying is a common stock index, and the dollar value of a stock index futures contract is the product of the futures price and the contract's multiple.
3. An interest rate futures contract is one whose underlying asset is a fixed-income instrument or an interest rate.
4. The listed interest rate futures contracts traded in the United States are the Eurodollar futures contract, the Treasury bill futures contract, the 30-day federal funds futures contract, and the Treasury bond and note futures contracts.
5. The Treasury bond and note futures contracts are unique in that the short is granted options as to which issue to deliver and, during the delivery month, when to deliver.

THE GENERAL ACCOUNTING OFFICE STUDY ON FINANCIAL DERIVATIVES

We have just explored our first derivative instrument. Some of these products are exchange traded, such as the futures contracts we discussed in this chapter. Other products are created by commercial banks and investment banking firms. These customized derivative products are called *over-the-counter* or *OTC derivatives*. Forward contracts are an example of an OTC derivative product. Swaps are another example of an OTC derivative. There are also OTC options.

There is public concern that commercial banks are creating OTC derivative products that put them in a position that could result in severe financial problems. Because it is the larger commercial banks that are creating OTC derivatives, this could have a rippling effect on the U.S. financial system. (One type of derivative, credit derivatives, did in fact have this effect.) Specifically, there is concern that banks creating OTC derivative products do not have the proper risk-management systems in place to effectively monitor their risk exposure. For example, a July 1993 report by a highly influential bank group—the Group of Thirty—recommended how to improve bank risk-management systems. However, the recommendations did not appear to be uniformly adopted since they did not carry the force of law. Moreover, end-users of derivatives—financial institutions and businesses—may not have the requisite skills and risk-management systems to use derivatives or might be using them for speculative purposes rather than controlling financial risk.

In May 1994, the General Accounting Office (GAO) prepared a report on *Financial Derivatives: Actions Needed to Protect the Financial System*. The study recognized the importance of derivatives for market participants. Page 6 of the report states:

Derivatives serve an important function of the global financial marketplace, providing end-users with opportunities to better manage financial risks associated with their business transactions. The rapid growth and increasing complexity of derivatives reflect both the increased demand from end-users for better ways to manage their financial risks and the innovative capacity of the financial services industry to respond to market demands.

Despite the importance of derivatives, the study goes on to state:

> However, Congress, federal regulators, and some members of the industry are concerned about these products and the risk they may pose to the financial system, individual firms, investors, and U.S. taxpayers. These concerns have been heightened by recent reports of substantial losses by some derivative end-users.

The GAO study was undertaken because of these concerns. The cover letter to the GAO report stated that the objectives of the report were to determine

> (1) what the extent and nature of derivatives use was, (2) what risks derivatives might pose to individual firms and to the financial system, (3) whether gaps and inconsistencies existed in U.S. regulation of derivatives, (4) whether existing accounting rules resulted in financial reports that provided market participants and investors with adequate information about firms' use of derivatives, and (5) what the implications of the international use of derivatives were for U.S. regulations.

Here are some of the principal conclusions of the study. First, boards of directors and senior management have primary responsibility for managing derivative risks and, therefore, should have the necessary internal controls in place to carry out this responsibility. Moreover, regulations should provide a legal framework that would require OTC derivative product dealers to comply with a common set of basic standards to effectively manage risk.

Second, financial reporting requirements for derivative instruments are inadequate and the Financial Accounting Standards Board should implement comprehensive accounting rules for derivative products. Third, improving regulations for derivatives in the United States without coordinating with foreign regulators will reduce the effectiveness of the regulations. Finally, policymakers and regulators should not stifle the use of derivatives. Rather, a proper balance should be struck between allowing the financial services to be innovative in creating products useful to end-users and protecting the safety and soundness of the financial system.

SUMMARY

The traditional purpose of futures markets is to provide an important opportunity to hedge against the risk of adverse future price movements. Futures contracts are creations of exchanges, which require initial margin from parties. Each day positions are marked to market. Additional (variation) margin is required if the equity in the position falls below the maintenance margin. The clearinghouse guarantees that the parties to futures contracts will satisfy their obligations.

A buyer (seller) of a futures contract realizes a profit if the futures price increases (decreases). The buyer (seller) of a futures contract realizes a loss if the futures price decreases (increases). Because only initial margin is required when an investor takes a futures position, futures markets provide investors with substantial leverage for the money invested.

A forward contract differs in several important ways from a futures contract. In contrast to a futures contract, the parties to a forward contract are exposed to the risk that the other party to the contract will fail to perform. The positions of the parties are not marked to market, so there are no interim cash flows associated with a forward contract. Finally, unwinding a position in a forward contract may be difficult.

Investors can use the futures market or the cash market to react to economic news that is expected to change the value of an asset. Well-functioning futures markets are typically the market of choice for altering asset positions and, therefore, represent the price discovery market because of the lower transactions costs involved and the greater speed with which orders can be executed. The actions of arbitrageurs assure that price discovery in the futures markets will be transmitted to the cash market.

Critics of futures markets believe that these contracts are the source of greater price volatility in the cash market for the underlying asset. Although this is an empirical question not fully discussed here, even if price volatility in the cash market were greater because of the introduction of futures markets, this does not necessarily mean that greater volatility is bad for the economy.

The financial futures contracts traded in the United States include stock index futures contracts (with the most actively traded contract being the S&P 500 futures contract), single stock futures contracts, narrow-based stock index futures, short-term interest rate futures contracts (Eurodollar futures, Treasury bill futures, and 30-day federal funds futures contracts), and Treasury bond and note futures.

The GAO study addresses the concerns of Congress and regulators regarding derivative products. There is concern that major banks and end-users do not have adequate risk-management systems in place. Inadequate accounting disclosure and the lack of coordination with foreign regulators were other concerns highlighted by the study.

KEY TERMS

- Cash settlement contract
- Cheapest-to-deliver issue
- Clearinghouse
- Conversion factors
- Daily price limit
- Equity
- Forward contract
- Futures contract
- Futures price
- Implied repo rate
- Initial margin
- Long position (long futures)
- Maintenance margin
- Most distant (deferred) futures contract

- Narrow-based stock index future
- Nearby futures contract
- Open interest
- Quality (swap) option
- Settlement date (delivery date)
- Settlement price
- Short position (short futures)
- Single stock futures
- Stock index futures contract
- Timing option
- Underlying
- Variation margin
- Wild card option

QUESTIONS

1. The Chief Financial Officer of the corporation you work for recently told you that he had a strong preference to use forward contracts rather than futures contracts to hedge: "You can get contracts tailor-made to suit your needs." Comment on the Chief Financial Officer's statement. What other factors influence the decision to use futures or forward contracts?

2. Explain the functions of a clearinghouse associated with a futures exchange.

3. Suppose you bought a stock index futures contract for 200 and were required to put up initial margin of $10,000. The value of the contract is 200 times the $500 multiple, or $100,000. On the next three days, the contract's settlement price was at these levels: day 1, 205; day 2, 197; day 3, 190.

   a. Calculate the value of your margin account on each day.

   b. If the maintenance margin for the contract is $7,000, how much variation margin did the exchange require you to put up at the end of the third day?

   c. If you had failed to put up that much, what would the exchange have done?

4. How do margin requirements in the futures market differ from margin requirements in the cash market?

5. "The futures market is where price discovery takes place." Do you agree with this statement? If so, why? If not, why not?

6. **a.** What is meant by a cash settlement futures contract?

   b. Identify at least three futures contracts traded in the United States that are cash settlement contracts.

7. **a.** What is meant by open interest?

   b. Why is open interest important to an investor?

8. What may be an alternative for an investor who wants to short the stock of a particular company instead of shorting in the cash market?

9. **a.** What was the motivation for the creation of a narrow-based stock index futures contract?

   b. How are the component stocks of a narrow-based stock index futures contract selected?

10. **a.** In a Treasury bond futures contract, there are choices or options granted to one of the parties to the contract. Which party has these choices, the buyer or seller?

    b. What are the options that are granted to the party?

11. On September 1, you sold 100 S&P 500 futures contracts at 1000 with multiples of $250, expiration date in three months, and an initial margin of 10%. After that date, the index fell steadily and you were not required to post any additional margin, but you also did not withdraw any of the cash profits you were earning. On November 1, the futures price of the contract was 900, and you reversed your position by buying 100 contracts.

    a. How much money did you make (ignoring taxes and commissions)?

    b. What was the rate of return on your invested funds?

    c. In those two months, the S&P 500 futures price fell 10%. Explain why your rate of return is so much higher than this level.

12. What is meant by an OTC derivative product?

13. What is the major concern with banks creating OTC derivative products?

Options Markets

LEARNING OBJECTIVES

After reading this chapter, you will understand

- what an option contract is, and the basic features of an option

- the difference between a call option and a put option

- why an option is a derivative instrument

- the different types of exercise styles for an option (American, European, Bermuda)

- the difference between an exchange-traded option and an over-the-counter option

- the difference between a futures contract and an option contract

- the risk/return characteristics of call and put options, to both the seller and the buyer of the options

- the hedging role of options in financial markets

- the extensive role that organized exchanges play in standardizing and guaranteeing option contracts traded on exchanges

- how stock options can change the risk/return profile of a portfolio

- the basic features of stock index options

- the basic features of interest rate options

- what an exotic option is

- some key aspects of non–U.S. options markets

- the basic features of options on futures or futures options

From Chapter 27 of *Foundations of Financial Markets and Institutions*, 4/e. Frank J. Fabozzi. Franco Modigliani. Frank J. Jones.

I n this chapter, we introduce a second derivative contract, an options contract, and we discuss the differences between the two.

OPTIONS CONTRACTS

There are two parties to an option contract: the *buyer* and the **writer** (also called the *seller*). In an option contract, the writer of the option grants the buyer of the option the right, but not the obligation, to purchase from or sell to the writer something at a specified price within a specified period of time (or at a specified date). The writer grants this right to the buyer in exchange for a certain sum of money, which is called the **option price** or **option premium**. The price at which the underlying (that is, the asset or commodity) may be bought or sold is called the **exercise price** or **strike price**. The date after which an option is void is called the **expiration date** or **maturity date**. Our focus in this chapter is on options where the underlying is a financial instrument or financial index.

When an option grants the buyer the right to purchase the underlying from the writer (seller), it is referred to as a **call option**, or simply, a **call**. When the option buyer has the right to sell the underlying to the writer, the option is called a **put option**, or simply, a **put**.

The timing of the possible exercise of an option is an important characteristic of the contract. This feature of an option is referred to as its **exercise style.** There are options that may be exercised at any time up to and including the expiration date. Such options are referred to as **American options.** Other options may be exercised only at the expiration date; these are called **European options.** A **Bermuda option**, also referred to as an **Atlantic option**, can be exercised only on specified dates.

Let's use an illustration to demonstrate the fundamental option contract. Suppose that Jack buys a call option for $3 (the option price) with the following terms:

1. The underlying is one unit of Asset XYZ.
2. The exercise price is $100.
3. The expiration date is three months from now, and the option can be exercised any time up to and including the expiration date (that is, it is an American option).

At any time up to and including the expiration date, Jack can decide to buy from the writer (seller) of this option one unit of Asset XYZ, for which he will pay a price of $100. If it is not beneficial for Jack to exercise the option, he will not, and we'll explain shortly how he decides whether or not it will be beneficial. Whether Jack exercises the option or not, the $3 he paid for the option will be kept by the option writer. If Jack buys a put option rather than a call option, then he would be able to sell Asset XYZ to the option writer for a price of $100.

The maximum amount that an option buyer can lose is the option price. The maximum profit that the option writer (seller) can realize is the option price. The option buyer has substantial upside return potential, while the option writer has substantial downside risk. We will investigate the risk/reward relationship for option positions later in this chapter.

There are no margin requirements for the buyer of an option once the option price has been paid in full. Because the option price is the maximum amount that the investor can lose, no matter how adverse the price movement of the underlying, no margin is needed. Because the writer (seller) of an option has agreed to accept all of the risk (and none of the reward) of the position in the underlying, the writer is generally required to put up the option price received as margin. In addition, as price changes occur that adversely affect the writer's position, the writer is required to deposit additional margin (with some exceptions) as the position is marked to market.

Options, like other financial instruments, may be traded either on an organized exchange or in the over-the-counter (OTC) market. **Exchange-traded options** have three advantages. The first is standardization of the exercise price, the quantity of the underlying, and the expiration date of the contract. Second, as in the case of futures contracts, the direct link between buyer and seller is severed after the order is executed because of the interchangeability of exchange-traded options. The clearinghouse associated with the exchange where the option trades performs the same function in the options market it does in the futures market. Finally, the transactions costs are lower for exchange-traded options than for OTC options.

The higher cost of an OTC option reflects the cost of customizing the option for the common situation where an institutional investor needs to have a tailor-made option because the standardized exchange-traded option does not satisfy its investment objectives. Investment banking firms and commercial banks act as principals as well as brokers in the OTC options market. Most institutional investors are not concerned that an OTC option is less liquid than an exchange-traded option because they use OTC options as part of an asset/liability strategy in which they intend to hold them to expiration.

Key Points That You Should Understand Before Proceeding

1. An option is a contract in which the writer of the option grants the buyer the right, but not the obligation, to purchase from or sell to the writer something at the exercise (or strike) price within a specified period of time (until the expiration date).
2. The price paid by the option buyer is called the option price or option premium.
3. A call option grants the option buyer the right to buy something from the option writer, and a put option grants the option buyer the right to sell something to the option writer.
4. The maximum amount that an option buyer can lose is the option price, while the maximum profit that the option writer can realize is the option price; the option buyer has substantial upside return potential, while the option writer has substantial downside risk.
5. The option contract will specify the exercise style (American, European, Bermuda).
6. Options may be traded either on an organized exchange or in the OTC market.

DIFFERENCES BETWEEN OPTIONS AND FUTURES CONTRACTS

One distinction between futures and options contracts is that one party to an option contract is not obligated to transact at a later date. Specifically, the option buyer has the right but not the obligation to exercise the option. The option writer (seller), though, does have the obligation to perform, if the buyer of the option insists on exercising it. In the case of a futures contract, both buyer and seller are obligated to perform. Of course, a futures buyer does not pay the seller to accept the obligation, while an option buyer pays the seller an option price.

Consequently, the risk/reward characteristics of the two contracts are also different. In the case of a futures contract, the buyer of the contract realizes a dollar-for-dollar gain when the price of the futures contract increases, and suffers a dollar-for-dollar loss when the price of the futures contract drops. The opposite occurs for the seller of a futures contract. Options do not provide this symmetric risk/reward relationship. The most that the buyer of an option can lose is the option price. While the buyer of an option retains all the potential benefits the gain is always reduced by the amount of the option price. The maximum profit that the writer (seller) may realize is the option price; this is offset against substantial downside risk. This difference between options and futures is extremely important because, as we shall see in subsequent chapters, investors can use futures to protect against symmetric risk and options to protect against asymmetric risk.

We will return to the difference between options and futures later in this chapter when we discuss the application of these derivative contracts for hedging purposes.

Key Points That You Should Understand Before Proceeding

1. Unlike a futures contract, only one party to an option contract is obligated to transact at a later date: the option writer.
2. Futures have a symmetric risk/reward relationship, while options do not because the buyer of an option retains all the potential benefits, but the gain is always reduced by the amount of the option price.

RISK AND RETURN CHARACTERISTICS OF OPTIONS

Here, we illustrate the risk and return characteristics of the four basic option positions: buying a call option (which market participants refer to as being **long a call option**), selling a call option (**short a call option**), buying a put option (**long a put option**), and selling a put option (**short a put option**). The illustrations assume that each option position is held to the expiration date and not exercised early. Also, to simplify the illustrations, we ignore transactions costs.

Buying Call Options

Assume that there is a call option on Asset XYZ that expires in one month and has a strike price of $100. The option price is $3. Suppose that the current price of Asset XYZ is $100. What is the profit or loss for the investor who purchases this call option and holds it to the expiration date?

The profit and loss from the strategy will depend on the price of Asset XYZ at the expiration date. A number of outcomes are possible.

1. If Asset XYZ's price at the expiration date is less than $100, the investor will not exercise the option. It would be foolish to pay the option writer $100 when Asset XYZ can be purchased in the market at a lower price. In this case, the option buyer loses the entire, original option price of $3. Notice, however, that this is the maximum loss that the option buyer will realize regardless of how low Asset XYZ's price declines.
2. If Asset XYZ's price is equal to $100 at the expiration date, again, there is no economic value in exercising the option. As in the case where the price is less than $100, the buyer of the call option will lose the entire option price, $3.
3. If Asset XYZ's price is more than $100 but less than $103 at the expiration date, the option buyer will exercise the option. By exercising, the option buyer can purchase

Asset XYZ for $100 (the strike price) and sell it in the market for the higher price. Suppose, for example, that Asset XYZ's price is $102 at the expiration date. The buyer of the call option will realize a $2 gain by exercising the option. Of course, the cost of purchasing the call option was $3, so $1 is lost on this position. By failing to exercise the option, the investor loses $3 instead of only $1.

4. If Asset XYZ's price is equal to $103 at the expiration date, the investor will exercise the option. In this case, the investor breaks even, realizing a gain of $3 that offsets the cost of the option, $3.

5. If Asset XYZ's price is more than $103 at the expiration date, the investor will exercise the option and realize a profit. For example, if the price is $113, exercising the option will generate a profit on Asset XYZ of $13. Reducing this gain by the cost of the option ($3), the investor will realize a net profit of $10 from this position.

Table 1 shows the profit and loss for the buyer of the hypothetical call option in tabular form, whereas Figure 1 graphically portrays the result. While the break-even point and the size of the loss depend on the option price and the strike price, the profile shown in

Table 1   Profit/Loss Profile for a Long Call Position

Assumptions:
Option price = $3
Strike price = $100
Time to expiration = 1 month

Price of Asset XYZ at Expiration Date	Net Profit/Loss*	Price of Asset XYZ at Expiration Date	Net Profit/Loss*
$150	$47	100	−3
140	37	99	−3
130	27	98	−3
120	17	97	−3
115	12	96	−3
114	11	95	−3
113	10	94	−3
112	9	93	−3
111	8	92	−3
110	7	91	−3
109	6	90	−3
108	5	89	−3
107	4	88	−3
106	3	87	−3
105	2	86	−3
104	1	85	−3
103	0	80	−3
102	−1	70	−3
101	−2	60	−3

* Price at expiration −$100 −$3.
Maximum loss = $3.

Figure 1   Profit/Loss Profile for a Long Call Position

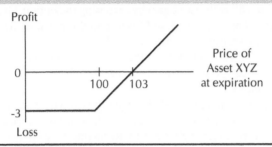

Figure 1 will hold for all buyers of call options. The shape indicates that the maximum loss is the option price and that there is substantial upside potential.

It is worthwhile to compare the profit and loss profile of the call option buyer to that of someone taking a long position in one unit of Asset XYZ. The payoff from the position depends on Asset XYZ's price at the expiration date. Consider again the five price outcomes given above (and again ignore transactions costs):

1. If Asset XYZ's price at the expiration date is less than $100, the investor in the call option loses the entire option price of $3. In contrast, a long position in Asset XYZ will have one of three possible losses:
   a. If Asset XYZ's price is less than $100 but greater than $97, the loss on the long position in Asset XYZ will be less than $3.
   b. If Asset XYZ's price is $97, the loss on the long position in Asset XYZ will be $3.
   c. If Asset XYZ's price is less than $97, the loss on the long position in Asset XYZ will be greater than $3. For example, if the price at the expiration date is $80, the long position in Asset XYZ will result in a loss of $20.
2. If Asset XYZ's price is equal to $100, the buyer of the call option will realize a loss of $3 (option price). Similarly, there will be no gain or loss on the long position in Asset XYZ.
3. If Asset XYZ's price is more than $100 but less than $103, the option buyer will realize a loss of less than $3, while the long position in Asset XYZ will realize a profit.
4. If the price of Asset XYZ at the expiration date is equal to $103, there will be no loss or gain from buying the call option. The long position in Asset XYZ, however, will produce a gain of $3.
5. If Asset XYZ's price at the expiration date is greater than $103, both the call option buyer and the long position in Asset XYZ will post a profit. However, the profit for the buyer of the call option will be $3 less than that for the long position. For example, if Asset XYZ's price is $113, the profit from the call position is $10, while the profit from the long position in Asset XYZ is $13.

Table 2 compares the long call strategy and the long position in Asset XYZ. This comparison clearly demonstrates the way in which an option can change the risk/return profile for investors. An investor who takes a long position in Asset XYZ realizes a profit of $1 for every $1 increases in Asset XYZ's price. As Asset XYZ's price falls, however, the investor loses dollar-for-dollar. If the price drops by more than $3, the long position in Asset XYZ results in a loss of more than $3. The long call strategy, in contrast, limits the loss to only the option price of $3 but retains the upside potential, which will be $3 less than for the long position in Asset XYZ.

Table 2 Comparison of Long Call Position and Long Asset Position

Assumptions:
Initial price of Asset XYZ = $100
Option price = $3
Strike price = $100
Time to expiration = 1 month

Price of Asset XYZ at Expiration Date	Net profit/loss for		Price of Asset XYZ at Expiration Date	Net profit/loss for	
	Long Call	Long Asset XYZ		Long Call	Long Asset XYZ
$150	$47	$50	100	−3	0
140	37	40	99	−3	−1
130	27	30	98	−3	−2
120	17	20	97	−3	−3
115	12	15	96	−3	−4
114	11	14	95	−3	−5
113	10	13	94	−3	−6
112	9	12	93	−3	−7
111	8	11	92	−3	−8
110	7	10	91	−3	−9
109	6	9	90	−3	−10
108	5	8	89	−3	−11
107	4	7	88	−3	−12
106	3	6	87	−3	−13
105	2	5	86	−3	−14
104	1	4	85	−3	−15
103	0	3	80	−3	−20
102	−1	2	70	−3	−30
101	−2	1	60	−3	−40

Which alternative is better, buying the call option or buying the asset? The answer depends on what the investor is attempting to achieve.

This hypothetical example demonstrates another important feature of options: their speculative appeal. Suppose an investor has strong expectations that Asset XYZ's price will rise in one month. At an option price of $3, the speculator can purchase 33.33 call options for each $100 invested. If Asset XYZ's price rises, the investor realizes the price appreciation associated with 33.33 units of Asset XYZ, while with the same $100, the investor could have bought only one unit of Asset XYZ selling at $100, realizing the appreciation associated with only one unit if Asset XYZ's price increases. For example, suppose that in one month

Figure 2   Profit/Loss Profile for a Short Call Position

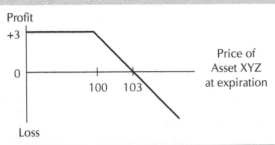

the price of Asset XYZ rises to $120. The long call position will result in a profit of $566.50 [($20 × 33.33) − $100] or a return of 566.5% on the $100 investment in the call option. By comparison, a $100 investment in the long position in Asset XYZ results in a profit of $20, for only a 20% return on $100.

It is this greater leverage that attracts investors to options when they wish to speculate on price movements. There are some drawbacks of leverage, however. Suppose that Asset XYZ's price is unchanged at $100 at the expiration date. The long call position (33.33 options) results, in this case, in a loss of the entire investment of $100, while the long position in Asset XYZ produces neither a gain nor a loss.

Writing (Selling) Call Options

To illustrate the option seller's (writer's) position, we use the same call option as in the example of buying a call option. The profit and loss profile of the short call position (that is, the position of the call option writer) is the mirror image of the profit and loss profile of the long call position (the position of the call option buyer). Consequently, the profit of the short call position for any given price of Asset XYZ at the expiration date is the same as the loss of the long call position. Furthermore, the maximum profit that the short call position can produce is the option price. The maximum loss is not limited because it is the highest price reached by Asset XYZ on or before the expiration date, less the option price; this price can be indefinitely high. These relationships can be seen in Figure 2, which shows the profit/loss profile for a short call position.

Buying Put Options

To illustrate the position of the buyer of a put option, we assume a hypothetical put option on one unit of Asset XYZ with one month to maturity and a strike price of $100. Assume the put option is selling for $2 and that the current price of Asset XYZ is $100. The profit or loss for this position at the expiration date depends on the market price of Asset XYZ. The possible outcomes are:

1. If Asset XYZ's price is greater than $100, the buyer of the put option will not exercise it because exercising would mean selling Asset XYZ to the writer for a price that is less than the market price. In this case, a loss of $2 (the original price of the option) will result from buying the put option. Once again, the option price represents the maximum loss to which the buyer of the put option is exposed.
2. If Asset XYZ's price at expiration is equal to $100, the put will not be exercised, leaving the put buyer with a loss equal to the option price of $2.

3. If Asset XYZ's price is less than $100 but greater than $98, the option buyer will experience a net loss on the position; exercising the put option, however, limits the loss to less than the option price of $2. For example, suppose that the price is $99 at the expiration date. By exercising the option, the option buyer will realize a loss of only $1. This is because the buyer of the put option can sell Asset XYZ, purchased in the market for $99, to the writer for $100, realizing a gain of $1. Deducting the $2 cost of the option results in a net loss of $1 to the position.

4. If Asset XYZ's price is $98 at the expiration date, the put buyer will break even. The investor will realize a gain of $2 by selling Asset XYZ to the writer of the option for $100, and this gain exactly offsets the cost of the option ($2).

5. If Asset XYZ's price is below $98 at the expiration date, the long put position (the put buyer) will realize a profit. For example, suppose the price falls at expiration to $80. The long put position will produce a profit of $18: a gain of $20 for exercising the put option less the $2 option price.

The profit and loss profile for the long put position is shown in tabular form in the second column of Table 3 and in graphical form in Figure 3. As with all long option positions, the loss is limited to the option price. The profit potential, however, is

Table 3 Profit/Loss Profile for a Long Put Position in Comparison to a Short Asset Position

Assumptions:
Initial price of Asset XYZ = $100
Option price = $2
Strike price = $100
Time to expiration = 1 month

Price of Asset XYZ at Expiration Date	Net profit/loss for		Price of Asset XYZ at Expiration Date	Net profit/loss for	
	Long Put*	Short Asset XYZ**		Long Put*	Short Asset XYZ**
$150	−$2	−$50	91	7	9
140	−2	−40	90	8	10
130	−2	−30	89	9	11
120	−2	−20	88	10	12
115	−2	−15	87	11	13
110	−2	−10	86	12	14
105	−2	−5	85	13	15
100	−2	0	84	14	16
99	−1	1	83	15	17
98	0	2	82	16	18
97	1	3	81	17	19
96	2	4	80	18	20
95	3	5	75	23	25
94	4	6	70	28	30
93	5	7	65	33	35
92	6	8	60	38	40

* $100 − Price at expiration.
Maximum loss = $2.
** $100 − Price of Asset XYZ.

Figure 3   Profit/Loss Profile for a Long Put Position

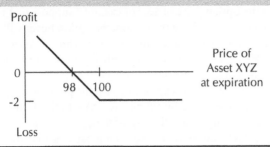

substantial: the theoretical maximum profit is generated if Asset XYZ's price falls to zero. Contrast this profit potential with that of the buyer of a call option. The theoretical maximum profit for a call buyer cannot be determined beforehand, because it depends on the highest price that can be reached by Asset XYZ before or at the option expiration date, a price that is indeterminate.

To see how an option alters the risk/return profile for an investor, we again compare it to a position in Asset XYZ. The long put position is compared to taking a short position in Asset XYZ because this is the position that would realize a profit if the price of the asset falls. Suppose an investor sells Asset XYZ short for $100. The short position in Asset XYZ would produce the following profit or loss compared with the long put position (without considering transactions costs):

1. If Asset XYZ's price rises above $100, the long put option results in a loss of $2, but the short position in Asset XYZ realizes one of the following:
   a. If the price of Asset XYZ is less than $102, there will be a loss of less than $2, which is the loss to the long put position.
   b. If the price of Asset XYZ is equal to $102, the loss will be $2, the same as the maximum loss of the long put position.
   c. If the price of Asset XYZ is greater than $102, the loss will be greater than $2. For example, if the price is $125, the short position will realize a loss of $25, because the short seller must now pay $125 for Asset XYZ that he sold short at $100.
2. If Asset XYZ's price at expiration is equal to $100, the long put position will realize a $2 loss, while there will be no profit or loss on the short position in Asset XYZ.
3. If Asset XYZ's price is less than $100 but greater than $98, the long put position will experience a loss of less than $2, but the short position will realize a profit. For example, a price of $99 at the expiration date will result in a loss of $1 for the long put position but a profit of $1 for the short position.
4. If Asset XYZ's price is $98 at the expiration date, the long put position will break even, but the short position in Asset XYZ will generate a $2 profit.
5. If Asset XYZ's price is below $98, both positions will generate a profit; however, the profit for the long put position will always be $2 less than the profit for the short position.

Table 3 presents a detailed account of this comparison of the profit and loss profiles for the long put position and short position in Asset XYZ. While the investor who takes a short position in Asset XYZ faces all the downside risk as well as the upside potential, the long put position limits the downside risk to the option price while still maintaining upside potential (reduced only by an amount equal to the option price).

Writing (Selling) Put Options

The profit and loss profile for a short put option is the mirror image of the long put option. The maximum profit from this position is the option price. The theoretical maximum loss can be substantial should the price of the underlying asset fall; at the outside, if the price were to fall all the way to zero, the loss would be as large as the strike price less the option price. Figure 4 graphically depicts this profit and loss profile.

To summarize these illustrations of the four option positions, we can say the following: Buying calls or selling puts allows the investor to gain if the price of the underlying asset rises; and selling calls and buying puts allows the investor to gain if the price of the underlying asset falls.

Considering the Time Value of Money

Our illustrations of the four option positions do not take into account the time value of money. Specifically, the buyer of an option must pay the seller the option price at the time the option is purchased. Thus, the buyer must finance the purchase price of the option or, assuming the purchase price does not have to be borrowed, the buyer loses the income that can be earned by investing the amount of the option price until the option is sold or exercised. In contrast, assuming that the seller does not have to use the option price amount as margin for the short position or can use an interest-earning asset as security, the seller has the opportunity to earn income from the proceeds of the option sale.

The time value of money changes the profit/loss profile of the option positions we have discussed. The breakeven price for the buyer and the seller of an option will not be the same as in our illustrations. The breakeven price for the underlying asset at the expiration date is higher for the buyer of the option; for the seller, it is lower.

Our comparisons of the option position with long and short positions in the underlying asset also ignore the time value of money. We have not considered the fact that the underlying asset may generate interim cash flows (dividends in the case of common stock,

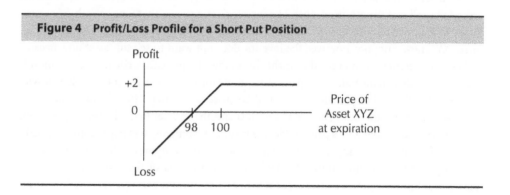

Figure 4   Profit/Loss Profile for a Short Put Position

interest in the case of bonds). The buyer of a call option is not entitled to any interim cash flows generated by the underlying asset. The buyer of the underlying asset, however, would receive any interim cash flows and would have the opportunity to reinvest them. A complete comparison of the long call option position and the long position in the underlying asset must take into account the additional dollars from reinvesting any interim cash flows. Moreover, any effect on the price of the underlying asset as a result of the distribution of cash must be considered. This occurs, for example, when the underlying asset is common stock and, as a result of a dividend payment, the stock declines in price.

Key Points That You Should Understand Before Proceeding

1. There are four basic option positions: buying a call option, selling a call option, buying a put option, and selling a put option.
2. An option can be used to alter the risk/reward relationship from that of a position in the underlying.
3. The buyer of a call option benefits if the price of the underlying rises; the writer (seller) of a call option benefits if the price of the underlying is unchanged or falls.
4. The buyer of a put option benefits if the price of the underlying falls; the writer (seller) of a put option benefits if the price of the underlying is unchanged or rises.
5. In determining the payoff from an option, the time value of money as a result of having to finance the option price must be considered.

ECONOMIC ROLE OF THE OPTIONS MARKETS

Futures contracts allow investors to hedge the risks associated with adverse price movements. Hedging with futures lets a market participant lock in a price, and thereby eliminates price risk. In the process, however, the investor gives up the opportunity to benefit from a favorable price movement. In other words, hedging with futures involves trading off the benefits of a favorable price movement for protection against an adverse price movement.

Hedging with options has a variety of potential benefits. For now, we provide an overview of how options can be used for hedging, and how the outcomes of hedging with options differ from those of hedging with futures. A good way to show the hedging uses of options is to return to the initial illustration in this chapter where the underlying for the option is Asset XYZ.

First, let's consider an investor who owns Asset XYZ, currently selling for $100, which she expects to sell one month from now. The investor's concern is that, one month from now, Asset XYZ's price may decline below $100. One alternative available to this investor is to sell Asset XYZ now. Suppose, however, the investor does not want to sell this asset now because either some restrictions prevent this or she thinks that the price may rise during the month. Suppose also that an insurance company offers to sell the investor an insurance policy providing that, if at the end of one month, Asset XYZ's price is less than $100, the insurance company will make up the difference between $100 and the market price. For example, if one month from now Asset XYZ's price is $80, the insurance company will pay the investor $20.

The insurance company naturally charges the investor a premium to write this policy. Let's suppose that the premium is $2. Holding aside the cost of the insurance policy, the payoff that this investor then faces is as follows. The minimum price for Asset XYZ that the investor can receive is $100 because, if the price is less, the insurance company will make up the difference. If Asset XYZ's price is greater than $100, however, the investor will receive the higher price. The premium of $2 that is required to purchase this insurance policy effectively assures the investor of a minimum price of $98 ($100 minus $2), while if the price is above $100, the investor realizes the benefits of a higher price (reduced always by the $2 for the insurance policy). In buying this policy, the investor has purchased protection against an adverse price movement, while maintaining the opportunity to benefit from a favorable price movement.

Insurance companies do not offer such policies, but we have described an option strategy that provides the same protection. Consider the put option on Asset XYZ with one month to expiration, a strike price of $100, and an option price of $2 that we discussed earlier in this chapter. The payoff to a long position in this put is identical to the insurance policy. The option price resembles the hypothetical insurance premium; this is the reason why the option price is referred to as the option premium. Thus, a put option can be used to hedge against a decline in the price of the underlying instrument.

The long put's payoff is quite different from that of a futures contract. Suppose that a futures contract with Asset XYZ as the underlying instrument has a futures price equal to $100 and a settlement date one month from now. By selling this futures contract, the investor would be agreeing to sell Asset XYZ for $100 one month from now. If Asset XYZ's price falls below $100, the investor is protected because she will receive $100 upon delivery of the asset to satisfy the futures contract. If Asset XYZ's price rises above $100, however, the investor will not realize the price appreciation because she must deliver the asset for an agreed-upon amount of $100. By selling the futures contract, the investor has locked in a price of $100, and fails to realize a gain if the price rises while avoiding a loss if the price declines.

Call options, too, are useful for hedging. A call option can be used to protect against a rise in the price of the underlying instrument while maintaining the opportunity to benefit from a decline in the price of the underlying instrument. Suppose, for example, that an investor expects to receive $100 one month from now, and plans to use that money to purchase Asset XYZ, which is selling currently for $100. The risk that the investor faces is that Asset XYZ's price will rise above $100 one month from now. Let us further suppose there is a call option such as we described earlier in the chapter. The option costs $3 and has a strike price of $100 and a month to expiration. By purchasing that call option, the investor has hedged the risk of a rise in the price of Asset XYZ.

The hedge outcome is as follows. If the price rises above $100 one month from now, the investor would exercise the call option and realize the difference between the market price of Asset XYZ and $100. Thus, if we hold aside the cost of the option for the moment, we can see that the investor is insuring that the maximum price she will have to pay for Asset XYZ is $100. Should the asset's price fall below $100, the call option expires worthless, but the investor benefits by being able to purchase Asset XYZ at a price less than $100. Once the $3 cost of the option is considered, the payoff is as follows. Regardless of the eventual price of the asset, the maximum price that the investor will have to pay for Asset XYZ is $103 (the strike price plus the option price). If the price of the asset declines below $100, the investor will benefit by the amount of the price decline less $3.

Compare this situation to a futures contract where Asset XYZ is the underlying instrument, the settlement is in one month, and the futures price is $100. Suppose that the investor buys this futures contract. If one month from now the price of Asset XYZ rises above $100, the investor has contracted to buy the asset for $100, thereby eliminating the risk of a price rise; if the price falls below $100, however, the investor cannot benefit because she has contracted to pay $100 for the asset.

It should be clear now how hedging with options differs from hedging with futures. This difference cannot be overemphasized—options and futures are not interchangeable instruments.

Although our focus has been on hedging price risk, options also allow investors an efficient way to expand the range of return characteristics available. That is, investors can use options to "mold" a return distribution for a portfolio to fit particular investment objectives.[1]

Key Points That You Should Understand Before Proceeding

1. Hedging with futures involves trading off the benefits of a favorable price movement for protection against an adverse price movement.
2. Hedging with options allows the option buyer to limit risk but maintain the potential to benefit from a favorable price movement.
3. Options allow the investor to mold a risk/return relationship.

U.S. OPTIONS MARKETS

There are a variety of options traded in the United States. Here, we provide a survey of the major ones.

Stock Options

Options on individual shares of common stock have been traded for many years. Trading of standardized call options on common stock began on the Chicago Board Options Exchange (CBOE) in April 1973. Since then, the Securities and Exchange Commission (SEC) has granted permission to other exchanges to trade options: the American Stock Exchange in 1974, the Philadelphia Exchange in 1975, the Pacific and the Midwest Stock Exchanges in 1976, the New York Stock Exchange in 1982, and the International Securities Exchange in 2000. SEC permission to trade put options on common stocks on organized exchanges was not granted until March 1977.

The SEC approved the creation of a national clearing system for options, the **Options Clearing Corporation (OCC)**, jointly established by the CBOE and the American Stock Exchange. Since its establishment in 1974, the OCC has issued, guaranteed, registered, cleared, and settled all transactions involving listed options on all exchanges.

Exchange-traded stock options have a standardized quantity: One contract applies to 100 shares of the designated common stock. While most underlying stocks are those of listed companies, stock options on a number of OTC stocks are also available. However, all the companies are large and their shares are actively traded.

---

[1] See Stephen A. Ross, "Options and Efficiency," *Quarterly Journal of Economics* (February 1976), pp. 75–89; and Fred Arditti and Kose John, "Spanning the State Space with Options," *Journal of Financial and Quantitative Analysis* (March 1980), pp. 1–9.

The OCC has established standard strike price guidelines for listed options. For stocks with a price above $100, option strike prices are set at $10 intervals; for stocks with a price below $100 and above $30, strike prices are set at $5 intervals; and for stocks priced between $10 and $30 the interval is $2.50. While the strike price of exchange-traded options is not changed because of cash dividends paid to common stockholders, the strike price is adjusted for stock splits, stock dividends, reorganization, and other recapitalizations affecting the value of the underlying stock.

All exchange-traded stock options in the United States may be exercised any time before the expiration date; that is, they are American options. They expire at 11:59 P.M. Eastern Standard Time on the Saturday following the third Friday of the expiration month. Exchange rules require that investors wishing to exercise an expiring option must instruct a broker about the exercise no later than 5:30 P.M. Eastern time on the business day immediately preceding the expiration date. Notices to exercise a nonexpiring option on a date other than the expiration date must be made between 10:00 A.M. and 8:00 P.M. Eastern Standard Time. When a nonexpiring option is exercised, the OCC assigns the obligation the next day to someone who has an outstanding short position in an option of the same exercise price, expiration date, and underlying stock. This assignment is on a random basis.

Options are designated by the name of the underlying common stock, the expiration month, the strike price, and the type of option (put or call). Thus, an IBM call option with a strike price of 125 and expiring in January is referred to as the "IBM January call."

The expiration dates are standardized. Each stock is assigned an option cycle, the three option cycles being January, February, and March. The expiration months for each option cycle are as follows:

Option Cycle	Expiration Months
January	January, April, July, October
February	February, May, August, November
March	March, June, September, December

In addition, the practice is to trade options with an expiration date of the current calendar month, the next calendar month, and the next two expiration months in the cycle. For example, suppose a stock is assigned the January option cycle. In February, options with the following expiration months would be traded: February (the current calendar month), March (the next calendar month), April (first next expiration month in the January option cycle), and July (second next option cycle month in the January option cycle). In May, the following expiration months would be traded for a stock assigned to the January option cycle: May (the current calendar month), April (the next calendar month), July (first next expiration month in the January option cycle), and October (second next option cycle month in the January option cycle).

Stock Index Options

In March 1983, a revolution in stock options and investments in general occurred. At that time, trading in an option whose underlying instrument was a stock index, the S&P 100 (originally called the CBOE 100), began on the CBOE. There are options on all the major stock market indexes. In the United States, the four most popular stock index options in terms of trading volume are the S&P 500 Index Option (ticker symbol SPX), S&P 100

Index Option (ticker symbol OEX), Dow Jones Industrial Index Option (DJX), and NAS-DAQ 100 Mini Index Option (MNX). All of these contracts are listed on the CBOE. Index options can have an exercise style that is American or European. As with stock index futures, all stock index options have a multiple. For the four popular stock index options, the multiple is $100.

The S&P 500 Index Option contract is European and the underlying is the S&P 500. The underlying for the S&P 100 Index Option is a capitalization-weighted index of the 100 stocks from a broad range of industries within the S&P 500. While there are both American and European style S&P 100 Index Options, the more popular is the American style. The Dow Jones Industrial Index Option has a European exercise style. The underlying index for the NASDAQ 100 Mini Index Option is a modified capitalization-weighted index composed of the 100 largest nonfinancial stocks listed on the Nasdaq stock market. The "Mini" version of this contract means the underlying is one-tenth of the value of the Nasdaq 100 Index.

There are also stock index options for components of the major broad-based stock market indexes, selected industries, and selected sectors. For example, the CBOE lists the Dow Jones Transportation Average Index Option, Dow Jones Utility Average Index Option, Dow Jones Internet Commerce Index Option, Dow Jones Equity REIT Index Option, CBOE Internet Index Option, CBOE Oil Index Option, CBOE Technology Index Option, and Morgan Stanley Retail Index Option. There are stock index options based on some attribute of the components of an index other than industry or sector. For example, the CBOE lists stock index options based on a classification of the component stock of the Russell 3000 in terms of value and growth. The Russell 1000 Growth Index Option and Russell 1000 Value Index Option include the 1,000 largest stocks in terms of market capitalization in the Russell 3000 that are classified as growth and value, respectively. The underlying for the Dow 10 Index Option includes the top 10 dividend-yielding stocks in the Dow Jones Industrial Average, with each component stock equally weighted in the index.

There are also stock index options based on the exercise style and the length of the expiration period. We already gave one example of the former: the S&P 100 Index Option is available in American and European exercise style. Examples of options with different lengths to expiration when first issued include the Weekly Short-Term S&P 500 Index Option and the Weekly Short-Term S&P 100 Index Option. These options, both listed on the CBOE, expire the Friday following the Friday of the listing of the option. Ordinarily, stock index options are not long term. The S&P Long-Dated Option listed on the CBOE can have an expiration of 24 months.

If a stock option is exercised, a stock must be delivered. It would be complicated, to say the least, to settle a stock index option by delivering all the stocks that make up the index. Instead, stock index options are *cash settlement contracts*. This means that, if the option is exercised, the exchange-assigned option writer pays cash to the option buyer. There is no delivery of any stock.

The dollar value of the stock index underlying an index option is equal to the current cash index value multiplied by the contract's multiple. That is,

$$\text{Dollar value of the underlying index} = \text{Cash index value} \times \text{Contract multiple}$$

Each stock index option has a contract multiple. For example, for the S&P 100 Stock Index the multiple is $100. So, if the cash index value for the S&P 100 is 600, then the dollar value of the S&P 100 contract is 600 × $100 = $60,000.

For a stock option, the price at which the buyer of the option can buy or sell the stock is the strike price. For an index option, the strike index is the index value at which the buyer of the option can buy or sell the underlying stock index. The strike index is converted into a dollar value by multiplying the strike index by the multiple for the contract. For example, if the strike index is 590 for an S&P 100 index option, the dollar value is $59,000 (590 $\times$ $100). If an investor purchases a call option on the S&P 100 with a strike index of 590, and exercises the option when the index value is 600, then the investor has the right to purchase the index for $70,000 when the dollar value of the index is $60,000. The buyer of the call option would then receive $10,000 from the option writer.

There are also options on stock index futures. These options are not as widely used as options on stock indexes. Options on futures contracts are the contracts of choice in the interest rate options market, so we will postpone our discussion of options on futures until later in this chapter.

Long-Term Equity Anticipation Securities

For an individual stock and a stock index, only the next two expiration months are traded on an exchange. Consequently, the longest time before expiration of a standard exchange-traded option is six months. **Long-Term Equity Anticipation Securities (LEAPS)** are option contracts designed to offer option contracts with longer maturities. These contracts are available on individual stocks and some indexes. Stock option LEAPS are comparable to standard stock options except the maturities can range up to 39 months from the origination date. Index options LEAPS differ in size compared with standard index options having a multiplier of 10 rather than 100.

Interest Rate Options

Interest rate options can be written on cash instruments or futures. At one time, there were several exchange-traded option contracts whose underlying instrument was a debt instrument. These contracts are referred to as **options on physicals**. For reasons explained later, options on futures that are based on debt instruments have been far more popular than options on physicals.

Market participants have made increasingly greater use of over-the-counter options on Treasury, agency debentures, and mortgage-backed securities.[2] Certain institutional investors who want to purchase an option on a specific Treasury security or a Ginnie Mae pass-through can do so on an OTC basis. There are government and mortgage-backed securities dealers who make a market in options on specific securities. Typically, the maturity of the option coincides with the time period over which the buyer of the option wants to hedge, so the buyer is not concerned with the option's liquidity.

Besides options on fixed-income securities, investors can obtain OTC options on a yield spread (such as the spread between mortgage pass-through securities and Treasuries or between double-A corporates and Treasuries).

---

[2] For a more detailed discussion of OTC options, see Chapter 2 of Mark Pitts and Frank J. Fabozzi, *Interest Rate Futures and Options* (Chicago: Probus Publishing, 1989).

FLEX Options[3]

A **FLEX option** is an option contract with some terms that have been customized. It is traded on an options exchange and cleared and guaranteed by the associated clearinghouse for the exchange. The need for customization of certain terms is a result of the wide range of portfolio strategy needs of institutional investors that cannot be satisfied by standard exchange-traded options.

A FLEX option can be created for individual stocks, stock indexes, and Treasury securities. The value of FLEX options is the ability to customize the terms of the contract along four dimensions: underlying, strike price, expiration date, and settlement style (i.e., American versus European). Moreover, the exchange provides a secondary market to offset or alter positions and an independent daily marking of prices.

The development of the FLEX option is a response to the growing OTC market. The exchanges seek to make the FLEX option attractive by providing price discovery through a competitive auction market, an active secondary market, daily price valuations, and the virtual elimination of counterparty risk. The FLEX option represents a link between listed options and OTC products.

Exotic Options

OTC options can be customized in any manner sought by an institutional investor. Basically, if a dealer can reasonably hedge the risk associated with the opposite side of the option sought, it will create the option desired by a customer. OTC options are not limited to European or American types. An option can be created in which the option can be exercised at several specified dates as well as the expiration date of the option. As noted earlier, such options are referred to as Bermuda options.

The more complex options created are called **exotic options**. Here are just two types of such exotic options: alternative options and outperformance options. An **alternative option**, also called an **either-or option**, has a payoff which is the best independent payoff of two distinct assets. For example, suppose that Donna buys an alternative call option with the following terms:

1. The underlying is one unit of Asset M or one unit of Asset N.
2. The strike price for Asset M is $80.
3. The strike price for Asset N is $110.
4. The expiration date is three months from now.
5. The option can only be exercised three months from now (that is, it is a European option).

At the expiration date, Donna can decide to buy from the writer of this option *either* one unit of Asset M at $80 or Asset N at $110. Donna will buy the asset with the larger payoff. So, for example, if Asset M and Asset N at the expiration date are $84 and $140, respectively, then the payoff would be $4 if Donna elects to exercise to buy Asset M but $30 if she elects to exercise to buy Asset N. Thus, she will exercise to buy Asset N. If the price for both assets at the expiration date is below their strike price, Donna will let the option expire worthless.

---

[3] For a more detailed description of FLEX options, see James J. Angel, Gary L. Gastineau, and Clifford J. Weber, *Equity FLEX Options* (1999).

An **outperformance option** is an option whose payoff is based on the relative payoff of two assets at the expiration date. For example, consider the following outperformance call option purchased by Karl:

1. Portfolio A consists of the stock of 50 public utility companies with a market value of $1 million.
2. Portfolio B consists of the stock of 50 financial services companies with a market value of $1 million.
3. The expiration date is six months from now and is a European option.
4. The strike is equal to

Market value of Portfolio B − Market value of Portfolio A

At the expiration date, if the market value of Portfolio A is greater than the market value of Portfolio B, then there is no value to this option and it will expire worthless. The option will be exercised if the market value of Portfolio B exceeds the market value of Portfolio A at the expiration date.

Key Points That You Should Understand Before Proceeding

1. There are options traded on individual shares of common stock and options traded on common stock indexes.
2. The dollar value of a stock index option contract is equal to the index value multiplied by the contract's multiple.
3. There are interest rate options in which the underlying is a debt instrument (called an option on a physical) and a futures contract (called a futures option).
4. Exchange-traded options on futures that are based on debt instruments have been far more popular than exchange-traded options on physicals.
5. There has been increased use by institutional investors of OTC options on Treasury and mortgage-backed securities.
6. Complex OTC options are called exotic options.

FUTURES OPTIONS

An option on a futures contract, commonly referred to as a **futures option**, gives the buyer the right to buy from or sell to the writer a designated futures contract at a designated price at any time during the life of the option. If the futures option is a call option, the buyer has the right to purchase one designated futures contract at the exercise price. That is, the buyer has the right to acquire a long futures position in the designated futures contract. If the buyer exercises the call option, the writer (seller) acquires a corresponding short position in the futures contract.

A put option on a futures contract grants the buyer the right to sell one designated futures contract to the writer at the exercise price. That is, the option buyer has the right to acquire a short position in the designated futures contract. If the put option is exercised, the writer acquires a corresponding long position in the designated futures contract.

There are futures options on all the interest rate futures contracts reviewed in the previous chapter.

Mechanics of Trading Futures Options

As the parties to the futures option will realize a position in a futures contract when the option is exercised, the question is: What will the futures price be? That is, at what price will the long be required to pay for the instrument underlying the futures contract, and at what price will the short be required to sell the instrument underlying the futures contract?

Upon exercise, the futures price for the futures contract will be set equal to the exercise price. The position of the two parties is then immediately marked to market based on the then-current futures price. Thus, the futures position of the two parties will be at the prevailing futures price. At the same time, the option writer or seller must pay the option buyer the economic benefit from exercising. In the case of a call futures option, the option writer must pay the difference between the current futures price and the exercise price to the buyer of the option. In the case of a put futures option, the option writer must pay the option buyer the difference between the exercise price and the current futures price.

For example, suppose an investor buys a call option on some futures contract in which the exercise price is 85. Assume also that the futures price is 95, and that the buyer exercises the call option. Upon exercise, the call buyer is given a long position in the futures contract at 85, and the call writer is assigned the corresponding short position in the futures contract at 85. The futures position of the buyer and the writer is immediately marked to market by the exchange. Since the prevailing futures price is 95, and the exercise price is 85, the long futures position (the position of the call buyer) realizes a gain of 10 while the short futures position (the position of the call writer) realizes a loss of 10. The call writer pays the exchange 10 and the call buyer receives 10 from the exchange. The call buyer, who now has a long futures position at 95, can either liquidate the futures position at 95 or maintain a long futures position. If the former course of action is taken, the call buyer sells a futures contract at the prevailing futures price of 95. There is no gain or loss from liquidating the position. Overall, the call buyer realizes a gain of 10. If the call buyer elects to hold the long futures position, then he or she will face the same risk and reward of holding such a position. But the call buyer still has realized a gain of 10 from the exercise of the call option.

Suppose, instead, that the futures option is a put rather than a call, and the current futures price is 60 rather than 95. If the buyer of this put option exercises it, the buyer would have a short position in the futures contract at 85; the option writer would have a long position in the futures contract at 85. The exchange then marks the position to market at the then-current futures price of 60, resulting in a gain to the put buyer of 25 and a loss to the put writer of the same amount. The put buyer, now having a short futures position at 60, can either maintain that position or liquidate it by buying a futures contract at the prevailing futures price of 60. In either case, the put buyer realizes a gain of 25 from exercising the put option.

The exchange imposes no margin requirements for the buyer of a futures option once the option price has been paid in full. Because the maximum amount the buyer can lose is the option price, regardless of how adverse the price movement of the underlying instrument, there is no need for margin.

Because the writer (seller) of an option has agreed to accept all of the risk (and none of the reward) of the position in the underlying instrument, the writer (seller) is required to deposit not only the margin required on the interest rate futures contract position if that is the underlying instrument, but, with certain exceptions, also the option price that is received for writing the option. In addition, if prices for the underlying futures contract adversely affect the writer's position, the writer would be required to deposit variation margin as it is marked to market.

Reasons for the Popularity of Futures Options

There are three reasons why futures options on fixed-income securities have largely supplanted options on physicals as the options vehicle used by institutional investors.[4] First, unlike options on fixed-income securities, futures options on Treasury coupon futures do not require payments for accrued interest to be made. Consequently, when a futures option is exercised, the call buyer and the put writer need not compensate the other party for accrued interest.

Second, futures options are believed to be "cleaner" instruments because of the reduced likelihood of delivery squeezes. Market participants who must deliver an instrument are concerned that the instrument to be delivered will be in short supply at the time of delivery, resulting in a higher price to acquire it. As the deliverable supply of futures contracts is more than adequate for futures options currently traded, there is no concern about a delivery squeeze.

Finally, in order to price any option, it is imperative to know at all times the price of the underlying instrument. As we mentioned in our discussions of the various bond markets, current bond prices are not easily available. In contrast, futures prices are readily available.

Key Points That You Should Understand Before Proceeding

1. A futures option gives the buyer the right to buy from or sell to the writer a designated futures contract at a designated price at any time during the life of the option.
2. If the buyer of the futures option exercises, the futures price for the futures contract will be set equal to the exercise price, but the position of the two parties is then immediately marked to market based on the then-current futures price.
3. There are several reasons why futures options on fixed-income securities have been used more by institutional investors than options on physicals.

SUMMARY

An option is a contract between two parties, the buyer and the seller (or writer). The buyer pays a price or premium to the seller for the right (but not the obligation) to buy or sell a certain amount of a specified item at a set price for a specified period of time. The right to buy is a call option, and the right to sell is a put option. The set price is the exercise or strike price. The period ends on the maturity or expiration date. If the right cannot be exercised until that date, the option is called a European option. If the option can be exercised at any time before the maturity date, the option is an American option. The item to which the

---

[4] Laurie Goodman, "Introduction to Debt Options," Chapter 1 in Frank J. Fabozzi (ed.), *Winning the Interest Rate Game: A Guide to Debt Options* (Chicago: Probus Publishing, 1985), pp. 13–14.

option applies is the underlying asset, and its value determines the value of the option. Hence, options are called derivative instruments.

Options traded on exchanges are standardized and guaranteed by the exchange and its clearinghouse, and trading in these options is monitored by the SEC. Customized options are traded in the unregulated OTC market.

Options differ from futures in several key ways. First, both parties to a futures contract accept an obligation to transact, but only the writer of an option has an obligation, and that occurs if the buyer wishes to exercise the option. Second, the option buyer has a limited, known maximum loss. Third, the risk/return profile of an option position is asymmetric, while that of a futures position is symmetric.

The risk/return profile of the option buyer is the mirror image of the risk/return profile of the option writer, whether the option is a put or a call, American or European. The purchase of a call option is like taking a long position in the underlying asset but with a fixed, maximum loss. The purchase of a put option resembles the short sale of the underlying asset but with a known maximum loss.

The essence of hedging with options is that it minimizes loss while reducing gains only by the price of the option. Thus, hedging with options is very much like taking out an insurance policy. Hedging with options differs from hedging with futures because the latter establishes a known, future price and does not allow the hedger to participate in gains that price changes might generate for the investor.

Options may be written on individual stocks or on bundles and groups of stocks. Those written on groups are called index options, the most popular being the S&P 100. Several stock index options are traded on major exchanges around the world. The exercise of stock options involves an exchange of cash for shares. By contrast, stock index options are cash settlement contracts, where the buyer receives the cash value of the difference between the exercise price (called the strike index) and the actual level of the stock market index. Options based on important government debt securities are also traded on major exchanges.

LEAPS and FLEX options essentially modify an existing feature of either a stock option, an index option, or both. LEAPS are designed to offer options with longer maturities. FLEX options allow users to specify the terms of the option contract.

An option on a futures contract gives the buyer the right to acquire a position in a futures contract—a long position in the case of a call option and a short position in the case of a put option. These options, referred to as futures options, are the option of choice in the fixed-income market.

OTC options can be customized in any manner sought by an institutional investor. Exotic options are the more complex options created in the OTC market. Two examples of exotic options are alternative options and outperformance options.

KEY TERMS

- Alternative option (either-or option)
- American option
- Bermuda option (Atlantic option)
- Call option (call)
- European option
- Exchange-traded option
- Exercise (strike) price
- Exercise style
- Exotic option
- Expiration (maturity) date

- FLEX option
- Futures option
- Long a call option
- Long a put option
- Long-Term Equity Anticipation Securities (LEAPS)
- Option
- Options on physicals

- Option price (option premium)
- Options Clearing Corporation (OCC)
- Outperformance option
- Put option
- Short a call option
- Short a put option
- Writer

QUESTIONS

1. Identify and explain the key features of an option contract.
2. What is the difference between a put option and a call option?
3. What is the difference between an American option and a European option?
4. Why does an option writer need to post margin?
5. Identify two important ways in which an exchange-traded option differs from a typical OTC option.
6. **a.** What are the main ways in which an option differs from a futures contract?
   b. Why are options and futures labeled *derivative securities*?
7. Explain how this statement can be true: "A long call position offers potentially unlimited gains, if the underlying asset's price rises, but a fixed, maximum loss if the underlying asset's price drops to zero."
8. Suppose a call option on a stock has an exercise price of $70 and a cost of $2, and suppose you buy the call. Identify the profit to your investment, at the call's expiration, for each of these values of the underlying stock: $25, $70, $100, $400.
9. Consider again the situation in question 8. Suppose you had sold the call option. What would your profit be, at expiration, for each of the stock prices?
10. Explain why you agree or disagree with this statement: "Buying a put is just like short selling the underlying asset. You gain the same thing from either position, if the underlying asset's price falls. If the price goes up, you have the same loss."
11. Why do stock index options involve cash settlement rather than delivery of the underlying stocks?

12. Suppose you bought an index call option for 5.50 that has a strike price of 200 and that, at expiration, you exercised it. Suppose, too, that at the time you exercised the call option, the index has a value of 240.
    a. If the index option has a multiple of $100, how much money does the writer of this option pay you?
    b. What profit did you realize from buying this call option?
13. How do LEAPS differ from standard stock options and standard index options?
14. **a.** What are the terms that can be customized in a FLEX option?
    b. Why was the FLEX option introduced by exchanges?
15. Suppose that you buy an alternative call option with the following terms:
    - The underlying asset is one unit of Asset G or one unit of Asset H.
    - The strike price for Asset G is $100.
    - The strike price for Asset H is $115.
    - The expiration date is four months from now.
    - The option can only be exercised at the expiration date.
    a. What is the payoff from this option if at the expiration date the price of Asset G is $125 and the price of Asset H is $135?
    b. What is the payoff from this option if at the expiration date the price of Asset G is $90 and the price of Asset H is $125?
    c. What is the payoff from this option if at the expiration date the price of Asset G is $90 and the price of Asset H is $105?

16. Suppose that you buy an outperformance call option with the following terms:
    - Portfolio X consists of bonds with a market value of $5 million.
    - Portfolio Y consists of stocks with a market value of $5 million.
    - The expiration date is nine months from now and is a European option.
    - The strike price is equal to

      Market value of Portfolio X −
      Market value of Portfolio Y

    What is the payoff of this option if at the expiration date the market value of Portfolio X is $10 million and the market value of Portfolio Y is $12 million?

17. Suppose you have a long position in a call option on a futures contract, and the strike price is 80. The futures contract price is now 87, and you want to exercise your option. Identify the gains from exercise, specifying any cash inflow and the futures position you get (and the price of the futures contract).

Pricing of Futures and
Options Contracts

LEARNING OBJECTIVES

After reading this chapter, you will understand

- the theory of pricing a futures contract

- how arbitrage between the futures market and the cash or spot market links the prices of those markets

- the meaning of the terms cost of carry and net financing cost

- the convergence of the futures and cash prices for a particular asset at the settlement date of the futures contract

- why the actual futures price may differ from the theoretical futures price

- how the market price of an option can be broken down into an intrinsic value and a time premium

- why arbitrage ensures that the prices of calls and puts on the same underlying asset with the same exercise price and expiration date have a certain relationship to each other

- the factors that affect the price of an option: the underlying asset's current price and expected price volatility, the contract's expiration date and exercise price, the short-term rate of interest, and any cash flows from the underlying asset

- the principles of the binomial option pricing model and how the model is derived

I n this chapter, we explain how to determine the theoretical price of these contracts using arbitrage arguments. A close examination of the underlying assumptions necessary to derive the theoretical price indicates how it must be modified to price the specific contracts.

PRICING OF FUTURES CONTRACTS

To understand what determines the futures price, consider the futures contract where the underlying instrument is Asset XYZ. We make several assumptions:

1. Asset XYZ is selling for $100 in the cash market.
2. Asset XYZ pays the holder (with certainty) $12 per year in four quarterly payments of $3, and the next quarterly payment is exactly three months from now.
3. The futures contract requires delivery three months from now.
4. The current three-month interest rate at which funds can be lent or borrowed is 8% per year.

What should the price of this futures contract be? That is, what should the futures price be? Suppose the price of the futures contract is $107. Consider this strategy:

Sell the futures contract at $107.
Purchase Asset XYZ in the cash market for $100.
Borrow $100 for three months at 8% per year.

The borrowed funds are used to purchase Asset XYZ, resulting in no initial cash outlay for this strategy. At the end of three months, $3 will be received from holding Asset XYZ. Three months from now, Asset XYZ must be delivered to settle the futures contract, and the loan must be repaid. This strategy produces an outcome as follows:

1. From settlement of the futures contract:
   Proceeds from sale of Asset XYZ to settle the futures contract   = $107
   Payment received from investing in Asset XYZ for three months   =   3
   Total proceeds   = $110

2. From the loan:
   Repayment of principal of loan   = $100
   Interest on loan (2% for three months)   =   2
   Total outlay   = $102

3. Profit: $ 8

Notice that this strategy guarantees a profit of $8. Moreover, this profit is generated with no investment outlay; the funds needed to buy Asset XYZ were borrowed. The profit is realized regardless of what the futures price at the settlement date is. In financial terms, the profit arises from a riskless arbitrage between the price of Asset XYZ in the cash or spot market and the price of Asset XYZ in the futures market. Obviously, in a well-functioning market, arbitrageurs who could get this riskless gain for a zero investment would sell the futures and buy Asset XYZ, forcing the futures price down and bidding up Asset XYZ's price so as to eliminate this profit.

This strategy that resulted in the capturing of the arbitrage profit is referred to as a **cash and carry trade**. The reason for this name is that it involves borrowing cash to purchase a security and "carrying" that security to the futures settlement date.

Suppose instead that the futures price is $92 and not $107. Let's consider this strategy:

Buy the futures contract at $92.
Sell (short) Asset XYZ for $100.
Invest (lend) $100 for three months at 8% per year.[1]

Once again, there is no initial cash outlay for the strategy: The cost of the long position in the futures contract is zero, and there is no cost to selling the asset short and lending the money. Three months from now, Asset XYZ must be purchased to settle the long position in the futures contract. Asset XYZ accepted for delivery will then be used to cover the short position—to cover the short sale of Asset XYZ in the cash market. Shorting Asset XYZ requires the short seller to pay the lender of Asset XYZ the proceeds that the lender would have earned for the quarter. Therefore, the strategy requires a payment of $3 to the lender of Asset XYZ. The outcome in three months would be as follows:

1. From settlement of the futures contract:
   Price paid for purchase of Asset XYZ to settle futures contract   = $ 92
   Proceeds to lender of Asset XYZ to borrow the asset   =   3
   Total outlay   = $ 95

2. From the loan:
   Principal from maturing of investment   = $100
   Interest earned on loan ($2 for three months)   =   2
   Total proceeds   = $102

3. Profit: $ 7

The $7 profit from this strategy is also a riskless arbitrage profit. This strategy requires no initial cash outlay, but will generate a profit whatever the price of Asset XYZ is at the settlement date. Clearly, this opportunity would lead arbitrageurs to buy futures and short Asset XYZ, and the effect of these two actions would be to raise the futures price and lower the cash price until the profit again disappeared.

This strategy that resulted in the capturing of the arbitrage profit is referred to as a **reverse cash and carry trade**. That is, with this strategy a security is sold short and the proceeds received from the short sale are invested.

At what futures price would the arbitraging stop? Another way to ask this question is this: Is there a futures price that would prevent the opportunity for the riskless arbitrage profit? Yes, there is. There will be no arbitrage profit if the futures price is $99. Let's look at what happens if the two previous strategies (cash and carry trade and reverse cash and carry trade) are followed, now assuming a futures price of $99.

Consider the first strategy (cash and carry), which has these elements:

Sell the futures contract at $99.
Purchase Asset XYZ in the cash market for $100.
Borrow $100 for three months at 8% per year.

---

[1] Consider the first strategy (cash and carry trade), which had these elements: Technically, a short seller may not be entitled to the full use of the proceeds resulting from the sale. We will discuss this later in this section.

In three months, the outcome will be as follows:

1. From settlement of the futures contract:

Proceeds from sale of Asset XYZ to settle the futures contract	= $ 99
Payment received from investing in Asset XYZ for 3 months	= 3
Total proceeds	= $102

2. From the loan:

Repayment of principal of loan	= $100
Interest on loan (2% for three months)	= 2
Total outlay	= $102

3. Profit: $ 0

If the futures price is $99, the arbitrage profit has disappeared.

Next, consider the strategy consisting of these actions:

Buy the futures contract at $99.
Sell (short) Asset XYZ for $100.
Invest (lend) $100 for three months at 8% per year.

The outcome in three months would be as follows:

1. From settlement of the futures contract:

Price paid for purchase of Asset XYZ to settle futures contract	= $ 99
Proceeds to lender of Asset XYZ to borrow the asset	= 3
Total outlay	= $102

2. From the loan:

Principal from maturing of investment	= $100
Interest earned on loan ($2 for three months)	= 2
Total proceeds	= $102

3. Profit: $ 0

Thus, if the futures price were $99, neither strategy would result in an arbitrage profit. Hence, a futures price of $99 is the equilibrium price because any higher or lower futures price will permit riskless arbitrage profits.

Theoretical Futures Price Based on Arbitrage Model

According to the arbitrage arguments we have just presented, we see that the equilibrium or theoretical futures price can be determined on the basis of the following information:

1. The price of the asset in the cash market.
2. The cash yield earned on the asset until the settlement date. In our example, the cash yield on Asset XYZ is $3 on a $100 investment or 3% quarterly (12% annual cash yield).
3. The **financing cost**, which is the interest rate for borrowing and lending until the settlement date. In our example, the financing cost is 2% for the three months.

To develop a theory of futures pricing, we will use the following notation:

F = Futures price ($)
P = Cash market price ($)
r = Financing cost (%)
y = Cash yield (%)

Pricing of Futures and Options Contracts

Now, consider the cash and carry trade:

Sell (or take a short position in) the futures contract at F.
Purchase Asset XYZ for P.
Borrow P at a rate of r until the settlement date.

The outcome at the settlement date would be:

1. From settlement of the futures contract:

Proceeds from sale of Asset XYZ to settle the futures contract	$=$	F
Payment received from investing in Asset XYZ	$=$	yP
Total proceeds	$=$	$F + yP$

2. From the loan:

Repayment of principal of loan	$=$	P
Interest on loan	$=$	rP
Total outlay	$=$	$P + rP$

The profit will equal

$$\text{Profit} = \text{Total proceeds} - \text{Total outlay}$$
$$\text{Profit} = F + yP - (P + rP)$$

The equilibrium futures price is the price that ensures that the profit from this arbitrage strategy is zero. Thus, equilibrium requires that

$$0 = F + yP - (P + rP)$$

Solving for the theoretical futures price gives this equation:

$$F = P + P(r - y)$$

In other words, the equilibrium futures price is simply a function of the cash price, the financing cost, and the cash yield on the asset.

Alternatively, let us consider the reverse cash and carry trade illustrated in our example above, which looks like this:

Buy the futures contract at F.
Sell (short) Asset XYZ for P.
Invest (lend) P at a rate of r until the settlement date.

The outcome at the settlement date would be

1. From settlement of the futures contract:

Price paid for purchase of asset to settle futures contract	$=$	F
Payment to lender of asset in order to borrow the asset	$=$	yP
Total outlay	$=$	$F + yP$

2. From the loan:

Principal from maturing of investment	$=$	P
Interest earned on loan	$=$	rP
Total proceeds	$=$	$P + rP$

The profit will equal

$$\text{Profit} = \text{Total proceeds} - \text{Total outlay}$$
$$\text{Profit} = P + rP - (F + yP)$$

Setting the profit equal to zero, so that there will be no arbitrage profit, and solving for the futures price, we obtain the same equation for the futures price as derived earlier:

$$F = P + P(r - y)$$

It is instructive to apply this equation to our previous example to determine the theoretical futures price. In that example, the key variables have these values:

$r = 0.02$
$y = 0.03$
$P = \$100$

Then the theoretical futures price is

$$F = \$100 - \$100\,(0.03 - 0.02)$$
$$= \$100 - \$1 = \$99$$

This agrees with the equilibrium futures price we proposed earlier.

The theoretical futures price may be at a premium to the cash market price (higher than the cash market price) or at a discount from the cash market price (lower than the cash market price), depending on the value of $P(r - y)$. The term $r - y$, which reflects the difference between the cost of financing and the asset's cash yield, is called the **net financing cost**. The net financing cost is more commonly called the **cost of carry**, or simply, **carry**. **Positive carry** means that the yield earned is greater than the financing cost; **negative carry** means that the financing cost exceeds the yield earned. We can summarize the effect of carry on the difference between the futures price and the cash market price in this way:

Carry	Futures Price
Positive ($y > r$)	will sell at a discount to cash price ($F < P$)
Negative ($y < r$)	will sell at a premium to cash price ($F > P$)
Zero ($r = y$)	will be equal to the cash price ($F = P$)

Price Convergence at the Delivery Date

At the delivery date, which is when the futures contract settles, the futures price must equal the cash market price because a futures contract with no time left until delivery is equivalent to a cash market transaction. Thus, as the delivery date approaches, the futures price will converge to the cash market price. This fact is evident from the equation for the theoretical futures price. As the delivery date approaches, the financing cost approaches zero, and the yield that can be earned by holding the investment approaches zero. Hence, the cost of carry approaches zero, and the futures price will approach the cash market price.

A Closer Look at the Theoretical Futures Price

To derive the theoretical futures price using the arbitrage argument, we made several assumptions. When the assumptions are violated, the actual futures price will diverge from the theoretical futures price. That is, the difference between the two prices will differ from the value of carry. Next, we examine those assumptions and identify practical reasons why the actual prices of all financial futures contracts tend to deviate from their theoretical prices.

Interim Cash Flows

Our theoretical analysis assumes that no interim cash flows arise because of changes in futures prices and the variation margin of the organized exchanges on which futures are traded. In addition, our approach assumes implicitly that any dividends or coupon interest payments are paid at the delivery date rather than at some time between initiation of the cash position and expiration of the futures contract. However, we know that interim cash flows of either type can and do occur in practice.

In the case of stock index futures, incorporating interim dividend payments into the pricing model is necessary because a cash position in a set of 100 or 500 stocks (the number of stocks underlying an index) generates cash flows in the form of dividends from the stocks. The dividend rate and the pattern of dividend payments are not known with certainty. They must be projected from the historical dividend payments of the companies in the index. Once the dividend payments are projected, they can be incorporated into the pricing model. The only problem is that the value of the dividend payments at the settlement date will depend on the interest rate at which the dividend payments can be reinvested from the time they are projected to be received until the settlement date. The lower the dividend, and the closer the dividend payments to the settlement date of the futures contract, the less important the reinvestment income is in determining the futures price.

It is important to note that, in the absence of initial and variation margins, the theoretical price for the contract is technically the theoretical price for a forward contract, not the theoretical price for a futures contract. This is because, unlike a futures contract, a forward contract is not marked to market at the end of each trading day, and therefore does not require variation margin and does not generate cash inflows from gains or outflows from losses.

Differences between Lending and Borrowing Rates

In deriving the theoretical futures price, we assumed that the investor's borrowing rate and lending rate are equal. Typically, however, the borrowing rate is higher than the lending rate. The impact of this inequality is important and easy to identify. We will begin by adopting these symbols for the two rates:

r_B = Borrowing rate
r_L = Lending rate

Now, consider the cash and carry trade:

Sell the futures contract at F.
Purchase the asset for P.
Borrow P until the settlement date at r_B.

Clearly, the futures price that would produce no arbitrage profit is

$$F = P + P(r_B - y)$$

Recall that the reverse cash and carry trade is

> Buy the futures contract at F.
> Sell (short) the asset for P.
> Invest (lend) P at r_L until the settlement date.

The futures price that would prevent a riskless profit is

$$F = P + P(r_L - y)$$

These two equations together provide boundaries between which the futures price will be in equilibrium. The first equation establishes the upper boundary, and the second equation the lower boundary. For example, assume that the borrowing rate is 8% per year, or 2% for three months, while the lending rate is 6% per year, or 1.5% for three months. According to the first equation, the upper boundary is

$$F(\text{upper boundary}) = \$100 + \$100\,(0.02 - 0.03) = \$99$$

The lower boundary according to the second equation is

$$F(\text{lower boundary}) = \$100 + \$100\,(0.015 - 0.03) = \$98.50$$

Thus, equilibrium is achieved if the futures price takes on any value between the two boundaries. In other words, equilibrium requires that $\$98.50 \leq F \leq \$99$.

Transaction Costs

In deriving the theoretical futures price, we ignored transaction costs of the elements in the arbitrage strategies. In actuality, the costs of entering into and closing the cash position as well as round-trip transaction costs for the futures contract do affect the futures price. It is easy to show, as we did previously for borrowing and lending rates, that transaction costs widen the boundaries for the equilibrium futures price. The details need not concern us here.

Short Selling

In the strategy involving short selling of Asset XYZ when the futures price is below its theoretical value, we explicitly assumed in the reverse cash and carry trade that the proceeds from the short sale are received and reinvested. In practice, for individual investors, the proceeds are not received, and, in fact, the individual investor is required to put up margin (securities margin and not futures margin) to short sell. For institutional investors, the asset may be borrowed, but there is a cost to borrowing. This cost of borrowing can be incorporated into the model by reducing the yield on the asset.

For strategies applied to stock index futures, a short sale of the stocks in the index means that all stocks in the index must be sold simultaneously. The stock exchange rule for the short selling of stock may prevent an investor from implementing the arbitrage strategy. The short selling rule for stocks specifies that a short sale can be made only at a price that is higher than the previous trade (referred to as an uptick), or at a price that is equal to the previous trade (referred to as a zero tick) but higher than the last trade at a different price. If the arbitrage requires selling the stocks in the index simultaneously, and the last transaction for some of the stocks is not an uptick, the stocks cannot be shorted simultaneously. Thus, an institutional rule may in effect keep arbitrageurs from bringing the actual futures price in line with the theoretical futures price.

Known Deliverable Asset and Settlement Date
Our example illustrating arbitrage strategies assumes that (1) only one asset is deliverable, and (2) the settlement date occurs at a known, fixed point in the future. Neither assumption is consistent with the delivery rules for some futures contracts. The case of U.S. Treasury bond and note futures contracts illustrates the point: An investor in a long position cannot know either the specific Treasury bond to be delivered or the specific date within the contract month when it might be delivered. This substantial uncertainty is a result of the delivery options that the short position in a futures contract has. As a reflection of the short positions' options and advantages, the actual futures price will be less than the theoretical futures price for the Treasury bond and note futures contracts.

The Deliverable Is a Basket of Securities
Some futures contracts involve a single asset, but other contracts apply to a basket of assets or an index. Stock index futures and the municipal bond index futures contracts are examples. The problem in arbitraging these two futures contracts is that it is too expensive to buy or sell every security included in the index. Instead, a portfolio containing a smaller number of assets may be constructed to track the index (which means having price movements that are very similar to changes in the index). Nonetheless, arbitrage based on this tracking portfolio is no longer risk-free because of the risk that the portfolio will not track the index exactly. Clearly, then, the actual price of futures based on baskets of assets may diverge from the theoretical price because of transactions costs as well as uncertainty about the outcome of the arbitrage.

Different Tax Treatment of Cash and Futures Transactions
The basic arbitrage model presented in this chapter ignores not only taxes but also different tax treatment of cash market transactions and futures transactions. Obviously, these factors can keep the actual futures price from being equal to the theoretical price.

Key Points That You Should Understand Before Proceeding

1. The equilibrium or theoretical futures price can be determined through arbitrage arguments.
2. The strategy that can be used to capture the arbitrage profit for an overpriced futures contract is the cash and carry trade; the strategy that can be used to capture the arbitrage profit for an underpriced futures contract is the reverse cash and carry trade.
3. The theoretical futures price depends on the price of the underlying asset in the cash market, the cost of financing a position in the underlying asset, and the cash yield on the underlying asset.
4. At the delivery date, the price of a futures contract converges to the cash market price.
5. The actual futures price will diverge from the theoretical futures price because of interim cash flows, differences between lending and borrowing rates, transaction costs, restrictions on short selling, and uncertainty about the deliverable asset and the date it will be delivered.

PRICING OF OPTIONS

The theoretical price of an option is also derived from arbitrage arguments. However, the pricing of options is not as simple as the pricing of futures contracts.

Basic Components of the Option Price

The option price is the sum of the option's **intrinsic value** and a premium over intrinsic value that is often referred to as the *time value* or *time premium*. While the former term is more common, we will use the term **time premium** to avoid confusion between the time value of money and the time value of the option.

Intrinsic Value

The intrinsic value of an option, at any time, is its economic value if it is exercised immediately. If no positive economic value would result from exercising immediately, the intrinsic value is zero.

Computationally, the intrinsic value of a call option is the difference between the current price of the underlying asset and the strike price. If that difference is positive, then the intrinsic value equals that difference; if the difference is zero or negative, then the intrinsic value is set equal to zero. For example, if the strike price for a call option is $100 and the current asset price is $105, the intrinsic value is $5. That is, an option buyer exercising the option and simultaneously selling the underlying asset would realize $105 from the sale of the asset, which would be covered by acquiring the asset from the option writer for $100, thereby, netting a $5 gain.

When an option has intrinsic value, it is said to be **in the money**. When the strike price of a call option exceeds the current asset price, the call option is said to be **out of the money**; it has no intrinsic value. An option for which the strike price is equal to the current asset price is said to be **at the money**. Both at-the-money and out-of-the-money options have intrinsic values of zero because it is not profitable to exercise them. Our call option with a strike price of $100 would be: (1) in the money when the current asset price is more than $100, (2) out of the money when the current asset price is less than $100, and (3) at the money when the current asset price is equal to $100.

For a put option, the intrinsic value is equal to the amount by which the current asset price is below the strike price. For example, if the strike price of a put option is $100, and the current asset price is $92, the intrinsic value is $8. That is, the buyer of the put option who simultaneously buys the underlying asset and exercises the put option will net $8 by exercising. The asset will be sold to the writer for $100 and purchased in the market for $92. For our put option with a strike price of $100, the option would be: (1) in the money when the current asset price is less than $100, (2) out of the money when the current asset price exceeds $100, (3) at the money when the current asset price is equal to $100.

Time Premium

The time premium of an option is the amount by which the option's market price exceeds its intrinsic value. The option buyer hopes that, at some time prior to expiration, changes in the market price of the underlying asset will increase the value of the rights conveyed by the option. For this prospect, the option buyer is willing to pay a premium above the intrinsic value. For example, if the price of a call option with a strike price of $100 is $9 when the current asset price is $105, the time premium of this option is $4 ($9 minus its intrinsic value of $5). Had the current asset price been $90 instead of $105, then the time premium of this option would be the entire $9 because the option has no intrinsic value. Clearly, other things being equal, the time premium of an option will increase with the amount of time remaining to expiration.

An option buyer has two ways to realize the value of a position taken in the option. The first way is to exercise the option. The second way is to sell the call option for its market price. In the first example above, selling the call for $9 is preferable to exercising, because the exercise will realize a gain of only $5 but the sale will realize a gain of $9. As this example shows, exercise causes the immediate loss of any time premium. It is important to note that there are circumstances under which an option may be exercised prior to the expiration date. These circumstances depend on whether the total proceeds at the expiration date would be greater by holding the option or exercising and reinvesting any received cash proceeds until the expiration date.

Put–Call Parity Relationship

There is an important relationship between the price of a call option and the price of a put option on the same underlying instrument, with the same strike price and the same expiration date. An example can illustrate this relationship, which is commonly referred to as the **put–call parity relationship.**

Our example assumes that a put option and a call option are available on the same underlying asset (Asset XYZ), and that both options have one month to expiration and a strike price of $100. The example assumes the price of the underlying asset to be $100. The call and put prices are assumed to be $3 and $2, respectively.

To see if the two prices have the right relationship, consider what happens if an investor pursues this strategy:

> Buy Asset XYZ at a price of $100.
> Sell a call option at a price of $3.
> Buy a put option at a price of $2.

This strategy generates these positions:

> Long Asset XYZ
> Short the call option
> Long the put option

Table 1 shows the profit and loss profile at the expiration date for this strategy. Notice that, no matter what Asset XYZ's price is at the expiration date, the strategy will produce a profit of $1. The net cost of creating this position is the cost of purchasing Asset XYZ ($100) plus the cost of buying the put ($2) less the price received from selling the call ($3), which is $99. Suppose that the net cost of creating the position for one month is less than $1. Then, by borrowing $99 to create the position so that no investment outlay is made by the investor, this strategy will produce a net profit of $1 (as shown in the last column of Table 1) less the cost of borrowing $99, which is assumed to be less than $1. This situation cannot exist in an efficient market. As market participants implement the strategy to capture the $1 profit, their actions will have one or more of the following consequences, which

Table 1   Profit/Loss Profile for a Strategy Involving a Long Position in Asset XYZ, Short Call Option Position, and Long Put Option Position

Assumptions:
Price of Asset XYZ: $100
Call option price: $3
Put option price: $2
Strike price 5: 100
Time to expiration: 1 month

Price of Asset XYZ at Expiration Date	Profit from Asset XYZ *	Price Received for Call	Price Paid for Put	Overall Profit
$150	0	3	−2	1
140	0	3	−2	1
130	0	3	−2	1
120	0	3	−2	1
115	0	3	−2	1
110	0	3	−2	1
105	0	3	−2	1
100	0	3	−2	1
95	0	3	−2	1
90	0	3	−2	1
85	0	3	−2	1
80	0	3	−2	1
75	0	3	−2	1
70	0	3	−2	1
65	0	3	−2	1
60	0	3	−2	1

*There is no profit because at a price above $100 Asset XYZ will be called from the investor at a price of $100, and at a price below $100, Asset XYZ will be put by the investor at a price of $100.

will tend to eliminate the $1 profit: (1) the price of Asset XYZ will increase, (2) the call option price will drop, and/or (3) the put option price will rise.

Our example clearly implies that, if Asset XYZ's price does not change, the call price and the put price must tend toward equality. But our example ignores the time value of money (financing and opportunity costs, cash payments, and reinvestment income). Also, our example does not consider the possibility of early exercise of the options. Thus, we have been considering a put–call parity relationship for only European options.

It can be shown that the put–call parity relationship for options where the underlying asset makes cash distributions and where the time value of money is recognized is

$$\text{Put option price} - \text{Call option price} = \text{Present value of strike price} + \text{Present value of cash distribution} - \text{Price of underlying asset}$$

Once more, we note that this relationship is actually the put–call parity relationship for European options. However, the values of puts and calls that are American options do conform approximately to this relationship. If this relationship does not hold, arbitrage opportunities exist. That is, investors will be able to construct portfolios consisting of long and short positions in the asset and related options that will provide an extra return with (practical) certainty.

Factors that Influence the Option Price

Six factors influence the price of an option:

1. current price of the underlying asset
2. strike price
3. time to expiration of the option
4. expected price volatility of the underlying asset over the life of the option
5. short-term, risk-free interest rate over the life of the option
6. anticipated cash payments on the underlying asset over the life of the option

The impact of each of these factors may depend on whether (1) the option is a call or a put, and (2) the option is an American option or a European option. A summary of the effect of each factor on put and call option prices is presented in Table 2. Here we briefly explain why the factors have the particular effects.

Current Price of the Underlying Asset

The option price will change as the price of the underlying asset changes. For a call option, as the price of the underlying asset increases (all other factors constant), the option price increases. The opposite holds for a put option: As the price of the underlying asset increases, the price of a put option decreases.

Strike Price

The strike price is fixed for the life of the option. All other factors equal, the lower the strike price, the higher the price for a call option. For put options, the higher the exercise price, the higher the option price. Table 3 shows this for the price of IBM call and put options on June 6, 2008, expiring in October 2008.

Time to Expiration of the Option

An option is a *wasting asset*. That is, after the expiration date the option has no value. All other factors equal, the longer the time to expiration of the option, the higher the option price. This is because, as the time to expiration decreases, less time remains for the underlying asset's price to rise (for a call buyer) or fall (for a put buyer), and therefore the probability of a favorable price movement decreases. Consequently, for American options, as the time remaining until expiration decreases, the option price approaches its intrinsic value.

Table 2 Summary of Factors that Affect the Price of an Option

Factor	Effect of an increase of factor on	
	Call Price	Put Price
Current price of underlying asset	Increase	Decrease
Strike price	Decrease	Increase
Time to expiration of option	Increase	Increase
Expected price volatility	Increase	Increase
Short-term interest rate	Increase	Decrease
Anticipated cash payments	Decrease	Increase

Table 3 Market Price on June 6, 2008, of IBM Put and Call Options Expiring October 2008

Call Options			Put Options		
Strike	Symbol	Last	Strike	Symbol	Last
70	IBMJN.X	53.8	70	IBMVN.X	0.2
75	IBMJO.X	42.7	75	IBMVO.X	0.2
80	IBMJP.X	44.9	80	IBMVP.X	0.2
85	IBMJQ.X	39.4	85	IBMVQ.X	0.4
90	IBMJR.X	28.0	90	IBMVR.X	0.5
95	IBMJS.X	34.7	95	IBMVS.X	0.7
100	IBMJT.X	28.5	100	IBMVT.X	1.2
105	IBMJA.X	24.5	105	IBMVA.X	1.8
110	IBMJB.X	20.5	110	IBMVB.X	2.5
115	IBMJC.X	15.3	115	IBMVC.X	3.4
120	IBMJD.X	12.1	120	IBMVD.X	5.1
125	IBMJE.X	8.7	125	IBMVE.X	6.2
130	IBMJF.X	6.2	130	IBMVF.X	9.0
135	IBMJG.X	4.1	135	IBMVG.X	12.4
140	IBMJH.X	2.7	140	IBMVH.X	14.8
145	IBMJI.X	1.7	145	IBMVI.X	18.9
145	TSBJI.X	0.3	150	IBMVJ.X	21.7
150	IBMJJ.X	1.2			

This can be seen in Table 4, which shows the price of IBM options on June 6, 2008, with different expiration dates.

Expected Price Volatility of the Underlying Asset over the Life of the Option

All other factors equal, the greater the expected volatility (as measured by the standard deviation or variance) of the price of the underlying asset, the more an investor would be willing to pay for the option, and the more an option writer would demand for it. This occurs because the greater the volatility, the greater the probability that the price of the underlying asset will move in favor of the option buyer at some time before expiration.

Table 4 Market Price on June 6, 2008, of IBM Put and Call Options with a Strike Price of 120 for Different Expiration Dates

Expires	Call Options Option Price	Put Options Option Price
June 2008	6.60	0.44
July 2008	8.30	2.00
October 2008	12.10	5.08
January 2009	14.40	6.90
January 2010	22.90	11.80

Notice that it is the standard deviation or variance, not the systematic risk as measured by beta that is relevant in the pricing of options.

Short-Term, Risk-Free Interest Rate over the Life of the Option

Buying the underlying asset ties up one's money. Buying an option on the same quantity of the underlying asset makes the difference between the asset price and the option price available for investment at an interest rate at least as high as the risk-free rate. Consequently, all other factors constant, the higher the short-term, risk-free interest rate, the greater the cost of buying the underlying asset and carrying it to the expiration date of the call option. Hence, the higher the short-term, risk-free interest rate, the more attractive the call option will be relative to the direct purchase of the underlying asset. As a result, the higher the short-term, risk-free interest rate, the greater the price of a call option.

Anticipated Cash Payments on the Underlying Asset over the Life of the Option

Cash payments on the underlying asset tend to decrease the price of a call option because the cash payments make it more attractive to hold the underlying asset than to hold the option. For put options, cash payments on the underlying asset tend to increase the price.

Option Pricing Models

We have shown that the theoretical price of a futures contract can be determined on the basis of arbitrage arguments. An option pricing model uses a set of assumptions and arbitrage arguments to derive a theoretical price for an option. As we shall see in the following text, deriving a theoretical option price is much more complicated than deriving a theoretical futures price because the option price depends on the expected price volatility of the underlying asset over the life of the option.

Several models have been developed to determine the theoretical value of an option. The most popular one was developed by Fischer Black and Myron Scholes in 1973 for valuing European call options.[2] Several modifications to their model have followed. We use another pricing model called the *binomial option pricing model* to see how arbitrage arguments can be used to determine a fair value for a call option.[3]

Basically, the idea behind the arbitrage argument is that if the payoff from owning a call option can be replicated by (1) purchasing the asset underlying the call option and (2) borrowing funds, the price of the option is then (at most) the cost of creating the replicating strategy.

Deriving the Binomial Option Pricing Model

To derive a one-period binomial option pricing model for a call option, we begin by constructing a portfolio consisting of: (1) a long position in a certain amount of the asset and (2) a short call position in the underlying asset. The amount of the underlying asset purchased is such that the position will be hedged against any change in the price of the asset at

---

[2] Fischer Black and Myron Scholes, "The Pricing of Corporate Liabilities," *Journal of Political Economy* (May–June 1973), pp. 637–659.

[3] John C. Cox, Stephen A. Ross, and Mark Rubinstein, "Option Pricing: A Simplified Approach," *Journal of Financial Economics* (September 1979), pp. 229–263; Richard J. Rendleman and Brit J. Bartter, "Two-State Option Pricing," *Journal of Finance* (December 1979), pp. 1093–1110; and William F. Sharpe, *Investments* (Englewood Cliffs, NJ: Prentice Hall, 1981), Chapter 16.

the expiration date of the option. That is, the portfolio consisting of the long position in the asset and the short position in the call option is riskless and will produce a return that equals the risk-free interest rate. A portfolio constructed in this way is called a *hedged portfolio*.

We can show how this process works with an extended illustration. Let us assume first that there is an asset that has a current market price of $80, and that only two possible future states can occur one year from now. Each state is associated with one of only two possible values for the asset, and they can be summarized in this way:

State	Price
1	$100
2	70

We assume further that there is a call option on this asset with a strike price of $80 (the same as the current market price), and that it expires in one year. Let us suppose an investor forms a hedged portfolio by acquiring two-thirds of a unit of the asset and selling one call option. The two-thirds of a unit of the asset is the so-called *hedge ratio* (how we derive the hedge ratio is explained later). Let us consider the outcomes for this hedged portfolio corresponding to the two possible outcomes for the asset.

If the price of the asset one year from now is $100, the buyer of the call option will exercise it. This means that the investor will have to deliver one unit of the asset in exchange for the strike price, $80. As the investor has only two-thirds of a unit of the asset, she has to buy one-third at a cost of $33 1/3 (the market price of $100 times 1/3). Consequently, the outcome will equal the strike price of $80 received, minus the $33 1/3 cost to acquire the one-third unit of the asset to deliver, plus whatever price the investor initially sold the call option for. That is, the outcome will be

$$80 - 33 \ 1/3 + \text{Call option price} = 46 \ 2/3 + \text{Call option price}$$

If, instead, the price of the asset one year from now is $70, the buyer of the call option will not exercise it. Consequently, the investor will own two-thirds of a unit of the asset. At the price of $70, the value of two-thirds of a unit is $46 2/3. The outcome in this case is then the value of the asset plus whatever price the investor received when she initially sold the call option. That is, the outcome will be

$$46 \ 2/3 + \text{Call option price}$$

It is apparent that, given the possible asset prices, the portfolio consisting of a short position in the call option and two-thirds of a unit of the asset will generate an outcome that hedges changes in the price of the asset; hence, the hedged portfolio is riskless. Furthermore, this riskless hedge will hold regardless of the price of the call, which affects only the magnitude of the outcome.

Deriving the Hedge Ratio

To show how to calculate the hedge ratio, we use the notation

S = current asset price

u = 1 plus the percentage change in the asset's price if the price goes up in the next period

d = 1 plus the percentage change in the asset's price if the price goes down in the next period

r = a risk-free one-period interest rate (the risk-free rate until
     the expiration date)
C = current price of a call option
C_u = intrinsic value of the call option if the asset price goes up
C_d = intrinsic value of the call option if the asset price goes down
E = strike price of the call option
H = hedge ratio, that is, the amount of the asset purchased per call sold

In our illustration, u and d are

$u = 1.250 \, (\$100/\$80)$
$d = 0.875 \, (\$70/\$80)$

Furthermore, State 1 in our illustration means that the asset's price goes up, and State 2 means that the asset's price goes down.

The investment made in the hedged portfolio is equal to the cost of buying H amount of the asset minus the price received from selling the call option. Therefore, because

$$\text{Amount invested in the asset} = HS$$

then

$$\text{Cost of the hedged portfolio} = HS - C$$

The payoff of the hedged portfolio at the end of one period is equal to the value of the HS amount of the asset purchased minus the call option price. The payoffs of the hedged portfolio for the two possible states are defined in this way:

State 1, if the asset's price goes up: $uHS - C_u$
State 2, if the asset's price goes down: $dHS - C_d$

In our illustration, we have these payoffs:

If the asset's price goes up: $1.250 \, H \, \$80 - C_u$ or $\$100 \, H - C_u$
If the asset's price falls: $0.875 \, H \, \$80 - C_d$ or $\$70 \, H - C_d$

If the hedge is riskless, the payoffs must be the same. Thus,

$$uHS - C_u = dHS - C_d \tag{1}$$

Solving equation (1) for the hedge ratio, H, we have

$$H = \frac{C_u - C_d}{(u - d)S} \tag{2}$$

To determine the value of the hedge ratio, H, we must know C_u and C_d. These two values are equal to the difference between the price of the asset and the strike price in the two possible states. Of course, the minimum value of the call option, in any state, is zero. Mathematically, the differences can be expressed as follows:

If the asset's price goes up: $C_u = \text{Max} \, [0, (uS - E)]$
If the asset's price goes down: $C_d = \text{Max} \, [0, (dS - E)]$

As the strike price in our illustration is \$80, the value of uS is \$100, and the value of dS is \$70. Then,

If the asset's price goes up: $C_u = \text{Max}\,[0, (\$100 - \$80)] = \$20$
If the asset's price goes down: $C_d = \text{Max}\,[0, (\$70 - \$80)] = \$0$

To continue with our illustration, we substitute the values of u, d, S, C_u, and C_d into equation (2) to obtain the hedge ratio's value:

$$H = \frac{\$20 - \$0}{(1.25 - 0.875)\$80} = \frac{2}{3}$$

This value for H agrees with the amount of the asset purchased when we introduced this illustration.

Now we can derive a formula for the call option price. Figure 1 diagrams the situation. The top left half of the figure shows the current price of the asset for the current period and at the expiration date. The lower left-hand portion of the figure does the same thing using the notation above. The upper right-hand side of the figure gives the current price of the call option and the value of the call option at the expiration date; the lower right-hand side does the same thing using our notation. Figure 2 uses the values in our illustration to construct the outcomes for the asset and the call option.

Deriving the Price of a Call Option

To derive the price of a call option, we can rely on the basic principle that the hedged portfolio, being riskless, must have a return equal to the risk-free rate of interest. Given that the amount invested in the hedged portfolio is $HS - C$, the amount that should be generated one period from now is

$$(1 + r)(HS - C) \tag{3}$$

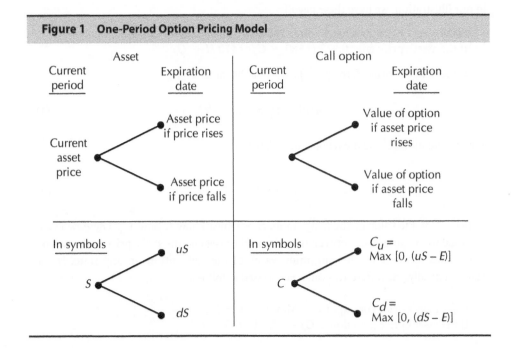

Figure 1 One-Period Option Pricing Model

Figure 2   One-Period Option Pricing Model Illustration

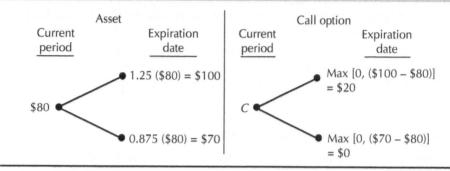

We also know what the payoff will be for the hedged portfolio if the asset's price goes up or down. Because the payoff of the hedged portfolio will be the same whether the asset's price rises or falls, we can use the payoff if it goes up, which is

$$uHS - C_u$$

The payoff of the hedged portfolio given above should be the same as the initial cost of the portfolio given by equation (3). Equating the two, we have

$$(1 + r)(HS - C) = uHS - C_u \tag{4}$$

Substituting equation (2) for H in equation (4), and solving for the call option price, C, we find

$$C = \left(\frac{1 + r - d}{u - d}\right)\left(\frac{C_u}{1 + r}\right) + \left(\frac{u - 1 - r}{u - d}\right)\left(\frac{C_d}{1 + r}\right) \tag{5}$$

Equation (5) is the formula for the one-period binomial option pricing model. We would have derived the same formula if we had used the payoff for a decline in the price of the underlying asset. This derivation is left as an exercise for the reader.

Applying equation (5) to our illustration where

$u = 1.250$
$d = 0.875$
$r = 0.10$
$C_u = \$20$
$C_d = \$0$

we get

$$C = \left(\frac{1 + 0.10 - 0.875}{1.25 - 0.875}\right)\left(\frac{\$20}{1 + 0.10}\right) + \left(\frac{1.25 - 1 - 0.10}{1.25 - 0.875}\right)\left(\frac{\$0}{1 + 0.10}\right)$$

$$= \$10.90$$

The approach we present for pricing options may seem oversimplified, given that we assume only two possible future states for the price of the underlying asset. In fact, we can extend the procedure by making the period shorter and shorter, and in that way calculate a fair value for an option. It is important to note that extended and comprehensive versions of the binomial pricing model are in wide use throughout the world of finance. Moreover, the other popular option pricing model, the Black-Scholes model mentioned earlier, is in reality the mathematical equivalent of the binomial approach as the periods become very short. Thus, the approach we have described in detail here provides the conceptual framework for much of the analysis of option prices that today's financial market participants regularly perform.

Fixed-Income Option Pricing Models

Because of the assumptions required for the binomial model described above, such models may have limited applicability to the pricing of options on fixed-income securities. More specifically, the binomial model assumes that (1) the price of the security can take on any positive value with some probability—no matter how small, (2) the short-term interest rate is constant over the life of the option, and (3) the volatility of the price of the security is constant over the life of the option.

These assumptions are unreasonable for an option on a fixed-income security. First, the price of a fixed-income security cannot exceed the undiscounted value of the cash flow. Any possibility that the price can go higher than this value implies that interest rates can be negative. Second, the price of an interest rate option will change as interest rates change. A change in the short-term interest rate changes the rates along the yield curve. Therefore, to assume that the short-term rate will be constant is inappropriate for interest rate options. The third assumption, that the variance of prices is constant over the life of the option, is inappropriate because as a bond moves closer to maturity its price volatility declines.

Fortunately, it is possible to avoid the problem of negative interest rates. We can develop a binomial option pricing model that is based on the distribution of interest rates rather than prices. Once a binomial interest rate tree is constructed, it can be converted into a binomial price tree by using its interest rates to determine the prices of the bond at the end of the period. We can apply to these prices the same procedure described earlier to calculate the option price by working backward from the value of the call option at the expiration date.

Although the binomial option pricing model based on yields is superior to models based on prices, it still has a theoretical drawback. All theoretically valid option pricing models must satisfy the put–call parity relationship. The problem with the binomial model based on yields is that it does not satisfy this relationship. It violates the relationship because it fails to take into consideration the yield curve, thereby allowing arbitrage opportunities.

The most elaborate models that take the yield curve into consideration, and as a result eliminate arbitrage opportunities, are called *yield curve option pricing models* or *arbitrage-free option pricing models*. These models can incorporate different volatility assumptions along the yield curve. They are theoretically superior to the other models we have described.[4]

---

[4] For a discussion of yield curve or arbitrage-free option pricing models, see Mark Pitts and Frank J. Fabozzi, *Interest Rate Futures and Options* (Chicago: Probus Publishing, 1989), Chapter 9; and Lawrence J. Dyer and David P. Jacob, "Guide to Fixed Income Option Pricing Models," in Frank J. Fabozzi (ed.), *The Handbook of Fixed Income Options* (Chicago: Probus Publishing, 1989).

> **Key Points That You Should Understand Before Proceeding**
>
> 1. The price of an option can be separated into two parts, its intrinsic value and its time premium.
> 2. The put–call parity relationship is the relationship between the price of a call option and the price of a put option on the same underlying instrument, with the same strike price and the same expiration date.
> 3. There are six factors that influence the price of an option: the current price of the underlying asset, the strike price, the time to expiration of the option, the expected price volatility of the underlying asset over the life of the option, the short-term, risk-free interest rate over the life of the option, and the anticipated cash payments on the underlying asset over the life of the option.
> 4. The theoretical price of an option can be determined on the basis of arbitrage arguments, but is much more complicated to determine than the theoretical price of a futures contract because the option price depends on the expected price volatility of the underlying asset over the life of the option.
> 5. Several models have been developed to determine the theoretical value of an option.
> 6. The value of an option is equal to the cost of creating a replicating hedge portfolio.

SUMMARY

Using simple arbitrage arguments, the theoretical or equilibrium futures price can be determined. Specifically, to capture the arbitrage profit for an overpriced futures contract a cash and carry trade can be implemented, and to capture the arbitrage profit for an under-priced futures contract a reverse cash and carry trade can be implemented. The ability of market participants to implement these two trades (or arbitrage strategies) results in the theoretical futures price being equal to the cash market price plus the cost of carry. The cost of carry is the net financing cost, that is, the difference between the financing rate and the cash yield on the underlying asset. The theoretical futures price will be less than the cash market price if the cost of carry is positive, equal to the cash market price if the cost of carry is zero, and more than the cash market price if the cost of carry is negative.

Developing the theoretical futures price with arbitrage arguments requires certain assumptions. When these assumptions are violated for a specific futures contract, the theoretical futures price must be modified. Because of the difference between borrowing and lending rates and because of transaction costs, there is not one theoretical futures price but, rather, a boundary around the theoretical futures price. So long as the actual futures price remains within this boundary, arbitrage profits cannot be realized.

The price of an option consists of two components: the intrinsic value and the time premium. The intrinsic value is the economic value of the option if it is exercised immediately. If there is no positive economic value resulting from exercising immediately, the intrinsic value is zero. The time premium is the amount by which the option price exceeds the intrinsic value. Six factors influence the option price: (1) the current price of the underlying asset; (2) the strike price of the option; (3) the time remaining to the expiration of the option; (4) the expected price volatility of the underlying asset; (5) the short-term, risk-free interest rate over the life of the option; and (6) the anticipated cash payments on the underlying asset.

The relationship among the call option price, the put option price, and the price of the underlying asset is known as the put–call parity relationship. The theoretical option price can be calculated with the binomial option pricing model, which also employs arbitrage arguments. Application of the binomial model to the pricing of options on fixed-income securities poses problems because of the model's underlying assumptions.

KEY TERMS

- At the money
- Cash and carry trade
- Cost of carry (carry)
- Financing cost
- In the money
- Intrinsic value
- Negative carry

- Net financing cost
- Out of the money
- Positive carry
- Put–call parity relationship
- Reverse cash and carry trade
- Time premium

QUESTIONS

1. Models for pricing futures and options are said to be based on arbitrage arguments.
   a. What does arbitrage mean?
   b. What is the investor's incentive to engage in arbitrage?
2. Suppose there is a financial Asset ABC, which is the underlying asset for a futures contract with settlement six months from now. You know the following about this financial asset and the futures contract:
   1. In the cash market, ABC is selling for $80.
   2. ABC pays $8 per year in two semiannual payments of $4, and the next semiannual payment is due exactly six months from now.
   3. The current six-month interest rate at which funds can be loaned or borrowed is 6%.
   a. What is the theoretical (or equilibrium) futures price?
   b. What action would you take if the futures price is $83?
   c. What action would you take if the futures price is $76?
   d. Suppose that ABC pays interest quarterly instead of semiannually. If you know that you can

reinvest any funds you receive three months from now at 1% for three months, what would the theoretical futures price for six-month settlement be?
   e. Suppose that the borrowing rate and lending rate are not equal. Instead, suppose that the current six-month borrowing rate is 8% and the six-month lending rate is 6%. What are the boundaries for the theoretical futures price?
3. **a.** Explain why restrictions on short selling of stocks would cause the actual price of a stock index futures contract to diverge from its theoretical price.
   b. Explain why creating a portfolio of stocks in which the number of stocks is less than the number of stocks in the index underlying a stock index futures contract would result in an arbitrage that is not riskless.
4. Why do the delivery options in a Treasury bond futures contract cause the actual futures price to diverge from its theoretical price?
5. "Of course the futures are more expensive than the cash price—there's positive carry." Do you agree with this statement?

6. Consider the following call option with three months to expiration:

> Strike price = $72
> Current price of underlying assets = $87
> Market price of option = $6

    a. What is the intrinsic value for this call option?
    b. What is the time premium for this call option?

7. Suppose the option in the previous question is a put option rather than a call option.
    a. What is the intrinsic value for this put option?
    b. What is the time premium for this put option?

8. You obtain the following price quotes for call options on Asset ABC. It is now December, with the near contract maturing in one month's time. Asset ABC's price is currently trading at $50.

Strike	January	March	June
$40	$11	$12	$11.50
50	6	7	8.50
60	7	8	9.00

Glancing at the figures, you note that two of these quotes seem to violate some of the rules you learned regarding options pricing.
    a. What are these discrepancies?
    b. How could you take advantage of the discrepancies? What is the minimum profit you would realize by arbitraging based on these discrepancies?

9. Indicate whether you agree or disagree with the following statements:
    a. "To determine the theoretical value of an option, we will need some measure of the price volatility of the underlying asset. Because financial theorists tell us that the appropriate measure of risk is beta (that is, systematic risk), then we should use this value."
    b. "If the expected price volatility of an option increases, the theoretical value of an option decreases."
    c. "It does not make sense that the price of a call option should rise in value if the price of the underlying asset falls."

10. Consider two options with the same expiration date and for the same underlying asset. The two options differ only in the strike price. Option 1's strike price is greater than that of Option 2.

    a. If the two options are call options, which option will have a higher price?
    b. If the two options are put options, which option will have a higher price?

11. Consider two options with the same strike price and for the same underlying asset. The two options differ only with respect to the time to expiration. Option A expires in three months and Option B expires in six months.
    a. If the two options are call options, which option will have the higher intrinsic value (assuming the options are in the money)?
    b. If the two options are call options, which option will have a higher time premium?
    c. Would your answers to (a) and (b) be different if the option is a put rather than a call?

12. In an option pricing model, what statistical measure is used as a measure of the price volatility of the underlying asset?

13. For an asset that does not make cash distributions over the life of an option, it does not pay to exercise a call option prior to the expiration date. Why?

14. Consider two strategies:

> **Strategy 1:** Purchase one unit of Asset M currently selling for $103. A distribution of $10 is expected one year from now.
> **Strategy 2:** (a) Purchase a call option on Asset M with an expiration date one year from now and a strike price of $100; and (b) place sufficient funds in a 10% interest-bearing bank account to exercise the option at expiration ($100) and to pay the cash distribution that would be paid by Asset M ($10).

    a. What is the investment required under Strategy 2?
    b. Give the payoffs of Strategy 1 and Strategy 2, assuming that the price of Asset M one year from now is
      (i) $120
      (ii) $103
      (iii) $100
      (iv) $80
    c. For the four prices of Asset M one year from now, demonstrate that the following relationship holds: Call option price ≥ Max [0, (Price of underlying asset − Present value of strike price − Present value of cash distribution)].

15. What is meant by a hedge ratio in developing an option pricing model?

16. a. Calculate the option value for a two-period European call option with the following terms:

Current price of underlying asset = $100

Strike price = $10

One-period, risk-free rate = 5%

The stock price can either go up or down by 10% at the end of one period.

b. Recalculate the value for the option when the stock price can move either up or down by 50% at the end of one period. Compare your answer with the calculated value in part (a).

17. What is the problem encountered in applying the binomial pricing model to the pricing of options on fixed-income securities?

OTC Interest Rate Derivatives: Forward Rate Agreements, Swaps, Caps, and Floors

From Chapter 30 of *Foundations of Financial Markets and Institutions*, 4/e. Frank J. Fabozzi. Franco Modigliani. Frank J. Jones.

OTC Interest Rate Derivatives: Forward Rate Agreements, Swaps, Caps, and Floors

LEARNING OBJECTIVES

After reading this chapter, you will understand

- what a forward rate agreement is

- what an interest rate swap is

- how an interest rate swap can be used by institutional investors and corporate borrowers

- why the interest rate swap market has grown so rapidly

- the risk/return characteristics of an interest rate swap

- two ways to interpret an interest rate swap

- reasons for the development of an interest rate swap market

- determinants of the swap spread

- what a swaption is

- what a forward start swap is

- what an interest rate/equity swap is

- what an interest rate cap and floor is

- how interest rate caps and floors and forward rate agreements can be used by institutional investors and corporate borrowers

- the relationship between an interest rate cap and floor and an option

- how an interest rate collar can be created

Interest rate futures and options can be used to control interest rate risk. Commercial banks and investment banks also customize other contracts useful for controlling interest rate risk for their clients. These include interest rate swaps, interest rate caps and floors, and forward rate agreements. In this chapter, we will review each contract and explain the way borrowers and institutional investors use them.

FORWARD RATE AGREEMENTS

A **forward rate agreement (FRA)** is the over-the-counter (OTC) equivalent of the exchange-traded futures contracts on short-term rates. Typically, the short-term rate is the London Interbank Offered Rate (LIBOR).

The elements of an FRA are the contract rate, reference rate, settlement rate, notional amount, and settlement date. The parties to an FRA agree to buy and sell funds on the settlement date. The FRA's *contract rate* is the rate specified in the FRA at which the buyer of the FRA agrees to pay for funds and the seller of the FRA agrees to receive for investing funds. The reference rate is the interest rate used. For example, the *reference rate* could be three-month LIBOR or six-month LIBOR. The benchmark from which the interest payments are to be calculated is specified in the FRA and is called the *notional amount* (or notional principal amount). This amount is not exchanged between the two parties. The *settlement rate* is the value of the reference rate at the FRA's settlement date. The source for determining the settlement rate is specified in the FRA.

The buyer of the FRA is agreeing to pay the contract rate, or equivalently, to buy funds at the settlement date at the contract rate; the seller of the FRA is agreeing to receive the contract rate, or equivalently, to sell funds at the settlement date at the contract rate. So, for example, if the FRA has a contract rate of 5% for three-month LIBOR (the reference rate) and the notional amount is for $10 million, the buyer is agreeing to pay 5% to buy or borrow $10 million at the settlement date and the seller is agreeing to receive 5% to sell or lend $10 million at the settlement date.

If at the settlement date the settlement rate is greater than the contract rate, the FRA buyer benefits because the buyer can borrow funds at a below-market rate. If the settlement rate is less than the contract rate, this benefits the seller, who can lend funds at an above-market rate. If the settlement rate is the same as the contract rate, neither party benefits. This is summarized as follows:

> FRA buyer benefits if Settlement rate > Contract rate
> FRA seller benefits if Contract rate > Settlement rate
> Neither party benefits if Settlement rate = Contract rate

As with the Eurodollar futures contract, FRAs are cash settlement contracts. At the settlement date, the party that benefits based on the contract rate and settlement rate must be compensated by the other. Assuming the settlement rate is not equal to the contract rate, then

> Buyer receives compensation if Settlement rate > Contract rate
> Seller receives compensation if Contract rate > Settlement rate

To determine the amount one party must compensate the other, the following is first calculated assuming a 360-day count convention:

If Settlement rate > Contract rate:

$$\text{Interest differential} = (\text{Settlement rate} - \text{Contract rate}) \times (\text{Days in contract period}/360) \times \text{Notional amount}$$

If Contract rate > Settlement rate:

$$\text{Interest differential} = (\text{Contract rate} - \text{Settlement rate}) \\ \times (\text{Days in contract period}/360) \times \text{Notional amount}$$

The amount that must be exchanged at the settlement date is not the interest differential. Instead, the present value of the interest differential is exchanged. The discount rate used to calculate the present value of the interest differential is the settlement rate. Thus, the compensation is determined as follows:

$$\text{Compensation} = \frac{\text{Interest differential}}{[1 + \text{Settlement rate} \times (\text{Days to contract period}/360)]}$$

To illustrate, assume the following terms for an FRA: Reference rate is three-month LIBOR, the contract rate is 5%, the notional amount is for $10 million, and the number of days to settlement is 91 days. Suppose the settlement rate is 5.5%. This means that the buyer benefits, since the buyer can borrow at 5% (the contract rate) when the market rate (the settlement rate) is 5.5%. The interest differential is

$$\text{Interest differential} = (0.055 - 0.05) \times (91/360) \times \$10,000,000 = \$12,638.89$$

The compensation or payment that the seller must make to the buyer is

$$\text{Compensation} = \frac{\$12,638.89}{[1 + 0.055 \times 91/360]}$$

$$\frac{\$12,638.89}{1.0139027} = \$12,465.58$$

It is important to note the difference of who benefits when interest rates move in an FRA and an interest rate futures contract. The buyer of an FRA benefits if the reference rate increases and the seller benefits if the reference rate decreases. In a futures contract, the buyer benefits from a falling rate while the seller benefits from a rising rate. This is summarized in Table 1. This is because the underlying for each of the two contracts is different. In the case of an FRA, the underlying is a rate. The buyer gains if the rate increases and loses if the rate decreases. In contrast, in a futures contract the underlying is a fixed-income instrument. The buyer gains if the fixed-income instrument increases in value. This occurs when rates decline. The buyer loses when the fixed-income instrument decreases in value. This occurs when interest rates increase. The opposite occurs for the seller of a futures contract.

Table 1 Effect of Rate Changes on Parties to an FRA and an Interest Rate Futures Contract

| | Interest Rates | | | |
| | Decrease | | Increase | |
Party	FRA	Futures	FRA	Futures
Buyer	Loses	Gains	Gains	Loses
Seller	Gains	Loses	Loses	Gains

INTEREST RATE SWAPS

An **interest rate swap** is an agreement whereby two parties (called *counterparties*) agree to exchange periodic interest payments. The dollar amount of the interest payments exchanged is based on some predetermined dollar principal, which is called the **notional principal amount**. The dollar amount each counterparty pays to the other is the agreed-upon periodic interest rate times the notional principal amount. The only dollars exchanged between the parties are the net interest payments, not the notional principal amount. In the most common type of swap, one party agrees to pay the other party fixed interest payments at designated dates for the life of the contract. This party is referred to as the **fixed-rate payer**. The other party, referred to as the **floating-rate payer**, agrees to make interest rate payments that float with some reference interest rate (or, simply, reference rate).

For example, suppose that for the next five years party X agrees to pay party Y 10% per year, while party Y agrees to pay party X six-month LIBOR (London Interbank Offered Rate). Party X is a fixed-rate payer/floating-rate receiver, while party Y is a floating-rate payer/fixed-rate receiver. Assume that the notional principal amount is $50 million, and that payments are exchanged every six months for the next five years. This means that every six months, party X (the fixed-rate payer/floating-rate receiver) will pay party Y $2.5 million (10% times $50 million divided by 2). The amount that party Y (the floating-rate payer/fixed-rate receiver) will pay party X will be six-month LIBOR times $50 million divided by 2. For example, if six-month LIBOR is 7%, party Y will pay party X $1.75 million (7% times $50 million divided by 2). Note that we divide by two because one-half year's interest is being paid.

The reference rates that are commonly used for the floating rate in an interest rate swap are those on various money market instruments: Treasury bills, LIBOR, commercial paper, bankers acceptances, certificates of deposit, federal funds rate, and prime rate.

As we illustrate later, market participants can use an interest rate swap to alter the cash flow character of assets or liabilities from a fixed-rate basis to a floating-rate basis or vice versa.

Risk/Return Characteristics of a Swap

The value of an interest rate swap will fluctuate with market interest rates. To see how, let's analyze our hypothetical swap. Suppose that interest rates change immediately after parties X and Y enter into the swap. First, consider what would happen if the market demanded that the fixed-rate payer must pay 11% in order to receive six-month LIBOR in any five-year swap. If party X (the fixed-rate payer) wants to sell its position, say, to party A, then party A will benefit by only having to pay 10% (the original swap rate agreed upon) rather than 11% (the current swap rate) to receive six-month LIBOR. Party X will want compensation for this benefit. Consequently, the value of party X's position has increased. Thus, if interest rates increase, the fixed-rate payer will realize a profit and the floating-rate payer will realize a loss.

Next, consider what would happen if interest rates decline to, say, 6%. Now a five-year swap would require the fixed-rate payer to pay 6% rather than 10% to receive six-month LIBOR. If party X wants to sell its position to party B, the latter would demand compensation to take over the position. In other words, if interest rates decline, the fixed-rate payer will realize a loss, while the floating-rate payer will realize a profit.

The risk/return profile of the two positions when interest rates change is summarized in Table 2.

Table 2	Risk/Return Profile of Counterparties to an Interest Rate Swap	
	Interest Rates Decrease	**Interest Rates Increase**
Floating-rate payer	Gain	Loss
Fixed-rate payer	Loss	Gain

Interpreting a Swap Position

There are two ways that a swap position can be interpreted: (1) as a package of forward/futures contracts, or (2) as a package of cash flows from buying and selling cash market instruments. We will evaluate both interpretations. Contrast the position of the counterparties in an interest rate swap in Table 2 to the position of the long and short futures or a forward contract shown in Table 1. An interest rate futures contract has an underlying fixed-income instrument. An FRA is one in which the underlying is a rate.

Consider first the FRA. As explained in the previous section, the buyer of an FRA gains if the reference rate rises above the contract rate at the settlement date (i.e., the settlement rate is greater than the contract rate) and loses if the reference rate falls below the contract rate at the settlement date (i.e., the settlement rate is less than the contract rate). The opposite is true for the seller of an FRA. Table 3 compares the position of the swap parties and the parties to an FRA if rates increase and decrease. Consequently, the buyer of an FRA realizes the same effect as a fixed-rate payer and the seller of an FRA the same effect as a floating-rate payer.

A swap can be viewed as a package of FRAs. In fact, an FRA can be viewed as a special case of a swap in which there is only one settlement date.

Now let's compare a swap to a futures or forward contract where the underlying is an interest rate instrument such as a Eurodollar CD. The long futures position gains if interest rates decline and loses if interest rates rise—this is similar to the risk/return profile for a floating-rate payer. The risk/return profile for a fixed-rate payer is similar to that of the short futures position: a gain if interest rates increase and a loss if interest rates decrease. Table 4 compares the counterparty positions for a swap, an FRA, and a forward/futures on a fixed-income instrument when rates change.

Consequently, interest rate swaps can be viewed as a package of more basic interest rate control tools, such as forwards. The pricing of an interest rate swap will then depend on the price of a package of forward contracts with the same settlement dates and in which the underlying for the forward contract is the same reference rate.

Table 3	Effect of Rate Changes on Interest Rate Swap Counterparties and FRA Counterparties		
Counterparties to		Interest Rates	
Swap	FRA	Decrease	Increase
Floating-rate payer	Seller	Gains	Loses
Fixed-rate payer	Buyer	Loses	Gains

Table 4   Effect of Rate Changes on Interest Rate Swap Counterparties, FRA Counterparties, and Futures and Forwards on Fixed-Income Instrument Counterparties

			Interest Rates	
		Futures/Forward on Fixed-Income		
Swap	FRA	Instrument	Decrease	Increase
Floating-rate payer	Seller	Buyer	Gains	Loses
Fixed-rate payer	Buyer	Seller	Loses	Gains

While an interest rate swap may be nothing more than a package of forward contracts, several important reasons suggest that it is not a redundant contract. First, the longest maturity of forward or futures contracts does not extend out as far as that of an interest rate swap. In fact, an interest rate swap with a term of 15 years or longer can be obtained. Second, an interest rate swap is a more transactionally efficient instrument. By this we mean that in one transaction two parties can effectively establish a payoff equivalent to a package of forward contracts. The forward contracts would each have to be negotiated separately. Third, the liquidity of the interest rate swap market has grown since its beginning in 1981; it is now more liquid than forward contracts, particularly long-dated (that is, long-term) forward contracts.

Package of Cash Market Instruments

To understand why a swap can also be interpreted as package of cash market instruments, consider the following. Suppose that an investor enters into a transaction to

- buy $50 million par of a five-year, floating-rate bond that pays six-month LIBOR every six months
- finance the purchase of the five-year, floating-rate bond by borrowing $50 million for five years with a 10% annual interest rate and payments every six months

The cash flow of this transaction is presented in Table 5. The second column of the exhibit sets out the cash flow from purchasing the five-year, floating-rate bond. There is a $50 million cash outlay and then cash inflows. The amount of the cash inflows is uncertain because they depend on future LIBOR. The third column shows the cash flow from borrowing $50 million on a fixed-rate basis. The last column shows the net cash flow from the entire transaction. As can be seen in the last column, there is no initial cash flow (no cash inflow or cash outlay). In all 10 six-month periods, the net position results in a cash inflow of LIBOR and a cash outlay of $2.5 million. This net position, however, is identical to the position of a fixed-rate payer/floating-rate receiver.

The net cash flow in Table 5 reveals that a fixed-rate payer has a cash market position that is equivalent to a long position in a floating-rate bond and borrowing the funds to purchase the floating-rate bond on a fixed-rate basis. But the borrowing can be viewed as issuing a fixed-rate bond, or equivalently, being short a fixed-rate bond. Consequently, the position of a fixed-rate payer can be viewed as being long a floating-rate bond and short a fixed-rate bond.

Table 5   Cash Flow for the Purchase of a Five-Year, Floating-Rate Bond Financed by Borrowing on a Fixed-Rate Basis

Transaction: Purchase for $50 million a five-year, floating-rate bond:
Floating rate = LIBOR, semiannual pay
Borrow $50 million for five years: fixed rate = 10% semiannual payments

| | Cash Flow (in millions of dollars) from: | | |
Six-Month Period	Floating-Rate Bond	Borrowing Cost	Net
0	$-\$50.0$	$+\$50.0$	$\$0$
1	$+(LIBOR_1/2) \times 50$	-2.5	$+(LIBOR_1/2) \times 50 - 2.5$
2	$+(LIBOR_2/2) \times 50$	-2.5	$+(LIBOR_2/2) \times 50 - 2.5$
3	$+(LIBOR_3/2) \times 50$	-2.5	$+(LIBOR_3/2) \times 50 - 2.5$
4	$+(LIBOR_4/2) \times 50$	-2.5	$+(LIBOR_4/2) \times 50 - 2.5$
5	$+(LIBOR_5/2) \times 50$	-2.5	$+(LIBOR_5/2) \times 50 - 2.5$
6	$+(LIBOR_6/2) \times 50$	-2.5	$+(LIBOR_6/2) \times 50 - 2.5$
7	$+(LIBOR_7/2) \times 50$	-2.5	$+(LIBOR_7/2) \times 50 - 2.5$
8	$+(LIBOR_8/2) \times 50$	-2.5	$+(LIBOR_8/2) \times 50 - 2.5$
9	$+(LIBOR_9/2) \times 50$	-2.5	$+(LIBOR_9/2) \times 50 - 2.5$
10	$+(LIBOR_{10}/2) \times 50 + 50$	-52.5	$+(LIBOR_{10}/2) \times 50 - 2.5$

Note: *The subscript for LIBOR indicates the six-month LIBOR as per the terms of the floating-rate bond at a particular time.*

What about the position of a floating-rate payer? It can be demonstrated that the position of a floating-rate payer is equivalent to purchasing a fixed-rate bond and financing that purchase at a floating rate, with the floating rate being the reference interest rate for the swap. That is, the position of a floating-rate payer is equivalent to a long position in a fixed-rate bond and a short position in a floating-rate bond.

Applications

So far we have merely described an interest rate swap and looked at its characteristics. With the help of two illustrations, we now explain how swaps can be used. Although we focus on basic or **plain vanilla swaps**, the illustrations will help us understand why other types of interest rate swaps have been developed.

Application to Asset/Liability Management

In the first illustration, we look at how an interest rate swap can be used to alter the cash flow characteristics of an institution's assets so as to provide a better match between assets and liabilities. The two institutions are a commercial bank and a life insurance company.

Suppose a bank has a portfolio consisting of five-year term commercial loans with a fixed interest rate. The principal value of the portfolio is $50 million, and the interest rate on all the loans in the portfolio is 10%. The loans are interest only loans; interest is paid semiannually, and the entire principal is paid at the end of five years. That is, assuming no default on the loans, the cash flow from the loan portfolio is $2.5 million every six months for the next five years and $50 million at the end of five years. To fund its loan portfolio, assume that the bank is relying on the issuance of six-month certificates of deposit. The interest rate that the bank plans to pay on its six-month CDs is the six-month Treasury bill rate plus 40 basis points (b.p.).

The risk that the bank faces is that the six-month Treasury bill rate will be 9.6% or greater. To understand why, remember that the bank is earning 10% annually on its commercial loan portfolio. If the six-month Treasury bill rate is 9.6%, it will have to pay 9.6% plus 40 basis points to depositors for six-month funds, or 10%, and there will be no spread income. Worse, if the six-month Treasury bill rate rises above 9.6%, there will be a loss; that is, the cost of funds will exceed the interest rate earned on the loan portfolio. The bank's objective is to lock in a spread over the cost of its funds.

The other party in the interest rate swap illustration is a life insurance company that has committed itself to pay a 9% rate for the next five years on a guaranteed investment contract (GIC) it has issued. The amount of the GIC is $50 million. Suppose that the life insurance company has the opportunity to invest $50 million in what it considers an attractive five-year, floating-rate instrument in a private placement transaction. The interest rate on this instrument is the six-month Treasury bill rate plus 160 basis points. The coupon rate is set every six months.

The risk that the life insurance company faces is that the six-month interest rate will fall so that it will not earn enough to realize a spread over the 9% rate that it has guaranteed to the GIC holders. If the six-month Treasury bill rate falls to 7.4% or less, no spread income will be generated. To understand why, suppose that the six-month Treasury bill rate at the date the floating-rate instrument resets its coupon is 7.4%. Then the coupon rate for the next six months will be 9% (7.4% plus 160 basis points). Because the life insurance company has agreed to pay 9% on the GIC policy, there will be no spread income. Should the six-month Treasury bill rate fall below 7.4%, the life insurance company will incur a loss.

We can summarize the asset/liability problem of the bank and life insurance company as follows:

BANK:

    1. Has lent long-term and borrowed short-term
    2. If the six-month Treasury bill rate rises, spread income declines.

LIFE INSURANCE COMPANY:

    3. Has effectively lent short-term and borrowed long-term
    4. If the six-month Treasury bill rate falls, spread income declines.

Now let's suppose that an intermediary offers a five-year interest rate swap with a notional principal amount of $50 million to both the bank and life insurance company. The terms offered to the bank are as follows:

1. Every six months, the bank will pay 10% (annual rate) to the intermediary.
2. Every six months, the intermediary will pay the six-month Treasury bill rate plus 155 basis points to the bank.

The terms offered to the insurance company are as follows:

1. Every six months, the life insurance company will pay the six-month Treasury bill rate plus 160 basis points per year to the intermediary.
2. Every six months, the intermediary will pay the insurance company 10% (annual rate).

What has this interest rate contract done for the bank and the life insurance company? Consider first the bank. For every six-month period during the life of the swap agreement, the interest rate spread will be as follows:

Annual Interest Rate Received:	
From commercial loan portfolio	= 10%
From interest rate swap	= 6-month T-bill rate + 155 b.p.
Total	= 11.55% + 6-month T-bill rate
Annual Interest Rate Paid:	
To CD depositors	6-month T-bill rate + 40 b.p.
On interest rate swap	= 10%
Total	= 10.40% + 6-month T-bill rate
Outcome:	
To be received	= 11.55% + 6-month T-bill rate
To be paid	= 10.40% + 6-month T-bill rate
Spread income	= 1.15% or 115 b.p.

Thus, regardless of what happens to the six-month Treasury bill rate, the bank locks in a spread of 115 basis points.

Now let's look at the effect of the interest rate swap on the life insurance company:

Annual Interest Rate Received:	
From floating-rate instrument	= 6-month T-bill rate + 160 b.p.
From interest rate swap	= 10%
Total	= 11.6% + 6-month T-bill rate
Annual Interest Rate Paid:	
To GIC policyholders	= 9%
On interest rate swap	= 6-month T-bill rate + 160 b.p.
Total	= 10.6% + 6-month T-bill rate
Outcome:	
To be received	= 11.6% + 6-month T-bill rate
To be paid	= 10.6% + 6-month T-bill rate
Spread income	= 1.0% or 100 b.p.

Regardless of what happens to the six-month Treasury bill rate, the life insurance company locks in a spread of 100 basis points.

The interest rate swap has allowed each party to accomplish its asset/liability objective of locking in a spread.[1] The swap permits each financial institution to alter the cash flow characteristics of its assets: from fixed to floating in the case of the bank, and from floating

---

[1] Whether or not the size of the spread is adequate is not an issue to us in this illustration.

to fixed in the case of the life insurance company. This type of transaction is referred to as an **asset swap.** The bank and the life insurance company could have used the swap market instead to change the cash flow nature of their liabilities. Such a swap is called a **liability swap.** While in our illustration we used a bank, an interest rate swap obviously would be appropriate for savings and loan associations that, because of regulation, borrow short term—on a floating-rate basis—and lend long term—on fixed-rate mortgages.

Of course, there are other ways that the two institutions could have chosen to match the cash flow characteristics of their assets and liabilities. The bank might refuse to make fixed-rate commercial loans and insist only on floating-rate loans. This approach has a major pitfall: If borrowers can find another source willing to lend on a fixed-rate basis, the bank would lose these customers. The life insurance company might refuse to purchase a floating-rate instrument. But suppose that the terms offered on the private placement instrument were more attractive than what would have been offered on a floating-rate instrument of comparable credit risk. Thus, by using the swap market, the life insurance company can earn a yield higher than what it would earn if it invested directly in a five-year, fixed-rate security. For example, suppose the life insurance company can invest in a comparable credit risk five-year, fixed-rate security with a yield of 9.8%. Given the funding through the GIC with a 9% rate, this investment would result in spread income of 80 basis points—less than the 100 basis point spread income the life insurance company achieved by purchasing the floating-rate instrument and entering into the swap.

Consequently, an interest rate swap performs two important functions: (1) It can change the risk of a financial position by altering the cash flow characteristics of assets or liabilities, and (2) under certain circumstances, it also can be used to enhance returns. Obviously, this second function arises only if there are market imperfections.

There is a final point to be made in this illustration. Look at the floating-rate payments that the life insurance company makes to the intermediary and the floating-rate payments that the intermediary makes to the bank. The life insurance company pays the six-month Treasury bill rate plus 160 basis points, but the intermediary pays the bank the six-month Treasury bill rate plus only 155 basis points. The difference of 5 basis points represents the fee to the intermediary for the services of intermediation.

Application to Debt Issuance

Our second illustration considers two U.S. entities, a triple-A rated commercial bank and a triple B rated nonfinancial corporation; each wants to raise $100 million for 10 years. For various reasons, the bank wants to raise floating-rate funds, while the nonfinancial corporation wants to raise fixed-rate funds. The interest rates available to the two entities in the U.S. bond market are as follows:

Bank: Floating rate = 6-month LIBOR + 30 b.p.
Nonfinancial corporation: Fixed rate = 12%

Suppose also that both entities could issue securities in the Eurodollar bond market, if they wanted to. Let us assume that the following terms are available in the Eurodollar bond market for 10-year securities for these two entities:

Bank: Fixed rate = 10.5%
Nonfinancial corporation: Floating rate = 6-month LIBOR + 80 b.p.

Notice that we indicate the terms that the bank could obtain on fixed-rate financing and that the nonfinancial corporation could obtain on floating-rate securities. You will shortly see why we did this. First, let us summarize the situation for the two entities in the U.S. domestic and Eurodollar bond markets:

Floating-Rate Securities		
Entity	**Bond Market**	**Rate**
Bank	U.S. domestic	6-month LIBOR + 30 b.p.
Nonfinancial corporation	Eurodollar	6-month LIBOR + 80 b.p.
		Quality spread = 50 b.p.
Fixed-Rate Securities		
Entity	**Bond Market**	**Rate**
Bank	Eurodollar	10.5%
Nonfinancial corporation	U.S. domestic	12.0%
		Quality spread = 150 b.p.

In this table, we use the term *quality spread*. This term simply means the differential borrowing costs that reflect the difference in the creditworthiness of the two entities.

Notice that the quality spread for floating-rate securities (50 basis points) is narrower than the quality spread for fixed-rate securities (150 basis points). This difference in spreads provides an opportunity for both entities to reduce the cost of raising funds. To see how, suppose each entity issued securities in the Eurodollar bond market, and then simultaneously entered into the following 10-year interest rate swap with a $100 million notional principal amount offered by an intermediary:

Bank:
Pay floating rate of 6-month LIBOR + 70 b.p.
Receive fixed rate of 11.3%
Nonfinancial Corporation:
Pay fixed rate of 11.3%
Receive floating rate of 6-month LIBOR + 45 b.p.

The cost of the issue for the bank would then be

Interest Paid:	
On fixed-rate Eurodollar bonds issued	= 10.5%
On interest rate swap	= 6-month LIBOR + 70 b.p.
Total	= 11.2% + 6-month LIBOR
Interest Received:	
On interest rate swap	= 11.3%
Net Cost:	
Interest paid	= 11.2% + 6-month LIBOR
Interest received	= 11.3%
Total	= 6-month LIBOR − 10 b.p.

The cost of the issue for the nonfinancial corporation would then be

Interest Paid:	
On floating-rate Eurodollar bonds issued	= 6-month LIBOR + 80 b.p.
On interest rate swap	= 11.3%
Total	= 12.1% + 6-month LIBOR
Interest Received:	
On interest rate swap	= 6-month LIBOR + 45 b.p.
Net Cost:	
Interest paid	= 12.1% + 6-month LIBOR
Interest received	= 6-month LIBOR + 45 b.p.
Total	= 11.65%

The transactions are diagrammed in Figure 1. By issuing securities in the Eurodollar bond market and using the interest rate swap, both entities are able to reduce their cost of issuing securities. The bank was able to issue floating-rate securities for six-month LIBOR minus 10 basis points rather than issue floating-rate securities in the U.S. domestic bond market for six-month LIBOR plus 30 basis points, thereby saving 40 basis points. The nonfinancial corporation saved 35 basis points (11.65% versus 12%) by issuing floating-rate bonds in the Eurodollar bond market and using the interest rate swap.

The point of this illustration is to show that, if differences in quality spreads exist in different sectors of the bond markets, borrowers can use the interest rate swap to arbitrage the inconsistency. Whether these differences do exist is another question, which we address below.

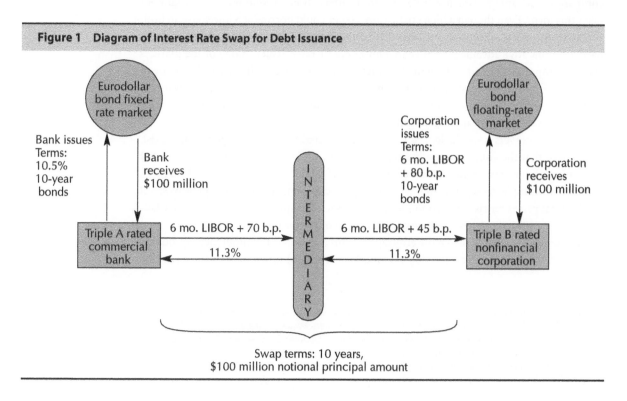

Figure 1   Diagram of Interest Rate Swap for Debt Issuance

Finally, look once again at the intermediary in this transaction. The intermediary pays a floating rate of six-month LIBOR plus 45 basis points to the nonfinancial corporation, and receives six-month LIBOR plus 70 basis points from the bank, realizing 25 basis points for its intermediary services.

Reasons for the Development of the Interest Rate Swap Market

According to the Bank for International Settlements, the interest rate swap market, which began in late 1981, is the largest component of the OTC interests rate derivatives market.[2] As of the end of 2007, the notional amount outstanding of interest rate swaps was $310 trillion of the $393 trillion interest rate OTC derivatives market. (FRAs made up $26 trillion of the market and option made up $57 trillion.)

What is behind this rapid growth? As our two illustrations have demonstrated, an interest rate swap is a quick way for institutional investors and corporate borrowers to change the nature of assets and liabilities or to exploit any perceived capital market imperfection.

The initial motivation for the interest rate swap market was borrower exploitation of what were perceived to be *credit arbitrage* opportunities. These opportunities were attributed to the fact that quality spreads, the difference in yields between lower- and higher-rated credits, were frequently not the same in the fixed-rate market as in the floating-rate market, and often the quality spreads were not the same in the U.S. debt markets as in the Eurodollar bond markets. Note that our second illustration assumes a spread of 50 basis points in the floating-rate markets and 150 basis points in the fixed-rate markets. Publications by dealer firms[3] and academic research have suggested this credit arbitrage motivation.[4]

Basically, this argument for swaps rested on the well-known economic principle of comparative advantage, which was developed in international economics. The argument takes this form: Even though a high credit-rated issuer could borrow at a lower cost in both the fixed-rate and floating-rate markets (that is, have an absolute advantage in both), it will have a comparative advantage relative to a lower credit-rated issuer in one of the markets (and a comparative disadvantage in the other). Under these conditions, each borrower could benefit from issuing securities in the market in which it has a comparative advantage and then swapping obligations for the desired type of financing. The swap market developed as the vehicle for swapping obligations.

Several observers have challenged the notion that credit arbitrage opportunities exist. They insist that the comparative advantage argument, while based on arbitrage, does not rely on irrational mispricing, but on assumptions of equilibrium in segmented markets. That is, two completely separate markets can be perfectly competitive unto themselves, but set different prices for risk. An economic agent transacting simultaneously in both markets would see an imperfectly competitive market and an opportunity to make money.

Those who challenge the credit arbitrage notion argue that the differences in quality spreads in the fixed-rate and floating-rate markets represent differences in the risks that

---

[2] Bank for International settlements, "Semiannual OTC derivatives statistics at end-December 2007," Table 19: Amounts Outstanding of Over-the-Counter (OTC) Derivatives, http://www.bis.org/statistics/otcder/dt1920a.pdf.

[3] See, for example, a January 1986 Salomon Brothers publication: T. Lipsky and S. Elhalaski, "Swap-Driven Primary Issuance in the International Bond Market."

[4] See, for example, James Bicksler and Andrew Chen, "An Economic Analysis of Interest Rate Swaps," *Journal of Finance* (July 1986), pp. 645–655.

lenders face in these two markets. Let us consider short- and long-term markets in this regard. The interest rate for a floating-rate note effectively represents a short-term interest rate, and the quality spread on floating-rate notes, therefore, is a spread in the short-term market. In contrast, the quality spread on fixed-rate medium- and long-term notes represents the spread in that maturity sector. There is no reason why the quality spreads across those two markets have to be the same.[5]

A serious obstacle to accepting the credit arbitrage explanation of the swap market is that opportunities for credit arbitrage should be rare in reasonably efficient international credit markets. Moreover, even if such opportunities arose, market participants would quickly exploit and eliminate them. How then can we explain the fact that the number of interest rate swap transactions has grown substantially over the past decade? The May 1984 edition of *Euromoney* contained a Citicorp-sponsored contribution that offered this interesting explanation of the swap market and its reason for being:

> The nature of swaps is that they arbitrage market imperfections. As with any arbitrage opportunity, the more it is exploited, the smaller it becomes. . . .
>
> But some of the causes of market imperfections are unlikely to disappear quickly. For example, insurance companies in many countries are constrained to invest mainly in instruments that are domestic in that country. That requirement, tending to favor domestic issuers artificially, is unlikely to be changed overnight. And even in the world's most liquid markets there are arbitrage opportunities. They are small and exist only briefly, but they exist nevertheless.[6]

As this opinion demonstrates, as early as 1984, some observers attributed the difference in quality spreads among markets to differences in regulations among countries. Similarly, differences in tax treatment across countries also create differences in the price of risk and in expected returns.[7] Thus, swaps can be used for regulatory or tax arbitrage and may be explained by such differences among national markets.

Finally, another argument suggested for the growth of the interest rate swap market is the increased volatility of interest rates that has led borrowers and lenders to hedge or manage their exposure. Even though risk/return characteristics can be replicated by a package of forward contracts, interest rate forward contracts are not as liquid as interest rate swaps. And entering into or liquidating swap transactions has been facilitated by the standardization of documentation published by the International Swap Dealers Association in early 1987. Moreover, a swap to hedge or manage a position costs less than a package of interest rate forward contracts.

---

[5] Two researchers demonstrate that differences in quality spreads between the fixed-rate and floating-rate markets are consistent with option-pricing theory. See Ian Cooper and Antonio Mello, "Default Spreads in the Fixed and in the Floating Rate Markets: A Contingent Claims Approach," *Advances in Futures and Options Research*, Vol. 3 (1988), pp. 269–290.

[6] "Swap Financing Techniques: A Citicorp Guide," Special Sponsored Section, *Euromoney* (May 1984), pp. S1–S7. Rather than relying exclusively on an arbitrage argument, one study suggests that the swaps market grew because it allowed borrowers to raise a type of financing that was not possible prior to the introduction of interest rate swaps. See: Marcelle Arak, Arturo Estrella, Laurie Goodman, and Andrew Silver, "Interest Rate Swaps: An Alternative Explanation," *Financial Management* (Summer 1988), pp. 12–18.

[7] This applies even more so to currency swaps, which we discuss in Chapter 32. Several examples of the way swaps can be used to exploit differences in taxes are given in Clifford W. Smith, Charles W. Smithson, and Lee MacDonald Wakeman, "The Evolving Market for Swaps," *Midland Corporate Finance Journal* (Winter 1986), pp. 20–32.

Consequently, we can say that the swap market originally developed around the purpose of exploiting real or perceived imperfections in the capital market, but eventually evolved into a transactionally efficient market for accomplishing asset/liability objectives.

Although there are no publicly available data on the users of swaps, a study by Leslie Lynn Rahl provides some insight into their identity.[8] She found that 25% of the end users of swaps are corporations, 60% are financial institutions that are not swap dealers, and 15% are government agencies and supranationals.

Role of the Intermediary

The role of the intermediary in an interest rate swap sheds some light on the evolution of the market. Intermediaries in these transactions have been commercial banks and investment banks, who in the early stages of the market sought out end users of swaps. That is, commercial banks and investment banking firms found in their client bases those entities that needed swaps to accomplish funding or investing objectives, and they matched the two entities. In essence, the intermediary in this type of transaction performed the function of a broker.

In the early years of this market, the only time that the intermediary would take the opposite side of a swap (that is, would act as a principal) was when it had to do so in order to balance out the transaction. For example, if an intermediary had two clients that were willing to do a swap but one wanted the notional principal amount to be $100 million while the other wanted it to be $85 million, the intermediary might become the counterparty to the extent of $15 million. That is, the intermediary would warehouse or take a position as a principal to the transaction in order to make up the $15 million difference between the clients' objectives. To protect itself against an adverse interest rate movement, the intermediary would hedge its position.

To explain how the intermediary's role developed over time, we need to address an important feature of the swap that we have not yet discussed. The parties to the swaps we have described had to be concerned that the other party would default on its obligation. While a default would not mean any principal was lost (because the notional principal amount had not been exchanged), a default would mean that the objective for which the swap was entered into would be impaired. As the early transactions involved a higher and a lower credit-rated entity, the former would be concerned with the potential for default of the latter. To reduce the risk of default, many early swap transactions required that the lower credit-rated entity obtain a guarantee from a highly rated commercial bank. Often, the intermediary in the swap was a bank of this type. Involvement as insurer or guarantor in this way led banks to accept the role of dealer or counterparty.

As the frequency and the size of the transactions increased, many intermediaries became comfortable with swap transactions and became principals instead of simply acting as brokers. As long as an intermediary had one entity willing to enter into a swap, the intermediary was willing to be the counterparty. Consequently, interest rate swaps became part of an intermediary's inventory of products. Advances in quantitative techniques and futures products for hedging complex positions such as swaps made the protection of large inventory positions feasible.

---

[8] Leslie Lynn Rahl, "Who Is Using Swaps?" *Bond Week* (October 14, 1991), p. 4.

Yet another development encouraged intermediaries to become principals rather than brokers in swaps. As more intermediaries entered the swap market, bid–ask spreads on swaps narrowed sharply. To make money in the swaps market, intermediaries had to do a sufficient volume of business, which was possible only if they had (1) an extensive client base willing to use swaps, and (2) a large inventory of swaps. Accomplishing these objectives necessitated that the intermediaries act as principals. A survey by *Euromoney* asked 150 multinationals and supranationals to identify the characteristics that make a swap house efficient.[9] The results indicated that the speed at which a swap could be arranged for a client was the most important criterion. That speed depends on client base and inventory. The same survey also revealed clients to be less interested in brokered deals than in transactions in which the intermediary is a principal.

Market Quotes

The convention that has evolved for quoting swaps levels is for a swap dealer to set the floating rate equal to the index and then quote the fixed rate that will apply. To illustrate this convention, we use the swap in our second example of the application of swaps. The terms for that 10-year swap are as follows:

BANK:

> Pay floating rate of 6-month LIBOR + 70 b.p.
> Receive fixed rate of 11.3%.

NONFINANCIAL CORPORATION:

> Pay fixed rate of 11.3%.
> Receive floating rate of 6-month LIBOR + 45 b.p.

The offer price that the dealer would quote to the nonfinancial corporation (the fixed-rate payer) would be to pay 10.85% and receive LIBOR flat. (The term *flat* means with no spread.) The 10.85% is obtained by subtracting from the fixed rate of 11.3% the 45-basis point spread over LIBOR. The bid price that the dealer would quote to the commercial bank would be to pay LIBOR flat and receive 10.6%. The 10.6% represents the payment to be received of 11.3% minus the 70-basis point spread over LIBOR.

The dealer determines or sets the quoted fixed rate by adding some spread to the Treasury yield curve with the same term to maturity as the swap. We refer to this spread as the *swap spread*. In our illustration, suppose that the 10-year Treasury yield is 10.35%. In this case, the offer price that the dealer would quote to the fixed-rate payer is the 10-year Treasury rate plus 50 basis points versus receiving LIBOR flat. For the floating-rate payer, the bid price quoted would be LIBOR flat versus the 10-year Treasury rate plus 40 basis points. In the terminology of the market, the dealer would actually quote this particular swap as "40–50." This swap spread means that the dealer is willing to enter into a swap on either side: to receive LIBOR and pay a fixed rate equal to the 10-year Treasury rate plus 40 basis points, or to pay LIBOR and receive a fixed rate equal to the 10-year Treasury rate plus 50 basis points. The difference between the fixed rate paid and received is the bid–offer spread, which is 40 basis points.

---

[9] Special Supplement on Swaps, *Euromoney* (July 1987), p. 14.

Primary Determinants of Swap Spreads[10]

Earlier, we provided two interpretations of a swap: (1) a package of futures/forward contracts, and (2) a package of cash market instruments. The swap spread is defined as the difference between the swap's fixed rate and the rate on a Treasury whose maturity matches the swap's maturity. Although a discussion of the valuation of interest rate swaps is beyond the scope of this chapter, it can be shown that they are valued using no-arbitrage relationships relative to instruments (funding or investment vehicles) that produce the same cash flows under the same circumstances.[11]

The swap spread is determined by the same factors that drive the spread over Treasuries on instruments that replicate a swap's cash flows (i.e., produce a similar return or funding profile). As discussed below, the swap spread's key determinant for swaps with maturities of five years or less is the cost of hedging in the Eurodollar futures market.[12] For swaps with a longer maturity, the swap spread is largely driven by credit spreads in the corporate bond market.[13] Specifically, longer-dated swaps are priced relative to rates paid by investment-grade credits in traditional fixed- and floating-rate markets.

Given that a swap is a package of futures/forward contracts, the shorter-term swap spreads respond directly to fluctuations in Eurodollar futures prices. A Eurodollar futures contract is an instrument where a fixed dollar payment (i.e., the futures price) is exchanged for three-month LIBOR. There is a liquid market for Eurodollar futures contracts with maturities every three months for five years. A market participant can create a synthetic fixed-rate security or a fixed-rate funding vehicle of up to five years by taking a position in a bundle of Eurodollar futures contracts (i.e., a position in every three-month Eurodollar futures contract up to the desired maturity date).

For example, consider a financial institution that has fixed-rate assets and floating-rate liabilities. Both the assets and liabilities have a maturity of three years. The interest rate on the liabilities resets every three months based on three-month LIBOR. This financial institution can hedge this mismatched asset/liability position by buying a three-year bundle of Eurodollar futures contracts. By doing so, the financial institution is receiving LIBOR over the three-year period and paying a fixed dollar amount (i.e., the futures price). The financial institution is now hedged because the assets are fixed rate and the bundle of long Eurodollar futures synthetically creates a fixed-rate funding arrangement. From the fixed dollar amount over the three years, an effective fixed rate that the financial institution pays can be computed. Alternatively, the financial institution can synthetically create a fixed-rate funding arrangement by entering into a three-year swap in which it pays fixed and receives

---

[10] The discussion in this section is adapted from Chapter 6 in Frank J. Fabozzi and Steven V. Mann, *Floating-Rate Securities* (New Hope, PA: Frank J. Fabozzi Associates, 2000).

[11] For an explanation of the valuation of swaps, see Jeffrey Buetow and Frank J. Fabozzi, *Valuation of Interest Rate Swaps* (New Hope, PA: Frank J. Fabozzi Associates, 2001).

[12] Naturally, this presupposes that the reference rate for the swap is LIBOR. Furthermore, part of the swap spread is attributable simply to the fact that LIBOR for a given maturity is higher than the rate of a comparable-maturity U.S. Treasury. For a discussion of non-LIBOR swaps and their valuation, see Buetow and Fabozzi, *Valuation of Interest Rate Swaps*.

[13] The default risk component of a swap spread will be smaller than for a comparable bond credit spread. There are two reasons for this. First, since only net interest payments are exchanged rather than both principal and coupon interest payments, the total cash flow at risk is lower. Second, the probability of default depends jointly on the probability of the counterparty defaulting and whether or not the swap has a positive value. See John C. Hull, *Introduction to Futures and Options Markets*, 3rd edition (Upper Saddle River, NJ: Prentice Hall, 1998).

three-month LIBOR. Other factors being equal, the financial institution will use the vehicle that delivers the lowest cost of hedging the mismatched position. That is, the financial institution will compare the synthetic fixed rate (expressed as a percentage over U.S. Treasuries) to the three-year swap spread. The difference between the synthetic spread and the swap spread should be within a few basis points under normal circumstances.

For swaps with maturities greater than five years, we cannot rely on the Eurodollar futures since liquid markets do not exist for these contracts at longer maturities. Instead, longer-dated swaps are priced using rates available to investment-grade corporate borrowers in fixed-rate and floating-rate debt markets. Since a swap can be interpreted as a package of long and short positions in a fixed-rate bond and a floating-rate bond, it is the credit spreads in those two market sectors that will be the determinant of the swap spread. Empirically, the swap rate for a given maturity is greater than the yield on U.S. Treasury securities and less than the yield for AA rated banks.[14] Swap fixed rates are lower than AA rated bond yields due to their lower credit due to netting and offsetting of swap positions.

In addition, a number of other technical factors influence the level of swap spreads. While the impact of some of these factors is ephemeral, their influence can be considerable in the short run. Included among these factors are (1) the level and shape of the Treasury yield curve, (2) the relative supply of fixed- and floating-rate payers in the interest rate swap market, (3) the level of asset-based swap activity, and (4) technical factors that affect swap dealers.[15]

Secondary Market for Swaps

There are three general types of transactions in the secondary market for swaps. These include (1) a swap reversal, (2) a swap sale (or assignment), and (3) a swap buy-back (or close-out or cancellation).

In a **swap reversal**, the party that wants out of the transaction will arrange for an additional swap in which (1) the maturity on the new swap is equal to the time remaining of the original swap, (2) the reference rate is the same, and (3) the notional principal amount is the same. For example, suppose party X enters into a five-year swap with a notional principal amount of $50 million in which it pays 10% and receives LIBOR, but that two years later, X wants out of the swap. In a swap reversal, X would enter into a three-year interest rate swap, with a counterparty different from the original counterparty, let's say Z, in which the notional principal amount is $50 million, and X pays LIBOR and receives a fixed rate. The fixed rate that X receives from Z will depend on prevailing swap terms for floating-rate receivers at the initiation of the three-year swap.

Although party X has effectively terminated the original swap in economic terms, there is a major drawback to this approach: Party X is still liable to original counterparty Y, as well as to the new counterparty, Z. That is, party X now has two offsetting interest rate swaps on its books instead of one, and as a result it has increased its default risk exposure.

The **swap sale** or **swap assignment** overcomes this drawback. In this secondary market transaction, the party that wishes to close out the original swap finds another party that is willing to accept its obligations under the swap. In our illustration, this means that X finds another party, say, A, that will agree to pay 10% to Y and receive LIBOR from Y for the next

---

[14] For a discussion of this point, see Andrew R. Young, *A Morgan Stanley Guide to Fixed Income Analysis* (New York: Morgan Stanley, 1997).

[15] For a further discussion of these technical factors, see Fabozzi and Mann, *Floating-Rate Securities*.

three years. Party A might have to be compensated to accept the position of X, or A might have to be willing to compensate X. Who will receive compensation depends on the swap terms at the time. For example, if interest rates have risen so that, to receive LIBOR for three years, a fixed-rate payer would have to pay 12%, then A would have to compensate X because A has to pay only 10% to receive LIBOR. The compensation would be equal to the present value of a three-year annuity of 2% times the notional principal amount. If, instead, interest rates have fallen so that, to receive LIBOR for three years, a fixed-rate payer would have to pay 6%, then X would have to compensate A. The compensation would be equal to the present value of a three-year annuity of 4% times the notional principal amount. Once the transaction is completed, it is then A, not X, that is obligated to perform under the swap terms. (Of course, an intermediary could act as principal and become party A.)

In order to accomplish a swap sale, the original counterparty, Y in our example, must agree to the sale. A key factor in whether Y will agree is whether it is willing to accept the credit of A. For example, if A's credit rating is triple B, while X's is double A, Y would be unlikely to accept A as a counterparty.

A **buy-back** or **close-out sale** (or **cancellation**) involves the sale of the swap to the original counterparty. As in the case of a swap sale, one party might have to compensate the other, depending on how interest rates and credit spreads have changed since the inception of the swap.

These methods for getting into or out of a swap leave much to be desired for market participants. It is this illiquidity in the secondary market that will hamper swap market growth. There have been proposals to create a swap clearing corporation, similar to the clearing corporations for futures and options, in which case swaps could be marked to market and credit exposure to a swap could be reduced. So far, these proposals have not been implemented.

Beyond the Plain Vanilla Swap

Thus far we have described the plain vanilla or generic interest rate swap. Nongeneric or individualized swaps have evolved as a result of the asset/liability needs of borrowers and lenders. These include swaps where the notional principal changes in a predetermined way over the life of the swap and swaps in which both counterparties pay a floating rate. There are complex swap structures such as options on swaps (called swaptions) and swaps where the swap does not begin until some future time (called forward start swaps). We discuss all of these swaps below. It may be difficult to fully appreciate the importance of these swap structures as a tool for managing the interest rate risk of a financial institution in this book because of our limited coverage of risk management. What is important to appreciate is that these swap structures are not just "bells and whistles" added to the plain vanilla swap to make them more complicated, but features that managers have found that they need to control interest rate risk.

Varying Notional Principal Amount Swaps

In a generic or plain vanilla swap, the notional principal amount does not vary over the life of the swap. Thus, it is sometimes referred to as a **bullet swap**. In contrast, for amortizing, accreting, and roller-coaster swaps, the notional principal amount varies over the life of the swap.

An **amortizing swap** is one in which the notional principal amount decreases in a predetermined way over the life of the swap. Such a swap would be used where the principal of the asset that is being hedged with the swap amortizes over time. For example, in our illustration of the asset/liability problem faced by the bank, the commercial loans are assumed to pay only interest every six months and repay principal only at the end of the loan term. However, what if the commercial loan is a typical term loan; that is, suppose it is a loan that amortizes? Or, suppose that it is a typical mortgage loan that amortizes. In such circumstances, the outstanding principal for the loans would decline and the bank would need a swap where the notional principal amount amortizes in the same way as the loans.

Less common than the amortizing swap are the **accreting swap** and the **roller-coaster swap**. An accreting swap is one in which the notional principal amount increases in a predetermined way over time. In a roller-coaster swap, the notional principal amount can rise or fall from period to period.

Basis Swaps and Constant Maturity Swaps

The terms of a generic interest rate swap call for the exchange of fixed- and floating-rate payments. In a **basis rate swap**, both parties exchange floating-rate payments based on a different reference rate. As an example, assume a commercial bank has a portfolio of loans in which the lending rate is based on the prime rate, but the bank's cost of funds is based on LIBOR. The risk the bank faces is that the spread between the prime rate and LIBOR will change. This is referred to as *basis risk*. The bank can use a basis rate swap to make floating-rate payments based on the prime rate (because that is the reference rate that determines how much the bank is receiving on the loans) and receive floating-rate payments based on LIBOR (because that is the reference rate that determines the bank's funding cost).

Another popular swap is to have the floating leg tied to a longer-term rate such as the two-year Treasury note rather than a money market rate. So one of the parties to the swap would pay the two-year Treasury rate, for example, and the counterparty would pay LIBOR. Such a swap is called a *constant maturity swap*. The reference rate for determining the yield on the constant maturity Treasury in a constant maturity swap is typically the Constant Maturity Treasury (CMT) rate published the Federal Reserve. Consequently, a constant maturity swap tied to the CMT is called a *Constant Maturity Treasury swap*.

Swaptions

There are options on interest rate swaps. These swap structures are called **swaptions** and grant the option buyer the right to enter into an interest rate swap at a future date. The time until expiration of the swap, the term of the swap, and the swap rate are specified. The swap rate is the strike rate for the swaption. The swaption can have any exercise style—American, European, and Bermudian.

There are two types of swaptions—a payer swaption and a receiver swaption. A **payer swaption** entitles the option buyer to enter into an interest rate swap in which the buyer of the option pays a fixed rate and receives a floating rate. For example, suppose that the strike rate is 7%, the term of the swap is three years, and the swaption expires in two years. Also, assume that it is a European-type exercise provision. This means that the buyer of this swaption at the end of two years has the right to enter into a three-year interest rate swap in which the buyer pays 7% (the swap rate which is equal to the strike rate) and receives the reference rate.

In a **receiver swaption**, the buyer of the swaption has the right to enter into an interest rate swap that requires paying a floating rate and receiving a fixed rate. For example, if the strike rate is 6.25%, the swap term is five years, and the option expires in one year, the buyer of this receiver swaption has the right when the option expires in one year (assuming it is a

European-type exercise provision) to enter into a four-year interest rate swap in which the buyer receives a swap rate of 6.25% (i.e., the strike rate) and pays the reference rate.

How is a swaption used? We can see its usefulness in managing interest rate risk if we return to the bank-insurance company example. The bank makes fixed-rate payments on the interest rate swap (10%) using the interest rate it is earning on the commercial loans (10%). Suppose that the commercial loan borrowers default on their obligations. The bank will not receive from the commercial loans the 10% to make its swap payments. This problem can be addressed at the outset of the initial swap transaction by the bank entering into a swaption that effectively gives it the right to terminate or cancel the swap. That is, the bank will enter into a receiver swaption, receiving fixed of 10% so as to offset the fixed rate it is obligated to pay under the initial swap. In fact, the borrowers do not have to fail for the swap to have an adverse impact on the bank. Suppose the commercial loans can be prepaid. Then, the bank has a similar problem. For example, suppose rates on commercial loans decline to 7% and the borrowers prepay. Then the bank would be obligated to make the 10% payments under the terms of the swap. With the proceeds received from the prepayment of the commercial loans, the bank may only be able to invest in similar loans at 7%, for example, a rate that is less than the bank's obligations.

Forward Start Swap

A **forward start swap** is a swap wherein the swap does not begin until some future date that is specified in the swap agreement. Thus, there is a beginning date for the swap at some time in the future and a maturity date for the swap. A forward start swap will also specify the swap rate at which the counterparties agree to exchange payments commencing at the start date.

Key Points That You Should Understand Before Proceeding

1. An interest rate swap is an agreement whereby two counterparties agree to exchange periodic interest payments based on a notional principal amount.
2. A position in an interest rate swap can be interpreted as a position in a package of forward contracts or a package of cash flows from buying and selling cash market instruments.
3. While the initial motivation for the swap market was borrower exploitation of what were perceived to be credit arbitrage opportunities, such opportunities are limited and depend on the presence of market imperfections.
4. The swap market has evolved into a transactionally efficient market for accomplishing asset/liability objectives to alter the cash flow characteristics of assets (an asset swap) or liabilities (a liability swap).
5. Commercial banks and investment banking firms take positions in swaps rather than act as simply intermediaries.
6. For swaps with maturities of less than five years, the swap spread is driven by rates in the Eurodollar futures market, but for swaps with maturities greater than five years, the spread is determined primarily by the credit spreads in the corporate bond market.
7. In addition to the generic swap structure where one party pays fixed and the other floating, there are swaps with varying notional principal amounts, basis swaps (floating payments made by both parties), constant maturity swaps, swaptions, and forward start swaps.

Interest Rate/Equity Swaps

In addition to interest rate swaps, there are currency swaps and **interest rate/equity swaps**. We will discuss the former in the next chapter. Here, we will explain interest rate/equity swaps.

Illustration of an Interest Rate/Equity Swap

To illustrate this swap, consider the following swap agreement:

- The counterparties to this swap agreement are the Brotherhood of Basket Weavers (a pension sponsor) and the Reliable Investment Management Corporation (a money management firm).
- The notional principal amount is $50 million.
- Every year for the next five years, the Brotherhood agrees to pay Reliable Investment Management Corporation the return realized on the Standard & Poor's 500 stock index for the year minus 200 basis points.
- Every year for the next five years, Reliable Investment Management Corporation agrees to pay the pension sponsor 10%.

For example, if over the past year the return on the S&P 500 stock index is 14%, then the pension sponsor pays Reliable Investment Management Corporation 12% (14% minus 2%) of $50 million, or $6 million, and the money management firm agrees to pay the pension sponsor $5 million (10% times $50 million).

Application to Creation of a Security

Swaps can be used by investment bankers to create a security. To see how this is done, suppose the following. The Universal Information Technology Company (UIT) seeks to raise $100 million for the next five years on a fixed-rate basis. UIT's investment banker, Credit Suisse, indicates that if bonds with a maturity of five years are issued, the interest rate on the issue would have to be 8%. At the same time, there are institutional investors seeking to purchase bonds but that are interested in making a play on the stock market. These investors are willing to purchase a bond whose annual interest rate is based on the actual performance of the S&P's 500 stock market index.

Credit Suisse recommends to UIT's management that it consider issuing a five-year bond whose annual interest rate is based on the actual performance of the S&P 500. The risk with issuing such a bond is that UIT's annual interest cost is uncertain, since it depends on the performance of the S&P 500. However, suppose that the following two transactions are entered into:

1. On January 1, UIT agrees to issue, using Credit Suisse as the underwriter, a $100 million, five-year bond issue whose annual interest rate is the actual performance of the S&P 500 that year minus 300 basis points. The minimum interest rate, however, is set at zero. The annual interest payments are made on December 31.
2. UIT enters into a five-year, $100 million notional principal amount interest rate/equity swap with Credit Suisse in which each year for the next five years UIT agrees to pay 7.9% to Credit Suisse and Credit Suisse agrees to pay the actual performance of the S&P 500 that year minus 300 basis points. The terms of the swap call for the payments to be made on December 31 of each year. Thus, the swap payments coincide with the payments that

must be made on the bond issue. Also, as part of the swap agreement, if the S&P 500 minus 300 basis points results in a negative value, Credit Suisse pays nothing to UIT.

Let's look at what has been accomplished with these two transactions from the perspective of UIT. Specifically, focus on the payments that must be made by UIT on the bond issue and the swap, and the payments that it will receive from the swap. These are summarized here:

Interest payments on bond issue:	S&P 500 return – 300 b.p.
Swap payment from Credit Suisse:	S&P 500 return + 300 b.p.
Swap payment to Credit Suisse:	7.9%
Net interest cost:	7.9%

Thus, the net interest cost is a fixed rate despite the bond issue paying an interest rate tied to the S&P 500. This was accomplished with the interest rate/equity swap.

There are several questions that should be addressed. First, what was the advantage to UIT to entering into this transaction? Recall that if UIT issued a bond, Credit Suisse estimated that UIT would have to pay 8% annually. Thus, UIT has saved 10 basis points (8% minus 7.9%) per year. Second, why would investors purchase this bond issue? As explained in previous chapters, there are restrictions imposed on institutional investors as to types of investments. For example, a depository institution may not be entitled to purchase common stock; however, it may be permitted to purchase a bond of an issuer such as UIT despite the fact that the interest rate is tied to the performance of common stocks. Third, isn't Credit Suisse exposed to the risk of the performance of the S&P 500? While it is difficult to demonstrate at this point, there are ways that Credit Suisse can protect itself.

Although this may seem like a far-fetched application, it is not. In fact, it is quite common. Debt instruments created by using swaps are commonly referred to as structured notes.

INTEREST RATE CAPS AND FLOORS

An interest rate cap and floor is an agreement between two parties in which one party, for an upfront premium, agrees to compensate the other if a designated interest rate, called the **reference rate**, is different from a predetermined level. When one party agrees to pay the other if the reference rate exceeds a predetermined level, the agreement is referred to as an **interest rate cap** or **ceiling**. The agreement is referred to as an **interest rate floor** when one party agrees to pay the other if the reference rate falls below a predetermined level. The predetermined level of the reference interest rate is called the **strike rate**. The terms of an interest rate agreement include:

1. the reference rate
2. the strike rate that sets the ceiling or floor
3. the length of the agreement
4. the frequency of settlement
5. the notional principal amount

For example, suppose that C buys an interest rate cap from D with terms as follows:

1. The reference rate is six-month LIBOR.
2. The strike rate is 8%.

3. The agreement is for seven years.
4. Settlement is every six months.
5. The notional principal amount is $20 million.

Under this agreement, every six months for the next seven years, D will pay C whenever six-month LIBOR exceeds 8%. The payment will equal the dollar value of the difference between six-month LIBOR and 8% times the notional principal amount divided by two. For example, if six months from now six-month LIBOR is 11%, then D will pay C 3% (11% minus 8%) times $20 million divided by 2, or $300,000. If six-month LIBOR is 8% or less, D does not have to pay anything to C.

As an example of an interest rate floor, assume the same terms as the interest rate cap we just illustrated. In this case, if six-month LIBOR is 11%, C receives nothing from D, but if six-month LIBOR is less than 8%, D compensates C for the difference. For example, if six-month LIBOR is 7%, D will pay C $100,000 (8% minus 7%, times $20 million divided by 2).

Interest rate caps and floors can be combined to create an **interest rate collar**. This is done by buying an interest rate cap and selling an interest rate floor. Some commercial banks and investment banking firms now write options on interest rate agreements for customers. Options on caps are called **captions**, and options on floors are called **flotions**.

Risk/Return Characteristics

In an interest rate cap and floor, the buyer pays an upfront fee, which represents the maximum amount the buyer can lose and the maximum amount the writer of the agreement can gain. The only party that is required to perform is the writer of the interest rate agreement. The buyer of an interest rate cap benefits if the underlying interest rate rises above the strike rate because the seller (writer) must compensate the buyer. The buyer of an interest rate floor benefits if the interest rate falls below the strike rate because the seller (writer) must compensate the buyer.

How can we better understand interest rate caps and interest rate floors? In essence, these contracts are equivalent to a package of interest rate options. The question is what type of package of options is a cap and what type is a floor. Recall from our earlier discussion of the relationship between futures, FRAs, and swaps that the relationship depends on whether the underlying is an interest rate or a fixed-income instrument. The same applies to call options, put options, caps, and floors.

If the underlying is considered a fixed-income instrument, its value changes inversely with interest rates. Therefore,

FOR A CALL OPTION ON A FIXED-INCOME INSTRUMENT:

1. interest rates increase → fixed-income instrument's price decreases → call option's value decreases
2. interest rates decrease → fixed-income instrument's price increases → call option's value increases

FOR A PUT OPTION ON A FIXED-INCOME INSTRUMENT:

3. interest rates increase → fixed-income instrument's price decreases → put option's value increases
4. interest rates decrease → fixed-income instrument's price increases → put option's value decreases

To summarize,

	When Interest Rates	
Value of:	Increase	Decrease
Long call	Decrease	Increase
Short call	Increase	Decrease
Long put	Increase	Decrease
Short put	Decrease	Increase

For a cap and floor, the situation is as follows:

	When Interest Rates	
Value of:	Increase	Decrease
Short cap	Decrease	Increase
Long cap	Increase	Decrease
Short floor	Increase	Decrease
Long floor	Decrease	Increase

Therefore, buying a cap (long cap) is equivalent to buying a package of puts on a fixed-income instrument, and buying a floor (long floor) is equivalent to buying a package of calls on a fixed-income instrument.

On the other hand, if an option is viewed as an option on an interest rate (underlying), then buying a cap (long cap) is equivalent to buying a package of calls on interest rates. Buying a floor (long floor) is equivalent to buying a package of puts on interest rates.

It is important to note that, once again, a complex contract can be seen to be a package of basic contracts, or options in the case of interest rate agreements.

Applications

To see how interest rate agreements can be used for asset/liability management, consider the problems faced by the commercial bank and the life insurance company in the illustration in the chapter of the application of interest rate swaps.

Recall that the bank's objective is to lock in an interest rate spread over its cost of funds. Yet, because it raises funds through a variable-rate instrument and is basically borrowing short term, the bank's cost of funds is uncertain. The bank may be able to purchase a cap so that the cap rate plus the cost of purchasing the cap is less than the rate it is earning on its fixed-rate commercial loans. If short-term rates decline, the bank does not benefit from the cap, but its cost of funds declines. The cap, therefore, allows the bank to impose a ceiling on its cost of funds while retaining the opportunity to benefit from a decline in rates. This use of a cap is consistent with the view of an interest rate cap as simply a package of call options.

The bank can reduce the cost of purchasing the cap by selling a floor. In this case, the bank agrees to pay the buyer of the floor if the underlying rate falls below the strike rate. The bank receives a fee for selling the floor, but it has sold off its opportunity to benefit from a decline in rates below the strike rate. By buying a cap and selling a floor, the bank has created a range for its cost of funds (or a collar).

Consider again from that same first example of the application of interest rate swaps the problem of the life insurance company that has guaranteed a 9% rate on a GIC for the next five years and is considering the purchase of an attractive floating-rate instrument in a private placement transaction. The risk that the company faces is that interest rates will fall so that it will not earn enough to realize the 9% guaranteed rate plus a spread. The life insurance company may be able to purchase a floor to set a lower bound on its investment return, yet retain the opportunity to benefit should rates increase. To reduce the cost of purchasing the floor, the life insurance company can sell an interest rate cap. By doing so, however, it gives up the opportunity of benefiting from an increase in the six-month Treasury bill rate above the strike rate of the interest rate cap.

Key Points That You Should Understand Before Proceeding

1. An interest rate agreement is an agreement between two parties in which one party, for an upfront premium, agrees to compensate the other if the reference rate is different from the strike rate.
2. A cap is an interest rate agreement in which one party agrees to pay the other if the reference rate exceeds the strike rate; an interest rate floor is an interest rate agreement in which one party agrees to pay the other if the reference rate falls below the strike rate.
3. A collar is created by buying an interest rate cap and selling an interest rate floor.
4. An interest rate floor can be used by a depository institution to lock in an interest rate spread over its cost of funds but maintain the opportunity to benefit if rates decline.
5. The buyer of a floating-rate asset can use an interest rate floor to establish a lower bound on its investment return, yet retain the opportunity to benefit should rates increase.

SUMMARY

An FRA is the over-the-counter equivalent of the exchange-traded futures contracts on short-term rates and is a cash settlement contract. Typically, the short-term reference rate is LIBOR. The elements of an FRA are the contract rate, reference rate, settlement rate, notional amount, and settlement date. The buyer of the FRA agrees to pay the contract rate and the seller of the FRA agrees to receive the contract rate. The amount that must be exchanged at the settlement date is the present value of the interest differential. In contrast to a position in an interest rate futures contract, the buyer of an FRA benefits if the reference rate increases and the seller benefits if the reference rate decreases.

An interest rate swap is an agreement specifying that the parties exchange interest payments at designated times. In a typical swap, one party will make fixed-rate payments and the other will make floating-rate payments, with payments based on the notional principal amount. There are more complex swap structures such as swaps with a varying notional principal amount, basis swaps, constant maturity swaps, swaptions, and forward start swaps. Participants in financial markets use interest rate swaps to alter the cash flow characteristics of their assets or liabilities, or to capitalize on perceived capital market inefficiencies. A swap has the risk/return profile of a package of forward contracts or a combination of positions in the cash bond market.

An interest rate cap and floor allows one party the right to receive compensation from the writer of the agreement for an upfront premium if a designated interest rate is different from a predetermined level. An interest rate cap calls for one party to receive a payment if a designated interest rate is above the predetermined level. An interest rate floor lets one party receive a payment if a designated interest rate is below the predetermined level. An interest rate cap can be used to establish a ceiling on the cost of funding; an interest rate floor can be used to establish a floor return.

KEY TERMS

- Accreting swap
- Amortizing swap
- Asset swap
- Basis rate swap
- Bullet swap
- Buy-back (close-out sale, cancellation)
- Caption
- Fixed-rate payer
- Floating-rate payer
- Flotion
- Forward rate agreement (FRA)
- Forward start swap
- Interest rate cap (ceiling)
- Interest rate collar
- Interest rate/equity swap

- Interest rate floor
- Interest rate swap
- Liability swap
- Notional principal amount
- Payer swaption
- Plain vanilla swap
- Receiver swaption
- Reference rate
- Roller-coaster swap
- Strike rate
- Swap reversal
- Swap sale (swap assignment)
- Swaption

QUESTIONS

1. Hieber Manufacturing Corporation purchased the following FRA from the First Commercial Bank Corporation: (1) reference rate is three-month LIBOR, (2) contract rate is 6% (3) notional amount is for $20 million, and (4) number of days to settlement is 91 days.

    a. Suppose the settlement rate is 6.5%. Which party must compensate the other at the settlement date?

    b. If the settlement rate is 6.5%, how much will the compensation be?

2. Explain whether you agree or disagree with the following statement: "Both the buyers of an interest rate futures contract and FRA benefit if interest rates decline."

3. At any time in the life of the interest rate swap, does the notional principal become a cash flow to either party or to the intermediary?

4. Consider a swap with these features: maturity is five years, notional principal is $100 million, payments occur every six months, the fixed-rate payer pays a rate of 9.05% and receives LIBOR, while the floating-rate payer pays LIBOR and receives 9%. Now, suppose that at a payment date, LIBOR is at 6.5%. What is each party's payment and receipt at that date?

5. A bank borrows funds by issuing CDs that carry a variable rate equal to the yield of the six-month Treasury bill plus 50 basis points. The bank gets the chance to invest in a seven-year loan that will pay a

fixed rate of 7%. So, the bank wants to engage in an interest rate swap designed to lock in an interest spread of 75 basis points. Give the outlines of two possible swaps: one designed to change the asset's cash flow into a variable rate, and the other designed to change the liability's cash flow into a fixed rate.

6. Identify two factors that have contributed to the growth of the interest rate swap market.

7. **a.** Describe the role of the intermediary in a swap.

   b. What are the two factors that led swap brokers/intermediaries to act as principals or dealers?

8. Suppose a dealer quotes these terms on a five-year swap: fixed-rate payer to pay 9.5% for LIBOR flat and floating-rate payer to pay LIBOR flat for 9.2%.

   a. What is the dealer's bid–ask spread?

   b. How would the dealer quote the terms by reference to the yield on five-year Treasury notes, assuming this yield is 9%?

9. Explain the three major ways in which a party to a swap can reverse that position in the secondary market for swaps.

10. Why can a fixed-rate payer in an interest rate swap be viewed as being short the bond market, and the floating-rate payer be viewed as being long the bond market?

11. **a.** Why would a depository institution use an interest rate swap?

    b. Why would a corporation that plans to raise funds in the debt market use an interest rate swap?

12. Suppose that a life insurance company has issued a three-year GIC with a fixed rate of 10%. Under what circumstances might it be feasible for the life insurance company to invest the funds in a floating-rate security and enter into a three-year interest rate swap in which it pays a floating rate and receives a fixed rate?

13. A portfolio manager buys a swaption with a strike rate of 6.5% that entitles the portfolio manager to enter into an interest rate swap to pay a fixed rate and receive a floating rate. The term of the swaption is five years.

    a. Is this swaption a payer swaption or a receiver swaption? Explain why.

    b. What does the strike rate of 6.5% mean?

14. The manager of a savings and loan association is considering the use of a swap as part of its asset/liability strategy. The swap would be used to convert the payments of its portfolio of fixed-rate residential mortgage loans into a floating payment.

    a. What is the risk with using a plain vanilla or generic interest rate swap?

    b. Why might a manager consider using an interest rate swap in which the notional principal amount declines over time?

    c. Why might a manager consider buying a swaption?

15. Suppose that a corporation is considering using an interest rate swap in conjunction with the offering of a floating-rate bond issue. That is, the corporation wants to use the swap to change the funding arrangement from a floating rate to a fixed rate.

    a. Would the corporation enter into a swap in which it pays or receives a fixed rate?

    b. Suppose that the corporation does not plan to issue the bond for one year. What type of swap can the firm's management enter into in order to set the terms of the swap today?

16. The Window Wipers Union (a pension sponsor) and the All-Purpose Asset Management Corporation (a money management firm) entered into a four-year swap with a notional principal amount of $150 million with the following terms: Every year for the next four years the Window Wipers Union agrees to pay All-Purpose Asset Management the return realized on the Standard & Poor's 500 stock index for the year minus 400 basis points and receive from All-Purpose Asset Management 9%.

    a. What type of swap is this?

    b. If in the first year when payments are to be exchanged, suppose that the return on the S&P 500 is 7%. What is the amount of the payment that the two parties must make to each other?

17. There are several depository institutions that offer certificates of deposit where the interest

rate paid is based on the performance of the S&P's 500 stock index.

    a. What is the risk that a depository institution encounters by offering such certificates of deposit?

    b. How do you think that a depository institution can protect itself against the risk you identified in part (a)?

18. Suppose a savings and loan association buys an interest rate cap that has these terms: The reference rate is the six-month Treasury bill rate; The cap will last for five years; payment is semiannual; the strike rate is 5.5%; and the notional principal amount is $10 million. Suppose further that at the end of some six-month period, the six-month Treasury bill rate is 6.1%.

    a. What is the amount of the payment that the savings and loan association will receive?

    b. What would the writer of this cap pay if the six-month Treasury rate were 5.45% instead of 6.1%?

19. What is the relationship between an interest rate agreement and an interest rate option?

20. How can an interest rate collar be created?

21. Acme Insurance Company has purchased a five-year bond whose interest rate floats with LIBOR. Specifically, the interest rate in a given year is equal to LIBOR plus 200 basis points. At the same time the insurance company purchases this bond, it enters into a floor agreement with Goldman Sachs in which the notional principal amount is $35 million with a strike rate of 6%. The premium Acme Insurance Company agrees to pay Goldman Sachs each year is $300,000.

    a. Suppose at the time that it is necessary to determine if a payment must be made by Goldman Sachs, LIBOR is 9%. How much must Goldman Sachs pay Acme Insurance Company?

    b. Suppose at the time that it is necessary to determine if a payment must be made by Goldman Sachs, LIBOR is 3%. How much must Goldman Sachs pay Acme Insurance Company?

    c. What is the minimum interest rate that Acme Insurance Company has locked in each year for the next five years by entering into this floor agreement and buying the five-year bond, ignoring the premium that Acme Insurance Company must make each year?

Market for Credit Risk Transfer Vehicles: Credit Derivatives and Collateralized Debt Obligations

LEARNING OBJECTIVES

After reading this chapter, you will understand

- what a credit risk transfer vehicle is

- what a credit derivative is

- the purpose of a credit derivative

- types and classification of credit derivatives

- how a credit event can be defined

- what a credit default swap is

- the different types of credit default swaps: single-name credit default swap, basket default swap, and credit default swap index

- what is meant by a collateralized debt obligation, collateralized bond obligation, and collateralized loan obligation

- the structure of a collateralized debt obligation

- the difference between an arbitrage and balance sheet transaction

- the economics underlying an arbitrage transaction

- the motivation for a balance sheet transaction

- what a synthetic collateralized debt obligation is and the motivation for its creation

- what a credit-linked note is

- what a structured finance operating company is

- concerns with the new credit risk transfer vehicles

From Chapter 31 of *Foundations of Financial Markets and Institutions*, 4/e. Frank J. Fabozzi. Franco Modigliani. Frank J. Jones.

The development of the derivatives markets prior to the turn of the century provided participants in financial markets with efficient vehicles for the transfer of interest rate, price, and currency risks, as well as enhancing the liquidity of the underlying assets. However, it is only in recent years that the market for the efficient transfer of credit risk has developed. Credit risk is the risk that a debt instrument will decline in value as a result of the borrower's inability (real or perceived) to satisfy the contractual terms of its borrowing arrangement. In the case of corporate debt obligations, credit risk encompasses default, credit spread, and rating downgrade risks.

The most obvious way for a financial institution such as a bank to transfer the credit risk of a loan it has originated is to sell it to another party. Loan covenants typically require that the borrower be informed of the sale. The drawback of a sale in the case of bank loans (more specifically leveraged loans) is the potential impairment of the originating financial institution's relationship with the corporate borrower whose loan is sold. Syndicated loans overcome the drawback of an outright sale because banks in the syndicate may sell their loan shares in the secondary market. The sale may be through an assignment or through participation. While the assignment mechanism for a syndicated loan requires the approval of the borrower, participation does not because the payments are merely passed through to the purchaser and therefore the borrower need not know about the sale.

Another form of credit risk transfer (CRT) vehicle developed in the 1980s is securitization. In a securitization, a financial institution that originates loans pools them and sells them to a special purpose vehicle (SPV). The SPV obtains funds to acquire the pool of loans by issuing securities. Payment of interest and principal on the securities issued by the SPV is obtained from the cash flow of the pool of loans. While the financial institution employing securitization retains some of the credit risk associated with the pool of loans, the majority of the credit risk is transferred to the holders of the securities issued by the SPV.

Two recent credit risk transfer vehicles are credit derivatives and collateralized debt obligations (CDOs). For financial institutions, **credit derivatives**, particularly credit default swaps, allow the transfer of credit risk to another party without the sale of the loan. A CDO is an application of the securitization technology. Credit derivatives can be used to create credit risk transfer products such as synthetic CDOs. In this chapter, we will describe credit risk transfer vehicles: credit derivatives, CDOs, synthetic CDOs, and credit-linked notes.

Although our focus in this chapter is on the transferring of corporate credit risk, credit derivatives and CDOs have been used to transfer sovereign credit risk and municipal credit risk.[1]

---

[1] For a discussion of the use of credit derivatives in the municipal bond market, see Frank J. Fabozzi, "Municipal Credit Default Swaps," Chapter 40 in Sylvan G. Feldstein and Frank J. Fabozzi (eds.), *The Handbook of Municipal Bonds* (Hoboken, NJ: John Wiley & Sons, 2008). The creation of CDOs backed by municipal bonds is in Rebecca Manning, Douglas J. Lucas, Laurie S. Goodman, and Frank J. Fabozzi, "Municipal Collateralized Debt Obligations," Chapter 41 in *The Handbook of Municipal Bonds*.

CREDIT DERIVATIVES

Credit derivatives are used by institutional portfolio managers in the normal course of activities to more efficiently control the credit risk of a portfolio or the balance sheet of a financial institution and to more efficiently transact than by transacting in the cash market. For example, credit derivatives allow a mechanism for portfolio managers to more efficiently short a credit-risky security than by shorting in the cash market, which is often difficult to do. For traders and hedge fund managers, credit derivatives provide a means for leveraging an exposure in the credit market.

The growth of the credit derivatives market has been documented by the British Bankers' Association (BBA), which periodically surveys market participants to gather information on the size of the market. According to the BBA surveys, the estimated size of the market was $180 billion in 1996. By the end of 2006, the estimated size of the market was $20.2 trillion, and it was expected to grow to $33.1 trillion by 2008.[2] This growth in the market followed the development of credit risk modeling.

There are several ways to characterize credit derivatives. One such categorization is shown in Figure 1. Some of the derivatives identified in the figure are not true credit derivatives in that they do not only provide protection against credit risk. Rather, they provide protection against both interest rate risk and credit risk. By far, the most popular type of credit derivative is the **credit default swap**. Not only is this form of credit derivative the most commonly used stand-alone product, but it is also used extensively in what is known as **structured credit products.** A credit default swap is probably the simplest form of credit risk transference among all credit derivatives, and according to the BBA it is the dominant form of credit derivative. Because of this, we will look at the different types of credit default swaps later in this chapter. In this section, we will discuss an important market development that fostered the growth of this market: the standardized documentation for the contract.

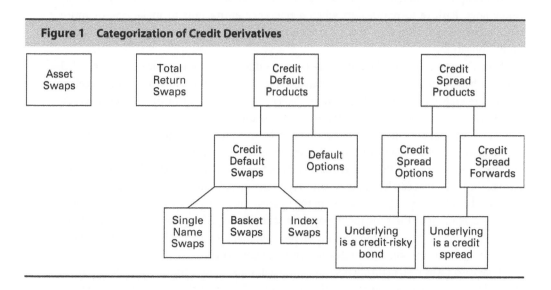

Figure 1   Categorization of Credit Derivatives

---

[2] British Bankers' Association, *Credit Derivatives Report 2006.*

International Swap and Derivatives Association Documentation

Prior to 1998, the development of the credit derivatives market was hindered by the lack of standardization of legal documentation. Every trade (i.e., the buying and selling of a credit derivative contract) had to be customized. In 1998, the **International Swap and Derivatives Association (ISDA)** developed a standardized contract that could be used by parties to trades of a credit derivatives contract. **ISDA documentation** is primarily designed for credit default swaps, but the contract form is sufficiently flexible so that it can be used for other types of credit derivatives.

Reference Entity and Reference Obligation

The documentation will identify the reference entity and the reference obligation. The **reference entity** is the issuer of the debt instrument and hence is also referred to as the **reference issuer**. It could be a corporation or a sovereign government. The **reference obligation**, also referred to as the **reference asset**, is the particular debt issue for which the credit protection is being sought. For example, a reference entity could be Ford Motor Credit Company. The reference obligation would be a specific Ford Motor Credit Company bond issue.

Credit Events

Credit derivative products have a payout that is contingent upon a **credit event** occurring. The ISDA provides definitions of credit events. The *1999 ISDA Credit Derivatives Definitions* (referred to as the "1999 Definitions") provides a list of eight credit events: (1) bankruptcy, (2) credit event upon merger, (3) cross acceleration, (4) cross default, (5) downgrade, (6) failure to pay, (7) repudiation/moratorium, and (8) restructuring. These eight events attempt to capture every type of situation that could cause the credit quality of the reference entity to deteriorate, or cause the value of the reference obligation to decline.

Bankruptcy is defined as a variety of acts that are associated with bankruptcy or insolvency laws. **Failure to pay** results when a reference entity fails to make one or more required payments when due. When a reference entity breaches a covenant, it has defaulted on its obligation.

When a default occurs, the obligation becomes due and payable prior to the scheduled due date had the reference entity not defaulted. This is referred to as an **obligation acceleration**. A reference entity may disaffirm or challenge the validity of its obligation. This is a credit event that is covered by **repudiation/moratorium**.

The most controversial credit event that may be included in a credit derivative product is restructuring of an obligation. A **restructuring** occurs when the terms of the obligation are altered so as to make the new terms less attractive to the debt holder than the original terms. The terms that can be changed would typically include, but are not limited to, one or more of the following: (1) a reduction in the interest rate, (2) a reduction in the principal, (3) a rescheduling of the principal repayment schedule (e.g., lengthening the maturity of the obligation) or postponement of an interest payment, or (4) a change in the level of seniority of the obligation in the reference entity's debt structure.

The reason why restructuring is so controversial is that a protection buyer benefits from the inclusion of restructuring as a credit event and feels that eliminating restructuring as a credit event will erode its credit protection. The protection seller, in contrast, would prefer not to include restructuring because even routine modifications of obligations that occur in lending arrangements would trigger a payout to the protection buyer. Moreover, if the reference obligation is a loan and the protection buyer is the lender, there is a dual benefit for the protection buyer to restructure a loan. The first benefit is that the protection buyer receives a payment from the protection seller. Second, the accommodating restructuring fosters a relationship between the lender (who is the protection buyer) and its customer (the corporate entity that is the obligor of the reference obligation).

Because of this problem, the *Restructuring Supplement to the 1999 ISDA Credit Derivatives Definitions* (the "Supplement Definition") issued in April 2001 provided a modified definition for restructuring. There is a provision for the limitation on reference obligations in connection with restructuring of loans made by the protection buyer to the borrower that is the obligor of the reference obligation. This provision requires the following in order to qualify for a restructuring: (1) there must be four or more holders of the reference obligation, and (2) there must be a consent to the restructuring of the reference obligation by a supermajority (66 2/3%). In addition, the supplement limits the maturity of reference obligations that are physically deliverable when restructuring results in a payout triggered by the protection buyer.

As the credit derivatives market developed, market participants learned a great deal about how to better define credit events, particularly with the record level of high-yield corporate bond default rates in 2002, and the sovereign defaults, particularly the experience with the 2001–2002 Argentina debt crisis. In January 2003, the ISDA published its revised credit events definitions in the *2003 ISDA Credit Derivative Definitions* (referred to as the "2003 Definitions"). The revised definitions reflected amendments to several of the definitions for credit events set forth in the 1999 Definitions. Specifically, there were amendments for bankruptcy, repudiation, and restructuring.

The major change was to restructuring, whereby the ISDA allows parties to a given trade to select from among the following four definitions: (1) **no restructuring**; (2) **full (old) restructuring**, which is based on the 1999 Definitions; (3) **modified restructuring**, which is based on the Supplement Definition; and (4) **modified modified restructuring**. The last choice is new and was included to address issues that arose in the European market.

Key Points That You Should Understand Before Proceeding

1. Two recent credit risk transfer vehicles are credit derivatives and collateralized debt obligations (CDOs).
2. Credit derivatives are used by institutional portfolio managers to more efficiently control the credit risk of a portfolio or the balance sheet of a financial institution rather than transact in the cash market.
3. A credit default swap is the dominant type of credit derivative.
4. The ISDA has facilitated the growth of the credit derivative market by introducing a standard contract that can be used in credit derivative trades.
5. The ISDA documentation for a credit derivative trade identifies the reference entity and what constitutes a credit event that sets forth when a payout must be made by the protection seller to the protection buyer.
6. There are eight types of credit events possible, the most controversial being restructuring.

CREDIT DEFAULT SWAPS

Credit default swaps are used to shift credit exposure to a credit protection seller. Their primary purpose is to hedge the credit exposure to a particular asset or issuer. A credit default swap in which there is one reference entity is called a **single-name credit default swap**. When there are multiple reference entities (e.g., 10 high-yield corporate bonds of 10 different issuers), it is referred to as a **basket credit default swap**. In a **credit default swap index**, there are multiple entities, as in a basket credit default swap. However, unlike a basket credit default swap, there is a standardized basket of reference entities.

In a credit default swap, the protection buyer pays a fee to the protection seller in return for the right to receive a payment conditional upon the occurrence of a credit event by the reference obligation or the reference entity. Should a credit event occur, the protection seller must make a payment.

The interdealer market has evolved to where single-name credit default swaps for corporate and sovereign reference entities are standardized. While trades between dealers have been standardized, there are occasional trades in the interdealer market where there is a customized agreement. For portfolio managers seeking credit protection, dealers are willing to create customized products. The tenor (i.e., length of time of a credit default swap) is typically five years. Portfolio managers can have a dealer create a tenor equal to the maturity of the reference obligation or have it constructed for a shorter time period to match the manager's investment horizon.

Credit default swaps can be settled in cash or physically. Physical delivery means that if a credit event as defined by the documentation occurs, the reference obligation is delivered by the protection buyer to the protection seller in exchange for a cash payment. Because physical delivery does not rely upon obtaining market prices for the reference obligation in determining the amount of the payment in a single-name credit default swap, this method of delivery is more efficient.

The payment by the credit protection seller if a credit event occurs may be a predetermined fixed amount or it may be determined by the decline in value of the reference obligation. The standard single-name credit default swap when the reference entity is a corporate bond or a sovereign bond is fixed based on a notional amount. When the cash payment is based on the amount of asset value deterioration, this amount is typically determined by a poll of several dealers. If no credit event has occurred by the maturity of the swap, both sides terminate the swap agreement and no further obligations are incurred.

The methods used to determine the amount of the payment obligated of the protection seller under the swap agreement can vary greatly. For instance, a credit default swap can specify at the contract date the exact amount of payment that will be made by the protection seller should a credit event occur. Conversely, the credit default swap can be structured so that the amount of the swap payment by the seller is determined after the credit event. Under these circumstances, the amount payable by the protection seller is determined based upon the observed prices of similar debt obligations of the reference entity in the market. In a typical credit default swap, the protection buyer pays for the protection premium over several settlement dates rather than upfront. A standard credit default swap specifies quarterly payments.

Single-Name Credit Default Swap

Let's illustrate the mechanics of a single-name credit default swap. Assume that the reference entity is XYX Corporation and the underlying is $10 million par value of XYZ bonds. The $10 million is the notional amount of the contract. The **swap premium**—the payment made by the protection buyer to the protection seller—is 200 basis points.

The standard contract for a single-name credit default swap calls for a quarterly payment of the swap premium. The quarterly payment is determined using one of the day count conventions in the bond market. The day count convention used for credit default swaps is actual/360, the same convention used in the interest rate swap market. A day convention of actual/360 means that to determine the payment in a quarter, the actual number of days in the quarter are used and 360 days are assumed for the year.

Consequently, the swap premium payment for a quarter is

$$\text{quarterly swap premium payment} = \text{notional amount} \times \text{swap rate (in decimal)}$$
$$\times \frac{\text{actual no. of days in quarter}}{360}$$

For example, assume a hypothetical credit default swap where the notional amount is $10 million and there are 92 actual days in a quarter. Since the swap premium is 200 basis points (0.02), the quarterly swap premium payment made by the protection buyer would be

$$\$10{,}000{,}000 \times (0.02) \times \frac{92}{360} = \$51{,}111.11$$

In the absence of a credit event, the protection buyer will make a quarterly swap premium payment over the life of the swap. If a credit event occurs, two things happen. First, there are no further payments of the swap premium by the protection buyer to the protection seller. Second, a **termination value** is determined for the swap. The procedure for computing the termination value depends on the settlement terms provided for by the swap. This will be either physical settlement or cash settlement. The market practice for settlement for single-name credit default swaps is physical delivery.

With **physical settlement** the protection buyer delivers a specified amount of the face value of bonds of the reference entity to the protection seller. The protection seller pays the protection buyer the face value of the bonds. Since all reference entities that are the subject of credit default swaps have many issues outstanding, there will be a number of alternative issues of the reference entity that the protection buyer can deliver to the protection seller. These issues are known as **deliverable obligations**. The swap documentation will set forth the characteristics necessary for an issue to qualify as a deliverable obligation. Recall that for Treasury bond and note futures contracts the short has the choice of which Treasury issue to deliver that the exchange specifies as acceptable for delivery. The short will select the cheapest-to-deliver issue, and the choice granted to the short is effectively an embedded option. The same is true for physical settlement for a single-name credit default swap. From the list of deliverable obligations, the protection buyer will select for delivery to the protection seller the cheapest-to-deliver issue.

Figure 2 shows the mechanics of a single-name credit default swap. The cash flows are shown before and after a credit event. It is assumed in the figure that there is physical settlement.

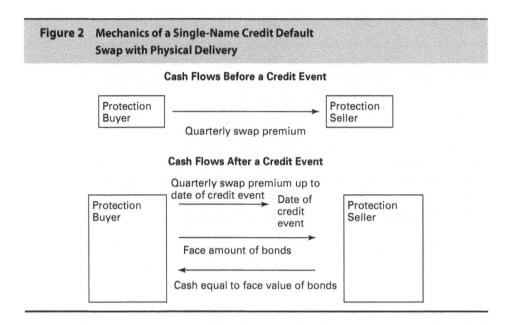

Figure 2   Mechanics of a Single-Name Credit Default Swap with Physical Delivery

Single-name credit default swaps can be used in the following ways by portfolio managers:

- The liquidity of the swap market compared to the corporate bond market makes it more efficient to obtain exposure to a reference entity by taking a position in the swap market rather than in the cash market. To obtain exposure to a reference entity, a portfolio manager would sell protection and thereby receive the swap premium.
- Conditions in the corporate bond market may be such that it is difficult for a portfolio manager to sell the current holding of a corporate bond of an issuer for which it has a credit concern. Rather than selling the current holding, the portfolio can buy protection in the swap market.
- If a portfolio manager expects that an issuer will have difficulties in the future and wants to take a position based on that expectation, it will short the bond of that issuer. However, shorting bonds in the corporate bond market is difficult. The equivalent position can be obtained by entering into a swap as the protection buyer.
- For a portfolio manager seeking a leveraged position in a corporate bond, this can be done in the swap market. The economic position of a protection buyer is equivalent to a leveraged position in a corporate bond.

Basket Credit Default Swaps

With a basket credit default swap, or simply basket default swaps, when a payout must be made must be specified. For example, if a basket credit default swap has 10 reference obligations, does a credit event for just one of the 10 reference obligations result in the triggering of a payment by the protection seller? It depends. Basket default swaps can be structured in different ways.

The simplest case is that if any of the reference obligations default, there is a payout and then termination of the swap. This type of swap is referred to as a **first-to-default basket swap**. Similarly, if a payout is triggered only after two reference obligations default, the swap is referred to as a **second-to-default basket swap**. In general, if it takes k reference obligations to trigger a payout, the swap is referred to as a k-to-default basket swap.

Unlike a single-name credit default swap, the preferred settlement procedure for a basket default swap is cash settlement. With **cash settlement**, the termination value is equal to the difference between the nominal amount of the reference obligation for which a credit event has occurred and its market value at the time of the credit event. The termination value is then the amount of the payment made by the protection seller to the protection buyer. No bonds are delivered by the protection buyer to the protection seller. The documentation for the basket default swap will set forth how the market value at the time of the credit event is determined.

Credit Default Swap Index

In a credit default swap index, the credit risk of a standardized basket of reference entities is transferred between the protection buyer and protection seller. For North America, the only standardized indexes are those compiled and managed by Dow Jones. For the corporate bond indexes, there are separate indexes for investment-grade and high-grade names. The most actively traded contract as of year-end 2008 is the one based on the North American Investment Grade Index (denoted by DJ.CDX.NA.IG). As the name suggests, the reference entities in this index are those with an investment-grade rating. The index includes 125 corporate names in North America. The index is an equally weighted index. That is, each corporate name (i.e., reference entity) comprising the index has a weight of 0.8%. The index is updated semiannually by Dow Jones.

The mechanics of a credit default swap index are slightly different from that of a single-name credit default swap. As with a single-name credit default swap, a swap premium is paid. However, if a credit event occurs, the swap premium payment ceases in the case of a single-name credit default swap. In contrast, for a credit default swap index, the swap payment continues to be made by the protection buyer. However, the amount of the quarterly swap premium payment is reduced. This is because the notional amount is reduced as the result of a credit event for a reference entity.

For example, suppose that a portfolio manager is the protection buyer for a DJ.CDX.NA.IG and the notional amount is $200 million. Using the following formula for computing the quarterly swap premium payment, the payment before a credit event occurs would be

$$\$200,000,000 \times \text{swap rate (in decimal)} \times \frac{\text{actual no. of days in quarter}}{360}$$

After a credit event occurs for one reference entity, the notional amount declines from $200 million to $199,840,000. The reduction is equal to 99.2% of the $200 million because each reference entity for the DJ.CDX.NA.IG is 0.8%. Thus, the revised quarterly swap premium payment until the maturity date or until another credit event occurs for one of the other 124 reference entities is

$$\$199,840,000 \times \text{swap rate (in decimal)} \times \frac{\text{actual no. of days in quarter}}{360}$$

As of year-end 2008, the settlement term for a credit default swap index is physical settlement. However, the market is considering moving to cash settlement. The reason is because of the cost of delivering an odd lot of the bonds of the reference entity in the case of a credit event. For example, consider a credit default swap index with a $10 million notation amount. If there is a credit event, the protection buyer would have to deliver to the protection seller bonds of the reference entity with a face value of $80,000 ($10 million times 0.8%). Neither the protection buyer nor the protection seller would like to deal with such a small position.

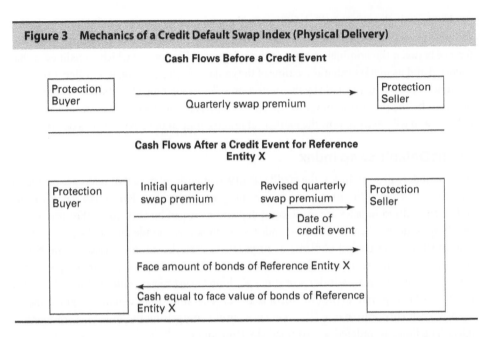

Figure 3 Mechanics of a Credit Default Swap Index (Physical Delivery)

Figure 3 shows the cash flow for a generic credit default swap index after a credit event for one reference entity. Because a credit default swap index, such as the DJ.CDX.NA.IG, provides exposure to a diversified basket of credits, it can be used by a portfolio manager to help adjust a portfolio's exposure to the credit sector of a bond market index. By entering into a credit default swap index as the protection seller, a portfolio manager increases exposure to the credit sector. Exposure to the credit sector is reduced by a portfolio manager being the protection buyer.

Key Points That You Should Understand Before Proceeding

1. The parties to a credit default swap are the credit protection buyer and the credit protection seller, the latter providing protection should a credit event occur for a reference entity or pool of reference entities during the life of the contract and the former making periodic payments for the protection.
2. There are three types of credit default swaps: single-name credit default swaps, basket credit default swaps, and credit default swap indexes.
3. With a single-name credit default swap, there is only one reference entity and once a credit event occurs, the protection seller must compensate the protection buyer (through either physical or cash settlement); payment by the protection buyer to the protection seller ends either when a credit event occurs or the maturity date of the contract is reached.
4. In a basket credit default swap, there are multiple reference entities, with the trigger determining when the protection seller must make a payment to the protection buyer being based on the number of reference entities that must default.
5. In a credit default swap index, the credit risk of a standardized basket of reference entities is transferred between the protection buyer and protection seller, with the contract continuing even if there is a credit event for any of the reference entities in the index but at a lower premium to reflect the credit protection for fewer reference entities.

COLLATERALIZED DEBT OBLIGATIONS

A **collateralized debt obligation (CDO)** is a security backed by a diversified pool of one or more of the following types of debt obligations:

- U.S. domestic investment-grade and high-yield corporate bonds
- U.S. domestic bank loans
- emerging market bonds
- special situation loans and distressed debt
- foreign bank loans
- asset-backed securities
- residential and commercial mortgage-backed securities

When the underlying pool of debt obligations consists of bond-type instruments (corporate and emerging market bonds), a CDO is referred to as a **collateralized bond obligation (CBO)**. When the underlying pool of debt obligations is bank loans, a CDO is referred to as a **collateralized loan obligation (CLO)**.

A CDO is an important credit risk transfer vehicle used by financial institutions and portfolio managers. In this section we explain the basic CDO structure, the reason they are created, and the types of CDOs.[3] The creation of these structures requires the use of derivative instruments, specifically interest rate swaps or credit derivatives, particularly credit default swaps discussed earlier in this chapter.

Structure of a Collateralized Debt Obligation

In a CDO structure, there is a **collateral manager** responsible for managing the portfolio of debt obligations. The portfolio of debt obligations in which the collateral manager invests is referred to as the *collateral*. The individual issues that comprise the collateral are referred to as the *collateral assets*. The funds to purchase the collateral assets are obtained from the issuance of debt obligations. These debt obligations are referred to as *tranches* or *bond classes*. The tranches include

- senior tranches
- mezzanine tranches
- subordinate/equity tranche

A CDO may or may not have a mezzanine tranche.

There will be a rating sought for all but the subordinate/equity tranche. For the senior tranches, at least an A rating is typically sought. For the mezzanine tranches, a rating of BBB but no less than B is sought. The subordinate/equity tranche receives the residual cash flow; hence, no rating is sought for this tranche. There are restrictions imposed as to what the collateral manager may do and certain tests that must be satisfied for the CDO to maintain the credit rating assigned at the time of issuance.

The ability of the collateral manager to make the interest payments to the tranches and pay off the tranches as they mature depends on the performance of the collateral. The proceeds to meet the obligations to the CDO tranches (interest and principal repayment) can come from

---

[3] For a more detailed discussion of CDOs, see Douglas J. Lucas, Laurie S. Goodman, and Frank J. Fabozzi, *Collateralized Debt Obligations: Structures and Analysis*, 2nd ed. (Hoboken, NJ: John Wiley & Sons, 2006).

- coupon interest payments from the collateral assets
- maturing of collateral assets
- sale of collateral assets

In a typical structure, one or more of the tranches has a floating rate. With the exception of deals backed by bank loans that pay a floating rate, the collateral manager invests in fixed-rate bonds. Now that presents a problem—paying tranche investors a floating rate and investing in assets with a fixed rate. To deal with this problem, the collateral manager uses interest rate swaps to be able to convert a portion of the fixed-rate payments from the assets into floating-rate cash flows to pay floating-rate tranches. An interest rate swap allows a market participant to swap fixed-rate payments for floating-rate payments or vice versa. A rating agency will require the use of swaps to eliminate any cash flow mismatches.

Arbitrage versus Balance Sheet Transactions

CDOs are categorized based on the motivation of the sponsor of the transaction. If the sponsor's motivation is to earn the spread between the yield offered on the collateral and the payments made to the various tranches in the structure, then the transaction is referred to as an **arbitrage transaction**. If the motivation of the sponsor is to remove debt instruments (primarily loans) from its balance sheet, then the transaction is referred to as a **balance sheet transaction**. Sponsors of balance sheet transactions are typically financial institutions such as banks seeking to reduce their capital requirements specified by bank regulators by removing loans from their balance sheet.

Economics of an Arbitrage Collateralized Debt Obligation Transaction

To understand the economics of an arbitrage transaction, we will use an illustration. The key as to whether it is economically feasible to create an arbitrage CDO is whether a structure can offer a competitive return for the subordinate/equity tranche.

To understand how the subordinate/equity tranche generates cash flows, consider the following basic $100 million CDO structure with the coupon rate to be offered at the time of issuance as follows:

Tranche	Par Value	Coupon Type	Coupon Rate
Senior	$80,000,000	Floating	LIBOR + 70 basis points
Mezzanine	$10,000,000	Fixed	Treasury rate + 200 basis points
Subordinate/Equity	$10,000,000	—	—

We will make the following assumptions:

- The collateral consists of bonds that all mature in 10 years.
- The coupon rate for every bond is a fixed rate.
- The fixed rate at the time of purchase of each bond is the 10-year Treasury rate plus 400 basis points.

Suppose the collateral manager enters into an interest rate swap agreement with another party with a notional principal of $80 million in which it agrees to do the following:

- Pay a fixed rate each year equal to the 10-year Treasury rate plus 100 basis points.
- Receive LIBOR.

Recall that an interest rate swap is simply an agreement to periodically exchange interest payments. The payments are benchmarked off a notional amount. This amount is not exchanged between the two parties; it is used simply to determine the dollar interest payment of each party. Keep in mind that the goal is to show how the subordinate/equity tranche can be expected to generate a return.

Let's assume that the 10-year Treasury rate at the time the CDO is issued is 7%. Now we can walk through the cash flows for each year. Look first at the collateral. The collateral will pay interest each year (assuming no defaults) equal to the 10-year Treasury rate of 7% plus 400 basis points. So the interest will be

$$\text{Interest from collateral: } 11\% \times \$100,000,000 = \$11,000,000$$

Now let's determine the interest that must be paid to the senior and mezzanine tranches. For the senior tranche, the interest payment will be

$$\text{Interest to senior tranche: } \$80,000,000 \times (\text{LIBOR} + 70 \text{ bps})$$

The coupon rate for the mezzanine tranche is 7% plus 200 basis points. So, the coupon rate is 9% and the interest is

$$\text{Interest to mezzanine tranche: } 9\% \times \$10,000,000 = \$900,000$$

Finally, let's look at the interest rate swap. In this agreement, the collateral manager is agreeing to pay some third party (called the swap counterparty) 7% each year (the 10-year Treasury rate) plus 100 basis points, or 8%, of the notional amount of the interest rate swap. In our illustration, the notional amount is $80 million. The collateral manager selected the $80 million because this is the amount of principal for the senior tranche. So, the collateral manager pays to the swap counterparty:

$$\text{Interest to swap counterparty: } 8\% \times \$80,000,000 = \$6,400,000$$

The interest payment received from the swap counterparty is LIBOR based on a notional amount of $80 million. That is,

$$\text{Interest from swap counterparty: } \$80,000,000 \times \text{LIBOR}$$

Now we can put this all together. Let's look at the interest coming into the CDO:

Interest from collateral	= $11,000,000
Interest from swap counterparty	= $80,000,000 × LIBOR
Total interest received	= $11,000,000 + $80,000,000 × LIBOR

The interest to be paid out to the senior and mezzanine tranches and to the swap counterparty includes:

Interest to senior tranche	= $80,000,000 × (LIBOR + 70 bps)
Interest to mezzanine tranche	= $900,000
Interest to swap counterparty	= $6,400,000
Total interest paid	= $7,300,000 + $80,000,000 × (LIBOR + 70 bps)

Netting the interest payments coming in and going out we have

Total interest received	= $11,000,000 + $80,000,000 × LIBOR
Total interest paid	= $7,300,000 + $80,000,000 × (LIBOR + 70 bps)
Net interest	= $3,700,000 − $80,000,000 × (70 bps)

Since 70 basis points times $80 million is $560,000, the net interest remaining is $3,140,000 ($3,700,000 − $560,000). From this amount any fees (including the asset management fee) must be paid. The balance is then the amount available to pay the subordinate/equity tranche. Suppose that these fees are $634,000. Then the cash flow available to the subordinate/equity tranche is $2.5 million. Since the tranche has a par value of $10 million and is assumed to be sold at par, this means that the potential return is 25%.

In our illustration, some simplifying assumptions were made. For example, it is assumed that there are no defaults. It is assumed that all of the issues purchased by the collateral manager are noncallable (or not prepayable), and, therefore, the coupon rate would not decline because issues are called. Moreover, as explained later, after some period, the collateral manager must begin repaying principal to the senior and mezzanine tranches. Consequently, the interest rate swap must be structured to take this into account since the entire amount of the senior tranche is not outstanding for the life of the collateral.

Despite the simplifying assumptions, the illustration does demonstrate the basic economics of arbitrage CDO structures, the need for the use of an interest rate swap, and how the subordinate/equity tranche will realize a return. In determining whether or not to create a CDO, dealers will look to see if there is a potential return available to the equity tranche of a minimum amount. The threshold return is based on market conditions.

Who are the buyers of the subordinate/equity tranche? In many deals, the sponsor will hold a certain percentage of the tranche. This is done so that the buyers of the other tranches in the structure will see that the sponsor's economic interests are also tied to the performance of the collateral. In addition, hedge fund managers are major buyers. The subordinate/equity tranche in the transaction is an equity-type leveraged security, the type of security that appeals to hedge fund managers. Recall the subprime meltdown in the mortgage market in the summer of 2007. The demand to originate subprime mortgages was driven by the demand from dealers to create subprime residential mortgage–backed securities. In turn, demand for subprime residential mortgage–backed securities came from CDO collateral managers for this product. As we just explained, an arbitrage CDO cannot be done if there is no demand for the subordinate/equity tranche. That demand came from hedge fund managers.

Types of Arbitrage Transactions

Arbitrage transactions can be divided into two types depending on the primary source of the proceeds from the collateral to satisfy the obligation to the tranches. If the primary source is the interest and maturing principal from the collateral, then the transaction is referred to as a **cash flow transaction**. If, instead, the proceeds to meet the obligations depend heavily on the total return generated from the collateral (i.e., interest income, capital gain, and maturing principal), then the transaction is referred to as a **market value transaction**. Most CDOs today are cash flow transactions.

Synthetic Collateralized Debt Obligations

A CDO is classified as a **cash CDO** or a **synthetic CDO**. The adjective *cash* means that the collateral manager purchases cash market instruments. Cash CDOs went a long way in providing banks with the opportunity to better manage their balance sheets. However, there were still two problems with cash CDOs. First, and this is a technical point, regulations allowed for more efficient ways for obtaining credit protection in order to reduce capital requirements.[4] Second was the problem of confidentiality. More specifically, if a loan is transferred into a CDO, borrower notification and borrower consent are required. Because borrowers do not always understand the motivation for the bank selling their loan, the potential for deterioration in customer relationships may make a bank reluctant to sell or transfer a customer's loan.

A synthetic CDO deals with these two limitations of a cash CDO. A synthetic CDO is so named because the collateral manager does not actually own the pool of assets on which it has the credit risk exposure. Stated differently, a synthetic CDO absorbs the credit risk, but not the legal ownership, of the reference obligations. Because the loans are not transferred or sold, the problem of confidentiality is overcome. The vehicle that allows institutions to transfer the credit risk, but not the legal ownership, of the reference obligations it may own in a synthetic CDO is a credit default swap. Synthetic CDO deals came to dominate the CDO market. There are both synthetic balance sheet and synthetic arbitrage CDO structures.[5]

A synthetic CDO works as follows: There are liabilities issued as with a cash CDO. The proceeds received from the tranches sold are invested by the collateral manager in assets with low risk. At the same time, the collateral manager enters into a credit default swap with a counterparty. In the swap, the collateral manager will provide credit protection (i.e., the collateral manager is the protection seller) for a basket of reference obligations that have credit risk exposure. Because it is selling credit protection, the collateral manager will receive the credit default swap premium.

On the other side of the credit default swap is a protection buyer who will be paying the swap premium to the collateral manager. This entity will be a financial institution seeking to shed the credit risk of assets that it owns and that are the reference obligations for the credit default swap.

If a credit event does not occur, the return realized by the collateral manager that will be available to meet the payment to the CDO bondholders is the return on the collateral consisting of low-risk assets plus the credit default swap premium. If a credit event occurs that requires a payout, the collateral manager must make a payment to the protection buyer. This reduces the return available to meet the payments to the CDO bondholders.

There are now standard synthetic CDO tranches that can be purchased by investors based on a standardized reference portfolio, the most common being the Dow Jones North American Investment Grade Index. Each tranche is denoted by two percentages. The first percentage is the subordination level. Once the realized losses exceed the subordination level, the investor in that tranche realizes a loss. The second percentage is the upper limit on the credit loss with the loss expressed as a percentage of the size of the underlying reference portfolio. For example, for the standard synthetic CDO in which the underlying is the Dow Jones North American Investment Grade Index, standard tranches are an equity tranche 0% to 3%, followed by a junior mezzanine 3% to 7%, a 7% to 10% senior mezzanine, a 10% to 15% senior, and a 15% to 30% super senior tranche. For example, consider the 7%

---

[4] For an explanation, see Chapter 12 in Lucas, Goodman, and Fabozzi, *Collateralized Debt Obligations: Structures & Analysis.*

[5] For a further discussion of synthetic balance sheet CDO structures and synthetic arbitrage CDO structures, see Chapters 12 and 13 in Lucas, Goodman, and Fabozzi, *Collateralized Debt Obligations: Structures and Analysis.* For a comprehensive discussion of the application of synthetic CDOs to balance sheet management for banks, see Chapter 7 in Frank J. Fabozzi, Henry Davis, and Moorad Choudhry, *Introduction to Structured Finance* (Hoboken, NJ: John Wiley & Sons, 2006).

to 10% senior mezzanine tranche. An investor in this tranche will only realize a principal loss if there are a sufficient number of defaults for the losses to exceed the subordination of 7% over the life of the tranche.

Key Points That You Should Understand Before Proceeding

1. A CDO is a security backed by a diversified pool of debt obligations.
2. CLOs and CBOs are types of CDOs.
3. The CDO collateral manager is responsible for managing the portfolio of debt obligations.
4. The funds to purchase the assets for a CDO are obtained from the sale of securities, and these securities include senior tranches, mezzanine tranches, and a subordinate/equity tranche.
5. In a cash flow CDO, payments to the tranches issued are generated from the collateral's coupon interest and principal from maturing or prepaid debt obligations.
6. CDOs are categorized based on the motivation of the sponsor of the transaction: arbitrage transactions and balance sheet transactions.
7. The motivation in an arbitrage transaction is to earn an attractive spread for the equity tranche.
8. The motivation in a balance sheet transaction is to transfer loans on a financial institution's balance sheet and obtain capital relief.
9. A synthetic CDO uses credit derivatives, most commonly credit default swaps, to create exposure to reference entities rather than purchasing the cash instruments of those reference entities themselves.

STRUCTURED FINANCE OPERATING COMPANIES

A **structured finance operating company (SFOC)** is a term used by Moody's to refer to an entity whose business activities and operations as well as its credit rating are based on detailed, predetermined parameters. Basically what an SFOC seeks to do is generate "arbitrage" returns by borrowing funds (i.e., employing leverage) and investing those funds in credit-risky debt instruments in such a way as to earn more than the cost of the funds. The reason we placed the term *arbitrage* in quotation marks is that it is not a true arbitrage where a risk-free return is generated without having to invest any funds. There is risk. Despite this risk, the terminology that has unfortunately been adopted is that arbitrage returns are sought.

An SFOC sounds much like an arbitrage CDO since both use borrowed funds to generate a return from investing in a pool of credit-risky assets. However, unlike a CDO, the manager of an SFOC can increase or decrease its leverage based on its expectation about factors that impact the return on its portfolio.

There are many types of SFOC. The most popular one is the **structured investment vehicle (SIV)**.[6] However, the survival of the SFOCs as an investment product is likely given the difficulties they faced in the credit crisis of 2007 and 2008.

---

[6] For a further discussion, see Garrett Sloan, "Structured Finance Operating Companies," Chapter 26 in Brian Lancaster, Glenn Schultc, and Frank J. Fobozzi (eds.), *Structured Products and Related Credit Derivatives: A Comprehensive Guide for Investors* (Hoboken, NJ: John Wiley & Sons, 2008).

CREDIT-LINKED NOTES[7]

A **credit-linked note (CLN)** is a security issued by an investment banking firm or another issuer (typically a special purpose vehicle), which has credit risk to a second issuer (called the reference issuer), and the return is linked to the credit performance of the reference issuer.

A CLN can be quite complicated, so we will focus on the basic structure only. The issuer of a CLN is the credit protection buyer; the investor in the CLN is the credit protection seller. The basic CLN is just like a standard bond: It has a coupon rate (fixed or floating), maturity date, and a maturity value. However, in contrast to a standard bond, the maturity value depends on the performance of the reference issuer. Specifically, if a credit event occurs with respect to the reference issuer, then (1) the bond is paid off, and (2) the maturity value is adjusted down. How the adjustment is made is described in the prospectus of a CLN offering. The compensation for the investor accepting the credit risk of the reference issuer is an enhanced coupon payment.

Typically, CLNs have a maturity of anywhere from three months to several years, with one to three years being the most likely term of credit exposure. The short maturity of CLNs reflects the desire of investors to take a credit view for such a time period.

CONCERNS WITH NEW CREDIT RISK TRANSFER VEHICLES[8]

As with any new complex financial product introduced by financial institutions, there are regulatory and supervisory concerns. The introduction of new credit risk transfer (CRT) vehicles, such as cash CDOs and credit derivatives that are employed to create synthetic CDOs, has elicited the same cautious response from overseers of the global banking system. As explained in this section, a good number of these concerns are the same as those identified for other derivatives such as interest rate and equity derivatives and securitized products, such as collateralized mortgage obligations.

Five studies have identified regulatory and supervisory concerns with CRT vehicles, such as credit derivatives and CDOs. The first is a study by the Financial Stability Forum of the Joint Forum (Joint Forum).[9] The Joint Forum consists of the Basel Committee on Banking Supervision, the International Organization of Securities Commissions, and the International Association of Insurance Supervisors. The second study was conducted by the European Central Bank (ECB),[10] which was a market survey based on interviews with more than 100 banks from 15 European Union banks, five large internationally active non-European Union banks, and securities houses operating in London. The last three studies are by rating agencies, two by Fitch Ratings[11] and one by Standard & Poor's.[12] From the five studies, the following four general issues were identified:

- clean risk transfer
- risk of failure of market participants to understand associated risk

---

[7] For a more comprehensive discussion of CLNs, see Chapter 9 in Fabozzi, Davis, and Choudhry, *Introduction to Structured Finance.*

[8] This section draws from Douglas J. Lucas, Laurie S. Goodman, and Frank J. Fabozzi, "Collateralized Debt Obligations and Credit Risk Transfer," *Journal of Financial Transformation,* 20 (September 2007), pp. 47–59.

[9] Joint Forum, "Credit Risk Transfer," Bank for International Settlements, 2005.

[10] European Central Bank, "Credit Risk Transfer by ECU Banks: Activities, Risk and Risk Management," May 2004.

[11] Fitch Ratings, "Global Credit Derivatives: A Qualified Success," September 24, 2003; and "Global Credit Derivatives Survey: Single-Name CDS Fuel Growth," September 7, 2004.

[12] Standard & Poor's, "Demystifying Banks' Use of Credit Derivatives," December 2003.

- potentially high concentration of risk
- adverse selection

Clearly, these concerns have been realized as was painfully evident by the financial crisis in 2008 due to bank positions in credit default swaps.

Clean Risk Transfer

As new vehicles for CRT have developed, increasing the market liquidity for corporate debt such as bonds and bank loans, the nature of the risks faced by market participants has changed in several ways. At one time, the focus of an investor in a corporate debt was on the ability of the corporation to meet its obligations. The issue with new CRTs is whether there is a "clean" transfer of credit risk.

The concerns with credit derivatives and, therefore, synthetic CDOs being used as CRT vehicles are threefold. First, there is a concern with counterparty risk—the failure of the counterparty selling credit protection would result in the buyer of credit protection maintaining the credit exposure that it thought it had eliminated. With respect to this concern, studies have noted that there are standard procedures available in risk management that can be employed to reduce counterparty risk. These risk management tools are equally applicable to over-the-counter derivatives used to manage interest rate and currency risk by regulated financial entities.

Second, while the development of standard documentation for credit derivative trades by the ISDA fostered the growth of that market, there remains a concern with legal risks that may arise from a transaction. Legal risk is the risk that a credit derivative contract will not be enforceable or legally binding on the counterparty to the trade or may contain ambiguous provisions that result in a failure of the contract to fulfill its intent. The most prominent example is what the credit derivatives market faced early in its life dealing with the issue of whether a credit event had occurred and, in particular, controversial credit events such as restructuring. The 2004 survey of financial institutions by Fitch investigated the frequency of disputed credit events and found that about 14% of the credit events captured in the survey were reported to involve some form of dispute. As for the resolution of those disputes, Fitch found that at the time the vast majority had been or were being resolved without the involvement of the court system. Another example of legal risk is whether the counterparty has the authority to enter into a credit derivative transaction. This is not unique to credit derivatives, but has been the subject of litigation in other derivative markets. For example, interest rates swaps between various dealers and local U.K. authorities were voided in 1991 because it was ruled the latter did not have the legal authority to enter into the contracts in the first place.

Risk of Failure of Market Participants to Understand Associated Risk

With the development of any market vehicle, there is the concern that market participants will not understand the associated risks. For example, there is evidence in the interest rate swap market of corporate entities allegedly failing to understand these risks, probably the two most well-known legal cases being that of Gibson Greetings and Procter & Gamble. The same is true for collateralized mortgage obligations. Both of these instruments have been important financial innovations, but there were users/investors who experienced financial difficulties/fiascos because product innovation may have run far ahead of product education.

In the case of a financial institution that seeks to make a market in the new CRT vehicles, there is a concern that in selling more complex products, such as synthetic CDOs, they may not be properly hedging their position and, therefore, are increasing the institution's risk. (While we have not discussed the pricing of synthetic CDOs, it fair to say that these instruments are not simple to price.) There is modeling risk. For example, in the case of a single-tranche CDO, the dealer will have an imbalanced position in credit defaults swaps and will try to hedge that position by delta hedging.[13] The risk, of course, is that the dealer has not hedged properly.

With respect to this issue, the recommendations of the report of the Joint Forum concentrated on the need for market participants to continue "improving risk management capabilities and for supervisors and regulators to continue improving their understanding of the associated issues." Given this focus, the report sets forth recommendations for market participants and supervisors in three areas: risk management, disclosure, and supervisory approaches, with particular emphasis on reporting and disclosure.

Potentially High Concentration of Risk

A CRT vehicle can result in either the transfer of the credit risk from one bank to another or from a bank to a nonbank entity. Within the banking system, the concern is whether there has become too much concentration of credit risk. For credit risk transferred out of the banking system, there is the concern with the extent to which credit risk is being transferred to nonbanks, such as monoline or multiline insurance companies and hedge funds. The overall concern is the impact on the financial system resulting from a failure of one or a few major participants in the CRT market.

The two studies by Fitch Rating reported the number of banks (North American and European) and insurance companies active in the CRT market and the relative size of each. In its 2003 market survey, Fitch surveyed about 200 financial institutions (banks, securities firms, and insurance companies), focusing on those it classified as protection sellers. Fitch found that through credit derivatives the global banking system transferred U.S. $229 billion of credit risk outside of the banking system. Most of this was to the insurance industry (monoline insurance companies/financial guarantors, reinsurance, and insurance companies). The insurance industry itself is the largest seller of credit protection. Fitch estimated that the insurance industry sold $381 billion of net credit protection (i.e., credit protection sold less credit protection purchased). Of that amount, insurance companies provided $303 billion in credit protection via the credit derivatives market and the balance, $78 billion in credit protection, by their participation in the cash CDO market. Within the insurance industry, the largest seller of credit protection is financial guarantors, insuring the senior tranches in synthetic CDO deals. Fitch concludes that bank buying of credit protection via credit derivatives "has significantly increased liquidity in the secondary credit market and allowed the efficient transfer of risk to other sectors that lack the ability to originate credit." There was a relatively high concentration of credit protection buying by large, more

---

[13] See Douglas J. Lucas, Laurie S. Goodman, Frank J. Fabozzi, and Rebecca Manning, *Developments in the Collateralized Debt Obligations Markets: New Products and Insights* (Hoboken, NJ: John Wiley & Sons, 2007).

sophisticated banks. Smaller and regional banks were net sellers of credit protection despite banks being net buyers of credit protection in the aggregate.

With respect to counterparty concentration, Fitch reported that the market is concentrated among the top 10 global banks and broker-dealers. While having investment-grade ratings, the risk is that the withdrawal of one or more of these firms from the market for financial or strategic reasons could undermine the confidence in the CRT market. This was one of the major concerns of the Federal Reserve in early 2008 in justifying the bailout of the investment banking firm Bear Stearns.

In its 2003 survey, Fitch attempted to collect information on hedge fund activities by writing to the 50 largest hedge funds in the world. None responded. In its 2004 survey, Fitch included questions for the major intermediaries as to their dealings with hedge funds. Fitch found that hedge funds represented between 20% and 30% of credit default swap index trading. Ultimately, counterparty risk exposure to hedge funds depends on the extent of the collateralization of the trades. While most of the intermediaries in the survey responded that their positions with hedge funds were fully collateralized, some stated that it was less than 100% collateralized.

Fitch also found that there is high concentration in the corporations that are the reference obligations in credit default swaps. Settlement problems could occur if there is a credit event for one of these reference entities, leading to a major market disruption. Moreover, because of the higher correlation of default that exists for counterparties and corporate references in the CRT market, in comparison to other derivative markets, there is a concern with the market facing multiple defaults.

Adverse Selection

The ability of originators to transfer credit risk via credit derivatives, CDOs, or securitization has raised concerns that a lending culture based on origination volume rather than prudent lending practices may be inadvertently adopted by banks. This is a concern about securitization in general.

SUMMARY

Interest-rate derivatives can be used to control interest rate risk with respect to changes in the level of interest rates. Credit derivatives can be used to alter the credit risk exposure of a balance sheet, an individual security, or a portfolio. The ISDA has standardized documentation for credit derivative contracts, and the documents define potential credit events. The most controversial credit event is restructuring.

The two most recent introductions into the credit risk transfer market that have made it possible to transfer large amounts of corporate credit risk exposure among banks as well as from the financial sector to the nonfinancial sector are credit derivatives and CDOs. By far, the most dominant type of credit derivative is the credit default swap, wherein the protection buyer makes a payment of the swap premium to the protection seller; however, the protection buyer receives a payment from the protection seller only if a credit event occurs. There are single-name credit default swaps, basket credit default swaps, and credit default swap indexes.

A CDO is a security backed by a diversified pool of one or more debt obligations. A CDO in which the collateral assets are bond-type instruments is called a CBO. A CLO is a CDO where the collateral assets are bank loans. A collateral manager is responsible for managing the collateral subject to restrictions imposed regarding the composition of the collateral. The funds to purchase the collateral assets come from the issuance of debt obligations. These debt obligations include senior tranches, mezzanine tranches, and a subordinate/equity tranche. The ability of the collateral manager to make the interest payments to the tranches and pay off the tranches as they mature depends on the performance of the collateral.

CDOs are categorized as either arbitrage transactions or balance sheet transactions. The categorization depends on the motivation of the sponsor of the transaction. In an arbitrage transaction, the sponsor seeks to earn the spread between the yield offered on the collateral assets and the payments made to the various tranches in the structure. In a balance sheet transaction, the sponsor's motivation is to remove debt instruments from its balance sheet. Interest-rate swaps are often used in CDO structures due to the mismatch between the characteristics of the collateral cash flow and some of the liabilities.

One variety of the CDO is the synthetic CDO, in which credit risk exposure is transferred via credit default swaps rather than the transfer of ownership of corporate debt obligations. A credit-linked note is a credit derivative that is in the form of a bond.

There are concerns raised by regulators regarding CDOs and credit default swaps, some of these being the usual concerns with the introduction of any new financial innovation.

KEY TERMS

- Arbitrage transaction
- Balance sheet transaction
- Bankruptcy
- Basket credit default swap
- Cash CDO
- Cash flow transaction
- Cash settlement
- Collateralized bond obligation (CBO)
- Collateralized debt obligation (CDO)
- Collateralized loan obligation (CLO)
- Collateral manager
- Credit default swap
- Credit default swap index
- Credit derivative
- Credit event
- Credit-linked note (CLN)
- Deliverable obligations
- Failure to pay
- First-to-default basket swap
- Full (old) restructuring
- International Swap and Derivatives Association (ISDA)

- ISDA Documentation
- k-to-default basket swap
- Market value transaction
- Modified restructuring
- Modified modified restructuring
- No restructuring
- Obligation acceleration
- Physical settlement
- Reference entity (reference issuer)
- Reference obligation (reference asset)
- Repudiation/moratorium
- Restructuring
- Second-to-default basket swap
- Structured credit products
- Single-name credit default swap
- Structured finance operating company (SFOC)
- Structured investment vehicle (SIV)
- Swap premium
- Synthetic CDO
- Termination value

QUESTIONS

1. What is the primary purpose of a credit derivative?
2. In a credit default swap, what is meant by
   a. a reference entity?
   b. a reference obligation?
3. What authoritative source is used for defining a "credit event"?
4. Why is "restructuring" the most controversial credit event?
5. Why may a bank be reluctant to sell a commercial loan that it has originated?
6. a. What is a basket default swap?
   b. When does the protection seller have to make a payment to the protection buyer in a basket default swap?
7. For a credit default swap with the following terms, calculate the quarterly premium payment.

	Swap Premium	Notional Amount	Days in Quarter
a.	600 bps	$15,000,000	90
b.	450 bps	$ 8,000,000	91
c.	720 bps	$15,000,000	92

8. All other factors constant, for a given reference obligation and a given scheduled term, explain whether a credit default swap using full or old restructuring or modified restructuring would be more expensive.
9. a. For a single-name credit default swap, what is the difference between physical settlement and cash settlement?
   b. In physical settlement, why is there a cheapest-to-deliver issue?
10. How do the cash flows for a credit default swap index differ from that of a single-name credit default swap?
11. a. Explain how a single-name credit default swap can be used by a portfolio manager who wants to short a reference entity.
    b. Explain how a single-name credit default swap can be used by a portfolio manager who is having difficulty acquiring the bonds of a particular corporation in the cash market.
12. How are credit default swap indexes used by portfolio managers?
13. What is a CLO?
14. What is meant by a balance sheet transaction CDO?
15. Why is the subordinate/equity tranche of a CDO not rated?
16. What are the sources of funds that are used in a CDO to pay bondholders?
17. Consider the following basic $150 million CDO structure with the coupon rate to be offered at the time of issuance as shown:

Tranche	Par Value	Coupon Rate
Senior	$100,000,000	LIBOR + 50 basis points
Mezzanine	$ 30,000,000	Treasury rate + 200 basis points
Subordinated/ equity	$ 20,000,000	None

Assume the following:

- The collateral consists of bonds that all mature in 10 years.
- The coupon rate for every bond is the 10-year Treasury rate plus 300 basis points.
- The collateral manager enters into an interest rate swap agreement with another party with a notional amount of $100 million.
- In the interest rate swap the collateral manager agrees to pay a fixed rate each year equal to the 10-year Treasury rate plus 100 basis points and receive LIBOR.

   a. Why is an interest rate swap needed?
   b. What is the potential return for the subordinate/equity tranche, assuming no defaults?
   c. Why will the actual return be less than the return computed?
18. a. How does a cash CDO differ from a synthetic CDO?

b. What is the advantage of a synthetic CDO over a cash CDO for a bank that wants to use this structure for balance sheet management?

19. a. What is the objective of a structured finance operating company?

b. What is the most common type of structured finance operating company?

20. In a basic credit-linked note, how does the maturity value differ compared to a standard bond structure?

21. What are the four major concerns that have been identified with new credit risk transfer vehicles?

The Market for Foreign Exchange and Risk Control Instruments

From Chapter 32 of *Foundations of Financial Markets and Institutions*, 4/e. Frank J. Fabozzi. Franco Modigliani. Frank J. Jones.
Copyright © 2010 by Pearson Prentice Hall. All rights reserved.

The Market for Foreign Exchange and Risk Control Instruments

LEARNING OBJECTIVES

After reading this chapter, you will understand

- what is meant by a foreign-exchange rate

- the different ways that a foreign-exchange rate can be quoted (direct versus indirect)

- the conventions for quoting foreign-exchange rates

- what foreign-exchange risk is

- a cross rate and how to calculate a theoretical cross rate

- what triangular arbitrage is

- the foreign-exchange market structure

- the fundamental determinants of exchange rates: purchasing power parity and interest rate parity

- the different instruments for hedging foreign-exchange risk: forwards, futures, options, and swaps

- the limitations of forward and futures contracts for hedging long-dated foreign-exchange risk

- how a forward exchange rate is determined and what covered interest arbitrage is

- the basic currency swap structure and the motivation for using currency swaps

The fundamental fact of international finance is that different countries issue different currencies, and the relative values of those currencies may change quickly, substantially, and without warning. The change, moreover, may either reflect economic developments or be a response to political events that make no economic sense. As a result, the risk that a currency's value may change adversely, which is called **foreign-exchange risk** or **currency risk**, is an important consideration for all participants in the international financial markets. Investors who purchase securities denominated in a currency different from their own must worry about the return from those securities after adjusting for changes in the exchange rate. Firms that issue obligations denominated in a foreign currency face the risk that the value of the cash payments they owe to investors is uncertain. The same is true if a firm is receiving a payment in a foreign currency from a customer.

In this chapter, we provide a review of exchange rates and the instruments that can be used to control the risk of an adverse movement in a foreign currency. These instruments include forward contracts, futures contracts, options, and currency swaps. We begin our discussion with a review of the euro.

THE EURO

The European Union consists of European member countries that engage in European economic and political activities. In February 1992, the Treaty on European Union of 1992 established that monetary union would take place by January 1999. The treaty, also called the Maastricht Treaty because its terms were agreed to at the European Council meeting in Maastricht (Netherlands) in December 1991, called for a single currency and monetary policy for member countries in Europe. Monetary policy was to be administered by the European Central Bank. The Economic and Monetary Union (EMU) represents the member countries that are part of the European Union that have adopted the single currency and monetary policy.

At the time of the treaty, the single currency was to be the **economic currency unit (ECU)**. It was the most widely used composite currency unit for capital market transactions. It was created in 1979 by the European Economic Community (EEC). The currencies included in the ECU were those of members of the European Monetary System (EMS). The weight of each country's currency was figured according to the relative importance of a country's economic trade and financial sector within the EEC. Exchange rates between the ECU and those countries not part of the EEC float freely. The exchange rate between countries in the EEC, however, may fluctuate only within a narrow range.

However, at a meeting of the heads of government in Madrid in December 1995, it was agreed that the name of the single currency would be called the **euro**. The reason that the ECU was not selected as the single currency was due to the opinion of Germans that the ECU was perceived to be a weak currency. The countries of the European Union electing to be members of the EMU are subject to a fixed conversion rate against their national currencies and relative to the euro. However, the value of the euro against all other currencies, including member states of the European Union that did not elect to join the EMU, fluctuates according to market conditions.

Members of the EMU are said to be part of "euroland" or the "euro zone" because the euro became the only legal currency. Initially, the member countries maintained their own physical currencies, although they were fixed in value relative to the euro, and the euro had no physical existence. The actual euro currency physically replaced the individual currencies of the participating countries on January 1, 2002. At that time, the relevant authorities of each member country began to withdraw their old national currency from circulation.

To qualify as a participating country in the EMU requires that a country satisfy certain economic standards. These standards set forth for fiscal policy were that the annual fiscal deficit could be no more than 3% of the gross disposable product (GDP), and total outstanding government indebtedness could be no more than 60% of GDP. Many other economic, political, and even social requirements for entry apply. Moreover, a provision of the treaty mandated that the voters of a country seeking membership had to approve the joining of the EMU by popular referendum. These objectives were also, more or less, achieved, and on January 4, 1999 (a Monday, the first business day of the year), 11 countries adopted the single currency, the euro. Other countries subsequently adopted the euro. The central banks of the 11 participating countries were discontinued and replaced by the European Central Bank.

The birth of the euro on January 4, 1999, was smooth and uneventful in terms of both market volatility and operations. Several notable outcomes resulted from this event. First, despite many skeptics, it worked; it proved viable and fairly stable. Second, it gave birth to a large public and corporate capital market denominated in the euro. With respect to the capital market, the governments of all the participating countries issue their government debt denominated in euros. Thus, the differences in the rate on the government debt are based only on differences in credit risk—because differences in currency risk were eliminated—and are quite small.

On the corporate side, the primary issuance of corporate debt denominated in the euro has become large and liquid. Both European and U.S. investment banks play significant roles in these fundings. The secondary markets in these issues have also become quite liquid.

FOREIGN-EXCHANGE RATES

An **exchange rate** is defined as the amount of one currency that can be exchanged for a unit of another currency. In fact, the exchange rate is the price of one currency in terms of another currency. And, depending on circumstances, one could define either currency as the price for the other. So exchange rates can be quoted "in either direction." For example, the exchange rate between the U.S. dollar and the euro could be quoted in one of two ways:

1. the amount of U.S. dollars necessary to acquire one euro, and this is the dollar price of one euro
2. the number of euros necessary to acquire one U.S. dollar, or the euro price of one dollar

Abbreviations are used for every currency throughout the world. Table 1 provides a list of selected currencies and their abbreviations. The three currency pairs that are most commonly traded are

- Euro against U.S. dollar (EUR/USD)
- U.S. dollar against Japanese yen (USD/JPY)
- British pound against U.S. dollar (GBP/USD)

The most traded currency pair is EUR/USD, which has captured about 30% of the global turnover. The USD/JPY and GBP/USD represent about 20% and 11%, respectively.[1]

---

[1] See Shani Shamah, "An Introduction to Spot Foreign Exchange," in Frank J. Fabozzi (ed.), *The Handbook of Finance: Volume I* (Hoboken, NJ: John Wiley & Sons, 2008).

Table 1   Selected Currency Abbreviations

Country	Currency	Abbreviation
Argentina	Pesos	ARS
Australia	Dollars	AUD
Bolivia	Bolivianos	BOB
Brazil	Real	BRL
Bulgaria	Leva	BGN
Canada	Dollars	CAD
Chile	Pesos	CLP
China	Yuan Renminbi	CNY
Colombia	Pesos	COP
Cyprus	Euro	EUR
Czech Republic	Koruny	CZK
Denmark	Kroner	DKK
Egypt	Pounds	EGP
El Salvador	Colones	SVC
Euro Member Countries	Euro	EUR
Hong Kong	Dollars	HKD
Iceland	Kronur	ISK
India	Rupees	INR
Indonesia	Rupiahs	IDR
Iran	Rials	IRR
Iraq	Dinars	IQD
Israel	New Shekels	ILS
Japan	Yen	JPY
Korea (North)	Won	KPW
Korea (South)	Won	KRW
Kuwait	Dinars	KWD
Latvia	Lati	LVL
Lebanon	Pounds	LBP
Malaysia	Ringgits	MYR
Mexico	Pesos	MXN
New Zealand	Dollars	NZD
Norway	Kroner	NOK
Pakistan	Rupees	PKR
Russia	Rubles	RUB
Switzerland	Francs	CHF
Thailand	Baht	THB
Turkey	New Lira	TRY
United Arab Emirates	Dirhams	AED
United Kingdom	Pounds	GBP
United States of America	Dollars	USD

Exchange Rate Quotation Conventions

Exchange rate quotations may be either *direct* or *indirect*. The difference depends on identifying one currency as a local currency and the other as a foreign currency. For example, from the perspective of a U.S. participant, the local currency would be U.S. dollars, and any other currency, such as Swiss francs, would be the foreign currency. From the perspective of a Swiss participant, the local currency would be Swiss francs, and other currencies, such as U.S. dollars, the foreign currency. A **direct quote** is the number of units of a local currency exchangeable for one unit of a foreign currency.

An **indirect quote** is the number of units of a foreign currency that can be exchanged for one unit of a local currency. Looking at it from a U.S. participant's perspective, we see that a quote indicating the number of dollars exchangeable for one unit of a foreign currency is a direct quote. An indirect quote from the same participant's perspective would be the number of units of the foreign currency that can be exchanged for one U.S. dollar. Obviously, from the point of view of a non–U.S. participant, the number of U.S. dollars exchangeable for one unit of a non–U.S. currency is an indirect quote; the number of units of a non–U.S. currency exchangeable for a U.S. dollar is a direct quote.

Given a direct quote, we can obtain an indirect quote (which is simply the reciprocal of the direct quote), and vice versa. For example, on November 21, 2007, a U.S. investor is given a direct quote of 1.4724 U.S. dollars for one euro. That is, the price of a euro is $1.4724. The reciprocal of the direct quote is 0.6792, which would be the indirect quote for the U.S. investor; that is, one U.S. dollar can be exchanged for 0.6792 euros, which is the euro price of a U.S. dollar.

If the number of units of a foreign currency that can be obtained for one dollar—the price of a dollar in that currency or indirect quotation—rises, the dollar is said to appreciate relative to the currency, and the currency is said to depreciate. Thus, appreciation means a decline in the direct quotation.

Foreign-Exchange Risk

From the perspective of a U.S. investor, the cash flows of assets denominated in a foreign currency expose the investor to uncertainty as to the actual level of the cash flow measured in U.S. dollars. The actual number of U.S. dollars that the investor eventually gets depends on the exchange rate between the U.S. dollar and the foreign currency at the time the nondollar cash flow is received and exchanged for U.S. dollars. If the foreign currency depreciates (declines in value) relative to the U.S. dollar (that is, the U.S. dollar appreciates), the dollar value of the cash flows will be proportionately less, leading to foreign exchange risk.

An investor who purchases an asset denominated in a currency that is not the medium of exchange in the investor's country faces foreign-exchange risk. For example, a French investor who acquires a yen-denominated Japanese bond is exposed to the risk that the Japanese yen will decline in value relative to the euro.

Foreign-exchange risk is a consideration for the issuer, too. Suppose that IBM issues bonds denominated in euros. IBM's foreign-exchange risk is that, at the time the coupon interest payments must be made and the principal repaid, the U.S. dollar will have depreciated relative to the euro, requiring that IBM pay more dollars to satisfy its obligation.

SPOT MARKET

The **spot exchange rate market** is the market for settlement of a foreign-exchange transaction within two business days. (The spot exchange rate is also known as the **cash exchange rate**.) Since the early 1970s, exchange rates among major currencies have been free to float, with market forces determining the relative value of a currency.[2] Thus, each day a currency's price relative to that of another freely floating currency may stay the same, increase, or decrease.

A key factor affecting the expectation of changes in a country's exchange rate with another currency is the relative expected inflation rate of the two countries. Spot exchange rates adjust to compensate for the relative inflation rate. This adjustment reflects the so-called **purchasing power parity** relationship, which posits that the exchange rate—the domestic price of the foreign currency—is proportional to the domestic inflation rate, and inversely proportional to foreign inflation.

Let's look at what happens when the spot exchange rate changes between two currencies. Suppose that on day 1 the spot exchange rate between the U.S. dollar and country X is $0.7966 and on the next day, day 2, it changes to $0.8011. Consequently, on day 1, one currency unit of country X costs $0.7966. On day 2, it costs more U.S. dollars, $0.8011, to buy one currency unit of country X. Thus, the currency unit of country X *appreciated* relative to the U.S. dollar from day 1 to day 2, or, what amounts to the same thing, the U.S. dollar *depreciated* relative to the currency of country X from day 1 to day 2. Suppose further that on day 3 the spot exchange rate for one currency unit of country X is $0.8000. Relative to day 2, the U.S. dollar appreciated relative to the currency of country X or, equivalently, the currency of country X depreciated relative to the U.S. dollar.

Although quotes can be either direct or indirect, the problem is defining from whose perspective the quote is given. Foreign exchange conventions in fact standardize the ways quotes are given. Because of the importance of the U.S. dollar in the international financial system, currency quotations are all relative to the U.S. dollar. When dealers quote, they either give U.S. dollars per unit of foreign currency (a direct quote from the U.S. perspective) or the number of units of the foreign currency per U.S. dollar (an indirect quote from the U.S. perspective). Quoting in terms of U.S. dollars per unit of foreign currency is called **American terms**, while quoting in terms of the number of units of the foreign currency per U.S. dollar is called **European terms**. The dealer convention is to use European terms in quoting foreign exchange with a few exceptions. The British pound, the Irish pound, the Australian dollar, the New Zealand dollar, and the euro are exceptions that are quoted in American terms.

Cross Rates

Barring any government restrictions, riskless arbitrage will assure that the exchange rate between two countries will be the same in both countries. The theoretical exchange rate between two countries other than the United States can be inferred from their

---

[2] In practice, national monetary authorities can intervene in the foreign market for their currency for a variety of economic reasons, so the current foreign-exchange system is sometimes referred to as a "managed" floating-rate system.

exchange rates with the U.S. dollar. Rates computed in this way are referred to as **theoretical cross rates**. They would be computed as follows for two countries, X and Y:

$$\frac{\text{Quote in American terms of currency X}}{\text{Quote in American terms of currency Y}}$$

To illustrate, let's calculate the theoretical cross rate between the Swiss franc and Japanese yen on November 21, 2007. The spot exchange rate for the two currencies in American terms was $0.8990 per Swiss franc and $0.009089 per Japanese yen. Then, the number of units of yen (currency Y) per unit of Swiss franc (currency X) is

$$\frac{\$0.8990}{\$0.009089} = 99.0098 \text{ yen per Swiss franc}$$

Taking the reciprocal gives the number of Swiss francs exchangeable for one Japanese yen. In our example, it is 0.0101.

In the real world, it is rare that the theoretical cross rate, as computed from actual dealer dollar exchange rate quotes, will differ from the actual cross rate quoted by dealers. When the discrepancy is large by comparison with the transactions costs of buying and selling the currencies, a riskless arbitrage opportunity arises. Arbitraging to take advantage of cross-rate mispricing is called **triangular arbitrage**, so named because it involves positions in three currencies—the U.S. dollar and the two foreign currencies. The arbitrage keeps actual cross rates in line with theoretical cross rates.

Dealers

The foreign-exchange market is an over-the-counter market that operates 24 hours a day. This means that market participants who want to buy or sell a currency must search different dealers to get the best exchange rate on a specific currency. Alternatively, market participants who want to transact can refer to various widely available bank/broker screens such as Bloomberg Financial Markets and Reuters. The prices cited on those screens are for indicative pricing only.

Foreign-exchange dealers, however, do not quote one price. Instead, they quote an exchange rate at which they are willing to buy a foreign currency and one at which they are willing to sell a foreign currency. That is, they quote a bid–ask spread. For example, on November 21, 2007, the bid–ask spread for the U.S. dollar in terms of Swiss francs was 1.1027 bid and 1.1029 ask. What this means is that one could exchange 1 U.S. dollar for 1.1027 Swiss francs or pay 1.1029 Swiss francs and receive 1 U.S. dollar. The bid–ask spread is 0.0002 in terms of Swiss francs.

Dealers in the foreign-exchange market are large international banks and other financial institutions that specialize in making markets in foreign exchange. Commercial banks dominate the market. There is no organized exchange where foreign currency is traded, but dealers are linked by telephone and cable, and by various information transfer services. Consequently, the foreign exchange market can best be described as an interbank over-the-counter market. Most transactions between banks are done through foreign-exchange brokers. Brokers are agents that do not take a position in the foreign currencies involved in the transaction. The normal size of a transaction is $1 million or more.

Dealers in the foreign exchange market realize revenue from one or more sources: (1) the bid–ask spread, (2) commissions charged on foreign exchange transactions, and (3) trading profits (appreciation of the currencies that dealers hold a long position in, depreciation of the currencies that they hold a long position in, or appreciation of the currencies that they have a short position in).

INSTRUMENTS FOR HEDGING FOREIGN-EXCHANGE RISK

Four instruments are available to borrowers and investors to protect against adverse foreign-exchange rate movements: (1) currency forward contracts, (2) currency futures contracts, (3) currency options, and (4) currency swaps.

Currency Forward Contracts

Recall that in a forward contract one party agrees to buy the underlying, and another party agrees to sell that same underlying, for a specific price at a designated date in the future. Here we consider forward contracts in which the underlying is foreign exchange.

Most forward contracts have a maturity of less than two years. Longer-dated forward contracts have relatively large bid–ask spreads; that is, the size of the bid–ask spread for a given currency increases with the maturity of the contract. Consequently, forward contracts are not attractive for hedging long-dated foreign currency exposure.

Both forward and futures contracts can be used to lock in a certain price, which in this case would be the foreign-exchange rate. By locking in a rate and eliminating downside risk, the user forgoes the opportunity to benefit from any advantageous foreign-exchange rate movement. Futures contracts, which are creations of an exchange, have certain advantages over forward contracts in many cases, such as stock indexes and Treasury securities. For foreign exchange, by contrast, the forward market is the market of choice, and trading there is much larger than trading on exchanges. However, because the foreign-exchange forward market is an interbank market, reliable information on the amount of contracts outstanding at any time, or open interest, is not publicly available.

Pricing Currency Forward Contracts

There is a relationship between spot prices and forward prices, and arbitrage ensures that the relationship holds. We now apply similar considerations to the pricing of foreign-exchange futures contracts on the basis of the spot exchange rate, using an extended example.

Consider a U.S. investor with a one-year investment horizon who has two choices:

Alternative 1: Deposit $100,000 in a U.S. bank that pays 7% compounded annually for one year.
Alternative 2: Deposit in a bank in country X the U.S. dollar equivalent of $100,000 in country X's currency that pays 9% compounded annually for one year.

The two alternatives and their outcomes one year from now are depicted in Figure 1. Which is the better alternative? It will be the alternative that produces the most U.S. dollars one year from now. Ignoring U.S. and country X taxes on interest income or any other taxes, we need to know two things in order to determine the better alternative: (1) the spot exchange rate between U.S. dollars and country X's currency, and (2) the spot exchange rate one year from now between U.S. dollars and country X's currency. The former is known; the latter is not.

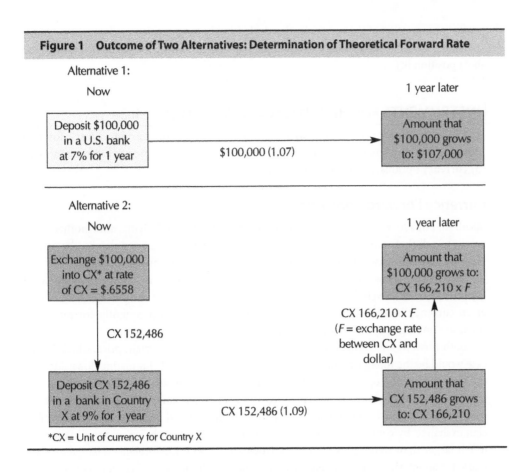

Figure 1 Outcome of Two Alternatives: Determination of Theoretical Forward Rate

Alternative 1:

Now

1 year later

Deposit $100,000 in a U.S. bank at 7% for 1 year

$100,000 (1.07)

Amount that $100,000 grows to: $107,000

Alternative 2:

Now

1 year later

Exchange $100,000 into CX* at rate of CX = $.6558

CX 152,486

Deposit CX 152,486 in a bank in Country X at 9% for 1 year

CX 152,486 (1.09)

Amount that CX 152,486 grows to: CX 166,210

CX 166,210 x F (F = exchange rate between CX and dollar)

Amount that $100,000 grows to: CX 166,210 x F

*CX = Unit of currency for Country X

We can determine, however, the spot rate one year from now between U.S. dollars and country X's currency that will make the investor indifferent between the two alternatives.

Alternative 1: The amount of U.S. dollars available one year from now would be $107,000 ($100,000 times 1.07).

Alternative 2: Assume that the spot rate is $0.6558 for one unit of country X's currency at this time. We denote country X's currency as CX. Then, ignoring commissions, $100,000 can be exchanged for CX152,486 ($100,000 divided by 0.6558). The amount of country X's currency available at the end of 1 year would be CX166,210 (CX152,476 times 1.09).

The number of U.S. dollars for which the CX166,210 can be exchanged depends on the exchange rate one year from now. Let F denote the exchange rate between these two currencies one year from now. Specifically, F denotes the number of U.S. dollars that can be exchanged for one CX. Thus, the number of U.S. dollars at the end of one year from the second alternative is

$$\text{Amount of U.S. dollars one year from now} = \text{CX166,210} \times F$$

The investor will be indifferent between the two alternatives if the number of U.S. dollars is $107,000:

$$\$107,000 = \text{CX166,210} \times F$$

Solving, we find that F is equal to $0.6438. Thus, if one year from now the spot exchange rate is $0.6438 for one unit of country X's currency, then the two alternatives will produce the same number of U.S. dollars. If more than $0.6438 can be exchanged for one unit of country X's currency, then the investor receives more than $107,000 at the end of one year. An exchange rate of $0.6500 for one unit of country X's currency, for example, would produce $108,037 (CX166,210 times $0.6500). The opposite is true if less than $0.6438 can be exchanged for one unit of country X's currency. For example, if the future exchange rate is $0.6400, the investor receives $106,374 (CX166,210 times $0.6400).

Let us now look at this situation from the perspective of an investor in country X. Suppose that an investor in country X with a one-year investment horizon has two alternatives:

Alternative 1: Deposit CX152,486 in a bank in country X that pays 9% compounded annually for one year.
Alternative 2: Deposit the equivalent of CX152,486 in U.S. dollars in a U.S. bank that pays 7% compounded annually for one year.

Once again, assume that the spot exchange rate is $0.6558 for one unit of country X's currency. The investor in country X will select the alternative that generates the most CX at the end of one year. The first alternative would generate CX166,210 (CX152,486 times 1.09). The second alternative requires that CX be exchanged for U.S. dollars at the spot exchange rate at this time. Given the spot exchange rate assumed, CX152,486 can be exchanged for $100,000 (CX152,486 multiplied by $0.6558). At the end of one year, the second alternative would generate $107,000 ($100,000 times 1.07). Letting F continue to denote the number of U.S. dollars in country X, following alternative 2 will realize the following amount of country X's currency one year from now:

$$\text{Amount of country X's currency one year from now} = \$107,000/F$$

The investor will be indifferent between the two alternatives if

$$\$107,000/F = \text{CX166,210}$$

The equation yields a value for F of $0.6438, the same exchange rate that we found when we sought the exchange rate one year from now that would make the U.S. investor indifferent between the two alternatives facing that investor.

Now suppose that a dealer quotes a one-year forward exchange rate between the two currencies. The one-year forward exchange rate fixes today the exchange rate one year from now. Thus, if the one-year forward exchange rate quoted is $0.6438 for one unit of country X's currency, investing in the bank in country X will provide no arbitrage opportunity for the U.S. investor. If the one-year forward rate quoted is more than $0.6438 for one unit of country X's currency, the U.S. investor can arbitrage the situation by selling country X's currency forward (and buying U.S. dollars forward for CX).

To see how this arbitrage opportunity can be exploited, suppose that the one-year forward exchange rate is $0.6500 for one unit of country X's currency. Also, assume that the borrowing and the lending rates within each currency's country are the same. Suppose that the U.S. investor borrows $100,000 for one year at 7% compounded annually and enters into a forward contract agreeing to deliver CX166,210 at $0.6500 per CX one year from now. That is, one year from now the investor is agreeing to deliver CX166,210 in exchange for $108,037 (CX166,210 multiplied by $0.6500).

The \$100,000 that was borrowed can be exchanged for CX152,486 at the spot rate of \$0.6558 to one unit of country X's currency, which can be invested in country X at 9%. One year from now, the U.S. investor will have CX166,210 from the investment in country X, which can be delivered against the forward contract. The U.S. investor will receive \$108,037 and repay \$107,000 to satisfy the bank loan, netting \$1,037. Assuming that the counterparty to the forward contract does not default, this riskless arbitrage situation results in a \$1,037 profit generated with no initial investment.[3] This riskless profit will prompt many arbitrageurs to follow this strategy and will, obviously, result in the U.S. dollar rising relative to country X's currency in the forward exchange rate market, or possibly some other adjustment.[4]

On the other hand, if the one-year forward exchange rate quoted is less than \$0.6438, an investor in country X can arbitrage the situation by buying CX forward (and by selling U.S. dollars forward). This riskless arbitrage again leads arbitrageurs to act, with the result that the forward exchange rate of U.S. dollars relative to CX falls.[5] The conclusion of this argument is that the 1-year forward exchange rate must be \$0.6438, because any other forward exchange rate would result in an arbitrage opportunity for either the U.S. investor or the investor in country X.

Thus, the spot exchange rate and the interest rates in two countries determine the forward exchange rate of their currencies. The relationship among the spot exchange rate, the interest rates in two countries, and the forward rate is called **interest rate parity**. The parity relationship implies that an investor, by hedging in the forward exchange rate market, realizes the same sure domestic return whether investing domestically or in a foreign country. The arbitrage process that forces interest rate parity is called **covered interest arbitrage**.

Mathematically, interest rate parity between the currencies of two countries, A and B, can be expressed in this way:

Let

I = amount of A's currency to be invested for a time period of length t

S = spot exchange rate: price of foreign currency in terms of domestic currency (units of domestic currency per unit of foreign currency)

F = t-period forward rate: price of foreign currency t periods from now

i_A = interest rate on an investment maturing at time t in country A

i_B = interest rate on an investment maturing at time t in country B

Then

$$I(1 + i_A) = (I/S)(1 + i_B)F$$

---

[3] An investor in country X could also arbitrage this situation.

[4] Actually, a combination of things may occur when U.S. investors attempt to exploit this situation: (1) The spot exchange rate of U.S. dollars relative to country X's currency will fall as U.S. investors sell dollars and buy CX, (2) U.S. interest rates will rise in the United States as investors borrow in the United States and invest in country X, (3) country X interest rates will fall as more is invested in country X, and (4) the one-year forward rate of U.S. dollars relative to CX will fall. In practice, the last will dominate.

[5] A combination of things may occur when country X investors attempt to exploit this situation: (1) The spot exchange rate of U.S. dollars relative to CX will rise as country X investors buy dollars and sell CX, (2) country X interest rates will fall as more is invested in the United States, and (3) the one-year forward rate of U.S. dollars relative to CX will rise. In practice, the last will dominate.

The Market for Foreign Exchange and Risk Control Instruments

To illustrate, let country A be the United States and country B represent country X. In our example, we have:

$I = \$100{,}000$ for one year
$S = \$0.6558$
$F = \$0.6438$
$i_A = 0.07$
$i_B = 0.09$

Then, according to interest rate parity, this relationship holds:

$$\$100{,}000(1.07) = (\$100{,}000/\$0.6558)(1.09)(\$0.6438)$$
$$\$107{,}000 = \$107{,}005$$

The \$5 difference is due to rounding.

Interest rate parity can also be expressed as

$$(1 + i_A) = (F/S)(1 + i_B)$$

Rewriting the equation, we obtain the theoretical forward rate implied by the interest rates and spot exchange rate:

$$F = S\left(\frac{1 + i_A}{1 + i_B}\right)$$

Although we referred so far to investors, we could use borrowers as well to illustrate interest rate parity. A borrower has the choice of obtaining funds in a domestic or foreign market. Interest rate parity provides that a borrower who hedges in the forward exchange rate market realizes the same domestic borrowing rate whether borrowing domestically or in a foreign country.

To derive the theoretical forward exchange rate using the arbitrage argument, we made several assumptions. When the assumptions are violated, the actual forward exchange rate may deviate from the theoretical forward exchange rate. First, in deriving the theoretical forward exchange rate, we assumed the investor faced no commissions or bid–ask spread when exchanging in the spot market today and at the end of the investment horizon. In practice, investors incur such costs, which cause the actual forward exchange rate to be plus or minus a small amount of the theoretical rate.

Second, we assumed that the borrowing and lending rates in each currency are the same. Dropping this unrealistic assumption eliminates the possibility of a single theoretical forward exchange rate, and instead implies a band around a level reflecting borrowing and lending rates. The actual rate should be within this band.

Third, we ignored taxes. In fact, the divergence between actual and theoretical forward exchange rates can be the result of the different tax structures of the two countries. Finally, we assumed that arbitrageurs could borrow and invest in another country as much as they wanted in order to exploit mispricing in the exchange market. It should be noted, however, that any restrictions on foreign investing or borrowing in each country impede arbitrage and may cause a divergence between actual and theoretical forward exchange rates.

Link between Eurocurrency Market and Forward Prices

In deriving interest rate parity, we looked at the interest rates in both countries. In fact, market participants in most countries look to one interest rate in order to perform covered interest arbitrage, and that is the interest rate in the Eurocurrency market. The **Eurocurrency market** is the name of the unregulated and informal market for bank deposits and bank loans denominated in a currency other than that of the country where the bank initiating the transaction is located. Examples of transactions in the Eurocurrency market are a British bank in London that lends U.S. dollars to a French corporation, and a Japanese corporation that deposits Swiss francs in a German bank. An investor seeking covered interest arbitrage will accomplish it with short-term borrowing and lending in the Eurocurrency market.

The largest sector of the Eurocurrency market involves bank deposits and bank loans in U.S. dollars and is called the Eurodollar market. The seed for the Eurocurrency market was, in fact, the Eurodollar market. As international capital market transactions increased, the market for bank deposits and bank loans in other currencies developed.

Currency Futures Contracts

Foreign-exchange futures contracts for the major currencies are traded on the International Monetary Market (IMM), a division of the Chicago Mercantile Exchange. The futures contracts traded on the IMM are for the euro, the Canadian dollar, the British pound, the Swiss franc, Japanese yen, and the Australian dollar. The amount of each foreign currency that must be delivered for a contract varies by currency. For example, the British pound futures contract calls for delivery of 62,500 pounds, while the Japanese yen futures contract is for delivery of 12.5 million yen. The maturity cycle for currency futures is March, June, September, and December. The longest maturity is one year. Consequently, as in the case of a currency forward contract, currency futures do not provide a good vehicle for hedging long-dated foreign-exchange risk exposure.

Other exchanges trading currency futures in the United States are the Midamerica Commodity Exchange (a subsidiary of the Chicago Board of Trade) and the Financial Instrument Exchange (a subsidiary of the New York Cotton Exchange). The latter trades a futures contract in which the underlying is a U.S. dollar index. Outside the United States, currency futures are traded on the London International Financial Futures Exchange, the Singapore International Monetary Exchange, the Toronto Futures Exchange, the Sydney Futures Exchange, and the New Zealand Futures Exchange.

Currency Option Contracts

In contrast to a forward or futures contract, an option gives the option buyer the opportunity to benefit from favorable exchange rate movements but establishes a maximum loss. The option price is the cost of arranging such a risk/return profile.

The two types of foreign currency options are options on the foreign currency and futures options. The latter are options to enter into foreign-exchange futures contracts. Futures options are traded on the IMM, the trading location of the currency futures contracts.

Options on foreign currencies have been traded on the Philadelphia Exchange (now owned by Nasdaq oms) since 1982. The foreign currencies underlying the options are the same as for the futures. Two sorts of options are traded on the Philadelphia Exchange for each currency: an American-type option and a European-type option. The former permits exercise at any time up to and including the expiration date, while the latter permits exercise only at the expiration date. The number of units of foreign currency underlying each option contract traded on the Philadelphia Exchange is one-half the amount of the futures contract. For example, the Japanese yen option is for 6.25 million yen and the British pound option is for 31,250 pounds. Options on currencies are also traded on the London Stock Exchange, the London International Financial Futures Exchange, International Securities Exchange, and the NYSE Archipelago.

In addition to the organized exchanges, an over-the-counter market exists for options on currencies. Trading in these products is dominated by commercial banks and investment banking firms. Over-the-counter options are tailor-made products that accommodate the specific needs of clients. Only options on the major currencies are traded on the organized exchanges. An option on any other currency must be purchased in the over-the-counter market.

One key factor that affects the price of any option is the expected volatility of the underlying over the life of the option. In the case of currency options, the underlying is the foreign currency specified by the option contract. So, the volatility that affects the option's value is the expected volatility of the exchange rate between the two currencies from the present time to the expiration of the option. The strike price also is an exchange rate, and it affects the option's value: the higher the strike price, the lower the value of a call, and the higher the value of a put. Another factor that influences the option price is the relative risk-free interest rate in the two countries.[6]

Currency Swaps

Interest rate swaps are transactions in which two counterparties agree to exchange interest payments with no exchange of principal. In a currency swap, both interest and principal are exchanged. The best way to explain a currency swap is with an illustration.

Assume that two companies—a U.S. company and a Swiss company—each seeks to borrow for 10 years in its domestic currency. The U.S. company seeks USD 100 million dollar-denominated debt, and the Swiss company seeks debt in the amount of CHF 127 million. For reasons that we explore later, let's suppose that each wants to issue 10-year bonds in the bond market of the other country, and those bonds are denominated in the other country's currency. That is, the U.S. company wants to issue the Swiss franc equivalent of USD 100 million in Switzerland, and the Swiss company wants to issue the U.S. dollar equivalent of CHF 127 million in the United States.

Let's also assume the following:

1. At the time when both companies want to issue their 10-year bonds, the spot exchange rate between U.S. dollars and Swiss francs is one U.S. dollar for 1.27 Swiss francs.

---

[6] To understand why, take a look at the payoff of a call option on an asset. A portion of the asset is purchased with borrowed funds. In the case of a currency option, it involves purchasing a portion of the foreign currency underlying the option. However, the foreign currency acquired can be invested at a risk-free interest rate in the foreign country. Consequently, the pricing of a currency option is similar to the pricing of an option on an income-earning asset such as a dividend-paying stock or an interest-paying bond. At the same time, the amount that must be set aside to meet the strike price depends on the domestic rate. Thus, the option price, just like interest rate parity, reflects both rates.

2. The coupon rate that the U.S. company would have to pay on the 10-year, Swiss franc-denominated bonds issued in Switzerland is 6%.

3. The coupon rate that the Swiss company would have to pay on the 10-year, U.S. dollar-denominated bonds issued in the United States is 11%.

By the first assumption, if the U.S. company issues the bonds in Switzerland, it can exchange the CHF 127 million for USD 100 million. By issuing USD 100 million of bonds in the United States, the Swiss company can exchange the proceeds for CHF 127 million. Therefore, both get the amount of financing they seek. Assuming the coupon rates given by the last two assumptions, and assuming for purposes of this illustration that coupon payments are made annually, the cash outlays that the companies must make for the next 10 years are summarized as follows:

Year	U.S. Company	Swiss Company
1–10	CHF 7,620,000	USD 11,000,000
10	CHF 127,000,000	USD 100,000,000

Each issuer faces the risk that, at the time a payment on its liability must be made, its domestic currency will have depreciated relative to the other currency. Such a depreciation would require a greater outlay of the domestic currency to satisfy the liability. That is, both firms are exposed to foreign-exchange risk.

In a currency swap, the two companies issue bonds in the other's bond market and enter into an agreement requiring that:

1. The two parties exchange the proceeds received from the sale of the bonds.

2. The two parties make the coupon payments to service the debt of the other party.

3. At the termination date of the currency swap (which coincides with the maturity of the bonds), both parties agree to exchange the par value of the bonds.

In our illustration, these arrangements result in the following:

1. The U.S. company issues 10-year, 6% coupon bonds with a par value of CHF 127 million in Switzerland and gives the proceeds to the Swiss company. At the same time, the Swiss company issues 10-year, 11% bonds with a par value of USD 100 million in the United States and gives the proceeds to the U.S. company.

2. The U.S. company agrees to service the coupon payments of the Swiss company by paying the USD 11,000,000 per year for the next 10 years to the Swiss company: the Swiss company agrees to service the coupon payments of the U.S. company by paying CHF 7,620,000 for the next 10 years to the U.S. company.

3. At the end of 10 years (the termination date of this currency swap and the maturity of the two bond issues), the U.S. company would pay USD 100 million to the Swiss company, and the Swiss company would pay CHF 127 million to the U.S. company.

This complex agreement is diagrammed in Figure 2.

Now let's assess what this transaction accomplishes. Each party received the amount of financing it sought. The U.S. company's coupon payments are in dollars, not Swiss francs; the Swiss company's coupon payments are in Swiss francs, not U.S. dollars. At the termination date, both parties will receive an amount sufficient in their local currency to pay off the

The Market for Foreign Exchange and Risk Control Instruments

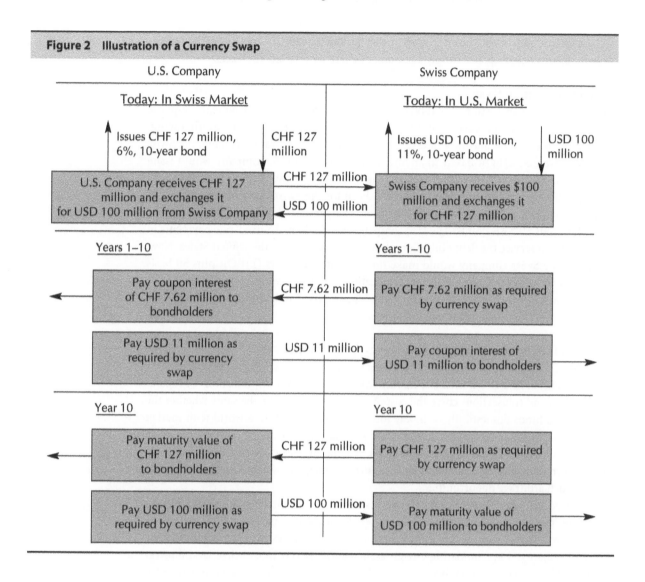

Figure 2 Illustration of a Currency Swap

holders of their bonds. With the coupon payments and the principal repayment in their local currency, neither party faces foreign-exchange risk.

In practice, the two companies would not deal directly with each other. Instead, either a commercial bank or investment banking firm would function as an intermediary (as either a broker or dealer) in the transaction. As a broker, the intermediary simply brings the two parties together, receiving a fee for the service. If, instead, the intermediary serves as a dealer, it would not only bring the two parties together, but would also guarantee payment to both parties. Thus, if one party were to default, the counterparty would continue to receive its payments from the dealer. Of course, in this arrangement, both parties are concerned with the credit risk of the dealer. When the currency swap market started, transactions were typically brokered. The more prevalent arrangement today is that the intermediary acts as a dealer.

An interest rate swap is nothing more than a package of forward contracts. The same is true for a currency swap; it is simply a package of currency forward contracts.

Currency Coupon Swap

In our illustration, we assumed that both parties made fixed cash flow payments. Suppose instead that one of the parties sought floating-rate rather than fixed-rate financing. Returning to the same illustration, assume that instead of fixed-rate financing, the Swiss company wanted LIBOR-based financing. In this case, the U.S. company would issue floating-rate bonds in Switzerland. Suppose that it could do so at a rate of LIBOR plus 50 basis points. Because the currency swap would call for the Swiss company to service the coupon payments of the U.S. company, the Swiss company would make annual payments of LIBOR plus 50 basis points. The U.S. company would still make fixed-rate payments in U.S. dollars to service the debt obligation of the Swiss company in the United States. Now, however, the Swiss company would make floating-rate payments (LIBOR plus 50 basis points) in Swiss francs to service the debt obligation of the U.S. company in Switzerland.

Currency swaps in which one of the parties pays a fixed rate and the counterparty a floating rate are called **currency coupon swaps**.

Reasons for Development of the Currency Swap Market

Now, we turn to the question of why the companies in this illustration may find a currency swap beneficial. In a global financial market without the market imperfections of regulations, taxes, and transactions costs, the cost of borrowing should be the same whether the issuer raises funds domestically or in any foreign capital market. In a world with market imperfections, it may be possible for an issuer to reduce its borrowing cost by borrowing funds denominated in a foreign currency and hedging the associated exchange rate risk, also known as an arbitrage opportunity. The currency swap allows borrowers to capitalize on any such arbitrage opportunities.

Prior to the establishment of the currency swap market, capitalizing on such arbitrage opportunities required use of the currency forward market. The market for long-dated forward exchange rate contracts is thin, however, which increases the cost of eliminating foreign-exchange risk. Eliminating foreign-exchange risk in our U.S.–Switzerland illustration would have required each issuer to enter 10 currency forward contracts (one for each yearly cash payment that the issuer was committed to make in the foreign currency). The currency swap provides a more transactionally efficient means for protecting against foreign-exchange risk when an issuer (or its investment banker) identifies an arbitrage opportunity and seeks to benefit from it.

As the currency swap market developed, the arbitrage opportunities for reduced funding costs that were available in the early days of the swap market became less common. In fact, it was the development of the swap market that reduced arbitrage opportunities. When these opportunities do arise, they last for only a short period of time, usually less than a day.

As another motivation for currency swaps, some companies seek to raise funds in foreign countries as a means of increasing their recognition by foreign investors, despite the fact that the cost of funding is the same as in the United States. The U.S. company in our illustration might be seeking to expand its potential sources of future funding by issuing bonds today in Switzerland.

SUMMARY

We reviewed the spot exchange rate market and markets for hedging foreign-exchange risk. An exchange rate is defined as the amount of one currency that can be exchanged for another currency. A direct exchange rate quote is the domestic price of a foreign currency; an indirect quote is the foreign price of the domestic currency. An investor or issuer whose cash flows are denominated in a foreign currency is exposed to foreign-exchange risk.

The spot exchange rate market is the market for settlement of a currency within two business days. In the developed countries, and some of the developing ones, exchange rates are free to float. According to the purchasing power parity relationship, the exchange rate between two countries—the price of the foreign currency in terms of the domestic currency—is proportional to the domestic price level and inversely proportional to the price level in the foreign country. Exchange rates are typically quoted in terms of the U.S. dollar.

The foreign-exchange market is an over-the-counter market dominated by large international banks that act as dealers. Foreign-exchange dealers quote one price at which they are willing to buy a foreign currency and one at which they are willing to sell a foreign currency. The difference between those prices is one cost a user of the market must pay; another cost is the explicit fee or commission to brokers arranging the purchase or sale of currency.

Currency forward contracts, currency futures contracts, currency options, and currency swaps are four instruments that borrowers and investors can use to protect against adverse foreign-exchange rate movements.

Interest rate parity gives the relationship among the spot exchange rate, the interest rates in two countries, and the forward rate. The relationship is assured by a covered interest arbitrage. Interest rate parity implies that investors and borrowers who hedge in the forward exchange rate market will realize the same domestic return or face the same domestic borrowing rate whether investing or borrowing domestically or in a foreign country. In implementing covered interest arbitrage, the relevant interest rates are those in the Eurocurrency market, the market for bank deposits and bank loans denominated in a currency other than that of the country where the bank initiating the transaction is located. The Eurodollar market is the largest sector of this market.

Exchange-traded options on major foreign currencies and futures options on the same currencies are traded in the United States. An option on any other currency must be purchased in the over-the-counter market.

A currency swap is effectively a package of currency forward contracts, with the advantage that it allows hedging of long-dated foreign-exchange risk and it is more transactionally efficient than futures or forward contracts. Currency swaps are used to arbitrage the increasingly rare opportunities in the global financial market for raising funds at less cost than in the domestic market.

KEY TERMS

- American terms
- Covered interest arbitrage
- Currency coupon swaps
- Direct quote
- Economic currency unit (ECU)

- Euro
- Eurocurrency market
- European terms
- Exchange rate
- Foreign-exchange risk (currency risk)

- Indirect quote
- Interest rate parity
- Purchasing power parity

- Spot exchange rate market (cash exchange rate)
- Theoretical cross rates
- Triangular arbitrage

QUESTIONS

1. A U.S. life insurance company that buys British government bonds faces foreign-exchange risk. Specify the nature of that risk in terms of the company's expected return in U.S. dollars.

2. Explain the difference between a spot exchange rate and a forward exchange rate.

3. These spot foreign exchange rates were reported on November 21, 2007.

	Japanese Yen	British Pound	Australian Dollar
U.S. Dollars	0.009218	2.0654	0.8709

The exchange rates indicate the number of U.S. dollars necessary to purchase one unit of the foreign currency.

a. From the perspective of a U.S. investor, are the preceding foreign-exchange rates direct or indirect quotes?

b. How much of each of the foreign currencies is needed to buy one U.S. dollar?

c. Calculate the theoretical cross rates between:
(1) the Australian dollar and the Japanese yen,
(2) the Australian dollar and the British pound,
and (3) the Japanese yen and the British pound.

4. a. What is the euro?

b. Comment on the following statement: "The exchange rate between the euro and the currencies of all major economic countries is fixed."

c. Comment on the following statement: "The euro was the first choice as the single currency for the Economic and Monetary Union."

5. Explain the meaning of triangular arbitrage, and show how it is related to cross rates.

6. On February 8, 1991, the U.S. dollar/British pound spot rate was U.S. $1.9905 per pound and the U.S. dollar/Japanese yen spot rate was U.S. $0.00779 per yen. The following forward rates were also quoted:

	British Pound	Japanese Yen
30 days	1.9908	0.007774
60 days	1.9597	0.007754
90 days	1.9337	0.007736

a. Explain what someone who enters into a 30-day forward contract to deliver British pounds is agreeing to do.

b. Explain what someone who enters into a 90-day forward contract to buy Japanese yen is agreeing to do.

c. What can you infer about the relationship between U.S. and British short-term interest rates and U.S. and Japanese short-term interest rates?

7. What is the drawback of using currency forward contracts for hedging long-dated positions?

8. How does covered interest arbitrage relate to interest rate parity?

9. Why are the interest rates in the Eurocurrency market important in covered interest arbitrage?

10. Suppose you know the following items: You can borrow and lend $500,000 at the one-year interest rate in the United States of 7.5%; in country W both the borrowing and lending rates are 9.2%; the spot exchange rate between the U.S. dollar and country W's currency is now $0.1725 per unit of currency of country W; and the one-year forward exchange rate is $0.2 per unit of currency of country W.

a. Explain how you could make a profit without risk and without investing any of your own money. (Assume commissions, fees, etc., to be equal to zero.)

b. Aside from assuming commissions, fees, and so on, to be zero, several unrealistic assumptions must be made in answering part (a). What are they?

c. Even if we incorporated realistic considerations regarding commissions and so on, the interest rate and exchange rate numbers in this question would probably produce a profit of some size. Why do you think opportunities like the one in this question are unlikely to come along often in the real world?

11. If the one-year borrowing and lending rates in Country ABC are 3%, and 4% in the United States, and if the foreign-exchange rate between dollars and the currency of Country ABC is $0.007576 per currency of Country ABC (i.e., $1 could buy 131.99 units of Country ABC), then what should the spot exchange rate of dollars for the currency of Country ABC be?

12. For which currencies are options and futures traded on organized U.S. exchanges?

13. What is the major difference between a currency swap and an interest rate swap?

14. The following excerpt appeared in the January 14, 1991, issue of *Wall Street Letter.*

> The Philadelphia Stock Exchange plans to list the first nondollar denominated options to trade in the United States, according to sources at the exchange. The Phlx will list cross-currency options based on the relationships between the Deutsche mark and the Japanese yen, as well as British pound/yen and pound/mark options, a spokesman confirmed. . . .

> The exchange currently lists currency options that are based on the relationship between that currency and the dollar, one Phlx member explained. "If you're not American," he added, "then the dollar doesn't do it for you." The three new cross-currency options should be attractive to the same banks and broker-dealers that currently trade dollar-based currency options, as well as non-U.S. entities that have interests in other currencies.

> Cross-currency options are "a very big part of international trade and international capital markets," and are big over-the-counter products, but none currently trades on an exchange. The advantage of exchange-traded options, the Phlx member said, is that "99% of the customers don't have the credit" to trade such a product over-the-counter with a big bank.

a. Explain what the representative of the Phlx means by saying, "If you're not American, then the dollar doesn't do it for you."

b. Why is the credit of customers critical in the over-the-counter market but not for an exchange-traded contract?

c. When the Philadelphia Stock Exchange filed with the SEC to list cross-currency options, the exchange indicated that the demand for this product has been "spawned by recent large fluctuations and dramatic increases in volatility levels for cross-rate options." Why would this increase the demand for cross-currency options?

Index

690